D0274676

ANGLO-SAXON ENGLAND AND THE NORMAN CONQUEST

Social and Economic History of England

Edited by Asa Briggs

Anglo-Saxon England and the Norman Conquest (2nd Edition)
  H. R. Loyn

Medieval England: Rural Society and Economic Change 1086–1348
  E. Miller and J. Hatcher

The Late Medieval Economy   *J. A. Tuck*

The Age of Plunder 1500–1547   *W. G. Hoskins*

The Age of Elizabeth 1547–1603 (2nd Edition)   *D. M. Palliser*

England's Apprenticeship 1603–1763 (2nd Edition)
  Charles Wilson

The Rise of Industrial Society in England 1815–1885
  S. G. Checkland

The Vital Century: England's Economy 1714–1815
  John Rule

Albion's People: English Society, 1714–1815   *John Rule*

ANGLO-SAXON ENGLAND AND THE NORMAN CONQUEST

Second Edition

H. R. Loyn
Professor Emeritus, University of London

Longman
London and New York

Longman Group UK Limited
Longman House, Burnt Mill, Harlow,
Essex CM20 2JE, England
and Associated Companies throughout the world.

*Published in the United States of America
by Longman Inc., New York*

© H. R. Loyn 1962. This edition © Longman Group UK Limited 1991

All rights reserved; no part of this publication may be
reproduced, stored in a retrieval system, or transmitted in
any form or by any means, electronic, mechanical,
photocopying, recording, or otherwise without either the
prior written permission of the Publishers or a licence
permitting restricted copying in the United Kingdom issued
by the Copyright Licensing Agency Ltd, 33–34 Alfred Place,
London, WC1E 7DP.

First published 1962
Second edition 1991

British Library Cataloguing in Publication Data

Loyn, H. R. (Henry Royston)
 Anglo-Saxon England and the Norman Conquest. –2nd ed.–
 (Social and economic history of England).
 1. England to 1066
 I. Title   II Series
 942.01

 ISBN 0–582–07297–2
 ISBN 0–582–07296–4 pbk

Library of Congress Cataloging-in-Publication Data

Loyn, H. R. (Henry Royston)
 Anglo-Saxon England and the Norman Conquest. —2nd ed.
   p.   cm. — (Social and economic history of England)
 Includes bibliographical references and index.
 ISBN 0–582–07297–2 (cased) : £25.00. —ISBN 0–582–07296–4 (paper) :
£12.95.
 1. England—Economic conditions—Medieval period, 1066–1485. 2. England—Social conditions—Medieval period, 1066–1485. 3. Great Britain—History—Anglo-Saxon period, 449–1066. 4. Great Britain—History—Norman
period, 1066–1154. 5. Normans—England—History.
 6. Anglo-Saxons—History.
 I. Title.   II. Series.
 HC254.L6 1991
 942.01—dc20

                                                                90–48513
                                                                    CIP

Set in 10/12pt Linotron Baskerville

Produced by Longman Singapore Publishers (Pte) Ltd.
Printed in Singapore

Contents

For P.B.L.

List of Maps

List of Abbreviations

Generally accepted abbreviations such as J. for Journal, Proc. for Proceedings, Trans. for Transactions, are not listed below.

Aelfric's Catholic Homilies: *The Homilies of the Anglo–Saxon Church*, part I, Catholic Homilies, ed. B. Thorpe, London, 1844.

Alcuin, 'Versus de Sanctis': 'De Pontificibus et Sanctis Ecclesiae Eboracensis', ed. J. Raine, *Historians of the Church of York*, R.S., I, 1879.

A.S. Chronicle: Anglo–Saxon Chronicle, consulted in the edition of C. Plummer, *Two of the Saxon Chronicles Parallel*, Oxford, vol. I, 1892, vol. II, 1899, unless otherwise stated.

A.S.E.: *Anglo–Saxon England*, ed. P. Clemoes, Cambridge, (1971–).

Asser's Life of Alfred: *Asser's Life of King Alfred*, ed. W. H. Stevenson, Oxford, 1904. 2nd imp. 1959.

B.A.R.: *British Archaeological Reports*.

Bede, *Hist. Eccl.*: Bede's *Historia Ecclesiastica Gentis Anglorum*, consulted in the edition of C. Plummer, *Venerabilis Baedae Opera Historica*, 2 vols., Oxford, 1896, unless otherwise stated. This edition also includes Bede's letter to Archbishop Egbert, and his Lives of the Abbots of Jarrow and Wearmouth.

Bibl. der angelsachs. Prosa: Bibliothek der angelsachsischen Prosa.

B.N.J.: *British Numismatic Journal*.

Boniface, *Epist.*: M.G.H., *Epistolae Selectae, I*, ed. M. Tangl, Berlin, 1916.

Brit. Mus. or B.M.: British Museum.

C.B.A.: Council for British Archaeology.

C.S.: *Cartularium Saxonicum*, ed. W. de Gray Birch, 3 vols., London, 1885–93.

Darby, *Eastern England, Midland England*, etc: the appropriate volume in H.C. Darby, *The Domesday Geography of England*, 5 vols. and gazetteer, Cambridge, 1952–75.

D.B. I, II, III, and IV: Domesday Book, Record Commission, the first two volumes ed. Abraham Farley, London, 1783, the last two by H. Ellis, London, 1811 and 1816. D.B. I deals with most of the country; D.B. II with Essex and East Anglia; D.B. III provides Ellis's valuable indexes; D.B. IV gives various surveys allied to the main Domesday.

Econ. H.R.: *Economic History Review.*

E.E.T.S.: Early English Text Society.

E.H.D. I: *English Historical Documents*, ed. D. Whitelock, London, 1955, 2nd ed., 1979.

E.H.D. II: *English Historical Documents*, ed. D. C. Douglas and G. W. Greenaway, London, 1953, 2nd ed., 1981.

E.H.R.: *English Historical Review.*

E.P.N.S.: English Place-Name Society.

Florence of Worcester: *Florentii Wigorniensis Monachi Chronicon ex Chronicis*, ed. B. Thorpe, 2 vols., London, 1848-9.

Haddan and Stubbs: *Councils and Ecclesiastical Documents relating to Great Britain and Ireland*, ed. A. W. Haddan and W. Stubbs, 3 vols., Oxford, 1869–78 (reprint 1964).

Harmer, *Select Documents*: *Select Documents of the Ninth and Tenth Centuries*, ed. F. E. Harmer, Cambridge, 1914.

H.M.S.O.: Her Majesty's Stationery Office.

Hist. Eccl., I, II: See Bede, *Hist. Eccl.*

Kemble, C. D.: *Codex Diplomaticus Aevi Saxonici*, ed. J. M. Kemble, 6 vols., London, 1839–48.

Liebermann I, II or III: F. Liebermann, *Die Gesetze der Angelsachsen*, 3 vols., Halle, 1903–16. References to individual royal law-codes are given according to the name of the kings, and refer to this edition where not otherwise stated.

M.A.: *Medieval Archaeology.*

*M.E.C.*I. : P. Grierson and M. Blackburn, Medieval European Coinage, I, *The Early Middle Ages, 5th – 10th Centuries*, Cambridge, 1986.

Mon. Ang.: W. Dugdale, *Monasticon Anglicanum*, rev. ed., London, 1849.

M.G.H.: Monumenta Germaniae Historica; *Ep. (Epistolae), SS (Scriptores)*.

M.H.B.: *Monumenta Historica Britannica*, ed. H. Petrie, London, 1848.

Num. Chron.: *Numismatic Chronicle*.

Pastoral Care: *King Alfred's West Saxon Version of Gregory's Pastoral Care*, ed. H. Sweet, E.E.T.S., 1871.

R.S.: Rolls Series.

T.R.E.: *Tempore Regis Eadwardi*, in the time of King Edward.

T.R. Hist. S.: *Transactions of the Royal Historical Society*.

V.C.H.: Victoria County History.

W.A.M.: *Wiltshire Archaeological and Natural History Magazine*.

W. Malms., *Gest. Regum and Gest. Pont.*: William of Malmesbury, *Gesta Regum*, ed. W. Stubbs, R.S., 1887–9; and *Gesta Pontificum*, ed. N. E. S. A. Hamilton, R.S., 1870.

Wulfstan, *Collected Homilies*: A. S. Napier, *Wulfstan: Sammlungen der ihm zugeschriebenen Homilien*, Berlin, 1883.

Wulfstan's Homilies: *The Homilies of Wulfstan*, ed. D. Betherum, Oxford, 1957.

Wulfstan's Institutes: *Die 'Institutes of Polity, Civil and Ecclesiastical', ein Werk Erzbischof Wulfstans von York*, ed. K. Jost, Berne, 1959.

Introductory Note

Interest in economic history has grown enormously in recent years. In part, the interest is a by-product of twentieth-century preoccupation with economic issues and problems. In part, it is a facet of the revolution in the study of history. The scope of the subject has been immensely enlarged, and with the enlargement has come increasing specialization. Economic history is one of the most thriving of the specialisms. Few universities are without an economic historian. New research is being completed each year both in history and economics departments. There are enough varieties of approach to make for frequent controversy, enough excitement in the controversy to stimulate new writing.

This series, of which Mr. Loyn's volume is the first, is designed to set out the main conclusions of economic historians about England's past. It rests on the substantial foundations of recent historical scholarship. At the same time, it seeks to avoid narrow specialization. Economic history is not lifted out of its social context, nor are the contentious borderlands of economics and politics neglected. The series is described as 'a social and economic history of England'.

The bracketing together of the two adjectives is deliberate. Social history has received far less scholarly attention than economic history. A child of the same revolt against the limited outlook of the political historian, it has grown less sturdily. Its future depends on the application of greater discipline and more persistent probing. Developments in recent years are encouraging, and many of them will be reflected in these volumes. So too will developments in historical geography and, where they are illuminating, in demography and sociology. There is hope that just as the economist has provided useful tools for the study of economic history, so the sociologist may be able to provide useful tools for the study of social history and the demographer valuable quantitative data. There is no need, however, for economic and social historians to work in separate workshops. Most of the problems with which they are concerned demand co-operative effort.

However refined the analysis of the problems may be or may become, however precise the statistics, something more than accuracy and discipline are needed in the study of social and economic history. Many of the most lively economic historians of this century have been singularly undisciplined, and their hunches and insights have often proved invaluable. Behind the abstractions of economist or sociologist is the experience of real people, who demand sympathetic understanding as well as searching analysis. One of the dangers of economic history is that it can be written far too easily in impersonal terms: real people seem to play little part in it. One of the dangers of social history is that it concentrates on categories rather than on flesh and blood human beings. This series is designed to avoid both dangers, at least as far as they can be avoided in the light of available evidence. Quantitative evidence is used where it is available, but it is not the only kind of evidence which is taken into the reckoning.

Within this framework each author has had complete freedom to describe the period covered by his volume along lines of his own choice. No attempt has been made to secure general uniformity of style or treatment. The volumes will necessarily overlap. Social and economic history seldom moves within generally accepted periods, and each author has had the freedom to decide where the limits of his chosen period are set. It has been for him to decide in what the 'unity' of his period consists.

It has also been his task to decide how far it is necessary in his volume to take into account the experience of other countries as well as England in order to understand English economic and social history. The term 'England' itself has been employed generally in relation to the series as a whole not because Scotland, Wales or Ireland are thought to be less important or less interesting than England, but because their historical experience at various times was separate from or diverged from that of England: where problems and endeavours were common or where issues arose when the different societies confronted each other, these problems, endeavours and issues find a place in this series. In certain periods Europe, America, Asia, Africa and Australia must find a place also.

One of the last volumes in the series will be called 'Britain in the World Economy'.

The variety of approaches to the different periods will be determined, of course, not only by the values, background or special interests of the authors but by the nature of the surviving sources and the extent to which economic and social factors can be separated out from other factors in the past. In Mr. Loyn's volume archaeological and literary evidence, for example, must necessarily have a different relative place from that in the volumes on the eighteenth and nineteenth centuries. For many of the periods described in this series it is extremely difficult to disentangle law or religion from economic and social structure and change. Facts about 'economic and social aspects' of life must be supplemented by accounts of how successive generations thought about 'economy' and 'society'. The very terms themselves must be dated.

Where the facts are missing or the thoughts impossible to recover , it is the duty of the historian to say so. Many of the crucial problems in English social and economic history remain mysterious or only partially explored. This series must point, therefore, to what is not known as well as what is known, to what is a matter of argument as well as what is agreed upon. At the same time, it is one of the particular excitements of the economic and social historian to be able, as G. M. Trevelyan has written, 'to know more in some respects than the dweller in the past himself knew about the conditions that enveloped and controlled his life'.

ASA BRIGGS

Preface

This book has been written as an introduction to the social and economic history of England from the time of the Anglo-Saxon invasions to the Norman Conquest. There has been no attempt to tell the political story, but the first chapter is intended to act as a chronological guide to the main events of the age, and the second chapter to help to fit the Anglo-Saxon scene into its wider European setting. The book then deals with more specialized topics, until in the seventh chapter some analysis is made of general social developments during the Anglo-Saxon age. The last chapters treat of the Norman Conquest and the state of society in eleventh-century England. Over such a long and involved period a writer's debt to others is necessarily great, and I would like to make special mention of the work of Professor Whitelock, Dr. F. E. Harmer, Miss A. J. Robertson and Dr. F. L. Attenborough, whose critical editions and translations of so much essential diplomatic and legal material have made lighter the task of the general historian. To Sir Frank Stenton all workers in the field owe a great debt for his sure guidance, in detail and in general, towards an accurate interpretation of the period.

There are many personal acknowledgments to be made in connection with the preparation of this book, but it is right and most pleasant to begin at the beginning and to pay tribute to my teachers, later my colleagues, Professor William Rees, Miss G. B. M. Whale and Dr. Dorothy Marshall of the History Department at Cardiff; and to Professor E. C. Llewellyn, who introduced me to the study of the Anglo-Saxon language. To Sir Frank Stenton go my warmest thanks for his support during my graduate studies, and for his constant encouragement. My greatest debt in relation

to the present book is to Professor Whitelock, who read the
typescript, and who gave generously of her time, knowledge and
deep understanding of the period to suggest many improvements
and corrections. The typescript was also read by Professor Asa
Briggs, the general editor of the series of which this volume is
part, who made many helpful criticisms; and by my friend, Mr.
M. C. Ede, who did much to improve the style. My very grateful
thanks go to Professor S. B. Chrimes, who generously read through
all the page-proofs, and who helped to clarify expression and to
remove many ambiguities. Among others whose assistance I wish
to mention in particular, are Mr. R. H. M. Dolley of the British
Museum for his ready contributions on all matters concerning
Anglo-Saxon coinage, and for reading some sections of the book
in proof; and Mr. Lionel Williams and Dr. Michael Jarrett who
read part of the proofs. I am pleased also to acknowledge the
patience and courtesy of many librarians, particularly those of my
own college.

I thank Professor Jackson and the Edinburgh University Press
for permission to reproduce the map of British River-Names;
Professor Whitelock and Messrs. Eyre & Spottiswoode for permission to incorporate some of the information in the map of
Scandinavian Settlement; Mr. R. H. M. Dolley for the information
upon which the map of Anglo-Saxon mints is based; Professor the
Rev. Dom David Knowles and the Cambridge University Press for
permission to use the material contained in the map of the Monastic
Revival in Late Anglo-Saxon England, and Professor Barlow and
Messrs. Longmans, Green & Co., for permission to use some of
the information in the map of England at the end of the eleventh
century. My thanks also go to the Cambridge University Press for
allowing me to use on p. 97 the long quotation from Miss A. J.
Robertson's translations *The Laws of the Kings of England from
Edmund to Henry I.* I also wish to recognize the courteous help
given by all departments of Longmans, Green & Co., who have
guided the book through the press.

Last, but far from least, my thanks go to my wife, whose
preparation of the index — that traditional wifely chore — is
merely a material indication of her constant and indispensable
support.

H. R. LOYN
University College of South Wales and Monmouthshire
16 January 1962

Prefatory Note to the Second Edition

An attempt has been made to bring the text up to date without losing the substance of the original arguments over the development of the Anglo-Saxon economy and society. In the course of the last thirty years much advance in knowledge has been achieved, especially by archaeologists and numismatists. The complexity of patterns of settlement, including a pronounced middle-Saxon shift in settlement sites, is better understood. Refinement of techniques of coin description and analysis has confirmed the importance of the evidence drawn from the coinage in telling us of the growing coherence of the late Anglo-Saxon monarchy and society. A firmer knowledge of Domesday Book, resulting from the 900th anniversary celebrations in 1986, has facilitated work on the Norman Conquest and eleventh-century conditions in general. Additions to footnotes and to the bibliography have necessarily been selective, but made with a view to clarifying argument and bringing the reader into touch with constructive modern work on a complex but rewarding period of English social history. My special thanks go to Mark Blackburn who has read the numismatic sections for me, has helped to bring them up to date, and has saved me from several errors. Those that remain, in these sections as in others, remain of course my own responsibility.

H. R. L.

St Albans 1990

CHAPTER ONE
Settlement and Peoples

1. SOURCES AND POLITICAL OUTLINES OF EARLY SETTLEMENT

The centuries from the withdrawal of the Roman garrisons to the consolidation of Norman feudal mastery saw the making of England. In later centuries there were accretions of population from overseas, English institutions received profound modification, and the economy was transformed. Yet the Anglo-Norman England of A.D. 1100, for all its appearance of exotic alien culture at court and in the Church, contained the essential ingredients of England: a monarchy which had grown with the community, and a people compounded of elements drawn from the four major historic groups that had in their different ways contended for and with the soil of England – from the Romano-Britons, the Anglo-Saxons, the Scandinavians and the Norman conquerors. In the eleventh century the last successful hostile settlements were made in England, and even these were in a sense superficial. The main colonizing efforts were complete by mid-tenth century, and it is with the two chief settlements achieved, the Anglo-Saxon and the Scandinavian, that the present chapter is primarily concerned.

There is no single problem in English history more perplexing than that which surrounds the first settlement of the peoples who gave their name to the land. Enough written evidence has survived to make interpretation a possibility, though one studded with its own peculiar perils relating to reliability of sources such as Gildas, the Anglo-Saxon Chronicle and Nennius, to say nothing of Frankish or Byzantine accounts which dismiss the settlement in a phrase, or embroider the story with fanciful tales of dragons or monsters. Bede himself, whose works provide the major source for the early period, had to rely on traditions of settlement not all of which were sound. Archaeological evidence is plentiful but one-sided, so much of it coming from grave-sites. We know more of the Roman living, more of the Saxon dead. Patient work on habitation sites such as Mucking in Essex, Chalton in Hampshire or West Stow in Suffolk is beginning to redress the balance, and acceptable archaeological evidence is now available to support the view that the Germanic immigrants came in substantial numbers and that they were used to a stratified society. The halls of West Stow stand side by side with the admittedly dominant sunken huts just as the jewels, weapons, and imported bronze and glass of the finest burials off-set the simple pre-Christian interments devoid of grave-goods. Yet it is increasingly recognized that the relationship between the archaeological and the historical record is complex and that much more careful local investigation is needed before firm conclusions can be drawn on the nature of the early Anglo-Saxon settlement.[1]

The most helpful line of approach still comes from a field which, in spite of its somewhat treacherous nature, gives the firmest and most tangible evidence relating to some of the settlement problems: that of place-name study and the study of language. The references that will be made in the following pages to the work of the English Place-Name Society, and to the work of Professor Jackson on the language and history of early Britain, pay only too inadequate tribute to the help that is being given from these sources to all students of our early history.

In one respect, however, the writer whose concern lies in the social and economic aspects of history has an advantage. He is not bound to the worrisome discussion of minute detail that plagues the political historian. Disputes over the existence of Hengest and Horsa, or over the exact date of the Adventus Saxonum or of the battle of Mount Badon, are not relevant directly to his purpose. There might have been two Vortigerns, and then again there might not. He asks for a reasonable general framework in which to conduct a discussion of the nature of settlement, and there has emerged from the hard work of the last decades an agreed general picture of the political background sufficient for his needs.

[1] Catherine Hills, 'The archaeology of Anglo-Saxon England in the pagan period: a review', *A.S.E.* 8, pp.297–330, provides the best modern guide to the problem.

There is one certain fact to start with: the withdrawal of the garrisons from Roman Britain in the first decade of the fifth century. This did not mean the end of Roman Britain, which still remained part of the Roman world. The provincials continued to regard themselves as Roman, though political predominance probably passed away from the more Romanic to the more Celtic elements in the population. The tyrants, of whom the sources tell, are likely to comprise tribal chieftains drawn from the more backward areas of the province, and brought into prominence by their success in resisting Picts and Scots. Ecclesiastical contact with the Continent was maintained. As late as A.D. 455 the Church in these islands was still in administrative and doctrinal touch with the Church in Gaul.

Then in the middle years of the fifth century heathen Germanic peoples, known generically to the British as Saxons, who had for long been troublesome pirates to the inhabitants of Britain, altered the nature of their intentions towards the island. The settlement proper began. By the end of the fifth century a firm foothold had been established along the eastern shores of Britain from the Humber and the Wash to the Thames Estuary and Kent. Sussex became a Saxon kingdom in the last quarter of the century. The whole movement was bound up politically with the slow consolidation of Frankish power in the north-east of Gaul, and possibly with the failure to set up a Saxon Normandy.

This initial advance was halted. At the battle of Mount Badon, fought at some time between the years 490 and 516, the invaders received a serious check. The first half of the sixth century was a time for consolidation. There was no hard and fast political frontier, and to talk in such terms is misleading. Perhaps the true significance of this period of uneasy balance is missed without an appreciation of the magnetic attraction of the coast in troubled times for Celt to the west as well as for German to the east. On the eastern coastal settlements, however, the Germanic peoples intensified their hold, welcoming new immigrants from the Continent and spawning off important new secondary settlements such as that of the Jutes in the Isle of Wight and South Hampshire, or that of the 'Men of the March' in the Middle Trent, the nucleus of historic Mercia, which appeared to gain coherence in the middle of the sixth century. In the Upper Thames valley the Saxons held their ground to form the main spearhead for political advance in the succeeding half-century. In the valley of the Warwickshire Avon there survived another important early sixth-century Germanic settlement which was to prove an important base for fresh advance.

Meanwhile in the west, Celtic tribal kingdoms sorted themselves out uneasily, losing their Romanic features though retaining, or possibly in many instances acquiring, the Christian faith. The intensification and consolidation of Christianity among the Celtic peoples under the impulse of a strong ascetic movement is a major characteristic of the whole period of political disaster. Nor were these kingdoms without political energy. The slowness of the Saxon advance and the tangled violence of the Celtic scene itself contradict such a view. It used to be held that the complex systems of earthworks known as Wansdyke (Woden's dyke) were the work of British communities facing the pressure of thriving Saxon populations from the Upper Thames. These fortifications, with their ditches to the north, stretched, impressively if intermittently, from the Kennet valley to near the Bristol Channel. Archaeologists now attribute the two major sections of Wansdyke to the pagan Saxons, probably in the later sixth century,[2] but it is evident that the British communities were quite capable of such effort. Gildas, writing to all appearance in the mid-sixth century, places the chief blame for the woes of Britain on the shoulders of the quarrelsome princes, on their lack of discipline rather than on their lack of resource or on their timidity.

Conditions in these islands cannot have been easy during this period. Procopius tells of reverse migrations back to the land of the Franks from the mysterious island of Brittia.[3] Traditions among the Old Saxons on the Continent deal with a movement of *Angli* from Britain to the Cuxhaven district about A.D. 531.[4] The colonization of Brittany by Celtic peoples from Britain was well under way by the end of the first half of the sixth century, and already by that date coherent groups from Devon and from Cornwall constituted an important element in the new Breton population.[5]

[2] Cyril and Aileen Fox, 'Wansdyke Reconsidered', *Archaeological Journal*, 1958; H. S. Green, 'Wansdyke: Excavations, 1966–70' W.A.M., vol.66,1971,pp.129–46. J. N. L. Myres, whose opinion demands respect, maintained to the end the likelihood that East Wansdyke was constructed by some sub-Roman authority, *The English Settlements*, Oxford, 1986, p.156.
[3] Procopius, *The Gothic War*, Book IV, c. 20; Loeb Classical Library, Procopius, vol.V, p.254. See below p. 27.
[4] H. M. Chadwick, *The Origin of the English Nation*, Cambridge, 1907, p.92.
[5] K. Jackson, *Language and History in Early Britain*, Edinburgh, 1953, pp.14–15, and on p.26, where he suggests that the south-west element was intensified by mass migrations in the latter half of the sixth century.

In the succeeding century, A.D. 550–650, occurred the main political advance, marked traditionally by the triumph of the West Saxons at the battle of Dyrham near Bath in 577, and by the battle of Chester, which was fought between 613 and 616, when the dwellers north of the Humber announced their political maturity. Under Penda (632–54), the settlers in the Midlands achieved similar consolidation. By the middle of the seventh century the England of the Heptarchy had received its major bold outlines. With Wessex, Mercia, Northumbria, the kingdoms which could still expand against the independent Celt, lay the political hope of the future. The achievements of St Augustine and his successors and the energy of the Celtic missionaries, particularly in the north, brought it about that most of the kingdoms of this new England were Christian, or subject to Christian influence, though Penda of Mercia himself remained a steadfast heathen.

Such in brief outline appears to be the accepted political pattern for these centuries. It is naturally subject to modification year by year as scholars throw emphasis on this or that facet of the evidence. At the moment the tendency is, if anything, to antedate the coming of the Saxons, to stress the fact that in Britain, as elsewhere in the Roman West, Germanic federate troops had settled, and that from their settlements around York, Lincoln, Cambridge, Caistor-by-Norwich, or Canterbury they prepared the way for slow infiltration by their countrymen quite early in the fifth century. Be this as it may, from the general picture there emerges one firm and undisputed fact that is of fundamental importance to a discussion of early Anglo-Saxon England. The Anglo-Saxon conquest and settlement of the lowlands of Britain was slow. The implications of this fact are great. If there is added to it the further fact that over much of England the Anglo-Saxons were agriculturalists rather than mere tribute-takers, a basis is given for understanding why these centuries saw the true foundation of England.

Yet vast problems remain. What happened to the native inhabitants, to the Romano-British as they may be called? Who were these newcomers that are labelled Anglo-Saxons? Why did they come? What stage of economic development had they reached, and what form of social organization did they bring with them? Is generalization possible at all about social structure or economic wealth in the kingdoms of the Heptarchy? Are the sweeping generalizations, Germanic tribal communities to the east, Celtic tribal communities to the west, no more than masks for ignorance? In fact the outlook is not as despairing and dark as we might think in face of the difficulties. A surprising amount of evidence is accumulating which enables something to be said of the variety of life and institutions in early Anglo-Saxon England.

2. THE CONTINUITY QUESTION

(a) Survival of inhabitants

There is first the question of the survival of native inhabitants. This is a desperately contentious problem, but on its solution rests a satisfactory interpretation of the institutions of early Anglo-Saxon England.[6] On one extreme it has been argued that the Anglo-Saxons came in great numbers, exterminating or at best driving westwards the unfortunate natives whom they met in the course of the migration. On the other extreme it has been argued that the Anglo-Saxons were few in number, consisting of aristocratic warriors and exalted free tribesmen, accompanied by few women, and imposing upon a large subject population of slaves and rustics the language, institutions and customs of a new military aristocracy. Neither of the two arguments is convincing in its entirety for the whole of England, though truth lies nearer to those who favour substantial Germanic migration with all its consequences than to those who stress the social importance of British survivors. The case against wholesale extermination rests primarily on interpretation of archaeological and place-name evidence. The case against wholesale survival of Britons in coherent social groups rests primarily upon the formidable evidence of the Anglo-Saxon language itself, which is singularly free from British influence. The smallness in number of words of British origin relating to agriculture or to domestic economy, to general household goods and services, is strong evidence against a substantial survival of British peasants and womenfolk in Anglo-Saxon England. Peasants in the North Riding at the end of the seventh century were accustomed to sing, and presumably to think and talk, in the English tongue. Felix in his early eighth-century account of the Life of St Guthlac emphasized that Guthlac did not learn his Celtic speech among the East Angles, nor by inference among the Middle Angles where he was brought

---

[6] A balanced view of the evidence, particularly of the implications of the place-name evidence, is given by R. Lennard, 'From Roman Britain to Anglo-Saxon England', *Wirtschaft und Kultur*, Festschrift ... Alfons Dopsch, Leipzig, 1938.

up.[7] Much of the most interesting work of the last decades has helped to emphasize regional differences and to fill in the picture of Britons surviving in greater number to the west of England than to the east, possibly in enclaves in the east, certainly as slaves throughout the island. It has not dislodged the traditional picture of a new society formed by Germanic migrants who were primarily interested in good land for permanent agrarian settlement.

Yet valuable conclusions have resulted from modern examination of British survival. For example, recent intensive concentration on the classification of place-names is making it clear that the predominant German did not set up his settlements, his *-hams* and his *-tons*, and possibly a shade later his *-ingas* and *-ingahams*, on an empty board. It is hard to find a single district of size without names, if only of large rivers, prominent natural features, hills or forests, or above all of Roman towns, that go back well beyond the fifth century. Towards the west names bearing a Celtic origin increase in number up to the true Celtic fringe on the Cornish boundary, on the borders of Wales and in the Cumbrian uplands. A purist indeed will justly object to the use of the term 'Celtic' in relation to these names: non-Germanic would be safer, and in regard to the Celtic world itself Brittonic or Goidelic more precise. Perhaps the homelier word 'British' is adequate in this context to describe the inhabitants of Roman Britain who spoke an Indo-European tongue which was already in the fifth century undergoing changes that were to lead to the evolution of Early Welsh, of Cumbrian, of Cornish and of Breton. It is clear enough that in English England the degree of such British survival varied from district to district. The problem is to arrive at some criterion by which the intensity of settlement and of native survival can be judged. In this respect the evidence of river-names is particularly helpful. Names of large rivers are among the most conservative of all place-name elements, and even in the areas of heavy and early Anglo-Saxon settlement big rivers such as the Thames and the Trent preserve their pre-Saxon names. On the other hand names of small rivers and above all names of streams are not so conservative. A new language-speaking group, if settled in strength, will quickly rename minor water-ways. The river-names can therefore, if handled with care, tell much about the settlement of the newcomers and about the survival of the former predominant language-group. Professor Jackson has constructed a map, based

[7] Bede, *Hist. Eccl.*, IV, 24; *Felix's Life of Saint Guthlac*, ed. B. Colgrave, p.110.

Certainly or probably Celtic
Possibly Celtic

British river–names

on this evidence, which enables three principal areas in the history of English settlement to be distinguished.[8] These divisions are so important that a description of them at this point will be helpful in giving some idea of the geography, and also a little more of the chronology, of the settlement, before turning to further discussion of its nature.

The first area in question consists of, in modern terms, England east of a line drawn from the Yorkshire Wolds to the east of Salis-

[8] K. Jackson, op. cit., p.220. The analysis of river-name evidence is of great importance in sorting out the three main settlement regions of England (pp.221–3).

bury Plain and so to the Hampshire coast near Southampton. Essentially it comprises the river valleys, save in their highest reaches, that drain from the highland spine of England into the sea between Flamborough Head and the Solent. It includes the East Riding of Yorkshire, Nottinghamshire, Leicestershire, Northamptonshire, Oxfordshire, East Berkshire and South Hampshire. Within this area British survivals are rare, and consist, as Professor Jackson points out, of large and medium-sized rivers which, together with the names of towns and of major geographical features, would probably have been familiar to the invaders from the very earliest days of settlement, if not by hearsay before. This area as a whole corresponds very well to a region of primary English settlement, that is to say to an area where Germanic-speaking peoples came to predominate in the course of the century, A.D. 450–550.

The second area is more indistinct, consisting of England west of the line mentioned above, and east of a line running(*a*) with the eastern borders of the modern shires in Cumberland, Westmoreland, and Lancashire to the Ribble, and thence south-west to the sea; (*b*) from Chester roughly along the Dee and the Severn to the Bristol Channel; (*c*) along the eastern border of Somerset, thence along the valley of the Wiley to the boundary between Dorset and Hampshire and so to the sea. Geographically this is the highland spine of England, from the Pennines to the Cotswolds, to Salisbury Plain and the valley of the Hampshire Avon.

Within this area British survivals are more numerous, including many more names of hills, forests and of small rivers, than in the first area. Politically it would correspond very well to the territory absorbed by the rising kingdoms of Wessex, Mercia and Northumbria in the period A.D. 550–650.

The third area consists of Cumberland, Westmorland and the greater part of Lancashire; the Welsh Marches; the south-west to the Tamar. There is also reason to include the wild country between the Tees and the Tyne in this group.

Within this area British water-names are especially common, even applying to small streams. For the main part the river-systems drain west in this area, a fact that may help to explain the late British-speaking predominance suggested by this evidence. But on political grounds alone such a predominance in this area would be expected throughout the seventh century, and indeed in the south-west to the early eighth century. There are more British habitation names in the region, and it may be more than coincidence that, on the Germanic side, the major -*sætan* (or -*sæte*) names are to be found here: *Wreocensætan* in Shropshire, *Magonsætan* in Herefordshire, *Sumorsætan* in Somerset. They may serve as reminders of large-scale colonizing movements of the seventh century. The presence of the *Cilternsætan* in the Chilterns would agree with this general hypothesis if indeed there were, as many suppose, a late survival of a British enclave in the deserts of the Chilterns.

In this third area the north-west provides the most interesting problem. There is a tendency nowadays to regard the battle of Chester as something of an isolated incident, and to throw the date of colonization of the north-west forward to the latter half of the seventh century, the greatest effort coming during the reigns of Oswald and Oswy (633–70) and coinciding with the reception of Christianity from Celtic sources.[9] There are no pagan Anglian place-names in the north-west. Yet by 685 Anglian political control was firm, and settlement of the lowlands well advanced.

To the west of this area lie Cornwall and Wales, including Monmouthshire and part of Herefordshire, where the river-names are overwhelmingly Celtic.

Such an analysis is helpful, particularly as it does correspond so well with the broad outline of the political pattern of the conquest and settlement. Of course it cannot tell anything approaching the full story of settlement or of the survival of British peoples. What it does show is that the relative predominance of the new-comers' language in place-names moves with the pace of conquest, and in the main with the intensity of settlement from east to west. But the nature of conquest itself varied from area to area, from valley to valley. There were occasional massacres of native inhabitants such as that recorded in 491 in the Anglo-Saxon Chronicle at *Andredes ceaster* (modern Pevensey). It is reasonable to suppose some movement of Celtic peoples westwards in the early stages of the conquest. But even in the most heavily Germanized areas there are traces, at times strong, of native inhabitants who survived and came to terms, attracted valleywards by force or by superior agricultural technique, or living possibly for generations in remote enclaves in forest, fen or hill. These traces are of variable quality and, as the following discussion will show, are capable of various interpretations.

From the kingdom of Kent comes the best written evidence for the survival of the native inhabitants as social inferiors. The Laws of

---

[9] K. Jackson, op. cit, pp.213–18. H. R. Loyn, 'The Conversion of the English to Christianity: Some comments on the Celtic Contribution', *Welsh Society and Nationhood* ed. R. R. Davies *et al.*, Cardiff, 1984, pp.5–18.

Ethelbert discuss the status of a whole range of unfree conditions, from the half-free, or *læt*, through a hierarchy of slavery. The word *læt* itself, unique in Anglo-Saxon law, corresponds to continental German legal terms used occasionally of subjected people of alien race. In the Chilterns around Wendover a significant cluster of British place-names suggests independent survival at least until the campaigns of the West Saxon Ceawlin in the 570s.[10] At St Albans in the eighth century the Saxon inhabitants were aware of their neighbour *Verulamium* which they knew under its ancient name of *Verlamacæstir* or under their own hybrid *Vaeclingacæstir* (i.e. the fortress of the followers of Wæcla). The name of the site *Verulamium* had been transmitted to them in a good form, but they also remembered the name of the permanent English group that settled this conspicuous site. If the river-name *Bene ficcan*, which appears in the Anglo-Saxon Chronicle for 913, means what it appears to mean, that is 'the little Bene', 'Bene fychan', with Welsh order and inflexion, then a British tongue was still familiar to some inhabitants of Hertfordshire well after the first phase of settlement was over and after the change in position of adjective had occurred in the British tongue.[11] Further north the evidence for survival in enclaves in the Fens and West Suffolk is less satisfactory, though there is some anthropological evidence used by Professor Fleure to suggest British survival in the Brandon area, and T. C. Lethbridge has listed a formidable array of potsherds, combs, tweezers and iron-working to suggest Romano-British survival in the Cambridge area.[12] The kings of East Anglia found it expedient at one stage to place Caesar as well as Woden among their remote ancestors.[13] But Felix, writing in the early eighth century, showed – as was mentioned above – that Guthlac could understand the *strimulentes loquelas* of the British-speaking demons who haunted him at Croyland only because he had spent some time in exile among British-speaking peoples.[14] There are peculiarities in Lincoln which may be explained by native survival: the Germanic kingdom of Lindsey took its name from ancient Lindum; and in 625 Paulinus, the missionary, was received by the *praefectus* of

[10] E. P. N. S., *Buckinghamshire*, pp.xii–xiii.
[11] E. P. N. S., *Hertfordshire*, pp.xv–xvi.
[12] H. J. Fleure, *The Races of England and Wales*, Oxford, 1922, p.20, and T. C. Lethbridge, 'The Anglo-Saxon Settlement in Eastern England', *Dark Age Britain*, ed. D. B. Harden, London, 1956, p.118.
[13] W. G. Searle, *Anglo-Saxon Bishops, Kings and Nobles*, Cambridge, 1889, p.254.
[14] *Felix's Life of Saint Guthlac*, ed. B. Colgrave, Cambridge, 1956, p.110.

11

Lindum, though *praefectus* is the term most frequently used to translate *gerefa*, or reeve, and would spring naturally to the mind of an Anglo-Saxon writing in Latin without any formal classical over-tones.[15] Further north again the Celtic kingdom of Elmet around modern Leeds was still a force to be reckoned with in the early seventh century, while to the far north the kingdom of Bernicia provides the clearest example of an Anglo-British kingdom, if similarities in later institutions to medieval Welsh parallels may be presented as evidence in this connection.[16] General divisions into geographical areas are no more than rough approximations when it comes to the question of the survival of peoples. Even within the first of the main areas mentioned above there may have been enclaves of British peoples in the sixth century. The evidence for the district to the north-west of London, in Hertfordshire and Buckinghamshire, is particularly interesting and unexpected.

There is need, however, to guard against a modern tendency to look for Celts under every stone. The most scientific and aloof of philologists and historians is not immune from currents of opinion, and it must be admitted that at present continuity is fashionable, abrupt break is not; survival of Celtic peoples, even if culturally negative, is fashionable, emphasis on pure Germanic is not. Yet Bede himself, echoing Gildas, in an impassioned, rhetorical ac-count of the evils that overtook the British at the hands of the pagan Saxons, told of survivors, doomed it is true to lifelong slavery, or eking out a wretched and fearful existence among the mountains, forests and crags, ever on the alert for danger.[17]

Where modern scholarship is making genuine advance is in its demonstration that place-name survival did not occur merely in a dead, fossilized form. If it had done so one would expect, for example, very much greater distortion of those town names and names of great natural features than actually occurred. Evidence is mounting for the transmission of British place-names to Anglo-Saxon during a bilingual period, and there are definite signs of bilingualism on the part of Britons who made their place-names known to the Saxons. Sound-substitution in British names adopted in English was extensive and regular, enough to suggest that the natives learned Anglo-Saxon thoroughly and accurately. Inflexions were understood and transmitted as in the case of British *Dobras*, the waters, to Anglo-Saxon *Dofras*, modern Dover. Acute analysis

[15] Bede, *Hist. Eccl.*, II, 16.
[16] J. E. A. Jolliffe, 'Northumbrian Institutions', *E. H. R.*, 1926
[17] Bede, *Hist. Eccl.*, I, 15.

of Latin–elements in Old English place-names is tending to support the case for a phase of overlap and even of controlled settlement in many areas.[18] Occasionally a straight translation was attempted and *Lann San Bregit* (Herefordshire) became Bridstow, though the lateness of date of the Celtic forms vitiates this evidence in relation to problems of early Anglo-Saxon settlement. No one would deny some bi-lingualism in Herefordshire in the eleventh century. On the other hand some names were passed on to new inhabitants clearly unaware of the meaning of common British words, and Pen (hill) becomes Pendle Hill (Lancashire) with two extra synonyms tacked on to it at different times for good measure.[19] It is important, too, in this connection to remember that, in spite of all the mass of evidence available, it is impossible to give anything like a complete picture of the historic development of place-name forms. Later Anglo-Saxon charters sometimes show British names that did not survive, such as *Susibre* in a Mercian charter of 718. In other instances some British names such as the river Coln did survive, though stretches of it at least were known at one stage in the settlement under the Saxon form *Tillath* or *Tillnoth*.[20] Indeed language evidence, and place-name forms fall into a special category of such evidence and can be a deceptive guide. The language is so Germanic in its final official form of tenth- and eleventh-century West Saxon that it is only too easy to forget the vagaries and the influences to which it was subjected during the centuries that were not so well recorded. Yet the earliest Anglo-Saxon records show no more trace of Celtic vocabulary than the late West-Saxon.

There is one vital language problem which still demands discussion. If it is assumed that the Romano-British population surviving into Anglo-Saxon England was considerable enough to influence the place-name structure, why did not their language influence the tongue of the Anglo-Saxon conquerors? The greatest linguists have examined and re-examined the problem. Max Forster, whose

---

[18] Margaret Gelling, 'English Place-names derived from the compound *wicham*', M. A., 11, 1967, pp.87–104; 'Latin loanwords in Old English Place-names', A. S. E. 6, 1977, pp.1–14. Names in -*wicham* are associated with settlements near Romano-British *vici*, those in -*funta* with watercourses with a possible surviving distinguishing physical construction. The elements *eccles*, *port*, and *camp* are also sensitively discussed.

[19] K. Jackson, op. cit., pp.241–6, a section of fundamental importance on the question of bilingualism. For Bridstow, p.244; Pendle Hill, p.245.

[20] H. P. R. Finberg, *Roman and Saxon Withington*, Leicester, 1955, c. xi, p.35. Both Susibre and Coln are discussed in relation to a 'prolonged bilingual period'.

Keltisches Wortgut im Englischen (Halle, 1921) remains the basis for investigation, found no more than fourteen common words taken from Romano-British to Anglo-Saxon, and of those four he held to be doubtful. Ekwall contributed two more, but the list is still miserably thin. *Ass, bannock, binn, bratt* (a pallium), *brock, carr* (a crag in dialect), *cumb, hog, luh* (sea), *toroc* (a stopper), with *dun* (colour), *mattock, beck*(hoe) and *gavelock* as doubtful. To these Ekwall would add *torr* (tor: a high rock or pile of rocks) and *funta* (a spring), though the latter survives only in recorded Saxon place-names.[21] Even in this limited company there is room for great dispute, and to take one example, the Oxford English Dictionary refuses to accept a British derivation for *hog*. It has been held that the high proportion of animal, natural feature and tool names tells something of the occupations of the British speakers, though this seems slender ground for the ascription of superior metal-work technique on the part of the British smiths. It is more accurate to say that the influence of the British tongues on Anglo-Saxon was extremely slight.

This does not mean that the languages did not come into close contact; place-name evidence alone is sufficient to dispose of such a proposition. It does suggest that the British tongue was markedly the social inferior. A Breton today keeps his French free from Breton words; his Breton is often interlarded with French. Frederick the Great, when he wrote in French, would use no German words; when he turned to German then the more French he could introduce the better he was pleased.[22] Relationship between languages is sometimes determined by social custom, by the way in which one language is regarded as the natural vehicle for things cultural, the other as the everyday popular speech, sometimes by the sheer political or economic mastery of one language-speaking group over another. In early Anglo-Saxon England the political mastery achieved by the Germanic new-comers was sufficient to account for the phenomenon. The Anglo-Saxon master would not use the strident argot of British underling or slave, and the relative purity of the Anglo-Saxon language further suggests that marriages between the newcomers and women speaking a British tongue were not of widespread or frequent occurrence. Children take to their mother's tongue, and common British words would

---

[21] F. Ekwall, *Englische Studien*, 1920, pp.102 ff. On *funta*, Margaret Gelling, 'Latin loanwords . . . ', cf. footnote 18, above.
[22] O. Jespersen, *Growth and Structure of the English Language*, Oxford, 1935, p.36.

quickly have intruded themselves into Anglo-Saxon if the invasions and settlement had been matter for companies overwhelmingly masculine in composition.

Tangible material evidence of British survival is still not easy to identify, though great advances have been and are being made in the techniques of classification of types of ornament, brooch and pottery, and the interpretation of artistic forms. As Professor Leeds said, in the course of his intensive monograph on the so-called 'small-long brooches', there is some archaeological material which can be explained only by an assumption of the continued existence of unexterminated natives: female, it must be confessed, not male.[23] Some enamel-work, some metal-work, some pottery also speak of survival. In the case of enamel-work and of hanging-bowls, some of the richest work culturally of the whole settlement period may be attributed to Celtic craftsmen, though whether peripatetic artists or genuine native survivors remains a question for dispute. There is certainly not enough evidence yet to displace the view that the bulk of native survivors into Anglo-Saxon England was 'culturally negative' – a massive euphemism if ever there were one.[24]

(b) Survival of institutions

Indeed if there were significant survival of Romano-British population, the social historian has to ask further what of their institutions, of the towns and villas of Roman Britain, of the hill-top farms and tribal organization that underlay the Roman covering, and an approach to this problem is needed even before turning to look at the Saxon conquerors themselves.

On one major point it is possible to speak with certainty. In contrast to the situation in Gaul the break in the continuity of town-life and villa-life was sharp and dramatic, even more clearly so with the villa than with the town. This is not to deny the possibility of continuity in habitation sites at places such as London or York or Cambridge. London was an obvious site, the lowest point at which the Thames could be easily crossed and bridged, and

---

[23] E. T. Leeds, 'The Settlement of the Anglo-Saxons, Archaeologically Considered', *Archaeologia*, 1945, p.4.
[24] J. N. L. Myres, 'The Present State of the Archaeological Evidence for the Anglo-Saxon Conquest', *History*, 1937, p.328, a view sustained in his final considered judgement, *The English Settlements*, especially ch.8 'Change and Decay', pp.202–19.

terminus of so many Roman roads. Its virtues to a people coming by sea can perhaps be exaggerated, and Lethbridge has asked, with some rhetoric but also with practical sailing experience in mind, 'if London had been completely destroyed why is it there today? It is a horrid port to make'![25] Canterbury, although it changed its name from Durovernum, is one attested site for continuity, probably as a federate headquarters. But it is altogether unlikely that organized town-life can have survived through the troubles of the fifth and sixth centuries. Gildas lamented the destruction of the twenty-eight cities of Britain, and there is no reason to doubt the essential truth of his statement. Withdraw the imperial economy of Rome and you withdraw the life-blood of urban institutions in the fifth century. Even in Roman Britain, towns appeared a shade exotic, owing their reason for being more to the military and administrative needs of Rome than to any economic virtue. Destruction may have come as much from internal as from external reasons. Without the industrial and commercial resources to maintain to the full an urban civilization, Britain lacked the resource to sustain the savage attacks of barbarians out for loot in the fourth as in the fifth century. When settlement came there was no room in the Germanic economy for the town, as the Romans conceived it. We do not forget, late poetic flourishes though they may be, references to towns as *eald enta geweorc*, the old work of giants. The absence of a continuous urban episcopate, in itself the institution most responsible for the survival of towns in Gaul, speaks against such survival in Britain.

The villa provides an even more extraordinary example of lack of continuity. It is ironical now to read in the important pages of Seebohm's *English Village Community* that the 'archaeological evidence, gradually accumulating as time goes on, points more and more clearly to the fact that our modern villages are often on their old Roman and sometimes pre-Roman sites – that however much the English invaders avoided the walled towns of Roman Britain, they certainly had no such antipathy to the occupation of its villas and rural villages'.[26] The accumulation of archaeological evidence over the last century or so appears at the moment the decisive factor which leads to a very different conclusion, namely that the Roman villa did not survive into Anglo-Saxon England. About five hundred villa sites are known in Roman Britain, some great elabo-

[25] T. C. Lethbridge, 'The Anglo-Saxon Settlement in Eastern England', *Dark Age Britain*, p.122.
[26] F. Seebohm (4th ed., 1905), p.436.

rate centres of industry and the focal points of substantial estates, others little more than modest country houses. Their divorce from urban life has been exaggerated. Most are within a comfortable distance of town or posting-station.[27] There is evidence to suggest that some villas at least had an official status, possibly as centres for the collection of *annona*. Villas were more closely integrated into the Roman system of tax, road and town than has always been realized. The idea of the villa as a retreat from decaying towns has distorted the true picture.

Over a large part of Gaul the villa survived as a country estate, though there are instances in areas of Frankish settlement of the villa building itself being used merely as stabling for the new Germanic hall. Ownership often changed, of course, in areas of heavy settlement, but villa names showed a surprising tenacity. The modern map, particularly of South and Central Gaul, is dotted with names of townships that trace unbroken descent from the name of their eponymous Gallo-Roman estate-owners. In England in violent contrast there is not a single instance of a villa name surviving the period of conquest. The inference is that neither the buildings, nor the type of agrarian and industrial organization they represented, appealed to the taste of the invaders.

This is a remarkable fact. In order to explain it there are many who hold that the villa economy did not survive the disastrous attacks made by the Picts in A.D. 367 and in succeeding years; there is strong archaeological evidence for early destruction and collapse. It may be that before the legions left, the Roman villa had failed. Certainly Gaulish agrarian unrest and suggestions of similar happenings here in the latter half of the fourth century indicate deep-rooted economic decay. Organized slavery is no satisfactory way to ensure permanent tillage of the soil in times when the discipline of the state is crumbling from inner corruption and external barbarian attack. Compromise between new Germanic political masters and old senatorial aristocracy and church alone served to preserve the vestiges of the classical villa over most of Gaul.

However, even in Britain there are areas where peculiar economic conditions may have ensured a greater degree of continuity. H. P. R. Finberg appears to have found evidence for one such district in his account of the estate of Withington in the Cotswolds,

[27] A. L. F. Rivet, 'Distribution of Roman Villas in England', *Archaeological News Letter*, vol. VI, no. 2, 1955. J. Percival, *The Roman Villa*, London, 1976, pp.91–105.

though not all will be convinced by his claims that the bounds of the Saxon estate were identical with those of the Roman villa.[28] The importance of the ranch type of sheep run in this area, combined with relatively favourable political conditions, may have ensured continuous occupation with only minor dislocations. But if this is so, the circumstances that brought it about were exceptional. Roman villa sites have been subject to rigorous archaeological investigation. The fact that the top layer, vital for the fifth century, is often unsealed makes the task exceptionally difficult, but even so the paucity of Saxon objects found on villa sites is striking. Until a short time ago it was said authoritatively that scarcely a single Saxon object had been found on such sites. Now, with increased awareness of the nature of the hybrid pottery brought to our notice by J. N. L. Myres, it is no longer possible to sustain quite so sweeping a statement.[29] Perhaps, too, a distinction needs to be made between the institution of the villa and the arable fields that were associated with them. Little is known of the agrarian history of the Roman villas in Britain, but from sites at Silchester, at Great Chesterford, at Twyford Down in Hampshire, and in Gloucestershire proof has been given of the existence of a heavy plough with broad ploughshare and large coulter in Roman Britain. It used to be thought on purely technical grounds that great fields, ploughed into long strips, would be necessarily associated with the possession of such an instrument, but modern opinion stresses the nature of the traction and the length of the yoke rather than merely the weight of the plough. F. G. Payne has argued that, yoked abreast, four or six oxen require no more headland space to turn in than is needed for two oxen, and that in Wales eight animals are known from the early laws to have worked abreast. He concludes that there is no evidence to suggest that the Anglo-Saxons could have brought with them better ploughs or more advanced ploughing techniques than those already in Britain.[30] There are those who would go further and look to the Roman villa in northern climes rather than to the German forest as the home of the great field and the heavy plough. It may be that, for all the decay of the villa as a

[28] *Roman and Saxon Withington*, cf. footnote 20, p.13 above.
[29] J. N. L. Myres, 'The Survival of the Roman Villa into the Dark Ages', *Archaeological News Letter*, vol. VI, no. 2, 1955, *Anglo-Saxon Pottery and the Settlement of England*, Oxford, 1969. C. J. Arnold, *Roman Britain to Saxon England*, London, 1984, pp.61–71: examples of Germanic settlers on smaller villa sites.
[30] F. G. Payne, 'The Plough in Ancient Britain', *Archaeological Journal*, 1947, pp.82–111, esp. p.86 and p.108.

building and as an economic institution, the agrarian inheritance in the shape of methods and field-systems was far from negligible from Roman villa to Saxon village. E. Barger, with negative caution, denied our authority 'for supposing that the Anglo-Saxon invaders, living in their own fashion in villages not far from the ruined buildings of villas, did not take over in their own way the fields of the villas'.[31] There is evidence that some late Roman ditched fields were taken over, possibly even as going concerns, by Saxon settlers or at the least could be identified as boundaries when the takeover took place.[32] Such a view would accord well with a general belief in significant survival of a subjected British peasantry. But the difficulties of accepting it also seem considerable. It is not easy to envisage the separation of the agrarian apparatus of a villa from its institutional life; the association of strip-farming with villas is conjectural and socially unconvincing; and it seems certain that the villa as a social institution did not survive the transition from Roman Britain to Anglo-Saxon England. Indeed the question most often discussed is whether it failed to survive into the last years of Roman Britain itself.

But both town and villa are to a measure symptoms of Romanism. They might well have failed to survive the fifth century even without the Anglo-Saxon settlement. In unconquered Britain, the more backward part of the island it is true, there is less evidence of town life than in Saxon Canterbury, less evidence of villa survival than near Gloucester's Chedworth. What of the straggling Celtic 'villages', the hamlets and farms with the small rectangular-shaped fields now so familiar from aerial photography, the agricultural settlements on the chalk hillsides with light soil and light ploughs to till it, the Celtic tribal communities which continued to exist under the control of Imperial Rome very much as if she were not?

Towards a solution of this problem modern archaeology, and above all aerial photography, has made an immense contribution. The basic generalization has been, for him who dares to generalize about this period, that the Saxon invasions saw a radical alteration in agrarian habits in these islands, that old settlements were abandoned and new settlements appeared on new sites. In Roman days farms and settlements tended to cling to the higher contour lines. Lighter soils were favoured. The field patterns show the typical small rectangular fields of the Celts. The plough was

[31] E. Barger, 'The Present Position of Studies in English Field Systems', *E. H. R.*, 1938, pp.406 and 410.
[32] *Early Land Allotment*, ed. H. C. Bowen and P. J. Fowler, B. A. R. 48, 1978.

19

light and, though Romano-British agriculture has not been without its zealous defenders, so also were the crops presumably light. In Anglo-Saxon days a very different situation presented itself. Farms and settlements moved to the valleys. Light gravelly soils were favoured in the early days of settlement, and the Saxon showed a general fondness for gently sloping land at no great height, but heavy clay was no longer an insuperable barrier. Skill, matured in the German forests, at clearing woodland and waste was early employed. Field systems show great open fields divided in a way to suggest communal enterprise such as that involved in clearing new land. The plough was heavy; so relatively were the crops.

Some of this picture is pure conjecture. There is a tendency to trace the Saxon open fields further back than the evidence would strictly allow, to read parallel continental developments as indications of basic primitive Germanic practice instead of as parallel developments of people with a similar forest-clearing background to a similar challenge, to fail to recognize the existence of a heavy plough in the Roman villa. But elements of truth it does contain. In some parts of Britain, the apparent transformation of the agrarian situation was remarkable and complete.

Over much of the south, particularly in the chalk districts of Wessex and Sussex for example, there was a clear-cut division between Romano-British agriculture and Anglo-Saxon. On Salisbury Plain and in much of Cranborne Chase the old sites were abandoned, and the land-hungry Saxons settled anew on land that suited them. The county boundary between Wiltshire and Dorsetshire passed very near two Romano-British settlements at Woodcuts Common and Bokerly Junction, yet both these settlements appear to have been neglected by the Saxon new-comers. The difference in disposition between Romano-British and Anglo-Saxon settlement has indeed been held to mark a fundamental change in settlement pattern.[33]

This change was held to be essentially from smaller and more scattered British village settlement to more compact Germanic settlement. However, with modern investigation showing that many settlements formerly regarded as villages were in fact farmsteads, the words 'Romano-British villages' are themselves becoming suspect and subject to much qualification. In the first instance at least the villa was no more than a Romanized farm, and the neat dichotomy between villa economy and Romano-British

---

[33] O. G. S. Crawford, 'Our Debt to Rome', *Antiquity*, 1928, pp.179–80.

village economy seems to be going the way of so many other generalizations that are useful in illumining temporarily a social situation but prove incapable of sustaining the weight of additional evidence. Yet it remains true to say, as far as can be judged, that agrarian settlements tended to be scattered and small among the native populations in Romano-British days. The Saxons on the other hand preferred and needed a more compact settlement with the open fields stemming off one main centre. But where agriculture in Roman days had been practised in the valleys, then examples of continuity may be found. In the Upper Thames such examples are not infrequent. Occasionally, as at Shaftesbury, the Saxons favoured an upland site, and there again continuity was assured. No one clears new land for the joy of it as long as there is enough suitable cleared land available. There are examples, revealed by aerial photography, of Saxon fields overlying Celtic. Arable strips are not, of course, sure proof of the presence of Saxons. At Twyford Down in Hampshire strip fields have been disclosed contiguous with Celtic fields laid out in their chess-board fashion. Pre-Saxon strip farming has been recognized at sites in Wessex, at Housesteads, and in Cumberland, Northumberland and South Scotland, though not all are prepared to accept this evidence.[34] Archaeologists in the eastern counties, in East Anglia and in Essex, have confirmed the simple, common-sense fact that where the soil suited, the Saxon turned to cleared land before fen and forest. In the Thames valley itself aerial photography shows heavy concentration of agriculture in the vital area to the north and west of Goring, with apparent continuity from the Bronze Age to Saxon times, and of course through to the present day. Most modern investigators have the uneasy feeling that there was more to Romano-British agriculture than concentration on the Wessex upland farms, themselves possibly marginal, would suggest. We just do not know how much evidence of lowland farming has been obliterated, or to say the least obscured, by the later activities of the Saxon ploughmen.

There may be a sound agrarian solution to the problem posed by the apparent break in continuity. The Saxon economy placed more emphasis on cereals, on oats, barley and ale. The Romano-British economy emphasized the mixed nature of farming, cereals to be sure, but also and supremely, sheep. The pastoral element in the

---

[34] E. Barger, op cit., p.391. A. L. F. Rivet, *Town and Country in Roman Britain*, London, 1958, p.122.

latter economy was stronger than that to which the newcomers were accustomed. On the other hand some have looked to a deeper geological explanation, holding that there was a great lowering of the general level of the water-table in the chalk districts of south England from Romano-British times onwards. At Woodcuts itself there is a strong possibility that the site was abandoned in the course of the fourth century. The Saxons coincided with and accelerated a drift to the valleys already in motion in Roman days, and it is probable that the acceleration was considerable south of the Thames. The scarcity of post-Roman objects and easily recognizable Saxon objects in the Romano-British 'villages' of Wessex has often been remarked on, and recent excavations have done little to alter this view in relation to the lands later occupied by the West Saxons. The stream of continuity seems to have been broken over much of the south.

In the rest of England the evidence is not so clear-cut, but the impression remains of new land taken in, of new patterns imposed on agrarian settlement. Along the Trent, along the War-wickshire Avon, in eastern England, in the Vale of York, the lines of entry marked by the tangible remains of heathen graves and early habitation sites tell of a valley-seeking people, less pastoral than the British, more concerned with heavy arable that could be tamed and protected. When at a later stage, in the seventh century, new country was opened up further west in Cumberland, early place-name forms suggest an attraction to similar low-lying country. The contour lines of early settlement were remarkably consistent.

From the evidence of final settlement it appears, too, that, ex-cept in Kent and possibly in Lincolnshire, Roman roads were not particularly important in setting out the lines of settlement; certainly not compared with the importance of the river valleys. Between Essex and Cambridge there is a strong probability that the Roman road system fell into complete disuse. The Fenlands which from the first to the third century had been open to a relatively intense British settlement, presumably under direct im-perial stimulus, were described by the biographer of St Guthlac early in the eighth century as a most dismal fen, beginning at the banks of the Granta, not far from the *castellum* at Cambridge, and stretching north to the sea. It consisted of marshes, bogs, black waters overhung by fog, studded with woody islands and traversed by the windings of tortuous streams.[35] Along stretches of the Trent

[35] *Felix's Life of Saint Guthlac'*, ed. B. Colgrave, pp.86–7.

and particularly in North Lincolnshire, however, there are signs of regularity in establishment of nucleated villages, about a mile from the Trent on each bank except at crossings, in Lincolnshire approximately a mile apart and a mile to a mile and a half from Ermine Street. Some have even suggested that there is evidence for planning by central authority at one time in the regularity of Lincolnshire settlement.[36]

So much at least can be said. In the face of an agrarian movement, more settlement than mere political conquest, the Celtic hill farm and village disappeared as an effective social institution over the greater part of England. It is likely that where the British farms survived near Saxon settlements they were attracted by and subordinated to the newcomers' methods, with their own remote farms eventually deserted and left to decay. Only where geographical conditions were favourable did they survive; in Bernicia where later social customs show close analogies to those of medieval Wales itself, in Cumberland where the Briton was dislodged from his hill farm not by Saxon in the seventh century but by Norwegian in the tenth.[37]

3. THE ANGLO-SAXON SETTLEMENT

(a) Origins and nature

In some respects, however, discussion of British survival runs ahead of the main line of argument concerning the settlement. It may well be held that there was no significant institutional survival from Romano-British times. What of the new-comers, the Anglo-Saxons themselves? Where did they come from, and what did they bring with them in the way of social and economic institutions?

On the question of origin there are moments when one looks in despair to the certainties of the nineteenth century, or better still to the certainties of Bede. Bede knew where the Anglo-Saxons came from. He tells us in precise terms. They came from three of the very formidable races of Germany, the Saxons, Angles and Jutes.

---

[36] W. Page, *'Notes on the Types of English Villages and their Distribution'*, *Antiquity*, 1927, p.457.
[37] J. E. A. Jolliffe, 'Northumbrian Institutions', *E. H. R.*, 1926; E. P. N. S., *Cumberland* (part III), p. xxii.

From the Jutes are descended the people of Kent and the *Victuarii*, that is the people who hold the Isle of Wight, and those in the province of Wessex opposite the Isle of Wight who are called Jutes to this day. From the Saxons, that is the country now known as Old Saxony, came the East, South and West Saxons. And from the Angles – that is the country known as Angulus which lies between the province of the Jutes and the Saxons, and remains unpopulated to this day – are descended the East and Middle Angles, the Mercians, all the Northumbrian peoples, that is those people living north of the river Humber, and other English peoples.[38]

Corroboration for this view of the homeland of the Angles is provided in the account of the journey of the Norwegian sea-farer Ohthere who, more than a century and a half after Bede wrote, reported to King Alfred that for two days before reaching Schleswig on a journey from the Oslo fjord, Jutland, Sillende and many islands lay on his starboard bow. Alfred himself commented that 'on these islands dwelt the *Engle* before they came hither'.[39] Bede, wise in his generation, hazards no guess as to the precise location of the Jutes.

In our generation we are more ambitious. We struggle for prevision, and want to know how, when, at what stage, in what numbers the settlers came. Language experts are unhappy at a picture that throws too much emphasis on the Danish peninsula, too little on the Frisian lands. Archaeologists agree that to under-emphasize the importance of the lands at the mouth of the Rhine would be to distort the true nature of the movement of Germanic peoples. Those most familiar with boat-building techniques feel that mass migration by sea could most plausibly have been effected from the Frisian lands; as late as 793 the good Alcuin was horrified at the incredible and unheard-of crossing of the North Sea by merely one well-armed raiding party of brutal young ruffians.[40] There is justification for the belief that Bede simplified, but there is no cause for serious complaint. Bede was concerned with the origins of the predominant groups of Germanic invaders as they hardened out within these islands. He answered his own questions according to his own evidence. Indeed, as Professor Jankuhn has shown, on the very important question of the origin of the Angles he is almost certainly right. Recent archaeological work has proved a heavy concentration of population in the province of Angeln in the third and fourth centuries A.D. The number of cemeteries,

[38] Bede, *Hist. Eccl.*, I, 15.
[39] *King Alfred's Orosius*, ed. H. Sweet, E. E. T. S., 1883, p.19.
[40] Alcuin to Ethelred, king of Northumbria, *E. H. D.* I, p.776.

a reasonable test of population, decreased sharply in the fifth century, a fact which would well accord with a movement west over land and sea.[41]

Perhaps the first point of departure from Bede comes with doubts concerning the homogeneity and integrity of the units with which he was primarily concerned. It is generally thought that the tribal kingdoms were made in England, and that only in rare instances is there likelihood of strong tribal groups maintaining their integrity unbroken from continental days. A sea-crossing is perilous to tribal institutions. The very names of the kingdoms are geographical: the dwellers north of the Humber or Northumbrians, the men of the March, or Mercians, the various groups of Angles and Saxons arranged according to alignment on the river-systems and watersheds. Only among the smaller groups, whose often obscure names are recorded in the Tribal Hidage,[42] such as the Gyrwe, dwellers in the Fens, who were taxed at the assessment of three hundred households in the eighth century, and who had been ruled by their own princes in the seventh, is approach made to the tribal basis of heathen Anglo-Saxon England. Even these groups probably represent no more than the chance amalgamation of kindreds and of lords and dependants brought about by the necessities of invasion and settlement. Similar groupings, normally on a smaller scale, consisting of dependants as well as blood-relations, offer the most intelligible explanation for our early *-ingas* names, such as those surviving in modern Hastings, Reading and Sonning.

These *-ingas* names are very good evidence for early settlement, though they need to be handled with special care.[43] Not all modern names ending in *-ing* or *-ingham* are of great antiquity. The suffix *-ing* in Old English had many meanings. It could be a diminutive; it retained the sense of 'son of'; it could mean 'the place of' as in *bremling*, the place where brambles grow, or in Clavering (Essex), the place where clover grows. Even in plural form *-ingas* does not always indicate early date. As late as the tenth century the inhabitants of the Five Boroughs were called *Fifburgingas*. Yet, particularly when compounded with a rare and ancient patronymic, the element *-ingas* often provides good reason for suggesting early settlement. Continental parallels help, and in

---

[41] H. Jankuhn, 'The Continental Home of the English', *Antiquity*, 1952.
[42] For this document, see below, pp.316–18.
[43] A. H. Smith, *English Place-Name Elements*, E. P. N. S., xxv, '-ingas'. An essential guide to an immensely complicated topic.

Gaul the equivalents of Old English -*ingas* are taken as proof of Germanic settlement in the fifth and sixth centuries. The custom of so naming places after a group of settlers died out early in historic times, and the switch in fashion from naming places after groups to naming places after individuals has considerable social implication. These groups in England of Hæsta's people, of Reada's people and so on, who gave their names to Hastings (the only English example to retain its plural inflexion into the modern period) to Reading, to Goring and to Wapping may well have constituted the basic social unit during the pagan and early Christian pe- riod though not the earliest. A fine, authoritative analysis by J. McNeal Dodgson has put our understanding of names in -*ingas* and -*ingaham* on a new basis. A close examination of topography and of the known distribution of pagan cemeteries has led him to conclude that the -*ingas* communities are most likely to represent a social development contemporary with a colonizing process later than, but soon after, the immigration settlements recorded in the early pagan cemeteries.[44] They give insight into the network of kindreds and of lords and dependants that lies behind the tribal generalities.

There are other features of the -*ingas* name which tell by in- ference of the nature of early Anglo-Saxon settlement. Their dis- tribution is significant; they are concentrated most heavily to the east and to the south-east of England, which on other grounds is presumed to have been an area of primary settlement. Within that area they vary both in nature and in density. J. N. L. Myres has drawn attention to the contrast provided by Sussex and Essex. In the former kingdom they are numerous and packed together. Sometimes three or four are found within the bounds of a single modern parish. In the latter there is one group, the Rodings, which is spread out over an area of twenty square miles, suggesting a scantily populated district slowly brought into cultivation over a considerable period of time.[45] A high proportion of -*ingas* names applies to settlements of some substance and importance. They suggest that the early settlers chose their sites well. They also give a glimpse of the intense effort of small local groups needed to consolidate the settlement, and hint at considerable diversity in the social organization of the earliest settlements, from the small

[44] J. McNeal Dodgson, 'The Significance of the Distribution of the English Place-Name in -*ingas*, *inga*- in South-east England', *M. A.* x, 1966, pp.1–29.
[45] J. N. L. Myres, *The English Settlements*, Oxford, 2nd ed., 1937, pp.375–6; also further thoughts, *The English Settlements* Oxford, 1986, pp.37–44.

compact villages of Sussex to the more widespread and diverse community of Sonning or Roding. He would be a bold man who would postulate racial homogeneity as a general characteristic of these -*ingas* groups of early Anglo-Saxon England.

From the Continent also the evidence for the amorphous nature of the peoples of the north-west increases from year to year. The Saxons, like the Franks, were composed of many small tribes. Bede tells how the Old Saxons as late as the eighth century were ruled by many *ealdormen*, and that only when going to war did they submit temporarily to the overlordship of a single war-chief.[46] It seems likely that they were fused into a loose unity during the migration period only by economic necessity, by the land-hunger recorded in the multiplication of habitation sites and cemeteries in the fourth and early fifth centuries, and by the spasmodic military cohesion imposed upon them as they advanced west in search of new homes. The difficulty of drawing a line of distinction between them and the Angles, who were presumably their direct neighbours to the east, is so great that there have been those who advocate free use of the word Anglo-Saxon even in the fifth century to describe the masses of Germanic peoples on the move in the north-west from the Elbe to the Rhine, ready for new ventures, seeking new lands to till, their great assets their experience as clearers of forest and swamp and their prowess in war.

Perhaps such an advocacy goes a little too far. The term 'Anglo-Saxon' sprang up in historic days to distinguish the insular Saxons from those who stayed behind in north-west Germany, from the Old Saxons. Its literal meaning should not be pressed at this early stage, useful though it is as a loose description of a variety of peoples. For, as shall be seen, there is some archaeological evidence to sustain Bede's concentration on the two main stocks of Angle and Saxon.

A second point of departure from Bede concerns the importance of the Frisian lands. Procopius, writing from Constantinople in the sixth century, gave a garbled account of north-west Europe, possibly an echo of a report by a Frankish ambassador or by an Angle in the ambassador's entourage.[47] Too much weight must not be put on the mixture of fact and fantasy in the account, but the

---

[46] *Hist. Eccl.*, V. 10.
[47] *The Gothic War*, Book IV, c.20; Loeb Classical Library, Procopius, vol. V, p.252 ff.; a pleasant discussion of the problem appears in P. N. Ure, *Justinian and his Age*, London, 1951, pp.246–8. I wish to thank Professor B. R. Rees for help with this reference.

core of the story – which gives it some historical importance – is the record, however confused, of a populous island named Brittia, from which migrations took place into Frankish lands, and in which dwelt peoples with the highly significant names of *Angiloi, Phrissones,* and *Brittones,* that is to say Angles, Frisians and Britons. It is true that Procopius himself made a rigid distinction between Brettania (his normal term for Britain) and Brittia, which he says lay opposite the mouth of the Rhine and between the islands of Britain and Thule, but mention of a wall in Brittia, and of the fertility of the east of the island, may suggest some deep confusion between Britain and the semi-mythical island of Brittia, to which indeed the souls of the dead were ferried, no doubt by Frisian boatmen. Snakes and adders, absent from Ireland, appear in abundance in western Brittia. It is perhaps only the apparently authentic combination of names, Angles, Frisians and Britons, which demands hard attention to this interlude in serious Byzantine discussion of the Gothic wars.

The importance of Frisia does not, however, rest on dubious documentary evidence. Archaeology, language-study, and common sense are all inclined to emphasize the importance of Frisia. The boats were available, the pressure of land-hunger was acute, terpen building – the beginnings of attempts to come to terms with an encroaching sea – had intensified as early as the fourth century A.D., and the journey across to England was relatively easy. Frisia was also an area directly in contact with the formidable Franks, slowly coalescing into the groups that in the early sixth century achieved political supremacy over most of Gaul. These Franks blocked the way west to their pressing, more barbarous Frisian and Saxon neighbours. In the Frisian lands, too, is to be found the language group closest akin to modern English. Even the mysterious Jutes, no matter what their ultimate origin, passed through Frisian lands if evidence for their close affinity with culture groups of the Middle Rhine is as striking as it appears to be. Students of institutions have pointed to parallels between medieval East Anglia and medieval Frisia.[48] The free peasant of East Anglia resembled closely his Frisian cousin, east over sea. Open-field farming in its fully developed form did not predominate in East Anglia as over the great swathe of the Midland plain. Family holdings were concentrated on particular parts of the

[48] G. C. Homans, 'The Frisians in East Anglia', Econ. H.R., 1957, pp.189–206. This interesting article appears to underestimate the strength of Scandinavian influence on East Anglia.

village fields; partible inheritance was near to the Frisian and for that matter to the Kentish model. Indeed East Anglia was closer in its social organization to Kent than to other Anglian territories, and close links with the mobile Frisians provide a possible explanation of the peculiarities of both these major regions of England.

But above all perhaps there is modern resistance to Bede's simple answer to a simple question on this matter of origins because of a growing awareness that the question itself is so far from simple. The movement of peoples to this island was slow and spread over several generations. In itself it was an organic part of a yet slower social process, the movement of the Germanic peoples to the west, the whole Folk-Wandering, which had as a climactic moment the fall of the Rhine frontier in A.D. 406, and which did not reach its consummation till Charles the Great extended his rule over the mass of Christianized continental Germans at the turn of the ninth century.

Conscious therefore of the shifting sands that underlie the confident ascriptions of pieces of territory to Tacitus' German tribes and their successors, the modern student is a little inclined to play for safety, to emphasize the mobility of the peoples in this period, to say that immigrants into these islands came from the whole stretch of coast from the Rhinemouth to Schleswig, possibly even from South Sweden, and that the Frisian lands played a vital part at the mouth of the Rhine, possibly as a temporary halting place for many of the groups before they took to the venture of the sea. England received the full attention of the north-west wing of the migration of German folks. Even so it would be carrying scholarly caution too far to deny that Angles and Saxons constituted the two main stocks of the Germanic peoples who settled in these islands, though it must be confessed that the literary, linguistic and institutional evidence at our disposal is not sufficient to make the line of distinction between Angle and Saxon uniformly clear.

Uncertainty about origins is intimately connected with the changing picture of the very nature of the invasions themselves. Gildas, and therefore Bede in this instance, told of federate troops called in to help the Romano-British against the Picts, of quarrels over pay, of treacherous desertion and apocalyptic disaster. Such is a perfectly reasonable picture, and in some areas, notably in Kent, there is no reason to dispute it. The very name Cantium, Cent or Centland, was retained to describe the new kingdom. When they renamed the chief city, the *metropolis*, as Bede called it, they could find no better name than the fortress of the dwellers

29

in Kent, the *Cantwara-burh*, though the fact of renaming in itself, of course, testifies to the predominance of Germanic-speaking peoples in the area. To the north, in the Vale of York, the kingdom of Deira may well have owned its origin to a similar federate settlement.[49] Some archaeological evidence points to the possibility of federate settlements on a much larger scale. The distribution of early Germanic pottery, which Myres terms Anglo-Frisian, outside important Roman centres such as York, Ancaster, Lincoln, Caistor-by-Norwich, is perfectly consistent with the establishment of a whole network of German mercenaries well placed to help against the Pictish menace.[50] A rough alternation of protection and looting while their kinsfolk settled the arable would be a plausible description of their relationship with the provincials. There is precedent in plenty for such a picture, on the Continent in the late fourth and early fifth centuries, in Britain itself where Alemani were settled in substantial numbers after the disastrous Pictish raids of A.D. 367. Indeed the closer definition of Romano-Saxon pottery discovered in or about the main centres of the Saxon Shore and its hinterland, at Caister-by-Yarmouth, Burgh Castle, Richborough, and Bradwell-on-Sea, suggests the presence of Germanic warriors on the eastern shores well before the end of the fourth century.[51] The presence of such federates would explain why so little has survived in tradition and legend of the capture of York or Lincoln, to say nothing of London.

Be this as it may, at some stage substantial bodies of newcomers, with or without federate allies, banded together to campaign against provincials presumably more British than Roman. Reference to a shadowy overlordship in the south-east in the late fifth century by Aelle of Sussex suggests initial military regional hegemony which, possibly after Mount Badon, split up into component parts. In the Midlands and the north similar commands may have sprung up during the early days of invasion when military leadership was at a premium. From these commands may easily have developed the ruling kins capable of moulding the motley collection of peoples, now predominantly Angle, now predominantly Saxon, into their historic shape. But the settlement itself – and this point cannot be

[49] P. Hunter Blair, 'The Origins of Northumbria', *Archaeologia Aeliana*, 1947, pp.41–3.
[50] T. C. Lethbridge, 'The Anglo-Saxon Settlement in Eastern England', *Dark Age Britain*, p.116.
[51] J. N. L. Myres, 'Romano-Saxon Pottery', *Dark Age Britain* pp.16–39, esp. pp.35–7 Oxford, 1969; *Anglo-Saxon Pottery and the Settlement of England*, pp.62–83.

overstressed – was agrarian in nature. Land for settlement, not loot from decadent provincials, was the prime object of the invaders. The contrast with Vandal North Africa, or Ostrogothic Italy, or the greater part of Gaul is violent and spectacular. The Anglo-Saxons were primarily tillers of the soil, not takers of tribute.

(b) Routes and areas of early settlement

Their chief routes of entry can still be traced by the archaeologist. The three main lines of settlement lay along the Thames valley, along the river systems that drained into the Wash, and through the Humber, particularly along the long winding line of the Trent that led south and west from the Humber down into what was to be the heartland of Mercian power in modern Staffordshire. It is possible to exaggerate the navigable quality of these rivers. It is not possible to exaggerate the importance of the river-valleys themselves as routes, and also as providing the most suitable soil for settlement. The whole Anglo-Saxon movement was essentially a river-valley settlement.

The tests of the early nature of settlement lie primarily in the discovery of objects in grave-sites, particularly brooches which are known to be typologically early; in the presence of heathen burial sites, above all in the practice of cremation; and in the presence of early place-name forms, such as the *-ingas* names referred to above or heathen names such as Harrow (from *hearh*, a heathen temple) or Wednesbury, Staffs (the *burh* of Woden). None of these tests is absolute in itself. Typological analysis, of grave-goods or place-names, though brought to a very fine point of technical perfection, cannot give the historian the chronological accuracy he craves for. The flight from cremation, which is so marked a characteristic of the settlement period, was conducted at different speeds in different areas. The dating of place-name types is an intricate process, though one can be reasonably sure of the attested names in *-ingas*, and that names in the genitive plural *-inga* and *-ham*, such as modern Hensingham, also suggest settlement at an early date. Even there, however, allowance must be made for regional peculiarities, some areas retaining an archaic place-name structure later than others. Yet sufficient coincidence of tests of early settlement occurs to allow some precision on the question of pattern of settlement. From the river-name evidence alone it is possible to distinguish the main regions, the more Germanic east and south-east, the highland spine of England with its stronger

Celtic survival, the mixed westerly settlement with stronger Celtic survival again as we move towards the borders of Cornwall, Wales and Cumbria. Further evidence permits a more detailed picture again which has a direct bearing on the later political geography of Anglo-Saxon England.

First and clearest to define are three coastal areas that bear many of the marks of early, even of fifth-century, settlement. They are the natural points of entry, serving as centres into which immigrants poured and from which further intensive settlement progressed. Conspicuous among the three is the lower Thames valley with the Sussex coast from which were formed in historic times the kingdoms of Kent, Sussex, Essex and Middlesex. Secondly there is the important line of entry through the Fens from which were formed the kingdoms of the Middle and the East Angles. Thirdly, to the north, was the basin of the Humber from which developed in early days the kingdoms of Deira and of Lindsey. Nowhere were these historic kingdoms completely homogeneous. They were made in England. Even in Sussex, the most compact and the last to retain its heathenism, the people of Hastings provide, not only in their name, evidence of separate identity. Kent itself, apart from the astonishing variety of grave-goods which proves the presence of at least two radically different Germanic peoples, was divided historically into two kingdoms, and in Christian days into two bishoprics. Middlesex, of which Surrey may have been the southern part, has left only its name to us; already by the seventh century it was incorporated into the kingdom of Essex. Further north the men of East Anglia were divided into a north and south folk, though the men of Deira and of Lindsey show signs of greater cohesion. The Middle Angles on the other hand were a regular hotch-potch, exhibiting the characteristics of a confederation of small groups from their earliest days.

Archaeologists have come to stress the importance of the territory occupied in historic days by the Middle Angles in the story of the early Anglo-Saxon settlement, as important in its way as the apparently more spectacular and better-chronicled exploits of the Germanic peoples in the Thames valley. This district, the drainage area of the Ouse, the Nene and the Welland into the Fens, corresponding roughly to the modern shires of Northampton, Huntington and Cambridge, was heavily settled in heathen times, to such an extent as to suggest the arrival of many small tribal groups. Yet even here variety in racial awareness is a characteristic, with significant groups of Saxons to offset the appearance of Anglian predominance. It may well be, as Sir Cyril Fox has suggested, that the dyke systems of Cambridgeshire represent early tribal boundaries between Germanic folks.[52]

In the three coastal areas settlement was early and settlement was intense. We are dealing with a migration. In law, institutions and language the German was firmly planted in the east.

More interesting, and much more unexpected, than the coastal settlements are the inland areas which show proof of early settlement. Three substantial groups are of particular importance in the political shaping of Anglo-Saxon England. First and foremost comes the settlement of the Upper Thames valley from Goring to Oxford, in the modern shires of Berkshire and Oxfordshire, with Dorchester-on-Thames as the focal point. The archaeologist can prove that here there was early pre-500 settlement, and that the Saxon tribesmen settled in force. This Upper Thames settlement became the heartland of the greatest of all Anglo-Saxon political units, the kingdom of Wessex. The second inland area is later in date, probably not fully stable until the mid-sixth century, extending along the Middle and Upper Trent beyond Newark and Nottingham, stemming for the most part from the settlements on the Humber with a strong admixture of Germanic peoples from the Middle Angles. This settlement formed the basis of the powerful confederation that was to consolidate the central English plain in the seventh century under the name of Mercia. The third inland area of early settlement lies between the two main groups, on the Warwickshire Avon. It was settled by the Saxons of the Thames valley in the first instance, though it certainly received a strong Anglian admixture at an early stage. Its recorded history is obscure, but its major task is clear enough. This group, settled on the Warwickshire Avon, directed the advance to the west and the Severn valley. They created the kingdom of the Hwicce, a kingdom overshadowed by the rise of Mercian authority, but which at its height probably stretched from Worcester to Wychwood in Oxfordshire. A sub-kingdom under West Saxon control in the early seventh century, the land of the Hwicce passed under Mercian lordship in 628.

On the composition of these inland 'nuclear areas' it has been suggested that there is a great contrast between them and the coastal settlements.[53] The former, it has been held, represent es-

[52] *Archaeology of the Cambridge Region, Cambridge*, 1923, pp.392–3.
[53] S. W. Woolridge, 'The Anglo-Saxon Settlement', *Historical Geography of England*, ed. H. C. Darby, London, 1936, p.123.

sentially the survivors of war-bands living on terms, if not in amity, with the native inhabitants, while the latter represent more purely Germanic creations, constantly reinforced by immigration from overseas. That there is a measure of truth in this picture is hard to deny. Common sense would speak of the importance of constant reinforcement to the reception areas on the coast, and the contrast between coastal and inland fits well with the evidence to be drawn from the place-name structure. But there is a danger of underestimating the number of settlers concerned in these inland groups. Certainly in the Upper Thames evidence of pagan settlement is sufficient to suggest colonization in large numbers at a very early stage.

Awareness of this concentration of settlement on the Upper Thames has provided one of the formative historical problems for the last generation. Here was a clear-cut case where archaeological evidence clashed with the documentary evidence of the Anglo-Saxon Chronicle. The Chronicle attributed the foundation of Wessex to the landing of Cerdic and his three ships on the Hampshire coast in the early sixth century.[54] A series of campaigns was then outlined, giving details of a hard struggle through Hampshire and Wiltshire to the Thames. To the archaeologist this did not make sense. His evidence pointed to a line of entry for the so-called West Saxons from the Wash along the ancient track known as Icknield Way into the Upper Thames. There was also a possibility, made plausible by the alignment of East Saxon, Middle Saxon, and West Saxon, that the Thames itself provided a major means of entry. A lacuna in evidence of early finds on the Middle Thames made some unwilling to accept the alternative route, but the negative evidence was not insuperable. On the other hand there was no intelligible likelihood of a mass movement from the south coast to the Thames such as had been inferred by some from the Chronicle account. Hampshire and Wiltshire are both shires well known to the archaeologist and both are singularly unproductive in finds suggestive of early Anglo-Saxon settlement. The solution of this problem which is now generally accepted is that the Chronicle relates the story of a ruling kin, while the archaeologist reveals the mass of settlement. Cerdic and his kin, a warrior band, fought their own way north but achieved their

[54] The Chronicle first mentions Cerdic's arrival in the annal for 495, but F. M. Stenton, *Anglo-Saxon England*, pp.19–25, gives evidence of double entries of single events in the Chronicle which suggests an early sixth-century date for Cerdic's landing.

historic mission when they welded the heavy concentration of Saxon settlers on the Upper Thames into the kingdom of the West Saxons. The crucial political events occurred in the reigns of Cuthwine and Ceawlin in the second half of the sixth century when successful campaigns were waged, first against British enclaves to the north-east in the Chilterns, then in 577 to the west when the capture of Gloucester, Cirencester and Bath opened the way for the steady movement to the south-west. This movement which brought the West Saxon kingdom to the Tamar early in the eighth century, laid the economic basis of the strength of Wessex, and gave a prime reason for her leadership in England in the following centuries. The success of this expansion to the south-west, coupled with the loss of lands north of the Thames to Mercia in the eighth century led to a somewhat distorted picture of the origins of their nation at the West Saxon court itself.

On the Mercian nucleus there is not the same measure of agreement. It does appear, however, that a *modus vivendi* was successfully reached with the Celtic peoples. Indeed evidence of trade along the Severn valley is steadily increasing. It may be that the Cotswold-Severn area remained an important 'bastion of Romano-Celtic culture' for the first three quarters of the sixth century. Metal-work of sub-Roman or Irish origin reached the Saxon midlands in good quantities. H. N. Savory even puts forward the suggestion – and there is nothing intrinsically implausible about it – that survivors of settlers after Mount Badon may have taken service under Celtic princes.[55] Such an hypothesis would at least explain the nature of the Warwickshire Avon settlement which otherwise intrudes into the geographical picture like a sore thumb. When Penda in the seventh century built his greater Mercia, mostly at the expense of his fellow Germanic peoples, above all by a savage thrusting-back of intrusive Northumbrian power, he did so with the active help and co-operation of British kings. When he marched to his final campaign and death at Winwæd Heath, he was accompanied by thirty war-leaders, some drawn from other Midland folk, including the king of the East Angles, but others Welsh princes.

The Mercian nucleus at all events gave opportunity to the settlements further east to thrive. It fulfilled the function of a March. Along the valley of the Trent in our modern shires of Derbyshire and Nottinghamshire early settlement appears to have been con-

---

[55] H. N. Savory, 'Some Sub-Romano-British Brooches from South Wales', *Dark Age Britain*, pp.56–8.

fined to the river-valley, expansion into the heavy forest of Sher-wood for example not coming until the seventh or eighth century at the earliest. In Leicestershire, apart from the valley of the Soar, there is little trace of intensification of settlement in the sixth century, but further east in Northamptonshire, Cambridgeshire and East Anglia there was heavy settlement, and it is reasonable to suppose that in turn, the expansion to the west was helped and hastened by an increase in population in the lands of the Middle Angles and of East Angles.

North of the Humber the situation was interesting. The East Riding of Yorkshire and the Vale of York itself were settled early and thoroughly. From this district came the slave-boys seen and questioned by Pope Gregory in the Roman slave-market. Deira was the name of their kingdom, and *de ira dei* the good Gregory promised to redeem them.[56] Yet the unmistakably British kingdom of Elmet remained its near neighbour in the upper reaches of Wharfe and Aire, around the modern city of Leeds. Further to the north in the middle of the sixth century, to be reckoned as part and parcel of the movement of expansion that followed the period of consolidation, there was established yet a further nucleus of Anglo-Saxon settlement, probably from Deira but just possibly from further south, around the grim rock of Bamborough and in the valleys of Tyne and Tees. The complex archaeology of Yeavering at the entrance to the Cheviots strengthens the hypothesis that the kingdom of Bernicia was primarily the creation of political conquest, and can indeed be interpreted as evidence for the relatively peaceful assumption by Germanic rulers of lordship over a British aristocracy and peoples. The strategic position of the royal halls at Yeavering, with a grandstand shaped like a *cuneus* of a Roman amphitheatre, fits with a tribute-taker's fortress rather than an administrative centre for an agrarian community.[57] Pastoral farming must have predominated in the lands of the Cheviots though where the coastal plain gave arable there the Germanic peoples settled. The union of this bare upland kingdom with the more populous and prosperous Deira set Northumbria on its path to greatness in the seventh century. When the men from the north marched to free Britain from the Saxon in the last decades of the sixth century, they ignored the Bernicians and made their great

[56] *Hist. Eccl.*, II, 1.
[57] B. Hope-Taylor, *Yeavering: an Anglo-British centre of early Northumbria*, H. M. S. O. 1977 (1979), a readable and vastly important report by the director of excavations at this key site.

effort against Deira.[58] At Catterick they fell. But it is possible that a strong British element remained in the Northumbrian kingdom, east as well as west of the Pennines.

Concentration on these areas of intense and early settlement gives a sounder impression of the somewhat fitful colonization movement from specially favoured settlements than any account of swift-moving armies and battles for political predominance. The making even of early Anglo-Saxon England was a big enterprise, involving considerable stretches of country and a long period of time. Unified command of the whole enterprise at any one stage is unlikely. Even for the very earliest ventures which resulted in the establishment of successive footholds in Deira, the Fenlands and the Thames, an overall unified authority is not seriously to be considered. A strong probability remains, however, that before the consolidation of the kingdoms unified regional commands were common. Archaeological similarities between Surrey and Sussex, in spite of the difficulties of the forest country separating them, help to substantiate the claim of Aelle the South Saxon to be the first *Bretwalda* in the Thames valley. Such regional commands were probably not long-lasting. Variety in the intensity of settlement itself would lead to variety in political predominance among the groups of settlers. Where pagan cemeteries are thick on the ground and cremation retained late, a larger group of warrior-farmers may have settled, resisting, as Myres puts it, the leaven of the British. But archaeologists cannot always point to such groups in places where on political grounds we might expect them. Essex, apart from the great site at Mucking, is poor in archaeological remains, a poverty which is accounted for in part by the presence of so much wood and waste and marsh in the Essex topography. On the other hand Essex contains many place-names of early form, and rose to be a dominant political power in the early seventh century. Energetic military leadership capable of controlling London, Middlesex and parts of eastern Hertfordshire may have led the East Saxons to their brief moment of success. In the northern Home Counties, in the modern shires of Buckinghamshire, Bedfordshire, and Hertfordshire, place-names indicate a slow settlement, of a secondary nature, proceeding from the major river valleys to the north and to the south. Consolidation of the Lower Thames valley and of the Cambridge region preceded expansion in this area. As so often the story of Anglo-Saxon settlement, when

[58] A point made by K. Jackson, op.cit., p.213.

looked at in depth, yields more of the saga of man against forest than of Saxon against Celt. It was a colonizing movement in the true sense of the word. Where soil was suitable settlement took root, and slowly extended the rule of the plough over cleared lands. Regional commands were ephemeral. In the south-east and to a considerable extent all along the eastern seaboard, it was the smaller historic kingdoms that drew the loyalties of the newly settled agrarian communities.

(c) Angles, Saxons and Jutes

Finally, on the problems of early settlement a word is needed once again on the traditional divisions of the English settlers into Angle, Saxon and Jute. For all the reservations and hesitations the modern student comes back to Bede's definitions with a recognition that there is reality behind them. As far as language peculiarities are concerned, use is made quite freely of distinctions between Anglian and Saxon, though linguistically at least these peculiarities were evolved within these islands. In Oxfordshire, for example, marked Anglian influence can be seen in place-names in a strip of country some two-and-a half to three miles from the western boundary of the county.[59] It has been held with justice that this is further indication of strong Anglian influence in the people of the Hwicce. Attempts have been made to show that some personal names are distinctively Anglian, others distinctively Saxon. Most important of all is the contribution of E. T. Leeds to a solution of this problem. His essay, 'The Distribution of the Angles and Saxons, Archaeologically Considered', was based on an intensive examination of brooches of the fifth and sixth centuries, especially of the small-long brooches.[60] He was able to show by means of a magnificent series of maps that there is a marked difference in the distribution of the various types of brooch, indicating regional peculiarities that may stem from a variation in racial origin, or from tribal peculiarities which existed when the Angles and Saxons still dwelt on the Continent. For example, cruciform brooches appear characteristic of the group known historically as Anglian; saucer and applied brooches appear Saxon. Taking such criteria he provided a composite picture of a rough frontier between Angles and Saxons, although he stated clearly that in the earliest days of

[59] E. P. N. S., *Oxfordshire* (part I), p.xix.
[60] *Archaeologia*, 1945, pp.1–107.

invasion 'one is hardly justified in speaking of any particular part
of the whole area south of the Wash, and this may be true further
north, as specifically Anglian or Saxon'.[61] The Cambridge area,
which in production and development of the small-long brooch
played a dominant part, is particularly mixed. From it, however,
he projected a line along the Via Devana to Godmanchester and
thence beyond the Ouse along the Roman road towards Leicester.
The line did not reach Leicester, but near Rothwell in Northamptonshire, that is between the tributaries of the Nene and the
headwaters of the Warwickshire Avon, it swung west to the Severn
between the Avon and the tributaries of the Trent. 'This is, on the
evidence of the brooches, the Anglo-Saxon line'.[62]

Carrying the analysis further he showed that there is considerable overlap, that the Anglian admixture south of his line is
strong, that the Saxon elements in Cambridgeshire only gradually
lost ground, heavy Anglicization having occurred in the latter half
of the sixth century. Some corroboration is given to the view
that the Cambridgeshire dykes were tribal boundaries of the pagan period; some evidence is given of inter-tribal warfare in the
skeletal remains found at Bran Ditch on the Icknield Way; the
Icknield Way itself formed the main route for the West Saxons
who moved along it from Cambridgeshire to their home in the
Upper Thames.

E. T. Leeds therefore accepted and, within the limits of his type
of archaeological evidence, confirmed Bede's general attribution
of, at all events, predominant stocks to the various kingdoms of
England. In so doing he looked back behind the formal outlines
of the Heptarchy to a time when the groups were coalescing and
before the regional peculiarities were fully stabilized. The presence of a strong Saxon element and the presence of at least a
strong Anglian element in the Hwicce suggest that side by side
with larger groups that eventually predominate there also existed
smaller groups drawn from the land-hungry population of North
Germany. The peoples of England fell into their historic heptarchic
pattern during the two centuries of settlement. Stocks, Anglian or
Saxon, came to predominate socially in each of the areas out of
which were carved the kingdoms. Beyond this broad general division it is doubtful if one can move further towards homogeneity.

Most difficult of all the racial questions that vex the student of
this period is the problem of the Jutes. It is known that Kent was

61 Ibid., p.78.
62 Ibid., p.80.

39

different. Indeed the difference of Kent from the rest of England is a constant theme of English social history. Kent was also conscious of its individuality, and in historic times used a Jutish ancestry to explain it. Other groups felt the same difference, and reached the same conclusion about their origin. Bede tells of Jutes in the Isle of Wight and South Hampshire. Archaeologists confirm that similarities in grave-finds suggest affinity to Kent in these districts, and that the Meon Valley and the Isle of Wight probably represent areas of secondary settlement from a Kentish base. As late as the twelfth century Florence of Worcester (*sub anno* 1100) refers to the New Forest which in the tongue of the English is called Ytene, i.e. 'Jutish' or 'of the Jutes'. But straightway there must be dismissed any notion of a coherent tribal group fresh from Jutland, or even of such a group that had lingered near the Middle Rhine on its long journey from Jutland to Kent. In no area of England is the evidence for the presence of diverse cultures so clear-cut and definite as in Kent. If only the chronology of the cultures was equally clear-cut there would be no 'Jutish problem'.

The most rewarding approach to the question still lies in the pages of J. N. L. Myres who, basing his analysis on material from the Kentish cemeteries, enabled us to "distinguish at least two principal cultures and several minor groups". The first of these, by no means homogeneous, and with several related sub-groups, was much of a piece with other grave-finds that may be attributed elsewhere to the earliest phase of settlement. Cremation was still occasionally practised, and their material equipment, pottery and brooches, suggests affinities both with Saxons and Frisians. The other culture is a different matter 'marked by inhumation, by wheel-made pottery of sub-Roman character and strongly Frankish technique, by the use of precious metals, garnets, glass, crystal, shells, amethyst beads and other luxuries in personal adornment, and by a skilful employment of enamel, niello and filigree techniques unparalleled in any other part of Britain'.[63] The poorer of the two cultures is represented mainly in settlements on the north coast of Kent along the Thames estuary, though more recent excavations at Canterbury have shown traces of their presence there. The richer culture, which is thought of inevitably as typically Kentish, is stronger in the Isle of Thanet and along the line of

---

[63] J. N. L. Myres, *The English Settlements*, p.361, Oxford History of England; and in richer form in *The English Settlements*, ch.8, Oxford, 1986, with further emphasis on the importance of the *Litus Saxonicum* as a determining factor in the nature of the Germanic settlement in south-east Britain.

Watling Street, exhibiting a more barbaric strain in Thanet, a more 'delicate and luxurious' tradition in the vicinity of Watling Street.

It used to be assumed that the poorer culture was the earlier, but it is more likely that the two main cultures overlapped, the richer representing the remains of federates and their successors, the poorer the remains of immigrants drawn mostly from Saxon and Frisian stock, setting up farmsteads under the protection of a warrior-aristocracy. It is also clear that pagan archaeology in West Kent tends to be poorer than that of the east with links to cemeteries in Surrey and Essex. Attempts to establish a firm chronology have not been completely successful. E. T. Leeds advanced one possible sequence which, modified by C. F. C. Hawkes and later scholars, fits well with the material evidence though is suspect in relation to racial terminology.[64] This would suggest a Jutish phase extending over the first two or three generations of settlement, characterized by considerable advance in skills notably in the Isle of Thanet, and followed by a Frankish phase from about 525 to at least the end of the reign of Ethelbert, in 616. The richest products of Kentish culture, including the finest jewellery, would then fall into place to coincide with the rise to political predominance of the Kentish kingdom under Ethelbert (560–616), and continuing well into the seventh century. Following this line it is tempting then to associate Ethelbert's prestige with the consolidation of a Kentish kingdom along the Thames estuary, taking in West Kent as far as London from an originally federate base in East Kent, the Isle of Thanet and Canterbury.

A critical unsolved problem of Kentish history lies in this so-called 'Frankish' phase and in the relationship of the Franks to the settlement of Kent. Similarities in material culture, and also similarities in institutional development, between Kent and the district from Dusseldorf to Coblenz are so close that it has even been held that the bulk of settlers in Kent were Ripuarian Franks led by a Jutish/Frisian aristocracy. There are difficulties in accepting this view. It is odd that some breath of tradition has not come down relating to Frankish provenance. The Franks were proud of their race and, as they triumphed on the Continent, one would expect some reference on one side or other of the

[64] C. F. C. Hawkes, 'The Jutes of Kent', *Dark Age Britain*, pp.91–111. Also a rejoinder in the posthumous note by E. T. Leeds, 'Jutish Art in Kent', *Medieval Archaeology*, vol. 1 (1957), 1958, pp.5–26, and a note in the same volume, p.173, by H. Arbman, drawing attention to the uncertainties of Continental typological chronology upon which some of Professor Hawkes's conclusions are based.

Channel to so spectacular an exploit as the settlement of Kent
if it had indeed been a Frankish venture. Instead tradition takes
us back consistently to Hengest, a Jutish leader of federates, and
archaeology emphasizes the diversity of settlement. It may be that
the importance of trade with Frankia in the sixth century has been
consistently underestimated, so distorting the view of the nature
of the settlement itself. On the other hand, the case for material
relationship with the Franks by trade would not be weakened by
the presence of actual Franks settled in Kent.

The hub of the problem lies in the interpretation of the institutional evidence originally presented by J. E. A. Jolliffe and
further analysed, with rejection of some of his conclusions, by K.
P. Witney and N. P. Brooks.[65] Drawing his material, of necessity,
from a later period, Jolliffe argued that the dominant note in the
social structure of Kent was radically different from that elsewhere
in England, save for a Kentish fringe in Surrey and Sussex, and in
South Hampshire. To these areas some modern investigators are
now inclined to add East Anglia. The unit of settlement was the
hamlet of free peasant cultivators, not the nucleated village. The
unit of cultivation was the ploughland tenement and the custom of
tenure was the common right of kindred in *gavelkind* inheritance.
Administratively the Kentish *lathe*, each with its *villa regalis* at the
centre and each with its share in the forest of the Weald, was
the dominant institution. In detail Jolliffe's interpretation of the
lathes of Domesday Book has been shown to be faulty, notably
his attempts to uncover a primitive yet enduring tax system of
substantial regularity, 80 sulungs to the lathe; but his suggestion
that the administrative structures of the historic kingdom of Kent
owed something to sub-Roman arrangements has proved helpful.
Joliffe was able further to comment on a marked similarity between
the Kentish social scene and that in parts of the Rhineland, even the
relation of the *wergeld* or blood-price of noble and ordinary freeman bearing the same proportion of three to one. The possibility
that these institutional peculiarities may be attributed to a powerful
substratum of Celts is particularly attractive on the Kentish scene,
and is supported in some measure by the complexity of the social
scene revealed to us in the earliest legal codes. But the further
problem is then raised that Celtic influence may have been present

[65] J. E. A. Jolliffe, *Pre-Feudal England: The Jutes*, Oxford, 1933. K. P. Witney,
Kingdom of Kent, 1982. N. P. Brooks, 'The Creation and early structure of
the kingdom of Kent', *The Origins of Anglo-Saxon Kingdoms*, ed. Steven Bassett,
Leicester, 1989, pp.55–74.

in the immigrants even before they settled: the Istevonian Franks having a stronger leaven of the Celt than the Herminones of the Elbe or the Ingaevones of the North.

There is danger, however, in attributing to racial causes what can be better explained on economic grounds. Even the most backward settlers would benefit quickly from the richness of the soil of Kent and from its proximity to the Continent. This proximity was coupled with excellent communication from the Channel ports to the Thames estuary. Watling Street in Kent, unlike so many other stretches of Roman road, proved an attractive means of ingress to the Germanic migrants. As the settlements in the Thames estuary were consolidated, so did opportunity increase for the adventurous packman from Frankish cultural circles. The archaeological case for the presence of Franks in Kent rests in large part on material goods which may have been transmitted as merchandise, as marriage gifts or as ceremonial presents from Frankish ruler to Kentish prince. There is a growing body of evidence for such intercourse in the fifth and sixth centuries between north Gaul and Kent.

It is important also to remember that Kent early achieved a measure of political stability. The story of federates rebelling against their paymasters is plausible, and the possibility that more of the structure of the 'Roman-Britain of the tyrants' survived in Kent than elsewhere is not unlikely, and that the Anglo-Saxon kingdom was formed, as Nicholas Brooks has expressed it, 'not simply by the coalescing of groups of English settlers'.[66] Brooks has also advanced a plausible explanation of the problem of the lathes by suggesting that the four lathes of East Kent (based historically on Wye, Canterbury, Lympne and Eastry) may represent divisions present from the very earliest days of the kingdom or even earlier, while the more amorphous arrangements of the West (a possible three lathes dependent initially on Rochester) may preserve something of the structure of late sixth-century conditions as Ethelbert took over. Be that as it may the new dynasty, proud of descent from Hengest, regarded itself as Jutish, and that in itself was sufficient to give a label to a multi-racial community, consisting of subjugated provincials, Saxons with their typical saucer-brooches, Frisians, possibly some Franks, probably many Jutes. In Hampshire and the Isle of Wight Kentish men led by royal princes carried on the 'Jutish' tradition. But the relative wealth and prosperity of the first English kingdom to welcome Christian missionaries were made in

[66] N. P. Brooks, 'The creation and early structure of the kingdom of Kent', p.57.

Kent. Resemblance to Ripuarian Franks may then be due to direct trading contact and, as regards institutions, to a similarity in the rate of economic and social development. The hamlet-type society of Kent may owe its predominant position to the simple fact that from very early days cultivation of arable and defence of nucleated village was less essential to the survival of the community than was the case elsewhere. Relative political security and contact overseas with Frankia may be the real key to many Kentish puzzles.

(d) Stage of development

Such speculations lead to a discussion of a fundamental point in relation to the settlement. What stage of economic and cultural development had these settlers reached? The first impression is of tremendous decline from the days of Roman Britain, a decline not to be explained solely by the fact that the Romans built in stone and the Saxons in wood. This impression is correct, although a fair contrast would demand concentration on Roman-British rural society as against Saxon settlement, or on the poverty and devastation of the early fifth century rather than on the town and villa in the heyday of Empire. J. N. L. Myres long ago stated forcibly that the settlers were illiterate and economically in a very primitive condition, that they left no inscriptions, in marked contrast to the Celtic peoples of the west, and that they used no coinage.[67] All this is true, but there is a danger of exaggerating the primitive nature of their economy. They lacked the trappings of Romanic civilization, but they did not lack skill in agriculture. There is little to go on save the results, but that may be enough. By the seventh century the Anglo-Saxon had so tamed the land that it could support expanding and thriving communities capable of sustaining powerful kings, a prosperous aristocracy and a new Church that made heavy demands upon the faithful.

What little there was to go on in 1937, when J. N. L. Myres wrote, fully justified his statement. The only full-scale excavations of an early habitation site had taken place at Sutton Courtenay in Berkshire.[68] These showed a community living at a low level of subsistence agriculture in huts little better than temporary shelters. Some thirty-three house sites were explored, covering an area of

---

[67] J. N. L. Myres, 'The Present State of the Archaeological Evidence for the Anglo-Saxon Conquest', *History*, 1937, pp.317–30.
[68] E. T. Leeds, *Archaeologia*, vol. LXXIII (1922–23), pp.147–92; vol. LXXVI (1926–27), pp.59–80; vol. XCII (1947), pp.79–94.

390 by 290 yards. There were signs of planning about the settlement. The houses were roughly aligned. They consisted of only
one storey, and often only of one room. They were of primitive
construction, built of wood, many no more than a rough rectangle
twelve feet by eight. Some were on a larger scale. In House X,
for example, in which was found the skeleton of 'a well-built and
muscular man of superior rank' there were three rooms, one of
which served as a kitchen. In another a partly sunken room was
discovered which, to judge from the amount of clay found in it,
was probably used as a workshop for the potters. Though ignorant
of the potter's wheel the Saxons of Sutton Courtenay produced
'better pottery than perhaps has hitherto been suspected'. The
village as a whole, however, was poorly furnished with material
goods. Iron knives, iron combs, loom-weights, cattle-bells, bone
pins and combs made up the bulk of the finds. Miserable squalor
seemed a fitting phrase to describe the conditions unearthed. Since
then there have been a few major excavations and many minor
that have helped fill in the picture, though the gaps in knowledge
are still painfully obvious. Many groups of sunken-floor huts have
been discovered in eastern England, and the important sites at
Mucking in Essex on the Thames estuary, West Stow in Suffolk,
and Chalton in Hampshire provide a more rounded picture of the
earliest settlements with clear evidence of rectangular hall-houses
and associated workshops and lesser habitations.[69] At Chalton
excavation of an Anglo-Saxon village dated to the sixth and seventh
centuries disclosed a complex of such hall-houses, though the ancillary buildings included only one sunken-floored hut. Analogies
with substantial Norwegian farmhouses of early modern times with
their small outlying ancillary buildings are not inappropriate. Such
halls provide links in the social chain that leads to the sensational
twentieth-century discoveries at Sutton Hoo and at Yeavering. The
sheer weight of precious possessions found in the great ship burial
at Sutton Hoo in Suffolk told of a prosperity in the East Anglian
kingdom undreamed of previously outside Kent. At Yeavering in
Northumberland the skill and ingenuity of new techniques, pho-

[69] Catherine Hills, 'The archaeology of Anglo-Saxon England in the pagan period',
A. S. E. 8, pp.297–329, esp. p.310. Good accessible guides to the principal sites
appear in P. V. Addyman, 'The Anglo-Saxon House: a New Review', A. S. E. 1,
1972, pp.273–307; P. V. Addyman and D. Leigh, 'The Anglo-Saxon Village at
Chalton, Hampshire', M. A. xvii, 1973, pp.1–25; S. E. West, The Anglo-Saxon
Village of West Stow, M. A. xiii, 1969, pp.1–20; M. U. Jones, 'An early Saxon
landscape at Mucking: Anglo-Saxon settlement and landscape at Mucking', B. A.
R. 6, 1974, pp.20–35.

tography from raised platforms and subtle interpretations of post-hole evidence, disclosed a series of royal halls that fitted in well with the world of epic poetry. A steady accumulation of contributary evidence from continental sources has already confirmed that final judgement on the nature of early English settlement will be kinder than was thought possible in 1937.

Continental archaeologists have certainly helped enrich under-standing of the state of society during the Migration age by their work at cemetery and settlement sites, for example, at Wijster in Holland, Feddersen Wierde near Bremerhaven, and Liebenau in Hanover.[70] The best insight, however, is still that given by the excavations at Warendorf near Münster a Saxon village which flourished c.650–850.[71] It consisted in the first place of a number of stoutly built long rectangular houses, eleven of which were traced, measuring from fourteen to twenty-nine metres in length and from four and a half to seven metres in breadth. Some were dwelling houses, some agricultural buildings, barns and the like. The dwelling houses had entrances with projecting porches near the centre of the long side and a hearth towards the end of the central area. Such a house is what might be expected from an Anglo-Saxon *ceorl*. It could serve as a model on a modest scale for a typical lord's hall which within its more ample recesses, would offer space for the feasting and ceremonial so lovingly described by epic poets. Surrounding the substantial dwelling houses were a number of lesser houses and buildings including some huts very like those upturned at Sutton Courtenay. Indeed it appears more and more that Sutton Courtenay, excavated under exceedingly difficult circumstances, may have revealed only the less salubrious side of a Saxon agricultural settlement. There must have been migration entry points - and Mucking with its mass of low quality hutments may have been one such - but once a regular agrarian routine was stabilized, native skills in handling wood and carpentry must have come into play from folk who had just completed a successful move in boats which they themselves had built to weather the North Sea. Warendorf and now analagous English sites give a likely model for the general pattern of English settlement at a very early stage: long, rectangular hall-houses, the homes of prosperous free farmers, a network of agricultural buildings, and lesser houses declining into hovels possibly for slaves.

It must be remembered, too, that the Anglo-Saxons were a pio-

[70] J. N. L. Myres, *The English Settlements*, 1986, p.52.
[71] C. A. Ralegh Radford, 'The Saxon House', M. A. i, 1957, pp.27–38.

neering people. Variety is to be expected. Their conquest of the soil depended on the industry and skill of comparatively small groups and individuals. These groups and individuals varied enormously one from the other. It would be rash to generalize too emphatically from the unfortunate clusters of sunken-floor huts. By the seventh century the society could support a colourful aristocracy and a lively Church. That fact alone speaks well for the agrarian achievements of the new settlers.

4. INTENSIFICATION OF SETTLEMENT

There can be no doubt that the succeeding two centuries, that is from *c.* 650, when Penda's triumphs were complete, to *c.* 850 and the first wintering of the Danes in these islands, saw an intensification of these processes of settlement and colonization. The Anglo-Saxons, with a greater or lesser admixture of Celtic blood, strengthened the hold of man upon nature in England. Place-names show a multiplicity of settlements stemming from original *-ings* and *-ingahams* and *-hams*. Apart from the elements denoting forest clearing, particularly well-marked in the Midlands, the numerous names in *-ington* probably in the main stem from this period.[72] Estate names compounded of aristocratic personal names and *-ton* became common, and of course remain so throughout the Anglo-Saxon period. The political boundary was extended westwards, to be fixed first at the Tamar and then in the early tenth century to incorporate all Cornwall in the south-west; in the Midlands by Offa in the eighth century to the great dyke that still bears his name; in the north to an uneasy and fluctuating border with the Brittonic kingdom of Strathclyde that gave Anglo-Saxon settlers opportunity to intensify their hold on the lowlands of Lothian and Cumberland. Edinburgh probably passed into English hands in A.D. 638.[73] Behind this moving frontier, in spite of all civil wars and disputes of turbulent dynasties and aristocracies, the real wealth of England increased as these unrecorded generations of forest-clearers laid the pattern of *-hams* and *-tons* which may still be traced so clearly on the map of England.

[72] A. H. Smith, 'Place-names and the Anglo-Saxon Settlement', *Proc. British Academy*, 1956, p.80, where he shows the formation to have been a living one until at least the ninth century.
[73] K. Jackson, 'Edinburgh and the Anglian Occupation of Lothian', *The Anglo-Saxons*, ed. P. Clemoes, Cambridge, 1959, pp.35–42.

Politically the two centuries were characterized by the consolidation of the three big kingdoms of Anglo-Saxon England, Wessex, Mercia and Northumbria. The smaller kingdoms of the east and the south-east, East Anglia, Essex, Kent and Sussex, were demoted to the status of sub-kingdoms. One precious document, the Tribal Hidage, to which reference has already been made, gives a momentary and partial insight into a grouping of peoples that was yet more remote.[74] Essentially a tribute-taker's survey, and probably in final form of the Mercian court in the eighth century, the Tribal Hidage assessed the taxable capacity of a whole range of groups of people subordinate to a greater Mercian kingdom. Mention was made of the big groups themselves, the Mercians proper with their thirty thousand hides, the men of Kent with fifteen thousand and, as a later interpolation, Wessex with no fewer than a hundred thousand. Of more importance for our immediate purpose are the smaller groups, some of whose names are lost in the mists of obscurity. Most, however, are intelligible enough, and some speak clearly of settlement in territorial groups such as the *Wreocensætan*, the men settled around the Wrekin and assessed at seven thousand hides, the *Pecsætan* of twelve hundred hides, settled in the Derbyshire Peak district, or the *Elmetsætan* of six hundred hides, men settled in the old Celtic kingdom of Elmet in south Yorkshire, the Elfed of later Welsh record. Others speak rather of tribal groups whose names are otherwise known only because they are embedded in fossil form in place-names, like the *Herefinna* of Hurstingstone Hundred in Huntingdonshire or the *Hicce* of Hitchin in Hertfordshire. A tribal name that is given by Bede reappears in the Tribal Hidage as the *Feppingas*, a small Middle Anglian folk, assessed at three hundred hides. It is reasonable to attribute to these groups a tribal cohesion that was retained for fiscal purposes as the larger territorial kingdoms developed. The absorption of such groups into the larger kingdoms of Anglo-Saxon England is probably in itself a sign of the general economic advance of the period. The widening scope of royal government would not be possible without a firmer and more secure agrarian base to support it.

Perhaps the best way of illustrating this advance is to look closely at the map of one particular region, examining place-name and archaeological evidence in relation to the settlement problem. A

[74] Wendy Davies and Hayo Vierck, 'The Contexts of the Tribal Hidage: Social Aggregates and Settlement Patterns', *Fruhmittelalterliche Studien*, 8, 1974, pp.223–93.

whole generation of modern local historians has sprung up whose regional surveys give the general historian his clearest insight into the tangle of problems surrounding this matter of intensification of settlement. Two modern shires, very different in nature, seem particularly well suited to illustrate this process at work: Leicester and Devon. The first represents an area not vastly important in the first days of settlement, by-passed to a considerable extent; the second represents an area virtually untouched by the English until this period, substantially settled during the eighth and early ninth centuries.

Leicestershire was not particularly attractive to the first settlers. Its boulder clay, heavy to work, difficult to drain, covered with oak and ash forest, did not lend itself to primary settlement by peoples not yet sure of their political position. Early settlements tended to be founded on glacial sand and gravel which capped the clay in patches of varying size with soil that was lighter and easier to clear and drain. The valley of the Soar offered some such attractions to the Middle Angles even in the pagan period, but it was between 650 and 850 that the true advance was made. Village sites to the east of the Soar were settled and advance was made to the west of the Soar, especially around Leicester itself. At a later stage what Hoskins calls the 'sombre landscape of North and South Leicestershire' was settled from nuclear settlements at Lutterworth and probably at Loughborough.[75] By the time the Danes arrived the greater part of Leicestershire was occupied, the east and the Soar valley fairly densely, the north and south thinly, the west densely around Leicester and more thinly towards the Staffordshire border. The extreme north-west was unsettled till the Danes arrived. A similar pattern may be discerned elsewhere in England during these two centuries. In the more westerly shires of Stafford, Shropshire and Worcester, as in the eastern shires, the place-names structure yields evidence of intensified settlements. Devon in the south-west gives an excellent example of this movement of expansion. Politically the conquest of Devon was late and probably swift, set in motion by the West Saxons about 660 and virtually complete by the death of King Ine in 725. After a battle, fought in all probability at Penselwood in 658, the Saxons advanced to the river Parrett; by 682 they had reached the Quantocks and were pushing into the coastal plain between the Quantocks and Exmoor; their king Centwine is said

[75] W. G. Hoskins, 'The Anglian and Scandinavian Settlement of Leicestershire', *Trans. Leicestershire Archaeological Society*, vol. XVIII, 1934–5, p.125.

to have driven the Britons to the sea. King Ine himself in 710 defeated the last recorded independent British king of Devon, and the Laws of Ine made provision for the Wealhas, the Welsh, some of whom occupied a responsible position in the society of the kingdom. To some degree settlement preceded final political conquest. The Saxons were in firm possession of Exeter itself by the 680s; a monastery existed there before 690, and St Boniface received his early training at Exeter; and the distribution of the main villages of South Devon suggests some settlement by sea. For, in spite of the fact that a British kingdom existed in Devon as late as the first decade of the eighth century, the shire cannot have been thickly populated. British place-names are not as numerous as one would expect, and it seems that mass migrations to Brittany in the sixth century had permanently modified the population structure of the south-west. Indeed there are indications that much of the Saxon occupation of Devon was a comparatively peaceful affair. References in the tenth-century laws by King Athelstan to his subjects at Exeter, Britons and Saxons; traces of British enclaves, such as the Treable estate on Tavistock lands, in districts otherwise Saxon;[76] the nature of the final move into Cornwall; the conclusion of the anthropologist that pre-Saxon stocks predominate in Devon: all these are pointers to a ponderous wave of colonization, faithfully recorded in the solemn -*tons*, -*stocks*, -*watleys* and -*hangars* of Devon. It is probable that political disintegration attendant on extreme poverty in the west – certainly if archaeological excavations at Mawgan Porth are any criterion – coupled with the political resilience of the West Saxon dynasty gave opportunity to the Saxons to push forward their colonizing frontier into the fertile lands of North and South Devon. What British names survive are scattered, speaking possibly of some continuity in hamlet and upland farm. The habitation sites in general are overwhelmingly English, varied in character, as numerous to the west as to the east, including even local names of Dartmoor.

There is one further feature of the settlement of Devon that demands attention. Peculiarities in the ecclesiastical history often throw light on secular affairs, and the size of the Devonshire parishes, averaging six square miles against Norfolk's two square miles, for example, is a fact of considerable significance. In the earliest days Saxon clergy dwelt at *mynsters* such as those whose names are preserved at Axminster and Exminster. As the settle-

---

[76] H. P. R. Finberg, *The Early Charters of Devon and Cornwall*, Leicester, 1953.

ment was stabilized so did the parish system develop, and the parish therefore often gives us the shape of settlement in a somewhat fossilized form. It appears that, large as the parishes are, they were at one stage much larger. River names like Taw and Plym were used of river-valley settlements 'deliberately super-imposed on a landscape dotted with small communities of native hamlets and farms'.[77] The suffix -*ton* was added to the river name to describe the central nucleated village on the Germanic patterns surrounding an open square or rectangle with the nobleman's house at one side. The estates on the Taw and Plym may have extended to thirty square miles or more. On the Tavy, the Culm, the Coly, the Claw, the Creedy, the Clyst and Teign similar -*tons* were set up from which subsidiary settlements grew. These villages, the real nuclei of separate river-valley settlement, may have been the result of 'rapid military conquest and immediate settlement'; they may have preceded military conquest in some areas.[78] As shall be seen later the concern of the Laws of Ine with the nobleman settled on an estate may be due in part to the immediate situation in Devon. Royal direction is likely, and as late as the time of Domesday Book nearly all these early villages belonged to the king or had been granted to the Bishop of Exeter by him. The topography of Devonshire settlement would speak for strongly controlled occupation by Saxons under the direct supervision of the king and his close military followers. It is probable that the magnet of good arable, particularly of the fertile redlands of the Exe valley, drew the political ambitions of a powerful king anxious to provide his people with compensation for lands north of the Thames lost to the Mercians in previous generations. Many of the villages gave their names to later hundreds. Devon became a county where nucleated villages, and apparently open-field agriculture, symbolized the power and the growing wealth of the West Saxon dynasty.

5. THE SCANDINAVIAN INVASIONS AND SETTLEMENT

To this process of slow, unspectacular advance an immense stimulus was given in the last two centuries of Anglo-Saxon England by

[77] W. G. Hoskins, 'The Making of the Agrarian Landscape', *Devonshire Studies*, London, 1952, pp.308–9.
[78] Ibid., p.309. This section draws heavily on the work of W. G. Hoskins and H. P. R. Finberg.

the advent of a people whose first appearance seemed to threaten utter disaster: the Scandinavians. Of the place of immediate origin of these peoples there is no problem. The Danes came from Denmark and South Sweden, and the Norwegians from Norway. The bulk of the latter had an intermediate stay of a generation or more in lands where a Celtic tongue was spoken, the islands to the north-west of Britain, Ireland itself and the Isle of Man, before their colonizing groups arrived in England. Nor is there real difficulty over the impulse behind the attacks nor over the nature of the attacks. Pressure of peoples from the more barren lands to the fertile crescent is one of the major facts of recorded history. The early Germanic onslaught, of which the Anglo-Saxon invasions were part, and the seventh-century Arab conquests may be read in the same context. Land-hunger prevailed. Political consolidation back home, in itself a symptom of a prosperity sufficient to produce an excess population, contributed to unrest and helped provide the aristocratic spearhead for attack. Maturity of boat-building techniques gave the northerners a mobility that terrorized the civilized world. In Norway there is evidence of land-hunger as early as the eighth century when the move to colonize the islands to the north of Britain began. The peaceful, thorough and well-recorded settlement of Iceland in the ninth century indicates the strength of the economic urge that drew an intrepid and skilful people to seek new lands to till. For it must be remembered that the onslaught against England was only part, though an important part, of a much larger movement that resulted in the establishment of a whole range of fortified markets under Scandinavian control from Rouen and Dublin to Novgorod and Kiev. To the west the most adventurous reached Vinland the Good on the American coast in search of land to settle; to the east the magnet of the great city, Constantinople, drew Scandinavians to man the Varangian Guard of the emperors. The Mediterranean came to know them as traders and raiders. Their ravaging of the Frankish kingdoms did not ease until they had received the duchy of Normandy from Carolingian hands in 911. The late ninth and tenth centuries were truly the Viking Age, an age when an iron cap of fortified strongholds was placed over the whole of northern Europe.

On England successful Scandinavian attacks occur at two periods. It is with the first of these that our principal concern lies, between 865 and 954, that is between the beginning of the first effective onslaught of a great Danish army against the Mercian and Northumbrian power and the date of the final overthrow of a Norwegian kingdom at York. The second attack occurred during the reign of Ethelred and ended with the conquest of England by Canute who reigned as King of the English from 1016 to 1035. Politically it would be foolish to deny the importance of this second movement, but from the point of view of settlement and the actual structure of population, it was secondary in significance to the changes made during the earlier period. A Scandinavian element was reinforced in the aristocracy and court; some settlers 'observing that the land was most excellent chose to take up residence in so fertile a country';[79] but there was not the same folk-movement that made so fundamental an alteration to so great a part of the country in the late ninth and early tenth centuries.

The Scandinavian invasions are naturally much better recorded than the Anglo-Saxon. Indeed with the help of the Anglo-Saxon Chronicles it is possible to trace the movements of hostile armies, and follow the triumphs first of the West Saxon house and later of Sweyn and Canute in surprising detail. But again, apart from a few vital hints given in the written evidence, in the Chronicles and the Laws, any discussion of the problem of settlement has to rely for the main part upon evidence brought to light by the ancillary sciences of language and place-name study, of archaeology and numismatics, supplemented by legitimate inference from later institutional development, record of which has been preserved for us in Domesday Book and allied documents.

The political story of the first settlement necessary for our purpose is soon told. It falls into two main parts, the late ninth century when the Danes make their tremendous effort to conquer all England, and the first half of the tenth century when the centre of interest passes to the less spectacular Norwegian infiltration into the north-west of England. The great Danish armies of 865-80 gained rapid control of the greater part of Northumbria, eastern Mercia and East Anglia. Even London passed temporarily into their hands, and they ravaged deep into Wessex itself. The brilliant recovery by Alfred, drawing deep on his reserves in the south-west, led to stabilization of the political border along Watling Street and the river Lea that is roughly along a line from Chester to Shrewsbury to Lichfield to Bedford to Hertford and so to London itself which was reclaimed and placed under the lordship of the Mercian *ealdorman* who was also Alfred's own son-in-law. To the far north some Northumbrians maintained a precarious autonomy

---

[79] *Encomium Emmae Reginae*, ed. A. Campbell, London, 1949, pp.16–17.

in Bernicia but the rest of England to the east of the Pennines passed under effective Danish military control. Some districts were heavily settled under the leadership of petty Danish kings and earls; others saw merely the Scandinavian element dominate the local aristocracy and the law-courts. The name Danelaw came to be applied to the whole area, and a very suitable name it was. Essentially the Danelaw was the area in which Danish legal custom predominated.

The violent Danish success against Northumbria and Mercia left something of a power vacuum in the north-west, never a very stable region of England. Scandinavians, particularly those of Norwegian origin, had already settled the islands and the Isle of Man. Danes and Norwegians together, sometimes in unity, sometimes not, had set up important permanent settlements on the east coast of Ireland at Dublin, Wexford and Waterford, from which they raided the whole west coast of Britain, Celtic and Saxon. In the first decade of the tenth century the Norwegians, with presumably a strong Celtic interlacing, began their settlements in the north-west from the Wirral to Carlisle, settlements that have left a permanent impress on the map of England west of the Pennines. Politically their influence extended further east, and it was not until the death of Eric Bloodaxe in 954 that the danger of a northern kingdom stretching from York to Dublin and the isles was finally removed.

It is possible that the relative backwardness and ferocity of the Norwegians had one further important effect that should be noted at this point. The first three-quarters of the tenth century saw the golden period of West Saxon monarchy. The Danes, settled in eastern Mercia and East Anglia, submitted to Edward the Elder, Alfred's son. His son, Athelstan, himself a great figure in Old Norse saga, exercised a virtual *imperium* over most of the island. The Norwegian return to York proved evanescent, and under Edgar the Peaceful, 959–75, the authority of the West Saxon king was exercised on Wessex itself, English Mercia and the whole of the so-called Danelaw, including the whole of the lands of a reconstituted Northumbria. Fear of the Norwegians prompted the more advanced Danes, quick to accept Christianity, to accept also the Christian kingship of revived Wessex.

For in spite of their proud military triumphs these English kings did not so much reconquer Scandinavianized England as absorb it. The monarchy remained the prime agent of unity together with the Christian Church to which it was closely bound. Nevertheless the social changes brought about by the new settlements proved permanent. In the early twelfth century the 'Leges Henrici Primi' could still refer to the three laws into which England was divided: Wessex, English Mercia and the Danelaw.

The nature of the Scandinavian settlements varied from region to region in the Danelaw. In the actual campaigns there was devastation and destruction, probably all the greater because of a feeling of kinship among peoples whose very languages at this stage were not unintelligible one to the other. But when it came to settlement, one general feature of a distinctly unexpected nature stands out: there was apparently no major displacement of existing population. Where the Dane or Norwegian settled, he supplemented rather than superseded the existing community. There was still at this stage room for clearings to be made and good arable to be found in England. The Scandinavians, ultimately of the same stock as the Anglo-Saxon, with the same agrarian needs, and probably with the same basic equipment, settled relatively quickly and smoothly into the agrarian and social pattern of English life. Without idealizing overmuch this Scandinavian conquest one can say that their powers of assimilation, and power to be assimilated, were much in evidence in later Anglo-Saxon England.

On the problem of density of settlements place-names give the most reliable evidence. Sir Frank Stenton has shown how they illustrate the whole pattern of colonization that went on behind the protective screen of Danish armies drawn up to the north of Watling Street.[80] In the belt of country that stretches from Grimsby to Leicester Danish names are exceptionally strong. They are numerous but not so concentrated in the East and West Ridings of Yorkshire, very strong again in the North Riding, but with merely a trickle further north into Northumberland. In East Anglia, Norfolk produces its due measure of *-bys* and *-thorpes* though certainly no more than could be expected from its recorded history as a point of early Danish settlement, while Suffolk has only a few Danish names to the north and the west of the country. It is possible, however, that the minor names of East Anglia, which have not yet been systematically collected, will be more productive. In the south-east Danelaw Danish names are rare. Essex has no more than a cluster in the north-east corner of the shire; Hertfordshire is practically Dane-less, though the Hundred of Dacorum to the south of Watling Street and the name Tring (*priding*, a third part as in the modern Yorkshire Ridings) show the mark of the Dane.[81]

[80] *Anglo-Saxon England*, Oxford, 3rd ed., 1971, pp.524–5.
[81] E. P. N. S., *Hertfordshire*, pp.25 and 51.

The pattern of colonization is clearly varied, from a few noble-men who would impose their legal custom upon the moots of Hertfordshire, Essex and possibly Suffolk, to the more formidable

The Scandinavian settlement

The shadings are approximate only, and it is clear that some Danes settled in 'Norwegian' districts just as some Norwegians settled in 'Danish'. Among *burhs* still unidentified are *Scergeat* and *Weardbyrig* on the western Mercian border.

settlement of Danish farmers and their households in Lincolnshire and Leicestershire.

There has properly been much discussion of the nature, indeed of the very existence, of these Danish farmers. P. H. Sawyer, for example, has argued in stimulating fashion that the numbers involved in invasion and settlement were small.[82] He has made a case for the smallness of the armies in the field in late ninth-century England, but the present writer is not convinced that substantial migration did not occur behind the screen of the protecting armies. The traditional view has been that the migrants have left proof of their existence in the sokemen of Domesday Book. These men, bound to a personal lord, but enjoying considerable tenurial freedom, exercised important functions as doomsmen in the litigious Danelaw. They were numerous. In Domesday Book nearly 11,000 of them are recorded in Lincolnshire alone, amounting to close on fifty per cent of the recorded population of the shire. Elsewhere in the Danelaw forty per cent was not an unusual figure. We have been warned, however, to handle our Dane with care, and not to seize on a racial explanation of free status which may more intelligibly be explained on economic or institutional grounds.[83] In East Anglia, for example, attempts have been made at an intepretation of society that would stress hard work and good soil rather than intrinsic virtue attached to immigrant Danes. Norfolk had over forty per cent, and Suffolk more than forty-five per cent, of its recorded population described as freemen or sokemen in 1086, and R. H. C. Davis has suggested that the grounds for ascribing this freedom to Danish ancestry are slender. Some scholars would trace East Anglian freedom to Frisian rather than to Danish sources, and read the Danish conquest as an interlude in the course of which the Dane, far from reorganizing East Anglian society, was steadily assimilated to the already existing peculiarities of that society. Such arguments are ingenious but not convincing. Against them may be brought the strong objection that the Danish peculiarities apply not only to East Anglia but also to Mercia north-east of Watling Street where no case can be made for difference in social structure from 'English' Mercia in pre-Danish days. It remains noteworthy that in

[82] P. H. Sawyer, 'The Density of the Danish Settlement in England', *University of Birmingham Historical Journal*, vol. VI, 1958, pp.1–17, an argument, developed and modified in his *The Age of the Vikings*, London, 2nd ed., 1971.
[83] F. W. Maitland, *Domesday Book and Beyond*, Cambridge, 1897, p.139, a warning reinforced by R. H. C. Davis, 'East Anglia and the Danelaw', *T. R. Hist. S.*, 1955, p.39.

Leicestershire there were two thousand sokemen in the late eleventh century, while across Watling Street in English Warwickshire there was none. Sokemen were not unknown in English England, but their presence in significant number is a characteristic of areas, though not of all areas, which had passed under Danish control in the late ninth century. They may not have been the descendants of free Danish settlers, but it still seems reasonable to explain their presence, together with other signs of direct Danish influence, as the result direct and indirect of an immigration on a large scale from Scandinavia.

These other signs of direct Danish influence speak strongly in favour of the intensity of settlement. Profound modification was made over much of England in the very language itself, in the style of personal names, in the field names and lesser habitation site names, in systems of land measurement, in methods of accounting and in the basic fabric of institutional life, legal and political as well as agrarian. The fact that the English word *law* is of Scandinavian origin is no mere terminological accident, and while it is possible to argue that many of the institutional changes were brought about by the action of a dominant aristocracy, it is not easy to explain on these grounds basic alterations in speech habits sufficient to lead to the naming of even small streams and fields in the new tongue, and the introduction of Scandinavian words into the language. Indeed the social and institutional evidence still points to the view that Danish colonists, radiating from the old highways of entry, the Humber and the Wash, came in numbers large enough to warrant the description of a migration. Against this must be noted the scarcity of archaeological discovery relating to these colonists. There are few Viking burials recorded in England or on the Continent, though a rapid conversion to Christianity offers a possible explanation of this apparent anomaly. The Anglo-Saxon Chronicle tells of land allotted to Danish soldiers as the army settled on the defeated countryside. There was a time when parallels with the settlement of Normandy in the early tenth century appeared to support the view that this land division amounted to a partition of arable among the successful warrior-farmers, but more recent investigation of the Norman situation suggests that lordship of dependent villages was more often in question in the duchy.[84] Yet in England at times,

[84] L. Musset, 'Les Domaines de l'Époque franque et les destinées du régime domanial du IXᵉ au XIᵉ siècle', *Bulletin de la Société des antiquaires du Normandie*, vol. XLIX, 1946, particularly pp.9–17 and a very shrewd note on p.79. My thanks go to Dr. E. B. Fryde for drawing my attention to this important article.

perhaps notably in Derbyshire, the very pattern of place-names suggests something in the nature of a deliberate plan of settlement at some distance from the main army headquarters, but protected by a screen of fortified posts.[85] Notably in parts of the Northern Danelaw the Danes appear to have been true colonizers, opening up new land and presumably taking readily and easily to an open field system. The Danes did not diminish the prosperity of the land. Initial destroyers they often were, but they quickly adapted themselves to the superior cultural and religious habits of the English. Socially they preserved their customs. In the early eleventh century complaint was made that even in Wessex people were adopting a Danish style of hair-cut with bared neck and blinded eyes.[86] That by their coming the Danes intensified differences which already existed between English England and parts of the 'Danelaw' is perfectly possible. But to ignore the linguistic and social evidence in favour of Danish migration itself seems to lead to serious distortion of the pattern of settlement of England.

The Norwegian infiltration was not on the same scale as the Danish. In one respect it was very different in nature. Reference has already been made to the fact that in the main there was no major displacement of existing population. This is substantially true even in Leicestershire and Lincolnshire. But the military nature of the initial entry was unquestionably stronger on the Danish side of the Pennines. The fighting was hard and well recorded. Particularly in the area of the Five Boroughs the settlement was organized on a military basis. The Danish armies of Lincoln, Stamford, Nottingham, Leicester and Derby turned to the soil. As early as 876 the Danes divided the land and allotted shares to successful warriors. Northampton and Cambridge were also important army headquarters. Army organization was maintained. For forty years, from 877 to 917, the warrior-farmers of the Boroughs provided the spearhead of attack and the shield of defence in uneasy political relationships with English England. Not that relationships even at that stage were universally hostile. Trade persisted. Regulations were drawn up to protect Danish traders in Wessex and English traders in the Danelaw. By the end of Edward the Elder's reign Englishmen were encouraged to buy property in the Danelaw, no doubt with a view to increasing English influence in territories only

[85] F. T. Wainwright, 'Early Scandinavian Settlement in Derbyshire', *Derbyshire Archaeological and Natural History Society*, vol. LXVII (for the year 1947), p.102.
[86] *E. H. D.* I, pp.895–6, fragment of an Old English letter.

freshly brought back under political lordship.[87] Under Athelstan, Archbishop Wulfstan of York, the King's own nominee, was given the great tract of Amounderness which had been bought back from the pagans with the King's own money.[88] These lands had special strategic importance, and by 1066 had passed into the earl's hands. Watling Street was no impenetrable curtain. But it is true to say that the military might, in particular of the men of the Five Boroughs, provided a screen behind which a migration of Danish farmers, their wives and families, could take place.

There is little of this military nature in evidence in the main area of Norwegian penetration. There was some overlap, of course. A heavy concentration of Norwegian elements in the place-names of parts of the North Riding suggests settlement there. The Normantons of the Danelaw – there are no fewer than five in Nottinghamshire alone – betray the presence of Norse enclaves in an otherwise predominantly Danish venture, and some Scandinavian place-names authorities would go further, and would bring much of the East Riding also under heavy Norwegian influence. Careful analysis of the place-name structure of Rutland suggests that its Normanton, near the splendid hill-top site of Hambleton, may represent a Viking Norse presence in an area where English husbandmen for the most part continued to exploit the soil.[89] Inversely, west of the Pennines, there are areas around Manchester and in the Lake District where the Dane rather than the Norwegian has left his mark. But in the main Norwegian effort came in the north-west along the coast from the Wirral peninsula to Carlisle, heavily in Cumberland and Westmoreland and North Lancashire, spilling over the Pennines into the west of the North Riding and the north-west of the West Riding. Political factors alone are sufficient to account for the relatively peaceful nature of the Norwegian move. The Danes forced their way to Watling Street and beyond in a generation of hard campaigning. The Norwegians infiltrated into an area where there was little left of the political authority of the dispirited kingdom of Northumbria. They came later on the scene than the Danes and only in the north-west tip of Mercia did they encounter strong resistance. It is precisely there, at Chester in 907, that they were engaged in their hardest battles.

---

[87] F. M. Stenton, *Latin Charters of the Anglo-Saxon Period*, p.30.
[88] D. Whitelock, 'The Dealings of the Kings of England with Northumbria in the Tenth and Eleventh Centuries', *The Anglo-Saxons*, ed. P. Clemoes, p.72.
[89] Barrie Cox, 'Rutland and the Scandinavian settlements: the place-name evidence', A. S. E. 18, pp.135–48.

The Norwegians came east and south over sea, from Ireland, the Isle of Man, and the islands to the north-west and west of Britain. Their place-names, like Aspatria in Cumberland (Patrick's ash tree) were often modified by Celtic influence in order and vocabulary.[90] They came in the first half of the tenth century, and in the main their settlements represent peaceful penetration, the opening up of new lands and the reinvigoration of old. As F. T. Wainwright says of the situation in Lancashire, '*parallel* not *superimposed* is the adjective required to describe the relationship of the Norse settlement to that of an earlier age'.[91] This was not a military conquest; battles and skirmishes were certainly fought but the main nature of the movement was colonizing. Over most of Lancashire and Cheshire English remained the dominant element in place-names. Only in the upland districts of lake and fell, probably not settled by the English, are Anglian elements absent.

Of the extent and depth of the settlement there can be little doubt. Over a hundred major place-names in Lancashire bear Scandinavian names, and if field names and names of minor natural features are taken into account the tally runs into four figures.[92] In Cheshire place-names reveal an intensive Norse settlement in the Wirral peninsula, in contrast to the rather faint overlap of Danish penetration into the east of the country. Dialect peculiarities and some evidence of the knowledge of Scandinavian inflexions point to familiarity with a Scandinavian tongue as late as the twelfth century. Certainly when the fine alliterative poetry of the north-west was produced in the fourteenth century, of which 'Sir Gawain and the Green Knight' and the 'Pearl' are outstanding examples, there was a strikingly heavy Scandinavian influence on the vocabulary, still markedly West Scandinavian rather than East.

Most interesting and spectacular of all these Norwegian settlements, scantily chronicled but well recorded in place-names, were those to the north of north-west England, in the modern shires of Cumberland and Westmoreland, linking up with the settlements in north Lancashire, in the Lake District, in Lonsdale and Amounderness. Here in country not utterly dissimilar to their land of origin the Norwegians set up their farmsteads and *sætrs*, settling heavily in the valley of the Derwent, the uplands of the ward of Leath, taking by second nature to the mixed farming

[90] E. P. N. S., *Cumberland* (part III), pp. xxii–xxvii.
[91] F. T. Wainwright, 'The Scandinavians in Lancashire', *Trans. Lancashire and Cheshire Antiquarian Society*, vol. LVIII, 1945–6, p.78.
[92] Ibid., p.74.

dictated by the spectacular contour lines, to the cultivation of some arable and to the tending of sheep. Racially the upland districts had been virtually untouched by the English. It was a British population which the Norseman met in the Cumbrian hills.

Of course, at this early stage in the development of the language it is not easy to distinguish between Danish and Norwegian elements in place-names, or to be more precise, between Old East Scandinavian and Old West Scandinavian. There are elements common to both, and there are others which can rarely be distinguished from Old English cognates, like *tun* and *dalr* and *hyll* (Old English, *tun, dæl* and *hyll*). Fortunately each group has its peculiarities. The common element *thorpe*, used in England of a secondary settlement often less pretentious than a village, is a mark of Danish nomenclature and not of Norwegian. On the Norwegian side, words like *gil* (ravine) and *skali* (a mountain hut) indicate the presence of western rather than eastern Scandinavians. Vocabulary acquired in a district familiar with a Goidelic tongue, like the element *-erg*, also signifying a mountain hut or a shieling, betrays the Norwegian. Phonology sometimes gives the essential clue. The Old Danish *hulm*, a water-meadow, is paralleled by the Old Norwegian *holmr*; the Old Danish *both* (a booth) by the Old Norwegian *buð*. Assimilation of *nk* to *kk* and of *rs* to *ss* distinguishes Danish *brink* from Norwegian *brekka* and Danish *fors* from Norwegian *foss*. As this change is held not to have taken place until the eleventh century it is possible to infer that the Scandinavian tongues remained alive in England until the end of the period, and that the differences between Danish and Norwegian persisted. Although the differences are often minute they are precise; and the resulting shading off of Norwegian from Danish is a major fact to be taken into account in any description of the peoples of England.

Most interesting of all the place-name elements introduced by the Scandinavians is the suffix *-by*. It had a long history as a living form in England. Long after the Conquest *-bys* were still in use even compounded with typical Norman names. The element was thoroughly naturalized. Originally it meant a farmstead, and in Denmark was used freely of a secondary settlement away from a parent village. But in England it appears from the earliest days to have been used more frequently of a village or even of a substantial township like Derby. Yet it retained its less distinguished function, and in particular was used with personal names in a fashion analogous to the use of English *-ton* in the south. Professor A. H.

Smith has shown that close on two-thirds of the names ending in -*by* are compounded with personal names, in marked contrast to conditions in the Danish homeland.[93] Without over-emphasis on the point, this may suggest a strengthening of the middle type of man, the small landowner of the Danelaw, at a time when King and Church were making increasing demands on his corresponding number's person and purse in the south.

The effect of Scandinavian settlement on the English may often be traced from the map itself. Some English names were changed to Danish, including a name as famous in ecclesiastical history as *Streoneshalch* which became Whitby after an intermediate period as *Prestebi* (monastery). There are other hybrid names, like the so-called Grimston hybrids with Scandinavian personal names and English -*ton*. In this numerous group there may be signs of political upheaval as the former English owner's name was replaced by that of the successful Dane, though the element of fashion must not be forgotten in dealing with personal names. Many Englishmen assumed Scandinavian names, particularly in the eleventh century when Canute and his sons sat on the English throne. It is only very rarely that a complete district is Scandinavianized. Normally Danish -*thorpes* and -*bys* are found interspersed with English -*hams* and -*tons*. In parts of the Danelaw the central settlement of a district sometimes retains its English name, to be surrounded by a mixture of English and Danish secondary settlements. For example English Grantham, Bolingbroke, Sleaford, Newark, Mansfield, Rothley and Melton Mowbray, to choose instances from the Five Boroughs alone, had many Danish and English settlements dependent upon them, bearing the mark, as Sir Frank Stenton puts it, of 'minor local capitals'.[94] Only occasionally, as in the Wreak valley to the north-east of Leicester, is there overwhelming Scandinavianization of the place-name structure, and it is quite possible that much of this was newly colonized land. No one who knows the Wreak with its Rotherby, Frisby, Kirbys and Sysonbys can fail to be aware that intensive colonization took place.

Place-name evidence is well supported by our knowledge of the laws and language of late Anglo-Saxon England. The Danes were a litigious people, and King Edgar found it wise and just to insist that their own laws and customs be observed. One of the most famous law codes promulgated in Anglo-Saxon times was that put out by Ethelred for the men of the Five Boroughs. Significant

[93] A. H. Smith, *English Place-Name Elements*, E. P. N. S., xxv, the element '-by'.
[94] F. M. Stenton, *Anglo-Saxon England*, p.525.

differences existed, even in reunited England, between the laws that applied in the Danelaw and those that applied in English England. Fines were heavier and in some instances were laid on districts, on territorial neighbourhoods. The King's own peace was valued more highly in the Danelaw. This does not mean that the Danelaw was necessarily more law-abiding than the rest of England, probably quite the reverse. There was a tendency also to stereotype fines for lesser offences under the name of a general *lahslit*, or penalty for breaking the law, which suggests a simplification of existing custom at the hands of a new political aristocracy.[95] The simplification remained even after the unification of England by the House of Wessex.

The language gives clearest proof of all that these Scandinavian settlements were migrations. Even the pronoun structure, notoriously conservative, was modified. Legal terms abound, but much more impressive are the common words in modern English that have a Scandinavian origin. *Take, call, window, husband, sky, anger, low, scant, loose, ugly, wrong, happy*, even grammatical words like *hence* and *thence, though* and *till*, are Scandinavian. As Jespersen says, an Englishman cannot *thrive* or be *ill* or *die* without Scandinavian words; they are to the language what *bread* and *eggs* are to the daily fare.[96] This influence is much more marked in modern English than in classical Anglo-Saxon, not because of later accretions of Scandinavian peoples in the post-1066 period, but simply because the basis of modern English is the East Midland dialect where the mingling of English and Danish was so complete. It seems evident that we had in that area the unusual co-habitation of two languages, similar enough to be mutually intelligible with some patience and forbearance, different enough to have a contribution to make one to the other. Questions of social prestige seem not to have arisen; questions of political mastery were not important save in the legal sphere; the two languages grew together to the great enrichment of the dominant partner. If a late Scandinavian source may be trusted, survivors from the battle of Stamford Bridge were still intelligible to peasants of the East Riding in 1066, though their manner of speech betrayed their origin.[97] Another late Scandinavian source brings home vividly the intelligibility of these Germanic speakers

[95] Ibid., p.507.
[96] O. Jespersen, *Growth and Structure of the English Language*, p.74.
[97] Harold Hardrada's Saga, c.94, *Snorre Sturlason, Kongesagær*, ed. G. Storm, Oslo, 1900, embodying older material preserved in the Fagrskinna.

one to the other, when it tells that there was only one speech in the north until William the Bastard won England.[98]

These legal and language facts help to suggest that the Scandinavians had sought and found in England a social pattern similar to that which they desired. Their ambitions were primarily agrarian; to assuage land-hunger was their object. In a later chapter mention will be made of one other contribution which they made in England, as in all Europe, and that is their contribution to urban development. They had a greater mobility than the Anglo-Saxons, kept in touch with their homeland east over sea, helped to build up the thriving little markets of Thetford, Lincoln, above all York, until these really deserved the name of town. On one count we can be sure. In agrarian as in commercial fields they brought prosperity to England. In 1086 the three richest shires were in the Danelaw: Lincolnshire, Norfolk and Suffolk. In Lincolnshire and in parts of Norfolk Scandinavian influence was notably strong.

Indeed over a great swathe of England in the eleventh century Anglo-Scandinavian rather than Anglo-Saxon becomes a more precise term of description. The epithet becomes yet more apposite with the success of the second Danish invasion of the early eleventh century. Under Canute and his jarls the old dynasty was replaced by a Scandinavian ruling house. Even with the restoration of the dynasty in the person of Edward the Confessor, the composition of the royal court remained strongly Scandinavian. Yet this second invasion had not the permanent impress of the first. Settlements were made. Men like Thorkell found the land prosperous, and settled their followers upon it. Danish housecarls were rewarded with estates in English England as frequently if not more so than in Danish. But these were drops in the ocean. There was no migration on the scale of the late ninth and early tenth centuries. Canute's triumph was essentially political.

6. THE NORMANS

With more reservation the same can be said of the Norman Conquest itself. In relation to the problem of settlement the Norman invasion, spectacular though it was, did not alter radically the settlement pattern of England. There were areas, notably in towns,

98 Gunnlaugs Saga, quoted by R. W. Chambers in his introduction to the facsimile of Exeter Book, London, 1933, p.2.

where French population on a reasonably heavy scale was introduced. In Norwich we hear of the new *burg* occupied by French settlers, the Franci de Norwich, of which there were forty-one in the demesne of king and earl.[99] In some country districts Frenchmen were numerous, and their activities in legal processes were highly important. But the essential contribution of the French lay in providing a new aristocracy for England. The population that came, and it would be wrong to dismiss the leaven as negligible, came as followers of their lords, as military servants, as household servants, burgesses, artificers, priests and clerks. Their influence was disproportionate to their number, but they left the essential structure of settlement untouched, except in those westerly districts where they pressed back still further the political control of the Celt, extending Englishmen into the Marches, introducing churlish folk to resettle part of Cumberland recovered from resurgent Strathclyde. Of the enormous contribution made by the Normans, directly and indirectly to the regularization and consolidation of English society more must be said later. They do not constitute one of the major elements in English population, certainly not by the side of Celt, Saxon and Dane.

We have now looked at the main themes in the story of English settlement over six hundred and fifty years. The emphasis has been solidly agrarian. Little has been said of urban development, and this emphasis has been deliberate. The main achievement of the whole period was the settlement of the soil of England, the slow building-up of a predominantly agrarian community, capable of supporting monarchy, aristocracy and Church. The last two centuries of this period saw impressive development in urban spheres, and no picture of society and economy in Anglo-Saxon England is complete without adequate discussion of the part town and market have to play. But it is the less spectacular work of woodsman and ploughman that gives permanence to the English scene. Not all settlements survive: bad choice of sites was made; but the tally of villages and hamlets recorded in Domesday Book in 1086 bears a striking correspondence to the tally of villages and hamlets of pre-eighteenth-century England. In itself this simple geographical fact pays great tribute to Anglo-Saxon and Scandinavian achievement.

[99] D. B. II, 118.

CHAPTER TWO

The European Setting and Overseas Trade

1. THE PROBLEM OF CONTACT OVERSEAS

The fragmentary nature of the written sources which limits the treatment of the problem of settlement similarly affects the question of its wider setting. Not until Bede's *Ecclesiastical History*, written in the early eighth century, is there an account of conditions in these islands sufficient to give anything like a continuous picture of the kingdoms and churches of England. Bede's primary concern was with ecclesiastical conditions, but he threw light also on the political nature of the so-called Heptarchy. His overriding purpose, however, was to show the success of the missionary enterprises that were directed to the pagan Germanic kingdoms of England in the course of the late sixth and early seventh centuries, and it is only incidentally that he advanced knowledge of the social and economic conditions of England, or of the relationships between England and the Continent in these fields.

It is often held that the missionaries, inspired in the first place by Pope Gregory and led by St Augustine, brought England back into the orbit of a civilized Europe from which she had been isolated for a century and a half. This is substantially true if civilized Europe is thought of as Rome and the Mediterranean world with its extension north through Gaul, excluding the areas settled by the Germanic barbarians. If instead we see the fifth and sixth centuries as a time which brought the Germanic barbarians within the orbit of the civilized world then the perspective changes. The old Mediterranean unity crumbled and finally fell apart in the seventh century. As compensation the north and the east, Scandinavia and Germany, to use modern terms, were slowly brought into the Romanic orbit. From the intermingling of the German and the Roman the civilization of Western Europe in the Middle Ages drew its strength. England's part in the conversion of Germany in the eighth century and of Scandinavia in the tenth and eleventh centuries was of vital importance to this process of intermingling. It may also be argued, though not without a touch of irony, that during the so-called period of isolation from 450 to 600 Britain was in closer touch, both personally and culturally, with the world of the North Sea littoral than ever before or since in her long history.

Even the lack of contact with the Romanic world grows less certain, at least from the south-east of Britain, the closer the problem is examined. The Merovingian kings of the later sixth century knew much about Kent, enough to make it worth their while to arrange a marriage between the daughter of King Charibert (d.567) and Ethelbert of Kent. A Christian Bishop, Liudhard by name, accompanied the princess, and a gold coin survives, probably a token not a current coin, which bears his name. His church, dedicated to St Martin, was built on a foundation established in Roman times; the dedication to St Martin is in itself probable indication of high antiquity. Canterbury, the capital city of the Kentish kingdom, the *urbs metropolitana, Doruuernensis* or *Doruuernis civitas* as it was called by Bede, the *Cantwaraburh* of the eighth-century annals in the Anglo-Saxon Chronicle, probably bore a marked resemblance to many of the smaller Merovingian towns. But contact is a ague term, and there are indications that contact with the world of Mediterranean civilization was fitful and indirect. Procopius, writing in mid-sixth century at Constantinople, could tell tales of 'Britain' reminiscent of the fancies of writers concerning *ultima Thule*. St Augustine himself was unhappy at the prospect of visiting a strange and terrible land. To Rome, for all the information at Gregory's disposal concerning London and York, Britain was the lost province. Slavers knew the routes well enough, reaping the benefit of tribal war and unrest, though whether they visited the eastern or the western shores of Britain is a matter for speculation. The slave boys from Deira on sale at the Roman slave market may have passed quite as easily from British hands to Bordeaux as from Germanic hands through Frisia or Quentovic. Slavers were as secretive about their source of supply as later Arab slavers about their African reserves. Yet this ignorance abroad of conditions in England does not necessitate the postulation of miserable clusters of mud huts and utter barbarism in England: the Kentish jewellery alone would speak against that. It does seem fair, however, to state that the peoples of England were preoccupied at this time with their own colonizing problems. The social achievement of the late fifth and sixth centuries lay in the formation of groups that we know historically as the tribes of England. Overseas trade, while not non-existent, can have played little significant part in the economic life of these settlers and consolidators.

To some degree this is true of the whole period. The great achievement of the Anglo-Saxon period lay in the colonization and settlement of England. By 1066, as was stated in the previous chapter, most of the village and hamlet settlements familiar to pre-industrial England had been etched into the countryside. In spite of recurrent civil wars and foreign invasions the Anglo-Saxons cleared forests and drained swamps to such an extent that in shire after shire the pattern of permanent agricultural settlement was drawn. Solid tracts of wasteland remained, of course: the Weald, the Fens, the deserts of the Chilterns; but even there the outlines of settlement were clearly marked.

Similarly in the social field the great achievement consisted in the creation of a territorial state out of a network of kindreds, some palpably artificial; and both achievements were made possible only by the skill and care of generations of unnamed peasant farmers working under a social system which slowly evolved more effective techniques for the maintenance of general peace. Above all in importance was the work of the House of Wessex in its great days under Alfred and his successors. They, in the course of the tenth and eleventh centuries, bound together the communities of England by assuming responsibility at the highest level for communications and for the maintenance of law and order.

These developments in both the economic and the social fields were essentially indigenous. Right through to the end of the eleventh century foreign trade was something of an exotic, and its record, though not without interest, is fragmentary and elusive.

Nevertheless, after the conversion to Christianity in the seventh century, England remained an integral part of Western Christendom, and was affected by the ebb and flow of the Western economy generally. It is sad to see one of the most acute of modern French observers, M. Latouche, confessing that he had almost completely omitted Great Britain from his masterly survey of the European economy in the period that stretches from the fifth to the eleventh century, because English evolution was so different from that of the Continent, and also because it would have

69

been difficult to incorporate it in his own synthesis.[1] Yet on occasion after occasion English economic conditions mirror, admittedly with some distortion, those of the Continent: the currency changes from gold to silver of the seventh century, the currency reforms of Charles the Great and Offa, the impact of the Vikings upon the economy, and the slow evolution of the town by way of the *burh*. Perhaps it is preoccupation with the evolution of feudal society that leads French historians to regard England as something of a conservative eccentric; perhaps too it is the contrast between the richness of Carolingian documents and the poverty of our own inadequately edited Anglo-Latin charters that leads to neglect.

2. THE EARLY MEDIEVAL ECONOMY: THE WORK OF HENRI PIRENNE

It is a tribute to one of the greatest historians of this century that all investigations of early medieval economy start overtly or secretly with the work of the Belgian historian, Henri Pirenne,[2] who, by the vigour and lucidity of his pen, gained a mastery over his field such as is granted to few men. Not that he was without astringent critics in his own day. Professor Dopsch of Vienna, his only co-worker of equal stature, disagreed violently on some essential points in Pirenne's synthesis, though on others there was complete accord. To Pirenne the economy of the Middle Ages, which to him began in the eighth century, was an economy of regression or even of decadence. The interruption of Mediterranean trade by the Moslems provoked the change from classical to medieval; the consequences were the extinction of urban life, of significant commerce and industry, and of the specialized merchant class. There arose in Europe a medieval economy which substituted for an economy of exchange, still functioning to that point, an economy completely dedicated to the cultivation of the soil and to the immediate consumption of its products. In one way Pirenne, by thus throwing his emphasis on the Moslem invasions as the critical turning point in the economic development of Western Europe, added a fresh dimension to thought concerning the early

[1] R. Latouche, *The Birth of Western Economy*, London, 1961 (first published as *Les Origines de l'économie occidentale*, Paris, 1956), pp.xvi–xvii.
[2] A short bibliographical guide to the Pirenne theses is provided by F. Havinghurst, *The Pirenne Thesis*, Boston, 1958.

Middle Ages. In essentials, though simplification does harm to the work of a profound and subtle thinker, Pirenne's theses that have strict bearing upon the questions here under consideration may be stated under the following heads:

(a) That there was no substantial break in continuity in economic development as a result of the Germanic invasions in the fifth and sixth centuries.

(b) That such a break occurred late in the seventh century as a direct result of the Mohammedan success in the Mediterranean.

(c) That in consequence there was an economic decline in Western Europe, the Carolingian Age being on the whole poorer than the Merovingian.

The first of these propositions provoked intense discussion; Professor Dopsch himself arrived at similar conclusions, though for different reasons.[3] On the whole the view is still maintained. There are few advocates of the old catastrophic view which attributed the fall of Rome to Alaric or to Attila or to the removal of Romulus Augustulus. Continuity is the text for many a sermon in learned periodicals or lecture-hall, and many and varied are the examples used to illumine the theme: Theodoric the Ostrogoth aping the Roman, Justinian's recovery of the Mediterranean littoral, the numerical inferiority of Vandal, Visigoth, Lombard and Frank, the sheer weight of Romanism in population, language and religion. To some it is the failure of any barbarian king to assume the imperial title that provides the vital clue to the puzzle; to others it is the reception of orthodox Trinitarian Christianity by the enduring German dynasties. Pirenne himself analysed the situation in typical epigrammatic style, drawing the contrast between happenings in the north of the Empire and those of the Mediterranean south by arguing forcibly and truly that the small group of Arabs assimilated the culture of the peoples they conquered, while on the other hand the Germans were assimilated by the culture of the peoples they conquered.[4]

In relation to Gaul itself – and Gaul to the north of the Loire and the west of the Rhine was very close in structure to Roman Britain, composed of the same peoples and moulded by the same social forces – Pirenne and his followers have argued that

[3] A. Dopsch, *The Economic and Social Foundations of European Civilization* (translation, London, 1937).
[4] H. Pirenne, *Mahomet and Charlemagne*, London, 1939, esp. pp.150–3.

the Merovingian kings of the sixth and seventh centuries ruled not as barbarian warrior kings but as successors to Roman governors. Their resources were extensive: imperial lands, the fisc, forests, waste, mines, ports, highways, taxes, and mints. One of them, Theodebert, even struck gold coins under his own name as early as A.D. 539; to Procopius this was a scandalous usurpation of an imperial right. Their servants were counts, Latin-speaking in districts to the south of the Loire; only in the north-east is there any recession of the Romance language border. The crack household troops of the Merovingians, the *bucellarii*, were nearer to the Byzantine model than to the German hearth-troop; they were paid from the treasury. Commerce still flowed through the Mediterranean. Groups of Syrian traders resided in places as far north as Orleans. Jews and Syrians passed constantly through the kingdom, trafficking in spices and fine stuffs from the East, papyrus and other precious goods, small in bulk but great in profit. The gold coinage of Byzantium ran current through the realm. The king preserved the resources to maintain a shadowy territorial state under the aegis of an imperial shade. The state was weak, the kings enervated, luxurious, fratricidal, but the officials, the bureaucrats of the secular Merovingian state, maintained the taxes and general machinery of government of the late empire; an unbroken line of descent has been traced from imperial imposts to some feudal dues. The Merovingians governed a state more akin indeed to Byzantium than to that of the Carolingians who succeeded them. Gregory of Tours in the late sixth century wrote in a society where the *civitas* remained important, where the Christian bishop preserved some of the function of a Roman magistrate. Up to the end of the seventh century, *romanitas* and *civilitas* were not overwhelmed. The society for the main part spoke and thought in Latin: the heritage of Rome (though barbarized) was preserved. The senatorial aristocracy shared their vast estates with the German warriors; the warriors were slowly assimilated by the superior culture of the Romans.

Attacks on this picture of Merovingian Frankia have been intense. Many think that the death agonies of imperial Rome have been unmercifully prolonged. The political historian sees Merovingian Frankia as a final stage in the disruption of the unity of Rome, an expression of a disintegrating tendency in full evidence as early as the third century A.D. The economist asks if the Syrian traders truly represent survival of the grand commerce of Rome. Do they not rather symbolize the decadence and sloth of the Westerner? The Syrians are adventurers out for quick profits, carrying luxury goods that promise quick returns. Their affinities lie, as M. Latouche picturesquely suggests, with the North African pedlar in modern-day metropolitan France, not with the solid merchant of Rome.[5] The gold coinage, papyrus, fine stuffs and spices point to the existence of a luxury-loving aristocracy, not to a healthy economic interchange of goods between East and West. The deplorable condition of the lesser bronze coinage is a firm indication of economic decay, while the good gold coinage tells only of aristocratic need and of means of supply that made no great impact on the economy as a whole. All these questions and counter-propositions have been put forward with subtle earnestness. Pirenne may have exaggerated the continuity and unconsciously masked the decadence of the late empire itself; no one can deny him credit for rejuvenating the problem.

Yet to this continuity of Romanism – and that the West remained Romanic cannot be denied by one with ears to hear and eyes to see – Britain remained an exception. To the Celtic west Christianity survived, but not in its characteristic Roman territorial guise. Recent work on the extravagant vocabulary of Celtic scholarship points, it is true, to continued awareness of the Latin heritage, though the latinity bears the mark of an esoteric group of scholars rather than a significant vigorous cultural survival.[6] In the Germanic east there was an astonishing lack of continuity with Roman Britain: institutions, laws, language, and religion were Germanic when Augustine and his missionaries landed in Kent in 597.

In the course of the spectacular conversion of the seventh century, however, part of the Roman heritage was recovered. Indeed it has been suggested that the apparent speed and thoroughness of the conversion may be explained by the presence of a submerged Romano-British population, ineffective against their German overlords but ready to flock to the altar in their thousands once the lead was given by the master aristocracy. However this may be – not proven and scarcely provable would seem the only verdict – the simple fact that the organization of the English Church was undertaken by Theodore, Archbishop of Canterbury 668–88, and by Adrian, Abbot of St Peter and St Paul at Canterbury 668–709, the former a citizen of Tarsus, the latter from the restored province of North Africa, is an important pointer to Pirenne's general picture of the sustained unity of Mediterranean civilization. In ecclesiastical

[5] Op.cit., p.123.
[6] P. Grosjean, 'Confusa Caligo', *Celtica*, 1956.

affairs England was drawn back to the ancient world of Rome; in 679–80 and again in 704, Wilfrid, Bishop of York, was present and active at Papal Councils in Rome itself. But this must not hide the fact that the Germanic invasions had made infinitely deeper onslaught against Roman institutions in Britain than elsewhere in the West. From the point of view of Pirenne's proposition England can provide no more than a negative touchstone by which to test continental developments.

Pirenne's second proposition, that the Moslems disrupted the ancient unity of the Mediterranean, has been more severely handled. There is a certain massive common sense of political history behind it. At the beginning of the seventh century the Emperor at Constantinople could send his garrisons to ports in Visigothic Spain, to Carthage, or to the Italian coast. An exarch ruled at Ravenna; Pope Gregory the Great himself had spent fruitful years as papal emissary at the imperial court at Constantinople. In 634 when Pope Honorius sent a pallium to the new Archbishop of Canterbury he dated his accompanying letter 'the 24th year of the reign of our lord Heraclius Augustus, and the 23rd after his consulship; and in the 23rd year of his son Constantine, and the third after his consulship; and in the 3rd year of the most illustrious Caesar Heraclius, his son: the 7th indiction, the year of our Lord, 634.'[7]

A century after this letter was written the followers of an obscure Arabian prophet, by name Mahommed, of whom Pope Honorius had probably never heard, were in full possession of the whole southern half of the fertile crescent. From the Pyrenees to the Indus a new vigorous world religion welded that enormous stretch of country into a loose unity. The commerce of the Mediterranean flowed from Cordova to Alexandria, no longer from Marseilles to Constantinople. Travellers from Gaul to Rome followed the overland routes through the Alps in place of their accustomed sea-journey from Marseilles. The Moslems so controlled the Western Mediterranean that navigation on it became an exceedingly perilous undertaking for a Christian. In consequence the Western world, deprived of its commercial highway, sank into rural stagnation.

The political facts of the Moslem invasions are clear beyond dispute. Controversy has raged over Pirenne's emphasis on the Moslem irruption as the cause of major economic change. It has

[7] Bede, *Hist. Eccl.*, II, 18.

been pointed out, for example, that Provence was in desperate plight before the Moslems came; that the cessation of the sea-route may be attributed to a more orderly state of affairs along the highways of the Lombard kingdom; that more attention should be given to internal strife in Frankia as cause of decline than to external attack; that the closing of the Mediterranean was not as absolute as Pirenne made out. M. Lombard has argued, reversing the Pirenne thesis, that the Moslem invasions served as the crack of a whip to stimulate the slothful Westerners to economic reorganization.[8] Many of the criticisms fail to do justice to Pirenne by over-simplifying his case. A simple statement that the Moslem invasions, the cutting of the Mediterranean, the conversion of that sea from a highway to a barrier, led to the evolution of the land-locked empire of Charles the Great, has something of historical truth to it though it fails to do justice to a highly complicated social situation in which questions of the extent to which Western Europe was already ruralized must be asked.

The English situation is interesting, and there at first sight, as on the Continent, the eighth century presents a broad contrast to the seventh. This contrast lies between a society in contact through Gaul with the Mediterranean world, gold-loving, capable of producing the luxury of Sutton Hoo, and a society in the eighth century whose main external efforts were directed east rather than south, to the conversion of the continental Germans rather than to the well-springs of Mediterranean culture. Emphasis on such contrast must not lead to neglect of the continued close relationship between England on the one hand and Frankia and Rome on the other during the eighth century. Historians of art and of letters stress the unity of the Carolingian world. Yet to some considerable measure both England and Frankia suffered jointly a literal reorientation in the course of the eighth century.

The third of Pirenne's major propositions has not stood the test of time so well. It was tempting, and by no means too divorced from reality, to see the land-locked empire of the Carolingians as retrogressive economically over against the luxurious Merovingian world. Luxury goods from the East still passed to the aristocracy and the great churchmen in the seventh century; this was no

[8] M. Lombard, 'Mahomet et Charlemagne. Le problème économique', *Annales, Économies, sociétés, civilisations*, 1948. Also R. Latouche, op. cit., p.168. R. Hodges and D. Whitehouse follow this line in *Mohammed and Charlemagne, and the Origins of Europe*, London, 1983, arguing that Islamic expansion was a symptom of the social and economic decline of the Roman world, not a cause.

longer true, at all events on the same scale, in the eighth. The fisc still operated in the seventh century; payments in solid gold coins were normal; in the eighth wealth came to depend almost entirely on land. The mercenary *bucellarii* of the Merovingians were replaced by the embryo feudal vassals of Peppin and Charles. The triumph of the Carolingians was the triumph of the more Germanic ruralized east of the Frankish realm against the more Romanic Neustrian west. The essentially secular nature of the Merovingian state contrasted sharply with the theocracy of the Carolingians. Rome in decline departed with the Merovingian; in its place emerged the forerunner of the new medieval world whose major institutions were to be theocratic kingship and the great estate, whose economy was to be rural to a degree difficult for ancient or modern to comprehend.

But do these facts imply that the eighth century was poorer than the seventh? From the first it was argued that they did not. Dopsch disagreed violently with Pirenne on this point; many French historians felt that Pirenne did less than justice to the Carolingians; even his own pupils tended in the product of their detailed research to show that he had exaggerated the decline. There is firm evidence for intensified craft production in pottery and glass. E. Sabbé, for example, proved that trade in fine stuffs, silks embroidered with gold, and brilliantly coloured fabrics, continued throughout the Carolingian period, coming from North Africa, Egypt and Persia as well as from Sicily and Constantinople. He agreed that it would be wrong to exaggerate the importance of the exchange economy that the presence of these goods suggests, but asserted that it would be equally wrong to deny outside commerce its proper place in Carolingian civilization.[9] The luxury trade continued, and was extended to German lands. Well-worn trade routes existed within the Carolingian world, to England, to Moslem Spain, to the Baltic, to the Slavonic world, above all through Italy (especially through Venice) to Byzantium and the Moslem East. R. S. Lopez showed that the inferences drawn from the disappearance of papyrus in the Merovingian chancery should not be attributed to the Moslem invasion.[10] Egypt was overrun in 639–41: papyrus was used by the chancery until 692 and known in Gaul to at least the middle of the

[9] E. Sabbé, 'L'Importation des tissus orientaux en Europe occidentale au haut moyen âge', *Revue belge de philologie et d'histoire*, vol. XIV, 1935, pp.811–48 and 1261–88.
[10] R. S. Lopez, 'Mohammed and Charlemagne: a Revision', *Speculum*, 1943, pp.14–38.

eighth century. The reason for the change was simple expediency; parchment was infinitely cheaper and as convenient. Similarly, the final blow to papyrus production in Egypt was given by the more widespread use of paper.

All of which reads like, and is, legitimate scholarly sniping. A point of central importance emerges with discussion of an economic fact that to Pirenne provided the greatest single indication of a decline in the economy of the West: the disappearance of a native gold currency.

The Merovingians had in the course of the late sixth and seventh centuries come to issue a gold imperial coinage of respectable gold content at the mints of Merovingian Frankia. This coinage was not completely without suspicion in the civilized Mediterranean world. Pope Gregory the Great himself reports that the *solidi* of Gaul were not accepted in Italy. The *solidus* (or sou) was of essentially the same weight and content as the imperial coin reformed by Contantine; more frequent in Gaul was the *tremissis* (or *triens*), the third part of a sou. These coins were copied in England in the first half of the seventh century, and gold coins bearing the name of the London mint were struck. Merovingian gold coins also were current in England; thirty-seven of them, the latest of which is dated to the 620s (and three blanks), were in the Sutton Hoo find. Contained in a purse adorned with garnets, mosaic glass and gold (itself one of the wonders of the jeweller's art), these coins were products of numerous identified mints scattered over Merovingian Frankia from Uzès, Arles and Bordeaux in the south to Huy and Dinant in the north, no two coins from the same mint. Merovingian coins from the Crondall hoard – the other major English seventh-century gold hoard – are more concentrated in their provenance, many coming from Quentovic and nearly all from the north-east of Frankia.

At some time during the last quarter of the century, however, both Frankia and Anglo-Saxon England ceased to mint gold coins. From that time forward to the thirteenth century no regular gold coinage was struck by a Western monarch. There were one or two minor issues, possibly at Duurstede for Louis the Pious; a few coins have survived from the Duurstede mint of the time of Louis the Pious, probably an indication of a move to reorganize coinage for the northern markets; there were, too, occasional sports such as the celebrated sous of Uzès struck in the name of the same monarch; for special occasions a gold coin was sometimes minted. But for the whole of this period the native currency of the Western world was overwhelmingly silver; the *denarius* of Charles the Great and the penny of Offa in England coming to set the pattern favoured for the succeeding centuries. The economy itself has, with some contempt, been labelled a denarial economy.

There are a number of possible reasons why this change should have taken place. To Pirenne it came as a symptom of decline in Mediterranean commerce: the West ceased to trade with the market where gold was the essential medium of exchange, that is with Constantinople and the East; it was a sign of economic decay. There were also other obvious reasons for the disappearance of a native gold currency, some of which Pirenne took into account. The supply of gold was limited. A gold-mine was not a field to be tilled but a sack to be emptied, and the native supplies of gold were emptying fast in the post-Augustan period. An adverse balance of trade with the East, the ancient bogey of trade with India, the burying of treasure in troubled times, of which the Anglo-Saxon Chronicle preserves for us a fifth-century memory,[11] all these factors served to drain the limited gold resources of the West. The existence of the Church, wealthy and well endowed, locked up an appreciable portion of the gold of the West in gold vessels, ornaments, even gold embroidery on robes. Nor was there any commodity in the West sufficiently powerful to attract back gold from the East. The bulk of the slaves went to Moslem Spain, and Spain itself switched over, though for little more than the critical period 755–912, to a native coinage in silver.[12] When the commercial balance was redressed, as occurred in the twelfth century with the export of arms, wood, wheat and cloth from the West, then supplies of gold re-entered the West and in the early thirteenth century, starting in Italy and spreading along the main continental trade-route, native gold coins were again struck at Venice, Verona, above all at Florence, and finally in the mid-thirteenth century in the western monarchies of France and England. Pirenne's logic, as always, is clear and incisive. The Mediterranean ceased to be a highway and became a barrier in the seventh century: the need for a gold coinage disappeared from the West; the Mediterranean was reopened to commerce in the eleventh and twelfth centuries: gold currency came back to the West.

[11] A. S. Chronicle, *sub anno* 418: the Romans collected all the treasures which were in Britain, and hid some in the ground so that no one could find them afterwards, and took some with them into Gaul.
[12] Religious reasons, respect for the religious authority of the Eastern Caliphs, may be the true cause of this change, as is suggested by F. Mateu y Llopis, *La moneda española*, Barcelona, 1946, pp.108–9.

It does not follow, however, that a lack of native gold coinage implies economic decay. Other factors enter into the question. Though native coins were no longer struck, gold coins continued to be known and used in the West during these centuries. They came from two sources; from Byzantium and from the Moslem world. The idea was embodied in the Theodosian Code that money is struck for the service of the public, that it is an instrument of exchange, official in nature. The emperors of the East persisted in this belief. One of the glories of the Byzantine world consisted in its standard of gold coinage. In spite of all vicissitudes the ancient *aureus* survived the ages victoriously. Towards 1200 the Byzantine *hyperperon* still equalled, in weight of pure gold, three-quarters or thereabouts of the weight of its Roman ancestor.[13] References to *besants* are found throughout the West. In the eleventh century they occur particularly along the overland commercial route of the Danube into Bavaria. The Moslems also continued to strike gold coins of good quality. There is one example, the so-called dinar of Offa, which shows the eighth-century Mercian king striking a gold coin, with Arabic religious inscription maintained, but bearing the Latin name and title *Offa Rex*. There are many references in Western texts to a coin – it could also be a unit of account – known as the *mancus*. At one time it was thought that these coins were Arabic: indeed a derivation from the Arabic *man-qash*, meaning struck, was invented. It is now generally accepted that *mancus*, a word philologically connected with its successor the French *manqué*, meant no more than a defective *solidus*, one that had been struck, probably in the first place in Byzantine Italy in the course of the eighth and ninth centuries, a *solidus*, a Byzantine *solidus*, that was not quite as good as the real thing. It was a light-weight coin in use at Rome itself, and from there the word spread even to Moslem Spain. The myth of the *mancus* has been exploded: a mystery still remains.[14] The coins must have circulated in sufficient number to be accepted as a unit of account throughout the West. In England, as will be shown later, the *mancus* was well known as a unit of account equal to thirty pence and also as a coin, though in the latter guise it was clearly rare and minted only on special occasions.[15]

[13] M. Bloch, 'Le Problème de l'or au moyen âge', *Annales d'histoire économique et sociale*, 1933, p.2.

[14] P. Grierson, 'Carolingian Europe and the Arabs: the Myth of the Mancus', *Revue belge de philologie et d'histoire*, vol. XXXII, 1954. Also an important note on the general significance of the currency changes, *Numismatics and History* (Historical Association pamphlet), London, 1951, pp.9–10.

[15] See below, Chapter 3, pp.128–9.

The predominance of coins from the great commercial empires reminds us of one fundamental fact concerning all coinage. Convenience is the first reason for the striking of coins; confidence is a close second. In particular confidence in the weight of precious metal in the coin could be given by the authority of the king or ruler in whose name it was struck. Such confidence in gold came to the Westerners from the ancient empire and the infidel, not from their own rulers.

Fashion also played a considerable part in determining the nature of a currency. Tacitus tells that as far back as the first century A.D. the barbarians preferred silver to gold.[16] Sensible men in their way, they preferred the metal that was precious enough to use in local marketing, but not too precious to express the values of their everyday transactions. Gold was the essential commodity for interregional exchange in the Mediterranean context: in the Baltic and North Sea areas a fondness for silver currency persisted even after the introduction of native gold.

In assessing the significance of this general swing away from native gold currency there is one positive point that should be established. As indicated above, there was at least a temporary slackening of trading contact with the East, but it is not right to assume that this slackening was caused by increased poverty. An economist could read the transition from gold to silver currency in the latter half of the seventh century as an answer to deflationary tendencies which had led to the farming of treasure and a slackening of exchange. In other words there was a wholesale adaptation of monetary symbols to a fall in prices and to a corresponding appreciation in value of the precious metals used in coining. From Anglo-Saxon England there is just not enough information about prices to sustain or reject such a thesis. The coin evidence itself has a direct bearing on this question, and numismatists are now inclined to put stability before mere metal content as a symptom of health in a society and in an economy. In some ways the reformed silver currency of the Carolingian empire, and the associated reformed silver currency of Offa in England, show precisely the reverse of Pirenne's argument; that is to say economic revival on the all-important local scale. To say only that the Merovingians continued to mint gold is to falsify the picture. At the lower level of currency their coins marked an appalling regression from the days of imperial Rome.[17] The petty bronze coins that have sur-

---

[16] *Germania*, c. v.
[17] P. Grierson, *Numismatics and History*, pp.9–10.

vived indicate confusion and general disruption. Gold coins would buy luxury for the few, would give the confidence without which interregional trade was impossible; the lesser currency of the fifth, sixth and to a considerable degree the seventh centuries speaks of impoverished local markets loosely supervised, of an economy which may be called an exchange economy only at risk of distorting the term. The Carolingian peace gave a chance to the local market to thrive; and the local markets with their demand for a stable silver currency are a truer index of a country's prosperity than are the visits of Eastern merchants bearing luxury goods for aristocratic churchmen, Germanic lords and survivors of the senatorial class.

The further consequences of Pirenne's arguments which, though at times negatively, have been the formative influences on modern thought, were quite revolutionary. To him the Dark Ages were still dark but came late. Western Europe still knew the grand commerce of the Mediterranean, was still Roman in essence, to the end of the seventh century. Change came with the Moslem invasions, the true dark beginning of the Middle Ages. The succeeding three centuries found the West at its poorest. Only the achievements of Charles the Great illumine a dark age, and his merit lay in a realistic effort to attain political equilibrium in a land-locked economy. His success was temporary only, and followed by the savage ninth and tenth centuries which brought economic localism and ruralism at its most miserable to a Western Europe racked by invasion from Northman, Magyar, Slav and Moslem. The economy of the early Middle Ages was not a primitive economy, but indeed this economy of regression or decadence of which we spoke earlier. The very education of the times supposed the non-existence of a civilized, lettered, merchant class. Carolingian minuscule was a scholarly, clerical achievement of no use to the merchant, the clerk or the agent. Not until the eleventh century did revival begin, first in Italy, then throughout the whole of the West as a merchant class arose.

Modern scholars are rapidly modifying this interpretation of the period both on the grounds that Pirenne has painted too rosy a picture of the seventh century and too gloomy a picture of the tenth. For the economist the greatest advances have been made in the fields of rural history under the inspiration of the great and lamented Marc Bloch. His synthesis, *Les caractères originaux de l'histoire rurale française*, Oslo, 1931, and later *La Société féodale*, Paris, 1939–40, supplemented by regional surveys by other scholars relating to Lorraine, to Burgundy and to Bavaria, bring out the vitality of these centuries during which there evolved the medieval manor. This manor was no mere fossil but a living economic and social institution brought into being to deal successfully with the difficult conditions of the age. Some of the veil that covers the tremendous effort in which man achieved a permanent conquest of his environment has been lifted. Many signs of advance are now known, such as those involved in the extensive use of water-mills, of superior harness for farm-beasts, of more skilful use of the motive power of water, ox and horse. Man was less dependent in Western Europe on geographical and geological conditions at the end of the tenth century than at the beginning of the eighth. The social consequence of such technical advance is connected with one of the most strangely neglected of major social themes in Western history: the rejection of classical slavery. In Merovingian Frankia the great estate still relied to a large extent on slave labour; by the end of our period the slave was an anomaly, as a social class insignificant. Behind the new commerce of the eleventh century is traced the slow plodding advance of corporate agriculture. During these centuries the peasant was fixed on his plot though his hold might be disguised under manorial forms. Anglo-Saxon England played its own part in these general Western developments, more advanced in some respects, notably in its achievement of political unity, more backward in others such as its late adherence to slavery.

3. ANGLO-SAXON ENGLAND AND OVERSEAS TRADE

(a) The pre-Viking period

For the moment, however, our concern lies with one aspect of Anglo-Saxon England; its overseas trade and the qualification of the picture of a stagnant, land-locked Europe that is necessitated by the very existence of that trade. As in so many fields there is a broad division of the whole period into two, with a breach occurring towards the middle of the ninth century: into a pre-Danish and post-Danish period or, if full provision is made for a considerable overlap, into a Frisian and a Danish period.

It is difficult to keep a sense of proportion in dealing with this question. A statement to the effect that overseas trade played a small but not negligible part in the Anglo-Saxon economy might be adequate up to a point, as long as it is recognized that that point is soon reached. It would be too cautious for the late tenth and eleventh centuries when London was a thriving centre of international trade; it would probably be too cautious for some centres, London in particular, but also York and Canterbury, throughout the whole period.

The problem arises in distinguishing significant trade from mere contact incidental to religious or cultural life. Indeed many would say that much of the so-called evidence of Dark Age trade tells of gift-exchanges, tribute and even plunder rather than of free trade.[18] It is only too tempting to read more into the journeys of pilgrims and missionaries than is justified by the facts. The pre-Alfredian period is rich in reference to Anglo-Saxon saints and scholars. Englishmen played a greater part in continental affairs in the eighth century than they were to play again until the eighteenth. England had received benefits from the Continent in the course of the seventh century; these gifts were repaid with interest during the succeeding hundred years. Yet the repayment came primarily in the cultural and the ecclesiastical spheres: the Conversion of Germany and the Reform of the Frankish Church, in both of which considerable enterprises Anglo-Saxons played a leading part. References to the islanders specifically as traders, however, are few, though significant, especially significant when the preponderant interest of the sources with religious and cultural matters is taken into account.[19]

For example a charter of Childebert III, of 710, referring to conditions in the middle of the seventh century, mentions *negociantes aut Saxonis vel quaecumquelibet nacionis*. These Saxons, and they are more likely to be islanders than continental Saxons, are singled out in this way for special reference in connection with the merchants visiting the annual fair at the monastery of St Denis near Paris (founded c.634). At the same monastery in the middle of the eighth century a certain *Saxo transmarinus* stopped to recover his health (*ex eis qui Angli dicuntur*). About the same period an English *negociator* named Botto was settled at Marseilles. Other references in Lives of Saints suggest that merchant ships from Britain called regularly at points along the north coast of France and off the mouth of the Loire, probably already by the end of the sixth century and

[18] In particular, P. Grierson, 'Commerce in the Dark Ages: a Critique of the Evidence', *T. R. Hist. S.*, 1959, pp.123–40.
[19] The following paragraph draws heavily on W. Levison, *England and the Continent in the Eighth Century*, Oxford, 1946, esp. pp.4–14.

certainly by the end of the seventh.[20] Wilfrid when he undertook his journey to Rome in 679–80 travelled by the Frisian port of Duurstede because he was afraid of falling into his enemies' hands if he chose the *via rectissima* through the port of Quentovic. St Boniface in 716 crossed the Channel from London to Duurstede, and in 718 from London to Quentovic. Willibald in 720, at the start of a journey that led to the Holy Land and Constantinople, to Rome and to Monte Cassino, took a different route, from *Hamwih* near Southampton to Rouen, at both of which settlements markets existed.[21] Terminology concerning these markets was still not completely standardized in Latin or in Anglo-Saxon. In one passage Bede referred to London as an *emporium* visited by many peoples coming by land or sea.[22] *Mercimonium* was the term used of the market near Rouen. In Anglo-Saxon *port* was in customary use, and also *burh* even at this early stage was used of a collection of dwelling houses (possibly, it is true, defended by a wall or an earthwork), as is shown in an eighth-century continental description of the English quarter at Rome, 'which in their language is called burh', the present-day Borgo San Spirito.[23] One point is evident. On both sides of the Channel – and it is well to remember that in Roman days the *litus Saxonicum* lay to the south as well as to the north of the Channel – there lived seamen who were accustomed to cross from Anglo-Saxon England to Merovingian Gaul.

Of the art of ship-building little is known of this pre-Viking Age, but enough to recognize that technical advance on the Nydam ship of the Migration Age was steady and consistent.[24] The Kvalsund ship of c. 600 was made with keel and rudder, fully capable of crossing the North Sea under mast and sail with cargo. The fine ship of Sutton Hoo, which was buried in its mound in the 620s, a generation or so after it was built, was eighty feet long and of slender build. It was not as well advanced as the Kvalsund ship, but it was still capable of a sea-going voyage. There was no sign of a mast or sail at Sutton Hoo, though some allowance must be made

[20] A. A. Lewis, 'Le commerce et la navigation sur les côtes atlantiques de la Gaule du Vᵉ au VIIIᵉ siècle', *Moyen Âge*, 1953, pp.249–98. E. Sabbé, 'Les Relations économiques entre l'Angleterre et le Continent au haut moyen âge', *Moyen Âge*, 1950, pp.167–93, esp. p.173.

[21] Eddius Stephanus, *Life of St Wilfrid*, ed. B. Colgrave, Cambridge, 1927, c. 25; W. Levison, op. cit., p.6: Vita Willibaldi episcopi Eichstetensis, M. G. H., SS.XV/1, p.91.

[22] Bede, *Hist. Eccl.*, II, 3.

[23] W. Levison, op. cit., p.41.

[24] H. Shetelig and A. W. Brøgger, *The Viking Ships*, Oslo, 1953.

for the ceremonial nature of the mound and its contents. In the North spectacular achievements were made in boat-building in the period 600–900, and the Frisians also had their own part to play, as the effigy of a sailing ship on a ninth-century coin from Duurstede demonstrates. The broad-beamed *kog* was known by that name in the ninth and tenth centuries, and until the slow maturity of Scandinavian techniques the Frisians remained the master seamen of this period in the North Sea and the Channel. It was to them that Alfred turned in his need for help against the Danes in the late ninth century. When the Anglo-Saxon poet lamented the anxiety of a sailor's wife, that wife was significantly enough a Frisian.[25]

The geographical position of the *Frissones* or Frisians was considered in the previous chapter. They remained heathen until the success of Willibrord's mission to them of 690–739; they retained independence or partial independence until the harsh campaigns of Charles the Great against the continental Saxons brought absorption in the Carolingian empire to them also. They travelled extensively through the Baltic and to them has been ascribed the fostering of important mercantile settlements such as those at Hedeby, near the modern Schleswig, and at Bjørko in Sweden. Their chief function in the European economy was to act as middlemen, carrying the products of the Rhineland and even of Italy into England and Scandinavia and bringing back in return slaves and furs. The height of their early medieval trade was reached in the period 750–850, when firmer Frankish control gave better conditions under which the merchants could thrive in their homeland. A Frisian colony at York, and further colonies at Worms, Xanten, Duisburg, Birken and Mainz, show the intensity of the trade contacts during this period.[26]

Evidence of close interest in England is found, however, at an earlier period than this mid-eighth century, indeed to some extent it had never been absent from the days of migration. Bede mentioned a Frisian trader at London who was ready to take charge of a captured prisoner of war brought down by his Mercian captor.[27] Perhaps most significant of all is the evidence of the coinage. The late seventh century saw emerge a silver currency that was used extensively in trade between Anglo-Saxon England

---

[25] This point is made by Professor Whitelock, *The Beginnings of English Society*, London, 1952, p.124.
[26] Dirk Jellema, 'Frisian Trade in the Dark Ages', *Speculum*, 1955.
[27] Bede, *Hist. Eccl.*, IV, 22.

and the Frisian lands. The coins, the *sceattas*, as they are usually called though it is more accurate to refer to them as pennies even at this early stage, were struck both sides of the Channel, and were of similar weight and type whether drawn from English or from Frisian mints.[28] Indeed it is difficult to say whether some types are Frisian or English, and the custom has grown of referring to them as Anglo-Frisian. Artistically the coins show influence from Roman, Merovingian and Northern sources; some such as the Woden-Monster or Dragon type have an honourable place in any discussion of the development of zoomorphic style. This Anglo-Frisian coinage reached its peak in circulation during the first half of the eighth century, and had a wide distribution; examples have been discovered as far afield as Scandinavia and in the great hoard at Cimiez near Marseilles. There are over a thousand provenanced finds from England itself, mostly in the south and east, especially in Kent and East Anglia, though some appear as far north as Whitby; over sixteen hundred have been discovered in Frisia, of which half came from Domburg on the island of Walcheren.[29] The Anglo-Frisian commerce, suggested by the existence of the *sceat* coinage, and confirmed by analysis of its distribution patterns, needs to be taken into account as a most important factor in the general economic picture of the late Merovingian and of Carolingian days.

The centre of activity of Frisian commerce was the *emporium* known as Duurstede. Lying on the Rhine, this centre was admirably suited to traffic from the Cologne district through into the north. It was also well placed in that the hinterland could provide articles for export, hides and probably some proportion of the *pallia Frisonica*, that are so often mentioned in the Carolingian records. Wine, precious goods from the East, and glassware from the Rhine passed through this Frisian town long before it came under direct Frankish control. With the Frankish conquest, however, coincided its most prosperous period. It became one of the chief toll stations of the empire, and the mint under Frankish control regulated the coinage for the whole of the middle Rhine. Excavations show that it covered an area of about thirty acres, taking on the appearance in the early ninth century of a typical Frankish *castellaria*. There were many houses spread out for more than half a mile along the

[28] See below, pp.118–19.
[29] P. Grierson and M. Blackburn, M. E. C. I.; S. E. Rigold and D. M. Metcalf, 'A Revised Check-list of English finds of sceattas' in *Sceattas in England and on the Continent*, ed. D. Hill and D. M. Metcalf, *B. A. R.*, 128, 1984, pp.245–68.

bank of the Rhine; palisade walls filled in with earth protected the settlement; a long dock stretched out along the river. In time the new settlements, originally temporary camps of passing merchants, outstripped in importance the old habitation-site. The new name of Duurstede made its appearance for the first time in the ninth century, the *vicus* by Duurstede (Wijk-bij-Duurstede). The Viking raids hit Duurstede hard and the town was destroyed in 863. Even more deadly was the continuous presence of Viking pirates at their island lair of Walcheren. Predominance even in the Frisian lands passed away especially to Tiel, where English merchants are heard of at the beginning of the eleventh century, and where the native merchants warned the Emperor Henry II that their dues would not be forthcoming unless he maintained proper peace, since otherwise they would not be able to visit Britain *causa negotiandi*, nor would the Britons be able to dwell with them. By the end of the tenth century the great days of Duurstede were over.[30]

Of equal importance for England, although not as central to this North Sea economy, was the port of Quentovic. Situated on the river Canche at the head of a network of Roman roads leading through Neustria to the Boulonnais, Quentovic in the fifth and sixth centuries replaced Boulogne as the important point of departure for Britain. In the seventh century its importance as the main Christian point of entry rivalled that of heathen Duurstede. It retained its importance in spite of severe Viking attacks in 842 and again in 900 until, probably as a consequence of the silting up of its harbour, Wissant in the mid-tenth century became the chief port in the region, a position it was to hold until the rise of Calais in the twelfth century. It is possible that Frisian seafarers had considerable influence at this point even at this early period. The most valuable information comes, however, again from the Carolingian period when Carolingian discipline in the way of edicts and capitularies regulating trade left a permanent impress on the economy. In the reign of Charles the Great an important dispute sprang up between the Frank and Offa of Mercia. The two intermediaries used at one stage in the dispute were a certain Grippo, *praefectus* or, as the English might say, reeve of the *emporium* of Quentovic, and also Gervaldus, a *procurator super regni negotia*, who had for many years supervised royal rights in various markets and cities and above all in Quentovic. Gervaldus was the Abbot of St Wandrille, and a good friend of Offa in Mercia. Like

[30] F. Keutgen, *Urkunden zur Stadtischen Verfassungsgeschichte*, Berlin, 1901, p.44. On Duurstede generally, cf. Jellema, op. cit.

Duurstede Quentovic was a very important centre for tolls, and indeed the most important mint after the palace itself.[31] According to the *Praeceptum negotiatorum* of 828 which was probably, as Sabbé suggests, an attempt to safeguard professional merchants from the exactions of unscrupulous landlords en route, exemption was granted from all tolls except the imperial tolls at Quentovic, Duurstede and the Mont Cenis.[32] The empire systematized and channelled the flow of trade, especially that coming from the north. On the English side of the Channel foreign merchants were welcomed, provided that sureties could be found for them. The royal interest in tolls can be seen from both the laws and the charters that have survived. Eadbert of Kent remitted tolls on ships at Fordwich and Saare. Ethelbald of Mercia considered the remission of tolls at London on a ship a fitting gift for a favoured monastic house or bishop's see, evidence incidentally that English merchants handled carrying trade within the islands.[33] A Frisian would not have had much, if any, language difficulty in these days: no more than an American has in England today. As late as the sixteenth century Dekker, the Elizabethan dramatist, could introduce whole scenes in the argot of the Dutch and Frisian coast into his *Shoemaker's Holiday*, confident that his audience would be able to follow it.

Fortunately there is further documentary evidence from the time of Charles the Great of Frankish concern with English trade. On two occasions late in the reign of the great Mercian king, Offa, in 789–90 and again in 795–6, there were strained relations between the two monarchs, and on the first of these occasions the dispute (over the breakdown of a marriage agreement) led to a temporary embargo on English trade into Frankia. At the end of 790 the Frankish ports were still closed, and Alcuin expected to be sent to England to make peace. It is possible that the later dispute, in the last year of Offa's life, did not reach the point of open rupture, and in the correspondence that has survived Charles showed anxiety on two scores: that merchants should not escape dues because they enter his realm disguised as pilgrims, and that the mantles imported into Frankia, the *sagæ*, should be of accustomed length. A slightly later narrative account told of Charles's indignation at a

[31] Ex miraculis S. Wandregisili, M. G. H. SS. XV/1, p.408. E. Sabbé, op. cit., p.180. E. H. D. I, p.341.
[32] E. Sabbé op. cit., p.179.
[33] C. S. 149. The king claimed the tax on the port of London, jure publico; C. S. 152, 171, 188 and 189.

new-fangled custom of rounding cloaks at the knees, which might have been old-fashioned prejudice or just hard economic sense. The Frisians, it is said, were selling those miserable little cloaks, *illa palliola*, at the same price though they did not contain so much cloth. 'What is the use', said Charles, 'of these *pittaciola*: I cannot cover myself up with them in bed, when riding I cannot defend myself against the wind and rain, and getting down *ad necessaria naturæ tibiarum congelatione deficio*'.[34] In his letter to Offa Charles was more guarded, but stated that if the Mercians complained about the size of the stones that were sent to them (probably from Tournai for use in fonts), then he in turn must complain about the length of the cloaks.[35]

Although the origin of these disputes may well have been personal and dynastic, the importance of the complaints and of the methods employed in conducting the quarrel is considerable to the economic historian. Charles used the economic weapon of forbidding access to a market and Offa in turn attempted a reciprocal embargo. The mention of cloaks from England is the first indication of the importance of English sheep and English wool; the anxiety of the statesmen concerned suggests that there is a significant trade involved. Both rulers were concerned that their merchants should have the protection of the other's courts.

Other eighth-century sources hint at considerable export of textiles from England. The Abbot of Wearmouth in 764 reported that he had sent two pallia of the most ingenious workmanship, the one plain and the other coloured, together with books relating to the life of St Cuthbert, and a bell to the Bishop of Mainz; in 800 the Abbey of St Bertin reserved a portion of its revenue to buy English cloth, *drappos et kamisias quae vulgo berniscrist vocitantur*; Paul the Deacon referred to the *vestimenta linea, qualia Angli-Saxones habere solent ornata institis latioribus vario colore contextis* – the idea of a drably dressed community needs to be dispelled.[36] Even the Moslem world knew of the reputation of the English cloth and from the ninth to the eleventh century many Arabic sources referred to its fame. Some scholars go so far as to hold that the bulk of the *pallia Frisonica* came from England. This is an exceedingly difficult problem. It seems likely that the phrase refers to cloaks carried by the Frisians rather than cloaks made by them. But it also seems

[34] Monarchi Sangallensis, Gesta Karoli, M. G. H., *SS.* II, p.747, cited by E. Sabbé, op. cit., p.183.

[35] *E. H. D.* I, p.849, letter of Charles the Great to Offa, A.D. 796.

[36] *E. H. D.* I, p.832; Cartulaire de l'abbaye de Saint-Bertin, p.65. E. Sabbé, op. cit., p.184; Paul Diaconus, *Historia Langobardorum*, IV, 22.

highly probable that they did not come exclusively from any one quarter, but merely give an indication of Frisian dominance in the carrying trade with the cloaks coming from Flanders, to be sure, as well as from England and possibly Frisia itself.

The evidence is not powerful enough to sustain more than the bare exciting hint of the beginning of English textile activity. To England was brought glassware, rare pottery, wine and some precious goods from the East. What, apart from cloth, was taken back in return? One grim and certain answer is: slaves. Right to the end of its days, Anglo-Saxon England was a slave-owning community. Some of the earliest knowledge of England comes from Bede's story of Gregory and the fair slave-boys from York; Gregory also made provision for the purchase of young slaves who could be trained to take part in his mission to England. Rich Christians in Frankia took it as a special Christian duty to redeem shiploads of captive slaves – even up to a hundred as the life of St Eligius says – especially of the Saxon race who at that time (some years before 641) were suffering disturbances which caused them to be driven hither and thither like sheep. One of these slaves, Balthild, became consort of Clovis II (639–57) and later Regent, ending her days in 677 as a founder of monasteries particularly the house at Chelles. As Dr Levison comments, this was 'truly an extraordinary career for an English slave sold to the Continent'.[37] Opinion under ecclesiastical influence hardened against the sale of slaves overseas, and a law of Ine stated that anyone selling his own countryman, bond or free, across the sea, was to pay his own wergeld as a penalty even though the man so sold was guilty.[38] The regulation was not closely observed. Even in the eleventh century there were still slavers trading from Bristol.[39] Anselm, in 1102, was still legislating hard against the *nefarium negotium*, by which hitherto in England men had been sold like brute beasts.[40]

The sources of supply of slaves were maintained throughout the Anglo-Saxon period, to some extent by warfare, but much more significantly by legal penalties and economic pressures. Defeat in battle could lead to enslavement, that is if the prisoner were fortunate enough to escape the sword of an avenger. Failure to meet the obligations of a freeman, to render a geld or a fyrd service, could lead to reduction to slavery. According to the laws

[37] W. Levison, op. cit., p.10.
[38] Ine II.
[39] *Vita Wulfstani*, ed. R. R. Darlington, pp.43 and 91.
[40] D. Wilkins, *Concilia*, I, London, 1737, p.383, c.xxviii.

of Ine, a thief and his household were to be enslaved, if the theft were performed with their knowledge.[41] Default in payment of due legal penalty led to slavery. Men could sell themselves for want in troubled times. It may be that the number of slaves, particularly in seventh- and eighth-century society, has consistently been under-estimated.[42] The free ceorls were well advanced in the social scale.

Continental evidence also exists for the slave-trade. Neither in England nor on the Continent was the Church concerned directly with the institution of slavery as such, but with the possibility of the selling of a Christian to an unbeliever. Why should it be? David was a better man as a *servus* than as a king. Pride was the deadly sin against which the theologian directed his shafts. The slave stood better chance than most of avoiding that sin. The indirect concern of the Church with slavery was, on the other hand, of great significance, and is dealt with in a later chapter in connection with the social thought of the Church. Throughout Gaul there existed a well-worn slavers' route to Marseilles and thence to Italy, North Africa and Spain. The advent of the Moslems may well have fostered rather than hindered this unsavoury trade. As early as the seventh century Franks established themselves in the Slav communities, and captives in tribal wars flooded the market that led to Spain where the very word *Slav* was the term from which the uglier 'slave' was derived. England with its inter-tribal war provided a parallel market, even after conversion. Marc Bloch was of the opinion that successful slave-trading accounted for the amount of gold that was drawn back to England in the shape of mancuses in the late Anglo-Saxon period.[43] This seems an exaggerated view-point, but it is probably true that fitfully and spasmodically the slave-trade operated to feed the needs of two distinct communities: the Moslems who remained a slave-owning people, and the Scandinavians whose colonization of Iceland was undertaken with the aid of many thralls from these islands.

Of products that were brought into these islands wine was probably the most profitable. Sherds of pottery from amphorae such as those customarily used for transporting Rhenish wine have been discovered at *Hamwih* in the same layer as a hoard of eighth-century coins. In the following century such pottery is common in London,

[41] Ine 7.1.
[42] For the Domesday figures, see below, pp.351–2. Also below, p.337.
[43] M. Bloch, 'Le Problème de l'or', op. cit., p.19.

91

and is known to some extent in *Hamwih* and Canterbury.[44] Ecclesi-astical use demanded wine, and probably more wine than could be produced in this country. The vine had spread north from Italy to the south of France and thence to Bordeaux in the early centuries of imperial Rome. As Christianity extended to areas where the climate was not particularly suitable for vine-growing, such as parts of Belgium, abbeys were endowed with lands from richer vine valleys.[45] Domesday Book shows a fair but not heavy scattering of vineyards throughout the southern half of England, but the unit of measurement, the *arpent* was a Norman term, and it is likely that most of these recorded vineyards were associated with the new Norman lords. The fact that vines were grown in higher latitudes than at present is sometimes held to be a symptom of a finer and drier climate in the first millenium A.D. As M. Latouche wryly remarks, it may better be ascribed to less sophisticated palates.[46] Wine was still much of a luxury. Aelfric, the great English scholar of the late tenth and early eleventh centuries, wrote a colloquy as an exercise for schoolboys, one of whom is made to say that he is not wealthy enough to drink wine – and that wine is not a drink for children or fools but for old and wise men.[47]

To conclude, it can be said that there is adequate evidence for continuous and regular movement of traders back and forth across the Channel transporting in their vessels slaves, textiles and wine. The distribution of Anglo-Saxon coinage found on the Continent suggests major routes through the Rhine and Duurstede, to the Neustrian lands through Rouen and Quentovic. There is also some evidence of contact with Bordeaux and through the Garonne to the Rhone valley and to Marseilles. For all the perils of journeying Anglo-Saxon pilgrims, churchmen and also traders were more footloose in the early period than might at first thought be ex-pected. By the third quarter of the ninth century they had gained an unenviable reputation for cupidity among the Franks.[48]

---

[44] G. C. Dunning, 'Trade Relations between England and the Continent in the late Anglo-Saxon Period', *Dark Age Britain*, p.219.

[45] H. Pirenne, 'Un grand Commerce d'exportation au moyen âge: les vins de France', *Annales d'histoire économique et sociale*, 1933, pp.229–30. Also the work of Van Werveke, *Revue belge de philologie et d'Histoire*, vol. II (1923), pp.643–62, and vol.IV (1925), pp.136–41, and a note by P. Grierson, 'Commerce in the Dark Ages', *T. R. Hist. S.*, 1959, p.128.

[46] R. Latouche, op. cit., p.94.

[47] *Aelfric's Colloquy*, ed. G. N. Garmonsway, London, 1938, p.47.

[48] E. Sabbé, op. cit., p.186; M. G. H., *Ep.*, Kar. Aevi, t. IV., p.190.

(b) The Viking Age and after

It was during the ninth century that the boat-building techniques of the Northerners came to fruition. Between 600 and 900 the skill of the Norsemen perfected the use of the true keel which gave full strength and solidity to the craft, so that it could sail with proper mast raised in practically all weathers. Coupled with political and social pressures in Scandinavia, that matrix of nations, these technical achievements opened the way for a vast movement of devastation and expansion which was to be a dominant political theme of European life from the early ninth century to the end of the eleventh century. The Vikings came to dominate the North Sea not only as pirates, raiders and settlers but also as merchants. Theirs was not an exclusive domination. Frisian trade still continued, and Frisian coins have been found along the main Varangian route, even in Kiev itself on the way to Constantinople.

The coming of the Vikings began a new phase of economic life, and sufficient emphasis has not always been placed on the extraordinary widening of horizons that they brought to the western world. It is true that interest in cosmography had been aroused early. Benedict Biscop had brought with him from Rome in the late seventh century a precious book on cosmography which he presented to King Aldfrith of Northumbria. In the middle of the eighth century Bishop Lul attempted to get from York *libros cosmografiorum*, though his correspondent, Coena, reported that he had only damaged copies.[49] The writings of Adomnan and Bede on the Holy Places and the 'Life of Willibald', written by an Anglo-Saxon nun at Heidenheim, also give proof of the curiosity of the age concerning distant places. Missionary activity in Germany and pilgrimages to Rome and further east to the Holy Land increased the fund of knowledge of other parts of the world and other peoples. With the Viking Age came greater precision and extension of knowledge. At the end of the ninth century Alfred inserted in the translation of Orosius two accounts of northern voyages, the one by a Norseman, Ohthere, who voyaged around the North Cape, further north than man had travelled before.[50] Ohthere had a firm eye to economic advantage and described the wealth in walrus and whale products, in furs, birds' feathers (eider-down?), and sealskin for ropes, which was available then

[49] *Boniface, Epist.* 124, p.261: W. Levison, op. cit., p.42; Haddan and Stubbs, vol. III, p.437.
[50] *King Alfred's Orosius*, ed. H. Sweet, E. E. T. S., 1883, pp.17–21.

in the north. The other traveller, probably an Englishman, was named Wulfstan, and his trip ran to Hedeby and thence to a port near the modern Gdansk. Modern archaeologists, particularly Professor Jankuhn of Kiel, have revealed the tangible remains of the tremendous vitality of the Baltic and North Sea world in the ninth and tenth centuries. The fury of the Northerner was great; he could be a cruel, cunning ravager and destroyer. Yet against that should be placed his opening up of the northern world to an intense economic activity. The longship has stolen much of the thunder that rightly belongs to the less spectacular trader. A long series of fortified markets was set up from Dublin to Kiev, and often navigation points are found to bear names, the earliest forms of which are Scandinavian in origin. For example, in the Bristol Channel, Flatholm, Steepholm and Skokholm show that here, as in so many other parts of the northern, world, it was a people speaking a Scandinavian tongue who first opened up the ports to continuous and regular transmarine navigation.

On their achievement in England itself something has already been said in the opening chapter. For the moment it is enough to note that England was richer and more advanced than the backward homelands of these new-comers. They settled, probably in large numbers, but were relatively quickly assimilated, politically and socially. The regular use of coinage was unknown to them in their own lands but they rapidly acquired the techniques from their hosts, and reputable coins were struck by Viking kings in East Anglia and York at quite an early stage in their settlement. The great hoard of some seven thousand coins deposited at Cuerdale in Lancashire in the opening years of the tenth century, whether it be a Viking treasure or not, illustrates vividly the mercantile vigour of the world in which these Scandinavians were operating. Containing coins from the Moslem world and from all parts of the Carolingian empire including Italy, the hoard also offers some five thousand coins from the Danish mints of East Anglia and York. In the political field the West Saxon dynasty emerged in the tenth century, strong from the fire of Viking invasion; it crumbled again in the eleventh century, and England became part of Canute's Scandinavian empire. It was an articulate and assimilative world. England, more so even than north Germany, was the chief source of cultural inspiration and religious conversion, and played a leading part in the civilizing of the North.

There are good texts upon which a discussion of the general effect of this Viking movement upon the development of English overseas trade can be based. The tenth and eleventh centuries saw the emergence of a merchant class in England, even at this stage fitting uneasily into the traditional social pattern of a predominantly rural community. Aelfric, in his colloquy referred to above, introduced a merchant who, called on to justify his ways, declared that he was useful to all men because he climbed into his ship with his goods, and sailed beyond the seas to sell his goods and buy precious things which were not found in this land, bringing them back in great peril of shipwreck, at times scarcely escaping with his life. He admitted that he took a profit, else how would he feed himself, his wife, and sons?[51] This type of seafarer/merchant participating directly in the perils of his enterprises was one familiar and not completely distasteful to the theologian. A private text of the eleventh century revealed how he was fitted into the general scheme of society. If he covered the sea three times with his own ship, he would thrive to thegnright.[52] There is no good reason to doubt the general validity of this statement; such a man would be well able, financially and in personal daring, to support the higher rank.

Indication of the extent to which the trading life of the community had developed is given, not only by incidental reference in ecclesiastical literature to a wealth that must have come in part from overseas, but also from a very important treaty that was made between Ethelred and Olaf Tryggvasson after the onslaught of 991. Elaborate precautions were taken to see that the truce was observed. Further it was laid down that if a subject of King Ethelred came to a land not covered specifically by the truce, protection was to be accorded his ship and goods. As an appendix to this agreement was added a long statement, the fullest there is, concerning the process of vouching to warranty. It is true that this appendix may have been accidentally tacked on to the agreement, which does read as if it is self-sufficient in itself. But internal freedom from theft may have been an important supplementary object of those who drew up the agreement, the prime purpose of which was the regulation of overseas traffic and freedom from piracy.[53] As Sir Frank Stenton says, the agreement in itself is clear proof that English merchants were to be met with in continental ports. Eleventh-century evidence points to an intensification of

---

[51] *Aelfric's Colloquy*, p.34.
[52] Geþyncðo, 6; Liebermann I, p.458.
[53] II Ethelred.

trade along the route that led from Cologne to Bruges and it seems certain that this was further connected with a vigorous and vital trade between Flanders and England.[54]

Of the origin of towns it seems wiser to speak in connection with the internal trade of Anglo-Saxon England. In the main the towns were more closely connected with internal than with external development. There are, however, exceptions. Southampton, and we may well believe other south-coast and east-coast ports also, from the first had important contacts overseas. One town demands treatment in connection with external trade, and that is of course London. It is so much the focal point of internal road communication, and at the same time so convenient a point of departure for overseas trade. Whether direct by sea from London Bridge – and such is the haphazard nature of our information that even the first clear mention of London Bridge in Saxon times comes in the tenth century when a witch was thrown from London Bridge for pin-sticking[55] – or by a route overland through Canterbury to Dover, goods were concentrated in town houses and warehouses at London as an essential preliminary to their shipment overseas. Long before 1066 many churchmen and powerful lay nobles found it expedient to have their town houses in London. Colonies of merchants from overseas dwelt within its walls. The Scandinavians had, not unnaturally, special privileges even against the merchants from Germany and from France. The most important information concerning London's trade comes from a difficult Latin document that has been attributed to the reign of Ethelred, but which may be as late as the last years of the reign of Canute. This document, known from Liebermann's arrangement as Ethelred IV, bore the form of a regular royal set of ordinances though it is not issued in a royal name. Apart from the antiquarian interest aroused by the first reference to names as familiar as Billingsgate and Cripplegate, it gives vital information which shows a thriving mercantile element at work in London. The document did the work of a royal ordinance, combined with detailed statement of toll and precautions against theft that tell of active co-operation with civic authorities. Aldersgate and Cripplegate were to be under armed guard. Tolls levied at Billingsgate were described in great detail in a clause of such importance that it is reproduced below in full.

[54] P. Grierson, 'The Relations between England and Flanders before the Norman Conquest', *T. R. Hist. S.*, 1941, pp.71–112.
[55] D. Whitelock, *The Beginnings of English Society*, p.144; A. J. Robertson, *Anglo-Saxon Charters*, no. xxxvii, a Winchester document, A.D. 963–975.

Penalties were decreed for those evading toll, for those committing serious breaches of peace including assault on an innocent man on the King's highway, and elaborate precautions were taken for the purification of the currency.[56]

It is the Billingsgate clauses, however, that give clearest indication of the scope and extent of trade. I quote Miss Robertson's translation of the crabbed Latin:

> If a small ship came to Billingsgate, one half-penny was paid as toll; if a larger ship with sails, one penny was paid.
>
> If a barque [*ceol*] or a merchantman [*hulcus*] arrives and lies there, fourpence is paid as toll.
>
> From a ship with a cargo of planks, one plank is given as toll.
>
> On three days of the week toll for cloth [is paid] on Sunday and Tuesday and Thursday.
>
> A merchant who came to the bridge with a boat containing fish paid one half-penny as toll, and for a large ship one penny.
>
> Men of Rouen who came with wine or blubber fish paid a duty of six shillings for a large ship and 5% of the fish.
>
> Men from Flanders and Ponthieu and Normandy and the Isle of France exhibited their goods and paid toll.
>
> Men from Huy and Liège and Nivelles who were passing through [London] paid a sum for exhibition and toll.
>
> And subjects of the Emperor who came in their ships were entitled to the same privileges as ourselves.
>
> Besides wool which had been unloaded and melted fat they were also permitted to buy three live pigs for their ships.
>
> But they were not allowed any right of pre-emption over the burgesses, and [they had] to pay their toll and at Christmas two lengths of grey cloth and one length of brown and 10 lbs. of pepper and five pairs of gloves and two saddle-kegs of vinegar, and the same at Easter.
>
> From hampers with hens, one hen [is given] as toll, and from one hamper of eggs, five eggs as toll, if they come to the market.
>
> Women who deal in dairy produce [i.e. cheese and butter] pay one penny a fortnight before Christmas and another penny a week before Christmas.[57]

The variation between the market-women dealing with cheese and butter and the merchants of Rouen who paid a substantial duty on their cargo of wine or fish is quite remarkable, and a reminder of the rural conditions that obtained even in the greatest of the ports. It is clear from the list of tolls that merchants still came along the old regular tracks and even if Quentovic and Duurstede no longer appeared by name their successors were present in

[56] See below, pp.130–1.
[57] A. J. Robertson, *The Laws of the Kings of England from Edmund to Henry I*, Cambridge, 1925, IV Ethelred 2.

this document. Some merchants stayed at London throughout the winter. In the twelfth century special privileges were still accorded to Danish and Norwegian merchants who were permitted to stay in the city for a year, though other foreign merchants were restricted to forty days. The Danes had the further privilege of access anywhere in England to other fairs and markets.[58]

Not all the products mentioned in these clauses came from overseas, and it seems likely that even at this early stage London was acting as the entrepôt on a scale that was considerable. The fact that the men of the Empire gave as their toll lengths of cloth as well as pepper, gloves and vinegar does not necessarily imply that they were importing cloth on any large regular scale. Gloves were very much a symbol of market-rights in medieval Germany. Some of the merchants were merely passing through London on their way further into the country presumably with wine and precious goods. Cologne was a very important point of departure for England. An interesting and unusual indication of contact with Cologne is given by the history of the Peterborough Sacramentary and Psalter, which was given to Canute, presented by him to Cologne, then returned a generation later to Ealdred of York and Worcester, and so ultimately to Wulfstan of Worcester in whose life the story is preserved.[59]

From other sources there is evidence of mercantile contact even further afield. Danish merchants were settled in great numbers in Anglo-Scandinavian York as well as in London, and there is clear proof of commercial intercourse with Scandinavia from the vast number of silver pennies from this country that have been discovered in Scandinavian soil, particularly in Sweden and in the Isle of Gotland which was then, as in later Hanseatic days, a centre for trade still further east to the Russian lands. Not all these coins were the product of forced exaction of danegeld. Some represent payment of heregeld, and others again, if one is to judge from the evidence of coins found with them, the product of trade; they are merchants' hoards. A preponderance of eastern towns figures among the mints represented on these coins, notably Lincoln, York and Norwich, as well as London itself. The products of the north, blubber oil, fish and wood, flowed to England in the eleventh century as during the rest of the Middle Ages, and indeed well on into the modern period.

[58] A. L. Poole, *From Domesday Book to Magna Carta*, Oxford, 1951, pp.88–9. M. Bateson, *E. H. R.*, 1902, pp.496 and 499.
[59] *Vita Wulfstani*, pp.5 and 16.

There is reason to believe also that direct trading contact with the Mediterranean countries was re-established during this later Anglo-Saxon period. Peter's Pence was paid to Rome, and Anglo-Saxon pilgrims and traders were known along the whole route across the Alps and into the Italian peninsula. Aelfric says that English traders were accustomed to take their goods to Rome.[60] The question must not be thought of in too modern terms. These packmen were far from the polished merchants of Roman days, and quite as far from the solid bourgeois of the central Middle Ages. Some indication of the scope of their activities is given by the actions of King Canute when he visited Rome in 1027 to attend the coronation of the Emperor Conrad II.[61] He negotiated successfully with the Emperor and the Burgundian king for relaxation of the heavy tolls which burdened English traders. The evidence which has survived from the city of Pavia is particularly illuminating. English traders were to compound for their tolls over a three-year period. Fifty pounds of pure silver was the largest item in the composition, suggesting a considerable volume of trade over the Alps. Other items such as two greyhounds and two fur coats, the latter for the officer in charge of the custom-house, suggest a man-to-man personal relationship, but does not perhaps augur well for the permanent nature of the settlement. Pilgrimages to Rome were still frequent; the routes were well known, and freedom of movement through Pavia, a key point in such a route, was a matter of considerable importance to the Anglo-Saxon ruler.

Finally, can anything definite be said about the goods which were carried back and forth between England and her neighbours? Aelfric, who was interested in the imports, not at all in exports, gave as his list: purple cloth and silks, precious gems and gold, various and coloured garments, wine and oil, ivory and copper, bronze and tin, sulphur and glass, and such articles.[62] There is an exotic quality to these goods, and even when other products are added such as fish from the Norman fishing grounds and furs, hides and cloth, the impression is left that imports were still somewhat superficial, applying in the main to luxury goods. At Beverley Ealdred's pulpit, for example, was described as *opere Teutonico*.[63]

---

[60] *Aelfric's Catholic Homilies*, vol. II, p.120.
[61] *M. G. H., SS.*, XXX (1934), p.1444. Discussed by R. W. Southern, *The Making of the Middle Ages*, Oxford, 1953, pp.43–4.
[62] *Aelfric's Colloquy*, p.33.
[63] *Historians of the Church of York*, ed. J. Raine, vol. II, p.354; I wish to thank Professor Whitelock for this reference.

In return, the merchants could take back with them good English silver, metalwork of which the fame of English craft was widespread in the eleventh century, precious embroideries and gold stitchwork, and above all English cloth. Reference was made soon after the Conquest to fine textiles as *opus Anglicanum*, and these special skills were presumably the product of long maturity.[64] Slaves in the eleventh century were still shipped from Bristol and went to the Ostmen of Dublin, but it is probably unwise to suggest that the slave trade bulked large in the economy at this stage. 'Irish' traders were certainly known at Cambridge as early as the time of Edgar or shortly afterwards.[65] Agricultural products, particularly cheese, found a ready market overseas, and it is pleasing to hear that the French and the Frisians record a steady trade in English cheeses. Among the tolls appertaining to the abbey of St Vaast in Arras in 1036 were those on salt, honey, oil, butter and cheese (English or Flemish).[66]

The influence of the Norman Conquest upon England will be considered later but, to anticipate a little, it may be said that the first generation of Conquest saw some intensification of English trade, but little obvious extension of range. Indeed in some respects the break with the Scandinavian countries, temporary only it is true, had something of a deleterious effect on Anglo-Saxon urban economy. The main routes of trade were already well established when the Conqueror came. However we may feel about the pre-Alfredian period, the merchant was now a familiar figure in the Anglo-Saxon economy. Predominantly agrarian that economy certainly was, but it seems unwise to exaggerate the isolation and rural backwardness of Anglo-Saxon England.

[64] P. Hunter Blair, *Anglo-Saxon England*, p.300; *The Bayeux Tapestry*, ed. F. M. Stenton, pp.44–5.
[65] *Liber Eliensis*, II, 32, ed. D. J. Stewart, p.148; they came *cum variis mercibus et sagis de Hybernia*.
[66] G. W. Coopland, *The Abbey of St Bertin, 900-1350*, Oxford, 1914, p.51.

CHAPTER THREE
Internal Trade:
the Coinage and the Towns

1. TRADE AND THE KING

If it is agreed that the merchant was a familiar figure in the England of 1066, then what conclusions are to be reached concerning his activities within these islands as opposed to his overseas ventures? Evidence comes particularly from legal sources that deal with the position of the king, and prominent among the royal rights in late Anglo-Saxon England were those exercised over the means of communication. Twelfth-century lawbooks, such as the so-called Laws of William I, declared that the four great highways of Watling Street, Ermine Street, the Fosse Way and Icknield Way were particularly under the king's peace.[1] This declaration represents a late extension of an early and virtually primary aspect of kingship: the ability to secure safe transit throughout the kingdom. The charters with their insistence on the maintenance of bridges as a condition of tenure point in the same direction; so too do the lawbooks with their decisive assertion of royal rights over *burhs* and coinage. Ideally the king's peace lay tranquil throughout his whole realm, over coastal seaways and waterways as well as the roads. No king was worth the name until he could protect those moving about his kingdom on lawful business. The high praise given by Bede to King Edwin of Northumbria was that in his day 'a woman with a new-born babe could wander through the island from sea to sea without fear of molestation'.[2]

There are indications that this state of affairs prevailed in theory at least from the earliest times. Seventh-century laws declared that

[1] Leis Willelme, 26; Liebermann I, p.510.
[2] Bede, *Hist. Eccl.*, II, 16.

traders and strangers lay under the special protection of the king. In Kent and in Wessex a virtually identical decree, suggesting in itself close co-operation on this matter between the two kingdoms, laid down that a man who had come from afar, or a stranger, stood in peril of being treated as a thief if he wandered off the road without shouting or blowing his horn.[3] The apparatus of trading was firmly supervised; attempts were made in the early tenth century to confine trade to a royal port in the presence of a royal reeve. The reason for this royal concern was obvious. A primary duty of a Christian king lay in the maintenance of a general peace within his kingdom, and nothing contributed so readily to violence as theft. In an effort to prevent theft the king acted decisively. The process of vouching to warranty by which a man would give proof of origin of goods in his possession was formalized. This process demanded the presence of trustworthy witnesses recognized by the state power. The safety of the ports and boroughs where trading would take place, and of the routes along which the traders passed, and the means by which the authenticity of the trading transaction could be vouched, were matters of first concern to the Anglo-Saxon kings.

It was also natural that a king would wish to know the business of an unknown visitor who might not be the harmless stranger he professed to be. The reeve at Dorchester, during the reign of Beorhtric (786–802), on the first coming of the Danes, rode to the harbour, asked the newcomers their business, and was promptly killed by them. The Chronicle says that he wished to force them to the king's residence, for he did not know who they were, and they slew him.[4] A happier picture of a similar officer at work is recorded by the poet of 'Beowulf'. When Beowulf landed in the kingdom of the Danes he and his companions were met by a sea-ward who asked them to make known their kindred, lest they should go further into the kingdom of the Danes as spies. Beowulf replied that he was the nephew of the ruler of the Geats, and in a long high speech, formal and dramatic, set out his intention to rid the Danish kingdom of the monsters that haunted it. Assured of friendly purpose, the sea-ward then guided him to the king along a road that was *stan-fah*, paved with stone.[5] Passage after passage from the whole gamut of Anglo-Saxon law shows the

[3] Wihtræd 28 and Ine 20.
[4] A. S. Chronicle 789 (787). Ethelweard adds that the reeve, the *exactor regis*, rode to the port, *putans eos magis negotiatores esse quam hostes*, M. H. B., p.509. It is Ethelweard who tells us that the port was Dorchester.
[5] 'Beowulf', lines 229–324.

same royal concern. The king wished to protect merchants and friendly strangers. He was also anxious to obtain pledges of good behaviour. Merchants were to travel inland with their companions only after they have made known to the responsible officer their numbers. Their men were to be such as could be brought to justice in a public meeting. They should be taken under the protection of the king; their wergeld like that of the priest was a matter of concern to the king; in case of unfortunate accident to a foreigner, two-thirds of the compensation was to be paid to the king and one-third only to his kinsfolk at home, even though some of these pronouncements came from a time when a merchant of Canterbury would be an alien to the legislator at Winchester.[6] For foreign merchants did not necessarily come from overseas. The early concern of the Kentish kings to ensure the rights of their merchants at the metropolis of London, then part of the kingdom of Essex, points to a need for formalization of trading relations in an island divided into numerous political communities. When unity was achieved by the revived West Saxon monarchy in the tenth century it was in economic as much as in political fields that the unity was manifest. Standardization of currency was successfully brought about, and attempts were made by King Edgar to standardize weights and measures as in Winchester, and possibly at London. In the same law-code Edgar fixed a maximum price for wool at 120 shillings a wey, with penalties for both seller and buyer who dealt at lower prices.[7] In itself this action shows early concern to safeguard the interests of sheep-farmers and to ensure stability in price, and serves as an energetic reminder of the liaison between the disciplinary powers of the community and the trader. Edgar, conciliatory to the Danes as ever, punished the men of Thanet for offences they had committed against the merchants from York.[8]

2.   COMMODITIES OF TRADE

(a) Metalwork

What can such traders have dealt in? Something has been said of the more exotic merchandise brought from overseas. That is,

[6] Ine 23 and 25; Alfred 34.
[7] III Edgar, 8, 8.1, 8.2.
[8] *E.H.D.* I, p.284; Roger of Wendover, *sub anno* 974 (969): the merchants came by sea and might well have been Scandinavians.

however, only part of the story, for Anglo-Saxon England the less important part. What of the trade within these islands? One point should be made at the outset. The presence of such trade does not necessarily imply the presence of professional traders. Many of the transactions of which we are about to speak could be conducted directly from the seller to buyer without the need for a merchant in between. Royal concern with safeguarding the place of transaction and with the presence of good witness might speak in favour of such comparative informality. Yet even in the darkest of the so-called Dark Ages two commodities were in active circulation: iron and salt. Trading in both was a matter which called for some little specialization in function and knowledge. Archaeological evidence for the existence of some trade in pottery is also growing steadily from year to year. Glassware does not appear to have been an important article of commerce, though inquiry into trade in textile goods yields a more fruitful result. Trade in agricultural products may have assumed considerable importance, and fisheries were not insignificant. Above all, the existence of a stable silver currency in Anglo-Saxon England speaks for the presence of stable local markets, and indeed constitutes our clearest evidence for the presence of active local trading.

As far as iron-working is concerned the evidence from Anglo-Saxon England is disappointingly small. Technically there was no reason why iron should not be mined and worked in many parts of England. Ironstone is often found near the surface, capable of recovery by unskilled labour, and craftsmanship was certainly not lacking. Indeed towards the end of the period the English metalworkers were acquiring a European reputation for their skill. But only scattered references occur, even in Domesday Book itself, to the working of iron. In Kent a seventh-century charter attributed to King Oswin with confirmation by King Ethelred granted to Abbot Adrian and the Abbey of St Peter a ploughland 'in which an iron-mine is known to exist'.[9] In Sussex, where iron might be expected, if it was to be found anywhere, there is reference to only one iron-mine in Domesday Book, in the Hundred of East Grinstead and formerly appurtenant to the royal manor of Ditchling.[10] The West Country is a little more fruitful. There was a concentration of iron workings at Gloucester with supplies drawn from the Forest of Dean. Part of the render of Gloucester

[9] *C.S.*73.
[10] D.B.I, 22b.

to the king in 1066 was still paid in iron and rods of iron drawn
out for making rivets for the king's ships; a contributory burgess
to Gloucester still rendered iron in place of the customary cash
payment.[11] To the north there were some references to iron in
Northamptonshire, Lincolnshire and Yorkshire. The Northampton iron-works at Gretton and Corby were described as appendant to the manors there in 1066, though by the time of the
Domesday survey both works and the wood which presumably
supplied them were lacking.[12] A similar mystery surrounds the
metal-workers of Towcester, the smiths who in 1066 rendered the
substantial sum of 100 shillings but 'now render nothing', and the
smiths of Green Norton who used to render £7 in King Edward's
time.[13] The implication that these were settlements that could easily
be disrupted seems reasonable, and it must be remembered that
Northamptonshire suffered severely in the disturbances of late
1065. Lincolnshire provides another faint pointer in the same
direction. Of the three iron-works mentioned in Domesday two
were near well-wooded Bytham, and one at Stow-by-Gainsborough.
None was near the ironstone outcrop of the county, and the possibility is strong that they were little iron workshops (*fabricae ferri*),
rather than places where iron was mined or smelted, workshops
set up to provide a local need and capable or easy disruption.[14]
In Yorkshire there was only one reference to workers in iron, at
a manor in Hessle near Wragley in the West Riding, attached to
which were six *ferrarii*.[15] This manor had somewhat exceptionally
in its district increased its value since the Conquest; ironstone
was locally available there. It is as dangerous to argue from the
occasional reference in Domesday as from its silences but it seems
reasonable to assume that, even at the very end of the period,
iron-working in Anglo-Saxon England was local, small-scale, very
much in tune with the needs of the small local market.

Of other metals most information survives concerning lead and
to some extent silver. Lead was used even in the seventh century for
roofing churches and its value in other respects, as for example in
the making of saltpans for the salt industry, was also well known by
the end of the period. This is as might be expected on metallurgical

[11] Ibid., 162.
[12] Ibid., 219b.
[13] Ibid., 219b.
[14] H. C. Darby, *The Domesday Geography of Eastern England*, pp.84–5. D. B. I, 360b;
at *Westbitham* seven *francigene* had three *fabricas ferri*.
[15] D.B. I, 316.

grounds; lead with its low resolving temperature is easy to work. England was known on the Continent as a source of lead. Servatus Lupus wrote direct to a king of Wessex to beg for metal as a gift.[16] Silver, found in the lead strata that produced the galena type of ore, was in great demand as ornament and as standard of value. The needs of the coinage made it a metal peculiarly subject to royal control, and in Derbyshire an unusual and pointed reference to payment in pure silver in the Domesday Survey suggests that impure silver was not unknown in these lead-producing areas.[17] The most fruitful argentiferous ores occurred further west in the Mendips and in north-east Wales, areas that passed under English control at the very time when the switch from gold to silver currency was made in the course of the seventh century.

Derbyshire was, however, far and away the most important centre of lead workings. As early as 835 a charge was laid on an estate at Wirksworth to provide the Archbishop of Canterbury with lead to the value of 300 shillings a year.[18] Domesday Book recorded the existence of three *plumbariæ* at the same Wirksworth, and of three others on royal demesne at Metesforde, Bakewell and Ashford, and one on the land at Ralf Fitzhubert at Crick. The three manors of Bakewell, Ashford and Hope were farmed in King Edward's time at a render of £30, five and a half sestiers of honey and five cartloads of lead, consisting of fifty slabs.[19] According to the author of the tract, 'Gerefa' the skilled men on an estate whom the reeve would supervise would include a lead-worker.[20] The tinker has a long and honourable ancestry.

Of other metals it is harder to speak. Cornish tin may have been mined in some quantity, and it may be from this area that the tin was brought by Aelfric's merchant who brought among other precious things, copper and bronze, tin and sulphur, and glass. There is no reason for supposing, however, that there was anything like a large-scale metallurgical industry in Anglo-Saxon England, or that trading in metals occupied more than a few people, and even them only spasmodically. The key figure was

[16] Loup de Ferrières, *Correspondance*, ed. L. Levillain, vol. II, Paris, 1935, pp.70–4 quoted by P. Grierson, 'Commerce in the Dark Ages', *T. R. Hist. S.*, 1959, p.129.
[17] V. C. H., *Derbyshire*, vol. I, p.331 and comment by F. M. Stenton, p.316; D. B. I, 272b.
[18] *C. S.*414.
[19] D. B. I, 272b, 273, 276b; V. C. H., *Derbyshire*, vol. I, pp.330, 332, 333 and 349.
[20] 'Gerefa' 16; Liebermann I, p.455.

the local man, the smith, and the very fact that – though the story of Weland was well known – the smith does not bulk as large in Anglo-Saxon legend as in the folk-tales of continental Germans and the Scandinavians speaks of the familiarity with which he was regarded. Less mystery surrounded his craft, but even so, in the earliest law-code, that of Ethelbert of Kent, the king's smith like his messenger was protected by a special wergeld, a *leodgeld*, which to judge from context and the order of the document may have amounted to the substantial sum of a hundred Kentish shillings.[21] The smith together with a reeve and a children's nurse were the servants whom the laws of Ine allowed a *gesithcund* man to take with him when he moved to a new district.[22] By the eleventh century, in Aelfric's Colloquy, the smith was something of a figure of fun. This school textbook set out to instruct children by the use of dramatic dialogue. The fundamental problem was posed as to who was the most useful member of the community, and in turn each of the ranks and conditions of working man supplied the answer. With impeccable orthodoxy the monk was given pride of place, and among secular workers the ploughman was awarded the palm. The smith then protested; where would be the ploughman without his share or coulter, where the fisherman without his hook, the shoewright without his awl or the tailor without his needle? To which the retort came that the ploughman gives us food and drink, but that from the smithy come only sparks of fire, the sound of beating hammers and blowing bellows.[23] The smith was put firmly in his inferior and noisome place.

Of his work and the organization of his smithy there is little information. The word 'smith' is common enough, either as a simple translation of the Latin *faber* or in compounds such as goldsmith or silversmith or even ironsmith. But nothing is said of him in the 'Rectitudines Singularum Personarum', a mid-eleventh-century document that supplies plentiful material on most of the inhabitants of a great estate, even to beekeepers, cheesemakers and the like. Nor does the allied document concerning the duties of a reeve add further information; a great list is given of the tools which a reeve should look after, but nothing is said of the way in which they were made. Among the skilled workers are placed the miller, tailor and tinker, but no smith. Yet the needs of a farming community must have made the smith a rural specialist

---

[21] Ethelbert 7.
[22] Ine 63.
[23] *Aelfric's Colloquy*, lines 226–8, p.40.

at a very early date. Bede tells of an unworthy brother, a man of dark thoughts and deeds, whose drunkenness and devotion to his smithy rather than to church were tolerated only because he was such a skilled smith.[24] The status of a smith in England does not seem to have been particularly exalted. Good metalwork, it is true, was greatly treasured, even regarded with superstitious awe as the work of Weland, but this was scarcely the province of the ordinary smith. Charles the Great sent a seemly gift of a belt, a Hunnish sword and two silk palls to Offa of Mercia.[25] Prince Athelstan in his will drawn up 1014–16 left a sword which had belonged to the same great Mercian king to his brother Edmund.[26] Such a sword might well be ceremonial like that girded on King Athelstan himself by his grandfather Alfred.[27] References to the transmission of weapons from generation to generation, above all of swords, show that fine metalwork was rare, and the skill to make a fine sword extremely rare. In that part of the *Liber Eliensis* which is based on Old English charters special mention is made, among the goods stolen from Thorth, Oslac's son, of *sicam unam optime insignitam auro et argento*.[28] More prosaic weapons, plain swords, spears and shields, were plentiful enough; a king's thegn's heriot according to Canute would contain two swords, four spears and four shields; one can well see the smith's hand here.[29] It is certainly hard to envisage any military household without a smith attached to it. A weapon-smith is referred to in 'Beowulf', and again in the poem on the 'Endowments of Men'.[30] Some of the groups of smiths we find in place-names or in Domesday may be skilled armourers. It is impossible to imagine a village or a cluster of villages without a smith competent to see to the ploughshares and farm implements. By the end of the period there were occasional concentrations of smithies. At Glastonbury there were no fewer than eight smiths recorded in Domesday Book.[31] The genitive plural is the most common form of smith to survive, in place-names such as Smeaton and Smeeton, Smethcote

---

[24] *Hist. Eccl.*, V, 14.
[25] *E.H.D.* I, p.849.
[26] Ibid., p.595
[27] W. Malms, *Gest. Regum*, II, pp. lx ff.
[28] *Liber Eliensis*, II, c. 32 ed. D. J. Stewart, London, 1848, p.147. My thanks go to Professor Whitelock for drawing my attention to this reference.
[29] II Canute, 71.1.
[30] 'Beowulf', l. 1452; the 'Endowments of Men', E. H. D. I, p.805.
[31] D. B. I, 90.

and Smethwick, Smiddales and Smisby.[32] It is a question of the
immortal smiths rather than the immortal smith.

In one respect the techniques of warfare in pre-feudal England
led to an inferior status on the part of the smith. The absence of
cavalry with all that its techniques implied to the smith in the way
of special armour, harness and weapons, must have tended in that
direction. The skilled work that was needed was performed by
exceptional craftsmen under close royal or episcopal patronage.
The exotic goldsmith was sure of his reward, and from time to
time they are mentioned as beneficiaries, even receiving land, in
the course of the tenth and eleventh centuries. In Domesday Book
the goldsmith Teodricus was to be found among those holding a
group of ministerial estates to the south of Southwark.[33]

If such modern terms may be used about ancient arrangements,
it may be said in conclusion that the metal industry and trade were
on a small scale with some highly skilled craftsmen attached to the
great magnates but with the bulk of the work performed by men
of comparatively humble status in workshops attached to villages
and market towns.

(b) Salt

The salt industry and trade is better chronicled. Methods of
extracting salt from sea-water were well known and extensively
used around the coasts. The salt workers seem to have been
small men renting their own salt-pans. It is likely that many were
fishermen or closely associated with fishermen.

There were no fewer than sixty-one salt-pans mentioned in the
Domesday Survey of Norfolk; exactly one hundred are credited to
the unknown *Rameslie* in Sussex; Lyme in Dorset was very strongly
maritime in occupation, possessing twenty-seven salt workers and
some fishermen over against ten villeins and six bordars.[34] Inland there were greater difficulties, but by the end of the period
Droitwich had emerged as unquestionably the centre of a substantial salt industry. Concern for the provision of salt is seen at a very
early stage in the written records. Ethelbald of Mercia early in his
reign, in 716 or 717, gave to the church at Worcester a certain piece
of ground to the south of the Salwarp, on which salt was made, for

[32] A. H. Smith, *English Place-Name Elements*, E. P. N. S. xxvi, 'smiðe'.
[33] A. J. Robertson, *Anglo-Saxon Charters*, no. lxxi; D. B. I. 36b.
[34] Ibid., 17 and 75b.

the construction of three salt-houses and six furnaces. In return he received from the Worcester community six other furnaces in two salt houses to the north of the Salwarp.[35] From the eighth century examples occur of an exemption from toll of a ship bearing salt in favour of a Kentish nunnery. In 833 a grant of Egbert of Kent was made to Dunna, Abbess of Lyminge of land at Sampton in Kent, of saltworks near the river Limene and of wood *ad coquendum sal* in Andredes Wood.[36] Consumption of wood in the somewhat primitive processes employed for the extraction of salt was high, and at the time of Domesday Bromsgrove alone was sending three hundred cartloads of wood to Droitwich and receiving back three hundred loads (*mits*) of salt in return.[37]

The detailed account of Droitwich in Domesday Book gives a rare insight into the workings of an Anglo-Saxon industry.[38] The pre-eminence of Droitwich in salt manufacture is altogether striking, and only in some districts of Cheshire is there anything at all comparable. Droitwich itself was assessed at ten hides, shared among twelve tenants-in-chief, six ecclesiastical and six lay. It was an important source of royal revenue, and in 1086 the sheriff farmed the royal *salinæ* for £65 and two *mits* of salt, something of a drop in revenue from 1066 when £76 was received from the royal and comital *salinæ*. Many places both inside and outside the county of Worcester also possessed an interest in Droitwich, owning *salinæ* or controlling salt-workers. In Gloucestershire salt was mentioned in connection with ten places, six of which were linked directly with *Wick*. In Herefordshire all the eleven places where salt was mentioned were connected with Droitwich, six owning salt-pans there, the other five recording their right to a number of loads or measures. Similarly three references in Shropshire, two out of six in Warwickshire, two in Oxford and, most surprising of all, one at Princes Risborough in Buckinghamshire, all named Droitwich as their source of salt. Within the county of Worcester the pattern was even more impressive, and of the three hundred and one salt-pans mentioned in the Worcester Domesday more than half were attributed specifically to Droitwich. In other instances the fact was so self-evident that the Commissioners failed to recount it. Subsidiary centres there were, at Nantwich and in some of the

---

[35] *E. H. D.* I, p.489.
[36] *C. S.* 411. Also C. S. 148, A.D. 732, where Ethelbert gives land at Sampton suitable for the cooking of salt to Abbot Dun, together with a hundred and twenty laden wagons of firewood for the cooking of the salt. E. H. D. I. p.490.
[37] D. B. I, 172.
[38] Ibid., 172–8 *passim*.

villages around these centres, at Awre in Gloucestershire and at Brailes in Warwick. But Droitwich certainly provided the main source of supply for the western Midlands. Place-name experts have pointed to the multitude of names like Saltways, Saltridge Hill, Salford, Salters Hill and Salterby that still trace the roads or tracks to Droitwich. It is a point to bear in mind when considering the tenacity of West Midlands tradition, and the cohesion of its cultural life.

Later medieval authorities relate that the methods used to extract the salt were to brew the brackish water in leaden pans, and then finally to dry the product in barrows made of twigs and willow each of which could contain two bushels of salt. Already in the eleventh century the special terminology of the industry was firmly established. There were three measures in use, the horseload or *summa*, the sestier or *sextarius* and the *mit* probably equivalent to eight bushels. Tolls were exacted, and reference was made at the royal manor of Chedworth in Gloucestershire to the *theloneum salis.*[39] Some by-industries were growing up, even to the manufacture of the special lead pans at Northwich in the *fabricæ plumbi.*[40] It used to be thought that the ending -*wic* itself had some special connection with the manufacture of salt, but it is probably no more than coincidence that the major centres such as Droitwich and Nantwich should bear the place-name form. A confident opinion is rash. The coincidence extends to the Continent where Wich near Metz, owned by the Abbey of Prüm, was an important salt centre. It may be that further work on *wik* and *wich* and *vik* will help to clear up the puzzles which still remain great. That some confusion occurred between the Latin *vicus*, meaning simply place, and the Germanic *wik* and its cognates is beyond dispute. A recent suggestion is that *wik* was used more and more in the tenth century to designate temporary and provisional installations in process of becoming permanent settlements, a definition that would suit the agglomeration of buildings around a thriving little industrial centre like Droitwich. An Old Saxon gloss gives: *wik – vicus ubi mercatores morantur.*[41] Quentovic, Bardowik, Schleswig, Osterwick, Brunswick all appear in the records. Most significant of all, Duurstede itself, as we have seen, became *wik* (Wijk-bei-Duurstede).[42] In a charter of Otto I to Utrecht, of 968, land is spoken of *in villa quadam Dorsteti*

[39] D. B. I, 164.
[40] Ibid., 173b.
[41] R. Latouche, *The Birth of Western Economy*, p.289.
[42] See above p.87.

nunc autem wik nominata.[43] It seems likely that the -*vic* in Quentovic was perpetuated in a Romance equivalent. After destruction by the Vikings, the settlement was re-established on the other bank of the Canche and known in time as *étaples* or *stabulum*, the equivalent of the Germanic *Stapel* or *wik*.

The extent of the Worcester salt industry, even in the eleventh century, is remarkable. There is one important reservation to be made, however, that helps to demonstrate the subordination of industry in Anglo-Saxon England to rural economy. The ramifications of Droitwich salt are great, but the nature of the industry was very much conditioned by the nature of land-tenure within the borough itself. So that when places as distant as Princes Risborough claimed rights over Droitwich salt almost always some tenurial connection between the distant manor and the territorial possession of Droitwich can be traced to help explain the connection. To see Droitwich as a great industrial centre for the supply of salt in a modern sense is to distort the true picture. The initiative lay rather with the lords of the manors than with the producers of salt, and it is safer to see Droitwich as a complex of rights each a valuable appendant to one or other manor in the neighbouring or in the more remote districts. Profits came as much from the tolls en route as from the primary acts of production. The traditional penny a manload and a shilling a horseload demanded at Worcester, or the reference to the *theloneum salis* at Chedworth, illustrates how the system could work. Salt, it is true, was a necessity without which meat could not be preserved, vegetables savoured or cheese and butter be made. Arrangements for obtaining supplies lay, however on the basic economic unit of the rural estate, in much the same way as continental abbeys annexed properties in wine-producing areas or indeed as English estates established town-houses as convenient centres for marketing or for storehouses. Even in as productive a centre as Droitwich the needs of the rural estates directly connected with the centre would be met before that familiar figure, the salter, would set out on his travels on the mud or dust of the Anglo-Saxon roads.

Fortunately it is possible to supplement the account of the Worcestershire salt industry with information drawn from the Domesday account of Cheshire. Here again tolls and dues to the king and his representative, the earl, bulk larger than the cost of the salt itself. If the earl sold salt from the house that supplied

[43] R. Latouche, op. cit., p.250, where he quotes Dipl. I, p.181, no.98. Also p.161.

his manor of Acton, two-thirds of the toll went to the king,
one-third to himself. Other owners of salt had salt for their own
consumption free only from Ascension Day to Martinmas. Rates of
payment varied, normally fourpence on a cart drawn by four oxen,
twopence on a horse-load or on eight mens' loads. Preferential rates
were given to those within the hundred; salt-pedlars from the same
hundred had to pay a penny a cart. If they carried salt on horseback
then one penny was paid at Martinmas. Tait has described the salt
industry of Cheshire as 'little manufacturing enclaves in the midst
of an agricultural district'.[44] The concern of the documents lies not
unnaturally with the trade and the profits of the trade rather than
with the manufacture as such.

c) Pottery and glass

Of two other commodities that may have passed through the hands
of local traders it is also profitable to speak: pottery and glass.[45]

The Anglo-Saxons used wood in everyday utensils to a greater
extent than is always imagined, and the local wood-wright, very
much in demand as he was, has left few traces. Aelfric's Colloquy
refers to him as a man who made houses, vessels and ships. The
preface to the translation of the Soliloquies of St Augustine tells of
the building of a dwelling-house, timber by timber.[46] Presumably
the prohibition of wooden vessels for use in the Mass was occasioned by the prevalence of wood in everyday utensils. It is certain,
however, that from the beginning the art of the potter was well
understood in Anglo-Saxon England. The mass-produced articles
of imperial Rome, wheel-turned and kiln-hardened, disappeared
with the urban civilization that produced them. In their place
appeared the rough hand-made pottery of Saxon England. In
pagan times funerary urns were manufactured on a considerable
scale and in the full continental Germanic tradition. In Christian
times stories of plates and dishes smashed but made miraculously
whole are proof that the product of the potter was familiar to the
Anglo-Saxon. Not all households, even royal households, could
follow the example of Oswald who, according to Bede, dined off

[44] J. Tait, *The Domesday Survey of Cheshire*, Manchester, 1916, p.39.
[45] A useful guide to problems of Anglo-Saxon pottery is given by J. G. Hurst, *The Archaeology of Anglo-Saxon England*, ed. D. M. Wilson, London, 1976, pp.283–348. On glass see D. B. Harden, 'Anglo-Saxon and Later Medieval Glass in Britain: Some Recent Developments', *M. A.* XXII, 1978, pp.1–24.
[46] *Aelfric's Colloquy*, pp.40–41; E. H. D. I, p.917.

a silver platter which in generous piety he ordered to be divided up for the benefit of the poor at his gate.[47] It is difficult to believe in all the panoply of gold-encrusted goblets made familiar in 'Beowulf', though the finds at Sutton Hoo warn against excessive scepticism on this score. The ceremonial goblet would grace the board of any substantial nobleman, such as the *gesith* in the East Riding whose wife acted as cupbearer when they entertained Bishop John of Beverley.[48] Such goblets are examples of the metalworkers's not of the potter's art, and yet few Anglo-Saxon sites have been dug which fail to yield some sherds of pottery, often rough and excessively difficult to date, which may be attributed to these people. Only towards the end of the period does the evidence at the moment permit a cautious reference to regular trade in pottery. The so-called Stamford ware, utilizing a type of lead-glazing that may have originated in the Netherlands, appears to have spread from East Anglia, above all from Thetford, along the Icknield Way into the region around Oxford. As the evidence grows the distribution of Stamford ware will probably give proof of a well-authenticated example of regular internal trade in pottery in Anglo-Saxon England, incidentally along a route which would coincide well with the activities of the thegn's guild of Cambridge from the eastern counties to the Thames Valley and also into the Mercian lands, ultimately perhaps to Chester.[49]

Glassware remained always something of a special case, and Aelfric listed it among those precious things that a merchant brings with him, because they are not known in this land. Even when the comparative poverty of archaeological finds for the late Anglo-Saxon period is taken into account, it is surprising to note how little glass has survived from the eighth to the eleventh century, in contrast to the relatively numerous finds which have been attributed with increasing confidence to the seventh century, and particularly to early seventh-century Kent. This early glass comes from funerary remains, particularly from the Kentish cemeteries and above all from Faversham which may even have been in itself a glass-producing centre. The glass bowls and beakers that survive

[47] *Hist. Eccl.*, III, 6.

[48] Ibid., V, 4.

[49] G. C. Dunning, 'Trade Relations between England and the Continent (Glazed Pottery in England)', *Dark Age Britain*, pp.228–31; also *M. A.* III, pp.37–42, where Mr Dunning puts forward the suggestion – interesting in view of the twelfth-century date of the Southern Belgian finds – that the distinctive Stamford glaze may have been introduced *from* England into the Low Countries (pp.41–2).

point to the luxury nature of the articles. Indeed as D. B. Harden says, 'the richness of Kentish jewellery goes hand in hand with the richness of Kentish glass, and when rich gold and garnet jewellery and similar items occur, glass not infrequently is found there too'.[50] It is possible that the disappearance of glass vessels in significant numbers from Anglo-Saxon finds is associated with a general eclipse of luxury goods in the later seventh century, though a simpler explanation lies in the nature of the archaeo-logical deposits, as Christianity discouraged the practice, so useful to the historian, of burial with rich grave furniture.

As far as can be judged, in the following centuries the arts of glass manufacture and of glazing remained a rarity in England. Bede says that Benedict Biscop sent to Gaul for stone-masons and glass-workers because the art was not known in Northumbria.[51] In the early eighth century the Pictish King Naiton asked Abbot Ceolfrid to send him some highly skilled stone-masons so that he might build churches after the Roman fashion (though there is, not unnaturally, no mention of glass-workers).[52] The intention was to train English boys in the craft, and Wilfrid caused the windows at York to be glazed.[53] But the lesson was not well learnt. In 764, Cuthbert, the Abbot of Wearmouth, wrote to Lul, the English missionary who was Bishop of Mainz, to ask for a good glassmaker because 'we are ignorant and destitute of that art.'[54] The same letter, it is true, asks for a harpist because the abbot had a harp but no one to play it; Wearmouth's lack of skill does not necessarily mean that there were no men capable of glazing a window in England. The good abbot also coupled his request with a lament at the winter just passed which 'oppressed the island of our race very horribly with cold and ice and widespread storms of wind and rain, so that the hand of the scribe was hindered from producing a great number of books'. Windows must have been an attractive and exciting prospect in such circumstances. Excavations at Wearmouth itself and at Jarrow have now yielded hundreds of fragments of

[50] D. B. Harden, 'Glass Vessels in Britain and Ireland, A. D. 400–1000', *Dark Age Britain*, p.154; this article, pp.132–67, give the authoritative account of this difficult subject.
[51] Bede, *Historia Abbatum*, ed. C. Plummer, c.5. He sent for *vitri factores, artifices videlicet Brittaniis eatenus incognitos, ad cancellandas ecclesiae porticumque et caenaculorum eius fenestras.*
[52] Bede, *Hist. Eccl.*, V. 21.
[53] *Eddius's Life of St Wilfrid*, ed. B. Colgrave, c.16, p.163.
[54] *E. H. D.* I, p.832. The glassmaker was to be skilled in making glass vessels; the harpist to play a special type of harp known as the *rottae*.

Anglo-Saxon glass, and discoveries elsewhere, at the small church at Escomb as well as the great buildings of Winchester, Brixworth and Repton, imply that glazing in Anglo-Saxon churches was more common than we thought.

Archaeological evidence for the later Anglo-Saxon age naturally takes on a rather different aspect from that for the earlier, and deals with habitation sites rather than with cemeteries. D. B. Harden has pointed out that one highly significant result emerged from the excavations at Thetford and those at *Hamwih*, part of modern Southampton. From the Thetford site there was very little glass, a half-dozen fragments or so were recovered; from the port of *Hamwih* there emerged extensive finds of glass, probably imported. A similar preponderance of imported pottery from *Hamwih* over the East Anglian site suggests further that Thetford relied on the local producers while *Hamwih* enjoyed its advantages as a seaport.[55] Chance finds may yet modify the picture, but the further inference is also clear that there was comparatively little glass manufacture in early Anglo-Saxon England.

To the west, however, there are more hopeful signs. At Glastonbury evidence of the existence of glass furnaces has been produced, with the strong possibility that they were in operation during the tenth century or earlier.[56] In such a great advanced ecclesiastical establishment one might expect to find, if anywhere, up-to-date techniques in use; the presence of a surprising number of smiths at Glastonbury may also be remarked on in this connection.[57] From Domesday Book itself there appears no reference to glass-houses as a source of profit; where glazing was undertaken it was exceptional and the work of exceptional craftsmen. The manufacture of glass and regular trade in that precious commodity cannot be held to have played any significant part in the development of the internal markets of England.

(d) Textiles and agrarian products: the process of vouching to warranty

If the Anglo-Saxon merchants' tracks were as carefully beaten as many are beginning to believe, the reason for their activity must be found not in these commodities, important as they are, but in what was after all the staple activity of the Anglo-Saxon, in

[55] D. B. Harden, op. cit., pp.153–4.
[56] *M. A.* II (1958), London, 1959, pp.188–9.
[57] See above, p.108.

agriculture and its allied activities. The question of the existence of a land-market itself is a matter to consider in a later chapter, and something has already been said of the influences which suggest even at this early period an export trade in textiles. The natural advantages of the countryside were sufficient to guarantee a surplus of yarn and cloth. On a big manor the organization might be sufficient to justify talking of specific centres of industrial activity. A great estate in the West Country, for example, the exact site of which is unknown, has left a bald inventory of tools used for spinning and weaving, sufficient to imply a substantial stock of technical knowledge and ability. Some of the technical terms then used are still obscure to this day, as the following quotation makes plain:

> 7 fela towtola: flexlinan, spinle, reol, gearnwindan, stodlan, lorgas, presse, pihten, timplean, wifte, wefle, wulcamb, cip, amb, cranstæf, sceaðele, seamsticcan, scearra, nædle, slic.
> 'and many tools for spinning: linen flax, a spindle, a reel, a yarn-winder, a "slay" (dialect, studdles: M. E. *telarium*, glossed *lame de tisserant*), a weaver's beam, a press (glossed *pannicipium* and *vestiplicium*), a weaver's comb, a tool for carding wool, a weft and warp (glossed *panniculæ*, possibly a bobbin with thread for the warp attached), a wool-comb, a weaver's stock, a "reed" or "slay", a reel for winding thread, a weaver's rod, a seam-stock, shears, a needle, a hammer.[58]

It is possible, though by no means certain, that the presence of spindle, reel and yarn-winder implies the presence also of some form of spinning-wheel. Not for a further two hundred years, however, is there an unquestioned reference to this familiar instrument of household economy.

On a smaller scale possession of spinning and weaving facilities may be assumed in all manors and communities. In one respect the problems bring the social historian face to face with a subject that it is only too easy to evade. In primitive Germanic communities it is known that these tasks were the womens': man to the plough, to the spear; woman to the spindle. To the end of the Anglo-Saxon period that may be taken as the ideal. Yet in hard economic fact the more powerful resources of the manorial lord operated more stringently in matters such as these than in any other. In the course of time ability to insist on the exaction of spinning and weaving work from the women of peasant households became a mark of lordship over true servile tenants. It may be that in the tenth and

[58] 'Gerefa' 15; Liebermann I, p.455.

eleventh centuries this process was well under way as the great estate improved its equipment and, with its superior facilities for maintenance of that equipment, came to play an increasing part in the clothing of its dependent communities. The manor was never completely self-sufficient; but the great rural estate, ecclesiastical or lay, was moving towards a more self-sufficient state by the end of the Anglo-Saxon period.

Of commodities other than metals, salt, and textiles that passed into the hands of internal traders it is harder still to speak. Perhaps the question itself is scarcely fair. As Aelfric shows, the merchant was regarded as one who dealt in exotic goods, yet even so there must have been traders dealing in ordinary agricultural surplus, quite apart from our salters and metal carriers. The evidence of the laws is indisputable on this point and the strong probability is that the traders dealt in agricultural surplus and above all in cattle; in cheeses and butter from districts where pasture was good, in wheat and barley and rye. Athelstan legislated to prevent the export of horses, except as a gift, suggesting the presence of some internal trade in this precious commodity. In a list of standard values for compensation, incorporated in an important London text from the same king's reign, the value of a good horse is put at a hundred and twenty pence, four times that of an ox, while a cow is worth twenty pence, a pig tenpence, and a sheep a shilling (or fivepence).[59] Such legislation still treated of a time when there could be plenty in Dorset, but dearth in Wiltshire. Fisheries were important and by the time of Domesday rents from sea fisheries were normally expressed in herrings: 38,500 from Lewes, Sussex, and 60,000 from Dunwich, Suffolk. Eels were also important, and rights over inland fisheries jealously guarded: at Wisbech alone fishermen paid a rent of 33,260 eels. Salmon, lampreys, even porpoises were mentioned in the same way. Aelfrics's fisherman complained that he could not catch as many as he could sell in the towns because the demand was so high.[60]

Much of the trade was unspecialized, localized, dependent on the immediate situation. Much was not – if, for example, the vigorous efforts of the state to regularize such traffic through boroughs are taken into account. The constant concern of the law-codes, particularly in the late ninth century and the tenth century with trade in livestock and with cattle-thieving indicate the mobility

[59] II Athelstan 18; VI Athelstan 6.1 and 6.2.
[60] *Aelfric's Colloquy*, c.99. See also below, pp.373–5.

of these predominantly agrarian communities; and indeed this concern contributed greatly to the creation of one of the most familiar of English public institutions, the hundred itself.

In one particular respect the legal evidence throws light, though somewhat obliquely, on English economic institutions. The early law-codes try to insist on reasonable safeguards in any commercial transaction, particularly in the provision of suitable witnesses, preferably before a royal officer. As early as the laws of Hlothere and Eadric, kings of Kent, there appeared a reference to vouching to warranty. A man of Kent had to make sure that he had trustworthy witnesses before he bought property in London, so that he could vouch the vendor to warranty at the king's hall in that town.[61] Alfred was concerned acutely with the problem, and implied a substantial volume of internal trade when he laid down rules concerning good behaviour of merchants who travelled from district to district accompanied by bands of servants.[62] It is certain that the great concern shown over supervision of warranty would not have appeared, had not the volume of internal traffic been sufficient to justify the attention. In the tenth and eleventh centuries there occurred the gradual perfecting of this process. A man taken with stolen goods in his possession would vouch to warranty the vendor from whom he had bought in good faith and in the presence of witnesses. A Westminster cartulary has preserved record of one such transaction in the mid-tenth century.[63] Athelstan of Sunbury was vouched to warranty in the case of a stolen woman, found in the possession of Wulfstan. Athelstan agreed to carry on the process but failed by default, and so the woman was returned to her former owner together with two pounds in compensation. This was not the end of the story, however, for then the ealdorman, the king's officer, interfered and demanded Athelstan's wergeld. Athelstan could not pay. His brother, Edward, offered to pay if Athelstan would give him Sunbury but the stubborn offender refused this offer out of hand, saying that he would rather the estate perished by fire and flood. Edward tried to reason that it would be better if one of them held it, but Athelstan went into service under Wulfgar rather than accept, and on a later occasion in King Edgar's reign turned down Edward's offer. The ealdorman presumably took over the estate at Sunbury in lieu of wergeld. The interesting feature of the case, apart from the record of savage

[61] Hlothere and Eadric, 16 and 16.1.
[62] Alfred 34.
[63] A. J. Robertson, *Anglo-Saxon Charters*, no. xliv.

dissension inside the kin, lies in the fearsome consequence of a rash failure to refute the warranty process. The right to supervise this process under the name *team* became one of the common perquisites granted to a lord of an estate. In origin, however, it was royal, part and parcel of the general kingly duty of supervising the comings and goings of traders and their transactions. The interchange of cattle for breeding, the sale of seedcorn, the sale of honey, fish and specialist agricultural products: all these transactions, like the sale of precious goods brought from overseas, required careful supervision and required too, a simple point that nevertheless needs stating, the use of money. Indeed, Canute laid down specifically in his decree relating to the sale of goods that nothing worth more than fourpence was to be sold *up on lande* except in the presence of good witness.[64]

3. THE COINAGE

(a) Money economy and barter: the general picture

The existence of a money economy raises points that are fundamental in any discussion of the Anglo-Saxon economy. It is true that barter was not unfamiliar to Anglo-Saxon England as late as the eleventh century. Ethelred specifically legislated for such transactions, laying down rules for peaceful trading, whether by money or barter. Even later, Aelfric Bata's Colloquy suggested payment for a well-written book in the form of gold or silver or horses or mares or oxen or sheep or swine or provender or clothes or wine or honey or grain or vegetables.[65] The fact has to be taken into account that this passage constituted a vocabulary exercise, but it may be significant that the wise seller chose pennies or silver because with silver you can buy what you please. After hard bargaining a missal was brought down in price from two pounds in pure silver to twelve mancuses, a very satisfactory drop of twenty-five per cent.

Too much emphasis has been placed in the past on the subject of natural economy and barter in early English society. It is certain that money was in general use for the last four centuries of

[64] II Canute 24.
[65] I Ethelred 3; *Early Scholastic Colloquies*, ed. W. H. Stevenson and W. M. Lindsay, Oxford, 1929, p.50.

Anglo-Saxon England, and possible (though to my mind increasingly unlikely) that the idea of currency was never foreign to this island from Roman days onwards. One of the great achievements of Anglo-Saxon England, for which the kings have been given inadequate credit, lies precisely in the evolution of a stable currency which in its day was admired and copied by her less advanced neighbours,

Much valuable work has been done recently on the Anglo-Saxon currency. The picture of the coinage as it existed during the last two centuries of Anglo-Saxon England has been etched in with greater detail than would have appeared possible sixty years ago. A basic guide is now provided in the appropriate sections of *Medieval European Coinage*,[66] but important modifications in detailed dating and type sequence appear with astonishing regularity in the pages of the *British Numismatic Journal*, the *Numismatic Chronicle* and the proceedings of many symposia.

(b) Coinage in the pre-Viking age: sceattas and pennies

In spite of all the fluidity of detailed interpretation, the general pattern of the development of the coinage is clearer and easier to comprehend than ever it has been, most of all for the later period. Even on the vexed and uncertain fifth and sixth centuries there is now a firm consensus on essentials. There used to be a strong body of opinion that refused to recognize break of continuity in the use of coins, mostly on the grounds that once the habit of using coins is acquired it is difficult to uproot. But there were special conditions applicable to the English situation. Roman Britain had depended upon continental mints for her coinage. By the early fifth century this source of supply was cut off. During the succeeding century and a half all currency appreciated in value, gold and silver presumably to the point where their bullion value was higher than any conceivable use as an economic currency. Numismatists are now in general agreement that the barbarous *radiates* and *minimi* on which the case for continuity used to rest belong to the third and fourth centuries rather than to the sub-Roman period.[67] In the process of settlement and consolidation the English communities in Britain

[66] *M. E. C. I*, up to the tenth century. R. H. M. Dolley, *Anglo-Saxon Pennies*, British Museum, 1964, remains valuable for the whole period.
[67] Modern investigation is attributing the *minimi* and the barbarous *radiates* on which the case for continuity in coinage rests, to the fourth century rather than to the sub-Roman period, as is shown in J. P. C. Kent's article on the continuity problem in *Anglo-Saxon Coins*, ed. R. H. M. Dolley, London, 1961.

produced princes who were givers of rings or cattle, not strikers and hoarders of coins.

The consolidation of the English settlements in Britain was accompanied by increased contact with the Continent where gold coins were still in use. Such coins have been discovered by archaeologists, mounted in jewellery in a sixth century context. With the coming of the Augustinian mission in 597 the need for a convenient medium of exchange, acceptable on the Continent, became pronounced and it is clear that by the early seventh century Continental coins exercised some monetary role in Kent and the south-east. The established history of the native English coinage begins with the issue of imitations of Merovingian coins known as *tremisses*, which were valued at one-third of a *solidus* and were of gold of about 1.3 grams in weight. Native coins were struck at Canterbury and London, though it is possible that the earliest mintage from the reign of Ethelbert proved a failure. Indeed the extent and importance of the early mintage in gold is still matter for some speculation since knowledge of it comes almost entirely from a hoard deposited at Crondall in Hampshire towards the middle of the century, probably in the decade c.640–50.[68] Sensitive work on the die-links of the sixty-nine Anglo-Saxon coins in the hoard suggests that they belong to a few limited issues, possibly struck for a special purpose. The indigenous coinage developed further in the third quarter of the century gradually coming to dominate the mixed currency of local and imported coinage circulating in south-east England. However, English production was still small by the side of Frankish mintage. The value of the *tremisses*, or shilling as it was probably known in England, was high, and the uses to which such a currency could be put must have been limited to larger payments such as land purchase, fines, and bulk trade. Even so, the very fact that a gold coinage existed certainly emphasizes the close links between south-east England and Merovingian Gaul.

The last quarter of the seventh century saw the beginning – a matter of much more moment for English numismatic history – of a respectable silver currency which rapidly replaced the gold. This coinage consisted of coins generally known since the seventeenth century as *sceattas* which were initially of quite a high degree of purity. Philip Grierson has shown that they were in fact pennies, but for scholarly convenience it is useful to retain the old (if technically incorrect) name to distinguish them from the standard penny

[68] C. H. V. Sutherland, *Anglo-Saxon Gold Coinage*, Oxford, 1948; a splendid description of the Crondall hoard.

of the late eighth century.[69] They were somewhat thicker than that penny, although in theory they contained the same amount of silver. As was mentioned above, at one phase in its development, the *sceat* gave hints of a uniform commercial area in the seventh and eighth centuries embracing the North Sea region and dominated by the Frisian trader. Unlike the later penny the *sceat* did not bear the king's name. The test of purity for these coins lay in familiar designs, known both sides of the North Sea, rather than in overt royal authority: and these designs, geometric and zoomorphic, beasts and birds, wolves and falcons, indicate a common Germanic mythology and speak of powerful Germanic predominance in racial composition. The inference is that trading communities themselves played a much bigger part in the control and regulation of currency than in later days. Within the last generation numismatic knowledge of the *sceat* series has grown much more precise.[70] No fewer than twenty-six series have been identified, falling into three principal phases. Primary production, overlapping briefly with the last of the debased gold issues, is attributed to the last quarter of the seventh century. It was well-regulated and of good standard, and came essentially from two centres, probably Canterbury and London. There followed an intermediate stage in the early eighth century which saw a marked expansion in the volume of the currency, fuelled by a dramatic increase in imported coin from Frisia. The secondary phase is characterized by a proliferation of coin types and an expansion of minting into East Anglia, Wessex, and now consistently Northumbria, while progressive debasement brought the currency to the point of collapse in many regions by the 750s. The large number of individual finds of this latter phase is remarkable, especially those from the trading centres at *Hamwih* (modern Southampton), Ipswich, and the Fishergate area of York. Special developments took place in Northumbria where royal control, sometimes in conjunction with the archbishop after 735, was more open and obvious. Further savage debasement in the north during the ninth century led to mintage of coins of the same module and weight as the *sceattas* in brass, known as *stycas*. They continued to be used up to the time of the capture of York by the Vikings in 867. Developments of central importance to the

---

[69] P. Grierson, *Sylloge of Coins of the British Isles*, vol. I, Fitzwilliam Museum, Oxford, 1958.
[70] I am grateful to Mark Blackburn for advice. The following paragraphs draw heavily on his work and on that of Stuart Rigold, Michael Metcalf and Stewart Lyon. The essential modern guide is to be found in the relevant section of *M. E. C.* I, ed. P. Grierson and Mark Blackburn.

history of English coinage took place further south. It was no accident that when, for the first time since the days of Ethelbert, the prosperous south-east fell firmly under the control of a king who exercised direct authority over a great part of Germanic Britain, there occurred also a major reform of the English currency with the fine standardization of the penny during the reign of King Offa of Mercia (757–96).

The word penny in the form *pænig* first appears in the laws of Ine and glosses of the school of Theodore and Adrian, of the late seventh century, i.e. just after the date numismatists give for the introduction of a new silver coinage in England and on the Continent. There has been great dispute over the origin of the term, but it is now generally accepted to have a common Germanic origin, possibly associated with a basic significance of pledge (modern German *pfand*) or token for value. In or about 755 the first Carolingian king of the Franks, Pepin the Short, abandoned the small, thick fabric of the earliest pennies for the broader, thinner module that was to remain throughout the Middle Ages. Before long a similar reform was instituted in England. Until recently it was thought that the first English broad-flan pennies were minted by two little known Kentish kings, Heaberht and Ecgberht, but new finds, some as yet unpublished, have changed the picture dramatically. It appears as if the reform was initiated in part by Beonna of East Anglia and more effectively by Offa of Mercia himself, of whom some particularly early coins, dating perhaps from the 760s, have been attributed to East Anglia and perhaps London.[71] Later on in his long reign Offa reorganized the coinage south of the Humber, and established in essentials the silver penny that was to remain the staple coin of England for the succeeding four and a half centuries. As Sir Frank Stenton remarked, 'the continuous history of the English currency begins in Offa's time'.[72] In most of Offa's coinage the king's name appears on the obverse and the moneyer's on the reverse though coins were also struck in the name of his queen, Cynethryth, and jointly in the names of the king and his archbishops of Canterbury or his bishop of London. At their best the coins achieve a fineness and beauty in execution that suggest already a degree of sophisticated central

[71] C. E. Blunt, 'The Coinage of Offa', *Anglo-Saxon Coins*, ed. R. H. M. Dolley, pp.39–41, suggested that the inauguration of the change was due not to Offa himself but to his contemporary Kentish Kings, Heaberht and Ecgberht. Offa's name was substituted for Ecgberht's on Kentish coins, *c.* 784–5.

[72] F. M. Stenton, *Anglo-Saxon England*, p.223.

control. Canterbury and London were the principal mints, though there was also a significant East Anglian group, an indication of their economic role as centres for trade with the Continent. The coinage reforms themselves tell us much of the developing relationship between England and the nascent Carolingian empire. Of more moment to the immediate purpose is the inference that the stabilization of a silver coinage of good quality implies a steady demand throughout the small local markets of Offa's England. They were markets in a community accustomed to minted coins as an important medium of exchange: and royal concern confirms the general truth that steps towards political unity and steps towards stable and unified currency coincide.

(c) Coinage in the Viking age and after

The high artistic standards of the *sceattas* and Offa's coinage were not maintained. However, despite the vicissitudes of the ninth century, the organization and control of the mint system established under Offa was gradually built upon by his successors. The principal mints remained those close to the channel ports and it was not until Alfred and his son that the first serious moves were taken to establish a network of local mints throughout their kingdoms. Minting became an essential element in their constructive and imaginative burghal policy. During the first three quarters of the tenth century some of the unity achieved in the ninth was lost and the currency took on a stronger local flavour. But the mints established by the Vikings in the Danelaw were successfully transferred to Anglo-Saxon control so that by the early 970s there were some forty mints active in England. Throughout the kings insisted on the legal unity of the coinage. Athelstan pronounced in his Grately decrees that 'there shall run one coinage in the realm', a sentiment powerfully reinforced by his successors.[73] With Edgar occurred one of the great currency reforms of English history. His so-called sixth type marked a true revolution in English currency. On the obverse of this type the royal bust was standardized and remained the normal type, mostly facing the left, till the Norman Conquest. On the reverse appeared the name of the mint and moneyer. Most of the mints came to achieve standard abbreviations such as LUND(E) for London, WINT for Winchester, EOFE(R) for York. Royal control of the currency became exceedingly strict, legal

---

[73] II Athelstan 14, III Edgar 8: also VI Ethelred 32; and II Canute 8.

penalties against false coining grew increasingly severe, indeed violent. Pride and self-interest operated to maintain the standard of the currency, and the numismatist confirms the general success of the monarchs in their endeavours.

On occasion the minters could produce a coin of real beauty. As an exception to the general type, there was struck during the reign of Ethelred a coin known as the *Agnus Dei* with the symbol of the Lamb of God on the one side, and the Dove of Peace on the other. This beautiful little coin, possibly to be attributed to 1009 in association with a programme of national penitence, shows the technical excellence that the Anglo-Saxon craftsmen were capable of achieving at their best. Nor did the normal king's-head type lack character, and at times beauty. From the reform of Edgar technical improvements were made that ensured relatively straight striking of coins. Henceforward the die-axis was fixed at a relationship of 0°, 90°, 180° or 270° between obverse and reverse, which was an aesthetic improvement on the somewhat haphazard die-axis of many earlier issues.[74] Only the conservative northern mint at York fails to give substantial evidence of the success of this reform. The portraits, though conventional symbols of royalty, are attractive and some, such as those of Athelstan which call the King *rex to. Brit.*, a reminder of the high-flown titles of his charters, give incidentally interesting information about the nature of the kingship of the age. The lettering is usually clear and well-defined, and the astonishing lack of wear on some of the coins is a reminder again how effective was the whole currency system, which demanded a fairly rapid calling in of the old types as the new types were issued. It is no wonder that other peoples admired and copied. The Welsh prince Hywel the Good, a frequent attendant at Athelstan's courts, struck at least one issue, probably at the Chester mint. The Scandinavians drew information for their own coinage from England, and there were certainly plenty of English coins to copy in Scandinavia. English dies were taken to Denmark (and to Dublin) for use in local mints. The English model was important for Scandinavia.

More remarkable even than the extent and standard of the mintage was the firm royal control achieved over it during the last two Anglo-Saxon centuries. In earlier days archbishops, and possibly some bishops, had struck in their own names by their own moneyers, presumably from their own silver, and at times

---

[74] R. H. M. Dolley, 'The Significance of the Die-Axis in the Context of Later Anglo-Saxon Coinage', *B. N. J.*, 1954, pp.167–74.

(though rarely) even from their own gold. The king alone was now represented on the coinage, the ecclesiastical rights being limited to the receipt of profits from certain moneyers. Elaborate penalties were decreed to preserve the standard of the mintage. Athelstan laid down that the penalty for false coinage was the loss of a hand, a Carolingian penalty into which some have read ultimate Byzantine influence. Ethelred insisted on the death penalty for those who minted in strange places away from the *burh*, and further stated bluntly in his laws that no one save the king was to have a moneyer.[75] This last enactment probably meant no more than that all rights over moneyers stemmed ultimately from the king. The Bishop of Hereford, for example, at the time of the Domesday Survey owned one of the seven moneyers in the borough, and whenever the types were changed this moneyer paid twenty shillings to the bishop whereas the others paid theirs to the king.[76] Changes in type were frequent and profitable; apparently every six years or so from 973 to the end of Canute's reign, increasing to every two or three years by the time of the Conquest.[77] Just how regular the cycles were in practice is difficult to determine. It is even possible that by the end of the period the king himself was constrained by this custom, of great financial importance, regalian though the right continued to be.

Occasional attempts were made to limit the number of moneyers, presumably in order to increase their efficiency. Athelstan had laid down that no one, apart from the king and a few ecclesiastical magnates, was to possess a moneyer, but that every borough should be enabled to have its mint. In his Grateley decrees, Athelstan gave the following list of minting places in the south of England.

> In Canterbury [there are to be] seven moneyers; four of the king, two of the bishop, one of the abbot; in Rochester three, two of the king, one of the bishop; in London eight; in Winchester six; in Lewes two; in Hastings one; another at Chichester; at Southampton two; at Wareham two; [at Dorchester one]; at Exeter two; at Shaftesbury two; otherwise in the other boroughs one.[78]

Ethelred (or possibly his successor) went much further and attempted to limit the privilege of possessing more than one moneyer much more straitly, to the *summi portus*, the main towns, which

[75] II Athelstan 14; II Ethelred 16; III Ethelred 8.1.
[76] D. B. I, 179.
[77] R. H. M. Dolley, *Num. Chron.*, 1956, p.267.
[78] II Athelstan 14.2. Dorchester appears in the *quadripartitus* only.

Anglo–Saxon mints, 973-1066

Doubtful mint–signatures on which work is still in progress include: *Dyr* (Suffolk?), *Eanbyrh*,*Fro* (Frome?),*Gothanbyrh*, and *Niwan/Bry(g)gin*.

were to have three moneyers only.[79] The failure to achieve this, possibly unrealistic, aim is shown by the fact, already mentioned, that Hereford had seven moneyers. The numismatist, from his study of the coins that have actually survived, is able to give valuable information about the number of mints, as opposed to the number of moneyers. It can be said that during the reign of Ethelred there were at least sixty minting places ranging from London to an obscure little hill fort like Cadbury in Somerset where, as R. H. M. Dolley has been able to show, a temporary mint was established during the Danish troubles.[80] In this particular instance the minters

[79] IV Ethelred 9.
[80] R. H. M. Dolley, 'Some Late Anglo-Saxon Pence', *Brit. Mus. Quarterly*, 1954, p.63; also 'Three Late Anglo-Saxon Notes', *B. N. J.*, 1955, pp.99–105.

at Cadbury were ready to return home to Ilchester and Bruton and Crewkerne from their uncomfortable hill fortress when the Danish danger was past, but in the normal borough mint there was a solid continuity, some producing types of practically every issue of Ethelred and Canute. In 1066, coins were struck at no fewer than forty-four recorded mints during the short reign of Harold. Under William I there was a marked continuity in mintage, though the silver pennies of the early Norman kings were somewhat heavier than those of Edward the Confessor, and more stable in weight from type to type. The new Norman general tax, the *monetagium commune* – possibly in origin a levy to ensure that the king did not lose over the changing of coins from type to type – owed part of its efficacy and unpopularity to a royal control of mint and of exchange which was inherited from Anglo-Saxon days. Reputable numismatists say, not altogether in jest, that Henry I was the last of the English kings.

During the later Anglo-Saxon period there were in operation some sixty to seventy mints, receiving dies from a varying number of die-cutting centres but all supervised closely by the royal court. At times, particularly towards the end of the period, the centralization was even more complete, and the dies for new issues were sent out from one die-cutting centre alone; certainly the moneyers of Hereford went to London for their dies.

It is difficult to determine precisely the status and duties of the moneyers. In law the term *myneteras* appears to apply to the craftsmen, and the brutality of the punishments inflicted on those discovered infringing the law suggests a low social standing for the offenders. The legal documents may mislead in this respect, as the penal code is concerned with wrongdoers, the little man who set up a smithy-workshop *up on lande*, or the fake moneyer and counterfeiter, not the true *mynetere*. In an important code of Ethelred, however, infringement of coinage rights was associated quite closely with penalties for the infringement of the *trinoda necessitas*, and there is reason to suppose that the king, wishing to have this important function well performed, looked to men in responsible positions to ensure success.[81] The moneyers at Hereford had sake and soke. The financial rewards, even when substantial

---

[81] V Ethelred 26.1; cf. also II Canute 8–10. Further evidence of high status, prosperous burgers and the like, comes from the Winchester evidence examined by Martin Biddle and D. J. Keene, *Winchester in the Early Middle Ages*, Oxford, 1976, p.421 and from charter evidence examined by Ian Stewart, *Revue Numismatique*, 30, 1988, pp.166–75.

overheads had been paid in the way of dues to the king on the changing of dies and the payment of craftsmen and labourers, would be sufficient to attract men of good standing. The term *mynetere* itself may well refer both to the gentleman, who farmed the office, and to the craftsman working in the mint.

In the present state of knowledge, this can be little more than conjecture. There is one line of enquiry which may ultimately prove effective. The coins give the names of many thousands of moneyers; these names are often, much more often than not, of a type characteristic of the thegnly class, dithematic such as Wulfbold, Wulfhere, Leofric, and the like, rather than monothematic. R. H. M. Dolley has further drawn my attention to peculiarities in the distribution of names, the historical significance of which had not previously been noted. In Mercia the element Leof- is frequent: in Wessex the element Aethel-. It may be that these eleventh-century regional peculiarities represent genuine aristocratic customs among the inhabitants of the two provinces. Leof- in particular seems well favoured in earldoms governed by the house of Leofric. To have one's name on even the reverse of a coin is an honour as well as a dangerous privilege. Supervision of the coinage, so heavily regalian, may have ranked among the regular thegnly duties.

As to control of the flow of currency, there is not so much information. When the king went on expedition the matter was simple; ingots would be brought with him and the moneyer would turn out the coins for him, 'as many as the king would wish', as the Hereford Domesday puts it.[82] This procedure literally stamped the small silver coin with the royal guarantee of authentic weight and silver content; as such it was respected even well beyond the bounds of the kingdom. If people other than the king or royal officers wished to have bullion converted into coins, then it is probable that the moneyer made his own bargain. Royal concern was apparent, in theory, in all such transactions. Edgar, when repeating Athelstan's law about a single currency, added that 'no man is to refuse it'. The law-code known as IV Ethelred stated again that no one was to refuse pure money of proper weight, and the responsibility lay fair and square on the shoulders of the moneyer to see that such purity was achieved. This particular law-code gives the strongest evidence in favour of private exchange.[83] In its penal clauses false coiners were lumped together with merchants (*mercatores*) who bribed such

[82] D. B. I, 179a.
[83] IV Ethelred 5 and 6.

coiners with good money so that they should recast the good metal into many inferior coins. In the same category, also, were placed those who made dies in secret and sold them to coiners for money, engraving upon them the name of another moneyer. Faced with this hierarchy of offence the good men of London made no distinction between the false coiner, the merchant who prompted the forgery, and the die-forger who fed the false coiner with the instrument of his trade. But the law made such a distinction. The death penalty, rare in an age which extolled mutilation as giving time for repentance, was imposed on those who worked in the woods and other secret places; the more familiar striking off of a hand and setting it up over the mint was imposed on the other offenders. The die-forgers were singled out for special severity in this way. It was from false dies that false coins could most safely be struck. The state was greatly concerned with the maintenance of a pure coinage. Methods of blanching and assaying were well known to the Anglo-Saxons, as can be gathered from a twelfth-century account of the workings of the lower Exchequer.

As for the scale of operation, much depended on the size and nature of the transaction, and it may reasonably be assumed that an important moneyer of York or Lincoln or Winchester or London would be asked to guarantee a major piece of coining from bullion, while the little man at the isolated *burh* of Cadbury or Aylesbury would not. Indeed the flow of currency must have been intimately connected with the importance of the local market; a frequency count of the number of moneyers in operation at any one *burh* at any one period, even a rough and ready calculation of the number of coins discovered from any one mint, gives an intelligible picture of economic activity in England. These show the predominance of London and of the cities that lead to the North Sea such as York and Lincoln, or to the Irish Sea such as Chester. Sir Frank Stenton has taken the number of moneyers as a strong piece of collateral evidence for the size and importance of towns.[84] In the last generation of Anglo-Saxon England there were twenty known moneyers at work simultaneously in London; more than ten at York; at least nine in Lincoln and Winchester; eight at least at Chester; seven at least at Canterbury and Oxford; and at least six at Gloucester, Thetford and Worcester. As Sir Frank says, this

[84] *Anglo-Saxon England,* p.537. Developed further by Michael Metcalf, notably in the important papers on 'Continuity and Change in English Monetary History, c. 973–1086', *B. N. J.* 50 and 51, 1981–2.

method which depends to some extent on the arbitrary fortunes of coin discovery probably does less than justice to Ipswich and Norwich which on coin evidence were served by no more than four or five moneyers. Even so the value of the figures is beyond question.

In attempting to understand the reasons for the multiplicity of mints we are helped considerably by continental parallels. Charlemagne attempted at one time to centralize all the minting at the palace of Aachen. This proved too unwieldy and a system was adopted, apparently similar to that in Lombardy, by which mints were set up in every important centre. Moneyers were enlisted in public *ministeria* under supervision of masters, *magistri*, who would put their names to the coins. The penalty of striking off a hand originated with Louis the Pious and was restated by Charles the Bald. In the Edict of Pîtres, he attempted to limit the mints to nine, and ordered old coins to be withdrawn, new coins struck and a small amount of silver from the royal chamber was lent to start the minting process. Moneyers themselves took a proportion of coin minted as their perquisite, one out of every twenty-two deniers in the time of Pippin the Short, and it is likely that they made harder bargains than this when and where they could. Further profits came from judicial rights over forgers, trade in gold, and money changing. A similar economic background, a similar denarial economy led to similar experiments on the Continent and in England.

At all events it can be stated with something like certainty that England in 1066 possessed a sound stable silver currency, the fluctuations in weight of which were carefully controlled at the national level. It may be that the reason lies with the chance of discovery, but this currency appears in advance of the so-called debased feudal currency that was used in Gaul at that time. The German currency is better than the French. The Ottonian reforms in Italy and in Germany may on further investigation prove to be closer to Edgar's reforms than has yet been realized, and the Salian emperors, particularly Henry IV, were most anxious to retain Goslar as an imperial centre, situated as it was in the silver-bearing districts of the Harz Mountains. Yet in imperial Germany there is not the same direct evidence of central direction and technical skill as in Anglo-Saxon England. The English achievement in these fields indicates not only Danish stimulus but unusual central control within the community. It also implies the stabilization of small but not insignificant local markets.

d) The non-silver coinage; the problem of gold

There is little trace of gold currency in the later Anglo-Saxon period. A few coins have survived, of Offa, of Wigmund, Archbishop of York, 837–53, of Edward the Elder, of Ethelred and of Edward the Confessor, but all these may be accounted for as other than normal currency. General numismatic opinion holds that no regular gold coinage was' minted after the last quarter of the seventh century. Yet the Anglo-Saxons, though they did not mint gold coins, knew them and used them. Their mancus, the equivalent of thirty pennies, was not merely a unit of account. Wærferth, in his translation of Gregory's Dialogues, described *mancessos (aureos)*, gleaming as if new taken from the fire; the Leechdoms refer to treasure that is discovered in mancuses or pennies; Eadred's will expressly demanded that mancuses should be struck in gold, and two thousand of them sent to depositories under the charge of a bishop, for the well-being of the inhabitants and the sake of his soul.[85] When mancuses of gold *by weight* were specified in the will of the ætheling, Athelstan, a natural contrast is surely implied with mancuses of gold by tale.[86] Mancus, which is a term common to Western Europe, was used very freely in tenth- and eleventh-century England in contexts where the most rational meaning is that of a gold coin. There is, indeed, one passage in an eleventh-century Colloquy by Aelfric Bata where the mancus, at first sight, appears to be referring to a silver coin. 'Count out the coins into my hand', said the seller of a mass-book to the purchaser, 'so that I may see if they are good and of pure silver'.[87] The mass-book cost twelve mancuses, but the probability is that mancus signified in this context a unit of account worth thirty silver pence.

As was mentioned in an earlier chapter, it used to be thought that mancus was derived from an Arabic term, and thus afforded evidence of a balance of trade with the Mediterranean, redressed by the export of slaves and tin from this island, and of direct and frequent contact with the gold countries in Moslem and Byzantine hands.[88] This view is no longer tenable, and yet it is certain that some Moslem currency reached this country. In 774, a famous coin

---

[85] *Bischofs Wærferth von Worcester Übersetzung der Dialoge Gregors des Grosses*, ed. H. Hecht (Bibl. der angelsachs. Prosa, V), p.65, Leipzig, 1900; *Anglo-Saxon Leechdoms*, iii, p.170; Harmer, *Select Documents*, no. xxi.

[86] D. Whitelock, *Anglo-Saxon Wills*, no. xx, pp.57–63.

[87] *Early Scholastic Colloquies*, ed. W. H. Stevenson and W. M. Lindsay, p.50.

[88] See above, p.79.

was struck in Offa's name that had even the Arabic inscriptions and
date (A H 157 = 774 A.D.) of its Moslem prototype. Byzantine
coins, or imitations of Byzantine coins, also found their way to
England.[89] But native striking of gold seems to have been limited
to ceremonial occasions, such as those laid down in Eadred's will
or to special shrine offerings when presumably the ordinary silver
dies would be used on the more precious metal. There was no call
for a gold currency on the home market; the transactions were
not elaborate enough for that. Much of the overseas trade lay with
the traditional silver-loving communities of the Baltic. Gold had a
special appeal as ornament, and the probability is that, if Eadred's
mancuses were indeed struck, they never passed into currency. A
quick transference back to ornament was their more likely fate.
Gold retained naturally its standard of value *vis-à-vis* silver, and one
brilliant attempt to establish the ratio suggests a gradual increase
in value of gold from perhaps nine to one at the time of Offa, to
ten to one at the beginning of the following century, to eleven to
one in the reign of Athelstan.[90] In Frankia there appears to have
been maintained a steady twelve to one ratio, but it is difficult
to base a generalization on such minute, and in the last resort
conjectural, differences. Precise numismatic work by the Swedish
scholar, S. Bolin, has given rather different results. He argued
that, in Western Europe, at the beginning of the seventh century
the ratio of gold to silver was ten to one, that there was a sharp rise
between 700 and 850 to the ratio of seventeen to one, and then,
from the second half of the ninth century an inverse movement
steadying the ratio to twelve to one in the tenth century.[91]

But saying that gold had value and that gold was used as currency
are two glaringly different propositions. The poverty of the supply
of gold hit all the communities of Western Europe, perhaps most
of all England. The still workable mines in these islands lay well
beyond the Celtic frontier. It does not seem likely that gold coins
were minted as regular currency in Anglo-Saxon England after the
last quarter of the seventh century.

The quantity of goods coming from the Mediterranean countries
did not apparently demand the issue of a gold currency. There was

[89] P. D. Whitting, 'The Byzantine Empire and the Coinage of the Anglo-Saxons',
Anglo-Saxon Coins, p.33, reminds us in a concentrated and important article that
'the record of English finds of Byzantine coins is indeed a sparse one'.
[90] H. M. Chadwick, *Studies on Anglo-Saxon Institutions*, pp.47 ff., 54 ff., and 158
ff.
[91] É. Perroy, 'Encore Mahomet et Charlemagne', *Revue historique*, 1954, pp.232–8;
also cited by R. H. C. Davis, *A History of Medieval Europe*, London, 1957, p.184.

regular contact with Rome, and Peter's Pence was paid on the whole with regularity.[92] Payment was made in silver, and fresh light has recently been thrown on one of the numismatic mysteries of the age. There has long been speculation about a coin of Alfred, heavier than the customary silver penny, with the letters *Elimo* inscribed on the reverse. Taking the last two letters as a customary abbreviation for *monetarius*, some numismatists provided us with a moneyer of unquestionably Jewish origin, named Eli. However, by putting together two suggestions made separately and independently about the coin and the name, R. H. M. Dolley has suggested in convincing fashion that *Elimo* was indeed an abbreviation for *Elimosina*, that is for the alms sent by the King to Rome. The conclusive scrap of evidence lies in the weight of the coin, or rather coins, as a fragment of a second has been discovered. This weight corresponds to that of six Frankish *denarii*, and so the picture is complete. These are, indeed, Peter's Pence, and Alfred is seen, in R. H. M. Dolley's own words, as the inventor not only of the British navy but of the sixpence![93] If silver were used for the tribute to St Peter, and the evidence of the hoards, found at Rome is strong on this point, then for what was it not used?

Of metals other than the precious gold and silver there is little evidence except for the kingdom of Northumbria, where a currency made of a composition of copper, zinc and silver, and known to numismatists as *stycas*, was struck during the eighth and ninth centuries. This has been held with some plausibility to mirror social and political decline in the northern kingdom. With the establishment of the Viking kingdom of York after 867 a large and distinctive coinage of good silver was issued in the later ninth century. After the reabsorption of the kingdom in 954 there is more conformity to the general pattern, though some evidence remains of unorthodoxy at the major mint of York.

(e) Coinage and value; monetary reckoning

If problems concerning the tangible coinage are difficult, problems concerning the value of that coinage are, in some respects, almost insoluble. For the early period it is reasonably well established that the Old English term *scilling* which occurs frequently in the law codes was the small gold *tremissis* of the earliest Anglo-Saxon

[92] See below, p.242.

[93] R. H. M. Dolley, 'The So-Called Piedforts of Alfred the Great', *Num, Chron.*, 1954, p.82.

coinage. After it was superseded in the late seventh century by the silver penny it became a unit of account. Its value varied from kingdom to kingdom: in Mercia it was worth four pence, in Wessex five, in Kent a little later (as also on the Continent) it was worth twelve. The reason for such difference is probably that while the value of the *tremissis* fell during the seventh century because of its progressive debasement, its value became fixed in each kingdom as a unit of account at different levels, depending on when the provisions about wergelds and fines were codified. It must be stressed that the silver coins we refer to misleadingly as *sceattas* were silver pennies, and that they have nothing to do with the weight unit of 1/20th of a *scilling* mentioned in the laws of Ethelbert of Kent. The value of the silver penny would have fluctuated as the weight and fineness of the coin varied, but it was effectively the same denomination that continued throughout the Middle Ages, indeed down to 1968. Even the Northumbrian *styca* is properly a penny, although its value must have been a fraction of the contemporary silver penny of southern England.[94] It was in Northumbria, too, curiously enough, that the term *tremissis* itself was retained in the form þrymsa to express the unit in which wergelds were reckoned as late as the tenth and eleventh centuries, though these þrymsas, units of account not coins, were worth at this stage only three silver pennies. But evidence is lacking for any successful translation of these relative values into more tangible terms.

Over and above this, payment by pounds for major transactions became frequent from the beginning of the ninth century. In time these pounds, of pure silver as is sometimes specified, were reckoned as equivalent to two hundred and forty silver pennies; it is probable that this ratio was established at a very early stage. Already in the second half of the tenth century there is some evidence from the Liber Eliensis of a twelve-penny shilling in use in eastern England; Byrhtferth of Ramsey stated expressly that twenty shillings of twelve pence made up a pound; and Aelfric referred to shillings of twelve pence.[95] It may be that for the reckoning of wergelds and legal penalties the older system was retained while traders, at least in the eastern part of the country, conformed to up-to-date Frankish practice. After 1066 when the

[94] I am grateful to Mark Blackburn for personal communications on which this paragraph is based.
[95] *Liber Eliensis*, ed. D. J. Stewart; clear examples occur in Book II, 11 and 25, pp.130 and 138. *Byrhtferth's Manual*, ed. S. J. Crawford, p.66. Aelfric, Exodus 21: 10 refers to twelve shillings of twelve pence, *Heptateuch*, ed. S. J. Crawford, p.264.

Frankish method of taking twelve pence or *denarii* to the shilling was universally adopted, the convenience of a pound that would divide into twenty shillings of twelve pence was sufficient to stabilize what came in time to be accepted as a special English peculiarity.

The Scandinavian invasions and settlements also brought greater complexity into the system of monetary reckoning. Their basic high standard of value was the mark, a weight of precious metal that was in turn divided into eight sections or ores. In the course of the tenth century these were brought into line with the English system by equating the ore with a certain number of pence, at times with twenty, and at other times with only sixteen. In the laws of Ethelred fifteen *orae* were reckoned to the pound; in twelfth-century law-books twelve to the pound.[96] Domesday Book contains examples of both methods of accounting. But methods of accounting they are; the basic tangible coin current in England was the silver penny. It was by no means insignificant in value; thirty pence in the reign of Athelstan was the legal compensation price of an ox.[97] It is not possible to translate with accuracy scales of value in late Anglo-Saxon England into scales of value in twentieth-century England. But if an Anglo-Saxon penny is thought of in terms of a substantial banknote nowadays a better idea will be given not of real value, but of the way in which a penny was regarded in the pre-Conquest period. It possessed sufficient value to make complexities in the handling of it worth while. If, as seems certain, old coins were called in when a new type was struck, then a twenty-mile journey to the nearest mint would not seem out of the way to change a coin which represented a substantial value. The modern overtones of insignificance attached to the idea of a few pence can be most confusing. It also seems evident that, for the minor transactions of rural life, barter and natural exchange were common, eggs, hens, butter, cheese, and so on, all related, however, to the idea of a scale of value expressed in a currency of which the silver penny was the tangible expression.

4. THE BOROUGHS

(a) The burhs *of Alfred and Edward*

One feature of English coinage demands special attention. The rule was laid down firmly, in the tenth and eleventh centuries,

96 IV Ethelred 9.2; Edw. the Conf. 12.4; Leis Willelme 2.3 ff.
97 VI Athelstan 6.2; see above p.118.

that no coin was to be struck outside a *burh*. In itself this rule
is remarkable testimony to the efficacy of the royal hold over
the mints, and indeed over the network of communications in
the realm. Precautions were taken against the possibility of false
coining *up on lande*. All this is a product of the last century and
a half of Anglo-Saxon England, and leads to a discussion of one
of the key questions involved in any analysis of the economic and
social history of Anglo-Saxon England. What precisely were these
burhs, and what relationship did they bear to the development of
urban life in Anglo-Saxon England?

Technically this is not too difficult a question to answer. The
official documents of the tenth and eleventh centuries show that
the *burhs* originated in a conscious planned policy carried out by
Alfred, and fully implemented by his son Edward and his daughter
Aethelflæd, the lady of the Mercians, and her husband Ethelred. In
essentials the *burhs* were fortified townships, walled about in some
instances, protected by earthworks in others, defensible points on
the lines of communication, the prickles on the hedgehog's back.
Their reason of being was military and political; their success was
considerable. Ultimately they were to be institutions through which
royal control of an expanding economy could be exercised. No
burh that could not thrive economically developed into a borough.
To appreciate the situation accurately it is essential to emphasize
both the official military nature of the Alfredian *burh*, and the
fact that it represented only a stage, though a vitally important
one, in the evolution of the medieval English borough and of the
medieval town.

In Old English there were three terms in common use to describe
a community larger than a *ham* or a *tun*. There was *burh* itself, and
secondly there was *port*, which was used particularly of a town with
a market, whether inland or at the coast, and thirdly there was
ceaster, a loan word from *castrum*, which was used of towns well
known in Roman Britain.[98] *Burh* itself originally meant no more
than a fortified dwelling place belonging to king or noble, or even
a prehistoric fort, and it often survives in the dative form (*æt -byrig*
giving modern -bury) in English place-names.

Information about the *burhs* in the critical reigns of Alfred and
his son Edward the Elder comes from two main sources, the Anglo-
Saxon Chronicle and a curious document known as the Burghal
Hidage. The two sources are pleasantly complementary, as the

[98] P. Hunter Blair, *Anglo-Saxon England*, Cambridge, 1956, p.227.

Chronicle gives information on the Mercian developments, while the Burghal Hidage concentrates on Wessex and the South and only briefly touches on Mercian affairs. The Chronicle itself is a composite document for the reign of Edward the Elder. Much information about the west of Mercia comes from what is known as the Mercian Register, which was incorporated in some versions of the Chronicle, while the main Chronicle concentrates on the activities of King Edward himself, who operated in the east and north-east of Mercia where the Danish peril was most acute. The Mercian Register tells of the restoration of Chester, of the building of ten *burhs* by Aethelflæd, ranging from places as important as Tamworth and Stafford to still unidentified places like *Bremesbyrig* and *Scergeat*. It also tells of the recovery of Derby and Leicester, and of the building by Edward himself of a *burh* at Cledemuthe in 921. This *burh* can probably be identified with a spot near Rhuddlan at the mouth of the Clwydd.[99]

The main Chronicle gives a more elaborate account, following the active royal campaigns rather than the more passive defensive measures of his sister. Mention is made of two double *burhs*, one each side of the river, at Hertford and Buckingham, of five *burhs* recovered from the Danes, Bedford, Huntingdon, Colchester, Stamford and Nottingham (with additional *burhs* constructed to guard a route or dominate a rival encampment on the south side of Bedford and Nottingham), and of seven new *burhs* at Witham, Maldon, Towcester (which was also walled as a separate process), *Wigingamere*, Thelwall, Manchester (repaired and manned) and Bakewell. The building of such defensive fortifications emerges unmistakably from the Chronicle as a master defensive stroke, but it is too easy to have misconceptions about them. For example they were not castles; the area enclosed, as may still be seen at Witham and Eddisbury, was often over twenty acres in extent, obviously designed to hold a substantial garrison. In some instances old Roman walls were used; in others earth mounds; in others hill-forts; in others newly built stone walls. All, however, were effective defensive works and, where other conditions were favourable, it is no surprise to find town life flourishing on the chosen sites as peace was re-established.

These particular *burhs*, however, were built primarily with an eye to military strategy. As Professor Tait pointed out, only eight of them reached municipal status in the Middle Ages: Chester,

[99] F. T. Wainwright, 'Ingimund's Invasion', *E. H. R.*, 1948, p.166.

Bridgnorth, Tamworth, Stafford, Hertford, Warwick, Buckingham and Maldon. All of these, with the possible exception of Bridgnorth, had mints in the late Anglo-Saxon period, and it is possible now that to Bridgnorth may be attributed a series of coins bearing the inscription BRY(G)GIN.[100]

Fortunately it is not a matter of a mere list of names, impressive though that might be. Real insight into the burghal system at work is given by a document which has survived relating to the heartland of the West Saxon dynasty. This document, the Burghal Hidage, also reminds us that the burghal system was not a complete innovation of Edward the Elder. Precedent lay in his father's day and, indeed, further back again. What was new was the scale of operation and systematic implementation of a royal central policy.

The Burghal Hidage is a document which may be attributed to the period 911–19.[101] It sets out a list of *burhs* encircling Wessex and the south from an unidentified *Eorpeburnan* to the east of Hastings, through Southampton and Winchester to Exeter, Halwell and Lydford, then back through Somerset along the north of historic Wessex through Malmesbury, Cricklade, Oxford and Wallingford to Southwark. The inclusion of Porchester, which was not in royal hands until 904, coupled with the inclusion of Buckingham on the last stage of the survey are good grounds for attributing to the document a date of origin in Edward the Elder's reign rather than that of his father. Later copies of the manuscript add statistics referring to two further Mercian *burhs*, Worcester and Warwick. To each of the names was added a simple formula: to Hastings belong five hundred hides, to Winchester belong two thousand four hundred hides, to Bath belong one thousand hides and so on. An interpretation was then offered of the figures, and the calculations are accurate, business-like and reasonable – a remarkable feature in a medieval document.

For the maintenance and defence of an acre's breadth of wall, sixteen hides are required. If every hide is represented by one man (Athelstan in an ordinance relating to boroughs attempted to exact two well-mounted men from each hide[102]) then every pole of wall can be manned by four men. The sums were then

[100] R. H. M. Dolley, 'Three Late Anglo-Saxon Notes', *B. N. J.*, 1955, pp.92–9.
[101] A. J. Robertson, *Anglo-Saxon Charters*, Appendix II, no. I. D. Hill, 'The Burghal Hidage: the establishment of a text', *M. A.* XIII, 1969, pp.84–92.
[102] II Athelstan 16; this is more likely to refer to the special needs of the *burh* than to general military service.

carried on to suggest that for a circuit of twelve furlongs of wall nineteen hundred and twenty men were required, and a hundred and sixty men for each additional furlong.

Comparison of the figures with the fortifications still surviving gives astonishing results. The medieval wall at Winchester was about 3,318 yards in length; the Burghal Hidage made provision for defence of 3,300 yards. At Wareham the fortifications appear to have been about 2,180 yards; the Burghal Hidage made provision for 2,200. Not all the figures are as close as these. The odd number, 513, attributed to Watchet suggests some corruption in the text. Correspondence is close enough, however, to show that the Burghal Hidage was a serious document, seriously conceived and drawn up with assessment to a national burden in mind. The burden of defence of the *burhs* was laid on the countryside, and in the case of the big *burhs* a considerable area was affected. This system of levy for defence of *burhs* by hides was probably a major step towards the evolution of the hide as a unit of assessment from its original meaning as a measure of extent of arable land.

It cannot be doubted that here in the maintenance of the walls there is elaboration of the duty of looking after *burhs*, exemption from which was so rarely, if ever, granted to the holders of estates. In this equation of needs of defence with the obligations of a landholding *thegn*, Maitland discovered the germ of his brilliant though somewhat distorted theory of the origin of the English boroughs, known as the garrison theory. The agglomeration of population that appeared in some of the English *burhs* during the tenth and eleventh centuries was made possible by fortification and constant replenishment of garrisons from the surrounding countryside. Full credit must go to Maitland for recognizing the military nature of the *burhs* of the tenth century; they were military creations of a monarchy that was insisting on a national system of defence implemented by the landholders of the neighbourhood. But by the time of Domesday the attachment of town houses to rural manors, of which Maitland made so much, had lost its military connotation and had taken on solid economic coating.[103]

Indeed the general development of the English town and borough cannot be understood until a sharp distinction is made between the Alfredian *burhs* as such, and the towns of Anglo-Saxon England. In the course of the tenth century *burh* came to acquire, at least in official eyes, a significance which was later enjoyed by

[103] See below, pp.317–19.

the borough. But in the early tenth century it could still mean fortification; to the very end of the period it was possible to use the term of a nobleman's stockaded dwelling-house. It is none the less true that for many of the Alfredian *burhs*, a majority in Wessex a minority in Mercia, the reasons that made them desirable posts of defence also made them desirable centres of economic activity, so leading in the future to their development as important towns.

(b)*Towns and urban life in the pre-Viking age*

Before the Alfredian period information about towns and urban life is distressingly scanty. Something has already been said of the problem of continuity with Roman Britain, and the conclusion tentatively put forward that, while not denying that some probably survived as habitation sites, there was a break in continuity of urban life with the Anglo-Saxon invasions. It has also been argued that from the second half of the sixth century there was significant revival of urban life, connected with royal *tuns*, trade with Merovingian Frankia, and finally, in the seventh century, with the Christian Church. Missionaries certainly showed a preference for Roman sites, and there is plentiful evidence from Bede of concentrations of population meriting the description of towns. In one town fire swept through all the buildings, they were so closely huddled together. In Northumbria around the gaunt rock of *Bebbanburh* there existed a township well enough fortified to resist the onslaught of Penda's army for three whole days. York was an important urban centre by the end of the seventh century; at Carlisle Cuthbert's guide showed him the walls and fountain of the old city with the same pride that a modern mayor has in his local ruined castle or abbey. Quite early in the progress of the Conversion, in 628, Paulinus was received at Lincoln by an officer whom Bede calls the *praefectus* of the city, and Paulinus built a stone church there whose walls were still standing in Bede's own day.

It is in the south-east, however, as might be expected, that the evidence of town life is strongest. London is referred to as the emporium for many peoples coming by land and by sea, and it is known now that significant development took place to the west of the Roman city along the modern Strand into Aldwych.[104] Gregory

---

[104] *Hist. Eccl.*, III, 16; Anon. life of St Cuthbert, ed. B. Colgrave, c. VIII; *Hist. Eccl.*, II, 16, and II, 3. B. Hobley, 'Lundenwic and Lundenburh', *The Rebirth of Towns in the West, A.D. 700–1050*, C. B. A. Research Report 68, ed. R. Hodges and B. Hobley, pp.69–82, 1988.

intended originally to set up an archbishopric at this natural capital, but the political predominance of Kent drew Augustine south to Canterbury. Legal references to London suggest a town with a market, halls where business could be transacted, and containing houses belonging to the monarchs of Kent, a place where the apparatus of urban dealing was already familiar.[105] Canterbury itself, the metropolis of Ethelbert's kingdom, was a substantial settlement, walled but with buildings spilling beyond the walls, the home of a church reputed to have survived from Roman days and, after the great work of Theodore of Tarsus, it unquestionably became the ecclesiastical capital of the island. Rochester had a market, a port reeve and an early bishopric. Elsewhere in the south there is little sign of urban development, though bishoprics were established at the old Roman settlements of Winchester and Dorchester-on-Thames. In the strong Middle Kingdom, obdurately heathen until the middle of the century, there is no documentary evidence of town life. Even in its great days of the eighth century the Mercian court found its favourite centre against the rural background of Tamworth and Lichfield.

With the important exception of *Hamwih*, now part of modern Southampton, evidence is ambiguous for fresh urban development in the eighth and ninth centuries. *Hamwih* itself owed its foundation to the increased prosperity of Wessex under Ine and, once established, had an important continuous history which has now yielded part of its record to the archaeologist's spade.

Only the seventh-century centres can have retained anything of a true urban character, like Canterbury, Rochester, London and York, and it is possible that even they were altering their nature. Elsewhere the very designation of the bishops as Bishops of the East Angles or Middle Angles or of the West Saxons probably expresses the reality that lies behind the title. Yet even in this period of concentration on agriculture, some places specially favoured by economic circumstances were emerging from the ruck of rural settlements to form the nucleus of later towns. In particular small coastal settlements attracted settlers to good natural harbours. On the east coast from the Wash to London many of the inlets gave scope for substantial settlement in secure harbours not too difficult to defend. Ipswich, founded in the early seventh century, offers firm archaeological evidence for a degree of urban development in East Anglia with a substantial pottery industry. At Northampton

---

[105] Hlothhere and Eadric, 16–16.3.

carbon dating has shown conclusively that a network of royal palaces first in timber then in stone, associated with the minster church of St. Peter, should be dated to the period c.750–850.[106] Similar centres may also have grown up in Hereford, Chester, Worcester and Gloucester, founding at the least a pre-urban nucleus. It is no matter for surprise that in such Roman towns the new combination of Christian Church and royal headquarters should have been on or near the principal Roman municipal sites as at Lincoln where the site of Paulinus's missionary church lies within the courtyard of the Roman forum. To the south the excavations at *Hamwih* give indication of expanding urban settlement. On the whole, however, the Anglo-Saxon evidence suggests that Pirenne may well have been right to emphasize the seventh and eighth centuries as the period of true break between the classical and the medieval world. Towns of the type described by Bede were Roman though in decadence; towns of the Carolingian world and tenth-century England and Germany were more firmly rooted in the soil, more attuned to a predominantly agricultural world. In early seventh-century Canterbury there was barbaric splendour imitating the classical world of the past: gold coins and fine Kentish jewellery. In tenth-century Winchester, there was a solid market town benefiting from some overseas trade, a prosperous local market, silver currency, a rustic nobility enjoying the luxury of town houses and storeplaces for their rural surplus.

For the obscure eighth and ninth centuries it is the south-east which provides the most valuable documentary evidence. Charters survive relating to Canterbury and Rochester which show considerable advance in municipal order in this period. At Canterbury houses were being built too close together, and what amounted virtually to a by-law laid down that there should be a space of two feet clear for eavesdrip between the houses.[107] Both the Kentish cities were partitioned into substantial *hagae* or *tuns*, that is enclosures within the walls. The Canterbury charter which told of the eavesdrip, also gives the first reference to a guild among townsmen the *cnihtengild* of 858. Canterbury was indeed an agricultural unit a trading centre and a place of defence, and in itself offers proof enough that the Anglo-Saxon borough was not a new conception

---

[106] John H. Williams, 'From 'palace' to 'town': Northampton and urban origins' *A. S. E.* 13, 1984, pp.113–36, an acute analysis of problems connected with urban growth.
[107] *C. S.* 519. N. P. Brooks, *The Early History of the Church of Canterbury*, Leicester 1984, pp.15–36, on the urban setting of the city.

of the age of Alfred. As early as the reign of Offa a tenement in Canterbury was included among the appendages to a large rural estate.[108]

Further north it is only at York that there is unquestioned evidence of urban development. In 735 Gregory's scheme of a second archbishopric was brought to fruition. A great school and substantial library was founded at York. Alcuin left a description from the end of the eighth century which gives the impression of a populous town attracting men of many nations.[109]

(c) Towns and urban life in the Viking age and after

It is nevertheless true that, with the possible exception of Canterbury and the certain exception of London and York, there were few towns in the pre-Danish age which sustained a population beyond that which their own fields could feed. The Danes themselves – and their incursions can be dated for this purpose from 865, a date which R. H. Hodgkin called the 1066 of the Danish Conquest – contributed two great aids to the town life of England. They brought with them their own skill as seamen and traders; they provoked the establishment of defensible, often walled, *burhs*. For all the political trouble and general unrest in the tenth and early eleventh centuries the late Anglo-Saxon period was a period of growth in urban communities in Anglo-Saxon England.

Apart from the very important evidence of coins, information about late Anglo-Saxon *burhs* on their stages of growth into boroughs comes from the law-codes and fragmentary reference to guild regulations. There are also valuable charters which throw light on urban organization. Prominent among these is a document that serves as a very important link between the Alfredian *burhs* and later borough development: a Worcester charter which tells how, in the later days of Alfred's reign, the ealdorman Ethelred and his wife Aethelflæd at the instance of Bishop Wæferth ordered the construction of a *burh* at Worcester for the defence of all the folk and the security of the cathedral.[110] The ealdorman and his wife, when the fortifications were complete, granted to the bishop half the rights that belonged to their lordships in market-place or in street, reserving to the king the toll on goods brought to Worcester

[108] F. M. Stenton, *Anglo-Saxon England* pp.526–7, C. S. 248.
[109] Alcuin, M. G. H., *Ep.* IV, 42 ff.; E. Duckett, *Alcuin, Friend of Charlemagne* pp. 161–2.
[110] C. S. 579.

145

in wagons or on horses, and to the bishop the rights which had belonged to the church within the property owned by the church. The king shared with the bishop *landfeoh*, presumably a rent paid by properties surrounding the *burh*, legal fines for fighting, theft and dishonest trading, an imposition levied for repair of the wall and legal fines for crimes that involved compensation. Outside the market the bishop was to be entitled to his land and dues with the clear implication that within the market the king or his representative was all-powerful. Special reservation was made of royal dues paid at Droitwich of a shilling (four Mercian pence) on a wagon and a penny on a pack. Worcester was unusual in being founded on land not wholly or in large part royal demesne, and it is a fortunate chance that has preserved this document. It shows even at this early stage a *burh* where the market was a very important feature though, as Sir Frank Stenton reminds us, the impression given is that the market like the fortifications was comparatively new. The fact that the ealdorman, responsible for the fortifications, was able to give such economic rights to the bishop, also provides a hint that the traditional *eorl's* penny of the customs of a borough may be derived from the efforts made in the first place to make the *burh* defensible.[111]

Perhaps the most interesting information on urban development in the pre-Conquest period comes from the somewhat fragmentary reference to guild organization. Record of these has come from as early as the ninth century with the mention of the Canterbury *cnihtengild*. It is not possible to say precisely who were these *cnihts*. Like *thegn* and *vassus* and *gwas*, the term was capable of bearing many meanings. The *cnihts* were the boys, the servants, in time the military servants and ultimately men of high rank. The fact that they banded together implies a degree of organization among a defined section of the inhabitants of a town, whether they were responsible citizens concerned in trade or in the defence of this walled city. From the tenth century information grows more precise. It was an age of voluntary or semi-voluntary associations. In the face of outside perils the freeman readily commended himself to a lord who could protect him. Powerful men in a neighbourhood found it expedient to band themselves together to act against theft. From the mysterious *gegildan*, the artificial kindred, the 'fellow-payers' in the earlier law-codes developed voluntary frithguilds organized on a stabler territorial basis. J. E. A. Jolliffe considered

---

[111] F. M. Stenton, *Anglo-Saxon England* pp.534–5.

that such organizations had important effects on the growth of the tenth-century hundred, which represented government initiative in harnessing a general social movement.[112] Nor did hundred activity exhaust the force of this movement. In Cambridge there was a peculiar organization known as the thegn's guild. In name it is immediately reminiscent of the earlier *cnihtengild* of Canterbury. Regulations have survived from the pages of a gospel-book that are very like, in some respects, the statutes of later medieval guilds. Concern is shown with funeral dues, the transport of a member's body home if he is taken ill or dies outside the district, almsgiving and the payment of customary dues, or customary fines, in sesters of honey. The bulk of the document is taken up, indicative of its early date, with elaborate details concerning the blood-feud, a matter made more complicated by the consistent mobility of the group as well as by their high rank.[113] Guild statutes from Exeter are also interesting, making provision for corporate payment in money and in spiritual observance on various occasions such as the death of a member, or a member's pilgrimage to Rome, or offering, if a member's house burned down, a rudimentary fire insurance.[114] Similar regulations from Bedwyn tell that, if a man's house is burnt, each member shall contribute 2d. or a load of building materials. About 1040 a Dorset thegn of Scandinavian origin made a munificent gift of a guildhall and site to the guild at Abbotsbury.[115] This gift was followed by a recital of the guild statutes, spiritual duties, alms-giving, with particular attention directed to proper skill in the preparation of a brewing. Then followed a statement parallel to that already found in the Cambridge regulations: 'If any one becomes ill within sixty miles we are then to find fifteen men to fetch him, thirty if he be dead – and they are to bring him to the place he desired in his life.' The chance of documentary survival has left these social records that illustrate important corporate organization in the smaller *burhs*. The strong probability is that similar organizations existed also in towns that by 1066 were sizeable communities, where members, or the most important among them, would be well used to travelling freely around the realm of England.

Further valuable evidence of unusual activity in English boroughs of the tenth and eleventh centuries is given by the law-

[12] *Constitutional History of Medieval England*, London, 1937, pp.116–17.
[13] *E. H. D.* I. pp.604–5.
[14] Ibid., p.605.
[15] Ibid., pp.606–7.

codes, though in some ways, as for example in their reference
to borough-courts, the entries are disappointingly ambiguous or
jejune. A code promulgated by King Edgar during or shortly
after the plague of 962 tells that a primary distinction is made
admittedly in a commercial matter, between those who live within
a borough and those who live without. Standing witnesses were
to be appointed to vouch for commercial transactions, thirty-six
for each borough, but only twelve for small boroughs and hun
dreds unless more were desired.[116] The same basic distinction
between borough and country was made again in the laws of
Ethelred and of Canute. Legally the dweller in the town was coming
to have a special status. In 1018 the Bishop of Crediton dealt
with the *burhwitan* of the four Devon boroughs of Exeter, Totnes
Lydford and Barnstaple.[117] Efforts were made to standardize the
procedure for exculpation of accusation in boroughs throughout
the country.[118] In twelfth-century codes that purported to reflect
conditions either immediately before or after the Conquest, it is
stated that no market or fair was to be held outside a borough
and, a point remarkably well attested by surviving numismatic and
legal evidence, that the boroughs were to take special precaution
against the falsification of money.[119]

It is necessary to stress this recognition of legal difference be
tween the borough and the countryside because it brings out the
crux of the problems relating to the Old English borough. Without
wishing to rake over the ashes of dead controversy, we may still
state that a lively mode of entry into any discussion of the matter
lies through the scholarly differences of opinion in the early 1930
between Professors Carl Stephenson and James Tait.[120] Funda
mentally what Stephenson did was to apply the continental analysis
of urban institutions to the English situation. The classic division
into *bourgs* and *poorts* was brought to bear on a community which
as later critics were quick to point out, had not developed on line
strictly analogous to the Flemish and Lotharingian heartland of
the *thèse de Pirenne*. Convinced of the rudimentary organization
behind urban life in England, Professor Stephenson attempted

[116] IV Edgar 3.1, 4 and 5.
[117] *Crawford Charters*, ed. A. S. Napier and W. H. Stevenson, p.9.
[118] II Canute 34; for right of exculpation and to wergeld in hundred and tithing
II Canute 20.
[119] Leis Willelme, 21.1a; Edw. the Conf. 39.2; also II Athelstan 12, and recognitio
of the failure of the policy in IV Athelstan 2.
[120] J. Tait. *The Medieval English Borough*, c. vi; *E. H. R.*, 1933, pp.642 ff.

a reinterpretation of the Domesday evidence which stressed the agrarian elements in the so-called boroughs, leaving his reader with the impression that outside one or two rare concentrations of population such as London there were no towns in Anglo-Saxon England, merely extensions of the rural communities. The peculiar tenures of the Domesday boroughs were explained in rural terms, and the heterogeneity of tenure which Tait had already taken as a legal hallmark of the borough was dismissed as a natural outcome of a situation where several manorial groups met for purposes which were overwhelmingly agrarian in intention.

These ideas were in their way exciting and salutary. The borough, as depicted in Domesday Book, often appears to represent little more than a manorial economy of the usual type. As shall be seen in a later chapter, many surveys concerned themselves so much with villein service, rights in the open fields, pasture rights and meadow rights, rights over woodland, even with labour service for so-called *burgenses*, that it is hard to imagine that anything that could properly be called town life could have existed.[121] The formal meetings at which dooms were promulgated were not held inevitably at boroughs: Grately and King's Enham figure in the list as well as London, Winchester and Bath. But a distinction was firmly drawn between landright and borough right; a borough normally had a court though it is not certain that in all instances the court was its own; royal legislation under Edward the Elder, attempted, though with no enduring success, to confine commercial transactions to ports; at such a centre there would be a royal reeve and often a prison as well as a mint.[122] Some formidable buildings of stone were built like the characteristic late Saxon churches, a superb example of which may still be seen at St Benet's in Cambridge. It is likely that boroughs would have their fixed markets and possibly their seasonal fairs.

On the question of tenure it is certain that the essential characteristics of later borough tenure were present in the late Anglo-Saxon England, above all the holding of tenements at money rent with freedom to alienate or sell. It is probable that such tenure originated in conscious royal policy; the defensible area of a new borough would be divided into plots which were later to develop into the *hagae* and *mansurae* of Domesday Book.[123] A tenth-century

[121] See below, pp.382–3.
[122] I Edward I.
[123] F. M. Stenton, *Anglo-Saxon England*, p.529.

will tells of such *hagae* which had been bought at Ipswich.[124] These plots would then be taken by men who wished to take part in trade at a standard and reasonable rent; most of the Alfredian *burhs* were constructed on royal land, and it was in the royal interest to encourage and support settlers.

Realization that economic motives were important from the beginning and at times predominated over the needs of defence helps to clear up some of the rather arid controversies that surround the problem of borough origin. In some ways the equation *burh* plus successful market equals borough provides an interesting pointer to how the late Anglo-Saxon borough developed, useful as long as it is remembered that many *burhs* were markets even before they were formally fortified and that some places satisfying the formula were stunted in their growth and never developed into boroughs. Establishment of a market was a royal act, a colourful example of the way in which greater complexity of communal action demanded closer definition of rights, the closer definition in turn leading to clarification of royal authority. The very symbol of the protecting hand so prominent in Ethelred's coinage may be associated with the familiar medieval symbol of the glove as a sign of protection hoisted over a market, though it is possible, of course, that the hand on the coins is meant to represent the protecting hand of God. When all is said, the so-called burghal policy of the late ninth and early tenth centuries, the vital factor in any discussion of Anglo-Saxon urban development, did no more than create the conditions of defensibility in which it was possible for some favoured trading centres to grow into the typical medieval walled towns.

Finally there remains the question of the size of population of the late Anglo-Saxon boroughs. To anticipate a little, Domesday Book supplies a mass of statistics relating to English boroughs in 1066 and in 1086. Unfortunately London was not surveyed – or, to be more precise, its survey has not survived. To some extent this loss is balanced by other evidence from the Chronicle and from the laws and the charters. Twelve thousand would be a conservative figure for the population of London in 1066. The organization of the town was complicated. It was divided into wards for purposes of administration; it had a network of hustings courts to deal with petty offences, and a great folk-moot that met at the hill by the side of St Paul's. York, in 1066, had a population of at least eight

---

[124] D. Whitelock, *Anglo-Saxon Wills*, no. i.

thousand, Norwich and Lincoln of five thousand, Thetford of four thousand, Oxford of three thousand five hundred, Colchester of two thousand, Cambridge of sixteen hundred and Ipswich of thirteen hundred.[125] These figures err on the side of moderation, and yet they help to illustrate the importance of the Anglo-Saxon borough to the life of the community. These were no mere agrarian groups of much the normal manorial pattern.

To conclude, at the end of the eleventh century England possessed in London one town that for its period might well be called great, a number of substantial boroughs, particularly on the eastern half of England, and a network of other smaller boroughs that in one respect were outstanding in Western Europe: their royal nature. As the Norman castles sprang up, a strong hand was needed to enforce these royal rights. But in theory at least England was strictly united under the royal authority, with the boroughs as important manifestations of that royal hand. In the course of a century the boroughs were to show signs of outgrowing their royal origins; in 1100 they still provide one of our most spectacular illustrations of the unity of the kingdom of England.

---

[125] *Historical Geography of England before 1800*, ed. H. C. Darby, p.208 ff, esp. p.218; P Hunter Blair, *Anglo-Saxon England*, p.297.

CHAPTER FOUR
The Land

1. SOURCES AND TECHNIQUES

Though there are complications in detail, it is possible to give a general outline of the settlement of England, and to some extent of the external and internal trade patterns of Anglo-Saxon England, an outline that can be traced with reasonable chronological firmness from the fifth century to the eleventh. So much cannot be said at the moment for the study of agricultural developments, fundamental though they are for an understanding of Anglo-Saxon society. Yet it seems evident that this is a side of Anglo-Saxon studies most likely to yield important results, particularly as new archaeological techniques are developed, and as the picture becomes clearer of the agricultural implements generally in use in the Germanic world. There is of course an appalling dearth of written evidence: a few ambiguous clauses in the laws of Ine, a section of Aelfric's Colloquy dealing with the hardships of a ploughman's life, a little treatise on eleventh-century estate-management. Otherwise reliance has to be placed on inferences drawn from material the primary purpose of which lay not with the land and its cultivation, but with the legal or fiscal aspects of the ownership of that land: land charters, legal dooms, the great Domesday Book itself. The vocabulary of Anglo-Saxon England adds something of value. There is, for example, a list of agricultural implements in use on a great estate in the document known as 'Gerefa', that deals with the duties of a reeve. The fact that a lord, a *hlaford* or *hlaf-weard*, is literally a guardian of bread while his lady, a *hlaf-dige*, is a kneader of bread has possible social implications for very early times, before the weakening and obscuring of the second elements *-weard* and *-dige*.

152

But there are moments when the task of recording agricultural developments in Anglo-Saxon England seems almost as difficult as an attempt to construct the agricultural history of the south-west from, say, the cartulary of Tavistock Abbey and an imperfect series of fifteenth-century manorial records.

One factor naturally remains constant, and that is the geological structure of the land itself. The Place-Name Society is recognizing more and more the significance of this major factor, and geological sketch-maps make a welcome appearance in their recent surveys. In Oxfordshire, for example, where the bulk of the land was potentially fertile and suitable for agriculture, the spring-lines were the decisive geological features which determined the pattern of early village settlement. Considerable variety in geological formation can occur within very short space in England, a fact which makes generalization about settlement particularly difficult. But fertility, potential or actual, coupled with availability of water supply sufficient for the needs of relatively concentrated human population, lead again and again to the village or hamlets of the early Anglo-Saxon settlers, who, in many districts, appear to have been the earliest predominantly agricultural settlers. Careful topographical studies drawing on the evidence of geological structure, of place-names and an inference from knowledge of development of farm tools offer the best hope of understanding the early Anglo-Saxon agriculturalists and their fields.

For the very early period help is given from aerial photography. This is a skilled science in its own right, and the historian for the most part can do no more than cull the general conclusions that technical experts provide for him. Fortunately, the pioneers in these studies, from O. G. S. Crawford to Dr St Joseph, were acutely aware of the historian's problems, and so provided guides which enable even the beginner to distinguish the rectangular fields that are associated with 'Celtic' farms and the great open fields with their long strips that are associated with the Anglo-Saxons. Given favourable conditions, the right light and the right dampness of soil, aerial photography can reconstruct past habitation sites and field systems with a clarity altogether surprising. It was a brilliant piece of such photography that set in train excavations at Yeavering, the most promising development in Anglo-Saxon archaeology since the discoveries at Sutton Hoo.[1] In less specta-

---

[1] D. Knowles and J. K. S. St Joseph, *Monastic Sites from the Air*, Plate 126, pp. 270–1, Cambridge, 1952; see above, pp. 45–6. B. Hope-Taylor, *Yeavering. an Anglo-British Centre of Early Northumbria*, London, 1977.

cular vein the photographer reveals open fields and evidence of corporate agriculture where the written record is mute.

Further help can also come from sheer powers of observation. There are still visible at certain seasons and in the right conditions marks that tell how the fields were used, even after the lapse of many hundreds of years. Heavier vegetation growth and a resulting difference in colouration in growing crops can indicate disturbance of sub-soil, possibly dating to a remote past. The plough leaves permanent traces for the expert to interpret. Ploughing on sloping land can produce a slow displacement of soil from the top of the stint ploughed to the bottom, so creating a gradual terrace effect with the establishment of what the agrarian historian calls lynchets. The characteristic 'ridge and furrow' ploughing technique in which the ploughman turns a double furrow at the centre of the plough-stint to create the ridge, turning the final sod away from the last sod of the adjoining stint to create the 'furrow', can leave a permanent and clearly defined mark on the land. A line of poppies growing in the wheat can indicate more intense disturbance of sub-soil, and at times a characteristic line can appear in the shape of a reversed S, indicating the path of an ancient plough with the furrow line curved, possibly to facilitate entry of the plough-team from the headland, more probably to ensure satisfactory drainage of the strips. Within their limits these clues are of enormous benefit to the historian. Their weakness comes into prominence if we are rash enough to attempt a more exact chronology. From the standpoint of the twentieth century 'ancient', 'early', 'many hundreds of years' can apply equally to A.D. 1300, 1000, or even 600. One of the basic and still unsolved problems of the whole period lies in deciding if the open-field system of agriculture was brought, virtually lock, stock and barrel, from the Continent by the invading Germanic peoples; or if, with the germ of it certainly in being in their native institutions, the Anglo-Saxons followed a similar path of agrarian evolution to that practised on the Continent, a path that led ultimately in the 'Second Feudal Age', to the agrarian base of the so-called typical medieval manor.

One point is reasonably well established. There may have been uneasy interim periods when the Germanic warriors set up their primitive folks upon a favoured site, but with permanent settlement came concentration on clearing the soil for arable farming. As early as the first century A.D. Tacitus emphasized the part played by corn-growing in the Germanic economy, and there is no reason to doubt that the Anglo-Saxons conformed to the general practice of the mass of the Germanic peoples. There were areas, probably more numerous than has always been realized, where the Anglo-Saxons settled on land already cleared, and modified it to their own usage. But, even so, much of the settlement was a matter of pioneer communities establishing themselves in clearings in forest and scrub, and it is possible to distinguish two methods open to resourceful peoples by which they could wrest good arable from the countryside. The first, approximating to the Scottish *runrig*, was to take in land, to plough and crop it until exhausted, then to take in further land. The second, and much more advanced, was to adopt something approaching a two-field system, whereby the arable would be permanent, with one field left fallow while its companion grew the crops, spring and winter corn alike, for the community. This second scheme would demand more corporate effort but there are one or two pointers to its early adoption.

To begin with, the Germans owed much of their success in the fifth and sixth centuries to their capacity for corporate endeavour, in the economic probably to as great an extent as in the military field. The farming experience of the Anglo-Saxons on the Continent and in England was as clearers of forest and marsh. To such communities the *runrig*, infield-outfield, system, suitable for poor lands, easily cleared, and suitable also for communities where the weight of the economy inclined to the keeping of livestock and pastoral activity, would be utterly wasteful. Where arable was hard won on heavy cleared soil, there was every incentive to keep it as a permanent asset to the community.

Another important point can be established with reasonable certainty from the evidence provided by place-names and archaeology. As was said in an earlier chapter, the Saxon coming intensified, though it would be going too far to say that it inaugurated, a valley-ward movement.[2] There is no doubt much truth in the picture of hillside Briton and valley-dwelling Saxon. But slowly with the help of aerial photographs it is seen that Saxon fields sometimes overlay earlier rectangular fields in some of the valleys, and that some hillside sites taken as characteristically Romano-British may have been abandoned before the Saxons came. The Romans themselves in their villas certainly possessed the tools, notably the heavy plough, and the resources to make as firm inroad on heavy soil as did the Saxons. Even so, when all exceptions are made, it is just to give the Saxons their full due as the people who opened

[2] See above, p. 21.

up the damp, much-forested, heavy lowlands of England to the permanent subjection of the plough.

2. THE CROPS AND THE PLOUGH

There are two vital matters on which information, though fragmentary, gives opportunity for fuller discussion: on the nature of the crops grown, and on the nature of the plough used. Wheat, oats, barley and rye were all known and grown, and the fact that barley gave its name to the important institution of the berewick, the *bere-wic*, barley-wick, or outlying farm, indicates the importance of the barley-crop both for food and for drink. Perhaps the most rewarding approach at the moment, although it is still difficult to assess the full consequences of the results, is that adopted by a very able and industrious group of Danish scholars. They have painstakingly collected evidence relating to cereals cultivated from the Neolithic right through the Bronze and Iron Ages into historic times. Direct evidence is scanty, though the preserving qualities of peat provided them with some botanical remains. Their real triumphs came from their reconstruction of ancient ears of grain from impressions made in pottery, dating from a time when the potter's clay was moulded on the floor of hut and workshop. There are, of course, statistical limitations to the method, to which the scholars themselves are the first to point. For the whole of the Danish Neolithic period, extending over the best part of a thousand years, only 425 impressions were available for study when Sarauw and Jessen wrote. Nevertheless the fact that wheat predominated in these impressions over barley to the extent of seven to one took on special significance when the investigators showed an almost exact reversal of seven grains of barley, both husked and naked in about equal proportions, to only one grain of wheat for the later stages of the Bronze Age, 800–400 B.C. Taken further to the Roman Iron Age, that is to the period of four to five hundred years preceding the Anglo-Saxon invasions, investigation showed a similar predominance of barley over wheat, with the husked variety now predominating over the naked to the extent of three to one. It is reasonable to suppose that barley was, at the least, a very important crop to the Saxon invaders, and the impressions so far taken from Anglo-Saxon pottery, exceedingly few in number though they are, point to a similar conclusion, though of course there is always the horrid possibility that potters, possibly women, were more careless with barley grains than with wheat.[3]

Indeed there is some danger lest too much emphasis should be placed on barley, or on oats, or on rye, which gave its name to the Anglo-Saxon month of August, *Rugern*, to the neglect of wheat. The Saxons themselves prized greatly the *hwæten hlaf*, or wheaten loaf, and had, as P. Hunter Blair points out, an even better-regarded loaf, the so-called 'clean' loaf, which was probably made of specially sifted flour.[4] Terminology is far from clear, and it is likely that at times a mixture of cereals was sown, possibly a resowing taking place in spring if a staple winter-wheat crop looked like failing. There are some who believe that rye took the place of wheat as the soil grew impoverished. Later in the Middle Ages it was considered that rye gave a better render, a seven-fold render over against the five-fold render that could be expected from wheat.[5] No doubt regional custom and climate had much to do with the final predominance of one cereal over another. St Cuthbert in the Farne island proved more successful with his barley than he did with his wheat. Seeing that the wheat had failed, he planted barley in summer, 'after the proper season when there was no hope of it maturing', but nevertheless a rich crop quickly sprang up.[6] Yet it is well to remember that in Roman days south-east Britain already had something of a reputation as an exporter of corn to the Continent, and that again in the twelfth and thirteenth centuries shipments of corn were made from East Anglia and Lincoln to the Scandinavian lands. The Anglo-Saxons undoubtedly made enormous contribution to the mastery of arable farming in England, but their story in turn fits into a much longer period of endeavour which stretches from Neolithic times to the present day.

Perhaps the key to an understanding of their contribution lies in the vexed question concerning the plough. So much depended upon this basic agricultural implement, including possibly the very shape of the fields themselves. The major difference in field-shape

[3] K. Jessen and H. Helbæk, *Cereals in Great Britain and Ireland in Prehistoric and Early Historic Times*, Copenhagen, 1944. P. J. Fowler's important survey suggests the four principal cereals were naked and hulled wheats, hulled barley, and cultivated oats, with hulled barley the favoured crop. 'Farming in the Anglo-Saxon Landscape', *A.S.E.*, 9, 1981, p. 278.

[4] P. Hunter Blair, *Anglo-Saxon England*, p. 275. F. E. Harmer, *Select Documents*, no. i.

[5] *Walter of Henley's Husbandry*, ed. E. Lamond, London, 1890, p. 71.

[6] Bede, *Hist. Eccl.*, IV, 28.

between the rectangular so-called Celtic fields and the great open fields of the Saxon can be best explained not by any racial reason, but simply by the nature of the plough used to till the soil. Where the plough was light and merely cut a simple shallow furrow, cross-ploughing was necessary to break up the soil properly and to prepare the field for sowing. For such ploughing a rectangular small field was most convenient. Where the plough was heavy, pulled by oxen amounting to as many as eight in number as methods of harnessing improved, and particularly when the mould-board was evolved to cut under the sod and to turn it steadily over the length of the furrow, a long strip was the most convenient unit for ploughing, the length limited merely by the strength and convenience of the beasts pulling the plough. Though the irregularity of the strips in the open field has now become a commonplace, the old traditional account of an acre as a day's work unit and the later formalized picture of the acre as a ploughed strip 220 yards (a 'furrow long' or a furlong) in length, and 22 yards, the length of a cricket pitch, in breadth, has much to tell us of the nature of ploughing in the Middle Ages, and by inference in Anglo-Saxon days. There is of course a danger in such a formalized picture, and the Orwins have done good service by emphasizing time and time again that there is very little in the characteristic features of the Open Field which cannot be explained simply and naturally by the common sense of farming practice. They thus warn against looking for legal explanations where technical suffice, against looking for doctrines of primitive equality to explain the complicated divisions of the open fields, where technical explanations connected with the process of co-aration, in which the ploughing was conducted steadily stint by stint, are sufficient to account for the partition of the arable. Above all they, and perhaps they alone, have offered a fully intelligible description of the operation of the open-field system in its infancy and an explanation of how – a vital question for the Anglo-Saxon period – the needs of an expanding community might be met by such an agrarian system.

For the basis of their valuable contribution to the problem of Saxon open fields, they speak with approbation of Seebohm's suggestion that a man's share in the open fields depended upon the number of plough-beasts he was able to contribute to the teams of the community.[7] Opportunity was thus afforded to new-comers,

---

[7] C. S. and C. S. Orwin, *The Open Fields*, Oxford, 1938, pp. 5–8; F. Seebohm, *The English Village Community*, pp. 113–14 and 120–1.

either by growth to mature age within the existing community or of addition from without, to enter the existing groups. The amount of arable taken in would depend upon the number of plough-teams; the number of plough-teams would depend again presumably upon the number of free households and also upon the number of dependent households where the head of the household would be equipped and set up in business by a lord. It would also depend, and this is one of the incalculables for the early period, on the amount of arable ploughed directly on behalf of a lord by servile or semi-servile labour. At the end of the period, as we shall see, it was quite usual in the more heavily manorialized parts of the country for the number of *servi* to bear a direct relationship to the number of ploughs in demesne.

On the physical nature of the plough employed in Anglo-Saxon days much may legitimately be inferred but little is known with certainty. Archaeology helps the historian very little in this respect. There is one substantial fragment of a plough of considerable interest, an early tenth-century discovery from Thetford, now at the Castle Museum, Norwich, which may suggest the existence of something approximating to a 'normal mould-board plough', and which may indicate the 'use or continued use in eastern England of a one-way plough with movable mould-board'.[8] However, some expert opinion is inclined to attribute even this discovery to Dane rather than to Anglo-Saxon. There are drawings in tenth- and eleventh-century manuscripts which show wheeled ploughs in action, some pulled by two oxen, some by four. Incongruously enough the most famous representation of a plough, that which occurs in the Bayeux Tapestry, has the motive force supplied by a somewhat dejected mule.[9] Coulters and shares come out clearly in these drawings but the existence of the vital mould-boards is much more dubious. At all events the nature of this evidence may well be brought into question. A monkish scribe would be more likely to copy from another manuscript than to reconstruct from life. A riddle, possibly of the eighth century and preserved in the Exeter Book, tells nothing of mould-boards, though it refers to shares, coulters, share-beams and tails. But F. G. Payne has shown that there is archaeological evidence that the 'fixed mould-board had arrived in the Romano-British period'.[10] That oxen were used

[8] F. G. Payne, 'The British Plough', *Agricultural History Review*, 1957, p. 79.

[9] *The Bayeux Tapestry*, ed. F. M. Stenton, London, 1957.

[10] F. G. Payne, op. cit., p. 79. P. V. Glob, *Ard and Plough*, p. 123, suggests that a plough with mould-board and wheeled fore-carriage may have been in use in Denmark before a period towards the end of the Iron Age.

to pull the plough is of course beyond question. Later in the Middle Ages Walter of Henley gave a spirited defence of the ox against the horse: oxen were less expensive to feed, they could be eaten once work-time was over, and they were stronger on heavy land.[11] The author might have added that the slowness of pace of the ox was also a great asset to a ploughman concentrating on controlling the depth and direction of the cut made by his heavy and cumbersome implement. In Anglo-Saxon days when good horses were expensive, these factors applied with yet increased vigour.

The horse was not, however, as scarce as some would have us believe. References to studs of horses occur, as in a Worcester charter of the tenth century where a clearing for a stud of horses is mentioned in the bounds of a land grant. But a great Anglo-Saxon lady in the same century bequeathed horses, tamed and untamed, which does suggest that the horse was not yet the prosaic partner of husbandry into which he later developed. The Anglo-Saxon who wrote down what Ohthere had to say about Norway thought it odd that Norwegians should plough with horses.[12] There is mention of horse-racing; the horse was the normal beast for riding; horses were needed for hunting; but for the plough always the ox, rarely if ever the horse, was the rule in Anglo-Saxon days.

There is no direct tangible evidence, as yet, that the Anglo-Saxons introduced a better plough than had been in use in Britain during the Roman occupation. But from the nature of the settlement, from the sites chosen and developed, it is probable that their plough and ploughing techniques were better suited to the lowlands of Britain than were the plough and ploughing techniques of the Celtic peoples. Roman and Romanized villas presumably did as well technically, if not better, than the Anglo-Saxons, but as has already been suggested in an earlier chapter, the villas were closely tied to that civilized administrative level of the Romanic world that failed to survive the Germanic migrations. The best of Saxon villages can scarcely have approached in comfort the best of Roman villas. But the comparison is in itself meretricious. Where the Saxon excelled was in his introduction of a superior general level of agricultural technique, and with it a social system better calculated to develop into that sound agrarian basis upon

[11] *Walter of Henley's Husbandry*, pp. 10–12.
[12] A. J. Robertson, *Anglo-Saxon Charters*, no. lvii; D. Whitelock, *Anglo-Saxon Wills*, no. iii, The Will of Wynflæd; *King Alfred's Orosius*, ed. H. Sweet, p. 18.

which could be built the more elaborate social structures of feudal England.

Yet such development was of very slow growth. There is a period of over six hundred years between the first settlements in this country and the great survey of Domesday Book from which in the last resort the strongest impressions of rural society in early medieval England are based. In France, where survival from Roman days in some curious ways simplifies the problem, recent historians have tended to point to this vital half a millenium and more as the time in which the peasant was fixed on his plot. Disguised under manorial forms as this process may be, perhaps in the last resort similar analysis can apply to England. In spite of all the historical glamour and excitement that surrounds the evolution of theocratic kingship, the co-operation of Church and State, and the growth of a feudal nexus in the upper reaches of society, kingship and greater sense of public order meant little more to the mass of the communities of the West than greater security to till the fields and to render the surplus upon which medieval civilization was built. The stabilization of the agrarian community was the great triumph of the age.

Yet he would be a very bold man who would argue that the final product of this stability – the open fields, the careful allotment of arable and meadow, the regulated use of common and forest, and the curious blend of corporate endeavour and private ownership – existed in the early days of Saxon settlement. On the Continent the tendency is now to look to the politically troubled ninth and tenth centuries as an age of considerable technical development in the harnessing of beasts to the plough. There is no such evidence on the English side of the Channel, though it is reasonable to suppose that some improvements were made in the course of these long centuries. It is likely that by the eleventh century the eight-ox plough, with the oxen harnessed two by two in a long line, was common, though four-ox teams were also frequent. On royal demesne in twelfth-century Herefordshire a plough-team of six oxen was customary.[13] There is some evidence from the Welsh laws that the yoking of oxen there was generally in a more solid group of four or even more abreast. For the earliest period

---

[13] *Herefordshire Domesday*, ed. V. Galbraith and J. Tait, London, 1950, p. xxxi. R. Lennard has analysed the twelfth-century evidence in an important article in *E.H.R.*, 1960. He shows that eight-ox teams were common and widespread, that six-ox teams were also widespread, and that ten-ox teams were rare.

evidence of any sort is scanty, and it is from the laws of Ine, which relate to conditions in the late seventh century though they have survived only in an Alfredian recension, that the most important direct evidence of agrarian development comes. Of the ox itself, it is said (clause 60) that a *ceorl* who has hired another's yoke of oxen is to pay for the hire in fodder if he can; if not, then half in fodder and half in other goods. There is also (clauses 58 and 59) a mysterious scale of values concerning the horn of an ox (tenpence) and of a cow (twopence); of the tail of an ox (a shilling) and of a cow (fivepence); of an eye of an ox (fivepence) and of a cow (a shilling). Coming from an age when a ewe with her lamb was worth a shilling (clause 55) until twelve days after Easter, there is something distinctly odd about such a scale of values which, in any event, scarcely tie up with the accepted equation of five West Saxon pennies to the shilling. Apart from such detail, however, the code also presents information concerning the village organization itself, and to it we must turn to further the discussion of agrarian organization.

3. THE OPEN FIELDS IN EARLY ANGLO-SAXON ENGLAND

There are two sections of the Laws of Ine which are of crucial importance in connection with agrarian organization, the first a series of dooms relating to the making of fences and to rights in woodland (clauses 40 and 42), the second relating to movement of a nobleman from one estate to another (clauses 63–8). It is the first group only that adds to knowledge of the open fields, and from these clauses it is learned that a *ceorl* was responsible for the fencing of his own *worðig*, that is the enclosure around his own homestead, and that he had no redress if the cattle strayed through a gap which he himself had left. The case was very different if common meadow or land (presumably arable) held in common was concerned. The clause (42) is so important that it should be quoted in full because upon it rests the main documentary evidence for the existence of the open field in early Anglo-Saxon England:

> 42. If *ceorls* have a common meadow or other land divided in shares [*gedalland*] to fence, and some have fenced their portion and some have not, and (if cattle) eat up their common crops [*æceras*] or grass, those who are responsible for the gap are to go and pay to the others

who have fenced their part, compensation for the damage that has been done there. They are to demand with regard to those cattle such reparation as is proper.

42.1. If, however, it is any of the cattle which breaks the hedges and enters anywhere, and he who owns it would not or could not control it, he who finds it on his arable is to seize it and kill it; and the owner is to take its hide and flesh and suffer the loss of the rest.

As Sir Frank Stenton reminded us, this is no proof of common ownership of arable or meadow.[14] Indeed an intensely personal attitude to property shines through this clause. And the fact that the clause is conditional – *if ceorls* have a common meadow – may suggest that some enjoyed a more complete proprietary right, such as that already applying to the *worðig*. But it does tell of a corporate obligation to protect growing crops and meadow in fields which may be divided into many parts. The situation is so prophetic of that obtaining in later medieval days that it would be carrying scepticism too far to doubt the simple meaning of *gærstun . . . gemænne* (common meadow) and *gedalland*. If this is not open-field farming, it is hard to know what it can be. There may have been much individual enterprise, some individual clearing, some isolated farmers. But the major agrarian unit was, if it had not been from the days of settlement, the community of *ceorls*, the effective leaders of the village community over so much of England, who took a corporate responsibility for the ploughing, sowing and probably the reaping and harvesting, though the balance of loss and gain remained intensely personal to the individual holder of the land. It may be that the very cost of specialized equipment, above all the cost of plough and oxen, furthered this communal coalescence in historic times. The Orwins were probably nearer the truth when they reminded us of relentless struggle against want, and even famine, which demanded corporate endeavour.

Anglo-Saxon charters of the eighth and ninth centuries become more intelligible, if the existence of open-field farming at an early stage is taken for granted. These charters recorded grants to the Church, to the royal family and to great retainers, and were often simple enough in tenor. They handed over so many hides, so many *cassati, manentes* or *tributaria* under the threat of powerful anathema directed against anyone daring to infringe them. The arable was usually given freely with little flourish: *terram trium aratrorum in marisco qui appellatur Stodmerch iuxta Fordewicum; aliquam partem terrae, id est X manentes; aliquam partem terrae, id est X*

---

[14] F. M. Stenton, *Anglo-Saxon England*, p. 280.

cassatos; XXXIII cassatorum in jus aeclesiasticae libertatis Wigornensis; X tributaria, and so on. Much has been written on the vexed topic of the nature of these grants. Were they gifts of land, of immunity, or merely of usufruct of land? Perhaps there has been excessive caution in refusing to accept the first possibility. It was generally assumed that the land would rest in the recipient's possession for all perpetuity, and while some onerous burdens such as the king's *feorm* and associated rights were certainly lifted, others, notably the three invariable necessities, were reserved, namely service to the *fyrd*, service in building bridges, service in repairing fortifications.[15] The whole question of what was involved in gift of land is one of the utmost complexity. Ideas of ownership vary from generation to generation. Terminology derived from late and debased Roman law did not always meet the reality of Anglo-Saxon conditions. Yet it is clear that no matter what precise public and fiscal privileges were involved, power over the arable, and over those who cultivated the arable was a prominent feature of the charters.

But if the arable is at the centre of the land-grant, connected rights in meadow, pasture, common, marsh and wood were closely associated with it. To the record-making bodies, king, witan, great church or abbey, the arable as the most permanent and expensive-to-maintain portion of an estate naturally received first attention. As a result, the administrative terminology is solidly impregnated with reference to the plough: *sulungs* in Kent (from the Anglo-Saxon *sulh*, meaning a plough), carucates, ploughlands, bovates became terms in fiscal administration, even to the extent of losing their original earthy connotation. We talk of fiscal ploughlands and real ploughlands just as we talk of fiscal hides and real hides. Arable by itself, however, was not enough. Corn-growing was merely the central point of interest in a whole nexus of agrarian relationships. There were plough-beasts to keep and feed, meadows to enclose and reap, woods to provide mast for swine, pasture and common for beasts, little enclosures around the homestead for vegetables, fruit-trees, and possibly some special pasturage for young beasts. All the complicated routines of rural life, hurdle-hedges to enclose arable and meadow, rights in woodland, selection of stock for breeding, selection of seed for sowing, and the processes of drying

---

[15] E. John has points of interest to make on the imposition of the three necessities, which he sees as an innovation of the eighth-century kings of Mercia, *Land Tenure in Early England*, Leicester, 1960, pp. 64–79. W. H. Stevenson, 'Trinoda Necessitas', *E.H.R.*, 1914, remains essential reading on this difficult topic.

and milling grain demanded exacting, regular attention. It is only too easy to forget the importance of the non-arable land of the settlement and of the wasteland around the settlement. The laws of Ine indicate the importance of the forest when they tell of the penalties involved in the infringement of rights over woodland: a man felling trees paid thirty shillings a tree for the first three and no more; if he burned the tree he paid sixty shillings, and the same sum if he cut down a huge tree so big that thirty swine could stand under it. The nice distinction between burning and chopping has more than antiquarian interest. It expresses the primitive distinction between secret act and open act; as the laws themselves put it so well, 'fire is a thief . . . but the axe is an informer not a thief'.[16]

The charters also give proof of the importance of the non-arable land. In the earliest charter of which the original has survived, land in Thanet was given to the Abbot of Reculver and his monastery with 'everything belonging to it, fields, pastures, marshes, small woods, fens, fisheries with everything, as has been said, belonging to that land'.[17] No sign was given of the extent of the land; reference instead was made to the 'well-known bounds shown by me and by my agents' (*proacuratoribus*). Nearly a century and a half later Ceolwulf of Mercia gave five sulungs at 'Mylentun' near Kemsing in Kent, to Archbishop Wulfred, with fields, woods, meadows, pastures, waters, mills, fisheries, fowling-grounds, hunting-grounds, and whatever was contained in it. Later in the same charter provision was made for food and pasture for swine and cattle or goats in the Weald at places pertaining to the estate at Ewehurst, *Sciofingden* and *Snadhyrst*.[18] Such formulae quickly became standardized, but they serve to show how complicated rural organization could be.

Of course charters dealt with estates, and estates can be so much bigger or smaller than these units which emerge, somewhat dimly it is true, as the natural agrarian units, the village or the hamlet. The Orwins consistently remind us of the ceaseless struggle for bread and for meat. It is probably true to say, however, that there has been some exaggeration of the pure 'farming for sustenance' theme. The earliest law-codes give evidence both of the importance of a money-economy and of some interchange of agrarian goods, of some marketing. Yet in the main it is still a fact that the small community strove to be self-sufficing, and that within that com-

16 Ine 43.1.
17 *E.H.D.* I, pp. 482–3.
18 Ibid, pp. 514–5.

munity the peasant-household, the *ceorlisc* holding, strove also to supply its own bread and meat. In order to do so over much of the country two things were needed: space and corporate effort in clearing, ploughing, harvesting.

Great variety existed in the extent of the land cultivated. In the eleventh century, a hide, that *terra unius familiae* which had in the past ideally provided for the peasant household, consisted of 120 acres of arable in Cambridgeshire and over much of the eastern counties, but probably no more than 40 acres in parts of Wiltshire and the west and south-west.[19] A tenth-century will states specifically that land was reckoned at 120 acres to the hide with the implication that the measurement was not universal, even in the eastern counties to which this particular will applied.[20] Nor was there uniformity in the acre itself which varied according to the length of the rod used to measure the breadth of a strip of land. In Anglo-Norman days a quarter of the 120 acres, a virgate of 30 acres, became recognized as a normal villein holding. Meadow was generally apportioned according to the arable, in the classic open-field country of the Midland belt divided into strips corresponding, though on a smaller scale, to the strips of the arable, often in the case of meadow no more than a good sweep of the scythe in breadth. Pasture depended very much on the lie of the land. In some districts beasts would be taken considerable distances from the main settlement for summer pasture; in others rights to pasture in woodland, as in the Kentish example mentioned above, were jealously guarded.

One great problem in the arable itself was the difficulty of manuring. In the earliest days of agriculture this was met by taking in new land as the old grew exhausted, but the Anglo-Saxon had advanced beyond that stage, though naturally from time to time new settlements were made and new land taken in. In this connection, though we can look at some deserted villages of the Middle Ages, the general continuity of our main agrarian settlements is an economic fact of prime significance. Yet the means of sustaining fertility were not great. Chief reliance was placed on manure from the beasts, and the right to fold the beasts at night and so to collect the manure became a much-coveted dominical

---

[19] J. Tait, 'Large Hides and Small Hides', *E.H.R.*, 1902, pp. 280–2. Against this view of the 'forty'-acre hide in Wiltshire, but in possible support of the 'small' hide, is an important note by R. R. Darlington on the Wiltshire Geld Rolls, V.C.H. *Wiltshire*, vol. II, pp. 182–3.

[20] D. Whitelock, *Anglo-Saxon Wills*, no. ii, The Will of Ælfgar. Also below, p. 321.

right, so much so that in the later Middle Ages it was regarded as a *mauvaise coutume* by good Frenchmen. The use of compost was known on the Continent, and presumably in England, though the present writer has come across no reference to it in Anglo-Saxon days. Marl was known on the Continent in the ninth century, though apparently the value of lime was appreciated only late. Black marl, peat, was much coveted, and in those districts where it was common was probably in use in England. But the key to sustained fertility lay in the use of a fallow year, sufficient for the ground to recover itself from the task of bearing crops both winter and spring sown. This fallow year was no time of idleness, for good fallow needed to be ploughed and broken up and cleared as firmly as any arable.

As to the shape of the fields, everything depended upon the lie of the land, and there was probably variety from year to year as the agrarian community throve or failed to thrive. In charters of the tenth and eleventh centuries boundaries of estates were given in great detail, and from these bounds valuable information is sometimes given. For example, hidden in the topographical references to the boundaries of the estate of Hardwell in Berkshire is mention of headlands, that is to say of strips lying across the top of the furrows in which the plough-teams had room to manoeuvre, of furrows and of gore-acres, that is to say odd-shaped stretches of land, usually triangular, that are left to the open field after the straight ploughing has turned most of the furrows. The bounds of this particular estate can still be traced on the modern map, and even more remarkable than the proof it gives of a reasonably advanced state of arable farming in the tenth century is the astonishing equivalence that still exists between the twentieth-century bounds of Hardwell Farm and the tenth-century bounds of Hardwell in Compton Beauchamp. As the Orwins say, this Berkshire estate in itself is a good sign of the skill of the Saxon farmer. 'After a thousand years no better way than theirs has been found for the ploughing of this bit of England for the practice of husbandry.'[21]

The evidence for the existence of open-field farming in later Anglo-Saxon England is overwhelming, and for early Anglo-Saxon England it is strong. Yet there were regional peculiarities in field

[21] *The Open Fields*, p. 29. The tendency in the past was to read too technical a meaning into terms appearing in the Anglo-Saxon bounds to charters. Interesting pioneer work by T. R. Thomson appears in the *W.A.M.* vol. lvi (Ellandune) and vol. lvii (Wanborough and Little Hinton), 1956 and 1957, and in the collection of *Materials for a History of Cricklade*, Oxford, 1959.

systems at the end of the period which may reflect differences in origin. Over most of England south of and including the East Riding of Yorkshire and the Vale of York, open fields prevailed Over much of this area nucleated villages were the normal units of settlement, where conditions permitted. Even in Devon, which was excluded from the open-field area by the Orwins, the pattern of large arable fields, running into hundreds of acres, of holdings scattered in strips, of a second- or third-year fallow, and of grazing rights in common, was not unfamiliar.[22] But Kent was different and though open-field agriculture was practised in that kingdom there were peculiarities in assessing and organizing land which point to peculiarities in social organization. The normal unit of assessment was the *sulung*, or ploughland, which came to be taken as equivalent to two Mercian hides. The settlement was organized in scattered hamlets rather than in nucleated villages, and the arable was concentrated in fields held by groups of kinsmen, and passing by the form of inheritance known as *gavelkind*. This involved a partition of inheritance, and of rights that were attached to membership of a community, rather than associated directly with the holding of arable. Outlying rights in woodlands and in saltings were of special importance, and were apportioned according to the position of the farmstead within one or other of the ancient *lathes* into which the kingdom was divided. Family ownership was more tenacious in Kent than in Saxon or Anglian England; the result was a less rigid and more individualistic economy than existed in areas where the nucleated village and communal right were dominant. But over a great swathe of country, Deira, Mercia, and especially Wessex east of Selwood, open-field farming predominated. This does not mean that England was covered with institutions identical to the medieval manor. The manor is much more a legal and administrative institution than an agrarian. But there are firm signs of the existence of the agrarian base of the manor, almost as far back as written records go.

The earliest Anglo-Saxon settlements, however, go back beyond the written record. Can it be assumed that the two-field system, with plough-team and oxen distributed among the peasant community, was in operation within a generation or two of the first settlement? The archaeologist can help little in this respect through no fault of his own, but simply because the Germanic new-comers

---

[22] W. G. Hoskins and H. P. R. Finberg, *Devonshire Studies*, London, 1952, particularly pp. 265–88 and 314–15.

chose their habitation sites so well that later generations made little effort to move away from them: a tribute to the sagacity of the farmers, though a misfortune to the historian. Parish boundaries sometimes preserve very ancient agrarian divisions possibly going back to the earliest settlements, and in Lincolnshire, Berkshire and Devon, for example, where close study has been made of this problem, it is often possible to trace an equitable division of arable, pasture, upland and lowland, marsh and dry land, between neighbouring agrarian communities. According to lie of land the shape of settlements may be long and thin or short and broad. It seems likely that in areas such as those settled by the *Sonningas* or *Readingas* in Berkshire, where consciousness of cohesion existed long before the historic monarchies took shape, some corporate scheme for the allotment of land was early agreed on by the sub-groups of the small primitive folk.

This brings to the fore a question which is much easier to ask than to answer. Did the new Anglo-Saxon settlers of the fifth and sixth centuries allot lands to community after community as their boundaries advanced, or were the villages themselves the result of a natural growth from a pioneering centre? Did the leader of a successful war-band allot land to his warriors after victory, or did the free *ceorls*, peasant-warriors, with their *familiae* set up a group of farmsteads according to a scheme already known to them from their farming practice in north-west Germany? If, as has been suggested earlier in the volume, the Anglo-Saxon invasion is read as a true migration, a combination of both processes is likely, with military lordship in the ascendant as new land was won and defended, with peasant independence asserted as peaceful conditions were resumed and settlement deepened. The free German peasant-warrior has become something of a pasteboard myth, but it would be going too far to deny his existence. An early Anglo-Saxon England peopled by dominant soldiers, dragooning an unwilling subjected peasantry, is surely even more divorced from reality than an early Anglo-Saxon England peopled exclusively by free peasant farmers, the quintessence of German republican virtue.

4. THE ORIGIN OF THE MANOR

Indeed, the great question associated with the presence of open-field farming in the mind of the social historian is the extent of the existence of the manor. If the agrarian base existed, at what stage was the manorial superstructure erected? As Marc Bloch reminded us, 'all descriptions of medieval economy have the manor as essential base, at once a group of producers, a centre of exchange, and the source of a great number of goods thrown afterwards into the main streams of circulation'. And as Bloch consistently reiterated in a fashion typical of the warmth of his approach to economic and social problems, these manorial problems were personal as well as 'merely economic' puzzles: wealth did not consist only in land, in gold, in silver.

> *Mais est richoise de parens et d'amens*
> *Li cuers d'un homme vaut tout l'or d'un pais.*[23]

The most important written statement concerning the origins of the manor in Anglo-Saxon England comes from the second group of clauses from the laws of Ine, referred to above. These dealt with the nobleman who was moving away from an estate, and it is likely that the wise men of Wessex who framed these dooms were very aware of the difficulties attendant on the colonization movement to the south-west, into Devon. It is stated that a nobleman (a *gesith-born* man) who moved elsewhere could take with him his reeve, his smith and his children's nurse; that he who had twenty hides must show twelve hides *gesettes landes* when he departed, that he who had ten hides must show six, and he who had three must show one and a half. Further if a *gesith-born* man was evicted, he was to be evicted from the *botl*, the main dwelling, but not from the *setene*.[24] There is immediately a major problem of interpretation. What is the meaning of *gesett* land? The phrase has been interpreted as land actually sown with corn. The object of the clause is then interpreted as a desire to ensure continuity in the cultivation of the arable, and to make certain that an estate was not handed over, presumably to the owner who might be the king, in a neglected state. The twelfth-century translator had this in mind when he rendered *gesettes landes* as *vestite terre*.[25] This interpretation suggests strong royal interest in the intimate processes of colonization, and also strong dominical control of local and quite extensive estates. The hide, even at this early stage, becomes a measure of extent of arable as much as a measure of settlement. Against this T. H. Aston has suggested that *gesett land* might well mean land settled by tenants, a view that had previously been held by Seebohm and Vinogradoff,

[23] Marc Bloch, *Annales d'histoire économique et sociale*, 1929, p. 257, where quotation is given from *Garin le Lorrain*, ed. P. Paris, vol. II, p. 218.
[24] Ine 63–8.
[25] Liebermann I, p. 119.

and one which appears to be acceptable on linguistic grounds.[26] He argues that the *gesett land*, in a range of fifty to sixty per cent of the arable of the whole estate, represents the peasants' land as opposed to the forty or fifty per cent retained in what amounts to demesne, a proportion which would fit in with later evidence concerning the proportion of land kept in demesne on the manor.

The picture that emerges is of conscious settlement of the land by noblemen with resources in armed force, slaves, stock and other equipment, who attract to their settlements men of free legal status but of humble economic condition. These men take on shares in the open field, the lion's share of which remains with the nobleman. Similarities exist to arrangements disclosed in tenth- and eleventh-century evidence in the south-west. Estates, demesne and tenancy are the consistent features of the documentary evidence. The strong personal name element in place-names is linked with the idea of seignorial activity as a primitive force in the organization of rural society. Mr Aston has argued his case with great vigour, and any discussion of the origin of the manor in England must take his shrewd arguments into account. He reminds us in particular of the complexity of these problems of settlement, and of the danger of too uncritical acquiescence in the existence of the elusive communities of free peasants. He provides a useful warning against underestimating the extent of settlement by aristocratic lords of villages. But it must be confessed that 'tenanted land' seems a slightly forced interpretation of a clause that is simply explained on grounds of royal concern with good husbandry on great estates. It is hard to see why the king should be anxious over the proportion of land let out to tenants, only when the nobleman was on the point of departing. Whichever interpretation of *gesett land* is adopted, one point emerges with some force: that the king and the noble played a considerable part in the workings of the agrarian economy. Admittedly these particular regulations may have applied primarily to newly colonized land, but even so, in face of them, one may have to modify the view that there is no trace in Ine's laws of any private lord, 'able to compel observance of the routine of agricultural life'.[27]

[26] T. H. Aston 'The Origins of the Manor in England', *T.R. Hist. S.*, 1958, pp. 65–6; the whole article, pp. 59–83, gives a clear introduction to the problems.
[27] F. M. Stenton, *Anglo-Saxon England*, p. 280; though Sir Frank's further point (in connection with Ine 42), that the king and council dealt with matters that would have later been the preserve of a manorial court, has great force in relation to his picture of the free *ceorl* as the basic unit in society.

Perhaps the most important of all statements from the laws o' Ine comes from clause 67: 'If anyone covenants for a yardland o' more at a fixed rent, and ploughs it, if the lord wishes to increase for him the [rent of the] land by demanding service as well as rent he need not accept it, if he does not give him a dwelling; and he is to forfeit the crops (*æceras*).' Again it must be remembered that this statement may refer to new land taken in by the plough, bu' even with this reservation the implications are considerable. Three general conclusions seem perfectly admissible: (1) that a lord may if he so wishes, demand labour service (*weorc*: *opus*) in place of o' as well as rent (*gafol*: *gablum*); (2) that if he has not provided the tenant with a house then the tenant may refuse *weorc*, though at a loss of tenure and of seed; (3) by implication that a tenant who has a house, a *botl*, committed to him can be held to labour services.

It is impossible to tell how widespread this practice was, widespread enough at least to provoke legislation by king and witan But in this practice we surely have not the origin but a point o' progression along the paths to manorial organization.

Discussion of these problems brings to the forefront the whole problem of the power of the lord in Anglo-Saxon England and o' his relationship with the agrarian community. To Earle, writing in 1888, Anglo-Saxon historians were divided into two principal groups. There were those who concentrated on the legal record, and there were those who attempted to interpret the economic situation[28] To the former, the long agrarian story was a tale of slow but steady encroachment by the peasantry on the lord's power. To the latter, the agrarian history of at least the Middle Ages was a tale of steady unsurpation by lords of the rights of a peasantry originally free. In fact, the antithesis is not as sharp as Earle makes out, nor is the concept of freedom so simple. But if the choice has to be made, the second possibility is nearer the truth. Indeed, after due allowance has been made for the strength of seignorial activity, there is much to be said for the view that the manor is essentially the community of peasants with the lord's rights superimposed. The basic social unit in the earliest law-codes of Kent was the free *ceorl* with his wergeld, his blood-price of one hundred 'golden' shillings. This sum, which was a symbol of his membership of a folk, went to his kinsmen in case of his death by violence. His slayer had further to pay fifty 'golden' shillings as a compensation to the king.[29] But

[28] J. Earle, *A Handbook to the Land Charters and other Saxonic Documents*, pp. lvi–lvii, Oxford, 1888.
[29] Ethelbert 6.

here was no intermediate lord between the king and the *ceorl*. In
Vessex, if it had been normal for there to have been a lord between
he *ceorl* and the king, Ine would not have legislated directly with
egard to how *ceorls* farmed their homesteads. Care must be taken,
f course, not to fall prey to the overtones associated with the
vords *churl* and *peasant*. In Old Norse sagas, admittedly late and
not always reliable, men of the highest rank turned their hands
o agriculture when need arose, and the same may have been
rue of seventh-century Kent or Wessex. The *ceorl* in the laws
f Ethelbert was well up in the social scale with a wergeld of
s much as a third of that of a nobleman, and with a range of
ubordinate ranks below him: a *ceorl's* 'loaf-eater' i.e., presumably
dependent servant, is mentioned specifically to say nothing of
hree classes of *laets* or half-free, and a further three classes of
lave.[30] Kent, as always, had its peculiarities. Only in the Laws
f Ethelbert was there mention of an intermediate class between
lave and simple freeman. But Wessex, where a *ceorl's* substantial
vergeld of two hundred silver shillings was a sixth of that of the
noble, presented a similar general picture. These *ceorls* were not
by definition noblemen, but they were potential noblemen. They
vere not lords of villages, but they were substantial householders,
he key men in agrarian organization. Even the most prosperous
of the Domesday *villani* did not move as resolutely in public affairs
as the seventh-century Kentish *ceorl*.

The law-codes throw considerable emphasis on the wergeld of
he *ceorls*. From the earliest laws to the latest the declaration of
a man's blood-price was of great social importance. Nobility is
present, and apparently nobility by birth, from the time of the laws
of Ethelbert. Indeed, if archaeology is brought into the picture,
he excavation of the mound at Taplow proves the existence of a
chieftain early in the days of the Anglo-Saxon settlement. Wergeld
payments tell of personal status, not of landed possessions. It was
possible in late-seventh-century Wessex for a man to be nobly born,
yet to have little endowment in land.[31] But such endowment was
normally associated with the holding of superior rank. Many of
the great nobles mentioned by Bede held estates. In the course of
the eighth century, land-books, which in the initial stages were the

[30] Ethelbert 16 and 25; see below, p. 213.
[31] Ine 45 and especially Ine 51, where the penalty for failure to perform fyrd duty
is declared at 120 shillings and forfeiture of land for the land-holding nobleman,
at 60 shillings for the nobleman who does not hold land, and at 30 shillings for
the *ceorl*.

special preserve of the Church, were granted to secular lords as well. These land-books read more like grants of land and subordinate peasantry to church or great noble rather than simple grant of royal rights over a free peasantry. Ine's tenant (cf. clause 67 above), tied to labour-service if he took on a house, would equat well with an occupier of part of a *cassatus* or *manens* referred to in the land-books.

Perhaps it has not always been made clear that the existence of free peasants and of rudimentary manors is by no means exclusive Historians in their attempts to clarify the social structure of early Anglo-Saxon England can do disservice by obscuring the complexity of the social scene. The *ceorl*, the free tribesman, of free kindred the two-hundred-shilling man, was the typical agent and produc of a migration that was also a colonizing movement. The *gesith-born* man, the nobleman, owning land, was also a product of a migration that was in part a military conquest. Both *ceorl* and *gesith* lived in the same communities, under the same kings and the same laws.

It must be remembered also that manorial lordship was not the only means by which the energies of small, local communities could be directed into channels necessary to the health of large communities. In Scandinavia there existed, until at least the end of the twelfth century, a social system in which free peasant householders maintained their direct contact with folk-moots and so provided the essential basis of society. But the wealthier England lands and the more complicated political pressures fostered developments which led to greater emphasis on manorial lordship. Kings were active and kings dealt more naturally with men than with folk-moots From the earliest days lordship and the estate were closely associated with one another. Extensive use of personal names in place-names suggests personal leadership in settlement. In the written records of historic days we meet frequent mention of the *tun* of a certain nobleman, or the *villa* of a certain *ealdorman*, or the *ham* of a certain lord. There is as much information about the lords of estates in the seventh century as about free peasants.

Yet the social importance of the free peasant was great, and he has left his traces on later rural organization. A subjected agrarian community dominated by relatively few military overlords and their retainers would not have provided the social forms revealed in Domesday Book and in other eleventh- and twelfth-century sources. The variety within the manorial system, the tenacity with which the custom of the manor was observed, and above all the fact that the lord himself in law if not in fact was bound by custom, speak of the existence of agrarian communities upon which the lord's rights were grafted. These rights are best explained as delegated rights from the king as representative of the folk. And if dominical rights are, as it were, additional to the basic community even in the manorialized parts of the country, how much more is this true of areas like East Anglia and the Northern Danelaw where the social forms must be derived from a society of free peasant farmers? Danish freedom may be held to have preserved this character late in these eastern counties, though it may be that a simple administrative point may better give the true explanation. In the south and west, in English England, governmental activity was more highly specialized; the resources of the community were more tightly harnessed to the needs of the victorious West Saxon dynasty. And, as a general theme, common to all Western Europe at this period, one may say that kingship and secular lordship grew in strength in partnership together.

Indeed organization for war or for defence is the key to many social developments in this age. It cannot be doubted that the free *ceorl's* freedom depended in large part upon his skill as a warrior and upon the need for him as a warrior. Common to all north-west Europe is the combination of warrior-peasant. In Frankia the process by which a Germanic peasantry, originally free, lost its freedom is one of the main themes of historians who deal with the Merovingian and Carolingian age. It is reasonable to suppose that a similar process was in force in England. In Frankia the milestones are better marked, the main crisis points more dramatic. The survival of Romanism, the unification of most of Gaul under the Franks, campaigns against Moslem to the south, against German and Slav to the East, and the revival of Empire under Charles the Great, are well-documented themes that have enabled historians to distinguish stages in the advance from free tribesmen to feudal vassal and peasant. The English situation is more obscure because the Germanic settlement was so much denser and also because the familiar and spectacular features of feudal society, notably fighting on horseback, were late in developing. As late as the battle of Maldon in 991 an *unorne ceorl* played a prominent part in the fight against the Norse raiders, and although the poet commented on the fact that such a *ceorl* made a high speech, his presence in the battle was no occasion for surprise as may be seen from the care with which the poet describes the drawing-up of the *folc* in arms in the earlier passages of the poem that have survived.[32] But the brunt of the fighting at Maldon was borne by the picked fighting-men, the hearth-troop, and it i probable that as the need for a specially skilled army increased, so did any primitive equality among fellow tribesmen tend to decline And although it is not perhaps until after the Alfredian wars that the full development takes place in England, there are pointer in that direction from the earlier times. In the internecine war recorded by Bede there is some contempt shown by the aristocrati leader of warriors for the mere *rustici* though these, it is true, wer carriers of supplies not full fighting men.[33] The problem of the gradual loss of freedom of the *ceorl* is bound up with fundamenta questions concerning the source of authority in Anglo-Saxon Eng land. Did authority stem from the king, or from the groups o free peasants whose freedom consisted in the possession of a fre kindred, or from the groups of free peasants joined together i agrarian associations for the main part in open-field villages? Som trace of the three elements was surely present in most Anglo-Saxon lordship. There is little evidence of the importance of folk-moot exercising an independent authority which used to lie so thick on the Anglo-Saxon scene. When popular courts appear the roya hand is already strong within them. Yet it seems likely, if no in formal court then in relatively informal assembly, that earl Anglo-Saxon society looked for authority ultimately to the king but immediately in day-to-day affairs to meetings of the free *ceorl* of a neighbourhood. They are the repositories of the custom o a district, and also the memory of a district. The standing o these *ceorls* again depended on the possession of a strong kindred From their number emerged in more complicated and specialize days the wealthier and more competent kindreds who 'throve to thegn-right' in both the military and the economic spheres.

It is reasonable to propound the existence in the late seventh century of agrarian communities that knew no secular lord below the king, and also of agrarian communities that were, almost cer tainly to varying degree, under the control of secular lords. It i the development of the latter communities into the manor, and th general extension of manorial lordship which provide the majo themes of Anglo-Saxon agrarian history. An examination of th problems of land-tenure is the best path of entry into question concerning the Anglo-Saxon manor.

---

[32] 'Battle of Maldon', l. 256 and lines 17–24. *E.H.D.* I, p. 324 and p. 320.
[33] Bede, *Hist. Eccl.*, IV, 22.

5. LAND-TENURE

a) Seisin

The first and most complicated problem in connection with the development of the manor concerns the nature of the tenure of the land. There is much relevant material available for a study of Anglo-Saxon conditions. A mass of land-charters has survived, mostly through monastic cartularies. The charters were for the most part locked up for the student in the two substantial collections of de Gray Birch and Kemble, but the appearance in 1955 of Professor Whitelock's *English Historical Documents*, Volume I, and the publication in 1968 of P. H. Sawyer's admirable annotated list of *Anglo-Saxon Charters* for the Royal Historical Society have made the charter treasure infinitely more accessible. These charters were solemn and formal records of grants of land. Their wording shows that the King, the Church, and the witan were operating in this field of land-law with the object of rationalizing customs that dated literally from immemorial antiquity. The gift of land was often made by some symbolic act like the cutting of a sod or the handing over of a knife. The ceremony of taking seisin was made as public as possible. In 931, for example, Earl Athelstan granted a substantial estate at Uffington to Abingdon at the shire-court of Berkshire with the bystanders all saying, as anathema was pronounced on anyone acting against the gift, *sy hyt swa, amen, amen.*[34] Duke William when he became King of England gave a playful flourish, as he made a grant of land to the Abbot of Holy Trinity, Rouen, threatening to stab his hand with a dagger and so to seal the compact in blood. 'Thus', he jestingly exclaimed, 'ought land to be bestowed.'[35] It was authority and legality for the gift, not strictly speaking the gift itself, that was effected by the promulgation of a charter. But the charter bore witness to the vital fact that land could be given. Indeed the right to alienate the land given still further is often expressly recognized in the charter, though a gift or a lease could be limited to the kindred, or even to the 'spear-hand', the male side of the kindred.[36] This fact of alienation warns against the ascription of too powerful a mystique to land. There is evidence indeed for something approaching a land-market in late Anglo-Saxon England. In the eleventh century Aelfric, an East Anglian bishop,

---

[34] A. J. Robertson, *Anglo-Saxon Charters*, no. xxii.
[35] *E.H.D.* II, p. 984.
[36] *Anglo-Saxon Charters*, no. xxxv.

left in his will an estate at Walsingham to be sold as dearly a
possible, with the money so gained to be paid out according to
his directions.[37] Not that all land could be alienated. The line of
division between the two basic tenures of Anglo-Saxon England
bookland and folkland, makes sharp division between that which
can be alienated and that which cannot. The third distinctive form
of tenure, *lænland*, important as it is in the discussion of manoria
origin, was not strictly a primary term itself; it was land – normally
land held on the good title guaranteed by the presence of a book
– granted for a specific and limited space of time.

(b) Bookland

Bookland is the simplest form to deal with, land held by the
book. For the tenth and eleventh centuries the importance of
charters becomes increasingly evident, as the surviving document
increase in number. But the practice of attesting gifts by book
originated on analogy with the late Roman private deed in the
seventh century. Later forgers even took opportunity to record
grants purporting to have been made by Ethelbert of Kent to
St Augustine at Canterbury. As time went on all great religiou
houses collected estates. An obvious purpose behind the earlies
law-codes was to incorporate the new church into the existing socia
system, and the land-charter fulfilled a similar purpose. In the firs
instance concern was to prove sure title for land granted to abbey
or episcopal see. As the custom of granting land by charter to
laymen grew, certainly from the second half of the eighth centur
onwards, the advantages became apparent to donor and recipien
alike of a form of land tenure, of holding land by book or charter
which permitted estates to be freed from the customary rules o
transmission within the kindred, and incidentally allowed then
to be given or willed to ecclesiastical establishments. Complaint
were early made against excessive endowment which detracted
from a prime purpose of land gifts, sustenance for the warrior
Bede complained of monasteries that had fallen from their true
purpose so that they were useful neither to God nor man, 'in tha
neither is there kept there a regular life according to God's will
nor are they owned by thegns or gesiths [*milites sive comites*] of the
secular power, who defend our people from the barbarians'.[38] He

[37] D. Whitelock, *Anglo-Saxon Wills*, no. xxvi.
[38] Letter of Bede to Archbishop Egbert, *E.H.D.* I, p. 804.

also lamented the growth of sham monasteries, set up by laymen
with letters of privilege as hereditary possessions. Such laymen
were quit of service to God and man.[39] When Bede referred
to possessions granted to true monasteries, 'free from all care
of earthly warfare', it is possible that he had more mind than a
vague aspiration towards seclusion and dedication to the cares of
heavenly warfare.[40] As the kingship grew wider in range so did
the value of documentary proof of tenure in the royal name grow
more effective. In the days of Offa of Mercia ecclesiastics from all
lands south of the Humber lent the weight of their names to the
diplomatic documents drawn up by Mercian king and witan. To
King Alfred bookland and perpetual possession were the ultimate
reward of a dependent, to be earned by his lord's kindness after
the follower had dwelt long on land loaned to him by his lord.[41]
It was not until the eleventh century that the flexible writ came
to vie in importance with the more cumbersome formal charter.
Writs of the Confessor were adduced as proof positive of legitimate
tenure at the time of the Domesday survey. Even then the spate of
so-called forged charters in the following century was occasioned
by the desire of ecclesiastics to possess proof of their tenure of
lands which for the most part fairly belonged to them. In spite
of Archbishop Lyfing's lament to Canute that he had charters in
plenty if only they were good for anything, men were looking to
documentary evidence supported by the strongest agency in the
land as the surest title to land.[42]

Such firm title was badly needed. In Anglo-Saxon days possession was nine points of the law. *Agnung*, that is to say proof
of ownership, lay nearer to the one who had than to the one
who claimed, and such claim itself was subject to all the pitfalls
of a formal legalistic procedure.[43] The *talu*, or suit of claim, was
hedged with prickly safeguards which made it a somewhat perilous undertaking. At the time of Domesday Book we are still two
centuries from the Quo Warranto proceedings and the Earl of
Warenne's rusty sword: inversely it is well to remember that we

[39] Ibid., p. 805.
[40] *Hist. Eccl.*, III, 24.
[41] *König Alfreds des Grossen Bearbeitung der Soliloquien des Augustins*, ed. W. Endter
(Bibl. der angelsachs. Prosa, XI), Hamburg, 1922, p. 2. *E.H.D.* I, p. 918.
[42] F. E. Harmer, *Anglo-Saxon Writs*, no. 26, p. 182. Professor Whitelock has drawn
my attention to a passage in the *Liber Eliensis* (II, 25) which makes this point firmly:
proprior erat ille ut terram haberet, qui cyrographum habebat, quam qui non habebat.
[43] II Ethelred 9.4.

are more than six centuries from the date when the first Saxon householder set up his permanent home on English soil.

Yet of course one must guard against exaggeration of the extent of bookland. All clerics and possibly most great magnates made every effort to provide their estates with the sanction and freedom from dues that royal charter or writ could give. But there were still in 1066 many freemen, *alodarii* and sokemen who held land, and who could 'go with it where they willed', unanswerable for their land to any lord save the king. Their holdings represented tenures more ancient than those sanctioned by the royal clerks. Further, some of the estates held by the king or by the great churches represented parcels of land of great antiquity, territorial groupings that in some instances were probably identical with the original settlement area of a small folk. At Sonning in Berkshire the name, size and recorded history of the great manor held by the Bishop of Salisbury suggest that here was the nuclear area of an original *regio* or province. The biggest royal estates may represent very early allotments to the leaders of folks. But, given ignorance concerning the original or non-original nature of kingship, the argument cannot be taken back far enough to touch on the nature of original settlement. Perhaps there is danger in searching for conclusions that are too rigid from the fragments of evidence. Once the community started to grow as a community, then certainly kingship flourished. With the development of kingship there followed the endowment of kings: estates at strategic points; hospitality; the king's *feorm*; protection over lines of communication. Bookland represents an extension of this royal power into the innermost recesses of the social system, into the very ownership of land, and the exercise of authority over it. A grant by the Mercian king Ceolwulf I in 822 went into unusual detail over the burdens actually removed from an estate by royal grant.

> from all servitude in secular affairs, from entertainment of king, bishop, ealdorman, or of reeves, tax-gatherers, keepers of dogs, or horses, or hawks; from the feeding or support of all those who are called fæstingmen; from all labours, services, charges or burdens, whatever, more or less, I will enumerate or say ... except from these four causes which I shall now name: military service against pagan enemies, and the construction of bridges and the fortification or destruction of fortresses among the same people, and it is to render single payment outside, according to the custom of that people, and yet pay no fine to anyone outside, but it is ever to remain free and secure in its integrity ... for Wulfred the Archbishop and his heirs in the future.

Such a list is a reminder of the public burdens that pass under royal cognizance, a reminder of the way in which complexity in society and in kingship grew together. The occasion of this particular grant was exceptional, a gift made by king to archbishop on the very day of the royal consecration. Its practical and direct purport, quite apart from the sureness of title established, is sufficient to show why a land-book was so coveted a possession. It could be an expensive acquisition. Even on this particular great occasion the Archbishop himself gave to the King 'acceptable money, i.e. a gold ring containing 75 mancuses'.[44]

(c) Folkland

The central thought concerning the problem is contained in a famous article written by Vinogradoff[45] in which he states the apparently trite proposition that folkland is land held according to folk-law. Yet there was great fury of argument behind this simple statement. Elaborate theories concerning the holding of land and even the original settlement were constructed on the somewhat slender foundations of an endorsement to a charter, a clause in the will of the ealdorman Alfred, and a phrase in the laws of Edward the Elder.[46] Folkland was taken as equivalent to Scandinavian *odal*; a new and highly controversial term *ethel-land* was introduced into the dispute; the giants battled mightily over interpretation. Attempts have been made since Vinogradoff wrote to upset his theories, but they are securely established. The most promising line of approach to modify his conclusions is to emphasize the negative rather than the positive implications of his thesis. That is to argue that part of the object of booking land was to free it from communal obligations which fell *sui generis* on folkland, but to recognize that folk-law and folk-right are more intangible than Vinogradoff would always allow. The shading off of concepts of folk-law into concepts of royal law can be a very gradual process. It is not a mere quibble to recognize that folkland was indeed land not freed from royal charges by formal act, and yet to question a sharp cleavage between ideas of royal law and folk-law.

Such discussion takes us at first sight far from the agrarian realities of plough and open fields. But the growth of agrarian

---

[44] *E.H.D.* I, p. 515.

[45] 'Folkland', *E.H.R.*, 1893.

[46] A fourth reference to folkland helps to establish the basic fact that land was *either* bookland or folkland: R. Flower, 'The Text of the Burghal Hidage', *London Medieval Studies*, 1937.

communities is intimately linked with their response, forced or voluntary, to communal obligation. This is as true in the relationship of the rudimentary cluster of peasant householders to immediate defence of the immediate locality as it is in the relationship of the agrarian communities in general to the larger units, to the lathes in Kent, to the *provinciae* or *regiones* of Wessex and the Midlands, ultimately to the kingdom of England. The growth of kingship sharpened the idea of the larger community. The king was the agent by which consciousness of larger obligation was brought home to the basic agrarian units, more often than not in the shape of strong moots and oppressive gelds. And over much of the country, though not all, the growth in power of the secular lord in the localities was an organic part of the whole process of creation of a wider kingdom. Folkland, therefore, in so far as it concerns our present theme, represents land still subject to the vaguer and more loosely defined burdens of communal obligation associated with early Anglo-Saxon kingship. Bookland itself is further advanced again, exempting from the loosely defined burdens, but ultimately sharpening those that remained.

Service at *fyrd, burh* and bridge came to mean more as kingdoms grew in size and complexity.

(d) Lænland

To imply that land was merely a static form of wealth and power, however, would be to falsify the picture. It was not solely a question of food-rents, regalian rights, renders in cash and kind such as might be thought from a simple description of bookland and folkland. There were occasions when greater fluidity in wealth was required, such as, for example, when the demand of Danish invader or royal tax-collector made the land-owner draw more heavily on his resources actual and potential. It happened also that land-owners, in particular ecclesiastical land-owners, desired at times a more regular render than that which could be relied on from the more direct processes of demesne farming and insistence on customary rights. To meet such occasions the lease was the obvious answer, and grants of leases became common in Anglo-Saxon England. The phrase, *lænland*, is used of land leased in this way for a stated term but on variable conditions. The grant of a *læn* implies possession of a book. One of the distinctions between bookland and folkland appears to be that the former could be loaned in this fashion.

Leases were granted at an early date in Anglo-Saxon England. The first recorded example comes from the early eighth century (721–43), when Bishop Wilfrid granted five *cassati* of the episcopal lands of Worcester at Bibury to a *comes*, of not ignoble birth, and to his daughter for a period of two lives with reversion to the see after their death.[47] Worcester, owing to the preservation of so many of her records, continues to bulk large in the history of Anglo-Saxon leases. Over seventy leases have survived from the episcopate of the great Bishop Oswald alone (961–92). But other churches and abbeys were busy in the same way. The widespread nature of the practice is admirably illustrated by R. Lennard, who has been able to draw on evidence from eighteen shires, and from the lands of twenty ecclesiastical lords, in order to show the extent of land grants on a tenancy of one or more lives in the generation before the Norman Conquest.[48]

As far as period of lease is concerned, the best-known form is the lease for a term of three lives, that is to say for the lifetime of the original lessee himself together with the lives of two heirs, sometimes specified in the lease, sometimes not. This form was popularized by Bishop Oswald in the tenth century, who carried out a thorough reorganization of the existing Worcester estates, the main lines of which are straightforward and clear. The Bishop had great wealth in land; he needed service. A lease for three lives was well calculated to give him the service required. It was not feudal service. There was not sufficient clarity of definition to justify the use of that term. The Bishop was not supplying his fighting retainers with land in return for permanent hereditary service. But as his memorandum on the subject to King Edgar shows, he was anxious to reward past service and also to supply himself and his see with a more stable render of service and dues. A period of three lives suited his purpose. It was a tenure that offered a reasonable length of attachment. It also offered a possible safeguard against one great peril that faced the landlord in those centuries: he who grants land loses it.

In relying on this tenure Bishop Oswald was no innovator. A church council of 816 had forbidden abbots and abbesses to grant out monastic lands, *nisi in dies et spatium unius hominis*.[49] Yet terms of three lives were fully familiar to the church of Worcester in the

---

[47] *C.S.* 166. Bibury (Beaganbyrig) takes its name from this transaction. The estate fifteen hides by the river Colne, was leased to Leppa and his daughter Beage.
[48] R. Lennard, *Rural England*, p. 164.
[49] Haddan and Stubbs, vol. III, p. 582.

ninth and early tenth centuries as the records of Bishop Wærferth's episcopate show. Difficulties naturally arose. Hemming himself stated that many estates had been lost through the failure of third heirs to give up estates, either because of the action of their powerful friends or because of negligence on the part of the Church.[50] There is an example, dating from 1030–44, on Abingdon lands of a lease granted to the brother of a man who had held the same Berkshire estate as the last life of a lease granted for three lives during the reign of Canute.[51] Any conditional tenure of this type prepared the way for possible squabbles. A good example occurs, again on Worcester land, at Sodbury, where an eighth-century bishop had granted an estate on condition that a member of the kin receiving the estate should become a priest before entering into possession.[52] The dual position of the bishop is brought out sharply here. He needed retainers, but he also needed resources in order to supply his diocese with priests. In course of time the essential condition (possibly a stipulation in the original grant to Worcester) was ignored; Bishop Wærferth attempted compromise; the possible priests rejected with some fury the idea that one of them should accept ordination. It was only with difficulty that the Bishop was able to assert his undoubted right in this instance. But the scheme itself was sound: conditional tenure with the Bishop's bookland let out on *læn* to provide ministerial service on the one part and reasonable security on both. Leases for a term of three lives provided a simple and effective application of this principle. In the Domesday survey there was mention of Normans who had taken over the third term in such Anglo-Saxon leases.[53]

It seems apparent, however, that by the time of the Norman Conquest leases for the term of one life were more common than those for longer periods. There is a little evidence which goes to show that terms for shorter periods were not unknown. Hereward the Wake himself is said to have held land in Lincolnshire on a yearly tenancy, *sicut inter eos conveniret unoquoque anno*.[54] But such tenancies appear to have been rare, though it must be remembered, of course, that by their very nature record of them is not likely to survive.

[50] A. J. Robertson, *Anglo-Saxon Charters*, no. xxxiv, and notes, pp. 318–20.
[51] F. E. Harmer, *Anglo-Saxon Writs*, no. 3.
[52] Harmer, *Select Documents*, no. xv; negotiations between Wærferth and Eadnoth with regard to land at Sodbury, perhaps *c.* 903–4.
[53] D.B. I, 46b, 175; quoted by R. Lennard, op. cit., p. 170.
[54] Ibid., p. 165; D.B. I, 377.

The terms upon which leases were granted in Anglo-Saxon days varied considerably, depending naturally upon what the land-owner wanted to get from them. An annual rent was normally exacted, though this could vary from a nominal token render in honey or other produce to the substantial render given by Archbishop Stigand to the Abbey of Bath for the great manor of Tidenham in the years immediately preceding the Conquest.[55] Life tenancies could be granted in return for a loan, or as a reward for past service, or in hope of future friendship. An abbey or church could vary the tenancy to meet the case. It could receive estates as a gift, and then yield them back to the donor on a life-tenancy. Tenancies were sometimes offered in return for the ultimate reversion of the lessee's own lands. There are examples both from Bury St Edmunds and from Ramsey of the same tenancy being used twice on separate occasions as bait to draw a lessee's land into the abbey.[56]

The mobility of wealth implied in the leasing and reversion of such estates is at first sight one of the most surprising features of late Anglo-Saxon England. It suggests a considerable, though somewhat clumsy exploitation of wealth and economic advantage. The lord could and did exact from his leaseholders services and dues far in excess of the somewhat bald statement of the lease itself. In return the leaseholder found it to his profit to hold a tenancy, subordinate though it was, in for example, a prosperous Worcestershire village. The economic and financial weight of lordship did not decrease with the multiplication of tenancies. King and manorial lord in their several spheres harnessed the energies of the agrarian communities. At the very end of the period Norman feudalism welded the resulting political government yet more strictly together.

(e) Provision for heirs

There is distressingly little information about the transmission of estates in early Anglo-Saxon England. It has been generally assumed that land passed according to customary laws within the kindred, and that one of the objects of the early land-books was to free land from such customary burdens, so that it could be willed or given to great ecclesiastical establishments. But there

---

[55] A. J. Robertson, *Anglo-Saxon Charters*, no. cxvii.
[56] R. Lennard, *Rural England*, pp. 162 and 164.

is no record of the rules by which such customary transmission of land within the kin could be effected. Bede, it is true, in a warning to monks not to elect an abbot because of his birth, but because of his 'more abundant spiritual grace', draws an analogy with earthly succession, by which parents are accustomed to ac-knowledge their first-born as the chief of their offspring (*principium liberorum suorum*), and to consider him to be preferred to the rest when they divide their inheritance.[57] But he is at pains elsewhere to suggest that good fighting men were being lost to the country because adequate provision could not be made for noblemen's sons or veteran thegns at an age when they were anxious to marry and settle.[58] Epic poetry suggests that land was the personal reward for the successful warrior. The fighting lord, of whom the king was the chief representative, looked after his hearth-troop in hall, and made allowance there for the presence of the *gioguð*, or youthful retainers. If some of these were mere boys, then the long training in arms, so characteristic of the feudal age, had its origin in the heroic age of the Germanic past. The social habit of taking service with a superior lord would provide for some, at least, of a nobleman's sons.

Formal provision, however, is not easy to isolate. In the early Anglo-Saxon period difficulties came about, particularly at the royal level. Young princes like St Guthlac, in his unregenerate youth, or Ethelbald the future king of the Mercians, struck out for themselves in violent frontier style, living on the loot from ter-rorized villages. Their exploits provide a salutary reminder of the violence that lay close beneath the surface of Anglo-Saxon society. It is true that Guthlac and Ethelbald were of the royal stock, and that Ethelbald, and probably Guthlac, were exiles when they started their careers of pillage.[59] A more assured royal succession brought generally more peaceful conditions. But both princes gathered a band of lawless young men around them, and it is probable that the absence of a clear-cut form of hereditary tenure contributed to disorder. It was not until the institution of thegnage grew more formal in the tenth and eleventh centuries – and some would say not until the age of Norman discipline – that a curb was placed on the violent and dissatisfied young men; and generations of effort on the part of the Church and nascent State were needed to fit the curb securely in position.

[57] Bede, *Historia Abbatum*, c. 11 (Benedict Biscop), ed. C. Plummer, p. 376.
[58] Letter to Archbishop Egbert, *E.H.D.* I, p. 805.
[59] *Felix's Life of Saint Guthlac*, ed. B. Colgrave, p. 148 and p. 111.

In the last centuries of Anglo-Saxon England prosperous men drew up wills in which they declared their intentions concerning the disposal of their lands and property. The Hyde Register has preserved a copy of King Alfred's own will which contains also a statement of the disputes over inheritance which had occurred even in this most attractive of all Anglo-Saxon dynasties. Alfred and his brothers had tried to keep properties in joint ownership, so that the King would have sufficient resources to give substance to his authority – but they found it difficult to do so, and indeed his father Ethelwulf's will was read before the witan who were asked to declare what was folk-right 'lest any should say he had done wrong to his kinsman'.[60] Division of inheritance among kinsmen was clearly regarded as normal at this stage. To judge from other wills and charters that have survived, sons normally inherited, with provision made for the widow during her widowhood and for the daughters at marriage. The testamentary freedom involved in book-right was used freely, but sometimes with the express reservation of estates within the kin. It was no easy task, even late in Anglo-Saxon England, to build up a great landed inheritance.

Lower down in the social scale inheritance was not such a complicated problem. Genealogies and marriages of simple *geburs* were recorded with care at Hatfield in the eleventh century.[61] Old English leases at times specified that lands were to pass with stock and with men, which implies a regular order of succession to peasant tenements. It was generally true that land was plentiful, and men were scarce. The open fields could cope with local problems of increase in population. The main problem must have concerned the stocking of estates and the provision of seed. In the tenth and eleventh centuries it is probable that responsibility for the equipment of newly settled land rested on the shoulders of the lord; in the earlier period responsibility might well rest on the peasant householder, secure in his possession of a free kindred. In the smaller communities the lord must often have grown out of the kin, as the head of the kindred assumed the duty of acting as *borh* in the public courts, and was equated for practical purposes with the secular lord, in the eyes of the state taking on the function of lord rather than head of the kin. 'He was both my kinsman and

---

[60] Harmer, *Select Documents*, no. xi. Produced after his brother Ethelred's death.
[61] J. Earle, *A Handbook to the Land Charters and Other Saxonic Documents*, pp. 275–7. T. H. Aston reads this as a possible sign that the *geburas* were tied to the land no less than to the lord, *T.R. Hist. S.*, 1958, p. 72.

my lord', says the ealdorman's retainer in the poem of Maldon;[62] at a much lower level in society that same combination may have been as frequent and quite as powerful. The social historian is inclined to see the whole period as one in which the king and the territorial lord grew in authority over against the kindred: but from the point of view of the small man of the day such a generalization would be meaningless. The process by which land rather than blood became the dominant mark of status was gradual, confused, and intermittent.

On one special matter concerning inheritance and the transmission of land a reasonable amount of information has survived. Among the land-owning classes a wife was normally endowed with a portion of land, partly as her means of sustenance in case of widowhood. A third of the husband's estate was regarded as fitting provision, for unlike the situation in the feudal world it was the husband not the father of the bride who provided the endowment. Bede tells how the man returned from the dead divided his goods into three, the one portion for his own use, which was promptly given away, the second for his sons, and the third for his wife.[63] Such land remained her own, unless she contracted a marriage within a year from the death of the first husband. If she did so, the land was to revert to the first husband's kindred.[64] This custom was a fruitful cause of strife, and lies behind the troubles set out in some of the later Anglo-Saxon wills and charters. In addition to the endowment, though in the later period the distinction was on occasion blurred, the wife was also given a 'morning-gift' the day after the marriage night. In primitive times this would consist of a gift in jewellery or gold, but in more settled days the prosperous classes, who alone have left record, normally gave an estate or several estates. Such a gift was peculiarly the wife's own, and even in the absence of direct heirs the land would revert to her kindred in the case of a respectable widowhood. She could give it away, if she so wished.[65] The Church could do little more than confirm and ratify such arrangements, though in doing so it did much towards bringing about peaceful succession to landed wealth.

---

[62] 'Battle of Maldon', l. 224.
[63] *Hist. Eccl.*, V, 12.
[64] II Canute 73a.
[65] Ethelbert 81; Leges Henrici Primi, 11, 13, 13a and 12, 3; Harmer, *Select Documents*, no. xviii and D. Whitelock, *Anglo-Saxon Wills*, no. xv; Kemble. C.D. 704.

There have survived from the later Anglo-Saxon period a number of documents that help to illustrate the working out of these principles in practice. For example there are two interesting marriage agreements dating from the second decade of the eleventh century.[66] Both deal with the top rungs of society, the one a marriage agreement made on behalf of Archbishop Wulfstan's sister, the other a Kentish contract made by a powerful man, Godwin by name, and a thegn, Brihtric, when Godwin wooed his daughter. The Worcester agreement is the simpler of the two, and may represent the standard arrangement decided on by men of substance dealing with such matters. The archbishop's sister was to receive two estates for her lifetime; there was a promise to obtain for her a further estate for three lives from the Abbey of Winchcombe; yet a further estate was to pass to her, at Alton, with full power of alienation. Over and above the land she was promised fifty mancuses of gold, thirty men and thirty oxen. Two copies of the agreement were made. One went to the Archbishop at Worcester, the other to Athelstan at Hereford. The Kentish arrangement follows the same lines, but with more obvious anxiety to make the terms public and well known. The bride-to-be was given in the first place one pound of gold to induce her to accept Godwin's suit. Then she received an estate at Street, 150 acres at Burmarsh, thirty oxen, twenty cows, ten horses, and ten slaves. Sureties were taken, and it was agreed that whoever lived the longer was to succeed to all the property in land, given to her and her husband by her father, and everything else. Agreement was confirmed before Canute himself at Kingston, and all responsible men in Kent and Sussex were told of the terms. The formality of the proceedings and the authority of the wife over her new possessions are interesting features of this settlement.

The question of the authority possessed by women over land is closely associated with matters of inheritance, and the prestige of many of the English queens and abbesses both in this country and on the Continent must have contributed to a recognition of womanly capacity in this sphere. Legal records lay stress on the strength of the woman's kindred. There is revealing evidence in a record of a Herefordshire law suit in which a son sued his mother for a portion of land at a shire-moot where her spokesman, Thorkell the White, denied the suit.[67] Three thegns were chosen

[66] A. J. Robertson, *Anglo-Saxon Charters*, nos. lxxvi and lxxvii.
[67] Ibid., no. lxxviii.

to ride to her home at Fawley, some nine miles from Aylton near Ledbury, a possible though not certain identification of the place where the moot was in session. They had a strong reception from the mother who summoned to her presence her kinswoman Leofflæd, Thorkell's wife, and recognized her solemnly as the heir. The thegns were then sent packing with instructions to act like men (*doð þegnlice*) and to tell all that she had done. This they did, and Thorkell thereupon stood up in the moot and claimed successfully on behalf of his wife. This precious glimpse of an assembly at work, the power of the thegnly class, the tense public atmosphere reminiscent of northern saga, must not obscure the simple fact that the woman was able to choose her heir, in land, in gold, in raiment, in possessions, to the neglect of her unhappy son.

A concrete illustration of provision for widows and daughters involving the transmission of land is provided in the will of the thegn Wulfgeat which he made in the early eleventh century, and which was preserved by the church of Worcester.[68] After making allowance for burial fees, his soul-scot of a hide of land, a pound of pence and twenty-six freedmen, he bequeathed to Worcester a brewing of malt, to Hereford and to St Guthlac's at Hereford a half-a-pound of pence and various other minor bequests. To his men he gave a year's rent as a gift, and made allowances for the payment of his heriot in horses, swords, shields and spears. With the preliminaries cleared away, then came the provision for the transmission of his lands. The bulk of his estates were to go to his wife, to all appearance much more than the traditional third, with reversion to his nearest kin; to his elder daughter went Donnington and Thornbury which had been purchased with her mother's gold; other estates went to his grandson and to his second daughter, and there is a record of agreement to succession of an estate made with a kinswoman. Gold and six mares and six colts were to be given to Brun, whether or not a kinsman cannot be said; the rest of the horses were to be divided equally among his wife and daughters. The features of most interest in this will are the usufruct allowed the wife for life with ultimate reversion to the kin, and the specific mention in relation to the elder daughter's inheritance that part had been bought, and was therefore presumably not subject to the rules that governed inherited land.

Ultimate reversion to the kin was in itself a principle open to abuse, and before we leave the question, it will be wise to examine

[68] D. Whitelock, *Anglo-Saxon Wills*, no. xix.

two *causes célèbres* of the late Anglo-Saxon period, both of which resulted ultimately in the enrichment of the Church, in the first instance of the church of Rochester, in the second of the church of Winchester. The difficult Kentish suit gives real insight into the perils of landed settlements made on marriage, and also on the interest of the Church in such affairs.[69] A wealthy Kentish man, Aelfheah by name, had allowed his brother estates for life. The brother died before him, and Aelfheah made the estates (Erith, Cray and Wouldham) over to the brother's son, Eadric. Eadric in turn died before his uncle, leaving a widow but no children. Aelfheah now granted the widow the estate at Cray as her marriage-gift, but retained the other estates. On a tour of his property, to collect his food-rents, Aelfheah fell ill, and before he died granted the estates, presumably of Wouldham and Erith, to the church at Rochester. The widow, however, remarried, and her new husband, Leofsunu, broke the terms of the will and seized the estates. Great meetings of the shire court followed, resulting to all appearance in the vindication of the rights of Rochester. In 1086 the Bishop of Rochester held Wouldham with an assessment reduced from six sulungs to three.

The Winchester document is of special importance in emphasizing in grim fashion the part that a widow can play in the succession of estates, and in throwing into relief the conflict of interests that could so easily emerge between wife and husband's kindred.[70] A powerful land-owner, Wulfbold by name, had been guilty of a series of violent acts, usurping estates first from his stepmother after his father's death, then from his kinsman at Bourne (Brabourne) in Kent. He ignored repeated forfeit; but such was the position in the troubled reign of Ethelred that none was strong enough to act against him and he died peacefully in bed. On his death his cousin moved into the estate that had previously been in dispute, but he reckoned without the virago, Wulfbold's widow, who together with her son launched an attack on Bourne in which the cousin, Eadmer, and fifteen of his followers were slaughtered. The cousin whom they slew was a king's thegn, and in this, if not in the feud itself, they exceeded the bounds of decorum not to say common sense. Wulfbold's estates passed into the hands of the king, and eventually into the hands of the queen-mother (by exchange). The incident is

[69] A. J. Robertson, op. cit., no. xli.
[70] Ibid., no. lxiii. Also *E.H.D.* I, pp. 575–9, where Professor Whitelock suggests that the Queen (Ethelred's mother) may have entrusted her deeds to the care of the New Minster at Winchester.

a good pointer to the part a woman could play in these tangled problems of inheritance and family hatreds. It is also a good example of the perilous unsettled situations which the Church was endeavouring to resolve by its provision of more accurate records, by its perpetuation of the memory of mortal man.

Lower down in the social scale it is hard to see how women can have inherited land. In an agricultural society women had an enormously difficult and onerous set of tasks to perform: the dairy, storage for winter, the weaving of clothes and the provisioning of the larder for a household. It was laid down in the laws that a woman was to be judged as guilty as her husband if stolen property were found in her storehouse or in her store-chest; not otherwise, since she could scarcely be expected to resist her husband.[71] The implication is that her authority over the two stated hiding-places was complete. She held the keys. But rights and duties and limited authority are one thing, ownership of land another. Could a peasant own land that he did not plough? Could a man hold a household that he could not defend? Defence against enemies or against the king's dues was the first thing expected of a land-owner in the eleventh century. Provided that a woman were wealthy enough to employ a reeve, and provided that she had the support of a powerful kindred, the answer to these questions is probably, yes. Without that proviso the answer must be no, and many a widow or daughter must have of necessity fitted into a subordinate position in a holding formerly owned by husband or by father.

The records distort the picture to some extent by telling so much of cases where women succeed, and of cases where, by will or solemn charter, special steps were taken to ensure the peaceful transmission of land. These are the extraordinary occasions of Anglo-Saxon land-law, and it is more difficult to get in touch with the ordinary occasions. Later divergent customs of inheritance tell a certain amount about the Anglo-Saxon past. Over most of the open-field country partible inheritance among the sons, after the lord's rights had been satisfied, was commonplace. But the final word rested with the ubiquitous 'custom of the manor', which in this respect represented age-long traditions of the primitive agrarian community meeting corporately to arrange their routine and social problems.

[71] II Canute 76.

Most information comes from Kent, which in later years became famous as the home of peasant freedom, and also the home of a major form of that system of land-tenure known as gavelkind. The word itself is interesting, and to a point informative. Anglo-Saxon law made an important distinction between the *gafolgelda* and the *gebur*.[72] The former word is capable of more than one interpretation, and in fact had more than one meaning. Yet its root sense was that of a man who paid *gafol*, or rent, as opposed to the *gebur* bound to labour service. The form of inheritance associated with gavelkind, however, is not that which one would expect from land held on a strictly economic basis. Under Kentish gavelkind the landed inheritance came to be partible among heirs male, and the homestead normally passed to the youngest son, a feature characteristic also of Celtic tribal society. In many English boroughs a similar system of inheritance became common, usually with special provision made for the youngest son.

Of course the payment of *gafol* is a question of great complexity, and it may be unwise to associate a tenurial term like gavelkind with the Anglo-Saxon *gafolgelda*. *Gafol* can mean tribute as well as rent, and it is possible to interpret *gafolgelda* as one responsible for the payment of public exactions, notably the geld. T. H. Aston, for example, would draw the line of continuity from the tenant on *gesett land* of Ine's laws to the man, presumably a *gafolgelda*, who occupied the *neatland* of Edgar's laws. The tenant, the man who sat on *gafolland*, in his opinion was the man liable to public exactions as opposed to those who served the inland. In one important Anglo-Saxon will, however, we hear of *geburas* who dwelt on *gafolland*, and who could still be granted by testament to a religious house.[73] They were kept clearly separate from the estate itself which also passed on reversion to the same religious house of Shaftesbury. The granting by will of a non-servile group of peasants in this way speaks of an immobility in peasant-holding bound by fixed customary rules of descent. The association of *geburs* with *gafolland* reminds us of the complexity of the social scene, so often obscured rather than clarified by the attempted simplications of lawyers and fiscal agents.

---

[72] Ine 6.3; *E.H.D.* I, p. 399 and note in which Professor Whitelock associates both *gebur* and *gafolgelda* with the ceorl who occupies *gafolland* of Alfred's treaty with Guthrum.

[73] D. Whitelock, *Anglo-Saxon Wills*, no. iii, cited by T. H. Aston, *T.R. Hist. S.*, 1958, p. 71, who makes the interesting comment that these *geburas* may have been settled on this Somersetshire estate by Wynflæd (the testatrix) or her ancestor.

Certainly the Normans, when they appeared on the scene, found the agrarian patterns too complicated for their taste. Probably the variations in customs of inheritance troubled them little. In time the general acceptance of that most unnatural form of tenure primogeniture, was sufficient in the feudal world for the upper ranks of society to maintain its integrity within the new Honour of England. The diametrically opposite principle of inheritance in parage and gavelkind continued to operate at the lower levels of society, with its disintegrating tendencies checked by the tighter manorial control of the new Norman lords.

6. THE MANOR IN LATE ANGLO-SAXON ENGLAND; THE 'RECTITUDINES'

The Normans were conscientious recorders as well as firm masters, and the Domesday Commissioners in preparing the vast amount of information they had so painstakingly gathered for their royal masters wished to describe this society in intelligible terms. They therefore used freely the word *manerium*, manor, and so gave, much more neatly than was the case in reality, a picture of an England divided into manors, each under the control of a lord. Most common of all types of entry in Domesday Book are such as this from the survey of Huntingdonshire:

> M[anerium]: In Hartford, King Edward had 15 hides assessed to the geld. There is land for 17 ploughs. Ranulf the brother of Ilger keeps it now. There are 4 ploughs now on the demesne; and 30 villeins and 3 bordars have 8 ploughs. There is a priest; 2 churches; 2 mills rendering 4 pounds; and 40 acres of meadow. Woodland for pannage 1 league in length and half a league in breadth. T.R.E., it was worth 24 pounds; now 15 pounds.[74]

In one respect the choice of terminology was unfortunate, though it is hard to see how it could be bettered. There are so many overtones, however, connected with the word 'manor' in the post-Conquest period, that the general effect is misleading. So much so that modern scholars now hold that *manerium* was no technical term in 1086, and that the most acceptable translation for it would be simply 'manor-house', a delicious reversal of opinion when it is remembered how carefully the two concepts used to be kept

[74] *E.H.D.* II, p. 917.

apart.[75] Whatever else may be implied in the term, certainly the presence of a hall seems the most likely. It may be that the hall was the point to which geld was brought, so giving the *manerium* a special significance in the scheme of royal fiscal organization. It may even be that the hall was the point at which neighbours and tenants assembled to discuss agricultural routine and to settle grievances that could be settled in reasonable amity. The hallmoots of the twelfth century with their Saxon name might well be pre-Conquest institutions though there is no positive proof to that effect.

To recognize the existence of manor-houses is not of course the same as recognizing the existence of full manors with all the rights and appurtenances familiar from thirteenth-century days. In East Anglia, to mention one region that has been very thoroughly dissected by social historians, there still existed in 1086 a form of agrarian organization very different from that of the traditional manor. There were many East Anglian freemen of small estate free to go with their land wheresoever and to whomsoever they would. The incidence of taxation in East Anglia fell not on a manorial unit but on the sub-division of the royal territorial unit, namely on the leet, which formed part of the hundred. When one pound was contributed by the hundred, then the leet, consisting of several villages, gave a fixed proportion, in some cases a sixth of the hundredal contribution, or forty pence.[76] The basic agrarian unit was the village not the manor. In no area of England is the simplification attempted by the Domesday Commissioners more obvious or more misleading.

Similarly in the Northern Danelaw, while there were manors of the traditional pattern such as those attached to the great ecclesiastical complex of lands belonging to the Minster of Southwell, the general picture is far from simple. Over most of the area, from Tees to Welland, the soke and the berewick were only loosely associated with the *manerium*. The manor was still not sharply defined, nor did it coincide with the pattern of agrarian settlement.

But for the bulk of England the discrepancy was not so marked. We talk with justice of the more heavily manorialized south and west. What has happened here to strike such a contrast with the free lands of the Danelaw? Why is there so much closer an approximation here in the south and west to the agrarian base of feudal society? With these problems we must grapple later when

---

[75] See also below, pp. 351–6.

[76] F. M. Stenton, *Anglo-Saxon England*, p. 645; also below, p. 321 and p. 354.

we turn to a final survey of eleventh-century England. For the moment it is enough to record the major line of division in social organization which runs through the lands of open-field farming roughly along the line of Watling Street.

For parts of the manorialized west information is remarkably full. At Worcester a fortunate chance enabled Bishop Wulfstan to control the affairs of the diocese at a time when the scholar Hemming was available to collect the charter evidence into the great cartulary that still bears his name. There were other good landlords in the West Country who took anxious care to survey their lands, and it was one of them who went to the enormous trouble to produce that little gem of social history, the *Rectitudine Singularum Personarum*.[77]

The object of this document, dating from the generation before the Conquest, was to describe the conditions of men who might be found on a great estate. The author is quite modern in his desire to stress the inadequacy of generalizations to cope with agrarian conditions. In some places, he tells us, services are heavy, in others moderate; the cottar's right varies with the custom of the estate; and, heavily and sententiously, all customs are not alike. But scholarly caution did not prevent him from giving a firm picture of rural conditions as he knew them on his great estate, a picture which, with the removal of some terminological difficulties, squares not too unhappily with that given in Domesday Book itself. He divided the free inhabitants of rural England into four main groups. First came the thegn, whose services were altogether honourable. His holding, presumably from king, bishop, earl or abbot, should be protected by charter; he should be worthy of his book-right, *dignus rectitudine testamenti sui*, as the twelfth-century translator puts it.[78] He performed three services for his land, *fyrd-service*, *burhbot* and *brycgeweorc*, the three necessities referred to in so many charters as public burdens from which bookland was not exempt. On many estates further services were demanded of a thegn – at the king's ban. The list was headed by *deorhege to cyniges hame*; that is presumably maintaining the fences around a royal residence, though there may be a hunting significance involved. The thegn had a part to play in equipping a naval force; he was to keep watch on the coast, and to protect the king on his visits to the locality, and to see to the drawing up of the fyrd. But he

---

[77] Liebermann I, pp. 444–53; *E.H.D.* II, pp. 875–9.
[78] Liebermann I, p. 444.

was not in regular attendance on the king. He was a *thegn enchasé*, an estate owner of importance of the type recurring throughout tenth- and eleventh-century legal records. He paid his church-scot and *ælmesfeoh*. He was the type of man upon whom the safety of the Old English state rested.

There followed a statement of the right of the *geneat*. The term is interesting. In early days the *geneat* was often a powerful nobleman, a companion close to the king, but *geneat* in this sense had disappeared by the time of Domesday Book. The twelfth-century translator referred to him under the still vague name of *villanus*. He was in fact a man of some position. He paid rent for his land and a swine for his pasture, which suggests a holding of at least the traditional villein's quarter of a hide. The great characteristic of his service lay in its mobility. He was to ride and carry, to fetch strangers to the *tun*, hold guard on his lord's person, take charge of the horses, and to act as messenger from far or near. The so-called riding-knights, or *radcnihts* of the West Midlands, seem identical with this group. Where service lay in a more direct humble agricultural sphere there was still some distinction about his function. He reaped and mowed, cut wild-beast hedges, built and fenced up the *burh*, and had some responsibility for the hunting setts. The plough knew him not; and the picture of an active, skilled freeman of the type that developed into the manorial ministerial class may be near the truth. He paid the freeman's dues of *ælmesfeoh* and church-scot.

Then is described the cottar who, with his Gallicized brother the bordar, was to be so prominent in the Domesday survey. His status lay below that of the *geneat*, but he was a freeman paying church-scot and dues to the Church, and also 'his hearth-penny as every freeman should'. He was expected to work every Monday or three days a week during harvest for his lord. Indeed in some estates the whole of August was to be spent labouring for his lord at the rate of one acre of oats (or half an acre of other corn) a day, from which one sheaf was to be his own, as the reeve or lord's servant gave it to him. He paid no rent, and was to have at least five acres of his own in the arable; if less, that were too little land a sign that he was being overburdened.

His special function was to acquit his lord's inland from certain services if demanded, duties of sea-ward, duties in connection with the king's *deorhege*, and of such things as might be meted out to him. The cottar indeed seems to have been the agent by which many of the thegn's more menial obligations were met. The presence of some active men in a village, holding only a very small share in the village arable but bound directly to the lord's inland and to service laid on that inland would be of great advantage, indeed indispensable, to the lord. If the relatively varied life of the cottar made him the greatest grumbler, the concern of the writer of the 'Rectitudines' that their service should not be abused nor their free status forgotten is easy to explain.

The last of the major groups, the *gebur*, has much more the function connected with the typical medieval villein. The man who held the 'shire', that is in this context the man in charge of the estate, whether he was a king's reeve or a great lord's reeve, was told to make himself thoroughly acquainted with conditions, and to find out whether the *gebur* paid his tribute in honey, meat or ale. No mention was made of money-rent for land, and the weight of the document was thrown heavily on the duties and obligations of the *gebur*. For two days in every week and for three days in harvest time he had to labour on the lord's demesne. Only if he was on carrying service was he excused this labour. He was to pay ten pence as tribute (*gafol*-pennies) at Michaelmas, after the harvest, twenty-three sesters of barley and two hens at Martinmas, one young sheep or two pence at Easter. During the winter he was to do duty at the lord's sheepfold. From first ploughing to Martinmas he was to turn over one acre of land every week offering the seed himself at the lord's barn. As boonworks he had to offer a further three acres and two acres of pasturage. If he needed more grass he should plough more for it. He also took responsibility for a further three acres sown from his own barn as *gafolyrðe*, that is a tribute-ploughing, for his land. A *gebur* would need many active and lusty sons to help him before he could cover these obligations, and so leave himself time to concentrate on his own welfare. He paid his hearth-penny, but not church-scot nor *ælmesfeoh*. Together with one of his fellows he maintained one hunting dog for his lord. He provided the herdsman with six loaves when the lord's pigs were driven to mast.

A very significant and interesting passage gives insight both into the real status of the *gebur* and into the legal nets that were beginning to enmesh him. On the lands subject to these impositions a *gebur* should be set up with two oxen, one cow, six sheep, and seven acres sown from his yard of land. After a year all dues would be expected from him. He would be given tools for his work, and utensils for his house. When he died the lord would take what he left. The *gebur* was clearly very dependent. The new workers, a young man of age, just marrying, possibly a new-comer o the village unprovided with land of his own, would be set up in a holding, but subject to very onerous conditions. The man with means would take advantage of the man without means. The need for protection must have been great before such demands could be made of a class that was certainly numerous. Villeinage in the worst sense of the much-abused term lay very close.

Immediately after this primary discussion which treats of those directly concerned with rights in the arable comes what might be called a vocational analysis, treating of the agrarian specialists. The bee-keeper and the swineherd had pride of place. The lord could claim their possessions at death with the interesting reservation in the case of the beekeeper 'unless there be anything free'. These men were subject to discipline similar to that of a *gebur*, and were also to perform many tasks at the lord's bidding. They both kept a horse for the lord's use.

The slaves, male and female, were certainly subject to work at the lord's will, so much so that no mention is made of any limit to their obligations. The document's concern with slaves was with, perhaps ominously, the amount of food they had the right to receive, proof positive that the non-servile majority had land enough to provide their needs. Rations for a twelvemonth for a male slave were to be twelve pounds of good corn and two sheep carcasses, one good cow for food, and the right to wood according to the custom of the estate. The female slave did not do so well; she was to have eight pounds of corn, one sheep or threepence for winter provision, one sester of beans for Lent, and whey in summer or one penny. Special provision for all slaves was made at Christmas and Easter. A strip of land was set aside for their use, and a harvest handful. Even the slave was protected by custom, and mention was made of 'the rights that belonged to bondmen'.

The rest of the main part of the 'Rectitudines' concerned itself with special cases such as the *folgere*, that is the free peasant who worked for another without possessing a holding in the open fields himself, and who was entitled to the proceeds from two acres, the one sown, the other unsown but prepared by himself. Customary dues were stated in relation to such essential agrarian workers as the sower, the oxherd, the cowherd, the shepherd, the goatherd, the cheese-maker, the granary-keeper, the woodward and the hayward. The cheese-maker, for example, was entitled to a hundred cheeses and all the buttermilk except the shepherd's share; a formidable woman, no doubt, and one wonders at the relationship between her and the poor shepherd with his right to a bowlful of whey or buttermilk all summer. Some of these workers were servile, some free. As always, legal freedom could be associated with stringent economic subjection. The beadle was in a special category. He should be freer from work than other men because his services might always be required. He should have a little land in return for his toil.

This memorandum concerning the conditions of men is especially valuable not only for what it tells, but for what it is. The cautious concern with custom demonstrates the difficulty of establishing a tyranny over the producers of food. There also emerges a strong sense of the responsibility of office which is one of the more endearing features of the author. In a phrase which reached, as it was meant to reach, poetic heights, he admonished his readers:

> Forðam laga sceal on leode luflice leornian
> Lof se ðe on lande sylf nele leosan

'Wherefore he who does not wish to lose respect in the land must willingly learn the customs among the people.'[79]

The survey ends on a happy note. There are among many peoples the following customs: feasts at winter, at Easter, at reaping ploughing, mowing; a feast for the making of hay ricks, for the gathering of wood, for the making of the corn ricks. The ceremonies of the agricultural year were not unassociated with substantial celebration.

The author did not stop at the description of the estate. It is probable that to him was due the tract 'Gerefa', a supplement as it were to the 'Rectitudines'.[80] His comments on the functions and duties of this key manorial officer come down with a refreshing vigour and directness. He had no use for reeves who did not look both to their lord's interests and to the customs of the community and in making that vital distinction between *hlafordes landriht* (the land-right of the lord) and *folces gerihtu* (the customs of the folk) he gives a valuable clue to the whole sweep of manorial development. The reeve was enjoined to take special care over the sheep-pen and the threshing-floor. The idea of proper incentives was certainly present; he was to spur on the peasants with admonitions concerning the lord's needs, and also to reward them as they deserved. He was not to let the peasants boss him about, but to rule each one with a lord's strength and according to folkright.

[79] Liebermann, p. 452; 'Rectitudines', 21.3.
[80] Liebermann, pp. 453–5.

The tract 'Gerefa' gives much concrete information of general importance to an understanding of the agrarian economy. It gives a survey of the routine of the agricultural year, an account of the things that a good reeve will look to – 'I may not tell all that a good reeve will look to', says the author, but he then proceeds to do so – and an impressive list of the tools and chattels, weaving implements and domestic utensils that need a reeve's attention. These range from kettles and ladles and beer-tubs, bath-tubs and salt-cellars to besoms, hammers, rakes, forks, and ladders: tools for the specialists, millers, tailors and tinkers, as well as for the farm-workers. The account of the agricultural routine is particularly interesting. In summer, that is in May, June and July, men must harrow, spread out dung, make good the hurdle-hedges, shear sheep, build and construct, make good the fences and buildings, cut wood, clear the ground of weeds, build sheep pens, make fish-weirs and water-mills. At harvest-time they reap, mow, dig up woad, take home many good things, roof and thatch, clean out the fold, arrange the sheep-pen and pig-sties before hard winter comes to land, and also they follow zealously the plough. In winter they plough, and in great frost cut timber, prepare their orchards, do many indoor jobs, thresh, cut wood, make a stall for the oxen, sties for the pigs, make a kiln on the threshing floor. An oven and a kiln and many things are needful for a *tun* – and also a roost for the hens. Finally in spring there is more ploughing, and planting of young trees. Beans are sown and vineyards set. Ditches are made and hedges hewn against wild beasts. When the weather is favourable madder is planted, and linseed and woad are also sown. Vegetables are to be planted and many other things.

The tract tells little of the crops actually grown on the arable. Its concern lay with the jobs that needed to be done to keep the whole estate in order. Nothing was too small to escape notice, from a mouse-trap to a hasp. The author's last words ring true, a little tired after his labours but proud of them: 'I have spoken about what I know; he who knows better, let him speak more.'[81]

Such a full account helps to give reality and depth to what is otherwise the rather abstract legal picture of the estate obtainable from the charters and the laws. Only occasionally does a survey help to substantiate the ideal account presented in the 'Rectitudines' and in 'Gerefa'. A survey of the Gloucestershire estate of Tidenham, made possibly in connection with the lease of the estate to Archbishop Stigand, gave a very similar, though much briefer, account to that of the 'Rectitudines'.[82] Apart from peculiarities in fishing rights occasioned by topographical differences, there are major points of agreement with the bigger tracts notably the emphatic distinction between *geneats* and *geburs*, and the careful division of the estate into lord's demesne and, in this survey, the *gesettes landes*, which in this connection and at this date meant tenants' land. The evidence points conclusively to the existence of the 'typical medieval manor' in the West Country before the Norman Conquest. Domesday Book itself showed that the *manerium* often corresponded more closely to the village in the west and south-west, in English England, than in the Danelaw where it was not uncommon to find two, three or even more *maneria* in one village. The two institutions, the agrarian village and the legal manor, were most closely integrated in the south and west, a clue to the whole development of the complex institution of the medieval manor.

7. THE DEVELOPMENT OF THE MANOR: A SUMMARY

Finally, to sum up, it is suggested that the development of the manor may have taken place on the following lines.

(1) During the early Anglo-Saxon period, when emphasis in economic activities lay on colonization and the opening up of new lands, the predominant social group consisted of communities of free peasants, engaged corporately in the chief agrarian processes, bound politically to the king and by the bonds of kindred. Such free peasants constituted the tribesmen warriors of the first consolidated settlements.

(2) Side by side with these communities were townships where for strategic or for religious reasons, the power of the king and of the leading nobles was strong. It is likely that the estates surrounding the great hall of epic poetry were the true forebears of the manor.

(3) The spread, not uniformly but generally, of the impact of lordly power upon the free communities. This could take place in many ways. As the kingdom consolidated, so were the rights of the

[82] *E.H.D.* II, pp. 879–80.

king to his *feorm* defined. This fundamental right to hospitality and
to food-rent could be delegated to members of the royal kin and
to successful leaders of the folk. The laws of Ine (cl. 70.1) tell that
from an estate of ten hides food-rent should amount to: '10 vats
of honey, 300 loaves, 12 "ambers" of Welsh ale, 30 of clear ale,
2 full-grown cows, or 10 wethers, 10 geese, 20 hams, 10 cheeses,
an "amber" full of butter, 5 salmon, 20 pounds of fodder and
100 eels.' As Sir Frank Stenton reminds us, this is a considerable
imposition on a moderate-sized estate by any standard.[83] When
delegated, it could be further extended. As Christianity spread
and the conversion deepened, the delegation of estates and rights
was intensified to provide endowment for the new Church. In the
eighth and ninth centuries colonization was actively supported by
strong royal dynasties, and the division of an estate into the lord's
inland and the tenants' land, fully familiar to the laws of Edgar,
may already have been implied by the laws of Ine.[84]

(4) Particularly under the impact of the Scandinavian invasions
there was an intensification of this process. In an age of peril it was
indeed natural for men to seek lords, and lords to seek men. But
such seeking was no mere abstraction, nor was it normally merely a
matter of personal commendation to a lord, though in some areas,
notably in those under Danish control, it could be little more than
that. Commendation normally involved part at least of a man's
land, to such an extent that he would probably be unable to go
where he would with his land. The lords capable of defending the
community strengthened their hold and increased their demands
on the landed wealth of the community. To the natural perils of
want and unrest, which would find the lord in a more advantageous
position, were added the major complication of barbarian, heathen
invasion. With important reservations, notably the hold kept on the
changes by the king, England in the tenth and eleventh centuries
went through the same social difficulties that were to provoke the
formation of feudal society on the Continent. The basic social
results were the same: the territorialization of political power,
the increase in the authority of the landlord, the regularization
of the duties of the peasant and the sharper differentiation of
status between the peasant and the lord. From the point of view
of the free peasants, Danish England did not suffer from the same

---

[83] *Anglo-Saxon England*, p. 288; Ine 70.1.
[84] II Edgar 1.1; *of þegnes inlande ge of geneatlande*; Ine 67, according to which a
demand for service is made from a tenant covenanting for a yardland; see above,
p. 172 and p. 193.

depression to so great an extent. Although the Danes were content
to receive the protection of the West Saxon monarchy against the
Norwegians, and probably anxious, too, for the recognition of a
legitimate monarch as a convenient source of legal authority, they
would not accept the weight of royal and lordly authority as readily
as those who had seen the alternative in devastation and barbarian
triumph. Maitland held that the weight of geld was an important
contributory factor to the creation of a subordinate population,
and with this question of the weight of royal taxation we must
deal later in this volume.[85] For the moment it is enough to say
that modern enquiry fully substantiates his belief. Maitland also
held that the existence of great ecclesiastical estates was harmful
to the freedom of lesser men. Both these factors applied less in
the Danelaw than to Wessex and West Mercia. The very success
of the monarchy and the Church contributed enormously to the
creation of the English manor. A great diocese such as Worcester
with its leases and elaborate forms of dependent tenure provides
a good example of this process at work.

At this level, of course, a bishop was dealing with men of the
thegnly class. Control of estates meant a lord's control of revenues.
It would not be anachronistic to talk of the manors granted to
the *milites* of Worcester. What in the meantime was happening to
the free peasants hidden under this cloud of dominical right? In
the main, as the 'Rectitudines' shows, they maintained their legal
freedom. Their economic freedom, in so far as it had ever existed,
atrophied under the pressure of military necessity and of government protection. The process of commendation to lords has a long
and controversial history but the main facts are easy to isolate.
In the tenth and eleventh centuries hold-oaths were elaborated;
everywhere lesser men commended themselves to greater. They
did so for a variety of reasons. The process was not completely
one-sided. Possession of a lord, the higher in rank the better, meant
greater security in everyday living, in the lawcourts and in the
fields. The kindred was no longer able to afford protection, at least
on the scale demanded by the harsh and more complicated times.
Attempts to equate wergelds between Danes and Englishmen, of
which record survives, could not have been easy to enforce. And if
a man commended himself to a lord one can be sure that the lord
was not unrewarded. Furthermore the legal codes encouraged the
process. By the time of Athelstan it was recorded as obligatory that

[85] See below, pp. 315–25.

a man should have a lord.[86] It was still possible for this bond to remain personal, but it was highly probable that these free peasants who failed themselves to thrive to thegn-right would quickly fall into a state of economic dependence for their land also.

More general factors also entered into the problem, and as the State grew so did ideas of communal activity. With greater complexity came awareness of the convenience of dealing with relatively few lords rather than with relatively many peasants. This was well attuned to the political thought of the period. 'Let each lord', said Charlemagne in one of the most famous of all his capitularies, 'command his men, so that they obey, better and better, imperial orders and precepts.'[87] Ultimately obedience to God was the goal. Gregory's 'Pastoral Care' expressed the same sentiments in more elaborate fashion. Each should try to fulfil the duties of his office to the best of his ability: from serf to king. The cardinal virtue is obedience, typically Benedictine: obedience closely partnered by humility as the essential attributes of the Christian man.

It might therefore be said that under the dual pressure of the need to seek lords and of increased State activity the land of England passed more firmly into the hands of a territorial aristocracy than had been the case in the pre-Alfredian period. It is with the development of that aristocracy that the next chapter is concerned.

86 II Athelstan 2.
87 Marc Bloch, *Feudal Society*, p. 157; Charlemagne, Capitulary of 810, t. 1, no. 64, c. 17.

CHAPTER FIVE
Kingship and Nobility

1. GENERAL DEVELOPMENTS; THE QUESTION OF TERMINOLOGY

The earliest records from the Anglo-Saxon period give full proof of the existence of an aristocracy. The Laws of King Ethelbert of Kent, for example, carefully distinguished between the *eorlcund* man and the *ceorl*, the latter in himself no insignificant figure in the social scale. If anyone slew a man on the king's estate he was to pay fifty shillings as compensation; if on a nobleman's estate (*eorlcundman*) twelve shillings; for slaying a *ceorl's* dependant the penalty was only six shillings. It seems certain that the general penalties for breach of protection, or *mundbyrd*, lay in identical proportions at fifty shillings, twelve shillings and six shillings respectively, and it is highly probable, though we are not told so explicitly, that the wergeld of an *eorlcund* man was three hundred shillings in contrast to that of a *ceorl* which itself lay at the very respectable sum of one hundred Kentish shillings.[1] Indeed this earliest of English legal codes – and there is no good reason for not attributing it to the early years of the seventh century – displayed a most elaborately graded society. Archaeological evidence is confirming the legal picture. The latest investigation of the whole complex burial ground at Sutton Hoo demonstrates increasingly that the dramatic area of burial mounds, including the royal ship burial itself, was separate and exclusive, to all appearance a royal and aristocratic preserve. No ordinary interments have been found in the area, though there are bodies which suggest sacrificial victims, buried in pre-Christian days to accompany those aristocrats

[1] Ethelbert 5, 13, 25; 8, 15; 21. See below, p. 213.

worthy of commemoration in conspicuous mounds. Sutton Hoo may indeed in its burial practices bear witness to a unique moment in English history when ruling kindreds were acquiring mastery over more or less permanent political groupings. Certainly the student who approaches it in the hope of discovering primitive democracy is fated to receive a rude shock.

A legally defined and hereditary nobility existed at the beginning of the seventh century. The general movement during the rest of our period lay in the direction of a territorialization of the aristocracy, and of the construction of closer bonds between it and the Crown. These two processes were far advanced in 1066: the Normans with their feudal ideals carried them to their logical conclusion.

To say so much is helpful up to a point. It does give a framework suggested by the surviving evidence, and some of the theoretical implications of such a framework are treated in a later chapter. For the moment the chief purpose is one of straightforward definition. Can we at various points during the long story of Anglo-Saxon England define our terms relating to the nobility, and say something about their functions?

There are three periods which lend themselves particularly well to this treatment. These may be called, for the sake of convenience, the age of the Conversion, the age of Alfred, and the later Anglo-Saxon period generally. The Norman intrusion is of such importance that it has been left for separate treatment later in the book.

The first major problem to face concerns terminology. It is obviously unwise to read too much into terminological usage, though there are occasions, particularly during the reign of Alfred, when the Anglo-Saxons themselves strive for greater precision in their terms to describe the nobility. But there is need for something better than the loose 'earls and thegns', sometimes cavalierly employed to cover the whole period. There is an immense difference between the nature of nobility in the seventh century and that of the nobility in the eleventh, a difference parallel to and probably occasioned by a general decline in the power of the kindred and the rise in importance of kingship and territorial lordship.

2. THE AGE OF THE CONVERSION

The characteristic terms used of the nobility in the age of the Conversion, that is roughly the period *c.* 600–735, were the *eorl* and *gesith*. The former term is found in Kentish documents, and may have been something of an archaism by the end of the seventh century though, in the jingle *eorl* and *ceorl*, gentle and simple, it retained currency throughout the Anglo-Saxon period and achieved fresh popularity under Scandinavian influence. *Gesith*, semantically a companion on a journey, was the equivalent of the Latin *comes*. *Thegn* was the common word for servant, derived from the verb *thegnian*, to serve, but *cyninges thegn*, i.e. a specific *king's thegn* made its first appearance in the laws of Wihtræd, *c.* 694.[2] Such a thegn could clear himself of a charge by his unsupported oath, which in view of the lack of information about an *eorl's* oath may suggest that *thegn* was beginning to acquire something of a technical sense over and above its general significance of servant. The laws of Ine, which were promulgated between 688 and 694, the first legal document from the West Saxon kingdom, reveal society classified according to the sum paid as wergeld: in Wessex into twelve-hundred-shilling men, the *gesithcund* corresponding to the *eorlcund* of Kentish law, the six-hundred-shilling men, apparently corresponding to the *gesithcund* man owning no land though there are complications in relation to this group, and the two-hundred-shilling men or simple *ceorls*.[3] Ine had the special problem of a British nobility to deal with on his south-west border in Devon, and he fitted the Welsh nobility into his scheme by allotting them a wergeld of six hundred shillings, that is to say half of what they would have enjoyed, had they been English by birth. The qualification that Ine laid down for such recognition was not, however, a qualification by blood nor perhaps primarily by service, but the possession of land assessed to the value of five hides.[4] In similar fashion a Welsh peasant was afforded a lower wergeld than the two hundred shillings of an English *ceorl*, and again possession of land determined the proportion: a hundred and twenty shillings if he had one hide, eighty shillings if he had half a hide and sixty shillings if he had none. A Welsh rent-payer (*gafolgelda*) had a wergeld of a hundred and twenty shillings and his son of a hundred shillings. The king's Welsh horseman (*horswealh*) was placed on an equal footing with an English *ceorl*, and given a wergeld of two hundred shillings. Possession of land involved service, and it is likely that, in the late seventh century, connection by blood with a king, service to

[2] Wihtræd 20.
[3] Ine 70.
[4] Ibid., 24.2.
[5] Ibid., 32, 23.3, 33.

king, and particularly service at a royal court were important
actors in determining noble status. It may well be that they were
original factors, supplemented chiefly by depreciation in status of
former royal kins as tribal kingdoms were consolidated. Just as the
king's servants in the general sense, his smith, his cupbearer, his
spokesman, enjoyed special rights, so too did his picked warrior-
companions, his *wil-gesiðas*, or *thegns*, or *dryhtguman*, as the poet of
Beowulf called them. A simple freeman occupied an important
place in the social hierarchy. To rise above that stage special service
to the community, pre-eminently military service (though Ine also
puts 'wise counsel' as a special distinguishing mark) was essential,
and such service in these days of tribal kingship meant service to
the king.[6] Of the *principes* and *comites* (*gesiths*) mentioned by Bede in
his 'Historia Ecclesiastica' many were of the royal kin and most had
some service to perform at the royal court. But they are not only
courtiers in the literal sense. In one very illuminating passage Bede
gives sharp insight into the nature of the nobility of the age. After
one of the sporadic but severe battles between the Mercians and
the Northumbrians, Imma, a Northumbrian warrior, was badly
wounded and captured by the servants of a certain *gesith*. The *gesith*,
thinking his captive a mere rustic, who had been a non-combatant,
had him well treated. In time it became clear from the captive's
appearance, clothing and speech that he was of the noble class,
and he confessed as much to the *gesith* after the latter had given
an oath that he would not be slain. The *gesith* regretted his oath
because, as he says himself, many of his kin had fallen in that battle
and it was his duty to avenge them. He spared Imma's life but sold
him to a Frisian slaver in London.[7]

The first implication of this story is that a social gulf already
separated the skilled fighting-man from the peasant; manner of
speech and knowledge of courteous ways betrayed the man of
superior social status. Then again the *gesith* himself was a significant
figure. He was settled on an estate, in command of a powerful
section of the royal army, and a victor in battle. He possessed a
strong kindred of fighting men, and held the power of life or
death over his captives. He was loyal to his oath, even though loyalty
meant failure to take the correct vengeance for his kinsmen.

Other references in the 'Historia Ecclesiastica' build up a similar
picture of the typical powerful noble as a holder of land. When

6 Ibid., 6.2.
7 Bede, *Hist. Eccl.*, IV, 22.

King Sigebert of Essex was assassinated, Bede considered it as jus
retribution for his failure to correct moral abuses on the part o
two *comites* (translated *gesiths* in the Old English Bede) who were hi
kinsmen; he was slain in the *ham*, that is to say the substantial estate
of one of these *comites*. In Northumbria two *comites* are said to hav
founded churches on their own estates.[8] A picture emerges from
the narrative sources of a great nobleman as a powerful militar
leader, possibly of the royal kin, settled on an estate, possessing
hall, and surrounded by retainers. If the picture is a little barbari
and heroic it is probably all the more true to life. Nor is it unlikel
that a successful *comes* would aspire even higher to kingship ove
a folk. Degrees of kinship to a royal house within six or sever
knees cannot have been too difficult to discover. In Wessex the
career of Cædwalla (685–8) shows how such a contender for the
throne might flourish, while that of Cyneheard (757) indicates tha
failure was not unknown.[9] The former contended for the kingdom
with a few companions, reigned violently and successfully for three
years, and then journeyed to Rome to receive baptism, dying there
ten days after the Pope had received him from the font; the
latter made a partially successful rebellion, surprised and slev
King Cynewulf but failed because Cynewulf's retainers would no
accept the slayer of their lord as king. The great Offa himself wa
probably responsible for a deliberate fostering of the legends tha
surrounded the first Offa who had ruled when the Angles wer
still on the Continent. Yet Offa himself claimed descent through ar
undistinguished list of Mercian princelings from Pybba, the fathe
of Penda.

The acceptance of Christianity made a great difference to the
nobility. In one of the most famous set pieces of early Englisl
history Bede tells how the witan of Northumbria deliberated ove:
the acceptance or rejection of the new faith: the most judicious o
all the arguments is put into the mouth of a certain nobleman, ar
elder, *maior natu* or *ealdorman* as he is called in the late ninth-century
translation. The established nobility looked also for a more stabl
religion. But a greater difference still was made to the kingship. I
might not be too much to say that the king was no longer regardec
merely as in the folk but as over the folk. *Populus iuxta sanctione
divinas ducendus est non sequendus*, as Alcuin wrote to Charles th
Great.[10] The bond between noble and king, originally so mucl

[8] Ibid., III, 22: and V, 4 and 5.
[9] Ibid., V, 7: A.S. Chronicle, 755 (757).
[10] Alcuin, M.G.H., *Ep. Kar. Aevi*, vol. II, p. 199.

hat between household retainer and lord, was knit more strictly
y Christian oaths. The lordship of the king and of Christ lay over
he land and the people.

As far as the person of the king was concerned, from the earliest
days when the institution of kingship was known a belief in the
ymbolic efficacy of the blood royal was held by the Germanic
eoples. *Reges e nobilitate, duces e virtute* is a text upon which many
n historical sermon has been preached.[11] On the Continent the
Merovingian farce of Chilperic III, paraded in his ox-cart on
eremonial occasions, can be explained satisfactorily only by sur-
ival of this belief among the Frankish rulers, though possibly the
npopularity of the Carolingian upstarts also played its part. In
England there are plentiful indications of this sentiment at work.
Sigebert of East Anglia was forcibly dragged from his monastic
etirement because he had formerly been a brave battle-leader. The
pecial concern of the followers of St Guthlac on his reformation
- he was a doughty leader of bandits till his twenty-fourth year –
nay be ascribed in part to his possession of the blood royal. The
areer of Ethelbald of Mercia shows how a successful leader of
a war-band might aspire to the highest honours, provided that
e had good claim to possession of royal blood. Germanic heroic
oetry is laden with belief in the supernatural force of royal kin. A
ong and honourable genealogy was a sure earnest of a successful
eign. If royal blood did not exist it could be discovered. The
Anglo-Saxon Chronicle reiterates with emphatic monotony: 'His
in goes to Cerdic.'[12]

This belief was deep-rooted in pagan practice, yet the Christian
eligion did not reject it. Indeed Christianity emphasized rather
han denied the value of the blood royal. There was good sense
ehind this attitude. It was in the interest of the Church to have
order preserved, to seek for legitimate authority. This was so not
only because of the teachings of the Church but also for solid
economic reasons. The Church quickly became a substantial land-
owner, and seventh-century records are studded with references
o munificent gifts; its first material consideration was to protect
ts estates and the lands of the faithful from possible depredation
y bands of lawless young men. Established legitimate kingship
offered its greatest hope of success, accompanied too by established

---

[1] Tacitus, *Germania*, c. vii.
[2] *Hist. Eccl.*, III, 18; *Felix's Life of Saint Guthlac*, ed. B. Colgrave, c. xix, p. 83,
and *passim* for the early career of Ethelbald; A.S. Chronicle, 786, etc. The phrase
tself, 'kin goes to Cerdic', may be a product of the time of Ethelwulf.

legitimate nobility. The ability to exercise lordship over freemen
developed into the most obvious mark of nobility, and particularly
as the Church passed out of the initial converting stage, it became
increasingly desirable to ensure peaceful succession on the part
of the Church to estates and power in a locality. The strong and
colourful anathemas in the more prolix land-charters have more
than a mere antiquarian flavour; they state in the most picturesque
terms the ecclesiastical desire for security of land-tenure, bringing
down on the heads of those who fail to observe the terms of
the settlement the punishment of Judas and the sacrilegious Jew
who mocked Christ, that they may burn in 'eternal confusion in
the devouring flames of blazing torments in punishment without
end'.[13]

The law-codes that have survived from this early period indicate
how king, nobility and church were becoming more settled, though
in a context which naturally laid emphasis on more antique Germanic social features, particularly on blood-right. There are four
main codes which purport to come from the seventh century, and
though they survive only in later copies, so that some measure of
alteration is not excluded, they appear in essence to be genuine
enough.

The laws of Ethelbert start with a clause that fitted the new
Church into the society of wergeld, compensations for injuries
and fines for infringement of rights. The laws of Hlothhere and
Eadric of Kent (673–85) – the obscurity of the kings is in itself an
indication of the authenticity of the document – had a special concern with homicide, theft, legal procedure and trading regulation.
The laws of Wihtræd (694) of Kent dealt mostly with ecclesiastical
affairs, while the last and most important of these documents, the
laws of Ine (688–94), provided in its seventy-six clauses the first
deep insight into the social structure of Wessex. Although the 'Law
of Ine' survive only in a recension prepared at the court of King
Alfred, archaic features survive, and there is detailed evidence
particularly in the preface, to establish the stated provenance as
accurate.

These laws have enough in common to give a picture of aristocratic society in what was still a heroic age. Special privilege
accorded the nobles included higher payment for infringement
of their house peace, of their own personal surety, of the lives and
property of their dependants and above all for their own persons

[13] *C.S.* 1344, *E.H.D.* I, p. 549.

A wergeld was the payment made on the death of a man by the slayer and the slayer's kindred. It varied according to the rank of the victim and was normally paid to the kindred of the slain according to set customary divisions. The children enjoyed the same wergeld protection as the father, though the wife continued to enjoy her own kin-right. It was so important a mark of social status that the payments became the legal terms used to describe the major ranks of society; the laws of Ine, as was mentioned above, recognized twelve-hundred-shilling men, six-hundred-shilling men and two-hundred-shilling men, together with a variety of payments for Welshmen. Each folk possessed its own rules for payment, and although one can point to general similarities in organization it is difficult to generalize for the whole country, particularly in the early period when legal information is so heavily weighted in favour of the south, of Wessex and Kent. In Kent the *ceorl's* wergeld of one hundred Kentish shillings, each of which was worth twenty silver coins, was a higher price than was paid for a West Saxon *ceorl*, two hundred shillings of four or five silver pennies to the shilling, and there are other indications that a Kentish *ceorl* was more prosperous than his westerly namesake. The price paid for a nobleman was however much nearer, if not actually, an exact equivalence. The *eorlcundman* of Kent was a three-hundred-shilling man; that is to say six thousand silver *sceattas* were to be paid in the case of his death. If the later West Saxon ratio of five 'pennies' to the shilling were in force, the equivalence would be exact: even if there were no more than four pence to the shilling there is greater uniformity among the dead noblemen than among the dead *ceorls*.[14]

It must be remembered that the payment of wergeld represents a considerable advance on the blood-feud itself, and as such received active support from the Church. A splendid example is given by Bede, when he tells of the intervention of Archbishop Theodore who brought about a reconciliation between the Mercian and the Northumbrian kings after what is called the 'customary heavy payment'. In 678 the young Northumbrian prince Aelfwine had been killed in battle against his own brother-in-law Ethelred of Mercia. Before Theodore's action the stage was set for a classic situation in the German heroic style with dramatic tension playing around the Mercian queen, Osthryth, whose husband had slain her

---

[14] H. M. Chadwick, *Studies on Anglo-Saxon Institutions*, Cambridge, 1905, pp. 113–14, and p. 109.

own brother. But compensation paid to the elder brother and head of the kin, Ecgfrith, King of Northumbria, bought off the avenging spear.[15] It was probably more customary for a feud to follow it course: a violent age settled its problems violently.

The method of payment of wergeld presents special problems The law-codes assessed the payments consistently in currency, and there is reason to believe that payment was made in coin: the Crondall hoard for example of a hundred-and-one gold coins one of which has been shown to be spurious, looks suspiciously like a portion of a wergeld payment. But mixed payments in coin and in kind were still common. According to Ine a man paying a wergeld, could include in each of the 'hundreds' a slave a coat-of-mail and a sword.[16] The one hundred shillings of the Kentish *ceorl's* wergeld may originally have signified payment of one hundred oxen. Indeed some would go further and see in the difference between the Kentish and the West Saxon shilling a difference in reckoning between an economy where the ox was the unit and an economy where the sheep was the unit in which important transactions were reckoned.[17]

What happened to the noble and his kindred in the event of violent death was not the only information given by these law-codes concerning noble privilege. Special protection was given to them personally, to their houses and to their dependants. Under the title of *borgbryce*, the breaking of surety, or *mundbryce*, the breaking of protective rights, a whole series of penalties and compensations was graded according to rank. Whoever was present on an expedition made for the purpose of killing a man was to pay compensation for the expedition according to the wergeld of the slain man: fifty shillings was demanded if the wergeld was two hundred shillings and one is to proceed with the same proportion in the case of the nobler born. A man's standing in law, the value of his oath the gravity of offence against him, and the culpability of his own offences depended in large part upon the stratum of society into which he had been born. The wergeld itself is so much a mark of status that it is used freely by those who drew up the codes almost as a unit of account. He who was accused of taking part in the raid of any army had to redeem himself with his wergeld, or with an oath of value equivalent to his wergeld.[18]

---

15 *Hist. Eccl.*, IV, 21.
16 Ine 54.1.
17 H. M. Chadwick, op. cit., pp. 155–60.
18 Ine 34, 34.1: 15.

On one matter of considerable social significance valuable information is given by the laws of Ine; that is on the authority of a nobleman over his dependants and over his estate. Clause 50 of his code reads: 'If a gesithborn man intercedes with the king or the king's ealdorman or with his lord for members of his household, slaves or freemen, he, the gesith, has no right to any fines, because he would not previously at home restrain them from ill-doing.'

There are ambiguities in this difficult clause – it is not certain to whom the phrase 'his lord' refers, though the natural reading would suggest the *gesith's* lord – but it is clear that the nobleman has the double duty of preventing ill-doing on the part of his household, apparently by some form of judicial procedure which would involve a right to fines, and of interceding for them in the public courts, if such ill-deeds should be performed. Knowledge of such public courts is scanty. Presumably they owed much of their authority to the dignitary who presided over them, king, ealdorman or great lord. Yet it would be too rash to deprive them of all semblance of the traditional folk-moot. There were matters that demanded interpretation by wise men, by elders of the moots. At the highest level of the kingdom such men were drawn together in an assembly to give special sanction to the promulgation of dooms. In 'Beowulf' itself the good king is said to have distributed things to young and old, except the folk-share and the lives of men, that is to say, presumably, the land and people in general upon which the well-being of the kingdom depended.[19] It is likely that the well-being would be looked to, possibly with some informality, by the elders of the kingdom. Within limits the powers of the greatest lords may have been of a somewhat primitive type dependent on their princely rank, perhaps even on their ceremonial high seats or thrones, ultimately derived from a royal source. But the authority was not arbitrary, and the dooms themselves show anxiety at every turn to define the custom of the community. There is no need to believe in primitive democracy in order to recognize that the free farmers of a community are likely to have met at a traditional meeting place, an ancient barrow, a great stone, a central point on the trackways covering a district, from the earliest days of settlement when they wished to deal with problems of a military and of a legal nature that would affect the whole community. Well-attested analogy from Scandinavia, apart from the somewhat romantic accounts of Tacitus, speaks

---

[19] 'Beowulf', l. 73: *buton folcscare ond feorum gumena*, a very difficult phrase, probably bearing only a general significance.

against disbelief in folk-moots. But even so it must be admitted that the direct authority of king over community and of lord over dependant is much more in evidence from the law-codes than in the power of moots.

There is at this stage no simple antithesis to be made between nobility by blood and nobility by service. The nobility appears perhaps more entrenched in their noble kindreds than later in the Anglo-Saxon period. Service to the king remained one of the chief means of ennoblement, but kingship itself had not at this stage advanced to the state where the semi-permanent links between noble and king so characteristic of the post-Alfredian Age could be forged. There was already some differentiation which may be teased out of the legal codes: a differentiation between status and office. It may be significant that when dealing with infringements of the peace the laws of Ine (cl. 6) give the following list of penalties: for fighting in the king's house, forfeiture of all possessions and the question of life or death to rest with the king; for fighting in a church (*mynster*) a hundred and twenty shillings compensation; in the house of an ealdorman or other important councillor sixty shillings compensation and sixty shillings fine; in the house of a *gafolgelda* (rent-payer) or *gebur* one hundred and twenty shillings as a fine and six shillings to the *gebur*; in the midst of open country one hundred and twenty shillings as a fine. The nobleman as such did not enter the picture. It may be that the nobleman was well able to look after himself, or it may be that the scale of compensation between *ceorl* and nobleman was well understood. Alfred (cl. 39.2) in connection with the same offences stated that the compensation due to the six-hundred man was to be three times that due to the *ceorl*, and that the compensation to a twelve-hundred man was to be twice as much again. The compensation was to grow with the wergeld, as Alfred himself said (cl. 11.5). But the interesting feature of this clause of Ine is the emphasis on the fine of one hundred and twenty shillings in the case of the lesser men, and only sixty shillings in the case of the great officers. In rudimentary form the principle appears which is to be of such vast importance in English social development, namely that maintenance of the peace is primarily a matter for the king and his officers.

3. FROM CONVERSION TO THE REIGN OF ALFRED

During the period between the writing of the 'Historia Ecclesiastica' and the age of Alfred it is difficult – for lack of survival of a

Mercian law-code – to analyse this question of who were the nobles and what their functions. Some help is given to us by charters which begin to flow in considerable number from the age of Mercian supremacy, from Ethelbald and from Offa. To judge from charters which have survived embodying gifts of estates to the lay servants of Mercian kings, *meo comite* or *meo duce atque comite*, some advance was made during the eighth century towards stabilizing a nobility on the land, dependent directly on royal favour.[20] Many of these ministerial grants are made with reversion to monastic houses – else they would not have survived – and one remembers Bede's own admonition in regard to the Northumbrian situation that land which should have been used to provide the royal host with adequate resources was being squandered on monastic houses not of the finest reputation. Others among the grants are in the nature of concealed purchases. Noblemen paid the king for charters which would exempt them from the payment of the royal *feorm* and other dues. One set of charters preserved by the Worcester house is particularly revealing for a political as well as for a purely social reason. As late as 770 a charter was promulgated by Uhtred, *regulus* of the Hwicce, sub-king of his own people, with, it is true, the approval of King Offa, the Mercian overlord; but he and his sons subscribe also as *subreguli* and are clearly merging into the mass of nobles, *comites* and *ministri*, who surround the warrior Mercian king.[21] An earlier grant, in the reign of Ethelbald, had been made *ministro meo valde fideli qui est de stirpe non ignobili prosapia regali gentis. Hwicciorum Osredo*.[22] Perhaps directly as a result of the long reign of Offa, perhaps merely because of the type of charter material that has survived, the impression is given that these nobles in attendance on the king, joining in their subscriptions with clergy drawn from all over England, south of the Humber, in the greatest of the assemblies, are in process of acquiring more of a corporate and an official nature during this eighth century. The germination of the triumph of office over status may have taken place at the court of the king who, until recently, was least regarded of the great Anglo-Saxon monarchs.

In one respect an event of wide significance for the future of English kingship took place during the later days of King Offa.

---

[20] *C.S.* 146, 154, 157, etc.
[21] Ibid. 202, 203, 205, 218, 220, 223, 231, 232; *E.H.D.* I, pp. 502–3 (*C.S.* 203): Uhtred's own brother, Ealdred, subscribes as a *subregulus* to this charter.
[22] Ibid. 165.

Basing his action on Carolingian precedent, the Mercian king had his son Ecgfrith consecrated to the kingship, the first of the English kings so to receive Christian anointing. The early and tragic death of Ecgfrith only five months after his accession made the event of less significance than might otherwise have been the case, and there is no proof that the precedent was followed immediately in Mercia or in Wessex.[23] Not until the tenth century do the West Saxons, in this as in so much else, prove themselves true heirs of the Mercian kings.

The first seventy years of the ninth century was a period of little obvious progress in English political and social development. Evidence for the status of the nobility remains sporadic until with the reign of Alfred (871–99), a further period presents itself in which the material is plentiful. A mass of literature in the vernacular has survived from the reign, and a positive attempt was made to write an intelligible, precise prose in the works of translation prepared on the order of the King by scholars such as Asser from Wales, Grimbald from Flanders and John the Old Saxon, to say nothing of Wærferth, Bishop of Worcester, and Plegmund, Alfred's own mass-priest and afterwards Archbishop of Canterbury. The translation of Bede's 'Ecclesiastical History' is particularly informative: the word *gesith* still survived in it to describe nobles settled on their estates and somewhat remote from the court. Indeed, the term as such survived still later, and twelfth-century law-books translate the *gesiðcund* of Ine's laws as *siðcund*. In Northumbria there is also some tenth-century evidence for the survival of the term in law. But the type of nobleman characterized as *gesith* in the Old English Bede rapidly disappears under the joint effect of the Viking invasion and the resurgence of Christian kingship in the House of Wessex. It has been suggested that their independence could not be sanctioned in such perilous times.[24]

Already in Alfred's day the most common terms for nobility were *ealdorman* and *thegn*. Whenever reference was made to the nobility corporately in relation to the king, *ealdormen and thegns* was the phrase that came naturally to the writer's pen. They appear to have been more closely bound to the king than were the nobles in the earlier records, and this impression is borne out, too, by the legal records. In part the political conditions of the age alone were

[23] Ceolwulf of Mercia was consecrated king by Archbishop Wulfred on 17 September, 822; *E.H.D.* I, pp. 514–5; see above, p. 165 and p. 180.
[24] Liebermann II, *siðcund*; Norðleoda Laga, c. 11; H. R. Loyn, 'Gesiths and Thegns in Anglo-Saxon England', *E.H.R.*, 1955, pp. 529–49.

sufficient to account for this development. Egbert and Aethelwulf had built up the West Saxon dynasty, so that its prestige rivalled that of the Mercian house. The epic struggle with the Danes forced coalescence on the Anglo-Saxons. Under the inspired leadership of Alfred full advantage was taken of this, and in his reign came the pivotal point in the history of the Anglo-Saxon nobility when the monarchy proved of sufficient prestige to insist that duties took precedence over rights. To some measure throughout these centuries the same problem faced all rulers: how to provide for loyal retainers and how to keep them loyal. It was only too easy for a retainer who had received his reward to lose touch with the ruler who had rewarded him. Centuries of secular and religious effort were needed in order to bring about a satisfactory solution of the problem. Emphasis on regularity and a Christian conception of lordship provided the most realistic means of approach, and both forces were at work in the desperate days of Alfred's reign when the functional nature of the nobility was strengthened and its ornamental nature fell away. The ealdormen were royal officers, responsible for leadership of the army and good government in the localities. The thegns, though the term was still relatively unspecialized, were predominantly ministerial in nature. The whole spirit of the age, as reflected in the educational programme at Alfred's court, made nonsense of all idea of a nobility that would not fulfil its proper function of military defence, and of a monarch who would not be essentially a good shepherd to his flock, a protector of his people.

Indeed there is much more than mere theory to the ideas of Christian lordship that one finds, for example, so strongly expressed in the prologue to the laws of Alfred. The age was violent, but hardheadedness can lead to as gross distortion of the truth as can excessive reliance on the word of ecclesiastics. In moments of crisis when pagan Danes were on the attack a good soldier might seem a sounder asset than a good theory of Christian lordship, but of course the two were not incompatible. The Christian religion provided the most potent binding force known to Western society in the ninth century, and this was particularly true when the ruler was as good a Christian as Alfred. In him more than in any other rulers of the period, even the great Charles himself, we see the ideal of Christian kingship: a successful defender of Christian peoples against pagan onslaught and also an assiduous supporter of scholarship and of Christian missionary effort. And in order to make the basis of his authority better appreciated he drew with great wisdom upon the work of Gregory, the fortitude of Boethius, the world picture of Orosius and the theology of St Augustine of Hippo, from whose works he had sound and workmanlike translations made at his West Saxon court.[25]

4. THE NOBILITY IN LATE ANGLO-SAXON ENGLAND

As one consequence of the work of Alfred the Great, after the success of the dynasty and the gradual reconquest and absorption of the Danish settlements, there was a tremendous outburst of legislative activity in the course of which it is possible to trace a conception of nobility transformed by Christian ideals. Fortunately there have also survived a large number of charters and, from the turn of the eleventh century, a bulky corpus of homiletic writing that deepen our knowledge of the thought of the period. The pointers that emerge from this somewhat amorphous body of material lead to a positive conclusion that lordship by service was gaining ground on the idea of lordship by blood. This is not to deny that, to the end of our period and beyond, kinship played a very important part in determining social position. Wergeld remained an important test of status. Alfred and his successors continued to refer to twelve-hundred men, the nobility proper, to six-hundred men (who disappeared from the Anglo-Saxon legal records after Alfred's day) and two-hundred men, the ordinary, but not so common, freeman. 'I was of high kin among the Mercians', says Aelfwine at the battle of Maldon; but he adds to his boast, 'my grandfather was ealdorman', that is, in modern terms, held the highest secular office under the Crown.[26] But even through, and in some respects especially because of, the second Danish invasion and the conquest of England by Canute, the Anglo-Saxon noble developed into one of two groups, *ealdormen* or *thegns*, distinguished primarily by function and both in the highest sense of the term officers of the king.

The ealdorman is the simplest to deal with, and there is much information concerning his activities. Already in Alfred's day he was very much of a king's man, though in origin he may have

---

[25] See below, pp. 290–3.
[26] 'Battle of Maldon', lines 216–19; *E.H.D.* I, p. 323.

been a descendant, or successor, of a royal line. He was a royal officer placed in charge of a definite province, often corresponding to one particular shire. Over the shire he had rights as a royal deputy, summoning the shire levies and leading them to battle. He possessed subordinate officers, reeves, to whom routine duties could be delegated. In the course of the tenth century it became customary for several shires to pass under the control of a single ealdorman, and great figures like Athelstan Half-King, or Ethelweard the Chronicler, or Byrhtnoth of Maldon became the type of great magnate-ealdorman, patrons of learning and benefactors of monasteries. In Northumbria, in particular, they possessed vice-regal powers after the expulsion of the last independent king in 954. The English kings were happy, when they were able, to appoint men experienced in Anglo-Danish affairs, preferably with a territorial stake south of the Humber, to high office in the north. Ethelred appointed such a one in Aelfhelm, 993–1006, a Mercian nobleman, brother of the immensely wealthy thegn, Wulfric Spot. He was styled ealdorman, whereas his predecessor Thored had earlier borne the title *eorl*. But it is a measure of Ethelred's failure that Aelfhelm was murdered and his two sons blinded, apparently at the King's own command.[27] These ealdormen were drawing apart from the rest of the nobility. Effective extension of thegnage together with the effective evolution of the hundred were making the ealdorman's functions more exclusively military and ceremonial, though it was still customary throughout the tenth century for them to be very active in the law courts.

The accession of Canute saw a fresh twist, terminological and functional, given to the office. In English England the term *eorl* (after the early Kentish law-codes) was confined to use in poetry and in the compound phrase, *eorl* and *ceorl*. But Danish cognates brought about a revival in popularity and, under Danish influence, *eorl* replaced *ealdorman*, the latter term retaining its force only as senior, an elder, and as such developing into an alderman of a town. The new earls, as Sir Frank Stenton says, were akin to the provincial viceregents, and not only the routine but many of the principal legal and administrative functions in the shire passed to the shire-reeves, the later sheriffs.[28] The earls became of such

---

[27] D. Whitelock, 'The Dealings of the Kings of England with Northumbria in the Tenth and Eleventh Centuries', *The Anglo-Saxons*, ed. P. Clemoes, London, 1959, pp. 80–1.
[28] F. M. Stenton, *Anglo-Saxon England*, pp. 414–6.

importance that the greatest of them, Harold Godwinson, became king in that ill-starred year 1066.

Of the constitutional controversies surrounding the position of the earls there is no need to speak at length here. They did not appear to constitute a major danger to the monarchy, though the careers of Godwin and Harold show the ever-present temptation open to the overmighty subject. Perhaps socially the massing of landed wealth by these *eorlisc* families, particularly when accompanied by an attempt to canalize the loyalties of the local thegns, represents something of a disruptive force to the community of England as a whole, though much of this landed wealth remained comital in nature; the earl was in the last resort an officer who could be appointed and removed. There is no sign that the English *ealdordom* or earldom, was developing into a virtually independent principality bound by only nominal ties to a royal overlord, as was happening in the duchies and counties of contemporary France.

Indeed the pre-eminence of the monarchy, for all the political vicissitudes involving changes of dynasty, is the outstanding feature that strikes the careful student of eleventh-century England. To all who wrote or legislated, the king was supremely the symbol of the nation. It is sometimes forgotten how many sides of the life of the community were brought together under royal surveillance: the coinage, supervision of general administration of justice through shire and hundred and tithing, provision of good title to land by means of charters, and protection of the Church. It might be said of England in the tenth and eleventh centuries that king and community grew together. There is evidence of strong loyalty to the monarchy, and the Church helped to encourage this feeling. During the tenth century coronation rites were introduced that made the coronation of Edgar a splendid and symbolic moment in the life of the nation. The promises given by King Edgar at his coronation reappeared in the Coronation Charter of Henry I; indeed in essentials the ritual of this Anglo-Saxon ceremony remains the core around which has been constructed the elaborate detail of modern coronations.[29] Homilists gave full play to their theological ideas. Aelfric in his Easter Sunday homily provided a classic statement of what might be taken as the pre-Hildebrandine notion of kingship: 'No man can make himself king, but the people has the choice to choose as king whom they please; but after he is

[29] See also below, p. 241.

consecrated as king, he then has dominion over the people, and they cannot shake his yoke from their necks'.[30]

The king was expected to rule, and also to define law. Alfred said as much when he declared that in framing his code he chose what seemed to him to be the most needful of old laws: the others he set to one side. Abstractions based on distinction between old law and new law seem somewhat fanciful in face of this statement of purpose and evidence of action.

The Old English kingship had therefore a theocratic element, with the strength and the weakness that such a position implies. It is even possible that some clerkly play was made with imperial titles in an attempt to interpret the authority of the victorious West Saxon dynasty.[31] There are times when the contrast between theoretical claim and actual practice provides a warning against too abstract an approach. Edmund legislated against violence, yet died under the assassin's knife. Ethelred, under the guidance of Archbishop Wulfstan, claimed the full theocratic position, yet the Chronicle records a pitiful tale of treachery and duplicity. But the constant reiteration of the special powers of the king from generation to generation had a powerful effect upon the institutions of English nobility, and in no respect is this more apparent than in the firm relationship evolved in these centuries between kingship and thegnage.

The term *thegn*, like so many others that later come to fame and fortune, originally meant servant. In the Alfredian translations it could still bear that simple meaning. But as the tenth and eleventh centuries progressed so did its significance undergo a semantic change. Thegn came to mean more exclusively a nobleman, possessed of a special wergeld, a twelve-hundred shilling man. Yet some of the ministerial attributes of an exalted servant still clung to him, and homilists could write of thegns of bishops or of abbots where no more than an equivalent of the Latin *minister* was meant. He no longer had to be a personal servant in attendance at court, though arrangements by Alfred at his own court suggest that every thegn at some period saw service in the royal presence. Asser tells how the noble thegns of the royal household served at court for one month out of three, spending the other two months at their own homes, seeing to their own affairs. An eleventh-century

---

[30] *Aelfric's Catholic Homilies*, vol. I, p. 212; *E.H.D.* I, pp. 925–6.
[31] H. R. Loyn, 'The Imperial Style of the Tenth Century Anglo-Saxon Kings', *History*, 1955; see also E. John, 'An Alleged Worcester Charter', *Bulletin of the John Rylands Library*, 1958.

compilation placed an office in the king's hall among the attributes expected of a man aspiring to thegnhood.[32] But the law codes generally put much more emphasis on his obligations in his locality. He is normally a land-owner, or at very least, a potential land-owner. Five hides came to be regarded as the minimum holding of a thegn. He was a key figure in the local assemblies, in the shires and in the hundreds. It was his function to give a lead to the populace in military matters, and in the general preservation of peace. His oath was worth six times that of an ordinary ceorl and, in claiming exculpation from some offences, the oath of at least one thegn was obligatory. In part of the Danelaw what amounted to a jury of twelve leading thegns had to be summoned in the wapentake. They were to swear, with the reeve, that they would accuse no innocent man nor conceal any guilty one, and they were to seize men against whom the reeve had been taking action.[33] The general impression is given by the law-codes that responsibility for the maintenance of good order lay theoretically on the king, and in practice on his thegns in their localities. Nor were these functions confined to public assemblies. Of more moment in some respects was the responsibility laid on them for their estates and for their dependants. The grant of rights of jurisdiction, of sake and soke, grow frequent in the eleventh century. Even more than the great immunists such as the Abbot of Ely with his $8\frac{1}{2}$ hundreds and the Abbot of Bury St Edmunds with his $5\frac{1}{2}$ hundreds in Suffolk, the thegn exercising sake and soke in the royal name provides the backbone of the forces struggling for law and order in the community. The thegn retained his military importance: at Maldon and Hastings he fought around his lord in typical heroic fashion. But while Alfred had lamented in a telling aside that 'we had not thegns now such as there were then', the epic sentiment applied under his successors to the thegn as lord and head of an estate rather than simply as a fighting-man.[34] Loyalty to a lord had been a consistent theme of epic poetry. From the reign of Alfred it became the cardinal moving spirit in the moulding of society. You shall fight for your kinsman when he is attacked except against your lord: that we do not permit, said a law of Alfred.[35] Under his successors the lordless man was treated as more and more of an anomaly. Society was held together by bonds of loyalty from man

---

[32] *Asser's Life of Alfred*, c. 100: *E.H.D.* I, p. 301. Geþyncðo, 2, *E.H.D.* I, p. 468.
[33] Alfred and Guthrum 3; III Ethelred 3.1.
[34] *King Alfred's Orosius*, ed. H. Sweet, p. 192.
[35] Alfred 42.6.

to lord and from lord who was also a thegn to king. The bonds were at times inclined to slip; they lacked the earthy solidity of the feudal order. But the sanction of solemn hold-oaths and the teachings of the Church helped to keep them in place. The west of Europe generally in the tenth and eleventh centuries knew a state of society where men sought lords, and lords sought men. In no place was this so marked as in England, and in no area was the royal control of the powers so effective. The *thegn* was the key person, the royal servant in the localities, the local lord. When the Normans came to build their feudal state they built upon a foundation that had been well laid.

To say what the thegns did as fighting men and local lords and how they fitted into society is one thing; to say who they were and what manner of life they led is quite another, and more difficult, matter. The thegns were unquestionably members of a class, conscious that they were a class. In function, status, and wergeld they were different from the ordinary freeman, the *ceorl*, though as we have already seen a simple ceorl took a prominent part in the battle of Maldon, fighting to the death by the side of his fallen lord, in precisely the same fashion and with precisely the same spirit as the thegns. Thegnly rank was heritable and it could also be lost for cowardice or betrayal of one's lord, for promoting injustice or for pronouncing false judgements. But the class was not exclusive. Men could aspire to thegn-right, and the economic qualifications for the rank are laid down by an eleventh-century compilation: 'If a ceorl prospered, that he possessed fully five hides of his own, a church and kitchen, a bell and a castle-gate, a seat, special office in the king's hall, then was he henceforth entitled to the rights of a thegn'.[36]

A merchant who made a trip overseas three times at his own expense was also said to be worthy of thegn-right.[37] Corroborative evidence for this mobility in society comes from an extract from Wulfstan's writing where the homilist stated that a thegn might be made an eorl by the king's gift or a ceorl a thegn by the eorl's gift. The possibility is even put forward that a thrall might become a thegn. He is using these illustrations from life as simple evidence for his case that members of the clerical order should be given their due rank. A shepherd (David) could become a king; a fisherman

---

[36] 'Battle of Maldon', line 256; þiegenboren, Dunsæte 5; II Canute 70.1 and 15a.1; Geþyncðo, 2, *E.H.D.* I, p. 468, see p. 224, above.
[37] Geþyncðo, 6.

(Peter) could become a bishop.[38] It is refreshing to find Wulfstan accepting these possibilities of advancement, unlike Langland with his sophisticated lament that bondsmen's bairns be made bishops though Wulfstan himself had in mind the Pauline text, *sive servus sive liber, omnes in Christo unum sumus.*

Such an elevation in rank would imply some public ceremony, when one considers the obligations assumed together with the thegnly rank. Details of the investiture have not survived; possibly it involved the handing over of a ceremonial weapon, or the laying of the sword in the lap of the king or his representative, the ealdorman. It may even have involved a more elaborate bestowal of arms upon the new thegn. Canute gives an account of the heriot demanded on the death of a thegn:

> The heriots of king's thegns who stand closest to him shall be: four horses, two saddled and two unsaddled, and two swords and four spears and as many shields and a helmet and byrnies and fifty mancuses of gold.
>
> The heriot of ordinary [*medeme*] thegns shall be a horse, its trappings and his weapons or his *healsfang* in Wessex, and in Mercia £2, and in East Anglia £2.
>
> And among the Danes the heriot of a king's thegn who possesses rights of jurisdiction is £4;
>
> and if he stands in a more intimate relationship to the king; two horses, one saddled, the other unsaddled, one sword, two spears, two shields, and fifty mancuses of gold.
>
> For him who has less and is of lower position the heriot shall be £2.[39]

The list suggests that the king will have found the military equipment for those in regular attendance on him, though this, in the more complicated society of late Anglo-Saxon England, is only a part of the story. A bishop could find his own heriot in horses and weapons.[40] From the immediate point of view the lesser men, paying comparatively small sums as heriot, yet powerful enough in their locality, are even more interesting. Ethelred was empowered to state that he alone had jurisdiction over his thegns.[41]

Perhaps the best indication of the type of man a thegn would be, particularly in the more heavily manorialized south and west, comes from the *Rectitudines Singularum Personarum*, in a passage

[38] D. Whitelock, *E.H.D.* I, p. 59. M. Angström, *Studies in Old English Manuscripts,* Uppsala, 1937, p. 125; K. Jost, *Die 'Institutes of Polity, Civil and Ecclesiastical'*, Berne, 1959, pp. 256–7; cf. *Grið*, 21.2, Liebermann I, p. 472.
[39] II Canute 71.1–71.5; *E.H.D.* I, p. 465.
[40] D. Whitelock, *Anglo-Saxon Wills*, no. i.
[41] III Ethelred 11.

already referred to in an earlier chapter. The thegn was to be
worthy of his bookland, that is of land held by charter which
he could grant by will to whomsoever he pleased, and he was to
perform in return three things for his land: *fyrdfæreld, burhbot* and
brycgeweorc, that is to say military service, repair of fortifications and
bridge-works.[42] At Rochester, an elaborate scheme was in force to
ensure that the bridge was kept in good repair, the responsibility
for the maintenance of the various sections of the bridge falling on
the great estates of the neighbourhood.[43] In practice the thegn was
the agent through whose actions royal concern with peace, order
and ease of communication in a rural society, could be expressed.
Ideally the thegn was an active noble warrior, settled on an estate,
responsible for a variety of honourable services to the king.

5. THE MANNER OF LIFE OF THE NOBILITY

On the manner of life of the nobility information grows towards
the end of the period, and particularly as the series of tenth- and
eleventh-century Anglo-Saxon wills tells of the possessions of these
nobles. Perhaps inevitably there is a tendency to take too static a
view of their life, to see in the eleventh-century thegn the seventh-
century epic hero in his hall surrounded by his retainers, and to
see in the prosperous landowners, busy in the moots, with their
passion for hunting and their town-houses, the *gesiths* of the age
of the Conversion. Our picture throughout the whole period is
coloured by the work of the epic poets. They emphasize the heroic
virtues, military valour, feasting – and boasting – in hall, barbaric
splendour, gold-adorned goblets and jewel-adorned warriors. The
effect is somewhat overpowering, and the impression is left that the
nobleman's life is a steady progression from feast to battle and from
battle to feast – if fate so wills it. It would be wrong to reject utterly
the joy in arms which throughout the Middle Ages remained the
mark of a noble class. But in fact by the eleventh century the thegn
was as much a landlord as a warrior, as much a supervisor of reeves
as a cleaver of skulls. As Professor Whitelock says 'the joys of hall'
cannot have played a disproportionate part in his everyday life.[44]

[42] *E.H.D.* II, p. 813. See above, pp. 196–7.
[43] A. J. Robertson, *Anglo-Saxon Charters*, no. lii: a document which may be post-
Conquest or which may have been drawn up originally in the tenth century.
[44] *The Beginnings of English Society*, p. 92.

The royal court set the pattern for noble life. Earls and the most prosperous of the thegns modelled their existence on it whenever that was possible. Further down in the social scale, it was impossible for the lesser thegn to match the peripatetic exploits of his betters, but even he would try to establish his fortified residence, his hall surrounded by outbuildings used as storehouses and as sleeping quarters. The king himself, accompanied by great officers, chamberlain, dish-thegns, butlers and the like, still to the end of the period received part of his dues in kind. The *firma unius noctis* was a well-known and heavy burden, sometimes compounded for but sometimes not. The West Saxon dynasty spent much of its routine time in the favoured counties of Wiltshire Somerset and Dorset, as the profusion of boroughs and mints in these shires tells. To the north a clearer light has been shed on royal life in Bernicia by the excavations at Yeavering. A hall of traditional rectangular shape, much built on and added to, has been discovered, surrounded by smaller buildings all of wood and in their day stoutly made. There are sensational features about Yeavering, above all the uncovering of what appears to be a formal site for a folk-moot and of buildings that may have been Christian churches, but the halls themselves, to judge from their ground-plans, seem very much as might be expected from the description in 'Beowulf'. The hall would be furnished with fixed benches and movable trestle tables. The benches could be covered with pillows and used as sleeping quarters for retainers in hall. Estates throughout the land would have a centre very much on this model. From 'Beowulf' it is learned how labour would be recruited for the building of a great hall, from far and wide throughout the kingdom.[45] In the Cynewulf/Cyneheard episode in the Anglo-Saxon Chronicle, the king was trapped in one such *burh*, or fortified enclosure: his retainers were apparently in the hall and he was surprised in one of the smaller bowers where he had slept with his mistress.[46] The whole complex of buildings was surrounded by a stockade and the name *burh*, before and after it came to apply to the new towns of the tenth century, was used to describe the fortified enclosure. By the end of the period building in stone was known, particularly in the towns and where stone was easily available. Domesday Book shows a land where halls, *aulae*, were commonplace throughout the land. Indeed the possession

[45] 'Beowulf', lines 67–9, and 74–6.
[46] A.S. Chronicle, 755 (757).

of an *aula* was the mark of a thegn; in Nottinghamshire there
were ten thegns at Eaton, six thegns at Carlton, Godric and six
other thegns at Headon, some with minute estates valued at only a
couple of shillings, but all possessing their *aulae*.[47] It was probable,
too, that any noble of substance would possess a town-house, for
business purposes as much as for social purposes, as a storehouse
or as a meeting-place if he journeyed from one of his estates to
another. Some of the nobles were rich in landed possessions, and
had estates scattered through many shires. They and their officers
needed halting-places in their travels around their possessions just
as did the king on his larger scale.

As far as movable possessions are concerned, the Anglo-Saxon
wills suggest great wealth on the part of some of the ealdormen and thegns. They, or their widows, disposed of precious
possessions, fine clothes, jewels, tapestries, a remarkable amount
of gold. Women were often wealthy and quite able to dispose of
their own wealth. Precious cups, hall-tapestries, bed-clothes and
mancuses of gold were bequeathed in women's wills. In the reign
of Ethelred, Aelfflæd, Ealdorman Byrhtnoth's widow, left a fine
tapestry, depicting her husband's career, to the monastic house
at Ely.[48] It is impressive to see in this connection, as so often in
Anglo-Saxon records, what a powerful role was open to Anglo-
Saxon women, from the Abbess Hild in the seventh century to the
formidable Aelfgifu (Emma) mother of Edward the Confessor, in
the eleventh century.

It certainly is true to say that there was no lack of precious goods
and weapons in later Anglo-Saxon England, and it is interesting
to see that the value is often given in terms of gold: two swords
with sheaths, two armlets of fifty mancuses of gold; a sword worth
one hundred and twenty mancuses of gold with four pounds of
silver on the sheath; two buffalo horns, a horse, a red tent, and a
gold-adorned wooden cup so that he may enlarge his armlet with
the gold – or sixteen mancuses of red gold in exchange; a scab-
bard adorned with gold worth eighty mancuses, two armlets worth
one hundred and twenty mancuses each, another armlet of thirty
mancuses, a necklace of one hundred and twenty mancuses; four
armlets of three hundred mancuses, an armlet of thirty mancuses;

---

[47] D.B. I, 284b (Ættune and Hedune), 285 (Careltune). These are discussed by F.
M. Stenton, *Types of Manorial Structure in the Northern Danelaw*, p. 22 and p. 63.
[48] *Liber Eliensis*, II, 63, ed. D. J. Stewart, p. 183: *cortinam gestis viri sui intextam atque depictam.*

an armlet worth sixty mancuses.[49] A splendour lies behind these fragments that should not be obscured by the more prosaic account of a nobleman regulating local affairs, prominent in local moots taking his pleasure in hawking and hunting.

The emphasis, naturally stronger in women's wills than in men's on fine stuffs and linen cloths and bed-furnishings might at first suggest a material poverty, since such ordinary possessions should not require the sanction of expensive testamentary documents. Wynflæd left to Eadgifu two chests and inside them her best bed-curtain and a linen covering and all the bed-clothes that go with it, black tunics and veils, chests and a spring box, books and such small things.[50] But such bequests show rather the special nature of certain possessions; a will, after all, had as its prime purpose the successful transmission of landed wealth; it may be supposed that the movable property dealt with in such formal and expensive documents was the most valuable in terms of money or of sentiment.

Perhaps more vividly than any generalized statements, an examination of the will of one of the highest of the nobility will help to bring out the wealth of a great Anglo-Saxon household. In 1015, at an early age, Prince Athelstan died, the son of King Ethelred and brother of Edmund Ironside. After gifts for the redemption of his soul and that of his father, he stated that his penally enslaved men acquired in the course of jurisdiction were to be freed. To Christ and St Peter he commended his body and gave two estates, Adderbury, bought from his father for two hundred mancuses of gold and five pounds of silver, and Marlow, bought for two hundred and fifty mancuses. To the King he left most of his estate, a silver-hilted sword which belonged to Ulfketel, a coat of mail which Morcar had, 'a horse Thurbrand gave me and a white horse Leofwine gave me'; to his brother the sword that King Offa (presumably the great Mercian) owned, another sword, a *brand*, a silver-plated trumpet and his estates from which one day's food rent and one hundred pence were to go to Ely, and one hundred poor people fed. In default of this obligation to Ely, the estates were to be forfeit to the monastic house. Then followed more bequests: Weston to his foster-mother, bought from Ethelred for two hundred and fifty mancuses of gold; to Eadric

---

[49] D. Whitelock, *Anglo-Saxon Wills*, nos. ii, iii, viii, x, xi, xxi.
[50] Ibid., no. iii; a splendid example of a woman's testamentary power is available in Professor Whitelock's translation of *The Will of Æthelgifu*, Oxford (Roxburghe Club), 1968.

he sword on which the hand was marked. All these things were done for the soul of Ethelred and his own and his grandmother, Aelfthryth, who brought him up. The young man died before he was thirty, but an impression is given here of royal splendour, a mass of swords, houses and gold, a rich household.[51]

Other wills went into greater detail over individual bequests to officers of the household; others again, such as that of Ulf and his wife Madselin before they set out on their journey to Jerusalem, were more matter of fact and make arrangement for the distribution of land among the kinsfolk if the voyagers failed to return. This particular pair may have come home safely; the terms of the will were not enforced; though as Ulf's lands were seized by the Normans it is not right to read too much into the non-enforcement of the will.[52] The overall impression is left of surprising mobility of wealth, much land, much gold, many precious things. The age may have been perilous; it was certainly not drab.

Time and time again in these wills direct proof is given of the strength of the legal bonds between the king and his earls and thegns. A prayer to the king to see that the terms were observed; a reservation that the bequest is subject to the will of the king; a matter-of-fact, businesslike recognition that power of enforcement lies at the royal court: such are characteristics of the later Anglo-Saxon testaments that point to a degree of dependence in matters concerning land and personal wealth greater than existed in the early Anglo-Saxon period. The aristocracy in the eleventh century was almost certainly more numerous, absolutely and relatively, than it had been in the seventh century; it was more dependent on the king; it had more the nature of a territorial aristocracy in which the noble warrior was also the local landlord, and in which possession of land that could be willed by testament was a sure test of status.

[51] Ibid., no. xx.
[52] Ibid., no. xxxix.

CHAPTER SIX
Church, Learning and Literature

1. GENERAL ACHIEVEMENTS AND PROBLEMS

(a) The principal achievements

There is no aspect of Anglo-Saxon life more fully chronicled than that which concerns the Church, nor is there any aspect which does not in some measure impinge upon the life of the Church or which does not come under the direct surveillance of the Church. Bede, careful historian as he was in his choice of terms, found himself compelled to speak at length of political, military and social happenings in order to construct his 'Ecclesiastical History of the English People'.

It is from the 'Ecclesiastical History', completed in A.D. 731, that most of the information concerning the early days of the Christian Church in England is derived. From it, and also from the earliest Kentish law-codes, a picture emerges of a Church adapting itself to the needs of a society that was not yet fully formed. Most knowledge of that society comes in the early stages from the efforts of the alien institution of the Church to fit itself into it. And alien the Church was in the strict sense of the word, its inspiration as an institution coming from Roman ideas and Roman ideals of government.

In a survey of social and economic problems, and in limited scope, little more can be done than to point out the most critical matters in which the Church played a decisive part in shaping English society. Over the period as a whole the achievements of the Anglo-Saxon Church lay in three principal fields. The first consisted in the establishment of a form of territorial government which mapped out England into territorial divisions, until finally

he whole country was split up into parishes. The second resulted
from the freshness and vigour infused into Christianity by the
newly converted Anglo-Saxons, a vigour that, acting back on the
Continent, produced a period of prestige and success in the eighth
century for both the Anglo-Saxon Church and the papacy. The
third consisted in the peculiar contribution of the Anglo-Saxon
Church to learning and letters, not only in Latin but also in the
vernacular.

There are two general problems that need to be discussed in
order to give the setting in which such achievements were possible.
These are the problems of the nature of the conversion and the
problem of the general attitude of the Church, both to the state
and to society at large. The very question of organization cannot
be treated in isolation. The parish system itself was a creature of
very slow growth, far from complete at the time of the Norman
Conquest. Indeed it may well be argued that such considerable
success as was achieved could have been realized only as a concomi-
tant of deeper social movements associated with the growth and
standardization of landlord power and with the territorialization
of political power.

(b) The Conversion

It was the Conversion of the English to Christianity that accelerated the consolidation of the kingdoms, and gave hope of a
more ordered society. The germs of such order were present
from the start, certainly from the time of the Synod of Whitby,
in essence from the initial urge given by Gregory the Great. There
is much more than mere abstraction to the generalization that
in the Church appeared the true heir of Rome. The person of
Gregory himself, at first prefect of Rome, and then Pope, illustrates
forcibly how real this heritage could be. In face of at times most
savage difficulties the Gallic bishops kept alive the spirit of Roman
administration. Such continuity could not be maintained in these
islands, and even Celtic Britain, where Christianity flourished in
the sixth century, saw developments that broke with this Romanic
tradition. The episcopal system naturally survived; all priests were
ordained by a bishop. But the bishops themselves were monks, and
political governance fell into the hands of abbots whose abbeys were
organized on a semi-tribal basis. Awareness of such peculiarities
was probably in Gregory's mind when he arranged that the Roman missionaries should treat with, and take precedence over, the

existing British episcopate. Such differences made agreement hard to come by, as Augustine discovered when he failed to establish a working arrangement with the British bishops. But there is much truth in the view that the Roman missionaries, when they arrived in Kent at the end of the sixth century, brought with them some conception of human groupings that transcended kindred and tribe. Universal religions such as Christianity and the Moslem faith have the power to weaken traditional tribal conventions. In the same century in which Theodore from Tarsus and Adrian from the North African province brought to the English a stable organization for their new faith, the followers of Mohammed united the Near East under religious teachings that forbade tribal war, and so loosed against the Fertile Crescent the power long restive in the barren southern lands.

Yet if stress is laid on the latent organizational power of the Roman mission, it must not be forgotten that the spearhead of conversion, both from the Roman and from the Celtic side, consisted of monks. Roman organization remained in the Church but was subordinate at this stage to the Church's immediate purpose, the spread of the gospel and the administration of the sacraments. It is wrong to attribute to the papacy of the sub-Roman period the political ambitions of a Hildebrand or the administrative gifts of an Innocent III. The dominant ideal in ecclesiastical thought was that of withdrawal from the tarnishing effects of government and society; the monk was the embodiment of that ideal. Only gradually as the Church was drawn more and more actively into the workings of society did the idea germinate that to be effective the Church would need to control the secular power that shielded it. The Church awaited the second coming of Christ; its teaching laid stress not on this temporal world, not even on the institutions of the Church here on earth, but on the life to come. There were no inhibitions in supporting established secular authority, while maintaining some important reservations concerning the maintenance of pure doctrine and of reasonable discipline. In such circumstances it is not to be wondered at that the chief part in converting the pagans should be played by men expressly dedicated by the most manifest pledges to withdrawal from society.

On the actual course of the Conversion there is no need to dwell in this volume. The Roman mission of Augustine was successful in Kent and to a lesser degree in Essex. Under Paulinus it extended its teaching to Northumbria in 627, but the death of King Edwin in 632 checked its progress in the northern kingdom. From 633 a major role in converting the English was played by Celtic monks from Iona, particularly by those who settled at Lindisfarne. At the Synod of Whitby, in 663, differences between the two groups of Christians were resolved in favour of the Romans. Under the great Archbishop of Canterbury, Theodore of Tarsus, 668–90, the English Church was stabilized. At his death there were no fewer than fifteen dioceses, extending over all the English kingdoms. Even isolated Sussex received the faith at the hands of Wilfrid of York in 680. Councils were held to deal with matters common to the whole English Church, at Hertford in 672 when diocesan rearrangements were affirmed, at Hatfield in 679 when a solemn profession of allegiance to orthodox doctrine was made.

In this task of conversion both Roman and Celtic Christians took their full share. Bede, much as he disliked, and could even consider detestable, the practices of the Celtic Christians – on procedure in baptism, method of tonsure and, much more important, the dating of Easter, they differed from the Roman custom – gave full credit to them for their activities in pagan England. He was harsher to the Welsh Church than to the Scottish, partly because of what he considered to be its deliberate refusal to convert the English, and partly because it had not, at the time he wrote, acquiesced in the more up-to-date methods of computing Easter. There was no doctrinal cleavage between Rome and the Celtic world, and particularly in East Anglia, in Wessex, and in Northumbria itself the two groups of Christians worked together amicably. This fact alone made for the success of the conversion, though it is clear that there were more profound social forces at work. Apart from the kings who died in battle against the heathen there were no martyrs in this astonishing episode in English history. Even Penda of Mercia, an obdurate heathen, slayer of both Edwin and Oswald, permitted missionaries to operate within his kingdom, and he was presumably the strongest ruler in England, 632–54. He did not object when Peada his own son, a man worthy of a kingdom and in fact sub-king of the Middle Angles, accepted the new faith. He held it detestable, as Bede says, that a man should not hold to the faith he professes.[1] The relative ease of the conversion may be attributed in part to careful planning. The royal courts were approached first, and in many cases, as in Kent originally, in Northumbria and among the Middle Angles, the presence of a Christian queen helped the task of conversion immeasurably. On

[1] Bede, *Hist. Eccl.*, III, 21.

the Roman side, skilful use of the special position of the papacy and judicious gifts from the Pope himself proved powerful weapons in the Christian armoury. In dramatic form the Synod of Whitby saw papal prestige used with firm judgement. Wilfrid, the protagonist of the Roman cause, triumphed over his Celtic opponents. Accept your faith from them, he argued, and you conform merely with the practice of one obscure corner of one remote island. We have St Peter and the keys of the kingdom of heaven. If King Oswy was smiling as he asked about St Peter's powers and the Roman cause, who can blame him? He had no wish to offend the keeper of the keys 'lest when I come to the gates of heaven, he who holds the key may not be willing to open them'.[2] And Rome meant contact with the Continent, with the civilized world of the Mediterranean.

Most striking of all reasons for the success of the conversion is the inadequacy of German heathendom. There were aristocratic reversions, and royal second thoughts, recorded in the early days of the conversion. Ethelbert's death in 616 caused a weakening of the faith in Kent itself, while the king of Essex left his kingdom to three sons and pagan reaction. In East Anglia King Redwald attempted the best of two worlds, and housed both a pagan and a Christian altar in the same building. In times of great stress, such as visitations of the plague, there was unrest with the new faith. Near Melrose backsliders had recourse to 'the false remedies of idolatry' till corrected by St Cuthbert.[3] As late as the eleventh century legislation was needed against a recrudescence of superstition and of natural religion, the worship of rivers, woods and mountains and the like. Aelfric complained of foolish men who practised manifold divinations and who passed their lives in diabolic magic; and in spells and lays which have survived from the late Anglo-Saxon period the names of the high Gods of the North were sometimes invoked.[4] But of systematic popular reaction towards Woden and Thor there is no sign. Bede, again with superb dramatic sense, has left in his story of Edwin's conversion a graphic account of the arguments employed in deliberation upon the merits of the new faith. The pagan high-priest himself, Coifi by name, complained bitterly of the old religion. No one had served it more faithfully than he, yet many had better rewards. Riding in shocking state on the back of a stallion, bearing arms that were denied to his priestly

[2] Bede, *Hist. Eccl.*, III, 25; Eddius Stephanus, *Life of Wilfrid*, c. x.
[3] Bede, *Hist. Eccl.*, II, 5, II, 15; III, 30; Bede's *Life of St Cuthbert*, c. ix.
[4] II Canute 5.1: *Aelfric's Catholic Homilies*, p. 98, in connection with the celebration of January 1st; D. Betherum, *The Homilies of Wulfstan* VIIIc (Napier V), pp. 183–4.

tatus, Coifi was the first to hurl a spear of desecration against the
ald idols. A more temperate reason for accepting the new faith
was given by an unnamed ealdorman. Among the best known of
all the writings of Bede it deserves full quotation not only for its
own sake but also as an example of Bede's style at its best, lucid
yet not lacking in poetry:

> When we compare the present life of man with that time of which we
> know not, then it seems to me like the swift flight of a lone sparrow
> through the banqueting hall where you sit in wintertime to feast with
> your chief men and thegns. Inside there is a comforting fire to warm
> the room; outside the winter storms of snow and rain are raging. While
> he is inside, he is safe from the winter storms; but after a few moments
> of comfort he vanishes from sight, from winter into winter. Similarly
> man appears on earth for a little while. But we know nothing of what
> went before this life, and what follows. Therefore if this new teaching
> can reveal any more certain knowledge, it seems only right that we
> should follow it.[5]

How much of this is Edwin's ealdorman and how much Bede
may well be called in question. Yet poetic truth is surely embodied
in the speech. The old religion failed to give satisfactory answers to
the fundamental problems facing a settled people. Indeed it cannot
be emphasized too much that Christianity on its own merits had
much to offer the people of the age. It is easy to gibe at scandalized
disputes over theological niceties and forms of tonsure. But the
Christian faith itself was mature; it faced the ever-present problems
of life and death; it gave a framework of heaven and hell into
which to fit the mystery of human existence. It also provided a
social discipline with austere views on sexual behaviour and on
attitudes towards authority that strengthened the priesthood in
coping with the needs of an agrarian community. The list of
answers sent back by Pope Gregory to the questions of Augustine
has a strong and somewhat unexpected sexual element. A ruling
is given on the length of time a husband should abstain from
relations with his wife after childbirth, on the propriety of a woman
entering church or receiving communion during her menses, or
of a man after relations with his wife before he has washed. As
Augustine said, the uncouth English required guidance on these
matters, and in the ability of the teachers to give some admittedly
idealistic standards of behaviour lay a great deal of the strength of
Christianity. Gregory himself could give the philosophical backing
needed by missionaries operating in a strange land.

[5] Bede, *Hist. Eccl.*, II, 13.

237

The origin of sin, therefore, is in suggestion, its growth in pleasure, an its completion in consent . . . And although the body cannot experienc pleasure without the mind, yet the mind, in contending against th desires of the body, is to some extent unwillingly chained to then having to oppose them for conscience sake, and strongly regrettin its bondage to bodily desires . . . So one may say that a man is bot captive and free; free through the law of right which he loves, an 'captive through the law of bodily pleasure, of which he is an unwillin victim.[6]

Most important attribute of all, Christianity was a religion o a Book, and also a religion of many books. The provision o a permanent source of written evidence was an enormous, a overwhelming asset. Augustine's mission came fortified with books and later tradition associates the copy of the Gospels, written i a sixth-century Italian hand and now in the library of Corpu Christi College, Cambridge, with the name of St Augustine o Canterbury. Early mention of the establishment of schools and o the rapid accumulation of scholarship within English monasterie speaks also of the presence of many books. King Alfred considerec that a copy of Gregory's 'Pastoral Care' was among Augustine' possessions.[7] The authority and continuity ensured by the writter word guaranteed consistency of teaching and promised a reason able permanence.

Another factor that accounts for the success of the conversior lies in the fact that no compelling political forces were gatherec around the old pagan gods. Later genealogies, to be sure, trace the royal descent from Germanic heroes and gods, all save that o Essex which is derived from Seaxneat leading the royal kin bacl to Woden. In later Christian days these genealogies were pushec back further to Old Testament days, so that Woden appeared as a distinguished descendant of Noah himself. But these genealogie are comparatively late products containing more than a hint o antiquarian flavour. There seems to have been little actual attach ment of monarchy to pagan ancestors. Into a relatively unformec situation the Christian religion brought a new faith that, apart fron its ultimate promises, offered hope of stability and of firmer socia discipline. As the political units, the kingdoms of the Heptarchy took proper shape, so did Christianity promise a more rationa universe into which they could be fitted.

Indeed during this sub-Roman period the secular rulers an

---

[6] Ibid., I, 27.
[7] P. Hunter Blair, *Anglo-Saxon England*, p. 312. *E.H.D.* I, p. 889.

he Christian bishops had great need of one another. This mutual
need is well illustrated in all missionary enterprise, and is nowhere
more apparent than in seventh-century England. To the king the
new Church brought a discipline and a Book which served as an
example of kingship in action. The very monotheistic emphasis of
the faith made analogies possible even in the limited field of Saxon
England. The pagan religion proved inadequate with its multiplic-
ty of gods, and its tendency to acquire exclusive local peculiarities,
possibly because of its divorce from original indigenous Germanic
shrines. As the more settled kingdoms, such as those of Ethelbert
of Kent or Edwin of Northumbria or Redwald of East Anglia,
demanded a more settled basis and justification for government,
so did the value of Christianity towards an establishment of such
a secure basis become apparent.

c) Church, Society and State

   This brings into prominence a second and more general problem. Is it possible to distinguish any general attitude of the Church
to Society and State during the whole Anglo-Saxon period? It is a
matter to be approached with some hesitation. Of all institutions
a Church might be expected to have a clear view of its position in
society, but in this period, in particular, so much clearly depended
on the individual bishop or archbishop. For example, to say that the
Church co-operated with the secular rulers is generally true. Yet
the career of St Wilfrid of York with its storms and trials, impris-
onment and exiles, suggests that co-operation was not uniformly
smooth. Occasionally but very rarely a bishop was ranged in active
opposition, as was the case with Archbishop Eanbald II, who re-
sisted the tyrant Eardwulf of Northumbria in the opening years of
the ninth century.[8] The nature of the surviving evidence demands
a cautious approach. To judge the eighth-century Church by the
figures of the articulate Aldhelm, Bede, Boniface and Alcuin, and
to ignore the worldly bishops and undisciplined abbots, would be
to provide a false verdict. Fortunately the righteous tend to be at
their most articulate on the misdeeds of the unrighteous.
   The Church in England conformed closely to the general trend
throughout the Western world. The inspiration of its teaching
came from the Bible and from St Augustine of Hippo, with Pope
Gregory the Great as the chief intermediary. English scholarship

[8] *Haddan and Stubbs*, vol. III, pp. 535–6.

had much to do with the preparation of an authoritative text of the Vulgate in the late eighth century. Alcuin of Northumbria who together with Theodulf of Orleans, played the principal part in the preparation of such a text, used texts familiar in Anglo-Saxon England as the basis of his work.[9] Of the books that were well known in England during the seventh, eighth and ninth centuries none was more potent, save the Scriptures themselves, than the Dialogues of Gregory the Great and his 'Pastoral Care'. The heroic figures, after Christ and the Evangelists, were the great pope and the great monk: St Gregory and St Benedict of Nursia. Gregory himself had provided the standard biography of St Benedict in the second book of his Dialogues. The cosmological picture was that of a society, worldly and very much the province of the Devil. The Church itself was a pilgrim society on earth. The ideal, attainable only by the few, was that of the celibate withdrawn life of monk or hermit. No comment on Anglo-Saxon life would be adequate that omitted reference to the anchorite. Particularly where Celtic influence was powerful, as in Northumbria, the ascetic tradition of withdrawal, exemplified supremely in England by the career of St Cuthbert, was exceptionally strong. To withdraw to the wilderness, to the desolate isolation of the Farne islands like St Cuthbert or to the fastnesses of the Fenland like St Guthlac, and there to practise savage austerities of body and mind, remained one of the highest manifestations of religious life.

But this dominant ideal did not prevent the Church from active co-operation with secular rulers. There is danger in oversimplifying very complicated situations, but it may be true to say that up to the reign of Alfred the Church's part in society was moulding and formative, immensely important in the cultural and educational spheres but a minor partner as far as its relationship to the secular state was concerned; and that during and after the reign of Alfred the Church accepted a more positive role in the task of creating an ordered society. Perhaps a high point was reached in the early period when the son of the great Offa, Ecgfrith, received consecration at the hands of the Church. This first fully authenticated instance of an English prince receiving consecration after the Old Testament pattern owed much to immediate Carolingian precedent. But it suggests overt recognition of the authority achieved by the English Church, just as Offa's attempts to create a fresh archbishopric at Lichfield point to a similar recognition of influence in a more

[9] H. H. Glunz, *Britannien und Bibeltext*, Leipzig, 1930, pp. 97 ff.

mundane vein. Coronation itself did not imply investment with such power as to make all opposition unlawful; and it did not in any sense imply that the king was raised above the law. Consistently from the pontifical of Archbishop Egbert of York, from the full coronation *Ordo* of the tenth century, to the coronation of Henry I, a threefold promise was made by the King himself at the coronation: to protect God's Church and people, to forbid iniquity, to rule with justice and mercy. The Church could, and did, exercise a right of criticism on moral grounds, though notably it must be confessed by strong ecclesiastics safe in foreign parts, such as Boniface who stoutly arraigned the moral iniquities of Ethelbald of Mercia, or Alcuin who wrote in strong terms to Osbald whom he suspected of being implicated in the murder of Ethelred of Northumbria.[10] Yet the tendency was, determined in some measure by Old Testament example, to emphasize that the king was a man set apart. A great Council held in England in 787, in the presence of papal legates, was constrained to direct an order against the murder of kings; to plot against the Lord's anointed was especially wicked.[11]

But the Church was, willingly or not, drawn ever more closely into the workings of the secular state. The land-charter appeared very early as a guarantee of the ecclesiastical possession of land. Law-codes were prompted in the first instance by the need to fit this new virile institution into existing society; kings found that ecclesiastical support was not only moral and theoretical. The clergy supplied literate servants, gave government a memory. Not that clergy were used as royal deputies or as governors of provinces. Such ideas are completely false. The bishop was given a special personal status, so was the priest. They were important men at the local moots. But their weapons were spiritual, and their appeal was to the supernatural. The 'Penitential' attributed to Theodore of Tarsus, illustrates perfectly the part that the clergy were called on to play. They were pastors of flocks, in the case of bishops powerful pastors. They were not rulers of men or agents of government.

To some extent this was true of the whole Anglo-Saxon period, though the reign of Alfred sees something of a critical change in the relationships of bishops and King. The tendency lay towards the creation of a theocracy of the Carolingian type where the secular and spiritual estates were closely interwoven, and where a crime against the state tended to be confused with a sin against God. The West Saxon dynasty from Alfred to Edgar was well suited to further

[10] *E.H.D.* I, p. 817 and pp. 852–3.
[11] Ibid., pp. 837–8. c. 12.

this development. Of both Alfred and Edgar it has been held that
they were better bishops than the bishops. Certainly under Alfred
the bishops were brought into intimate contact with the court. The
needs of his educational programme dictated this to a point. But
simple political necessity also made such co-operation imperative.
Wessex led by Alfred fought the main battle for the preservation of
the Christian faith among the English. Resistance to the Danes was
resistance to paganism, perhaps no stronger a paganism than that
which had held the Anglo-Saxons three centuries earlier. Alfred
claimed no mastery of the Church, such as was exhibited, for
example, by Charles the Great at the Council of Frankfurt. He
showed the greatest respect to the papacy, and may have been the
first to make regular payments of Peter's Pence to Rome, in spite
of the tradition which has long associated the origin of the payment
with Offa's remorse for the slaying of Ethelbert of East Anglia
and as a parallel to the foundation of St Albans. The humility
of Alfred in face of God's servants was unmistakably genuine
though he himself had reason to consider that as King and as
active reformer of the Church he was not the least among the
thegns of God. When he sent his version of Gregory's 'Pastoral
Care' to Bishop Wærferth of Worcester he lamented the falling
off that had occurred in the state of learning, and set out his
picture of the golden age in the past:

> I often considered ... what happy times there were then among the
> English; and how the kings who had authority over the folk in those
> days honoured God and his messengers; and how they held within
> their boundaries their peace, their morality and their authority, and
> also extended their bounds without; and how they prospered in war
> and in wisdom; and how the godly estates were zealous in instruction
> and in learning and in all the services that they owed to God; and how
> men from without their bounds sought wisdom and instruction here
> and how now we must obtain it from outside if we are to have it.[12]

The pattern of Christian kingship is clearly traced. Good morals
good learning and good government are closely intertwined.

Some indication of the change that was coming over Church
State relations may be discovered in the history of ecclesiastical
councils in these islands. Theodore of Tarsus did his work well
He gave England an example of institutional unity long before
any king could hope to do so. Though the foundation of York as
an archbishopric in 735, and the attempt of the Mercian house to
set up a permanent archbishopric at Lichfield later in the century

[12] *Pastoral Care*, ed. H. Sweet, E.E.T.S., 1871, pp. 4–5; *E.H.D.* I, p. 888.

mark a reaction against unitary principles, in the main England remained one ecclesiastical body. Yet already under the Mercian kings the royal hand in ecclesiastical councils was strong. As Sir Frank Stenton wrote, 'no king or bishop of the eighth century would have understood an argument which tried to show that ecclesiastical legislation, or the protection of ecclesiastical interests, was a matter for churchmen alone'.[13] From the days of Alfred to the end of the Anglo-Saxon period, with one notable exception in the council held at Winchester during the reign of Edgar to deal with affairs of the newly vitalized monastic movement, it becomes even more difficult to separate ecclesiastical councils from royal councils. Already under Alfred himself his great code of laws show us the path along which development was to lie. The neglected prologue to his dooms is a mine of information to the political theorist and to the ecclesiastical historian. It is a reminder that the wrapping in which the Germanic dooms of Ethelbert, Ine, Offa, and indeed of Alfred himself, were presented, was thoroughly religious. To the dooms themselves were prefixed the Ten Commandments, a further selection of Mosaic law, extracts from the Gospel of St Matthew and the Acts of the Apostles, ending with the negative Golden Rule: 'On this one doom man must take thought if he will judge others aright; he needs no other doom-book. Let him consider that he judge no man other than he would wish himself to be judged, if the other sought (or held) judgement over him.'[14]

There, it seems, lies the law. The dooms themselves were no more than commentaries on certain instances, presumably on practical matters brought to the attention of the king as the guardian of law for his kingdom. A great deal has been written to show that the king was no legislator, but to Alfred belonged all the functions that were needed in practice by a legislator. He decided, acting with the advice of his wise men, what dooms of former kings should be accepted, and what set to one side. These statements of law were no pious antiquarianism but were meant to be observed. Similarly through the succeeding century and a half king after king framed law-codes, some for special occasions and to meet special needs, such as the dooms of Athelstan and of Edgar against theft, others of a more general nature, such as the elaborate code known as Canute II, which was taken as an authoritative statement of Anglo-Saxon law long after the Norman Conquest. To deny that

---

[13] *Anglo-Saxon England*, p. 238.
[14] Liebermann I, p. 44; *E.H.D.* I, p. 408.

these kings exercised some legislative function would seem to los
the substance for the hair-splitting shadow.

Corresponding to the increase in activity on the part of roya
legislators comes a pronounced blurring of the distinction betwee
witenagemots and ecclesiastical synods. As the kingdom of Englan
painfully acquired its unity so did the boundaries of provinces an
kingdom come to coincide. King Edmund, for example, sum
moned a great synod to London at Easter-tide. It was attende
by the two archbishops and many other bishops, who deliberate
about the health of their souls and of those subject to them. Yet w
are expressly told that there were present those of the secular orde
as well as those of the spiritual.[15] Many of the codes of Edgar and o
Ethelred are almost completely ecclesiastical in tone and conten
in particular the codes that are known as Ethelred V, VI, VIII an
IX are overwhelmingly concerned with the Church and religiou
affairs. Canute's first code of laws is often termed his clerical code
it was issued at the same time as the famous second and secula
code, and it was clearly meant to supplement the secular edict
This promulgation of ecclesiastical law was carried out by the king
with the advice of his wise men, lay and religious, through in fac
by what may be called the ecclesiastical side of the witenagemo
Subtle and intuitive work on the career of the great archbishor
Wulfstan of York, has helped to show how the law-codes wer
drawn up in practice.[16] This extraordinarily powerful archbisho
and homilist was responsible for the form of much of the legislatio
of both Ethelred and of Canute. The phraseology and sentimen
are his. Passages from the homilies are incorporated lock, stoc
and barrel into the laws. They provide us with a clue to wha
would otherwise be a legislative mystery. There is no confusio
in theory between a provincial council and a royal witan. It i
the purpose of these assemblies, not the nature of the personne
present, that gives us insight into their part in ecclesiastical histor
An England threatened by Scandinavians, who were only slowl
rejecting paganism, needed not the formal pronouncements o
ecclesiastical synods but statements of customs and laws obtainin
in the Church made by the one body capable of safeguardin
them, namely the monarchy. There was no need for a provinci
synod. Only with the sweeping reforms of the Normans and wit

[15] Liebermann I, p. 184.
[16] D. Whitelock, 'Wulfstan and the so-called Laws of Edward and Guthrum
E.H.R., 1941, pp. 1–21; 'Wulfstan and the Laws of Cnut', *E.H.R.*, 1948
pp. 433–52.

heir promise of more settled conditions was Lanfranc's series of
·eforming councils necessary or possible. What was needed was
ull account, made by authority able to enforce it, of the rights
of the Church, the taxes and imposts, the traditional dues and
payments, the place of the monks, the discipline to be applied to
·agrant monks, regulations for feasts, for fasts, for holidays. In
hat need lies the explanation of such a code as Canute I, where
ill of the twenty-six clauses are directly concerned with Church
iffairs.

Here, in the legislative field, there is an indication of the development of relationships between growing state and Church strongly
·eminiscent of continental development during the Carolingian
period. Indeed owing to the strength and tenacity of the West
Saxon monarchy in the tenth and eleventh centuries, theocracy
n England was even more fully extended, and survived later.
The writings of homilists in the late tenth and early eleventh
centuries bear out this conclusion. Reference has already been
made to the passage in which Aelfric refers to the god-given
·ight of a king to rule once he has been chosen as monarch, and
consecrated. Wulfstan is equally rewarding on a similar theme.
In homily after homily he reverted to the question of Christian
duty: obedience to the lord, above all to the king, was the greatest
virtue. He divided society into three groups: those who pray,
:hose who fight, and those who labour. It was the royal duty
:o hold the balance between these groups, and to deal out good
ustice to men.[17] In later Anglo-Saxon England, ideas of Christian
kingship and the sight of that kingship in action illustrate the
closer interdependence of the Church as an institution and the
state. This is a phenomenon common to the whole of the West,
ind one that came to assume peculiar importance in Germany
under the Ottonian and Salian kings. As the reformed papacy
in mid-eleventh century became conscious of its potentialities, the
difficulties inherent in such interdependence grew more acute.
It is tempting to speculate how papal relationships might have
developed in England had not the powerful William succeeded in
1066. There is evidence enough of the interest taken in England
by the reformed papacy in the generation before the Conquest:

[17] Wulfstan, *Collected Homilies*, ed. A. Napier, no. L, pp. 266–7. Full expression
of the idea is given in Wulfstan's *Institutes of Polity*, ed. K. Jost, pp. 55–6, where
the three foundations of a secure throne are said to be, *Oratores, Laboratores, et
Bellatores*. The theme is borrowed from Aelfric, *E.H.D.* I, p. 928, and also occurs
in Alfred's 'Boethius', ibid., p. 919.

Anglo Saxon England and the Norman Conquest

in confirming privileges to Chertsey and Wells, or in separating
the dioceses of York and Worcester. A papal bull confirmed to
Wulfwig of Dorchester the diocese of Lindsey and the churches o
Stow, with Newark, after Archbishop Aelfric of York had seized
them.[18] Certain features of English church practice were quite a
distasteful to a Hildebrand as anything to be found in Germany
But the German problem lay nearer home, involved vital North
Italian interests, and affected more acutely the new and vigorous
ideals of ecclesiastical freedom.

An interesting illustration of the way in which the late Anglo
Saxon Church was involved in secular affairs comes from a tract
called 'Episcopus' (possibly a product of Wulfstan's pen, and cer
tainly a product of his inspiration), which treats of the dutie
of a bishop and to a lesser extent those of a priest.[19] It is no
only a recognition but also a justification of the prominent par
that ecclesiastics were playing in the everyday workings of soci
ety. A bishop was to promote right-doing both in secular and
in spiritual things, to instruct the clergy concerning their right
and duties, to strive for the settlement of feuds and conflicts
to co-operate actively with secular judges who loved right and to
supervise vigorously the procedures of oath and ordeal. He was
to be active in the economic field as well as in the legal, to see by
his counsel and witness that each legal right was done according
to borough-right and according to land-right, and also to see that
each borough-weight and pound-weight was true according to his
instructions. Good faith in business was the bishop's concern. He
was to know his flock well, to exhort them to cling to the right and
to shun wrong, and to work with the secular judges in drawing up
laws that would prevent injustice from arising. The priest also was
to busy himself in the active pursuit of justice in social dealings
Within his 'shrift-shire', his shriving-district or parish, he even had
the duty of supervising the amount of work that a lord could
exact from his slaves. He had the further task of seeing that al
the measures and weights in his 'shrift-shire' were properly made
with the bishop called in to settle the matter in case of dispute
The document ended with an emphatic reminder to the lord of
his personal need to look after his slaves, because free and servile
were equal in the love of God, and He had redeemed them at the
same price. It is good policy to look after those who have to obey us

[18] C. W. Foster, *Registrum Antiquissimum*, vol. I, pp. 186 ff.; *E.H.D.* II, pp. 641–2.
[19] Liebermann I, pp. 477–79.

246

here on earth, since God in turn judges us even as we judge them over whom we now have the judgement. It is especially interesting to note how the clergy were, in theory at the least, looked to as men with the duty of safeguarding the equitable treatment of slaves and fair dealing in trade.

To conclude these general remarks on the relationships between Church and state and between Church and society it may be said, at the risk of overstating the obvious, that at the end of the Anglo-Saxon period England was still in that pre-Hildebrandine phase which continental scholars call Carolingian or Ottonian. The involvement of the Church in the workings of royal administration had grown steadily more intimate. From the reign of Athelstan charter evidence reveals the existence of a skilled writing office, completely clerical in composition. Clerks in its service aspired as a result of faithful performance of duties to a bishopric. It was common practice to use the higher clergy as ambassadors or envoys. Bishops were attracted from overseas, notably from Lorraine, to serve the English king as administrators or as diplomats. Edward the Confessor, for all his piety, favoured promotions of men who had been active about the king's business at his court or as his chaplains. In his reign, though not it is true at his desire, Stigand succeeded to the archbishopric of Canterbury itself, to all appearance as the very type of political bishop. Papal refusal to recognize the ecclesiastical and political *coup* that led to this translation indicates the strains latent in the situation. The papacy was particularly concerned in this instance because Stigand's predecessor, Robert, was still alive. Robert had fled into exile in 1052 together with Bishop Ulf of Dorchester – another bad appointment during the reign of the Confessor. The failure of English bishops to go to Stigand for consecration except during the brief five months of his recognition gives foretaste of the stress to come when the cry for ecclesiastical reform directed itself harshly against the conservative royal theocracy.

2. ECCLESIASTICAL ORGANIZATION

(a) The bishoprics and the bishops

While it is useful to discuss the general theory upon which Church action could be based, it is equally useful to the social historian to consider the Church in action, its organization, the composition of its hierarchy, the nature of its teachings on social questions and, as far as can be judged, the effects of its teaching At the highest, the metropolitan, level the system of organization is clear. Gregory intended two archbishops for the new province, one at London and one at York, intrinsically equal and taking precedence according to their seniority of appointment. For political reasons Canterbury was chosen as Augustine's headquarters, not London; and York remained without metropolitan dignity until 735. From then to the end of the period, apart from the brief Lichfield episode, there remained two archiepiscopal sees in England with Canterbury well placed to claim precedence because of its direct contact with Augustine and so with the great Gregory, because of its greater antiquity, and because of its greater wealth.

Historically, too, Canterbury had been fortunate to attract Theodore of Tarsus, 668–90, an archbishop who merits the title of the true organizer of the new Church. It was he who gave the diocesan system the essential shape that it was to assume for the rest of the period. In 672 there were only seven sees for the whole of England, of which York, Lichfield and Winchester were apparently coterminous with the extensive kingdoms of Northumbria, Mercia and Wessex. In face of considerable and at times bitter opposition Theodore succeeded in multiplying bishoprics so that at his death only Winchester remained in truly unmanageable proportions. York was divided into three dioceses, the Deiran kingdom remaining subject to York but with fresh sees set up for Lindsey and for Bernicia at Lindisfarne with an alternative seat at Hexham. By about 685 there were bishops both at Lindisfarne and at Hexham. East Anglia was partitioned between the two sees of Dunwich and North Elmham. The Mercian situation is more obscure. To the west Theodore instituted bishoprics at Hereford and Worcester, and there are also traces of the establishment of a see that later blossoms into continuous life at Leicester. There was a short-lived Mercian see at Dorchester-on-Thames, to which the bishopric of Leicester was transferred in the post-Viking Age. With the establishment of a diocese of Sherborne for Wessex, of Selsey for the South Saxons and of Whithorn for Galloway in the north-west, the number of English dioceses in the early Anglo-Saxon period was complete. Of the seventeen sees that existed in the middle of the eighth century York and Lichfield were still extensive though no doubt their apparent extent is misleading, stretching as it does towards

he thinly populated and newly settled north-west.[20] But in the
main the dioceses were compact manageable territorial areas.

In theory the bishop of such a diocese was elected by the clergy
and people of his church. Bishops were sometimes said to consecrate their successors. Alcuin wrote to Eanbald I, Archbishop of
York, when the latter felt that his days were numbered, entreating
him to see that the clergy had their freedom to elect a successor,
and at the same time Alcuin wrote a further letter to the clergy
of York, begging them to elect a prelate faithfully and wisely,
taking special care to avoid simony, for whosoever sells a church,
gains gold but loses the kingdom of God. In one classic instance
Bishop Helmstan of Winchester, in a profession of obedience to
the Archbishop of Canterbury of the day, is said to have been
elected by the pope, by the congregation of the city of Winchester,
King Ethelwulf and the bishops, nobles and people of Wessex'. He
tells how he had been consecrated, presumably in 839, at 'the
illustrious place, built by the skill of the ancient Romans, called
throughout the world the great city of London'. Yet Florence of
Worcester records, probably from original Winchester material,
that Helmstan's successor, Bishop Swithin, owed his position *iussu
regis*, to the command of the king.[21] However much the theory of
free election might be maintained, in practice the king normally
had a decisive voice in the selection of a new bishop. Royal control grew even stronger in the later Anglo-Saxon period as the
theocracy developed. In the eleventh century a royal writ to the
shire-court was the instrument used to enjoin consecration of a
bishop-elect. Consecration itself was a matter for the ecclesiastical
superior. There is a little dubious twelfth-century evidence which
states that Edward the Confessor invested Wulfstan of Worcester
with his episcopal staff, but – though argument from silence is
exceptionally dangerous in relation to this period – it appears that
investiture of prelates with ring and staff was not practised by the
Anglo-Saxon kings.

Within his see a great weight of work fell undoubtedly on the
bishop himself. In the early days of conversion the responsibility
for baptizing converts must have been largely his, as well as the
task of catechizing and confirming candidates. One of the most
familiar of Bede's portraits in the story of the Conversion is that

[20] P. Hunter Blair, *Anglo-Saxon England*, pp. 143–4.
[21] Alcuin to Eanbald I, *Epistolae*, ed. E. Dümmler, M.G.H., *Ep.* IV, 90; to the
clergy of York, ibid., 92. *Haddan and Stubbs*, vol. III, pp. 360–76. *C.S.*, 424.
Florence of Worcester, ed. B. Thorpe, p. 69.

of Paulinus, 'a tall man, somewhat bent, with black hair, an ascetic face, the nose somewhat attenuated, and a venerable and
majestic presence'. It is told how he spent thirty-six days at the
royal residence of Yeavering, constantly instructing and baptizing
from dawn to dusk.[22] As the faith was received and churches
sprang up, some of this enormous weight was shifted from the
bishop's burden. Even so it is clear from the correspondence of
Boniface, Lul and Alcuin that a successful bishop needed to be an
exceptionally vigorous and active man. Bishops were expected to
make annual visitations of their dioceses, to hold diocesan synods,
to report concerning abuse to a general synod, and to supervise
monasteries in their dioceses, including those under secular control.[23] Their privileges were great. Ethelbert had hedged around
their property with an eleven-fold protection. Their word alone,
with no solemn oath taken, was sufficient, like that of a king, to
clear themselves from an accusation. Often, though not inevitably,
they were drawn from aristocratic ranks. Wilfrid was a man of
good family whose father was accustomed to entertain friends of
the king. On the other hand Cuthbert tended his lord's sheep in
his early days.[24] The high standard of education achieved by the
Anglo-Saxon bishops helped, with some conspicuous lapse in the
middle of the ninth century, to act as something of a social solvent
in this respect. Many bishops were monks, trained in monastic
schools and often fully committed to a life by rule. Bede himself
urged that new sees should be created to be held by men elected
by, and if possible from, the convents of monasteries attached
to the sees.[25] Dom David Knowles has shown that as many as
three out of four of the Anglo-Saxon bishops during the period
960–1066 were monks.[26] At times of great vitality in monastic
institutions, such as the end of the seventh century and the middle
of the tenth, the proportion was surely great. The strength of the
Anglo-Saxon Church depended in large part on the close contact
maintained between monasteries and the episcopacy. Many of the
diocesan centres were monastic, as at Hexham and Lindisfarne
in the seventh century. Others were served by a clergy who lived
together and who drew from a common revenue, even if they did

---

[22] *Hist. Eccl.*, II, 14 and 16.
[23] The Synod of *Clofesho*, A.D. 747, *Haddan and Stubbs*, vol. III, pp. 360–76.
[24] Ethelbert 1; Wihtræd 16; Eddius Stephanus, *Life of Wilfrid*, c. ii; Anon., *Life
of St Cuthbert*, Book I, c. iv.
[25] Bede, Letter to Archbishop Egbert, *E.H.D.* I, p. 804.
[26] D. Knowles, *The Monastic Order in England*, Cambridge, 1940, pp. 697–701. P.
Hunter Blair, *Anglo-Saxon England*, pp. 181–2.

not live according to a monastic rule. In the seventh century at both Lindisfarne in the north and at Canterbury in the south the bishop and his monks followed a way of life 'practised by our forefathers of the primitive church, who did not regard any property as personal, but shared all things in common'.[27] When reform was needed in the tenth century, as at Worcester under Oswald and Winchester under Ethelwold, the method favoured was the replacement of the existing somewhat loosely bound community by a group of monks. From beginning to end the inspiration of St Benedict was a great force in determining the nature of the Church in England.

Yet this inspiration was not expressed uniformly throughout the period. During the first half of the eighth century the influence of monks, living to a Rule, reached great heights, but there was a steady decline in fervour in the ninth century. Danish attacks were savage on monasteries that had grown rich from the endowments and gifts of generations of the faithful. Alfred attempted to revive organized monastic life, which he confessed had been lost to England. His foreign plantation at Athelney was not a success, though a nunnery set up at Shaftesbury was more influential. In the early tenth century individuals were known as monks and abbots, but these designations applied to them by virtue of special vows and professions of chastity, not because of their membership of an organized body living according to the Rule. Monasteries, so called, where they existed, were akin to communities of secular clerks and the rule of St Chrodegang, expressly set up in the eighth century to regulate a régime of clerks who would share refectory, dormitory, and financial assets in common, was certainly known in late Anglo-Saxon England, as were also other Carolingian institutes on the conduct of canons. True revival came in the middle of the tenth century, partly from the inspiration of native piety, partly from contact with the reformed Benedictine observance of the Continent. Under St Dunstan, Abbot of Glastonbury from 943, Archbishop of Canterbury, 960–88, a tremendous reform movement took hold, the beginning of the continuous life of what now can clearly be called the Benedictine Order in England. By the early eleventh century there were more than thirty monasteries and half a dozen nunneries securely established in the country. One peculiarity of this revival is of great importance in relation to the episcopate. On the Continent the reformed monasteries,

---

[27] *Hist. Eccl.*, I, 27: letter of Gregory to Augustine. Also *Hist. Eccl.*, IV, 27, where it is cited in connection with Lindisfarne.

notably the Cluniac houses, were as anxious to seek exemption from the control of the secular clergy as to escape the clutches of aristocratic authority. In England there was no such anti-episcopal feeling. The leaders of the movement were all bishops: Dunstan himself, Ethelwold of Winchester, 963–84, and Oswald of Worcester, 961–92. The accompanying map shows how their episcopal authority helped to further the monastic cause from their main monastic centres of Glastonbury, Abingdon (and Winchester) and Westbury (overshadowed by Oswald's better favoured and vigorous community at Ramsey). The three powerful bishops enjoyed the full support of King Edgar, and willingly recognized the special patronage offered to the monasteries by the royal family. Monks of the new reform, when they controlled the head-minster of a diocese, claimed the right to elect the bishop, and with royal approval the influence of the monks on the episcopate, as was stated above, became an outstanding feature of the late Anglo-Saxon church, as it had been during the age of the Conversion. From the time of St Dunstan to the election of Stigand in 1052 all the Archbishops, of Canterbury and of York, and most of the bishops were monks. Ideas concerning the nature of the office were strongly affected by the training given in Benedictine discipline to so many of the occupants of the sees.

The homilist Wulfstan, who could speak from first-hand experience, gave in his 'Institutes of Polity' an account of an early-eleventh-century bishop's day-work, as he called it. First he emphasized prayer, and then bookwork, reading or correcting manuscripts, teaching or learning. There is a puritan distrust of idleness; proper manual work (*handcræftas gode*) was regarded as seemly, and so too was proper supervision of the episcopal household to make sure that they in turn were not idle. The bishop was to preach often goodly instruction to the people in their assemblies. He was to be sober, prudent and dignified in his behaviour. Wisdom and prudence were especially fitting to his condition.[28] There was great emphasis on the authority and the responsibility of the position, and elsewhere Wulfstan warned against foolish pride and worldly pomp, against fondness for hunting, for hounds and for hawks, and against cupidity. A bishop was enjoined to be patient if he was faced by a situation which he could not put right, and to wait for the king to rectify the wrong.[29] Wulfstan was something of a special case, a man acutely aware of the joint responsibilities

[28] Wulfstan's *Institutes*, ed. K. Jost, pp. 75–7.
[29] Ibid., pp. 213, 216 and 262–7.

The monastic revival in late Anglo–Saxon England

Some of the 'derivations' of houses are necessarily conjectural: for full discussion see
D.Knowles, *The Monastic Order*, pp.48-52 and p.721.

of Church and State, but in his delineation of the character and
function of the bishop he faithfully expressed the high ideals of
the late Anglo-Saxon Church.

(b) Parishes, priests and landlords

The bishop was the key figure in the life of the Anglo-Saxon
Church, but perhaps the most important development in the institution of the Church was the growth of the parish system. There
were no conspicuous milestones to mark its progress. Signs of its
existence are clear as early as the seventh century. The founding of
churches with the object of providing spiritual service for the small
territorial community, the village or the hamlet grouped around a
lord's residence, was a widespread practice in at latest the second

generation of the conversion. But the number of full priests was never large. The mass thegns and altar thegns of the legal codes were men of some standing. The value of their oaths was so great that a priest could by his own unsupported solemn oath exculpate himself from accusation brought against him. The laws of Ethelred stated expressly that a priest who conducted himself properly should have the wergeld of a thegn. Thirty was the canonical age at which one could enter full priesthood, and there is no reason to believe that the rule was not observed. Wilfrid was ordained priest after he had been ordained abbot at Ripon.[30] Indeed a man entering priestly orders in Anglo-Saxon days was truly one worthy to be a bishop. Below the priest were the deacons and the subdeacons of the secular church. Many of these must also have received their education at monkish hands. Complaints concerning the illiteracy of the clergy were not unknown, though often they came with the querulousness of the learned. Complaints at the end of the period of the non-observance of celibacy were frequent, though in this respect a sharpening in attitude of the Church itself towards the marriage of secular clergy must be taken into account. Energetic prelates would threaten the penalties of hell, or ask their clergy to choose between their wife or their church, but for the most part the age was content to see its clergy in minor orders safely attached. *Si non caste tamen caute* was a maxim capable of extension beyond its native archbishopric of Hamburg and Bremen.

Some insight into the standard of the priesthood in the early eleventh century is given by Wulfstan in his 'Institutes of Polity'. A man seeking ordination was to seek his bishop a month before the date of the ordination ceremony. The bishop was to satisfy himself that the candidate was a true believer, and capable of making known true belief to other men. He was to show understanding of church services, particularly of baptism and the mass. He was to know something of the (penitential) canon, and to have enough mathematics to calculate the ecclesiastical year. If he was proficient in these things he was worthy of ordination. If his knowledge was not up to standard, if he was only half-taught (*samlæredne*), ordination was still possible, provided that he could give a surety that he would continue to study.[31] Wulfstan, and others like him, clearly paid more than lip-service to the idea of an educated clergy.

The ideal of the English Church in organizational matters was truly Roman and territorial. But it would be false to present a

[30] Wihtræd 18; VIII Ethelred 28; Eddius Stephanus, *Life of Wilfrid*, c. viii.
[31] Wulfstan's *Institutes*, ed. K. Jost, pp. 219–21.

picture, even for the eleventh century, of an England dotted with
stone-built churches, the centres of local activity. Yet over some of
the country, the more prosperous east and south, this picture was
not far from the truth. Outside areas where royal influence was
exceptionally strong, religious foundation depended to a great extent on the generosity of the land-owning class. In the last century
of Anglo-Saxon England this generosity found its most spectacular
expression in the endowment of new or re-endowment of old
monastic foundations. The ealdorman Byrhtnoth, who died at the
battle of Maldon, and his kindred were great friends to monasteries
in the east country, notably to the newly vitalized Medeshamstede
(Peterborough) and to Ely.[32] Canute himself was responsible for
the foundation of Bury St Edmunds and of St Benet's Holme. The
secular church also received its share of benefaction. In East Anglia
there are traces of endowment and rebuilding of parish churches
by the efforts of quite small men of the land-owning class. At
Stonham in Suffolk nine freemen gave small parcels of land to the
church for the good of their souls.[33] These men were in the full
flood of tradition of Anglo-Saxon church-building. In the pages
of Bede there is mention of noblemen building what are referred
to as their own churches, and having them consecrated by bishops
such as John of Beverley.[34] The mode of thought that leads to
a landlord regarding a church as his property was exceptionally
deep rooted. Even in pagan days prominent men regarded shrines
as their own. In Iceland the dominant social figure in the early
days of settlement was the *goði*, the landlord-priest who would
offer sacrifice and take responsibility for the religious behaviour of
the settlement. Echoes of Germanic house-fathers are everywhere
to be found. The Germanic communities in England as on the
Continent carried forward these ideas into Christian days. In the
main the Church was well content that this should be so. There is a
realism about the ecclesiastical attitude, a sense of the possible that
surprises at first sight. Gregory himself laid down in his wisdom
that heathen shrines could be used, after purification, for the
performance of the Christian mysteries.[35] Every attempt was made
to fit the Church into unfamiliar Germanic surroundings.

[32] E. Miller, *The Abbey and Bishopric of Ely*, p. 22. A. J. Robertson, *Anglo-Saxon Charters*, pp. 315, 337, 430. D. Whitelock, *Anglo-Saxon Wills*, pp. 104–7.
[33] R. R. Darlington, 'Ecclesiastical Reform in the Late Old English Period', *E.H.R.*, 1936, pp. 413–14. D.B. II, 438.
[34] *Hist. Eccl.*, V, 4 and 5.
[35] Ibid., I, 27.

Inevitably there was a financial angle to the problem. Ever before the standardization of money payments in the form of customary gifts and ultimately of tithes, the gifts of the faithful were sufficient to account for much ecclesiastical concern at their just apportionment. Drawing on Germanic and pagan custom, those who built and endowed churches treated the profits of worship as adjuncts to the altar. At its worst this line of thought led to a church being regarded as a mere dominical right, like a mill or a wine-press. Grave concern is expressed from time to time lest episcopal authority should be wrecked by the insistence of landlords on their own choice of chaplain for their church. In the main the bishop was successful in this field, at least in a negative sense; he did not lose his right to consecrate and to ordain within his diocese. How firmly such a right could be exercised against the wishes of a powerful landlord is quite another matter. The laws of Ethelred insisted that no one should oppress the Church or make it an object of improper traffic, or turn out a minister of the Church without the bishop's consent.[36]

The question of the extent of landlord control of the Church is critical in relation to any assessment of its strength and weakness in the eleventh century. Professor Böhmer saw the Anglo-Saxon Church as a classic example of the Germanic territorial Church in action, and his picture of an official episcopate and a Church dominated at the lower levels by landlords cast a gloomy shadow over late Anglo-Saxon England.[37] Modern opinion is much more favourably inclined towards the Old English Church, and it is generally held now that culturally, and in so far as contact with the papacy was concerned, there were few sections of the universal Church so healthy in essentials. On the matter of landlord control, however, it is hard to strike a balance. The tenth and eleventh centuries were the critical period in the course of which a thegnly class came to exercise social control in manorial form over much of rural England: and a measure of control of local churches, for the physical building and endowment of which the thegns were often responsible, was a natural consequence of such a social process. Certainly in Domesday Book churches were treated like any other disposable property. Among the claims heard by the Commissioners in the course of their tour of Huntingdonshire was a cause relating to the church of St Mary. The jurors of

[36] V Ethelred 10.2.
[37] H. Böhmer, 'Das Eigenkirchentum in England', *Festgabe für Felix Liebermann*, Halle 1921, pp. 301–53.

Huntingdon ran through a brief history of the ownership of the church during the previous generation. The Abbot of Thorney had given it in pledge to certain burgesses; King Edward had sold it to two of his own priests; they had sold it back to his chamberlain who in turn sold it to two priests of Huntingdon; these priests held the seal of King Edward at the time of their plaint, but the sheriff held the church, without livery, without writ and without seisin.[38] St Mary's was an important church. It is not to be wondered at that the Domesday Commissioners took special note of it. Their general concern with churches as sources of revenue is brought out by the fact that no fewer than 187 fractions of churches, according to Böhmer's calculations, were recorded in Domesday Book, mostly in the eastern counties.[39] Unfortunately, as we shall see, treatment of churches in the great survey is erratic, and only in Huntingdonshire and in East Anglia is a thorough record presented. No satisfactory explanation has yet been given of the criterion used for inclusion or non-inclusion. The thesis, at first sight attractive, that a church whose value could be assessed in the overall value of a manor did not receive separate treatment, does not stand up to detailed analysis.

(c) The classification of churches and their landed endowments

Domesday Book concerned itself with three main types of church: the principal churches, entered in feudal form under the bishop or abbot who held their lands as tenant-in-chief; collegiate churches; and ordinary churches, some of which were parish churches while others were mere manorial chapels. This division corresponded accurately enough to the principal churches, the old minsters, and the thegns' churches, with or without graveyards, of Anglo-Saxon law. In the early eleventh century a slightly more elaborate classification had been attempted by Ethelred, and repeated by Canute, into four categories: a head-minster, whose *grithbryce*, or penalty for the infringement of special peace, was £5, a medium-sized minster where the penalty was 120 shillings, that is to say £2, a lesser church with graveyard where the penalty was 60 shillings, and finally a field church with no churchyard where the penalty was 30 shillings. That the head-minster was normally, though not inevitably, the seat of a bishop or of an abbot is further suggested by the mention in one manuscript of Kent as a special

[38] D.B. I, 208.
[39] Discussed by R. Lennard, *Rural England*, p. 320.

case where the penalty was raised to £5 to the king and £3 to the archbishop, and by the translation in the *Instituta Cnuti* as *principale. autem ecclesie, sicut episcopatus et abbatie*.[40] Substantial endowments were needed to maintain these central churches, the true heart of any diocese. In the early tenth century three hundred hides of land were regarded as suitable endowment for a bishop. Many of the greatest churches, such as that of Worcester, possessed landed wealth far in excess of this figure. Indeed the empire-building of great churches sometimes encountered the strongest of opposition. The anti-monastic reaction, that followed Edgar's generosity to the revival of the mid-tenth century, is a case in point, though this reaction may have been local and personal in nature. Among the records of dispute over land embodied in surviving charters there is plentiful evidence that Anglo-Saxon kindreds did not always take easily to the granting out of estates to the Church away from the kindred. For all the undying nature of these great ecclesiastical houses, land did pass away from them. Anglo-Saxon wills and charters tell us of grants made to the Church in pre-Conquest days that were firmly in the hands of laymen in 1066 as well as in 1086. There was clearly considerable mobility in land-owning in eleventh-century England. The enduring feature is that the Church remained wealthy.

The principal source of information concerning the distribution of ecclesiastical wealth naturally lies in Domesday Book itself. The feudal arrangement of the Book in its final form tends to concentrate the information on the great ecclesiastical houses, particularly on the monastic houses. Information concerning collegiate churches and parish churches is much more scanty and difficult to interpret. On the endowment of the great monastic houses Domesday Book records that about one-sixth of the total landed wealth in England south of the Humber was owned by the monasteries with a total rent-roll of over £11,000.[41] Glastonbury was far and away the wealthiest with an income of over £800 a year. The distribution of monastic houses reflects conditions of the preceding two centuries. In Northumbria, the great home of English monastic observance in the seventh and eighth centuries, there were no monasteries whatsoever. In Mercia there were seven, five clustered around the Severn/Avon watershed in unconquered English Mercia. These houses were of solid worth and value with rent-rolls mostly over

[40] II Edgar 1 and 2; I Canute 3.2; Liebermann I, p. 283.
[41] The following paragraphs are based on D. Knowles, *The Monastic Order in England*, particularly pp. 702–3 (Appendix VI), and pp. 100–2.

£80 a year. Wessex, with seventeen houses, showed much greater variety. Some of the foundations were very poor indeed with rent-rolls as low as £17. Others like Malmesbury with £178.50 and Cerne with £160.25 ranked among the more substantial houses of the realm. Of the several East Anglian monasteries Ely nearly £769 and Bury St Edmunds nearly £640 were very wealthy. So too were the great abbeys of Canterbury Christ Church, the cathedral, and St Augustine's, Westminster, and the Old Minster at Winchester. The house at St Albans, whose rent-roll amounted to £270, was prosperous but not yet in the class it was to occupy in the later twelfth and thirteenth centuries.

Not only the amount of the endowment but the distribution of the endowment has its special features of interest. St Augustine's of Canterbury, for example, had obviously appealed mostly to local men with the result that its landed wealth lay solidly within the county, most of it between Canterbury and the Isle of Thanet. Westminster, on the other hand, with the widespread benevolence of the king to its support, had lands spread over no fewer than fifteen counties. The number of monks was small, ranging from a minimum of twelve to not much more than fifty. They were aristocratic for the most part, and Anglo-Saxon in sympathy. Four of the cathedral sees, Christ Church, Canterbury, Worcester, Sherborne and Winchester, were served directly by monks. Their wealth and their sympathies made them a special problem for the early Norman rulers.

At such cathedrals, whether or not they were true monasteries, the prime purpose of the organization was to have a group of dedicated men at the centre of a diocese, a group upon which could devolve the duties of instruction of clergy and of young scholars, without which the hope of a competent ministry would die. The success of the venture in the late tenth and eleventh centuries was so great that attempts were made to associate other great abbeys with the direction of diocesan duties. The diocese of Bath and Wells bears in its name to this day evidence of successful association of a rich abbey with a rural cathedral centre. At Rochester Lanfranc and Gundulf were able to replace a somewhat moribund community of secular canons by regular monks.[42] Other associations or suggested associations were not so fruitful. Efforts to unite Lincoln with nearby Stow, and Sherborne with Malmesbury,

[42] R. A. L. Smith, 'The Early Community of St Andrew at Rochester', *E.H.R.*, 1945.

and Bury St Edmunds with an East Anglian see failed. Ely was eventually made into the head of an independent see, but only after much vicissitude. Even so, when Carlisle was created as a new cathedral in 1133, served by a college of Austin canons, half the cathedrals in England were served by monks.

Of the wealth of the non-monastic head-minsters it is harder to speak. The poverty of York was notorious, so much so that for two lengthy periods in the last century of Anglo-Saxon England it was held in plurality together with the rich diocese of Worcester. There may have been political reasons for this union of a southern diocese with York, and it has been pointed out that in the last century of Anglo-Saxon England the kings favoured the presence of ecclesiastics with a solid Southumbrian, particularly Anglo-Danish, connection at the great Northumbrian see.[43] It must be confessed that the landed wealth of York, extending deep into Nottinghamshire with the great minster of Southwell under its control, does not appear all that insignificant. At Southwell, a head-minster in its own right, Ealdred established prebends either just before or just after the Norman Conquest.[44] Edward the Elder, with his administrative ability, had increased the number of bishops in Wessex, aiming to give each shire its bishop. Under his son Athelstan this aim was finally achieved for the whole of the west, but presumably because of difficulty of endowment, in 1066, the new see of Ramsbury had again been reunited with the mother se : of Sherborne, and the see of St German's which Athelstan had created was placed under the Bishop of Devon. Without a monastic nucleus to draw on, diocesan organization was exceedingly difficult to arrange. There is no satisfying evidence for the existence of dean and chapter in pre-Norman days. Nor were there rural deans capable of supervising sections of the still considerable dioceses. Archdeacons existed but references to them are scattered both in time and place, the earliest references to them dating from the late eighth century and the clearest references from near the end of the period when the 'Northumbrian Priests' Law' stated that fines were to be laid on priests who refused the archdeacon's summons or continued to say mass in defiance of his prohibition. But, as Sir Frank Stenton says, 'the custom which gave to the bishop at least

[43] D. Whitelock, 'The Dealings of the Kings of England with Northumbria in the Tenth and Eleventh Centuries', *The Anglo-Saxons*, ed. P. Clemoes, London, 1958, pp. 73–5.
[44] *Historians of the Church of York*, R.S., vol. II, p. 353; cited by F. M. Stenton, *Anglo-Saxon England*, p. 436.

one archdeacon as his executive and judicial assistant is certainly of Norman introduction'.[45]

For the most part the cathedral clergy had to be maintained out of the revenues common to the church they served. These charges could be exceedingly heavy on ecclesiastical endowments. It has already been noted how in one Worcester *cause célèbre* the bishop had granted an estate on condition that there should be a priest in the family to which it had been granted, and that trouble came when this condition was not fulfilled.[46] A bishop then as now needed a clear head for business and for successful handling of revenues. All chief minsters controlled substantial estates. Even in as poor a county as Stafford the value of lands belonging to the Bishop of Chester exceeded £36 at the time of the Domesday survey. A wealthy see like Worcester demanded skill more natural to the head of a financial corporation than to a pastor of souls.

Apart from the head-minsters which served as the headquarters of a bishop or an abbot there were other great churches, some-times described as head-minsters, which shaded off gradually into important churches served by a community of canons, into old minsters that were on occasion the mother churches of extensive areas. These were normally organized on a collegiate basis, and in Cornwall, for example, such collegiate churches were the only ones mentioned in the Domesday account of the shire. They bear a marked resemblance to the *clas* churches of Wales, and may rep-resent a survival of the old order in the conservative west. Not that the existence of such churches is an indication of racial differences between Celt and Saxon. Such establishments are to be found in the east as in the west, and were exceptionally well suited to areas where the population was not concentrated but settled in hamlets scattered over a relatively wide district. They represent an older form of ecclesiastical organization than the more advanced parish system of the eleventh century, and their antiquity is suggested by the fact that they often served as centres to which tithes were delivered from a cluster of surrounding habitation sites. For a variety of causes, some of recent origin, these mother churches were not thriving in 1086. A manorial lord was empowered to send two-thirds of the tithe to the mother church of a district, but new Norman lords found that alienation of this tithe to distant monasteries over sea was a relatively painless method of rewarding

[45] *Norðhymbra preosta lagu*, 6 and 7; Liebermann I, p. 380. F. M. Stenton, op. cit., p. 440.
[46] See above, p. 184.

their favoured abbey or nunnery on the far side of the Channel. Sequestration of revenue, diversion of effort into new monastic channels, a general tightening of discipline, particularly concerning celibacy, towards those who lived according to rule, contributed to their decay. The status of parish priest became more to the taste of many who had served the collegiate churches before the Conquest.[47]

In other more direct ways the new Norman lords helped positively to further the process by which parish life was extended. There is evidence of energetic rebuilding of churches during the early Norman period, and there is incidental reference to the foundation of new churches. Wulfstan of Worcester considered it his ideal to establish a church on each one of his estates, and to encourage other estate owners to do likewise. At Whistley in Berkshire, the Abingdon chronicler tells of the foundation of a new church because the inhabitants found it difficult to cross the fords to reach the old church at Sonning three miles away.[48] To revert for a moment to the classification of churches given by Ethelred, it may be said that the object of the conscientious bishop was to elevate the status of the lesser churches so that they would serve as a permanent base for a permanently settled priest. Possession of a graveyard was clearly an important mark of status in a church, a significant step towards the creation of a parish church. The success or non-success of attempts to create parish churches of this type, with sufficient revenue to maintain a priest, with some portion at least of the tithes, and burial fees, depended very much on local conditions, on the presence or absence of a resident lord, on the extent to which population was concentrated in a given area. As far as generalization is possible from the difficult statistics of Domesday Book, it would appear that over much of the country the parish system was well advanced by the end of the eleventh century.

Domesday statistics are especially difficult in relation to the churches because of a lack of consistency on the part of the scribes. The Commissioners, with their concern for revenue well to the fore, did not always record separately clerks and priests and churches, whose renders might be accounted for elsewhere, at times, though only at times, in the total value of a manor. Scribal

---

[47] R. Lennard, *Rural England*, pp. 300–2. A reminder of the complexities, which does justice to the continued vitality of the 'special churches' of Domesday Book, is given by John Blair, 'Secular Minster Churches in Domesday Book', *Domesday Book: a Reassessment*, ed. P. Sawyer, London, 1985, pp. 104–42.

[48] Ibid., p. 296 and p. 287; *Vita Wulfstani*, p. 52.

practice varied from circuit to circuit. As has already been mentioned, Huntingdonshire and East Anglia were particularly well favoured. In Huntingdonshire no fewer than fifty-three churches were recorded out of a total of eighty-three habitation sites; in East Anglia there are three hundred and forty-five churches mentioned out of six hundred and thirty-nine recorded places.[49] Elsewhere the record is more scanty but the overall impression remains that England was well served with ecclesiastical buildings, and that no Englishman lived an impossible distance from a church. Supplementary information sometimes is available to fill the gaps left by Domesday Book. In Kent the churches listed in the records of the monks at Christ Church, and preserved in the so-called 'Domesday Monachorum', amount to two hundred and twelve in number, more than half of which are not mentioned in Domesday itself. Further lists show that even this total is far from complete, and Dr Ward has argued that there were probably more than four hundred churches in Kent in 1066.[50] They were not all elaborate structures; some, lacking patrons, may have been no more than chapels served occasionally by priests from ancient mother churches like Dover, Lyminge or Folkestone. But their presence is enough to indicate the intensity and the variety of Anglo-Saxon religious experience. From the rough field-church, a cross, an altar and a primitive shelter, through the middle-sized church with or without graveyard, to the splendours of an Earl's Barton, to the head-minsters whose pattern can clearly be traced at North Elmham or at St Augustine's, Canterbury: all the evidence points to vitality and to depth in Anglo-Saxon and early Norman religious life. The great administrative, building bishops and abbots of the late eleventh century added their own peculiar crown of solid Romanesque achievement to very stable foundations.

(d) Ecclesiastical revenues: tithes and dues

It is probable that the permanent endowment in land, vast as it was and representing something over a quarter of the wealth of England in 1086, constituted only the smaller fraction of the total ecclesiastical revenue. Apart from the land and from extraordinary donations there were two principal sources of income to the Anglo-

[49] R. Lennard, op. cit., p. 294. VII Ethelred, the call to repentance, suggests that a church was within everyone's reach.
[50] D. C. Douglas, *Domesday Monachorum*, p. 15; G. Ward, *Archæologia Cantiana*, vol. XLV, p. 89; R. Lennard, op. cit., p. 294.

263

Saxon church, tithes and customary dues, both stemming from the
free offerings of the faithful. Tithes were in origin gifts made by
the laity to their local church. To judge from tenth-century legisla-
.tion the gift was often made to or through the local head-minster
or minster, and was presumably collected by some member, or
possibly by some reeve, of the ancient minster. Church-scot was
compulsory already in the laws of Ine, with a fine of sixty shillings
imposed for non-payment, and a threat that the defaulter would
have to pay twelve-fold.[51] It is probable that even at that early
stage, *church-scot* signified the first fruits of the grain crop, and
was often paid in grain. In the tenth and eleventh centuries a
land-owner who had set up a church on his own bookland was
permitted to pay a third of his tithe direct to that church, the
remainder passing to the head-minster. Canute in his ordinance
of 1027 stated that in the middle of August the tithe of the fruits
of the earth, and at the feast of St Martin the first fruits of the grain
(*primitie seminum*) should be paid to the church of the parish where
each man resided, and the twelfth-century translators, by whose
hands knowledge of the document has survived, took these dues
(or possibly the last alone) to mean church-scot; even though Edgar
on the other hand had declared that all church-scot should go to
the old minster.[52] Old Testament precedent had much to do with
the adoption of tithes. By the end of the seventh century a tenth
of the corn produce was regarded as a reasonable contribution to
the Church. The concern of the legislator in those days was to
affirm the legitimacy of such gifts. True compulsion and formal
penal legislation entered the field later, probably not until the
tenth century. Athelstan ordered tithes to be paid from his own
land and from the land of his ealdormen, bishops and reeves.
Edmund invoked the spiritual penalty of excommunication for
non-payment. Edgar insisted that tithes should be paid to old
minsters from all land under the plough, both thegn's inland
and geneatland. Edgar also introduced true penal legislation, later
reaffirmed by Ethelred and Canute, to the effect that in case of
refusal a king's reeve, a bishop's reeve and a priest were to visit
the culprit, set to one side without his consent the tithe, leave him
another tithe for his own use, and divide the remainder, four tenths
to the bishop, and four tenths to the landlord.[53] If such legislation

[51] Ine 4.
[52] I Canute 11 and 11.1 (II Edgar 2 and 2.1); Canute 1027, 16; I Canute 11.2
(II Edgar 2.2).
[53] I Athelstan, Prologue; I Edmund 2; II Edgar 1.1; II Edgar 3.1.

had come from Ethelred alone, it might suggest an excess of desperation rather than hope of effective government action. But the government itself played a most active part in the distribution of tithe. Ethelred and his witan declared that a third of the tithe should be spent on the repair of churches, a third on the servants of God and a third on the poor and poverty-stricken slaves.[54] If all the regulations were observed, even spasmodically, there is something surely to be said for Maitland's view that the presence of great ecclesiastical estates was associated with the depression of freemen. Tithes were so much a commonplace that Aelfric in his homily for the First Sunday in Lent could liken the fast of Lent to tithing-days, when we tithe our bodies with abstinence 'even as God's law enjoins us that we should of all the things which accrue to us from our yearly tillage give the tithe to God'.[55]

In the tenth century a distinction was already drawn between the great tithe, levied on the corn crop, and the lesser tithe, on the young animals, on vegetables and poultry, on the products of agrarian life, essential but regarded as subordinate to the yield of the arable. The lesser tithes were more personal in many ways than the great tithe, and in time came to be more bitterly resented. Faint echoes of discontent have reached us from the Anglo-Saxon age in the fourth code of Edgar which attributed the outbreak of plague to non-payment of tithes, and from the querulous tone of Ethelred's legislation which attributed even the success of the Danes to the evasion of legitimate church dues.[56]

There are also a whole host of minor dues, which were gradually built up into regular exactions. The most complete list is given in the first code of Canute: plough-alms, fifteen days after Easter, the lesser tithe by Whitsun, and the harvest offering by All Saints' Day. Peter's Pence was to be paid by St Peter's Day, and church-scot by St Martin's Day, the latter to be paid by each free household direct to the chief minster. Light-dues were to be paid three times a year: a halfpenn'orth of wax from each hide at Easter, and again at All Saints' Day and on the feast of the purification of St Mary (2 February). Soul-scot or burial due was to be paid at the open grave.[57]

This list shows well how the Church was involved in the workings of the agricultural year at every stage and with utter regularity

54 VIII Ethelred 6.
55 *Aelfric's Catholic Homilies*, vol. I, no. i, first Sunday in Lent.
56 IV Edgar 1; VII Ethelred 7.1; a commonplace in Wulfstan's thought, as in his 'Sermo Lupi ad Anglos', *E.H.D.* I, pp. 928 ff.
57 I Canute 8.1, 9, 10, 11.2, 12, 13.

from Easter to Easter. The mere recitation of dues is a reminder how used the countryside was to transactions assessed and often paid in hard cash, in the familiar silver pennies known from late Saxon times. Payments must have been formidable in mass, and it is quite understandable why Domesday churches should be treated as property, pure and simple.

(e) The status of the clergy

Any attempt to obtain a fuller account of the clergymen themselves meets with failure until the time of Domesday Book. Not enough direct evidence has survived. From the earliest days the higher clergy were recruited predominantly from the aristocracy. Even in the seventh century royal princesses found it fashionable to enter nunneries, where some became abbesses, presiding over the double houses for which England was so famous. The solvent of education was, as we have seen, early at work. Exceptionally bright boys, provided that they could enter monastic schools, had the ecclesiastical hierarchy open in front of them. There is one famous example, that of Cædmon the poet, of a peasant rising, through the natural gifts of his poetry, to become a monk. The fact that St Peter, though only a fisherman, became a bishop was well known and often spoken of. Recruitment to the lower positions among the clergy is exceptionally difficult to discuss. Wulfstan was very concerned that an 'altar-thegn' should be given great respect, and should in fact be fully worthy of a thegn's wergeld, both in life and in death. Even a thrall could aspire to become a thegn, and to Wulfstan it was clearly the office of altar-thegn that merited respect and rank. Only one example of an unfree priest has been preserved in the Anglo-Saxon records.[58] Possibility of advancement was not cut off from a boy, orphan or of good kin, who showed special aptitude. Even the taint of unfree birth could be overcome, though legal insistence was still strong that no illegitimate child should become a full priest.

More tangible conclusions concerning the social status of the priest can be made, however, from the facts and figures available in Domesday Book, fragmentary and partial though they are.[59] There is obviously great variety among the priesthood. The most prosperous of the village clergy held land that would have been

[58] See above, pp. 225–6. VIII Ethelred 28; ed. D. Whitelock, *The Will of Æthelgifu*, p. 32.
[59] R. Lennard, op. cit., pp. 306–32.

ufficient to qualify for thegnhood under the old dispensation.
There were also very poor priests holding a bare and pathetic
acre of land. In general the priest seems to have been a man
of something more than average wealth in his community. The
Domesday Commissioners expected to be able to take evidence
from him, as they made their enquiry, a fact which in itself shows
that it was regarded as normal that the priest should be a familiar
figure in any rural community. More often than not he possessed
some glebe land, a share at times extensive in the village arable.
He normally possessed plough-beasts. It is not known how much
of the great tithe would come to him, probably little save in some
specially favoured fat livings. These fat livings, such as Bosham
in Sussex, were at times held by rich pluralists, chancellors or
bishops-to-be, busy at the king's court. It is taken as a special
mark of sanctity in Wulfstan that he refused, when young, such
a rich living in order to take on the arduous habit of the monk.
Service could be extracted from a priest, though of an honourable
kind. The priests of Archenfield, the Welshry of Herefordshire,
were empowered to act as the king's messengers when such were
needed in Wales. Rent was normally paid from the glebe-land to
the lord of the church.[60]

As far as his relationship with his natural kindred is concerned
the Anglo-Saxon laws declare that the monk has no kin. The priest
was not in a similar position, nor were of course the lower orders of
clergy.[61] The pledge to celibacy may have been vital in this respect,
and the simple fact that the priest was still tied to his kin-law may
be a valuable pointer to a widespread non-observance of the rule
of celibacy. Pope Gregory himself, when he wrote to St Augustine,
gave permission to those clerics who were not in Holy Orders
and who did not wish to remain single, to marry and to receive
their stipends separately. He enjoined Augustine to make sure
that they observed the Church's discipline so that by God's help
they might 'preserve themselves in thought, word and deed from
anything unbecoming to their office'.[62] In later years much came
to depend on the bishop's own views as to what constituted good
order, but there is no reason to suppose that the rule of celibacy was
applied with any vigour in Anglo-Saxon England. Aelfric himself,
paraphrasing the extract from Gregory's letter to Augustine, said

---

[60] D.B. I, 17; R. Lennard, op. cit., p. 318; *Vita Wulfstani*, ed. R. R. Darlington,
p. 45; D.B. I, 179.
[61] VIII Ethelred 23.
[62] *Hist. Eccl.*, I, 27; the answer to the first of Augustine's questions.

somewhat ambiguously that to priests of common order (*gemæne hades*) it was permitted chastely to enjoy wedlock. But to other serving God's altar, that is mass-priests and deacons, all sexual intercourse was wholly forbidden. Wulfstan perhaps gives a more realistic insight into affairs when he complains that though it is forbidden that mass-priests should marry nevertheless some have two or more wives; and some put aside their wife and take another while the first is still alive. These men bring their order to such wretchedness that they, mass-priests as they are, live like ceorls. 'A priest's wife is the devil's snare', was his rigid summary of the situation.[63] The eleventh-century 'Northumbrian Priests' Laws' laid it down bluntly that a priest was to be cursed if he left his wife (*cwen*) and took another.[64]

(f) *The Church and the administration of law*

There were no separate ecclesiastical courts, as such, though the bishop by nature of his office exercised a disciplinary jurisdiction over his clergy in matters which did not come under the surveillance of public courts. His penitential discipline could be severe. King Edmund forbade anyone guilty of homicide to enter his household till he had begun to make amends to the king and had submitted to every legal penalty prescribed by the bishop.[65] Moreover, time and time again we hear that if a priest is guilty of a capital crime the case is to be reserved to the bishop. The *Liber Eliensis* has an interesting case of the bringing of a thieving priest before a bishop.[66] But it seems evident that such serious causes would be heard in the public courts of shire or hundred. An ordinance of Edgar laid down that the bishop of a diocese and the ealdorman should be present at the shire courts and should direct the observance of both God's law and secular law.[67] Indeed in late Anglo-Saxon England the bishop, together with the earl or his deputy, became the most prominent figure at the local shire court, taking on the virtual leadership of the moot.

The income of the Church was greatly augmented by the fines received for offences that came within its purview at these public courts. It was not only a question of matrimonial offences, or

---

[63] *Aelfric's Catholic Homilies*, p. 94; Wulfstan, *Collected Homilies*, ed. A. Napier, p. 269; *Wulfstan's Institutes*, p. 122.
[64] *Norðhymbra preosta lagu*, 35; Liebermann I, p. 382.
[65] II Edmund 4.
[66] *Liber Eliensis*, II, 32, ed. D. J. Stewart, London, 1848, p. 147.
[67] III Edgar 5.2.

icest, or perjury, but practically anything that could be classified
s moral passed under its control. The Archbishop of Canterbury,
y special franchise it is true, so extended the normal privilege that
ie penalties inflicted on both man and woman guilty of adultery
assed to him. The custom was, as we shall see, for the woman's
ine to pass to the church, the man's to the king.[68]

Above all the Church played a role of utmost importance in
rocedures relating to ordeal and to compurgation. Documents
ave survived telling us of the care with which the ordeal was
onducted. Elaborate arrangements were made to ensure that the
ccused approached the ordeal suitably prepared. He was to fast
or three days on bread, water, herbs and salt, to receive the
acrament and to make formal declaration of innocence. The in-
truments of ordeal, iron or water, were then hallowed, the litany
ung and the trial begun. The accused either plunged his arm
ito boiling water to draw out a stone, or seized a bar of glowing
ron of stated weight and carried it a specified number of paces
ccording to the gravity of the offence. The state of the injuries
fter three days indicated guilt or innocence.[69] For all its apparent
arbarity one cannot but be impressed by the religious trappings
nd formality of the proceedings. A guilty man must have passed
hrough a particularly bad three days before such ordeal: but
hen, to be innocent in such circumstances cannot have been a
appy situation. The classic but not altogether convincing defence
f ordeal is that the innocent rarely reached that unfortunate stage.
t is evident too that in causes where compurgation was adopted,
ntailing the counting of the value of the oaths paraded by this
itigious people, the clergy played a most prominent part. The
ishop was to see that profits arising from all religious offences
vere to be put to good use 'to pay for prayers, to the maintenance
f the indigent, to the repair of churches, to education, to clothing
nd feeding those who serve God, and to the purchase of books
nd bells and ecclesiastical vestments'.[70]

g) The Church and finance in general

During the last centuries of Anglo-Saxon England the Church
ertainly improved beyond measure its financial organization. Ex-

---

[8] D.B. I, 1: *De Adulterio vero per totum Chent habet rex hominem et Archiepiscopus
iulierem, excepta terra Sanctae Trinitatis et Sancti Augustini et Sancti Martini de quibus
ex nichil habet.*
[9] *Ordal*, Liebermann I, p. 386, and in particular *Iudicium Dei*, ibid., p. 407.
[0] VI Ethelred 51.

perience in matters such as the collection of Peter's Pence prove
a permanent asset. It is possible that churches were used mor
extensively than has been appreciated in the collection of norma
geld. King Eadred relied on his bishops, and on Abbot Dunstar
to take charge of the charitable bequests that he ordered in h
will.[71] There can be no doubt but that, for all the exhortations t
apostolic poverty, ecclesiastics were regarded as men most likely t
be competent and honest in financial transactions.

This effectiveness was, however, limited by the general attitud
of the Church towards money and usury. Failure to make a clea
distinction between interest and usury proved to have disastrou
social effects. The Church set its face against anything that smacke
of usurious transaction. The accretion of wealth in ecclesiasti
cal hands led therefore to little general economic improvemen
Church lands were not notably better cultivated than those in la
hands. Church wealth was locked up in valuable vestments, chal
ices, ornaments. Only perhaps in increased frequency of manumis
sion did the Church make a decisive step towards the amelioratio
of the material condition of her tenants. In general she acted a
a brake on the economy rather than as a stimulus to economi
advance.

3. THE CHURCH AND SOCIETY

(a) Marriage laws

The Church – regarded purely and simply as an institution –
can be seen at the end of the period as a great land-owner, i
receipt of vast revenues, possessing financial and judicial right
over the inhabitants of dioceses and parishes on a very large scale
Yet this picture would be false if it were taken as complete. Th
Church was more than its institutional shell. The Anglo-Saxor
Church made great impact on English society, particularly in it
attitude to marriage and inheritance, and in this respect at leas
the Anglo-Saxon Church fulfilled those functions expected from
any branch of the Catholic Church in the West.

The Church systematically attempted to clarify the existing
anomalous customs of the Anglo-Saxons in relation to marriage
and inheritance, and to give a measure of protection to the widow

---

[71] Harmer, *Select Documents*, no. xxi.

and orphans. Something has been said in an earlier chapter of marriage agreements in so far as they affected the holding of land. From record of such settlements together with the royal law-codes and the one anonymous tract that has survived, it is possible to trace a development towards a more rational and systematic treatment of marriage arrangements. The earliest law-codes tell of men buying wives, and also give the impression that divorce was as simple as purchase. In the middle of the tenth century an estate was forfeited to Archbishop Oscetel in compensation for illicit cohabitation – there were two brothers who had one wife. Even as late as the early eleventh century a homilist could arraign with indignation those who banded together to buy one woman to be owned in common.[72] The Church's teachings themselves, austere in theory, were tempered by circumstance. The marriage customs of the Anglo-Saxons were older than the Church, and fitted only uneasily into an ecclesiastical framework. There were two principal steps to a marriage, the formal betrothal, at which a settlement was reached of questions relating to property and endowment, and the ceremony of giving the bride to the groom. Neither demanded the presence of a priest, but the Church strove, in the main successfully, to be represented at the marriage where 'there should by rights be a priest, who shall unite them together with God's blessing in all prosperity'.[73] Lanfranc was still struggling after the Norman Conquest to prevent men from giving their daughters or kinswomen in marriage without a priestly benediction. The Church was not successful in another of its objects: to prevent marriage between partners within its neatly drawn tables of affinity. Even the great Maitland threw up his hands in despair at this aspect of ecclesiastical marriage law which he characterized as 'a maze of flighty fancies and mis-applied logic'.[74] Attempts to limit marriage to the sixth or seventh knee were unrealistic in a predominantly rural community, and readily explain the charges of incest put forward by the homilists of the eleventh century.

The fact that to the end of the period, and beyond, a marriage could be made validly without the blessing of the Church helps to make intelligible the apparent lack of rigidity in ecclesiastical rulings on matters where rigidity was later to be the order of the day. Divorce was permitted by Theodore of Tarsus in cer-

---

[72] Ethelbert 77; *E.H.D.* I, p. 565 (memoranda on the estates belonging to the see of York); Wulfstan, 'Sermo Lupi ad Anglos', *E.H.D.* I, p. 931.
[73] 'Concerning the Betrothal of a Woman', 8, ibid., p. 468.
[74] F. Pollock and F. W. Maitland, *History of English Law*, vol. II, p. 387.

tain instances, notably in case of desertion for five years and in the case of a partner being carried off into hopeless captivity, again with a five-year period before a second marriage could be made. Only a year's delay was insisted on for a wife who had not been married before and whose husband had been reduced to penal slavery.[75] This probably conformed to secular practice, and Professor Whitelock has drawn attention to evidence for easy divorce in eleventh-century Northumbria, where Earl Uhtred is said by a Durham authority to have married and divorced two wives in succession, the first of the wives also remarrying only to achieve a second divorce.[76] No doubt in more sophisticated times the ruling of nullity on the grounds of consanguinity could be put forward to protect the legal position of the Church. But in fact the Church was probably more concerned with the part it felt called on to play in the making of marriages to worry unduly about the breaking of marriages. Its penitential discipline showed some anxiety over various sexual perversions, and its general attitude favoured normality even if the legal position was blurred. 'It is better to marry than to burn' was the great text that haunted the mind of the ecclesiastical thinker on such questions.

The Church's reaction to adultery was not as savage as was the case in many communities, pagan as well as Christian. Boniface held it as a reproach to King Ethelbald and the Mercians that the heathen Old Saxons were more rigorous in their treatment of offenders than were the Christians.[77] Even so the penalties ecclesiastical and secular, were far from negligible. A wronged husband, a father catching a married daughter in adultery, or a son his mother in his father's lifetime, could slay the offender without incurring a feud.[78] In a Winchester charter, supposedly of the early tenth century, an adulterer is said to have forfeited his lands. King Edmund at his great London synod decreed that an adulterer should be treated like the seducer of a nun and forbidden Christian burial until he had made amends, just like the slayer of a man; that is to say made amends with the payment

---

[75] F. M. Stenton, *Anglo-Saxon England*, p. 140. Some ecclesiastical opinion was rigid enough. Pope John VIII wrote to the Archbishop of Canterbury, 877/878, and stated that no man was to marry whilst his former wife was still alive, *E.H.D.* I, p. 882.

[76] D. Whitelock, *The Beginnings of English Society*, pp. 150–1; Simeon of Durham (ed. T. Arnold), vol. I, pp. 215–20. His first wife was the daughter of Bishop Aldhun, the second a daughter of a rich citizen of York, named Styr, Ulf's son.

[77] *E.H.D.* I, p. 819.

[78] Leis Willelme 35, 35.1; Liebermann I, p. 514. Alfred 42.7.

of his wergeld. Heavy fines were certainly inflicted; according to the *Leges Henrici Primi* a married man guilty of fornication should pay his wergeld.[79] Penalties were even heavier on the wife found in adultery than on the husband. Canute stated that the judgement on the woman taken in adultery rested in the bishop's hands. Her property was to pass to her lawful husband, and the physical penalties involved mutilation, the cutting off of the nose and ears. Where public authority entered the affair, and fines were imposed, it was customary for the king to take the fine from the man, and the archbishop or bishop from the woman. As has already been said, the Archbishop of Canterbury enjoyed the double privilege in special localities, taking the proceeds from both offenders.[80] An important text, preserved in a late copy, implies that penal slavery was also imposed on the offenders as well as fines, when it declares: 'Concerning *æbricas* which you asked about, whether with nuns or laywomen, the convicted woman always goes to the bishop's see with her third part, and the male to the lord, whether it be bookland or folkland, whether it belongs to the king himself or any man. Then the man goes with his two parts to the lord if he commit adultery, and they are both convicted [*forworhte*]'.[81] But infringement of marriage law still remained in large part a matter for private settlement, into which Church and State intruded only partially and with difficulty.

Yet it is true to say that Christian teaching on marriage and on the permanent nature of the union between man and wife helped to bring further stability to Anglo-Saxon society, though marriage itself remained much of a secular contract, preceded by negotiation between kin and kin, and guaranteed by strong oaths and pledges.

In the matter of transmission of land at marriage settlements the Church played an increasingly powerful part as the body responsible for the making and the preserving of records. Above all in the solemn sanction given to wills ecclesiastical influence was very powerful. There are examples of death-bed wills made in the presence of important ecclesiastics.[82] The Church was especially concerned with such testamentary dispositions because of the need of the testator to make provision for his soul, by gifts to the Church

[79] *C.S.*, 623 and 1150; I Edmund 4; *Leges Henrici Primi* 12.3.
[80] II Canute 53, D.B. I, 1; see above, p. 269.
[81] B.M. (Add. MS. 43703, f. 225), printed by Robin Flower, *London Medieval Studies*, 1937, p. 62. Liebermann II, p. 365.
[82] A. J. Robertson, *Anglo-Saxon Charters*, no. xli; *Liber Eliensis*, II, 11, ed. D. J. Stewart, p. 122 and pp. 124–5.

and charitable bequests. To die intestate was, in some measure, a sin. Examples have been given above of ecclesiastical concern with proper provision for widows and daughters, and it is notable that some of the most celebrated land disputes of the period resulted in the ultimate enrichment of the Church.[83]

As in feudal days marriage could be used as an important diplomatic weapon, and it is clear that churchmen played a prominent part in the arrangement of such affairs. At the highest level in society are what truly amount to the matrimonial policies of Offa of Mercia or of Edward the Elder and his son Athelstan. The latter policy was particularly successful; Athelstan could boast of three sisters exceptionally well married, the one to the great Otto of Germany, the second to Hugh the Great, *dux Francorum*, the third to the Carolingian, Charles the Simple. Athelstan was, through this last marriage arrangement, uncle of Louis IV, Louis d'Outremer. Similarly the queens of Anglo-Saxon England often exercised great influence, particularly in the ecclesiastical field, and often represented in reverse diplomatic alliances of the type aimed at by Edward the Elder. Judith, the stepmother of Alfred the Great, and also most scandalously his sister-in-law, seems to have brought with her important notions concerning the special title and position of the queen, from her native Frankish sources. But throughout the period there is ample evidence that the queen played an active part in affairs, subscribing to charters, advising on matters as varied as the appointment of clerics and the bestowal of estates. By the end of the period special provision was made for the queen as a matter of course, part of the royal revenue in towns such as Exeter being apportioned for her use, and certain estates, notably those going to make up the bulk of the anomalous shire of Rutland. Queenly reputations were not always of the best. Offa's queen, Cynethryth, as far as can be seen a matron of sober life, was much blamed by later chroniclers for the assassination of the young King Ethelbert of East Anglia; stories more fitting to Thryth, the Atalanta of Anglo-Saxon legend, the perilous maiden, were told of this Mercian queen. The death of the young King Edward, the Martyr, was attributed by many to his stepmother, Queen Aelfthryth. In the eleventh century Emma of Normandy, queen first of Ethelred, then of Canute, played a dubious part in political intrigues at the beginning of the reign of her son by Ethelred, Edward the Confessor. The healing of the breach between Edward

---

[83] See above, pp. 188–92.

imself and the powerful Earl Godwin was symbolized in the
marriage, possibly not consummated it is true, between Edward
nd Godwin's daughter, Edith. Among the nobility in general
marriage was a common, though dangerous, way of publicly
nnouncing the end of a feud. Old memories aroused at marriage
easts form one of the steady perils to peace referred to in Anglo-
axon poetry: 'the murderous spear rests for but a little while,
hough the bride be good', sang the poet of 'Beowulf' anxiously.[84]
Vhen the Norman earls conspired with Waltheof against King
Villiam at a disastrous marriage feast in 1075 they were in the
ull tradition, though in this instance vengeance fell from outside,
om the King:

> There was that bride-ale
> Many men's bale.[85]

From the purely social point of view perhaps the most important
ngle fact, and in some respects the most likely to cause disturb-
nce, was that the wife remained worthy of her own kinright.
Marriage did not mean that a woman lost the protection of her
wn kin. In the earliest phase from which record has survived the
ws stated that, in the case of a marriage breaking up, the woman
as entitled to half the goods of the household if she departed with
er child. There was no mention of rights in land at this stage, but
is clear from the rights of the woman's kin in the important
natters of custody of orphans and protection of widows that the
omen continued to enjoy their own status apart from that of their
usbands.[86] According to the treatise concerning marriage, a wife's
indred was to be allowed to stand next in paying compensation,
 she committed an offence and had not possessions with which
he could pay.[87] In such complicated matters the rights were often
omewhat vague, and it is precisely where such vagueness existed
nat the royal and ecclesiastical power, flourishing and extending in
ne course of the tenth and eleventh centuries, exercised itself over
nose fields where authority was ill-defined and indeterminate.

It is reasonable to suppose that the general influence of the
Church in matters such as these, concerning inheritance and pro-
ection of widows and orphans, was towards the peaceful settle-
nent of dispute and the recognition of agreed principle in the

---

[84] 'Beowulf', lines 2030–1, and the Ingeld episode, lines 2032–69.
[85] A.S. Chronicle, 1075.
[86] Ethelbert 78 and 79.
[87] *E.H.D.* I, p. 468.

transmission of land. Great contribution to this end was made b
the evolution of the solemn charter and the formal will, both o
them exhibiting ecclesiastical draftsmanship and the religious hold
exercised by the Church over such fundamental social activities
Perhaps the explanation is that the Church alone could afford
permanence and consistency in such matters to a settled society
The Christian faith and Roman territorial organization were well
adapted to a settled agrarian community. It is more than coin
cidence that as permanent settlement was achieved in new land
so did the barbarians turn to the Roman faith: generally on the
Continent in the fifth and sixth centuries; in Anglo-Saxon England
among the Scandinavians; among the Avars and the Huns. The
only notable exception, where heathenism proved tough to con
quer, lay in Old Saxony, and there the strong political reason o
hatred of the Christian Frank was sufficient to account for the
phenomenon.

(b) The moral pattern

In England there is little unusual about the moral patter
preached, as far as it can be disentangled from homiletic writing
and extracts from law-codes, lives of saints and so on. The Christian
story itself was deeply tinged with the heroic assumptions of society
Christ was portrayed almost as a young warrior-prince, the apostle
as his hearth-troop. The one theme that emerges with constan
iteration, a result of the influence of Gregory the Great, and
through him of St Augustine of Hippo, is an emphasis on the
need for humility and obedience. Discipline of belief was crude
Visions of hell, the whale's mouth, were used freely, and one
imagines effectively. Visions of heaven appeared less frequently
usually of a fair and fertile plain where fruits are to be had fo
the picking, Marvell's garden. Teaching on the Incarnation and
the Atonement was fully in accord with the spirit of the epic age
The justice of God was so great that he would not forcibly take
mankind from the Devil. But the Devil was tricked into slaying
Christ, like a greedy fish that sees the bait, that is to say the
humanity of Christ, but not the hook, that is to say the divinity
and it is by the divinity that the Devil is choked and deprived o
all mankind who believe in God.[88] On most articles of belief such
elaboration was not attempted. A simple call to belief and obedience
was enough. The homilists stress that those who hold to the tru

[88] *Aelfric's Catholic Homilies*, vol. I, p. 216.

aith do not know how lucky they are. But the obligations are correspondingly greater. God expects more from them than from hose who have not heard his word. Both Aelfric and Wulfstan wrote homilies, the former's derived largely from the works of Augustine, Gregory and Bede, that were copied and presumably used well into the twelfth century. They make for vigorous, direct and concentrated sermons. The themes were age-old: the seven deadly sins, above all pride, the relation of this temporal world to he next, submission to one's lot in this world, and so on. Wealth was regarded as a positive danger. 'It is one thing that a man be rich, if his parents have bequeathed him possessions, another if hrough cupidity he becomes rich.'[89] The comforting doctrine was preached that the rich and the poor are needful to each other. The rich should spend and give: the poor should pray for the giver. In so doing the poor give more than they receive. But the simplicity and force of the approach says much for the authors, for the priests and clerks who were to use them, and indeed for he laity who were to receive them.

Perhaps they supply the best evidence we have for the view that the late Anglo-Saxon Church was fulfilling the function expected of a Christian Church in any age. And the modern view is that its work was well done in spite of the disrepute into which anachronisms and political figures like Stigand have brought it. There was probably more chance of an Anglo-Saxon receiving a reasonable religious education than any corresponding Westerner of his age. The Church, according to Alcuin, appeared to the Avars more as a collector of tithes than as a spreader of good news. In England it may be said without undue cynicism that a balance of both was judiciously achieved.

4. EDUCATION, LEARNING AND LITERATURE

(a) Roman and Celtic: the Northumbrian renaissance

Intimately connected with the health and nature of the Church is the development of education and learning and to a great extent of literature. Gibes are now no longer made at the 'illiterate Anglo-Saxon'. Indeed one of the shrewdest writers on the Norman Conquest has given the considered judgement that 'perhaps the two greatest achievements of medieval England were Anglo-Saxon

---

[89] *Ælfric's Catholic Homilies*, vol. I, p. 256.

vernacular culture and Anglo-Norman executive administration'.[90] There is still matter enough of course, for controversy, and there are critics who complain with much force and some justice of an excess of 'gidding and yelping in hall'. But the quality of 'Beowulf' alone is sufficient to assert the strength of the vernacular poetry, to say nothing of the surprisingly sensuous element that may be dis tinguished in some of the religious verse, notably in the 'Dream of the Rood' and in 'Judith'. Nor have accidents of survival succeeded in concealing the astonishing vitality and vigour of Anglo-Saxon intellectual life.

Schools were set up in the very earliest days of the conversion. To this very day King's School, Canterbury, lays claim to A.D. 604 as its foundation date. But for the first three quarters of the seventh century the intellectual life of England was fed from abroad, from the monasteries and nunneries of Gaul and from the Scottish and Irish monks of the north and west. The first considerable body of evidence of native achievement comes from a period that is some-times called the age of the 'Northumbrian renaissance', extending from *c.* 670 to *c.* 735. For a decisive generation following the death of Penda in 654 the Northumbrian kingdom achieved sufficient political stability for substantial monasteries to be established. The groundwork was thus prepared for a real intellectual ferment, in which scholarly and artistic traditions from Rome, from the Celtic lands and even from the Greek-speaking world, were enabled to mingle. Theodore himself was brought up in the Greek observance. His successor Berhtwold could consecrate to Rochester Tobias who is described as 'a scholar of Latin, Greek and Saxon'.[91] That wealth as well as political stability contributed to this end is shown by the remarkable speed with which an educated generation was created. Benedict Biscop, a man of noble birth, made no fewer than six journeys to the Continent, from all of which he brought back books and other precious things for his foundations of Jarrow and Wearmouth.[92] An incident from the early eighth century which shows Aldhelm prowling for books at the quayside at Dover indicates that the southerners also played their share in massing formidable libraries.[93] It was the presence of these books that attracted teachers and students to Jarrow, to Canterbury, and

[90] D. C. Douglas, *British Historians and the Norman Conquest*, Glasgow, 1946 p. 34.
[91] *Hist. Eccl.*, V, 8.
[92] Bede, *Hist. Eccl.*, esp. *Historia Abbatum*, c. 6 and c. 9, pp. 369 and 373.
[93] E. Duckett, *Anglo-Saxon Saints and Scholars*, p. 85: *W. Malms., Gest. Pont.*, pp. 376 ff.

o York, and made possible the intellectual activity of the age. Indeed particularly in Northumbria, the heart of the so-called renaissance', political stability contributed little during the first flowering period. From 685 the political outlook was black in the north. Yet there flourished a group of men, patronized by the royal court, steeped in monastic observance, who could adapt in their monasteries an attitude to learning capable of producing work as impressive as the original and scholarly writings of the Venerable Bede.

Indeed, in spite of all the wealth of artistic creation, of stone-carving, of book-illumination, of calligraphy, it is Bede who has firmly stamped his personality on the age for future generations. His life was quiet enough in externals. He entered the new monastery at Jarrow as a boy, was one of the few survivors of plague that hit the community, wrote his first works *c.* 700 and then gradually added to his astonishing output until a climax was reached with his magnificent 'Ecclesiastical History of the English People' in 731. At his death in 735 he was working on a translation of St John's Gospel into English. The range of his work is most impressive. There is a mass of commentary on the Scriptures, a selection of volumes that showed interest in scientific things, notably his erudite treatise *De Temporum Ratione*, and much exegesis that indicated both his learning and his freshness of approach. His knowledge of books was certainly not confined to Scripture and the works of the Fathers, well read though he was in these. M. L. W. Laistner in a brilliant piece of reconstruction gives a list of close on a hundred works known to Bede, including books by St Ambrose, St Augustine, St Gregory and St Jerome, together with some of the works of Cassiodorus, of Gregory of Tours, of Isidore of Seville, of Orosius, Pliny, Prudentius, Salinus, Vegetius and Virgil himself. Boethius alone is conspicuously absent, although he and through him Aristotle were familiar to Northumbrian scholars a generation after Bede's death.[94]

It is interesting to reflect that to Bede himself his commentary on the Scriptures was probably the most important of his work. Yet to future generations it was the 'Ecclesiastical History' that made his reputation. Over a hundred and fifty manuscripts or fragments of manuscripts of this remarkable work have survived, two of which

94 M. L. W. Laistner, *The Library of the Venerable Bede*, pp. 237–66, esp. pp. 263–6; *Bede, Life, Time and Writings*, ed. A. H. Thompson. Also J. D. A. Ogilvy, *Books Well-known to Anglo-Latin Writers from Aldhelm to Alcuin* (670–804), Cambridge (Mass.), 1936. P. Hunter Blair, *The World of Bede*, London, 1970, pp. 282–95.

may be ascribed to the generation immediately following Bede's own death.[95] From the distribution of these manuscripts and fragments it appears that the old view of the 'Ecclesiastical History' as of insular interest only is completely erroneous. It was copied extensively throughout the Christian world, and was well known on the Continent by the end of the eighth century. A translation of part of it was made into Old Irish, and an Old English version was prepared, apparently by a Mercian scholar, which provides a very important source book for ninth-century linguistic studies. The Latin of the original is so good that even classical scholars pay it homage. The grammar of classical Latin has been simplified, but the essential quality of the language has not been lost. The capacity for epigrammatic compression has been retained, and a new flexibility and simplicity acquired which brought the written language nearer the ease of the spoken, without degenerating into mere Romance vulgar tongues. Perhaps, of its period, only the Vulgate itself approached Bede's masterpiece for simplicity and power. The contrast with the strictly contemporary affectations of the West Saxon scholar, Aldhelm, is altogether astounding.

The 'Ecclesiastical History' is not only good Latin; it is good history. It performed what it set out to do simply and economically. Personal bias against the Celtic Church at times comes out strongly, but Bede was capable of fair and dispassionate judgement which does credit to himself, his order and his Age. Credit was given even to Penda for his fairness in permitting the conversion of Peada. Celtic Christians were harshly criticized for their failure to see the light of Roman reason, but criticism was tempered by genuine praise, as in the following charming and moving comment on Aidan.

> He cultivated peace and love, purity and humility; he was above anger and greed, and despised pride and conceit; he set himself to keep and to teach the laws of God, and was diligent in study and prayer. He used his priestly authority to check the proud and powerful; he tenderly comforted the sick; he relieved and protected the poor. To sum up in brief what I have learned from those who knew him, he took pains never to neglect anything that he had learned from the writings of the apostles and prophets, and he set himself to carry them out with all his powers.[96]

The miraculous element was kept reasonably low, and often qualified by phrases such as 'it is said', 'a certain man reported', 'it is

[95] D. Whitelock, *After Bede*, Jarrow Lecture, 1960, pp. 11–12.
[96] *Hist. Eccl.*, III, 17; also III, 3 and 5.

generally believed'. No modern scholar could be more anxious than Bede to show his authorities, and to give the reader chapter and verse for the conclusions reached. His prefatory letter to King Ceolwulf carefully set out a most impressive list of people who had helped him, drawn from all the kingdoms of England and including especially his 'principal authority and adviser in his work, the most reverend Abbot Albinus, an eminent scholar educated in the Church of Canterbury by Archbishop Theodore and Abbot Adrian'.[97] The letter gives proof of an educated climate of opinion without which such a scholar as Bede could not have thrived. And his consciousness of high Christian purpose did not obscure the thinking, reflective man: a fact which has endeared Bede to a host of surprisingly Pelagian admirers.

Bede himself, however, was only part, though the finest product, of the intellectual activity of his time, an activity to which he bore impressive testimony in his own writings. In the south there emerged another fine scholar of some originality in the person of Aldhelm, Abbot of Malmesbury and later Bishop of Sherborne. Trained by Celtic and Roman masters he represented a very different aspect of intellectual life from the clarity and Roman directness of Bede. His chief works consisted of a long and most involved poem on the theme of virginity, and a tract in prose on the same subject. He also delighted in elaborate forms of word-play embodied in riddles, an amusement that proved consistently popular to the Anglo-Saxons in the vernacular as well as in Latin. It is odd to find him explaining, as he does on occasion, that verbose garrulity or garrulous verbosity is execrable to God. The following short extract gives a fair impression of his style, on the whole not as obscure in verse as in prose. The answer to the riddle of which this particular passage is an extract is 'writing-tablets'.

Nunc ferri stimulus faciens proscindit amaenam
Flexibus et sulcos obliquat adinstar aratri,
Sed semen segiti de caelo ducitur almum,
Quod largos generat millena fruge maniplos.[98]

'An iron point in artful windings cuts a fair design, and leaves long twisted furrows like a plough. From heaven unto that field is borne the seed of nourishment which brings forth generous sheaves a thousandfold'.

97 Ibid., Preface.
98 Aldhelm, 'De Laude Virginitatis', c. xix. Aldhelm, 'Riddles', no. xxxii, *The Riddles of Aldhelm*, ed. J. H. Pitman, pp. 18–19. M. Winterbottom perceptively places Aldhelm's style in a central tradition of classical rhetoric, 'Aldhelm's prose style and its origins', *A.S.E.*, 6, 1977, pp. 39–76.

For the obscurity, the Celts are generally blamed. It has been held as axiomatic that Celtic love of fine imagery led to peculiar distortion of language. To write was a great adventure, and elaborate vocabulary lists of the fifth and later centuries provided the raw material out of which could be woven the finery of Gildas or the obscure majestic garments of Aldhelm. Two centuries later the style and vocabulary reappeared in the writing-office of King Athelstan, the cry of Celtic influence again rises up. Indeed elaborate theories concerning simple German and tortuous Celt are built back into this contrast between Aldhelm and Bede. Racially the theories are so much nonsense. From the point of view of educational theory, however, the contrast does acquire some significance in any attempt to analyse the two main elements of the Northumbrian Renaissance, the Celtic and the Roman.

In the Celtic world there was a long and strong tradition of education. From schools in Wales, notably Llantwit Major in the early sixth century, scholarship spread to Ireland, thence to the Continent, out to Scotland, and back into now English England from Iona to Lindisfarne, and from Glastonbury and Malmesbury into Wessex and Kent. The special strength of Celtic education, completely monastic, was aesthetic rather than intellectual. There were social reasons why this should be so. The Christian faith had been accepted, but as the faith of a remnant with little hope of social good in this world, with something of a survivor complex in a hostile world. The Celts were surrounded by pagan barbarians. A heritage of exclusiveness from their own paganism intensified their feeling of isolation. In turn they emphasized the esoteric elements in their new faith. So the mysteries of religion, not the social arts of deliberate exposition, discussion and organization, occupied their attention. A school of exquisite penmanship grew up. The half-uncial hand of Irish scribes was developed, to be later adopted by the English; art forms such as the twisted scroll work and animal-motifs of the illumination to the Lindisfarne Gospels, came to flourish in a Christian milieu. The highest ideals in society were aesthetic in a universal, abstract sense divorced from social reality; the ideal for the Christian individual was rigidly and harshly ascetic. From a combination of both ideals appeared the apparent paradox of ascetic craftsmen, of withdrawn artists; of men capable of achieving work of the standard found in the Book of Kells or the Book of Durrow. Yet, to further the paradox a little, one of the great practical achievements of Anglo-Saxon England, the insular hand, which reached its peak of perfection in the calligraphy of the Exeter Book in the late tenth or early eleventh century, was essentially a derivative of the Irish and of the Hiberno-Saxon school of penmanship. The uncial of the early Roman mission had no lasting effect on English handwriting; the half-uncial triumphed for all the Roman political victory at Whitby.

On the Roman side the tradition was very different. Willy-nilly the papacy had assumed the moral leadership of a worn and defeated Romania. In the *civitates* of Gaul the bishop emerged as the characteristic social leader in place of the Roman official. Starting with matters that seemed, directly or indirectly, to concern the moral leadership of the Church such as alleviation of distress, distribution of charities, points of marriage law and inheritance, the Church found itself involved in the maintenance of social discipline to such an extent as to suggest it was the true heir in many aspects of the Roman magistracy. With such a background it was natural that Roman ideals of education should differ fundamentally from those of the Celts. The Roman was an administrator; he needed a language and an attitude to thought, even in monastic spheres, that would enable him to get things done. Training was more closely geared to the needs of the world than was that of the Celt. Monastic organization brought out the difference sharply. The Celtic monasteries emphasized the cell within the institution, the whole monastery often tied to the tribal unit. The Roman accepted readily a rule of the type that ultimately developed into the Rule of St Benedict, the little code for beginners that gave order, discipline and work to the Western monasteries. Emphasis on orderliness found expression in the scheme of education. Clarity of expression was a special Roman virtue. The Roman clerics moved in a world where men were accustomed to close regulation of life; regulation demanded men capable of framing and understanding rules. Such administrative experience extended far outside the cloister. A great gulf separated the ascetic of the Irish observance from the cenobite of the Roman, though neither was the complete antithesis of the other. Enthusiasm was common to both, but in a more regulated orderly form when practised by men like Wilfrid, Bede, Egbert and Alcuin. Celtic otherworldliness and extravagance predominated in figures like Cuthbert and Aldhelm, both presumably Germanic in race.

It appears that the Celtic monks concentrated more on the education of the mature man whereas the Romans concentrated greatly on the education of children. This attitude to the education of children, dictated in the first place by cenobitic needs, in training choirs, and also by needs of the mission field, entailed the teaching of a generation that would accept, and think in, Latin. Celtic training on the other hand led to a somewhat esoteric attitude on the part of scholars who had trained themselves in an artificial vocabulary.

Historians of art and of architecture and of book-illumination have attempted similar analysis of Celtic and Roman elements, but have generally concluded with a note on the fortunate blend that was achieved in late seventh- and early eighth-century England. The surviving stone crosses of Northumbria, notably the great Ruthwell cross, far north in Dumfriesshire, and an occasional glimpse of skill in ecclesiastical architecture either rarely in the stone itself or in description in Bede or in lives of saints, and above all a study of one or other of the great illuminated manuscripts that have survived, all suggest that the high appraisal of cultural activity at this period is not misplaced. Important churches were certainly normally built in stone. The roofless walls of the splendid church at Lincoln were still standing in 731, a century after their construction. Bede tells of Edwin's church of St Peter at York, made of timber but then planned in stone on a larger scale to enclose the original oratory. It was left to Oswald to complete this building. The fact that Finan at Lindisfarne built his church not of stone but of hewn oak thatched with reeds was a matter for adverse comment. A later bishop, Eadbert, removed the thatch and covered both walls and roof with lead.[99] It is still possible to examine some of the skill of the early Anglo-Saxon builder in the church at Brixworth in Northamptonshire, a building which must have been most impressive when its arches opened into its original *porticus*. Architectural skill was not lacking, and the literary outburst was no isolated phenomenon. The Northumbrian renaissance alone is testimony to the vigour and indeed to the resources of these newly converted Germanic kingdoms. That the effect was long-lasting may be seen from Alcuin's description of the wealth of books available in the great library of York later in the eighth century. He himself paid steady and graceful tribute to the education he had received in Northumbria. In an elegant letter to King Charles the Great he tells how he has worked to bring into France the flowers of Britain: that not in York alone there may be 'a garden enclosed', but that in Tours also there may be 'the plants of Paradise with the fruit of the orchard'.[100]

---

[99] *Hist. Eccl.*, II, 16; III, 25.
[100] Alcuin, 'Versus de Sanctis', 1535 ff. *Bede, Life, Time and Writings*, p. 237; E. Duckett, *Alcuin, Friend of Charlemagne*, p. 21. *E.H.D.* I, p. 854.

(b) Vernacular poetry

The latter part of the seventh century saw also the recorded beginnings of a written literature in the vernacular. It can no longer be stated with confidence that the great epic 'Beowulf' or even 'Widsith' was written at this early date.[101] The tendency is to push the date of 'Beowulf' forward to late in the eighth century, and there are even those to whom the certainty that the poem was written before the great Danish invasions of the ninth century no longer appears compelling. It has been suggested also that 'Widsith' itself, for all its archaic flavour, is no more than a poet's catalogue of set pieces, possibly to be ascribed to a reign as late as that of Athelstan, though the evidence for a late date for the main substance of the poem is not convincing.[102] There are indeed enormous, and still unsolved, difficulties to be faced in connection with the dating of Anglo-Saxon poetry. It is Bede who gives the first account of the writing of an Anglo-Saxon poem, when he tells how the divine gift of poetry descended on the cowherd Cædmon.[103] His first poem, as it is recorded in the early manuscripts of the 'Ecclesiastical History', shows within its brief compass many of the general characteristics of Anglo-Saxon verse; particularly the alliteration, and the use of carefully calculated epithet which adds progressively to the image. It is a simple enough little poem of the creation, the beginning of things, the earth encompassed by the heavens without. But simple as it is in thought, in form it suggests an already well-matured poetic technique. Bede states that Cædmon had many passages of Holy Scripture read over to him and that after ruminating over them 'like a cow chewing the cud', he would produce the most satisfactory Anglo-Saxon verse. He says further that Cædmon had many imitators, but none as good.

Naturally enough many of the religious poems that have survived have been attributed at one stage or another to Cædmon, to such an extent indeed that one of the four major Anglo-Saxon poetic manuscripts has been called the Cædmon manuscript. A similar accretion of religious poetry has gathered around the name of the other certain Anglo-Saxon poet, Cynewulf in the eighth century. Modern scholarship is very suspicious of such ascriptions, so much so that nothing apart from the poem recorded in the Bede manuscripts is now with certainty attributed to Cædmon,

---

[101] D. Whitelock, 'Anglo-Saxon Poetry and the Historian', *T.R. Hist. S.*, 1949.
[102] R. L. Reynolds, 'Le poème anglo-saxon Widsith', *Moyen Âge*, 1953, pp. 299–324.
[103] *Hist. Eccl.*, IV, 24.

while Cynewulf's poems are limited to those four poems, 'Juliana', 'The Ascension', 'Elene', and 'The Fates of the Apostles', where his name appeared in simple cryptogram.

There is one characteristic that remains constant throughout the whole period: the very rhythm and alliterative form of the poetry. The span of time is considerable. From Cædmon to the poem of 'The Battle of Maldon' was over three hundred years. The elegy on the death of Edward the Confessor brought the span to near four centuries. Yet the conservative quality of the poetic forms is quite unmistakable. Alliteration was the key to the verse-form. Rhyme was rarely used. Each line of verse was broken by a caesura, and the sentence could stop either at a caesura or at the end of the line. The two half-lines, normally consisting of two stressed syllables apiece and a varying number of unstressed, were bound together by the alliteration. Scansion recognizes at least five main types, closely related.[104] The following lines from 'Beowulf' will give some indication of the importance of alliteration and stress:

> . . . cystum cuðe. Hwilum cyninges þegn
> guma gilp-hlæden, gidda gemyndig,
> se ðe eal-fela eald gesegena
> worn gemunde, word oðer fand
> soðe gebunden. Secg eft ongan . . .

The sense of the passage also adds to knowledge of poetic habits and techniques. The kennings build up progressively a picture of the king's thegn who is also a poet. He is a *guma gilp-hlæden*, a man laden with proud sayings; he is *gidda gemyndig*, mindful of songs; and he remembered a great many *eald gesegena*, or old lays. On his technique it is said that 'he composed new words, bound with truth' which expresses the feeling of the 'right word' known to all connoisseurs of spoken poetry. The highly sophisticated poet of 'Sir Gawain' would express similar approbation many centuries later when he talked of words 'correctly locked together'.[105]

Indeed the method and type was well suited to a society in which the art of the poet was closely connected with the art of declamation. Elaborate poems, particularly 'Beowulf' itself in final form, must have been written in the quiet of the study. But the stuff of which they were made was derived from an oral tradition. Even pieces as exquisite as 'The Seafarer' or 'The Wanderer' could well have been declaimed in hall. Poetry and song were part of the very

---

[104] D. Whitelock, *The Beginnings of English Society*, pp. 207–8.
[105] 'Beowulf', lines 867 ff. *Sir Gawain and the Green Knight*, line 35.

fabric of social life. This was true not only at aristocratic levels but among humble folk as well. No fact is better substantiated: the very episode referred to earlier tells us that Cædmon was in the habit of sneaking away from evening meetings at the monastic farmsteads as soon as the harp was handed round – because he could not sing. Aldhelm himself was so proficient at singing that he used to sit on the bridge at the entrance to the township and attract the people to him by singing of religious things. The emphasis with Aldhelm was very much on 'religious things'. He talked of the folly of those who concerned themselves with pagan poetry, turning from the pure waters of Holy Scripture 'to quench their thirst in muddy pools, swarming with a myriad of black toads, noisy with the guttural bark of frogs'. Alcuin, too, warned energetically against minstrelsy that dealt of pagan men and pagan times. What had Ingeld to do with Christ? But Asser says that King Alfred liked nothing better than to have Saxon poems recited to him.[106] Of the substance of the songs only fragmentary knowledge remains. Aelfric, for example, said that the passion of St Thomas was left unwritten because it had long since been turned from Latin into English poetry.[107] Again in a treatise on the Old Testament Aelfric referred to the story of Judith 'as an example to you that you may defend your country against an invading army'. This has been taken as a reference to the poem on Judith in the Beowulf manuscript (B.M., Cotton Vitellius A.xv), but it probably refers only to Aelfric's own writing on Judith.[108] That the clerical filter has choked back many choice specimens we may be sure. But enough remains to tell that the Anglo-Saxons were great lovers of song. It is highly probable – though none has survived or stood much chance of survival – that some were of the roistering type that might be expected to predominate in lordly halls filled with gorged and boastful fighting men.

Special interest has been aroused recently in the fragments of epics that have survived, proof apparently that there is a vast lost body of Beowulfian literature dealing with epic themes of the type merely hinted at in that scop's catalogue known as 'Widsith'. 'Beowulf' itself implied knowledge on the part of the reader of

---

[106] W. Malms., Gest Pont., v. 190 and v. 375, cited by E. Duckett, *Anglo-Saxon Saints and Scholars*, p. 39. Alcuin to Hygebald, *Alcuini Epistolae*, ed. E. Dümmler, p. 81. *Asser's Life of Alfred*, p. 59.

[107] *Aelfric's Catholic Homilies*, vol. II, p. 520.

[108] *The Old English Version of the Heptateuch*, ed. S. J. Crawford, E.E.T.S., 1922, p. 48. I am indebted to Professor Whitelock for this necessary word of caution on the Judith reference.

a considerable body of literature. It also implied, as Professor
Whitelock has pointed out, some maturity in Christian beliefs on
the part of such an audience.[109] The high allusiveness of references
to Finn and Hengest, to Eormenric's necklace, or to the ominous
marriage of Ingeld still escapes complete and certain interpretation. For all his ingenuity the modern critic lacks inevitably the
background of knowledge needed to unravel the incidents completely. That familiar poems lay behind these allusions is highly
probable. When Eddius Stephanus tells of Wilfrid's success in battle
against the pagans of Sussex at high odds the flavour of German
saga comes from the somewhat crabbed Latin.[110] The deeds of that
Offa who ruled the Angles on the Continent provided material
for one such saga. It is altogether probable that the deeds of his
distinguished descendant, the Mercian Offa, provided the basis
for yet another. His brutality to the young East Anglian king,
Ethelbert, is dismissed by the Anglo-Saxon Chronicle in the phrase
'in this year Offa ordered the head of Ethelbert to be struck off'.
By the thirteenth century a long and elaborate story had grown
up around this incident. It is a fine progression from the simple
Anglo-Saxon statement to the involved plot woven by the St Alban's
chronicler or by the rival houses of Westminster and Hereford.
Somewhere along the line of progression probably lay a solid piece
of alliterative verse.[111]

Again the very poems of the Chronicle, notably that dealing
with Athelstan's great victory at Brunanburh in 937, are reminders
that there is a tradition of great strength living throughout the
Anglo-Saxon period. The usual laconic entry in the Chronicle
over long periods of time should be read as little more than a
shorthand note to place in chronology a whole mass of material
relating to the incident. The very full account under the annal 755
of the deaths of Cynewulf and Cyneheard is altogether exceptional,
but similar detailed knowledge must have lain behind many brief
phrases. If, by unfortunate chance, the poem of Maldon had not
survived independently, little more would be known from the
Chronicle than that Ealdorman Byrhtnoth fought against Olaf
and his horde, and was killed by them at Maldon. Volumes could
be written, and indeed some have been, on the lost literature of
Anglo-Saxon England.

[109] D. Whitelock, *The Audience of Beowulf,* Oxford, 1951.
[110] Eddius Stephanus, *Life of Wilfrid,* c. xiii.
[111] A.S. Chronicle, *sub anno* 792; and a note by C. Plummer in his edition, *Two of the Saxon Chronicles Parallel,* vol. II, p. 61.

It may be wise at this point, after stressing the uniformity of
the vernacular verse and the strength of its tradition, to speak
of the way in which that verse has been preserved. Apart from
a few fragments and from the verse of the chronicle, the poetry
of the period is known from four great manuscripts, all of late
tenth- or early eleventh-century provenance, and all written in the
scholarly West Saxon dialect of the late Anglo-Saxon age. These
manuscripts are the Beowulf manuscript, the Exeter Book, the
Junius manuscript, and the so-called Vercelli manuscript which
was presumably taken to that Italian town, very much on the
normal pilgrim route, in the baggage of an abbot or some other
distinguished Anglo-Saxon traveller, ecclesiastical or lay, in the
eleventh century. The predominance of West Saxon may perhaps
be held to indicate scribal and social custom rather than to point to
the origin of the poems. The tendency among scholars of an older
generation was to suggest that Mercian or Northumbrian originals
lay behind the West Saxon transcriptions, but nowadays students of
Anglo-Saxon are reconciled to the idea that Wessex also produced
its poets. In bulk the preservation of this mass of poetry speaks well
of the standards of the scribes who copied such fine work.

In range of subjects, the body of poetry shows the inevitable
emphasis on religion and war. The heroic spirit is consistently
evoked. There is a haunting sense of loss in much of the poetry
which suggests that to the Anglo-Saxons the Golden Age did indeed lie in the past. Lament for lost joys was a dominant theme.
The peril of the kinless man is brought out vividly in the poem,
'The Wanderer':

> Where is the mare, where is the young man? Where is the giver of
> treasure?
> Where are the banquet-benches? Where, the joys of hall?[112]

Exile was regarded with only little less dread than death itself.
The hardships of life, the dangers and discomforts of the sea, the
savage fortune of the man doomed to spend his life in foreign
lands, the joylessness of the man who fails in his duty to his
lord: these were consistent themes. The *Ubi sunt* echoes resound
throughout poetry and homily.[113] 'Ever the longer the worse' is
one of Wulfstan's favourite comments on the temporal world.
Pilgrimage is common but penitential in nature, lacking the joyous

112 'Wanderer', lines 92–3.
113 J. E. Cross, ' "Ubi sunt" Passages in Old English Sources and Relationships',
Vetenskaps-Societetens i Lund Årsbok, 1956.

seeking of later centuries. Yet the mood of the Anglo-Saxon wa not consistently sad.[114] But without accurate dating there is littl that a social historian can isolate from the poetry in discussing th development of society. Indeed there is a danger that concentratio on heroic uniformity will lead to neglect of the great social growtl attributable to the period.

(c) Vernacular prose

More rewarding to the social historian both in itself and in wha it represents is the vernacular prose. In itself it shows from th end of the ninth century onwards an educated and articulate clerg not afraid to use the mother tongue for their own purposes. Wha it represents is a social attitude towards language of absorbing interest. There can be no doubt that during the early centurie of Christianity in England, Latin was the recognized language o culture. Yet the early law-codes were framed in English, in marke contrast to the situation on the Continent where barbarian legisla tion attempted the Latin tongue. Of course there is fundamenta difference between the comparatively simple exhortations of a law-code and the more elaborate ideas sought in theological work and lives of saints. The vocabulary and structure of the Old Englisl language could cope with the former, but not with the latter. Ther must have been some works in English in the early part of the nintl century, or else Alfred's statement that many could read what wa written in English would be meaningless. But even as late as the reign of King Alfred the language of the Alfredian translation wa only painfully moving towards an assimilation of technical abstrac terms, essential if the niceties of theological exposition were to be indulged in.

It is, however, to those translators that we owe the true formatior of an English literary language as a vehicle capable of transmitting the thought of the age. Their enterprise is of such importance tha it demands close examination.

The inspiration behind the educational programme was un-doubtedly Alfred himself. In an open letter to his bishops at the beginning of the translation of the 'Pastoral Care' he analysed the state of learning in England.[115] At his accession he could remember

---

[114] Jean Young, 'Glaed waes ic gliwum: Ungloomy aspects of Anglo-Saxon poetry', *The Early Cultures of North-West Europe*, ed. Sir Cyril Fox and Bruce Dickins, Cambridge, 1950.
[115] *E.H.D.* I, p. 888.

not a single man south of the Thames capable of apprehending their services or of translating a letter from Latin into English; there were very few this side of the Humber and not many to the north of the Humber. In bemoaning this falling off among the English he justified his task of translation. His object was to provide these texts which it was most needful for his people to know. He wished 'all the youth now in England, born of free men who have the means they can apply to it' to be devoted to learning 'as long as they cannot be of use in any other employment', until they can read well what is written in English. Then those who are likely to go further to Holy Orders could be instructed in the Latin tongue. He tells how he himself had set about the task of translation, sometimes word for word and sometimes sense for sense. He pays graceful tribute to his teachers, to Archbishop Plegmund, to Bishop Asser, to 'my priest Grimbald' (of St Bertin's) and to John (of Old Saxony). It is a matter of high note that at a moment of immense political difficulty the West Saxon king thought it fit to direct some of his precious energies and resources to the preparation of a planned educational programme. It is a tribute to his wisdom that he realized the need of such a programme. For all his laments one notes too that, though the state of Latin learning was still inadequate, there were many men who could read in the English tongue.

King Alfred's selection of the works most needful to know also indicates the wisdom of this most attractive of English rulers. In texts of various ages a number of major works have survived from the pens of translators. The latest authoritative account of vernacular prose literature that can safely be ascribed to the period before 900 allots two or three major texts to Mercian scholars (Gregory's 'Dialogues', Bede's 'Ecclesiastical History', and possibly an Old English Martyrology), and perhaps seven or so to the West Saxons.[116] Of the West Saxon contributions five were probably produced by King Alfred himself and his circle: Gregory's 'Pastoral Care', Boethius, '*De Consolatione Philosophiae*' (together with a rather disappointing verse rendering of much of the text), St. Augustine's 'Soliloquies', the prose psalms, and the introduction to the Laws. The translation of the world history of Orosius, which includes the graphic account of the northern voyages of Ohthere and Wulfstan, and the Chronicle account of the Danish wars of the 890s complete the corpus in the strictest sense, though there are hints of other

[116] Janet Bately, 'Old English Prose before and during the reign of Alfred', *A.S.E.*, 17, 1988, pp. 93–138.

texts, including a lost Handbook. The assembling of the Chronicle itself and the substance of the laws that pass under the name of Alfred and Ine make formidable additions to a truly remarkable literary output, exceptionally so, coming as it does at a time when danger from heathendom was still present. This danger in itself of course helped to provoke the need for intelligible texts.

Consciously or not, Alfred provided, either directly or by support and inspiration in the translations, the ideological basis for the Christian kingdom of England. In a sense the whole production, if a little loosely and with seemly hesitation over precise dating, may indeed be called the Alfredian translations. First in time came Bishop Wærferth's translation of the 'Dialogues' of Gregory, containing in its second book the Life of St Benedict. This had been expressly commissioned from the Mercian bishop of Worcester by the King himself. The 'Pastoral Care' itself was in many ways the most important work of all, and in it may be seen the historical and social strength of Christianity. Submission to lordship and legal authority, the place of Christianity in world history, and fortitude in face of secular disaster were recurring themes. And although those fighting the Danes must have been aware of more tangible and immediate issues, many, and above all the clergy, must have been fortified both in their resistance to the Danes and in the rapid, successful, and largely anonymous task of conversion by the availability of the pith of Christian doctrine in language which could easily be understood. Taken together with the earlier attempts at translating the Gospels, the whole programme assumes a maximum significance. A library of works relating to the Christian Church was now made available in English. Especially in the Boethius and in the 'Soliloquies' of Augustine, Alfred's concern with the deeper problems of divine Providence was vividly apparent, and vigorously expressed in a form capable of transmitting the thought to future generations.

The effect of this activity on the language itself was also far-reaching. Some of the passages attempted by the Alfredian translators demanded the utmost skill. It was no question of rendering merely the simplicity of the Vulgate, or the easier narrative passages of Bede. Some of Gregory's, and particularly of Augustine's, writing needed great care in rendering. The language matured as a literary vehicle in the attempts, slowly, painfully and at times awkwardly. At their best – and it must be admitted that Boethius when the King himself was busy does not represent their best work – the translators achieved a fine grasp and flexibility in making their meaning clear to the Anglo-Saxon readers. The method of approach varied from the Bede, and in the main the Gregory, where a translation close to the original was effected, to the Boethius, where it is rare to find more than a few lines consecutively rendered word for word.

Their enterprise established West Saxon as the chief literary dialect. With the reconquest of the Danelaw it came to predominate throughout all England. Indeed the dominance of West Saxon, from the reign of Alfred right through the early Norman period, as a literary language is a social fact of great significance. It makes the gap between Old English and Middle English so much more pronounced than might otherwise have been the case. After two centuries or so of English subservience it was a different dialect, the East Midland dialect, that became the true basis of Middle and so of Modern English.

For all its great achievement, the Alfredian literary output was not followed by a continuous stream of work in the vernacular. It was not until the end of the tenth century that a further productive period emerged, associated in particular with the names of Aelfric and Wulfstan, and with the detailed account of Ethelred's reign provided in the various versions of the Anglo-Saxon Chronicle. With Alfred the absence of Latin was a fact to be bemoaned, and his translations were intended in part as a means to an end, i.e. to the provision of a literate clergy competent in Latin. Aelfric and Wulfstan had different objects which may in themselves suggest the partial success of the Alfredian revival. They were concerned to give to congregations, inevitably ignorant of Latin, the essentials of the Christian faith in their own tongue. They were pre-eminently homilists, anxious to expound the Lord's Prayer, the Creeds, the Ten Commandments in Anglo-Saxon. Both of them achieve a firm grasp of the cadences and rhythms of the language. Aelfric had the finer mind, Wulfstan the greater strength. In the work of the latter, notably in the magnificent rhetoric of his most famous homily, 'The Sermon of the Wolf to the English', Anglo-Saxon prose reached its full maturity. Even in translation the vigour of the language comes out:

> Often two seamen or maybe three, drive the droves of Christian men from sea to sea, out through the people, huddled together, as a public shame to us all, if we could seriously and rightly feel any shame. But all the insult which we often suffer we repay with honouring those who insult us; we pay them continually and they humiliate us daily; they ravage and they burn, plunder and rob and carry on board; and

lo, what else is there in all these events except God's anger clear and visible over this people?[117]

From a later close and confidential adviser to Canute these are fine words.

In one important respect Aelfric's work marked a definite advance on what had gone on before. He recognized clearly that English was to be the vehicle for most of his work and that English was to be the language of instruction. His object was to bring about his effects, and above all to make the Gospels known, by simple speech using the pure and open words of the people's tongue rather than by the use of garrulous verbosity and unknown vocabulary. At times he seemed to be doing this immense labour unwillingly. In the Latin preface for the 'Saints' Lives' he stated: 'it is not fitting that many should be translated into our language, lest the pearls of Christ be had in disrespect'; there were books left untranslated because they contained subtle things which should not be disclosed to the laity, and which – as Aelfric confessed in engaging manner – he did not altogether grasp himself. In the preface to Genesis, he said: 'I say now that I dare not and I will not translate any book after this from Latin into English.' Indeed in the latter instance he told his patron, the ealdorman Ethelweard, that he had translated out of obedience to his wishes.[118] Yet to Aelfric must go the credit for the first systematic attempt to write in English a Latin grammar. Basing his work on the Latin models of Priscian and Cassiodorus, he strove to make his subject intelligible to pupils of his own school as well as others. He further produced the invaluable Colloquy, a series of reading exercises for boys, to which reference has been made in an earlier chapter, and a systematic series of Latin-English vocabularies, arranged according to subject-matter. The general impression given is of a sound and conscientious schoolmaster struggling to meet a very real need. In many ways his work represented the logical conclusion of the interest in education fostered by Alfred, and developed by the Benedictine revival of the tenth century associated with the names of Dunstan, Ethelwold and Oswald. Alfred sought to create a clergy educated in Latin, a laity educated in Anglo-Saxon. Aelfric provided means by which an educated clergy could communicate the basic Christian teachings to all inhabitants of Anglo-Saxon

[117] *E.H.D.* I, p. 932.
[118] The Latin Preface to the *Lives of Saints*, ed. W. W. Skeat, E.E.T.S., 1881, p. 2; *The Old English Version of the Heptateuch*, ed. S. J. Crawford, E.E.T.S., 1922, p. 80 and p. 76.

England. His success was so great that it has been suggested that his reputation stood as high as Aldhelm's in an earlier period and as Wycliffe himself in a later. In practice to Aelfric English was no longer a poor second-best. Latin was not a living language. His grammar was, as he said himself in his introduction, 'the key that unbinds the understanding of the books'.[119] He claimed no new learning in his 'Lives of the Saints'; he was merely anxious to reveal to the unlearned the truth that had long been locked up in the Latin tongue.

One consequence of this revived interest in education was the gradual creation of an educated laity. For all the emphasis on the vernacular Wulfstan considered it possible that a simple confirmed person could have a little Latin.[120] In the tenth century there were thegns to whom scholars could dedicate books in the full awareness that their work would be read. Ethelweard, a powerful member of the royal house it is true, actually produced a version of the Anglo-Saxon Chronicle in Latin. Emphasis on schools and on school-training led to a growth of a small but potent educated public capable of stimulating homiletic writing, even during the troubled reign of Ethelred the Unready. Thus a more competent priesthood and a revitalized monastic movement bore fruit in the so-called golden age of Anglo-Saxon prose at the end of the tenth century and the beginning of the eleventh.

Interest was also shown in non-theological matters. Aelfric himself produced an important tract on chronology, *De temporibus anni*. One scholar of great ability, Byrhtferth of Ramsey, attempted to gather together in his Manual a conspectus of scientific thought.[121] In depth of insight this represented no advance on Bede. The original genius of Bede was lacking. Nevertheless the material, culled from continental sources such as Hrabanus Maurus as well as from Bede, was well set out and clearly arranged. There was even some attempt at abstract mathematical analysis. He wrote with a strong didactic purpose and was anxious that men should understand his discourse on the *computus*, written in English, as he said, to help the clerks give up their dice-playing and obtain a knowledge of the art.[122] There was, however, none of the careful sorting out into categories characteristic of late eleventh-century

[119] *Aelfric's Grammar*, ed. J. Zupitza, introd., p. 2, lines 16–17.
[120] *The Homilies of Wulfstan*, ed. D. Betherum, p. 183; he should know the paternoster and creed in English, *buton he on Læden mæge*.
[121] *De temporibus anni*, ed. H. Hemel, E.E.T.S., 1942; *Byrhtferth's Manual*, ed. S. J. Crawford, E.E.T.S., 1929.
[122] *Byrhtferth's Manual*, p. 58.

work. But the fact that an important scientific work could be written in English in the early eleventh century is an indication of the progress made. At the same time, on a crude level, collections were made of folk-charms and lore concerning things medicinal that have survived in the form generally known as the 'Anglo-Saxon Leechdoms'. The most recent editors of the key manuscript have shown how Anglo-Saxon medicine, in its written form, was a compound of pagan material, of magic based on pagan and on Christian liturgical forms, of degenerate classical medical thought and of pure folk simples.[123] The leech himself seems most often to have been a lay figure. A bizarre satisfaction comes from observing the first use of the words 'petroleum' and 'treacle' in English, presumably from Byzantine sources. Botanists exercise themselves, often in vain, to give post-Linnaean forms to strongly pre-Linnean Anglo-Saxon generalized plant names. But *Lacnunga* can scarcely be held up as a tribute to Anglo-Saxon medicine, let alone to the Anglo-Saxon vernacular. Credit for the latter must rest squarely on the shoulders of ecclesiastical thinkers and homilists.

The development of Anglo-Saxon as a flexible literary instrument is a matter of extraordinary interest to the social historian. No other community in the West achieved such precocious progress. Continental German had to wait until the twelfth century for its first fine flowering period which was then chiefly poetic in inspiration. Only the Scandinavians surpassed the English among the Germanic peoples in their production of a prose literature, and it is the thirteenth century which sees their finest achievements. Indeed Icelandic pre-eminence itself is a question of subject matter rather than of beauty or variety of style. Even the more cultivated Romanic speakers – perhaps because of their cultivation which held them to regard the vernacular as no more than Latin badly spoken – did not achieve full fluency and flexibility until the twelfth century. Byrhtferth, writing in English in the early eleventh century, accused the French-speaker of *barbara lexis* for saying *inter duas setles cadet homo* when he should have said *inter duas sedes*.[124]

(d) General cultural achievements

It would be wrong to give the impression that Anglo-Saxon literary effort was made only in the vernacular. In Bede, Aldhelm

[123] J. H. G. Gratton and C. Singer, *Anglo-Saxon Magic and Medicine*, Oxford, 1952.
[124] *Byrhtferth's Manual*, p. 96.

and Alcuin England produced a formidable trio of Latin scholars in the eighth century. However, there was a definite falling off throughout the ninth century exacerbated rather than caused by Viking raids and wholesale destruction of monasteries, the depositories of books and of learning. Revival came in the mid-tenth century. In Wessex and East Anglia new or newly revived monasteries stimulated the production of books that were both useful and aesthetically satisfying. Continental influences brought a fine Carolingian minuscule into England to rival the mature insular hand, and gradually to oust it from predominance in the preparation of Latin ecclesiastical manuscripts. The version of the Benedictine office prepared *c.* 971 by Ethelwold and his helpers, and known as the *Regularis Concordia*, is a revealing example of the useful work produced.[125] It set out the Rule of St Benedict, making special allowance for the powers of the king, and ordering prayers to be said for him and his family. On the aesthetic side the 'Benedictional of Ethelwold' is perhaps the best example of the so-called Winchester School of Art.

Throughout the whole period Lives of Saints continued to be popular, and from the early lives of Cuthbert and Wilfrid to the post-Norman Conquest translation into Latin of the life of Wulfstan II, Bishop of Worcester 1062–95, indigenous saints received special attention. Often these 'Lives' were produced in Latin, though this was by no means universally the case. For example while Felix's 'Life of St Guthlac', written in Latin *c.* 730–40, was translated into Anglo-Saxon probably in the eleventh century, Wulfstan's life, where the evidence for an Anglo-Saxon original is particularly strong, was preserved only in a Latin translation of that work.

To conclude, it may be said that the literary output of Anglo-Saxon England, though not prodigious, was never negligible, and that a community capable of producing Bede and Aelfric, to mention the two outstanding geniuses of the age, was no community of illiterate barbarians.

Nor was the community lacking in achievement in artistic directions other than the purely literary. England was noted throughout the late tenth and early eleventh centuries as the home of fine manuscript illumination, of fine embroidery work, and of fine skilled metal-work. Examples have survived in the tomb of St Cuthbert of early tenth-century ecclesiastical vestments which

---

[125] *Regularis Concordia*, ed. Dom T. Symons, London, 1953.

show rich embroidery, splendid control of design and a surprising delicacy in colour, notably in the blue and green range.[126] Line-drawings are particularly revealing, exhibiting as they do a nervous sensitivity and vitality far removed from what might be expected of the stolid Saxon of historical fiction.[127] From the seventh and eight centuries came most impressive memorials of elaborate and beautiful carving in stone, an art which was not lost in the later centuries. The publication of a corpus of Anglo-Saxon stone sculpture is helping to bring home the quality of the best of the sculptors, notably in the eighth century[128]. Architecturally Anglo-Saxon England suffered inevitably from comparison with the great Norman period that followed, but in its own right it was capable of ecclesiastical buildings such as those built by Dunstan at Glastonbury, or those at Earl's Barton in Northamptonshire or at Winchester itself.[129] Of building for secular purposes there is much less information. Alfred is said to have constructed royal halls and chambers in stone and in timber, and to have moved royal residences in stone from their ancient sites to more suitable places.[130] It is probable that some of the more prosperous built houses of stone in the towns, but wood was the material in general use, and hazards of fire and decay brought inevitable impermanence of memory. There is no evidence whatsoever of advanced and elaborate techniques of home-building or of church-building in wood such as those which led to the creation of the stave-churches of the Scandinavian north. But there is strong probability that at their best the Anglo-Saxons could achieve solid and comfortable dwelling houses in wood, well calculated to withstand the damp and cold of the *insula brumosa*. By their nature these had less permanence than the written evidence of literary activity. It is by their word and intellectual prowess that these builders in wood deserve to be known. It is there that the true genius of the Anglo-Saxon bore permanent fruit.

---

[126] C. F. Battiscombe, ed., *The Relics of Saint Cuthbert*, Oxford, 1956.

[127] F. Wormald, *English Drawings of the Tenth and Eleventh Centuries*, London, 1952.

[128] Vol. 1, County Durham and Northumberland, ed. Rosemary Cramp, British Academy, 1984; vol. 2, Cumberland, Westmorland, and Lancashire North-of-the-Sands, ed. R. N. Bailey and Rosemary Cramp, British Academy, 1988.

[129] H. M. Taylor (with Joan Taylor for vols. 1 and 2) has produced a basic magisterial work, *Anglo-Saxon Architecture*, 3 vols., Cambridge, 1965–78.

[130] *Asser's Life of Alfred*, p. 77; *E.H.D.* I, p. 298.

CHAPTER SEVEN
The Major Social Changes

THE BACKGROUND TO THE GENERAL PROBLEM OF SOCIAL DEVELOPMENT

Before we turn to the Norman Conquest itself, an attempt must be made to evaluate the major social changes that occurred in England during the period that stretches from the advent of the Saxons to the coming of the Normans. This is by no means an easy task. Economists have tended in the past to dismiss the whole period, and indeed the greater part of the Middle Ages, as static or, audaciously, as relatively static. Anthropologists have been ready with the comparative method, and have therefore at times too easily rejected the immense differences in social growth between, for example, nineteenth-century Polynesia and seventh-century England. Historians and students of Anglo-Saxon literature are tied so close to the fragmentary nature of their evidence that they rightly hesitate to generalize. Conscious of the gaps in the evidence, they hesitate to postulate change and development for fear that they are only reflecting change in the type of evidence available. Indeed we have to look to the impressive work of Kemble as far back as 1849 to find a scholar so confident in his command of all aspects of his study as to attempt a complete picture of the society of the age.

Kemble himself, however, was so impregnated with Germanic liberal ideas that his masterpiece, the *Saxons of England*, valuable as it still is as a mine of information, reads strangely to the modern ear.[1] The assumptions of Tacitus are unquestioned. The basic

Two vols., London, 1849.

institutions of England were, as far back as could be seen, demo
cratic. Folk moots were essentially reasonable institutions. Th
primitive Germanic freeman-warrior was essentially a reasonabl
being, more at home in a deliberative assembly than as a member o
a blood-feud group. Yet Kemble himself held a reserve of commo
sense that helped him to avoid the more extravagant ideas of som
later Victorian scholars to whom Anglo-Saxon became almost
synonym for freedom, as opposed to Norman tyranny.

Not all scholars of that age, however, were led into accepting th
Anglo-Saxon period as the breeding ground of free institutions
Seebohm, whose occasional overstatements and rashness have re
sulted in much undeserved neglect of his work, held tenaciousl
to the view that late Roman influence survived the Anglo-Saxo
invasions. The *villae* of Bede were similar to the *villae* of th
fourth century, much nearer to those institutions than to an
primitive confederation of free tribesmen. Christian missionarie
in the seventh century came to England with knowledge of th
cities of Roman Britain. They favoured Roman sites for churches
Their buildings were set up on or near the Roman forts of th
Saxon shore, at Canterbury, London, Dorchester, Lincoln, an
York. Landlordship had never disappeared from these islands
The basic institution before and after the Saxon Conquest wa
the estate.[2]

Maitland had no difficulty in demolishing the most extravagan
ideas of Seebohm. Bede, it is true, referred to many *villae* in Eng
land. Some were owned by kings; others by noblemen, includin
noblemen known as *satrapae*. If the *villae* were Roman, commente
Maitland, then they were inhabited, no doubt, by satraps wh
were Persian![3] Constructively Maitland's brilliant pen did an im
mense amount towards stabilizing a moderate German position. O
analogy with continental development and from his own shrew
insight, he maintained that the fundamental unit in the earlies
recorded English society was the free peasant, warrior and head o
household, subject to the king, to the law, and to his own persona
obligations, but not normally to any secular lord. Maitland's genera
interpretation was modified very much by his approach from th
known world of Domesday Book to the unknown world that la
behind it, and the tenth- and eleventh-century material, which i
relatively so plentiful and which he knew so well, led him t

---

[2] Esp. his *The English Village Community*, London, 1883.
[3] *Domesday Book and Beyond*, p. 337.

mphasize the deterioration in status of a peasantry originally free
nder the twin pressures of royal and of ecclesiastical lordship.

Chadwick, Maitland's younger contemporary, blazed an original
rail which has still not been thoroughly explored. Particularly
n his modestly entitled *Studies on Anglo-Saxon Institutions*[4] he ap-
roached the fundamental social problems from careful analysis of
erminology, coins, weights and measures and like evidence. His re-
nains a pioneer work, in part for the simple reason that it stepped
utside the two major controversies that had torn Anglo-Saxon
tudies during the preceding decades: the question of Germanic
r Roman basis to English society and the question of feudalism in
ate Anglo-Saxon England. Starting from his profound knowledge
f Anglo-Saxon learning and literature, he was able to bring new
ight to what often proved to be new problems. From the point
f view of sheer straightforward analysis of difficult material it is
ard to find Chadwick's equal. On the other hand it is not easy
or the historian to isolate a clearcut conception of Anglo-Saxon
ociety from his work. The terminology favoured by historians –
ribalism, territorial states, and the like – was not that employed
y Chadwick. Where his contribution was of maximum importance
vas in that he showed a society in process of steady evolution. His
icture of the developing nature of institutions in Anglo-Saxon
ngland brought fresh vigour to studies somewhat bedevilled by
tatic analysis.

For a later generation Sir Frank Stenton has given an authori-
ative account of Anglo-Saxon society in a work to which frequent
eference has already been made. He preserves the best of the
Germanic assumptions, and by sheer weight of scholarship demon-
trates their soundness. Some of his arguments have already been
liscussed. At this stage it might be sufficient to reduce his analysis
o one basic point: that Anglo-Saxon England developed from an
early pioneering stage where the peasant householder was free but
ociety violent, into a more peaceful ordered community where
nuch of the earlier freedom had been lost. Professor Whitelock,
n the main in agreement with this account, has deepened the
nalysis at critical points and, as a true pupil of Chadwick, has
lone much to reconcile the assumptions of those who concentrate
heir attention on the heroic literature with the at first sight more
rosaic assumptions of the social historians.[5]

Cambridge, 1905.
Anglo-Saxon England, Oxford, 1943 (3rd ed. 1971); *The Beginnings of English
ociety*, London, 1952.

Before dealing with the particular themes that follow, therefore it is important to be aware of the weight of hard thought that has gone into the problem over the last century. Although modifications are now appearing from year to year, in the main Stenton's picture still holds the centre of the stage for the modern student.

In the course of treating the problems of settlement, of trade of social ranks and the Church we have had to deal with these processes of social development in so far as we can glimpse them. The question of definition in general terms presents a much more complicated problem. A peasant householder in newly conquered country could not live in isolation, and it is in analysing the bonds that tied him to his fellows that the best hope of a reasonable scheme of analysis lies. There was, indeed, a movement away from a tribal community where the major social bond was between kinsman and kinsman towards the emergence of a territorial state, but this generalization is deceptively simple. The bonds of society linking man and his kin, man and his lord, man and his fellows were very closely intertwined. In the eleventh century, kindred organization could still be powerful; in the seventh, territorial organization was not negligible. Yet the basic movement in these centuries was away from the tie of blood, and towards the tie of the territorial community.

In order to explore the reality that lies behind such generalization the bonds of society in Anglo-Saxon England may be examined under three heads: the power of the kindred; the power of the secular lord; the power of the community.

2. KINDRED

There appears to have been a slow decline in the significance of kindred ties during the period. There is also some evidence to suggest that kindred organization on the elaborate scale revealed in some of the twelfth-century Scandinavian law-codes did not exist in this country. It may be, as Dame Bertha Phillpotts urged, that kindred ties could not survive the sea-crossing from the homeland.[6] It may be that such elaboration is in itself the product of a society matured by different elements from those

---

[6] *Kindred and Clan*, Cambridge, 1913, pp. 264–5; the main disintegrating factor in the case of the Teutonic kindreds was migration, and especially migration by sea.

which operated in England: that the power of Christian kingship, territorial Church and landlord authority prevented the written formulation of what were still in the early seventh century vague concepts of kindred organization and of kindred responsibility. In the earliest law-code, that of Ethelbert of Kent, no more is said on this vital topic than that the kindred is responsible for the payment of half the wergeld if a homicide escapes.[7] Of the inner workings of the system surprisingly little is told.

The reason for this silence may be that everyone knew how the kindred system worked, and so there was no need for legislation. In these centuries written law was very much a product of doubt or of attempts to deal with new situations. The old and the familiar went without saying. Only where the rights of the Church or the rights of the developing state were infringed was direct statement in law-codes necessary. And, as a measure of the pertinacity of the kindred, it may be significant to note that one of the most important statements relating to payment of wergeld comes from the late (twelfth-century) compilation known as the 'Leis Willelme', the ninth clause of which stated that, after an initial payment of ten shillings to the widow and orphans, a man's blood-price is to be shared between the kindred and the orphans (*les parenz e les orfelins*). That this was no mere piece of antiquarianism is suggested by a table of price equivalents attached to the clause, in which, for purpose of reckoning a wergeld payment, a stallion was priced at twenty shillings, a bull at ten shillings and a boar at five shillings.[8]

The first problem is to distinguish kindred from family ties. The latter were social; the former were all-embracing. The latter were ill-defined; the former were normally capable of close definition. In a society where the kindred is dominant a man's status depends entirely on his possession of and his possession by a full kindred. Legal conceptions of torts and crimes would not be familiar to him. The presence of a kin capable of vouching for his good behaviour, and of taking vengeance if he were wronged or slain, is all-important. Anglo-Saxon law-codes yield plentiful evidence of the kindred principle at work in this way. If a man was in prison, his kindred fed him. If captured by his enemies after taking sanctuary, after siege in his own house, or after peaceful surrender in open country, his kindred were to be informed within thirty days. If

[7] Ethelbert 23.
[8] 'Leis Willelme', cl. ix.

he was taken in theft or accused of witchcraft or incendiarism
his kindred could stand surety for him. If the kindred refused
to do so, he was condemned to penal slavery or to death. If he
was slain during his first year as a penal slave, his kinsmen were
to receive his wergeld. If they failed to ransom him during that
twelve-month, he lost that precious right to wergeld, which came
to him as a member born of free kindred, and the kinsmen in turn,
of course, lost their right to receive wergeld if he were slain. As with
wergeld payments so also with marriage arrangements kinship was
a strong social force, and during the reign of Ethelred a man was
forbidden to marry within six degrees of kinship, that is within
four knees, or with the near kinsmen of his first wife. In case
of death at a young age the kindred took on responsibility for
maintaining the heir. According to the laws of Ine the widow was
to have the child and rear it, the father's kindred supplying six
shillings a year, a cow in summer and an ox in winter, the kin
also taking on the duty of keeping the *frumstol*, i.e. presumably
the father's residence and share in the arable, till the boy was
of age. The kindred certainly possessed extensive authority over
landed property. A famous statement of Alfred on the subject of
bookland declared that not even land subject to booklaw was to
pass out of the kin if there were evidence that the power to do
so were forbidden by the men who first acquired it or by those
who gave it. Under Canute if a woman married within a year of
her husband's death, the land and property that she had acquired
through her first husband were to pass to his nearest kin.[9]

But for all its importance in these social matters, in ensuring a
man's standing in law, in providing him with compurgators who
would swear to his innocence or to his good name in court, the
kindred took on its most spectacular aspect, and also its most significant, in relation to two closely related institutions: the payment
of wergeld and the waging of vendettas. If a man were killed by
violence then his kindred had the right to wage a feud against the
slayer and the slayer's kindred. Such a feud could be composed
the spear could be bought off; and the wergeld was the sum
payable by kindred to kindred for this composition. It was the
blood-price. Payment of wergeld was in itself an example of the

[9] Alfred 1.2, 5.3; II Athelstan 1.3, 6.1 and 2. II Edward 6; Ine 24.1; VI Ethelred
12; I Canute 7; Ine 38, Alfred 41; II Canute 73a. On the question of bookland
cf. also A.J. Robertson, *Anglo-Saxon Charters*, no. xxxv; D. Whitelock, *Anglo-Saxon
Wills*, nos. xi, xix; and King Alfred's own will preserved in the 'Liber de Hyda'
Harmer, *Select Documents*, no. xi.

steadying influence of community over kindreds. Even a king had a wergeld. For the murder of the West Saxon prince, Mul, in 694 King Ine exacted from the men of Kent the enormous sum of 30,000 sceattas. This amounted to 7,500 shillings, a sum, as Professor Chadwick pointed out, equal to the simple wergeld of a Mercian king, six times that of a nobleman, i.e. six times twelve hundred, with an extra amount for compensation for loss in weighing. The fragment of Mercian law that has survived set the king's simple wergeld at six times that of a nobleman. In addition a *cynebot*, equal to the simple wergeld, was also to be paid on the death of a Mercian king. It is possible that the simple royal wergeld applies also to a prince, to an *ætheling* such as Mul. In the Scandinavian kingdom in Northumbria in the first half of the tenth century, whose institutions were most probably those under discussion in the *Norðleoda Laga*, the king was hedged around with a protection of 30,000 thrymsas, no less than fifteen times the wergeld of an ordinary nobleman.[10] Men were normally classified according to the number of shillings in their wergeld, from the one thousand two hundred shillings of the noblemen, or *twelfhyndeman*, to the two hundred shillings of the ceorl. The concept was so familiar that the wergeld came to be used as a fine, with no idea of blood-composition to it. In the so-called 'Laws of Henry I', even a slave had a small wergeld allotted him.[11] As late as the reign of the Conqueror, wergelds were certainly paid, and complaints were made of some wild men in Gloucestershire who would not accept composition.[12] The constant care of the law-codes that the kinless man should be brought into the general pattern indicates how vastly important kindred organization was to the maintenance of general peace.

Indeed some of the most exact information about the working of kindreds comes precisely from that period when the revived West Saxon monarchy began to emerge as the active defender of peace throughout the whole domain of the new tenth-century England, and so to take over functions formerly exercised by the kin. Athelstan was particularly anxious to suppress violence, and took active steps against those men who were so rich or belonged

---

[10] H.M. Chadwick, op. cit., pp. 17–18; A.S. Chronicle, ed. G.N. Garmonsway, p. 40; Mircna Laga, 2, Liebermann I, p. 462; Norðleoda Laga, I, Liebermann I, p. 459.

[11] 'Leges Henrici Primi', 68.I, 70.7a, 76.2. Also 70.2, see below. p. 366.

[12] *Vita Wulfstani*, ed R.R. Darlington, p. 38; *nec a cognatis occisi ullo poterat pacto mercari amicitiam*, though the *cognati* were in fact five brothers.

to such a kin that they could not be punished. His answer was, in case of intransigence, to remove them lock, stock and barrel, noble or simple, with wives, children and all their goods to another part of the country. If they returned then they were to be treated as a thief caught in the act. Harbouring thieves by powerful kindreds was especially condemned, and reeves were to ride against such protecting kinsmen, to slay the thief and those who fought on his behalf.[13] Edmund – and it is one of the ironies of history that he should himself have been assassinated – took strong measures against the principle of vendetta itself. He laid down that the slayer should bear the vendetta alone, unless composition were arranged among the kindred. If, however, the kindred chose to abandon him and not to shelter the fugitive then the kindred was to be free from vendetta. Anyone taking vengeance on a kinsman of the offender was to incur the hostility of the king, of all the kin, and to forfeit all he possessed.[14] The community, acting through its wise men, was to put an end to feuding. The slayer himself was normally intended to give pledges and to pay wergeld. A homicide was to be refused the presence of the king until he had set about making amends for his ill deed. It is only in the exceptional days of Ethelred, when the king made a special pact with the Viking leader, Olaf Tryggvasson, that a royal law-giver, in an attempt to regularize relationships between English and Scandinavians within a borough, recognized in certain circumstances the right to settle a feud, 'head for head'.[15]

Regulations for the payment of wergeld have not survived in any great detail. The most complete statement comes from a short document of the tenth or eleventh century which has survived in two copies, one in Textus Roffensis (at Rochester), the other in a Corpus (Cambridge) MS, both twelfth century. It tells that a man, after he had pledged payment of wergeld for a slain nobleman, had to find guarantors, eight from his paternal kin and four from his maternal. The king's special protection thereupon stood over them. Arrangements were then made for regular payment at three-weekly intervals. First was paid the *healsfang* of one hundred and twenty shillings, that is the compensation to the immediate kin, the children, the brothers and the paternal uncle, and only within that knee. Secondly came the *manbot*, or compensation to the lord.

[13] III Athelstan 6, IV Athelstan 3, VI Athelstan 8.2 and 3.
[14] II Edmund I and 4.
[15] II Ethelred 6; for the two possible interpretations of this difficult clause see Liebermann I, pp. 223–5, and D. Whitelock, *E.H.D.* I, p. 438.

Then followed the *fyhtwite* or penalty for fighting which would normally go to the king. Finally the first instalment of the wergeld proper and so on until wise men should agree that full payment had been made. The insistence on the king's *mund* shows how important the royal power was in regulating such activities. The suggestion that wise men (*witan*) had some discretionary powers over the time in which the wergeld must be paid demonstrates the practical bargaining that must often have occurred in these instances. Most significant of all is the definition of the small inner group that received the *healsfang*. The *Leges Henrici Primi* give a rather different account of this group, saying that the *heaslfang* shall go to father or son or brother, or to whom is the nearer on the paternal side, if he has not the aforesaid kinsmen: if he has them all, they shall divide it among themselves. It may well be that the nearer kin in this way was the decisive active social agent. The wider kin, the *mægth* to seven degrees of kindred, may have been little more than a group that paid and stood guarantors. A man without near kin in practice might well be a kinless man, and as such assimilated easily to the world of territorial lordship and royal authority.[16]

From similar legal evidence it is learned that normally the paternal kindred was responsible for two-thirds of the payment, made or received, and the maternal kindred for one-third. The function of a kindred as a money-paying institution must have been very much in the contemporary mind. Where the kindred was lacking, artificial groups stepped in, and the associates, the *gegildan*, the 'payers', referred to in some of the law-codes belong to this category of artificial kindred. Alfred ordered that, if paternal kin was lacking, the associates should pay one-third, the maternal kin one-third, and the slayer himself one-third; if maternal kin also failed, then the associates were to pay one-half and the slayer himself one-half. In the case of a foreigner the king took two-thirds of the payment, the son or relatives one-third. Later in the period, under Ethelred, the king acted as kinsman and protector to all strangers and to men in Holy Orders if they had no other kin. Normally a man in Holy Orders, if charged with a feud, still had to clear himself with the help of his kindred. A monk, of course, was in different case. As the legal jingle put it:

> He goes from his kin-law
> When he bows to the Rule-Law.[17]

[16] Wergeld 5; *Leges Henrici Primi*, 76.7a.
[17] Alfred 27, 27.1 (30, 31); VIII Ethelred 33 and 25, I Canute 5.2d.

Indeed there is a danger of underestimating the achievements of the Anglo-Saxon monarchs, if we fail to realize how strong were these forces of kindred that they strove to harness to the good of the community. Behind Northumbrian royal history in the seventh and eight centuries lay tale after tale of feuding violence. When the Mercian nobleman captured Imma, the Northumbrian thegn, he told him that he deserved to die because 'all my brothers and kinsmen were killed in that battle'.[18] But it is not easy to get behind the wergeld group to the social nexus that linked people together in everyday affairs. Yet it is certain that the freeman, noble or ceorl, drew much of his standing from his kin, that he reckoned such kin from his mother's side as well as from his father's, and that nevertheless the father's kin was the more important of the two. He would often draw his name from the paternal kin, though the Anglo-Saxon also had a fondness for nicknames, not always of the most delicate nature. There is some evidence to suggest that respectable nicknames could be inherited.[19]

3. SECULAR LORDSHIP

From the earliest days of which there is record, however, it is difficult to examine kindred principles in isolation. Other social bonds, relationship with king and community, above all relationship with secular lords, are so closely entwined with them. The Anglo-Saxon Chronicle under the year 755 (757) gives in vernacular prose a classic story of divided loyalties. King Cynewulf of Wessex was trapped and slain by his enemy Cyneheard. Cyneheard, in turn, was trapped by Cynewulf's men. The two parties treated. Cyneheard offered the besiegers money and land at their own choice, if they would grant him the kingdom, adding that kinsmen of theirs were supporting him in the party that was being besieged. Cynewulf's retainers replied that 'no kinsman was dearer to them than their lord, and that they would never follow his slayer'. However they offered safe passage to their own kinsmen who were with Cyneheard. In turn these kinsmen remained loyal to their lord and were slain with him. The only one to survive – and he was severely wounded – was the besieging ealdorman's own godson.[20]

[18] *Hist. Eccl.*, IV, 22.
[19] A.J. Robertson, *Anglo-Saxon Charters*, no. lxx; examples given in notes.
[20] A.S. Chronicle, *sub anno* 755 (757).

In this victory of lordship principle over kindred tie, one of the great themes of epic poetry, there is given a pointer to English development, though it is well to remember how strong kindred ties remained throughout the period.

Yet it was the bond between lord and man that was to emerge as the strongest in society. That relationship can be traced back to immemorial antiquity. Heroic poetry treats it as one of the fundamental loyalties, specially reinforced if the lord is also kinsman-lord. In England the necessities of invasion and settlement strengthened this concept. Military leaders with a flair for directing defence and rallying colonizers came to the fore in every district, irrespective of the variations in depth and intensity of agrarian penetration. Permanent social units, as they formed themselves, often did so in the shape of rudimentary estate organizations. The free ceorls of Kent, for example, were men of substance and heads of households. The bond that held them together in the kingdom was primarily that of kinsman to kinsman. But the bond that tied them to the bulk of the population was as markedly that of lord to man as was that between the later Scandinavian free farmer and his estate-worker and slaves. The ceorl was also originally a fighting-man. In war, from the beginning of Germanic society, the social bond of loyalty was strong that drew *princeps* and *miles* together. At the highest it could achieve something of a spiritual quality. Already, in the heroic age, the relationship between a successful commander of men and his lord gathered about it much of the ceremonial that came later to be formalized in the feudal world. Beowulf on his return home to his kinsman-lord Hygelac received from his lord great estates, a princely stool and a ceremonial sword – the greatest of treasures in the shape of a sword.[21] 'Glory to the prince, and rewards to the warrior' was a constant theme in heroic writings. A strict and almost universally recognized code of conduct was expected both in the warrior and his lord. Acceptance into the hearth-troop of a lord was hedged with ritual and formality. It was disgraceful in a member of such a troop to survive his lord slain in battle with the lord unavenged. Tacitus said so, and so did the poet of Beowulf. 'Death is better for every *eorl*, than such a life of shame.'[22] The poem on the Battle of Maldon, as late as the end of the tenth century, expressed in unmistakable terms the feelings of a warrior aristocracy towards those who broke their troth to their

---

[21] 'Beowulf', lines 2190–6; *Sinc-maðpum selra on sweordes had.*
[22] Ibid., 2890–1.

lords and failed to fulfil the boasts they had sworn at banquets when they sat flushed with mead. The cowards fled. The ideal was expressed by the old companion Byrhtwold:

> Minds shall be harder, hearts the bolder
> Spirit the more resolute, as our number grows fewer
> Here lies our lord, all hewn down
> A good man on the ground; ever may mourn now
> He who thinks to turn from this battle-play.
> I am old in years: I will not turn hence.
> But I by the side of my lord
> By so dear a man, think to lie.[23]

Such a lordship is truly heroic, just as the relationship of estate-owner to estate-worker is mundane; yet both are fused into a clear social concept. The social attitudes engendered by the former could have its effects on the latter, and could so set the scene for the later complexities of feudal lordship. This heightened view of lordship, in the making of which Christian teachings played their part, was strongly in evidence in tenth-and eleventh-century society. The imposition of Norman feudalism was made possible by the creation in late Anglo-Saxon England of communities dominated by landlords bound closely in turn to the king. The trappings and institutional regularity of feudalism were to develop later, but a way of life that was apt and ready to receive and foster them clearly existed in late Anglo-Saxon England.

Time and time again in the legislation of the late Anglo-Saxon period there is insistence that responsibility for the maintenance of good order in the locality should fall on the landlord. In this respect the clearest sign is given that society was falling into a more complicated social pattern, in which the intangible relationship based on blood was yielding place to the tangible relationships based on land and associated lordship. As the community and the state grew more complicated, so did the ideas flourish together of kingship and territorial lordship. There was no conflict between kindred power and secular lordship, but the latter inevitably gained ground as the social order became increasingly complicated. Hold-oaths, emphasizing with strongest Christian sanction the closeness of man to his lord, point to the way in which more precise definition was achieved. As mutual obligations of lord and man received closer definition, so did more lords attract more men. The great achievement of the Norman lay in his concentration of territorial

[23] 'Battle of Maldon', lines 312–19.

power. The great achievement of the Saxon lay in the creation of such power.

The main evidence in this field comes again from the legislation of the resurgent West Saxon monarchy. Athelstan was concerned with the problem of the lordless man from whom no legal satisfaction could be obtained. He ordered the kin to settle such a man in a fixed residence where he would be amenable to public law, and to find him a lord at a folk-moot. If the kin chose not to do so, or if it found itself unable to do so, then the unfortunate man was declared an outlaw. The lordless man was already something of an anomaly. Every lord was to stand surety for his men, or to see that estate reeves did so on their behalf. Only if the reeve did not trust a man was the kindred to be brought in – with the object of bringing in twelve supporters to stand in the public eye as such security. A lord was responsible for the appearance of a man of his household in court on penalty of the man's wergeld paid to the king in case of escape. Plotting against a lord or deserting him at need were placed among the most heinous offences. If a man was slain a special *manbot*, or compensation for the loss of a man, had to be paid to the lord side by side with the *mægbot* to the kin. There were great advantages to be gained by the possession of a powerful lord; the lord's duties as well as his rights grew increasingly intensive. The Church, itself a formidable lord of men, fostered this development. Towards the end of the tenth century even a thegn's son found it expedient, through fear of God and of St Augustine, to bow down with his land to St Augustine's, Canterbury, to give a pound a year in token of submission, and to arrange for the reversion of his land to the abbey after his death. His father, Lifing the thegn, stood by when his son made his submission. Canute's first code gave clear expression to ecclesiastical beliefs when it enjoined men to be faithful and true to the king, 'for truly God shall be gracious to him who is justly faithful to his lord'. Inversely it was also the great duty of the lord to treat his men justly.[24]

4.   THE COMMUNITY

(a) Kingship and territorial units

But closely linked with this bond between lord and man was the third of the social ties, a tie which in some ways it is even

[24] II Athelstan 2.1; III Athelstan 7.2; III Edmund 7; III Edgar 6; III Athelstan 7; I Ethelred I. 10–13; II Athelstan 4; II Canute 64; VIII Ethelred 3; I Canute 2.5; A.J. Robertson, op. cit., no. lxii; I Canute 20.

more difficult to isolate and define: the bond of community. On the purely agrarian level something has already been said of the relationship between community and individual. It is likely that in the early days of settlement the community interfered only in those processes which demanded corporate endeavour: the ownership of plough and of plough-teams, the allotment of arable, and the partition of meadow. The provision of seed and ownership of crop remained private, and communal interest took a second place in these vital matters.

All agricultural settlement, however, demands defence, and when the cultivators of the soil themselves proved inadequate, a warrior aristocracy gradually developed among them. With the resulting aristocratic sense of cohesion came also a marked tendency to corporate growth. Above all, when monarchies were set up beyond the mere tribal bounds, the beginnings were made of a rudimentary but true state system. This development, perhaps the most important single institutional development of the Anglo-Saxon period, received constant stimulus from the active monarchical principle itself. The example of the monarchy and of the royal court spread slowly through the whole community. The royal kin was the first to be differentiated from all other kindreds. By intermarriage with the royal kin, and by natural prowess, other aristocratic kindreds sprang up. The royal court was aped at the local ealdorman's hall, and indeed at the bishop's *tun*. The Northumbrian queen complained bitterly of Wilfrid's enormous state, more befitting a warrior prince than a *miles Christi*.[25] As the royal court grew into a more efficient deliberative and administrative body, so did the like need develop for permanent institutions at the local level. It may well be that Anglo-Saxon institutional development came not so much from the community of neighbours up as from the royal household down. Certainly in the tenth century it is the royal court that emerges as the active agent, declaring in some detail measures for a general peace and stimulating local 'witans' such as that for Kent and that for London to put into effect the royal decrees. Athelstan laid the fine for disobedience to the king on anyone failing to attend a meeting three times, and ordained the same penalty for anyone failing to ride with his fellows against the defaulter. Edgar, in particular, made every effort to increase the efficiency of the local meetings. He specified that if a man of bad character failed to attend the moot on three

[25] Eddius Stephanus, *Life of Wilfrid*, c. xxiv.

occasions *even his kinsmen* were to join in riding against him.[26] The creation of a shire court as a permanent institution, and one that worked, must rank among not the least of the achievements of the tenth-century monarchs. The shire courts were accompanied again, at the same vital period by the regularization of permanent institutions on a smaller geographical scale. The hundred itself may derive often from a primitive *regio*; it may result from a chance rough grouping at a given time of a hundred households. As a permanent body, attended by regular suitors at regular and indeed frequent intervals, charged with special duties in the maintenance of peace, it owed its creation to the work of Edward the Elder or his immediate successors.[27] In the Danelaw the institution corresponding to the hundred was known as the wapentake. Already before the end of the tenth century a jury of twelve most senior thegns existed in many of these wapentakes.[28] There are traces before the Conquest of hundred and wapentake suffering penalties for failing to keep due order. In all facets of government the English realm was divided into geographical units held responsible for duties exercised in an earlier age by kindreds.

The growth of these territorial units reveals a very important social fact. By 1066 the Englishman considered himself in relation to many of his activities as an inhabitant of a region rather than as a member of a kindred. Even where his own personal status was concerned, his membership of a tithing, that is of groups of ten 'adult' men, was as important in the eyes of the law, certainly from the reign of Canute, as his position within the kin.[29] Bound by the ever-increasing and tenacious tie of lordship, which reinforced rather than slackened this territorial aspect, the local community had achieved before the Norman came some of that solid corporate sentiment that was to prove so characteristic of English society in the succeeding centuries.

Most active of all the forces operating towards this emphasis on community was the monarchy. And above all in its financial aspects the monarchy proved a true moulding force to English society.

---

[26] II Athelstan 20 and 20.2, III Edgar 7.2; also II Canute 25.2.

[27] II Edward 8, ordered each reeve to hold a moot every four weeks. The hundred is not mentioned by name until the time of Edmund: III Edmund 2, Liebermann I, p. 190. H.R. Loyn, 'The Hundred in England in the tenth and early eleventh Centuries', *British Government and Administration*, ed. H. Hearder and H.R. Loyn Cardiff, 1974, pp. 1–15.

[28] III Ethelred 3.1. See above, p. 224.

[29] II Canute 20 and 20a.

No examination of social bonds before the Norman Conquest can approach completeness until something is said about the monarchy and finance, particularly in relation to the exaction of geld which proved so formative an impost in the eleventh century.

(b) Royal exactions and the community

From the very earliest days of kingship positive payments were made to the king. His position did not depend merely upon the negative sanction of extra wergeld, a special personal peace, extra protection to his house and his servants, and the like. Probably the earliest of the payments, and certainly one that survived longest, was the obligation to provide for the king and his court on his journeys around the kingdom. Primarily this duty fell on his own estates. By the eleventh century the unit of assessment of this payment was known as the *firma unius noctis*, or the amount needed to support the king and his household for one day. But to keep a royal court in good trim was no easy task, and there is early reference to food-rents exacted from estates which were not purely royal. Indeed, as far as can be judged from strong circumstantial evidence, it seems established that contributions from all cultivated land to the king's *feorm* was substantially synonymous with the institution of Germanic kingship itself. This *feorm*, or food-rent, was probably not notably heavy, but it is an important pointer to the recognition of royal rights, the king as it were embodying the rights of the larger community to which estate and family land belonged. An interesting example occurs in eighth-century Mercian records. An estate, which was to be sure a former royal estate owned by Ethelbald of Mercia, had been granted by him to his kinsman Eanwulf. It consisted of land, assessed at sixty hides, at Westbury in Gloucestershire. From this estate the royal *feorm* was retained while the estate itself was granted by Offa, Ethelbald's effective successor and also Eanwulf's grandson, to the church at Worcester. The *feorm* amounted to the food-rent of 'two tuns of pure ale, a coomb of mild ale and a coomb of Welsh ale, seven oxen, six wethers, 40 cheeses, 6 long *peru*, 30 ambers of unground corn and four ambers of meal'. Although the full meaning of this passage is obscured by ignorance of the size of the measures in question, the render appears to have been modest from so large an estate.[30] It is highly probable that

[30] *C.S.*, 273; F.M. Stenton, *Anglo-Saxon England*, p.288. *E.H.D.* I, p. 507. This retention of a right, binding the land whoever owned it, resembles the later *profit à prendre*.

such a burden was normally removed from an estate by the act of booking land, and specific reference to the *cyninges feorm* among the burdens from which bookland was freed occurs occasionally, as in the complicated negotiation by which Ethelred of the Mercians endowed Berkeley during the reigns of his father-in-law Alfred and his brother-in-law Edward the Elder.[31]

Perhaps more impressive than the description of such *feorm* is the obvious anxiety of estate-owners to be freed from what are at times known as 'public burdens'. The most obviously weighty of these burdens, that of supplying men for the army, and contributing to the maintenance of bridges and of fortresses, were rarely if ever lifted. Contribution to the king's *feorm* and, equally as important, the duties of maintaining him, his ealdormen, and their servants, or those who had business with the king, were lifted by the act of booking land. Such freedom was highly prized. A grant by the Mercian king Brihtwulf in 843 or 844 to his ealdorman Aethelwulf of land at Pangbourne expressly freed it from 'the entertainment of ealdormen and from that burden which we call in Saxon *fæstingmen*; neither are to be sent there men who bear hawks or falcons, or lead dogs or horses, but they are to be freed perpetually for ever'. Food-rents and such expensive public rights formed quite a heavy burden on the land of the kingdom.[32]

As the kingdoms settled and matured so did it become common for these dues to be transposed into money payments, though there is evidence enough from Domesday Book to show that renders were still, if convenient, made in kind. The king's officers were responsible for the collection of such dues. The ealdorman developed by the end of the period into a great political officer, and it was on the king's reeves that the duties of collection fell. These reeves had as their primary function the charge of the king's estates. Among their number, one was gradually singled out as the earl's deputy in the shire. It was this shire-reeve who became the chief agent for the collection and transmission of all these traditional renders from all estates in the shire, both royal and private.

(c) The geld and the community

The renders together with the rents and services from his own extensive lands made up a considerable sum upon which the king

[31] Harmer, *Select Documents*, no. xii. See above, p. 180. The fact that bookland is freed of all burdens except three, of which *feorm* was not one, seems conclusive proof that *feorm* was removed at the creation of bookland.
[32] *C.S.*, 443; *E.H.D.* I, p. 521.

and his court lived. In addition rights over boroughs and notably minting rights brought to the king a considerable proportion of the trading wealth that was beginning to accumulate in England. Justice was, as always, a profitable business, and the offences for which the king himself took the fine helped to swell the funds which the royal officers had to provide for their masters. But over and above renders and customs and dues and legal perquisites lay the geld. The geld was a land-tax, the first regular and permanent land-tax known to the West in the Middle Ages. It was prompted by disastrous political events at the end of the tenth century. But it is also, as far as the instruments of collection are concerned, a product of the great efficiency of the monarchy, and of the greater cohesion and increased wealth of the community.

The Anglo-Saxon geld system of the eleventh century was undoubtedly an advanced institution of government for its day and age. Yet there are features of great antiquity to it that link the geld to the more primitive tribute taken by Anglo-Saxon kings in early days, and also with the system whereby food-rents were exacted from dependent estates. Charters reveal villages where a description given in the ninth, or even in the eighth century, corresponds to the assessment for geld recorded in Domesday Book. Sedgebarrow in Worcestershire is a village of four hides in a charter of Offa; it is assessed at four hides in Domesday Book. Hampton Lucy contained twelve *manentes* in 781; it is assessed at twelve hides in 1086.[33] The very methods used in the late eleventh century for the distribution of the burden of geld had roots far back in Anglo-Saxon history. In their finished form these methods reflect the social differences that existed between the various regions of Anglo-Saxon England. In no respect, for example, are the peculiarities of East Anglia and Kent more evident than in these matters of assessment to geld.

Information concerning the detailed working of the assessment comes primarily from Domesday Book. Fortunately there have survived also documents from the Anglo-Saxon period proper that help to give depth to the account of a land-tax that worked. Most ancient of all is a tribute-taker's document of the eighth century known as the 'Tribal Hidage', to which reference has been made in an earlier chapter.[34] It described in round figures the taxable

[33] F.M. Stenton, *Anglo-Saxon England*, p. 647; *Latin Charters of the Anglo-Saxon Period*. p. 74.
[34] C.R. Hart, 'The Tribal Hidage', *T. R. Hist. S.*, 21, 1971, pp. 133–57: Wendy Davies and H. Vierck, 'The contexts of the Tribal Hidage', pp. 223–93. See above p. 25 and p. 48.

capacity of an area roughly corresponding to the greater Mercia of the eighth century. Mercia itself was assessed at thirty thousand hides, and a later hand attributes one hundred thousand to the West Saxons. The subsidiary folks grouped around the Mercian core were treated in great detail, some of which can now no longer be interpreted. A figure of seven thousand hides was in general use to assess a powerful sub-group such as the dwellers in the Wrekin, and the (north) westerly parts of the Midlands, the men of Lindsey and Hatfield Chase, the unknown *Nox gaga* and *Oht gaga* peoples for whom a home may one day have to be found in the Middlesex area and Surrey, the Hwicce, the men of Essex, and the men of Sussex. Bede confirms that Sussex was held to contain seven thousand households. The same figure is mentioned when the hero Beowulf is granted his province on his return from his successful expedition to the land of the Danes. It is incredible that exactly seven thousand households can have existed severally in each of these areas, or that their arable capacity supported exactly seven thousand teams. The figure merely gives us an example of governmental financial reckoning in round terms from a very early stage.[35]

Lesser groups in the 'Tribal Hidage' were assessed on a basis of a three-hundred-hide unit, the men of the Peak in Derbyshire at twelve hundred hides, those of Elmet at six hundred, ten or eleven small folks in a swathe of country from the Fens to London assessed separately at between three hundred and twelve hundred hides, and similarly, possibly to the south of the Thames, a group of seven peoples was assessed in the same limited range. The document is impressive, coming from its remote period, as proof of an admittedly somewhat rough and ready but nevertheless systematic basis for royal exaction. Three hundred hides was later taken as a respectable endowment for a bishopric.

It is not until the early tenth century that the next general piece of evidence for a regular assessment system, the 'Burghal Hidage', makes its appearance. The 'Burghal Hidage' concentrates on the fortifications built and manned to protect English England, mostly south of the Thames, and to contain the Danes.[36] In relation to the immediate problem it shows the Anglo-Saxon employing the hide as a fiscal unit to determine responsibility for defence. But

[35] F.M. Stenton, *Anglo-Saxon England*, p. 295; J. Brownbill, *E.H.R.*, 1925, pp. 497–503; *Hist. Eccl.*, IV, 13; Beowulf, line 2195.
[36] See above pp. 138–42.

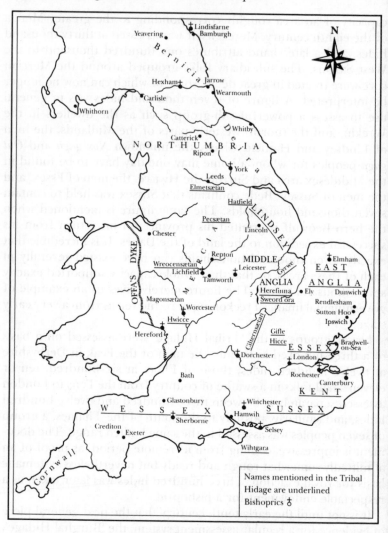

The England of the Tribal Hidage

A number of places mentioned in the Tribal Hidage have not been identified. The best up–to–date list (including locations for many small Fenland folk such as the *Bilmiga*) appears in David Hill, *Atlas of Anglo–Saxon England*, pp.76-7. *Syddensis civitas*, the seat of the bishop of Lindsey, has not been identified.

incidentally it reveals also that the shire of Worcester possessed for assessment purposes twelve hundred hides. This figure is confirmed in the third of our general fiscal documents, the so-called

'County Hidage' which set out, shire by shire, the taxable capacity of the greater part of the kingdom of Ethelred in the early eleventh century.[37] The 'County Hidage' has a special importance in any discussion of continuity of Anglo-Saxon territorial government for, as Maitland showed in his brilliant analysis of the document, in some instances the figures attributed to the various shires tally with the Domesday evidence to a remarkable degree. Of the thirteen shires dealt with in the 'County Hidage' eight, Bedford, Huntingdon, Gloucester, Worcester, Hereford, Oxford, Stafford, and, a shade less convincingly, Warwickshire have reasonable or exact equivalence with the Domesday estimates. There are discrepancies in the cases of Cheshire and Northamptonshire, but these can be explained, the former on grounds of variations in area, the latter on grounds of devastation and beneficial hidation. Wiltshire, another area about which there is discrepancy, seems to have been assessed at a very high figure in the Hidage (four thousand eight hundred hides to the four thousand or so of Domesday); Shropshire and Cambridgeshire have only half the number of hides in Domesday Book that they are held to possess in the Hidage, but again beneficial hidation, admittedly on a formidable scale, may have brought this result about. Even taking these anomalies and discrepancies into account, the impression remains of a continuity in shire assessment, connected in some instances directly with the number of hundreds in a shire, and coupled too with a flexibility that made possible a general reduction in taxation for areas that had suffered special political or natural disaster. The 'Tribal Hidage' brings us into contact with an age where royal impositions were linked to political superiority over many small folks; the eleventh-century fiscal documents disclose a kingdom in which the territorial division of the shire, itself a creation of royal government, was the key unit of fiscal administration.[38]

Over most of England the machinery for further subdivision of responsibility for geld within the shires bore certain common characteristics. Each shire was held to contain a round number of taxable units, hides or ploughlands or *sulungs*. Of these terms the

---

[37] P.H. Sawyer, *From Roman Britain to Norman England*, London, 1978, pp. 228–9, indicates reasons for having confidence in the figures of the County Hidage.
[38] For the 'Burghal Hidage', see *Anglo-Saxon Charters*, ed. A.J. Robertson, pp. 246–9. For the 'County Hidage', F.W. Maitland, *Domesday Book and Beyond*, pp. 455–7. The south-west geld rolls in D.B. IV; the Northamptonshire geld roll in Robertson, pp. 230–7 and also in *E.H.D.* II, F.M. Stenton, *Anglo-Saxon England*, pp. 643–8, is of fundamental importance to any discussion of geld and assessment.

first was the most common, and the most English. It had a cognate resemblance to the continental term *huf*, and signified the land occupied by one peasant household, at least in its original sense. Ploughlands and *sulungs* had an economic rather than a social basis to their meaning, signifying the land that could be cultivated by a full plough-team in one season. All these terms had advanced far from their original meaning by the time of the Domesday survey, when they possessed primarily a fiscal connotation, a description of a unit in a scheme of national taxation. In general the number of taxable units was smaller than the number of real ploughlands and of real hides.

The common practice was for the king and his court to decide on the amount to be paid to meet extraordinary need, above all extraordinary military need in providing for an army, the so-called heregeld, or the sum needed to buy off the Danes, the notorious danegeld. Terminology over these variants, geld, heregeld and danegeld is quite confused, and it is danegeld which survived as the common term in twelfth-century England. If for example, a levy of two shillings in the hide was needed, the order would go to the shire court to see to the collection. The hidage of the shire was fixed first, and as has been seen was normally the product of long custom: in the case of Northamptonshire, from which a geld roll of the reign of William I has survived, an assessment of 3,200 hides was assumed. This hidage was then divided among the hundreds, and the Northamptonshire Geld Roll preserves the accounts of the individual hundreds in the following form: 'To Cleyley hundred belong 100 hides, as was the case in King Edward's time, and of these 18 hides have paid geld and 40 hides are in demesne and 42 hides are waste.'[39]

Royal demesne did not pay geld as its services to king and community were performed in other ways. The inland of tenants by military service was similarly exempt from payment.

The 'Inquisitiones Geldi' for the south-western counties, incorporated in the Exeter Domesday, also gave the round number of hides for each hundred, the number held by king and barons in demesne, an account of those hides on which tax was not paid and of those on which it was paid, together with the amount.[40] It added the tax in arrears, and also the reason for the arrears. These documents have a pleasing immediacy as they refer to a particular

---

[39] *E.H.D.* II, pp. 517–20.
[40] D.B. IV, pp. x–xi.

geld of six shillings a hide and make their detailed assessments accordingly. In the hundred of Mere in Wiltshire fifty-one hides paid £15 6s., that is to say fifty-one times six shillings; in the hundred of Pinpre in Dorset thirteen hides paid £3 18s.; in the hundred of Conarditone in Cornwall ten hides paid £3. Valuable information is also given concerning the collection of geld. The collectors retained a small portion of geld for their own use. In Devonshire it was customary for the collector in each hundred to retain the geld on one hide. Somerset in all contributed £509, and those who took this sum to Winchester received forty shillings, and a further nine shillings and eightpence for the money they had spent on hiring baggage-men and a scribe and for buying containers and wax. But they could not account for 51s. 3d. which they had received, and had to give pledges that they would render that amount themselves to the royal commissioners.

Within the hundred, in turn, the allotment of hidage to villages was decided on, and to judge from twelfth-century evidence it was in the hundred court that the inevitable detailed disputes over the fairness of the assessment were hammered out. Over much of England, in Wessex, Essex, English Mercia and the southern Midlands villages were assessed at five hides or ten hides or some such number in a decimal system of reckoning. In the Northern Danelaw a duodecimal system was in force, the Danish carucates or ploughlands being grouped into units of six or twelve for fiscal purposes. The East Anglian system, as has been mentioned before, was different again. The liability of East Anglian villages was assessed, not in five-hide or six-carucate units, but in terms of the number of pence it was expected to contribute when its hundred paid a pound to the geld. East Anglian villages were further grouped into what were called 'leets', that is to say intermediate units between village and hundred that contributed forty pence when the hundred gave £1. In Kent the peculiar and archaic unit of the sulung persisted. This is again an economic unit, a ploughland, not a social 'hide' in origin, but it appears that in practice as early as the ninth century a sulung was taken as the equivalent of a double-hide, possibly a pointer to the superior wealth of the Kentish ceorl, though there were also double-hides, of two hundred and forty acres, in Cambridgeshire in the tenth century.[41] The grouping of sulungs within their hundreds follows very much the same decimal

[41] *Liber Eliensis*, ed. D.J. Stewart, II, 17, p. 132 and II, 31, pp. 145–7, *hydas de duodecies XL*.

pattern for assessment purposes as elsewhere in the south. The most startling features of the Kentish evidence were brought out brilliantly by J.E.A. Jolliffe who suggested that some vestiges of the system by which Kentish kings were maintained at the time of their independence were preserved in the distribution of sulungs grouped around royal *tuns* at the time of Domesday Book.[42]

From the general point of view the importance of the existence of such a tried and reasonably efficient assessment system is hard to exaggerate. The factors which stimulated it to maturity were grim: above all, the peril from the Danes in the late tenth century. To Archbishop Sigeric went the dubious credit of first recommending tribute to the Danes, and £10,000 was given to the slayers of Byrhtnoth in 991. Throughout the reign of Ethelred the heavy exactions continued, amounting to no less than £167,000 in formal payment alone by the end of the reign, if we may believe the figures given to us in the Anglo-Saxon Chronicle. It is worthy of note that in spite of these heavy burdens London itself was still capable of producing £20,000 in 1018 at Canute's command, apart from a tribute of £72,000 which the new king exacted from his kingdom.[43]

As well as tribute payment, true danegeld, extraordinary sums were collected by Ethelred for payment of the fleet for defensive purposes. The Chronicle declares that in 1008 the whole country was divided into districts of 310 hides, each of which contributed a warship of approximately sixty oars to the national force. The '310' hides, it has been happily suggested, may be explained as three hundred hides for the ship and ten hides for the dinghy. Others are more inclined to take it as a straight scribal slip.[44] Armour was supplied by a further levy, every eight hides contributing a helmet and a corslet. The three-hundred-hide units survived into the twelfth century in Warwickshire.[45]

Throughout the reign of Canute and his successors and for the first part of the reign of Edward the Confessor there were no Danes to buy off, but there were fighting men, Danish and English, to support. The names *heregeld*, or army geld, was given

---

[42] J.E.A. Jolliffe, *Pre-Feudal England: the Jutes*, pp. 43–7. See above pp. 42–4 for major modifications of Jolliffe's detailed figures.

[43] A.S. Chronicle, *sub anno* 1018.

[44] A.S. Chronicle, *sub anno* 1008, ed. G.N. Garmonsway, p. 138; but D. Whitelock, *E.H.D.* I, p. 241, accepts Plummer's reading of 310 hides.

[45] Ibid.; F.E. Harmer, *Anglo-Saxon Writs*, pp. 266–7; E.P.N.S., *Warwickshire*, pp. xix–xx.

to the exactions that were imposed to keep the fleet and army in being. Heregeld was heavy enough, and resented enough, to provoke one serious riot at Worcester in the reign of Harthacnut where the King ravaged violently in revenge for the murder of two unfortunate tax collectors. Hemming, writing with the Worcester tragedy well in view, gives the background when he tells of the almost insupportable geld laid on the whole country by Sweyn to the point that almost all the church ornaments and precious goods were lost, even lands and hamlets belonging to the church of Worcester being sold in an attempt to raise the money. Things were as bad under Canute, and even worse under Harthacnut who added yet heavier burdens to the already formidable weight of imposts. When the heregeld was abolished in 1051, in the thirty-ninth year of its existence according to the Anglo-Saxon Chronicle and to Florence of Worcester, the chroniclers expressed their relief.[46] Edward had earlier disbanded the standing fleet, nine crews being paid off in 1049, and the remaining five in the following year. Such reliefs no doubt did much to enhance his saintly reputation. Yet the levying of geld itself was so firmly established that the removal of these extra imposts can have done little to break the continuity of the land-tax. William made exceedingly good use of it. One of his first actions after his coronation was to lay a very heavy tax on the country, and again in the following year another heavy tax was laid on the unhappy people. Heavy but probably not unmerciful is the opinion of many scholars, and some of the strength of the system lay in the flexibility of the assessment scheme by which the hidage could be reduced for the benefit of impoverished communities. Over the south-eastern counties which suffered most from the campaigns that followed Hastings there is frequent reference to reduction in hidage on account of the waste and devastation.

   In conclusion, two particular considerations in connection with the geld and its relationship to the territorialization of political authority in England need to be emphasized. They tell us much of the way in which the monarchy and the community were growing into more complicated institutions. The first concerns the provincial figures for the assessment, the twelve hundred hides of Worcester or the thirty-two hundred hides of Northamptonshire; the second concerns the individual assessments of villages and estates within the shires.

---

[46] Florence of Worcester, 1041, *E.H.D.* I, p. 318; *W. Malms, Gest. Pont.*, Book II, p. 154; Hemming, *Mon Angl.*, vol. I, p. 593.

The round figures of the provincial assessments are interesting in themselves, proving as they do government action from above. What is even more interesting is the continuous history of these figures, in some areas at least, from the early tenth century to the end of the eleventh. Attempts to go beyond the early tenth century and to link up with the figures of the 'Tribal Hidage' have not been successful in practice. The 'Tribal Hidage' gives the men of Lindsey and Hatfield Chase seven thousand hides; the corresponding Domesday figures are 2,007 carucates for Lindsey.[47] Danish influx followed by negotiated recovery might make necessary slacker financial control in this area of the northern Danelaw. But in Sussex where Bede agrees with the 'Tribal Hidage' in attributing seven thousand hides, the corresponding figures for a period shortly before the Conquest will be no more than 4,250 hides.[48] The discrepancy is so great that serious attention has been given to the possibility that the hides of the earlier period were much smaller than the Domesday hides, representing virgates rather than hides. Certainly seven thousand *real* hides of a hundred and twenty acres each could not be squeezed into Sussex by any stroke of the surveyor's pen. It seems more likely that the hides of the early document, always assuming that the big figures are reasonably reliable, were more closely related to the idea of peasant households than to specific holdings in arable, and that possibly the question of military service occupied the Mercian overlord as well as the question of land taxation. An army of, say, fourteen hundred men from the kingdom of Sussex would not affront the historical imagination.

On the matter of assessments of villages within the shires the problem is more complicated, and more will be said about it in a later chapter. Domesday Book, the indispensable guide on these matters, was arranged feudally, that is according to the holdings of the tenants-in-chief with the basic unit the manor. It has taken the ingenuity of a remarkable series of Domesday scholars to reconstruct the so-called five-hide and six-carucate units, in so doing to reveal the territorial basis of English administration. The fact that financial imposts lay primarily on villages, not on estates,

---

[47] F.M. Stenton, *Anglo-Saxon England*, p. 648.
[48] J.H. Round and F. Salzmann, V.C.H., *Sussex*, vol. I, p. 360, where by great ingenuity the apparent chaos of the Sussex assessment is sorted out, and the 'original unreduced' figure is disclosed of forty-two and a half hundreds, which is remarkably close to the forty-three hundred and fifty hides attributed to Sussex in the 'Burghal Hidage'. See also F.W. Maitland, *Domesday Book and Beyond*, p. 502.

s of cardinal importance. Village and estate did not necessarily coincide, and it is by no means unusual to find two, three, even even so-called manors in the same village. It is only when the holdings of these manors are added together that the five-hide assessment plan stands revealed. The village not the manor was the institution of assessment with which the Anglo-Saxon monarchy treated.

Indeed it is the village which provided the fundamental unit of government in late Anglo-Saxon England. Kingship and royal government were powerful, more apt to lapse into fitful tyranny than into weak neglect. The power of the secular lord was great, and increasing in general in company with the power of the king. But above all, the major trend in the society of late Anglo-Saxon England was towards increased cohesion of society and towards the thorough territorialization of England through village, hundred, shire and monarchy. On the level of the person it was the bond between lord and man that emerged triumphant in late Anglo-Saxon England. On the level of government it was the power of the territorial community, symbolized in the person of the monarch, that flourished in full vigour.

CHAPTER EIGHT
The Norman Conquest

However much dispute there may be concerning the detail of the
Norman impact on England, there can be no doubt whatever
concerning the general importance of the coming of the Normans.
The Normans differed in many vital respects from the earlier
conquerors of English England, but the two main differences were
first, that their success was more complete, and second, that they
had more to offer. The Dane represented the barbarian who had
moved in from the outer fringe to the fertile lands. He was pagan
for the most part on arrival; the conquered were Christian. He
was a great seaman and something of a trader; the conquered
were primarily agriculturalists. But the Dane was also used to the
land and rapidly settled where cultivable land was available. It is
a consistent theme of the sagas that Scandinavian adventurers,
noble of blood and fighters by nature, showed willingness to settle
down and help with the routine agricultural work as a matter of
course during their stay in various ports of call in time of exile.
None of this was true of the Norman. He was a Christian and
his leader, Duke William, a devout Christian. That great weapon
of assimilation, the possession of a higher universal faith, was
not at the disposal of the Anglo-Saxons in their dealings with
the Normans as it had been in their dealings with the Danes.
Norman arrogance became proverbial, and to put the matter at
its mildest the Normans clearly felt no inferiority to the Saxons
they had conquered. Abounding self-confidence was a hallmark
of their race, and a principal reason for their success. Assimilated
they were in time, but the process did not approach completion till
the age of the Plantagenet Edwards. Gower as late as the fourteenth

:entury still faced the enviable task of choosing between French
and English for his poetic medium.

Yet even in its earliest stages the Norman Conquest was not the
arbitrary imposition of alien rule that is sometimes supposed. For
three years William attempted to preserve the substance as well as
the form of Edward's kingship. After 1072, with his success against
native rebellion, his rule became more arbitrary. The pattern of the
new feudalism was rigidly stamped upon the country. Defence and
landholding were neatly dovetailed. All land was held of the king.
A handful of great magnates saw to the military efficiency of units
supported by vast demesnes. Sub-infeudation, though slow to start
in the first instance, revealed the knight's fee as the basic unit in
the feudal hierarchy. An estate was still assessed at so many hides
accountable to the geld. The major concern of king and landlord
lay now much more in the obligation to send so many knights
to follow the feudal host. Socially the contract between king and
lord became of maximum importance. Military organization was
brought up to date, and while the Old English fyrd was retained,
the backbone of the army became a carefully trained cavalry,
professional and acutely class-conscious. The process of relating
land-tenure directly to military service was rapid and clear-cut.

In some respects, however, these innovations, startling as they
appear, were essentially superficial. The superstructure of Norman
England was undeniably feudal, but the basic institutions of Anglo-
Saxon England persisted. The kingship itself was the Old English
kingship, stiffened by the military prowess of the new king. It
gave William a legal position much superior to that which he had
occupied as Duke of Normandy. The territorial divisions into shires
and hundreds retained a paramount importance in administrative
and legal fields, though many hundreds fell into private hands.
One of William's early acts after the Conquest was to grant, in
a charter to the City of London, that the Londoners were to be
worthy of their laws as in the days of King Edward, that each
child was to be his father's heir after his father's day, and that
no man should offer any wrong to them.[1] The new king in effect assured the Londoners that there was to be no interference
with their rights. Among the landowning class the heavy casualties
at Hastings and in succeeding rebellions made such propositions
concerning inheritance of doubtful value. By 1086 there were only
two English tenants-in-chief of baronial rank in the whole of Eng-

[1] *E.H.D.* II, p. 1012.

land, Coleswain of Lincoln and Thurkill of Arden, both of whom
battened fat on the estates of dispossessed fellow-Englishmen.
Some of the best of the young men of thegnly class fled oversea
to Scandinavia or to swell the ranks of the Varangian Guard
at Constantinople, where they were able, under the banner of
the Greek empire, to fight against the hated Normans settled in
the south of Italy.[3] Some fled to Scotland to join the entourage
of the *ætheling* Edgar. Others lived on with a poor competence
to support them from what had previously been the substantial
renders of their estates. Aelfwine, son of Edwin, for example
appeared in Domesday Book as a modest sub-tenant of Walter de
Lacy for two manors in Herefordshire where his father had held
seventeen, including the great estate at Weobley.[4] In some case
estates devolved on heiresses who would be married to Norman
protectors. Some Englishmen overcame the social barriers erected
by the Conquest, learned the new arts of the feudal world, and
were assimilated to the Normans, occasionally adopting Norman
names. These were probably few in number, though evidence for
such interaction is marked in the case of wealthy London families.[5]
There can be no doubt that the years 1066–1100 brought about a
major social revolution in the upper classes of society.

How did this revolution express itself? In the first place by
the introduction of a new language which became peculiarly the
possession of the ruling and upper clerical class. The Norman
baron may have acquired sufficient English to satisfy his personal
needs: the Norman bishop, if conscientious, acquired enough to be
able to supervise the general working of the parishes in his diocese

[2] J.W.F. Hill, *Medieval Lincoln*, Cambridge 1948, p. 48. There are fifty-four entries
in Domesday Book relating to Coleswain's forty-four manors (no fewer than five at
Fillingham alone), eleven pieces of sokeland and seven berewicks. From the *valets*
and *valuits* of the manors, none of which had been held by Coleswain himself
in 1066, it appears that the value was nearly £80 in 1086, a little less than a
twenty-five per cent. increase on the corresponding value in 1066. Coleswain had
inherited four tofts in the city of Lincoln itself, and had received from the king a
stretch of waste land outside the city of Lincoln on which he had built thirty-six
new houses and had found inhabitants for them. He also built and possessed
two churches. Thurkill held seventy-one manors in 1086, only four of which
are known to have been his father's. Thurkill's descendants continued to hold
part of their inheritance, as military sub-tenants of the Earls of Warwick.
[3] F.M. Stenton, 'English Families and the Norman Conquest', *T.R. Hist. S.*,
1944.
[4] V.C.H., *Hereford*, vol. I, p. 275.
[5] D.C. Douglas, *The Domesday Monachorum of Christ Church, Canterbury*, London,
1944, pp. 62–3.

But English was relegated to a position of inferiority. Latin and French became the languages of culture. Government business hitherto conducted in English was now normally transacted in Latin. The effect on English was salutary in the long run. Already by the time of the Conquest the change from synthetic to analytic English was far advanced, more so in the spoken language than in classical Anglo-Saxon. The Conquest hastened the process, and the analytical Middle English which emerged from its period of quiescence was a more flexible instrument, unencumbered by the heavily inflected vesture of synthetic Anglo-Saxon. But to the Englishman of the day the inferior position into which their language sank must have appeared a disaster.

Then again there is the question of social manners. The Normans have been described as a rude and somewhat barbarous people, and certainly there is little in their eleventh-century history to justify the lavish praise that has been bestowed on them in the past. Courtoisie was of slow evolution, and William's barons and knights were not uniformly chivalric. What is more, it is utterly misleading to ascribe to the Normans all the credit for the fine flowering of intellectual life in the twelfth century, to the neglect of the English and continental roots that fed such flowering. The so-called 'age of the Investiture Contest' saw a remarkable revival of Western European civilization. Many of the most striking Norman achievements were rather cosmopolitan achievements. The scholarship of Lanfranc and of Anselm, in particular, was a cosmopolitan rather than a Norman or an insular phenomenon. Yet the fact that these two great scholars were able to exercise their talents in the highest ecclesiastical office in these islands was due to the sagacity of William. His success lay essentially in his ability to impose upon an ancient and civilized kingdom a means of defence uniquely suited to the needs of the day, and so to open the kingdom to fruitful influence from reviving continental Latin culture.

The social manners that were introduced were in the first instance those of the rough barbaric world of the first feudal age. The very oaths and gruffness suggest a vigorous, hasty-tempered military society. Great play has been made recently of a degenerate, effeminate element at Rufus's court where the King's favourites acquired notoriety for their long hair and sensuality. It is easy for such habits, particularly if associated with a group disliked by the Church, to be interpreted in the worst possible light.

Of luxuries and refinements in material culture there is little evidence in the first generation of the Conquest. A new breed

of horses seems to have been introduced, the destrier, capable of
carrying in battle the heavy-armed fighting man. The smith's work
for equine purposes grew more specialized and skilful. The armed
knight and the castle were the two most conspicuous innovations
of the Normans in the English scene, but the name 'castle' is
something of a misnomer. The Tower itself it is true, begun by the
Conqueror, was substantially constructed. Under the year 1097 the
Anglo-Saxon Chronicle stated that many shires which owed work
to London were greatly oppressed in making the wall around
the Tower. When completed, presumably before the death of
its chief architect, Gundulf, Bishop of Rochester, 1077–1108, the
Tower served as a model to be followed by most twelfth-century
keeps. It was bigger than any other English keep, save Colchester,
and measured a hundred and eighteen by ninety-eight feet at its
base.[6] Other royal castles placed at strategic points were from the
earliest days well and stoutly built of stone. Some of the great
tenants-in-chief followed the most ambitious royal plans. But in
the main the new Norman castles were little more than roughly
built shelters, the *motte* thrown up as a temporary means of defence,
the building of wood and small, the bailey in which subsidiary
buildings, smithies and storehouses would be set up of no great
extent. Only in the towns of strategic importance, where houses
were often demolished on a large scale to make room for the castles,
were ambitious schemes practicable in these early days of Norman
settlement. The function of the castle was to serve as a rallying
point, a loyal centre in times of danger, and as an administrative
headquarters for royal officer or head of an honour in times of
peace.[7] They were not comfortable dwelling places, being more
akin to barracks than to country houses. Most Norman barons,
even the greatest, were content to live much as their Anglo-Saxon
predecessors had done, only somewhat more lavishly.

The basic wealth of the community lay in land. It is evident
that considerable variation in land-values and in taxable capacity
occurred between 1066 and 1086, as is shown in every page of
Domesday Book. For example, the path of the avenging Norman
armies in their 'Harrying of the North' is only too easy to trace in

[6] E.S. Armitage, *The Early Norman Castles of the British Isles*, London, 1912, pp. 222–3.
[7] F.M. Stenton, *The First Century of English Feudalism*, 2nd ed., Oxford, 1961, p. 56: 'The honour, in the usual sense of the word, was essentially the fief of a great lord, charged with a definite amount of military service to the king.'

the entries recording waste and a significant drop in value of land that are to be found in the entries relating to Northamptonshire and to Yorkshire. Yet, taking the country as a whole, the apparent drop in value of land did not amount to much. The very thoroughness of Domesday sometimes conceals the fact that it was a survey at a given moment in time, that the conditions it described had been subject to immediate stress and strain, that it was indeed a record of a fleeting moment from which it is not possible to tease eternal answers to eternal questions. But there were fewer people to enjoy the surplus from land, and also a more closely defined surplus set aside for the lord's purposes. It has been estimated that estates were so consolidated in the generation after the Conquest that some four to five thousand thegns were replaced by no more than a hundred and eighty Norman barons. The situation was not quite as simple as these figure suggest. The barons themselves used their resources in order to equip an army quite as formidable, though probably somewhat smaller, than any the Anglo-Saxons could put into the field. But the barons made up a more compact group at the head of affairs than had the Anglo-Saxon earls and thegns. What is more, there existed among them a small powerful ring of inner nobility, interrelated and bound very straitly to the royal court, which controlled nearly a quarter of the landed wealth of England. The King himself controlled a fifth directly, the Church a further quarter and the remaining barons a further quarter. The whole group was extraordinarily compact. Wealth was much more tightly controlled in Anglo-Norman than in Anglo-Saxon days.[8]

In the ecclesiastical sphere William's approach was cautious. Archbishop Stigand himself was not deposed until after the death of Ealdred of York in 1069, and even then it was left to the papacy to take the initiative in the matter. But with the appointment of Lanfranc to Canterbury and the resulting reorganization, Normans were steadily appointed to abbacies and to bishoprics as the major ecclesiastical offices fell vacant. As a group the new men were distinguished not so much for spirituality as for administrative gifts. Almost to a man they were builders of the institutional Church in the material as well as in the spiritual sense. Their urge to build was infectious. Wulfstan, Bishop of Worcester, most prominent

---

[8] D.C. Douglas, introduction to *E.H.D.* II, p. 22, lists the ten men who between them held close on a quarter of England: Odo of Bayeux, Robert of Mortain, William Fitz-Osbern, Roger of Montgomery, William of Warenne, Hugh of Avranches, Eustace of Boulogne, Richard FitzGilbert, Geoffrey of Coutances, and Geoffrey of Manneville.

of the English prelates during William's reign, lies today in the crypt of the great church at Worcester to whose rebuilding he contributed so much. Gundulf of Rochester, with experience at the Tower behind him, and Paul of St Albans, Lanfranc's own nephew, were typical of the energetic building prelates of the age. St Albans is a particularly interesting example. In this church the massive simplicity of part of the Romanesque early Norman nave may still be enjoyed in the Gothic setting of later medieval achievement.[9] The full flowering of the architectural revival lies beyond our period. Yet it is right to mention here the first impetus which came from a concentration of ecclesiastical wealth in the hands of powerful churchmen, well able to insist on their financial rights and also to perform what they saw as their religious duties. To build a great church at the urban centre of a see was a symbol of Norman energy, magnificence, and political sense.

The secular lords used their concentration of wealth differently. Their great period of building did not come in this generation. Indeed it seems that the wealth was at this time used for what was the prime need of the country, defence against foreign invasion and internal upheaval. The solidarity of the aristocracy is a feature quite rightly remarked on. Enlightened self-interest is sufficient explanation for this solidarity, with occasional aberrations, as when the Earls of Hereford and Norfolk, together with the unfortunate Waltheof, rebelled in 1075, or when Odo of Bayeux himself defected. The new Norman rulers were men in possession of much new wealth; they were also men under obligation to defend that new wealth.

What of the men themselves who came with William to rule conquered England? The most important were Norman, and were drawn from William's immediate sphere of interest around Rouen. But they were not exclusively Norman, and William had other adventurers among his followers. His recruiting drive had embraced a good part of northern France. The Breton contingent was particularly strong, and its settlement in England in the south-west and in the Honour of Richmond was particularly concentrated. Even so the diversity of origin was more than counterbalanced by the feeling of unity found under the banner of William, and the diversity itself should not be emphasized except as a check on excessive adulation of the Norman. For all their hesitation and reluctance in council before the campaign the Normans provided

[9] Not to mention Victorian amendment.

he backbone of the army of invasion, and many, such as the
Bohuns and the Mowbrays, made their fortunes by it. Some of
he chief men in England had been great men in Normandy,
members of the ducal house or substantial tenants-in-chief of Duke
William. Others were drawn from relatively undistinguished stock,
vicomtes of obscure corners of the Cotentin, or sub-tenants, notably
sub-tenants of Bishop Odo of Bayeux. This latter, half-brother
of the Duke, became Earl of Kent as a result of the invasion,
and appears to have played the leading role in the allotment of
conquered English lands. To be a successful troop-commander
under Duke William and his half-brother was a sure path to success.
Many of the most illustrious twelfth-century families had no earlier
distinction to their ancestry.[10]

The strangeness of this new aristocracy in a conquered land
brought about an intensification in social cleavage more vigorous
than the old division into wergeld groups. Antiquarians such as
the author of the *Leges Henrici Primi* still clung to wergeld as the
mark of status, but in point of fact social cleavage ran sharper
along racial lines. The institution of the *murdrum* fine by William
I was of particular significance in making clear the distinction
between French and English. By it a hundred had to prove that
the victim of a murderous onslaught was an Englishman or else lay
themselves open to a corporate fine.[11] The humblest followers of
the Conqueror were well protected. Further up in the social scale
the distinction between knight and *villanus* was much greater than
that between thegn and ceorl had been. The aristocrat was now
a professional fighting man, ruling a household of professional
fighting men. As his household grew more specialized, so was it
natural that by means of sub-infeudation it should be stabilized
on the country. The baron was granted his fief by the Conqueror,
usually consisting of an agglomeration of estates held by many
Anglo-Saxon antecessors. In return he owed service of a stated
number of knights to the royal host. Detail of the provision made
for these knights was normally the baron's concern, though there
were instances of William's interfering in the fief of a great vassal
in order to make provision for a worthy follower. In time sub-
infeudation became the normal means of provision. The great
baronial fief, held together by an honorial court which met at the

---

[10] L.C. Loyd, *The Origin of Some Anglo-Saxon Families*, ed. C.T. Clay and D.C.
Douglas, Harleian Society, vol. CIII, Leeds, 1951.
[11] Willelmi I Articuli, 3; Liebermann I, p. 487.

baron's chief seat was divided (apart from demesne) among his military sub-tenants. Among the sub-tenants a hierarchy formed some prosperous men, notably the feudal officers, constables and the like, holding quite extensive lands not directly of the crown, but indirectly through a great baron. Some of these honorial barons, as they have happily been called, themselves achieved baronial rank in course of the twelfth century. The baron and the knight could not claim the long traditional tenures associated with Anglo-Saxon thegnage. Theirs was a new feudal tenure, and their fiefs were the new institutions introduced after 1066.

Not that we should see rigid medieval feudalism introduced at the stroke of the sword. There was much slow development before England was thoroughly feudalized, but the sure foundations of the final structure were laid before William was dead. It was still possible, however, in the reign of William I for as great a tenant-in-chief as the Abbot of Bury St Edmunds to be relatively vague as to his rights in the basic requirement of military service from a subordinate fief. 'Let it do service for three or four knights' was the phrase employed in a charter.[12] Nor was it a simple question of new lords slipping automatically into the position held by their predecessors. The shape of the old estates tended to remain the same, lands of Anglo-Saxon thegns falling to the Normans by forfeiture after battle and rebellion. But their nature was radically changed, the service due from them rigidly defined, and their part in the feudal hierarchy closely regulated. All land was subject directly to service, and the most significant service was that of a feudal military nature. The Anglo-Saxons contributed much to make the Norman success possible. But the Normans themselves contributed much, above all the tense solidarity attendant upon their position as a conquering army in hostile country. They had a new political vision, and a new energy to make it fact. Taken with their assertion of the right to rule the Saxons as successors of the West Saxon dynasty, this was to enable them to construct the most compact feudal monarchy in the West from the very promising material at their disposal.

It was a harsh world that these Normans introduced for all the brilliance and glitter. It is evident, for example, that the legal position of women was less favourable under the Normans than under the Anglo-Saxons. On the critical questions of inheritance and dower the world of the Anglo-Norman aristocrats was very

[12] *E.H.D.* II, p. 961.

much a man's world. There was little attempt to do more than prevent unscrupulous guardians marrying off heiresses to their own advantage and against the wishes and interests of the girl. The Queen continued to receive dues and renders which had accrued to her as a matter of custom in the last centuries of Anglo-Saxon England. According to Gaimar, Emma on her marriage with Ethelred received Winchester, Exeter and Rutland, though this was a somewhat garbled record based on gifts of estates around Exeter and Winchester.[13] Queen Edith, the Confessor's Queen and Godwin's daughter, had most extensive possessions according to Domesday Book, but it is hard to distinguish what came to her as Queen from what came to her as Godwin's daughter. The greater part of the peculiar, not to say anomalous, shire of Rutland was reserved for the Anglo-Saxon queen. Edith herself had extensive rights in the boroughs, including the royal profits from Exeter, Bath, Ipswich and Torksey, seventy houses free of all save baker's custom at Stamford, and a right to all custom from her tenants in Canterbury. Gifts from the shires are recorded as a hundred shillings from the counties of Worcester, Warwick, Northampton and Oxford, and gifts of gold are made from royal estates in Bedfordshire.[14] A queen did not normally wear a crown before the Norman Conquest; Aelfric stated expressly that Esther wore a crown on her head as was *their* custom.[15] Yet the queens of the last century before the Conquest played quite as formidable a part in affairs as they were to do in post-Conquest days. Of course at the royal level personality counted for much, and it is hard to imagine either Emma of Normandy or Eleanor of Aquitaine fading into insignificance no matter what her exact legal rights might have been. Of more general importance is the social fact that the Norman aristocrats expected their wives to bring land with them, whereas in Anglo-Saxon days more concern was shown that a man should arrange an equitable settlement with the kindred of his wife-to-be. Favour lay with the spear not with the spindle in Norman days.

Trade did not flourish immediately as a result of the Conquest, though increased regular contact with the Continent and an infusion of new blood were both characteristics that promised well

---

[13] *Encomium Emmae Reginae*, ed. A. Campbell, London, 1949, p. xliv.

[14] J. Tait, *The Medieval English Borough*, pp. 94–5. D. Whitelock, *The Beginnings of English Society*, p. 67.

[15] *Hester*, vv. 33–7, cited in Liebermann II, p. 550: Königin Id.

for the future. Feudal arrangements gave opportunity for communities of traders to thrive under the more secure protection of the new castles and of the new *capita* of feudal honours. But, as has already been suggested, only when the general European revival made itself felt in north-west continental Europe was England able to participate to the full in the increased commercial activity so characteristic of the age. The effects of this stimulus lie beyond our chronological scope. Lines of communication between Rouen and London were not as vital as those that lay further to the east outside King William's immediate control.

Clear cut as the general effects of the Norman Conquest appear to be at the aristocratic level, it is not easy to point to any accompanying revolution in costume that came with it. War accoutrements were certainly modified and the chain-mail, helmet, sword and lance of the Norman cavalryman took the place of the Anglo-Saxon helmet, sword, byrnie and spear. The most conspicuous military change came in relation to the equipment of the war-horse, and these trappings could be decorative and expensive. There is a case in Domesday Book, brought to our notice by Professor Whitelock, where a Norfolk reeve transferred the service of five sokemen worth 10s. 8d. a year in return for a bridle.[16] But everyday dress was only slowly altered. No clear distinction between Norman and Saxon civilian dress can be made from the evidence of the Bayeux Tapestry, which is the chief sourcebook. Classes were distinguished clearly enough, the manual workers in breeches with a shirt tucked into the waistband, the soldiers and better-class men, possibly just simply those who did not take off their coats to work, with tunics added, the nobles and kings distinguished by mantles clasped at the throat. Banded stockings with what have been described as 'puttee-like wrappings' and low shoes completed the outfit.[17] Linen and wool were the common materials in use throughout the period and the Conquest brought no change here. The long mantle, the true garment of distinction, persisted with its elaborate clasps and brooches as a mark of special dignity and rank. Women's clothes likewise underwent no immediate conspicuous change. A long gown, reaching to the ground, a mantle often fastened by shoulder clasps and a hood remained the standard features. Greater elaboration and richness of costume is a characteristic of the twelfth-century world, a general phenomenon which came to England a

---

[16] D. Whitelock, *The Beginnings of English Society*, p. 96.
[17] *Medieval England*, ed. A.L. Poole, Oxford, 1958, p. 301.

a somewhat earlier stage than might otherwise have been the case because of the stronger connection with the Continent under the Norman dukes. What cosmopolitan change occurred had its centre in London where merchant families bearing Anglo-Saxon names intermarried with the Norman conquerors during the reign of the first William.

The effects of the Norman Conquest on the lower grades of society are much more difficult to disentangle. The tendency was strong towards legal uniformity though it is hard to grasp the social complexity that underlay such apparent smoothness. In place of the heterogeneous terminology of Anglo-Saxon England was substituted a uniform *villani* to describe the peasantry. The term bore no unpleasing connotation at this stage. If it has to be translated, 'inhabitant of a vill', even 'villager', comes nearest to the sense. The pejorative sense of villein was acquired only after a century and more of proud Norman dominance. Indeed the whole question of whether there was an immediate depreciation in peasant status as a consequence of the Norman Conquest is still capable of harsh debate. In one respect the Normans made conditions better. The institution of slavery declined to such an extent under their rule that within a generation or two it became socially negligible.[18] A uniform serfdom took its place. It seems odd at first sight that the Normans, well-known for their stern government, should sacrifice advantages that would appear to accrue to a slave-holding society. Humanitarianism is not a quality normally associated with the great William, though one must always take into account strong feeling among more advanced ecclesiastical thinkers against chattel slavery. It appears that the thoroughgoing slavery of the Anglo-Saxon world was not familiar to the Normans. What is more, it was not necessary. Provided that manorial discipline was strong enough, the slave could be more nuisance than he was worth. To keep estates manned by a substantial portion of slave labour may well have been uneconomic in time of unstable prices with much local variation of market. The *servi* had their food provided for them by the lords. They may have been much less profitable than the free peasants bound to give hard labour service on the lord's demesne. Indeed the emphasis in Norman days is thrown squarely on the peasants' obligation to the lord. In that may be found one explanation for the apparent indifference of the new Norman lords to old Saxon distinctions between free and unfree. J.H. Round

[18] See below, pp. 362–6.

maintained, for example, that the great drop in number of *servi* in Essex between 1066 and 1086 was best explained on terminological grounds. Many of the *servi*, to whom service in charge of the lord's teams or demesne seemed a special function, were absorbed into the amorphous class of 'bordars'. Others, unfree ploughmen, often arranged two to the plough on a lord's demesne, appear in the Domesday survey as *bovarii*.[19] The Normans were not concerned with a man's standing towards his local community or with his legal obligations. Their concern lay in the economic field with a desire to benefit from his labour, to receive a share of the produce of his toil.

This attitude of mind could lead to extortion and to hardships. New men could take a much more clear-cut view of landed wealth as a source of profit. Analogies have been made, not completely seriously yet not in utter jest, between the Norman Conquest and a take-over bid in the modern industrial world. Increased efficiency usually means hardship for some. The huge rent-rolls of the great tenants-in-chief tell part, but only part, of the story. The rents came from estates only a fraction of which were kept actively in demesne under the direct care of a reeve or a bailiff. Much of the lord's revenue came from the farm of the manors, that is to say from a fixed sum paid by a *firmarius* who took on the responsibility of making a render in cash or kind or both to the lord, recouping himself from the profits of the demesne of a particular manor together with the less important customary dues. Such a *firmarius* could operate on a big scale with a host of minor officers under him. He could, on the other hand, be little more than a bailiff.[20] It seems likely that perhaps most of the *firmarii* of Domesday Book were lessees, taking on their duties for a fixed time and making what they could from the venture.

The king set the pattern, and it is plain that the farm of the royal manors was often though not always held by the sheriff of a shire who in turn would farm out individual manors, or have them administered direct by underlings. The Anglo-Saxon Chronicle retains some of the feelings of the conquered English

---

[19] V.C.H., *Essex*, vol. I, pp. 360–1.

[20] Professor Whitelock has drawn my attention to a section of the metrical Life of Saint Swithin which implies that a tenth-century reeve farmed a manor from his royal master. *Frithegodi Monachi Breviloquium vitae beati Wilfredi, et Wulfstani Cantoris Narratio Metrica de Sancto Swithuno*, ed. A. Campbell, Zurich, 1950, book II, lines 299–434.

when it tells of the results of the Conquest from the vantage point offered by the death of King William in 1087:

> The king gave his land for rent as dearly as he possibly could; then came some other and offered more than the other had given before; and the king let it to the man who had offered him more; then came a third and offered yet more, and the king gave it to the man who had offered most of all. And he paid no heed how very sinfully the reeves got it from poor men, nor how many illegalities they did.

There is sufficient evidence from Domesday Book to support the truth of this statement. Mr Lennard has made an exhaustive study of the problem, and has shown that in all the counties of the seaboard from Hampshire to Norfolk, and in Surrey and Berkshire, there were frequent references, as many as fifty-seven in Hampshire alone and thirty in Kent, to rents which exceeded the value of the land or which proved to be oppressive.[22] Such rents were not limited to royal land, and were to be found also on the estates of lay and ecclesiastical tenants-in-chief. Some were exacted from men of English name, and it is possible that a few members of the defeated race brought themselves back into a reasonable social position by this tortuous means. Such were marginal cases and of more social importance is the general impression that rents and farms were high. Ultimately the burden of such rents and farms fell on the peasantry.

For all this increased efficiency in the exaction of profit from land, the Norman Conquest did not cause a disastrous change in the general structure of rural society. There is an altogether astonishing continuity in rural institutions, as studies of East Anglia and Kent in particular have shown. Peculiarities in organization, notably in the unmanorialized or partly manorialized east, persisted for all the legalistic Norman attempt to fit anomalous areas into their ideal pattern of *manerium* and *villanus*. Major change came primarily in the person of lord and *firmarius*, whose hands lay heavier on the peasants than the hands of their Saxon predecessors. They expected more, and in return did more for the community. In some shires, especially in Cambridgeshire and Bedfordshire, there is strong evidence of a depression of the peasantry which was more than terminological.[23] Increased imposition of labour service

---

[21] A.S. Chronicle, *sub anno* 1087.
[22] R. Lennard, *Rural England*, pp. 155–6. Mr Lennard's analysis of the farming of Domesday manors is of fundamental importance to all students of eleventh-century social history.
[23] F.W. Maitland, *Domesday Book and Beyond*, pp. 63–5.

appears to have been enforced in some areas. Normally, however, it was probably by a clearer and more accurate definition of service that the new-comers made their demands more onerous.

On the question of the status of the peasantry more will be said in the succeeding chapter. For the moment it is enough to record that the beginnings of a process that was to lead to the gradual disappearance of slavery was the most vivid feature of change reflected into the Domesday survey. But, almost as startling, was the great drop in numbers of sokemen and freemen in many districts, notably in the eastern counties, where they were plentiful in 1066. Freedom is at times an ambiguous term. It may well be that in some instances an unfair imposition of labour services overrode a securely based tradition of freedom. In most cases the process was more natural and less arbitrary. Personal freedom was meaningful in two ways: in giving standing in law and access to public tribunals, and in relation to land-tenure. In connection with the former most of the Saxon peasants retained their freedom, a privilege that legally was counterbalanced by the special dues, notably church dues, that fell on the freeman. He was free who could afford to pay. But as kindred ties grew weaker, and the waging of feuds and the payment of wergelds became rarer, so did legal peasant freedom become more of an occasional privilege and less of a basic fact fundamental to his good standing and to his good name. In connection with the land question, the situation is more complicated. In Domesday Book, above all in the eastern counties, there is record time and time again of men of relatively humble position who could 'go with their land whither they would'. They were notably more common in 1066 than in 1086. Maitland thought that their tenure was too free.[24] They represented anarchical forces that might well have disrupted the community. To the Norman mind also this was a freedom that could not be tolerated. Land-holding had been an important test of status even in Anglo-Saxon days. It was much more than that to the Normans. In feudal society land was the essential means of providing and provisioning an army. It was the fundamental and indivisible source of power and political authority. In such a world it was undesirable that land should be capable of easy alienation. The whole conception of the feudal hierarchy was against it. From humble land-owner to baron there was a network of intricate relationship that was gradually fitted into the new feudal organization. Honorial courts dealt primarily with

[24] Ibid., p. 171.

military feudal questions and the small landowner had only indirect contact with so august a body. Yet socage tenure was developing fast, and the services upon which such land was held, while not expressly military, were often intimately connected with military affairs. Indeed by 1100 most land was held on definite service of a military or non-military nature. The idea of land unburdened by service gradually became unthinkable. Just as a hierarchy of lordship stretched from humblest to highest, to the king – and the mystical would say to God – so did a hierarchy of lordship in land lead to the honorial courts and ultimately to the king.

It is, however, important at this stage to remember that the feudal relationship was not the only relationship, personal or tenurial, that existed in Anglo-Norman times. There were other institutions apart from the fief. The shire courts and hundred courts, the territorial organization of England, persisted and gave the monarchy the institutional strength needed to overcome the disintegrating tendencies of feudalism. Yet it would be equally wrong to ignore the tenurial revolution that occurred after 1066, and which affected all land-holding, even to the little men with their half hide worth eight shillings in the Hundred of Lexden in Essex.[25] A tighter regulation of tenure is no mere abstraction. It involved a general tightening of personal relationship that, while permitting the ancient regional distinctions of England to survive, did not permit some of the uncertainties of Old English tenure to live on into the feudal world. The curiosity of William concerning his new kingdom was undoubtedly one of the factors that led to the production of Domesday Book. It may be that conscious efforts at closer definition were also important, and that the disappearance of an unencumbered market in land was among the chief changes wrought by the immense social upheaval of the Norman Conquest.

[25] D.B. II, 99.

CHAPTER NINE
England at the End of the Eleventh Century

I. THE RURAL ECONOMY

The time has now come to attempt a survey of England at the end of the eleventh century. Writer after writer has emphasized that the modern man would be appalled by the poverty even of tranquil England if by some fantastic means he found himself transported back to the England of William and his sons. In many respects this is true. The spectre of famine was never far distant in the eleventh century. Plague does not appear to have been so virulent, undergoing one of those recessive cycles that modern medical science has taught us to take seriously. Occasional outbursts of violence could devastate a community. Tyranny was too often the fortune of a village that sought over-zealously for protection. The national frontiers were vague and undefined. William Rufus effected an arbitrary border with the Scots that by historical accident still remains substantially unaltered. The Marcher Lords in their ascendancy were removing the Welsh menace which had been acute in the generation before the Conquest. Populations could still be transported like the peasants who were moved into Cumberland at the instigation of William Rufus.[1] But colonization now followed closely defined lines, and was directed against the soil and not against fellow settlers. The Normans were rulers, not peasants: therein lies the fundamental distinction between their Conquest and the first Danish onslaught. The Danes had been colonizers as well as conquerors, in some areas effecting considerable settlement, apparently without major displacement of indigenous population.

[1] A.S. Chronicle, *sub anno* 1092.

The Normans did little more than provide the ring of internal peace within which colonization could become more intense.

The word 'colonization' gives a clue to the nature of the society. After six centuries the Anglo-Saxon community had still some of the appearance of a rural and pioneering society with the hazards inevitably attendant upon that way of life. The expanding frontier lay not in the wide open spaces but in the heart of long-settled shires, in the Weald and among the forests and swamps of the heavy Midland clay soil. Although advances in the way of assart and encroachment on waste did not approach the concentrated intensity of the thirteenth-century expansion, there was much vigour and not a little prosperity in the rural organization of the eleventh.

For all the infusion of Viking blood England is not to be thought of as an outstanding maritime country in A.D. 1100. It is a familiar story. With outlet for energies inland, the pirates turn from the seafaring life. The Anglo-Saxon poet was near the heart of the matter when he lamented the life of exile led by the seafarer, and when he spoke of the rime-cold waves and the frozen night-watches.[2] Fishing was an important supplementary industry. Trade was not insignificant. But only with some reluctance did the Anglo-Saxon turn to the sea.

The great mass of the people of England lived on the land, and off the land. Over much of the country they toiled on the open fields of a type described in an earlier chapter. Their outlook tended to be limited to providing for their own needs and in meeting the demands of their lord's reeve and of the Church. Yet even in the more manorialized part of the country, reputedly unfruitful of individual enterprise, there is some hint of mobility within the rural community, of assarting and clearing, of the rise of successful families, of the decline of the unenterprising. Some throve to freedom and prosperity through the service of their lords; others even farmed their own manors like the *villani* who held Willesden, where there was no demesne, at farm from the canons of St Paul's.[3] Such farming on the part of a group of peasants was, it is true, rare and exceptional, as Professor Hoyt has shown from his collection of what he himself terms the meagre evidence for peasant farming of manors.[4] There is firmer ground,

[2] 'The Seafarer', lines 5–17.
[3] D.B.I. 127b. *Early Charters of the Cathedral Church of St Paul, London*, ed. M. Gibbs, London, 1939, p. xxiii.
[4] R.S. Hoyt, 'Farm of the Manor and Community of the Vill', *Speculum*, 1955, pp. 168–9.

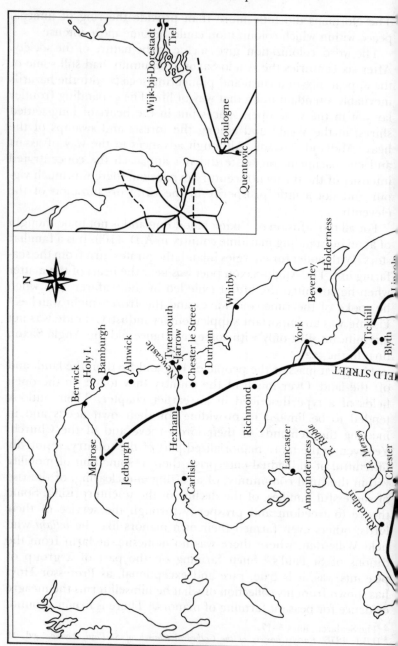

England at the end of the eleventh century

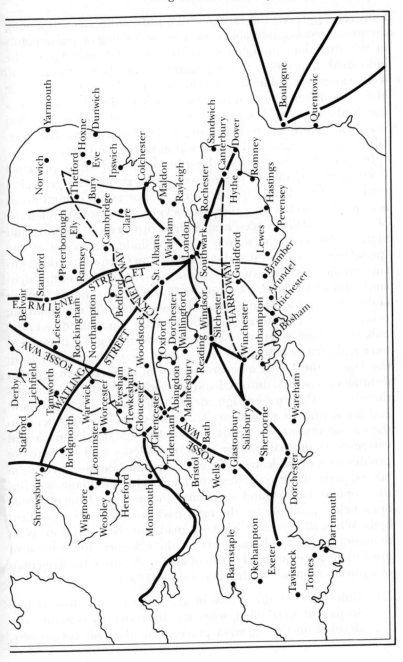

however, to suggest the existence of a prosperous element among the peasantry. Considerable variety in the holding of arable points in this direction, though the painful lack of knowledge of the individual obligations of the peasants in question diminishes to some extent the value of this evidence. Yet the entries for some of the Middlesex villages which show *villani* holding a whole hide, a hundred and twenty Domesday acres, side by side with other *villani* who held no more than half a virgate or fifteen Domesday acres, tell of some mobility and vigour within the peasant groups.[5]

In an earlier chapter something has been said of the principal features of agricultural organization in England. The geological structure of the land, together with racial or group custom which is in itself moulded by geological background, accounts for some of the obvious differences. Kent with its prosperous peasantry and high taxable unit, the sulung or double-hide, stands out as one special area. To the west and to the north, in Cornwall, in the highlands to the north-west of the Pennines, on the uplands of the highland spine of England, the emphasis lay on pastoral rather than on arable, and arable taken in from the moorlands did not attain the prime economic importance attributed to the ploughlands over the bulk of England, where the plough was indeed king. Yet these areas were truly fringe lands, and over a great swathe of country from the Tees to the Tamar a general picture of uniformity in agrarian techniques is not too distorted and misleading. Within this compass there was difference enough, dependent on the lie of the land and the density of settlement. The main social cleavages between the various regions were considerable. In some districts nucleated villages were normal and the modern tendency is to attribute the proliferation of nucleated villages to the post-Conquest period; in others, particularly to the west, the hamlet type predominated. But the economic background was similar, the emphasis lying on arable open fields, probably for the most part organized on a two-field basis. When all allowance has been made for the natural stress on dominical rights so characteristic of the evidence, the student of institutions is still justified in disentangling the three fundamentals of agrarian economy in the England of 1100 as:

(1) Cultivation of the arable in great open fields divided into strips that were tilled, sown and harvested by peasants who decided on the agrarian processes of the year corporately,

[5] F.W. Maitland, *Domesday Book and Beyond*, p. 40.

but who worked each on his plot and on his lord's plot indi-
vidually. The lord's demesne, normally consisting of diverse
not consolidated plots, fitted in naturally to this arable basis
of the community.

(2) Pasture and meadow, essential for the needs of the community, were very important, and rights in both were dependent
on the share in the arable.

(3) Rights in wood, water and waste, again essential for the needs
of the community, were also very important, and dependent
once more upon the share in the arable.

2. DOMESDAY BOOK

But while there is good reason to talk of a basic economic uniformity in agricultural technique over much of the country, it is
plain that a corresponding social uniformity did not exist. There
is much evidence available to treat of the economic and social
problems of the age. In earlier chapters mention has been made
of evidence from Domesday Book. It is time now to consider the
great record itself and the methods by which it was drawn up. The
Anglo-Saxon Chronicle tells how at Christmas 1085 King William
held a great council at Gloucester.[6] As a result of his deliberations
he sent his men all over England to see how many hundreds
of hides of land there were in each shire, how much land and
livestock the king possessed, and what annual dues were lawfully
his from each shire. He also had recorded how much land all the
other landholders possessed, how much livestock and how much it
was all worth. The Chronicler goes on: 'So very thoroughly did he
have the inquiry carried out that there was not a single hide, not
one virgate of land, not even – it is shameful to record it, but it
did not seem shameful for him to do – not even one ox, nor one
cow, nor one pig which escaped notice in this survey. And all the
surveys were subsequently brought to him'.

The result of all this immense activity was Domesday Book, to
say nothing of a host of other surveys, the 'Inquisitio Eliensis', the
'Inquisitio Comitatus Cantabrigiensis', the Exeter Domesday, the
'Domesday Monachorum' of the estates of Christ Church Canterbury, part of the Feudal Book of the Abbot of Bury St Edmunds,

[6] A.S. Chronicle, *sub anno* 1085.

to mention only the most important subsidiary or satellite production stimulated by the collection of material made by the Domesday Commissioners.[7] In Domesday Book itself the information, painfully collected from each shire and from each hundred by juries giving evidence on oath before Commissioners, is rearranged feudally so that a picture is given for each shire of the lands analysed under their feudal owners. The way in which the material was recorded territorially, but finally presented feudally, is a matter for some dispute. Some hold that the original returns (the survey of the Chronicle) were all sent to Winchester and that the work of editing and rearranging was all performed there. Others suggest that preliminary work of sorting and rearrangement was performed at local centres, an intermediate digest between original return and finished product being sent to Winchester. Exeter Domesday and even Volume Two of Domesday Book itself may represent such an intermediate stage. Volume Two, the Little Domesday, relating to the shires of Essex, Suffolk and Norfolk only, certainly presents a fuller, more detailed picture, closer in accord with the terms of reference set out by the Chronicle than Volume One of the main Domesday Book. On the other hand, while fuller, it is less systematic than Volume One. The clerks knew better what the royal master wanted when they prepared the first volume. However, no matter what the exact method used to achieve the finished product, complaint cannot be made of lack of information concerning the English of 1086, and indeed also of 1066, and in some instances, there is also full information concerning conditions at an intermediate date when the tenant of Domesday Book first took possession of his new estates. William's legitimate curiosity about his kingdom would certainly have been satisfied had he lived to see the final production of this survey, unique in its day and meritorious in any age.

Full though the information is, it is presented in a form that is often not convenient to the modern scholar. The historian has to tease his information out of Domesday Book. For the 'Book of Winchester' was a practical document, in time to be lodged in the Exchequer and referred to there in matters of dispute, a geld-book but more than that, and something of a feodary even though the military service due from the estates was not mentioned. Above all

---

[7] V.H. Galbraith laid the foundation for all recent work on the construction and nature of Domesday Book : *The Making of Domesday Book*, Oxford, 1961, and *Domesday Book : its place in administrative history*, Oxford, 1974.

348

it was an authoritative statement of the condition of landholding at the end of the first generation of Norman settlement, a record of the tenurial revolution that had been achieved by the success of Duke William. It tells much, but it does not always tell what is wanted. To take the most obvious example, the historian is naturally anxious to give a reasonable estimate of the Domesday population. Figures there are in plenty. Sir Henry Ellis painstakingly worked out that some 283,242 people were mentioned in the course of the survey.[8] From other contemporary evidence it is plain that, even within their terms of reference, the Commissioners did not always give as full an account as they professed. There were omissions within the districts covered. There were also districts untouched by the survey, particularly in the north and north-west and among the boroughs. London and Winchester were unhappily left out. Then again, not all the 283,242 were heads of households though it seems reasonable to suppose that close on a quarter of a million of them were. Upon largely subjective conclusions concerning probable size of families, omissions and needful interpolations, depends the final estimate of population. On the evidence available any figure between one million and two would seem likely, and most cautious observers move towards a figure somewhere in the middle of this vast range. Maitland suggested a population of 1,375,000 which seemed then as now on the lower edge of plausibility.[9]

Again, as shall be seen below on the question of the social classes, Domesday terminology can be deceptive. It is so tempting to give terms like *villanus* meanings that were not assumed till a later age. The Norman clerks were classifying a strange population in a terminology substantially new, and it was not easy for them to gauge the finer shades of meaning in old English social and legal rank.

Yet, for all the difficulties, enough emerges from the survey itself to hazard a few general statements, particularly on the regional peculiarities of England. The south and the west, the great part of Wessex and Western Mercia, were the home of a peasantry sub-

---

[8] *A General Introduction to Domesday Book*, London, 1833, vol. II, p. 514. Modern discussion of population is based on the more sophisticated statistics presented by H.C. Darby, *Domesday England*, Cambridge, 1977, pp. 57–94, especially pp. 87–91.
[9] *Domesday Book and Beyond*, p. 437. *Domesday Book : Studies*, ed. Ann Williams and R.W.H. Erskine, Alecto Historical Editions, London, 1987, pp. 26–7, where H.C. Darby suggests 1½ to 1¾ million. More recent demographers would be happy with a figure even over 2 million.

jected to manorial discipline. The north and the east, the Danelaw and Kent, were the home of a freer peasantry. Peasants in Lincolnshire, East Anglia and Kent are generally assumed to have been more prosperous than those elsewhere. Evidence for the survival of communities of free peasants is stronger in these regions than elsewhere.

It is also true that the basic legal and economic unit remained the village, whether nucleated or scattered. The territorial unit was more deep-rooted in English life than the manorial super-structure. Men were subject to lords; they were also members of a larger community. They paid dues and service to lords; they were also villagers, *tunesmen, villani*. Yet, at first sight, this is not the impression given by Domesday Book. There instead an England is revealed, divided into manors, sokes, and berewicks. The villages are criss-crossed with the pattern of lordship. Only painfully can the typical village be reconstructed from the bits and pieces of Domesday evidence, so as to make plain the five- and ten-hide assessments or six- or twelve-carucate assessments that were characteristic of many villages before the Conquest. The clerks of Domesday, concerned with men and their individual wealth and responsibilities, often conceal rather than reveal the 'territorial basis on which English feudalism rested'.[10] Their line of analysis followed the personal paths of lords, old and new, to the confusion of village and hamlet.

For example, there are no fewer than five entries relating to the Hertfordshire village of Wallington, and it is only by searching through the fiefs of Earl Alan, Robert German, Geoffrey de Manneville, Gilbert of Belvache and Harduin of Scalers that the village itself is discovered, hidden under the tenurial fragmentation. The earl held two hides less ten acres; Robert three hides less twenty acres; the thirty acres held by Geoffrey go to complete a neat five-hide unit. The other two parcels are assessed at three hides and forty acres, and at one hide and eighty-six acres – another neat five-hide unit apart, alas, from an odious and inexplicable supplement of six acres. There is justification enough for regarding Wallington as a territorial unit subject to a ten-hide assessment parcelled out in 1066 among Saxon holders, sokemen and men commended to the West Saxon and Mercian comital houses, now in 1086 parcelled along similar lines among the great Norman barons and their sub-tenants. Of the fragments

[10] F.M. Stenton, *Anglo-Saxon England*, p. 656. See above, p. 341.

350

only the land of Gilbert is referred to expressly as a manor. The entry is worth giving in full as an example of the information given in the Domesday Survey, with both its richness and its limitations. The hidage of course refers to assessment, not to real acres, and the three hides and forty acres of Gilbert's estate represent an exact two-thirds of a five-hide assessment unit. For a reasonable estimate of the prosperity of an estate the best guide is given by the number of plough-teams at work and by the value (*valet* or *valuit*), presumably the annual rent. The freedom to sell the land is a feature remarked on in all Wallington entries relating to 1066.[11]

> In Wallington Fulco holds of Gilbert 3 hides and 40 acres of land. There is land for five ploughs. In demesne there are two ploughs, and four *villani* with three ploughs. The bordars have two ploughs, and there could be three. There is one cottar and two *servi*. There is pasture for beasts, and wood for hedges.
> Altogether it is worth 50s. When he received it, 30s. At the time of King Edward, 100s. Edric, a man of Earl Aelfgar, held this manor, and he had the power to sell it, and of this land a certain sokeman held 24 acres, a man of Eddeva the fair, and he had the power to sell it. Of these earl Ralph had been seised: but at the time of his forfeiture he was not so seised according to the testimony of the hundred.

Similar examples of villages split up among many manors may be discovered in yet greater numbers to the east and north of Watling Street. The village of Harpswell in Lincolnshire, for example, was divided in the following fashion:[12]

The King held	2 carucates . 6½ bovates
The Archbishop of York held	. 5½ bovates
Jocelyn Fitz-Lambert held	2 carucates . 4 bovates
	6 carucates . 0 "

The assessment to geld of six carucates, a typical unit in these Danish areas, was laid on the village as a whole. In this respect the manorial divisions were more recent and superficial.

3. THE MANOR OF DOMESDAY BOOK

The question of the origins of the manor has been discussed in an earlier chapter. As for the word *manerium*, the manor of

---

[11] D.B. I, 140b. Cf. also, 137, 138, 139b, 141b.
[12] D.B. I, 338, 338b, 340, 359 (twice).

Domesday, by the time all qualifications have been made, one has a firmer impression of what it was not, rather than of what it was. Later in the Middle Ages there were three features that one would expect in every manor: a consolidated estate, the lord's rights of jurisdiction, a peasantry bound to labour service. It is impossible to prove that these elements preponderated in our Domesday *maneria*. Yet the subtlest of modern work in regional fields is helping to build up a steady picture of an England where agrarian economy was moving in that direction. Sir Frank Stenton looked to some tangible, material, Anglo-Saxon term underlying the Latin *manerium*, and suggested *heafod-botl*, or the like, the chief residence, the home of a lord.[13] If there were no such residence, no *aula*, then Domesday Book was quick to comment on the absence. This would link well with Maitland's neat definition that the manor was a hall to which peasants rendered their geld. Not that such a *manerium* would be as Maitland further suggested, the ultimate unit in geld.[14] Ease in collection, not legal responsibility, would explain the Domesday concern with the manor.

Perhaps the most incisive lines of inquiry are those inaugurated by scholars such as Sir Frank Stenton and Professor Douglas in their regional work on the Northern Danelaw and East Anglia respectively. In both areas the Domesday 'manor' was shown to have been very different from the manor as it was understood in Worcester or Wiltshire. Yet in both areas there were manors of a consolidated type; there were also what both scholars tend to refer to as 'incomplete manors'; and there were village communities relatively untouched by the hand of manorial lordship. Indeed, though it is not suggested that the hypothesis will meet all cases, the idea that the medieval manor consisted of the peasant community, originally free, with the lord's rights superimposed, receives much strength from these areas that were in an uneasy process of manorialization.

The Northern Danelaw proved a particularly rewarding stretch of country to examine, because in these shires it was still possible to trace the difficulties of the Domesday Commissioners as they applied their standard terminology of manor, berewick and soke to districts in which the idea of manorial lordship was something of a novelty. The district in question had a political individuality of its own, a distinctive form of assessment and a strong Danish

[13] *Anglo-Saxon England*, p. 480.
[14] *Domesday Book and Beyond*, pp. 120–8.

element in its population. It extended over the East and West Riding of Yorkshire, Lincoln, Nottingham, Derby, Leicester and Rutland. Within this district the term *manor* was used whenever a lord's house, an *aula*, existed. To such a house services would be paid and dues rendered. From such a house, presumably, geld would be paid to the royal officers responsible for its transmission to the king. Such a house, and it need not have been elaborate, was also the centre of an estate. Often to the estate were attached portions of what was known as sokeland, and also land known as berewicks. Sokeland consisted of land owned by the men seated upon it but subject, above all in matters of justice, to seignorial dues. A berewick was an outlying portion of a manor, a barleywick, separate geographically from the chief manor but 'owned, as to its soil, by the manorial lord'.[15] But though such manors with their outliers could comprise a formidable body of estates and rights, in the main they were far from consolidated in the Northern Danelaw in 1086. Such consolidation occurs in classic form where a village and a manor coincide, where the tenurial unit which was the manor could be equated exactly with the agrarian unit that was the village. Under pressure of lordship and of dominical responsibility for geld the tendency was for the two to grow together. But it was still possible to find as many as seven manors in one vill in the Northern Danelaw of 1086.[16] It may be that the geld did not lie as heavy nor for as long a period on the northern shires as it did in historic Wessex and in Western Mercia. Such an explanation of the more unconsolidated nature of the Danelaw manor is more acceptable than would be any undue emphasis on racial origins. To judge from place-name evidence, lordship over settlements was as prominent a feature of Danish agrarian institutional life as it was of Anglo-Saxon. Yet lordship does not appear to have been as all-embracing as in English England. There are many instances in Domesday Book of humble men owning no lord below king, earl, or bishop. In 1086 the term *manor* was used freely in the north and east. It clothed a much more unsubstantial and loose-knit body than was customary in the south and west. Yet, remote as they might be from the manorial idea, the Northern Danelaw manors were more

---

[15] F.M. Stenton. *Types of Manorial Structure in the Northern Danelaw*, Oxford Studies in Legal and Social History, vol. II, Oxford, 1910, p. 13. His introduction to *Documents Illustrative of the Social and Economic History of the Danelaw*, British Academy: Records of Social and Economic History, vo. V, 1920, is a further essential guide to the problems of the region.
[16] *Types of Manorial Structure*, pp. 63–6.

stable than, for example, the groups of freemen revealed in the shires immediately to the south and east, in Cambridgeshire and East Anglia.[17]

The structure of the East Anglian manors is still a matter for considerable controversy. But the fundamental analysis undertaken by Professor Douglas in the course of his survey of Bury St Edmunds gives ample material for a generalized account of the manorial structure. He held that the manor was even more artificial an institution in East Anglia than in the Danelaw proper.[18] And indeed he showed that, apart from the highly organized ecclesiastical manors, there was a complete disseverance of village and manor in East Anglia. The administrative system bears the stamp of an artificial imposition from above by royal agents on a countryside inhabited by free communities. The hundred, the soke, the manor itself were all late. None grow from the primitive structure of the East Anglian folk. The village, as elsewhere, constituted the unit of assessment to the geld, and its relationship to the assessment of the hundred was direct. It was the village that contributed so many pence to each £1 raised by the hundred. In no area of England was the territorial nature of the administration so clear; in none was the hand of the lord so slack. The village maintained its liabilities to royal imposts, even attesting charters and performing semi-legal acts in virtue of its economic unity. The free or lordless village was common. There was some tenemental disintegration, in itself a symptom of freedom, and a sign that there was no strong hand from the lord to check the process. The prosperity of East Anglia probably helped more than any other single factor to preserve its peculiarity. A gradual depression did take place, but even in the thirteenth century East Anglia conformed only very uneasily to the manorial pattern. Its characteristic agrarian institution became that of the large estate surrounded by a wide area occupied by a tribute-paying peasantry. An exceptionally careful distinction was maintained in East Anglia between manorial villeins and socage tenants who were scrupulously assessed to burdens separately.

The contrast is striking between these freer eastern shires and the heart of the more manorialized English England. In Wiltshire, for example, it was unusual for a village to be divided among

---

[17] Ibid., pp. 39–43.
[18] D.C. Douglas, *The Social Structure of Medieval East Anglia*, Oxford Studies in Legal and Social History, vol. IX, Oxford, 1927, pp. 209–10. Douglas also gives a most valuable introduction to *Feudal Documents from the Abbey of Bury St Edmunds*, British Academy: Records of Social and Economic History, vol. VIII, 1932.

several lords. The shire was highly manorialized, and the manors were large. No fewer than fifty-three estates were assessed at twenty hides or more; ten of these exceeded fifty hides.[19] Even taking a probable over-assessment into account – and factors other than arable may well have had a bearing on the assessment and value of such large estates – Wiltshire was undoubtedly the home of great estates which contained rather than merely impinged upon village communities. It might be agreed that in such a prosperous shire where the interest of the ancient dynasty was paramount, this is no more than one would expect. But in Staffordshire, one of the poorest and most scantily settled of the shires of English England, the same manorial pattern is in evidence. As a recent V.C.H. editor of the Domesday Staffordshire shrewdly remarks, there is no great difficulty where Staffordshire is concerned in reconstructing what Maitland called 'those villages . . . which the Norman clerks tore into shreds'.[20] In twenty cases only is a vill divided, and in seven of these the second and smaller part quickly disappears. Not of course that a simple equivalence of manor and village should be expected throughout the south and west of England. Manorial structure varied greatly, and in Staffordshire itself distinction has been made between composite estates consisting of a manor with at-tached berewicks and appendages, and single estates. The former, held by king, earl or bishop, were the older, set up on land which had been longer settled; the latter, 'the small unitary settlements', probably represented secondary settlement.[21] But small man or great, simple or composite manor, the relationship of estate to community is more clear-cut, precise and, it is probably correct to say, absorbing than is the general rule to the north and east of Watling Street.

But if the economic reality of the village is rightly emphasized, the social and institutional reality of the manor must not be ne-glected. For, in the very period of which Domesday Book gives record, the dominical authority of new Norman lords, exercised in financial and legal matters, was reshaping the units of English agrarian life, consolidating seignorial rights, extending the ideal of a manorial organization into parts of England which had known little of it in the past. It may well be that in much of the south and west the rights already possessed by Anglo-Saxon lords over their

---

[19] R.R. Darlington, V.C.H., *Wiltshire*, vol. II, p. 49.
[20] C.F. Slade, V.C.H., *Staffordshire*, vol. IV, p. II.
[21] Ibid., pp. 9–10.

peasants left the Norman successors nothing further to covet, and nothing further to add. But in East Anglia and also the greater part of the Danelaw the Norman definer certainly brought a stricter discipline into the collection of dues and the exercise of legal rights over the rural population.

4. THE PEASANTS OF DOMESDAY BOOK

The matter of manorial discipline raises again the problem of the general effects of the Norman Conquest upon the peasantry and, associated intimately with this, the question of the types of men to be found in rural society in the late eleventh century. As Maitland wisely declared, the weight of authority is in favour of a depression of the peasantry after 1066.[22] Most of his detailed evidence, it is true, was taken from the eastern parts of the country, notably from Cambridgeshire, and there are many who feel that too much weight was placed on the simple terminology. A free man living in squalor was not necessarily better off than a well-fed villein. Maitland himself was fully aware of this, and did his best to separate problems of status and wealth, and of status and tenure. To be free did not mean to be prosperous; to be servile did not mean to be utterly without rights. Yet, because the evidence relates to status so much more directly than to prosperity, there is an inevitable tendency to argue from the certain terminology to the uncertain economic reality that underlies it. Perhaps special care again is needed since the evidence for depression of the peasantry comes in some measure from the knowledge of extra duties imposed upon the peasants by manorial discipline and definition. It is possible that such duties could be performed only because of the increased efficiency of manorial farming over against the looser individualistic ties of, for example, the agrarian communities of East Anglia. The reeve is too easily portrayed as the oppressor of the poor, insisting that the allotted tasks on the lord's demesne shall be performed. It should not be forgotten that he is the earliest English specialist in estate management. The clarification of communal duty under a seignorial regime may have given more scope for individual advancement than has always been appreciated. All of which possibilities add extra hazards to the explanation of the division of rural society as revealed by Domes-

[22] *Domesday Book and Beyond*, pp. 61 ff.

day Book. Yet efforts have been made by economic historians, particularly by R. Lennard, to read the Domesday statistics in a new light, especially by concentrating on the figures, where given, of ploughs and teams belonging to villeins and sokemen in an attempt to assess the prosperity of these classes of people. The advantages of this approach are considerable. An alternative test of prosperity, given by a concentration on the amount of land, in terms of Domesday hides, virgates and acres, actually recorded as belonging to the peasants, is surer but is unfortunately available only for a very limited area of England, notably for Middlesex. Figures for ploughs and teams are spread over most of the country in a form sufficiently detailed and free from ambiguity to make generalization possible. The approach and the resulting generalizations have not been free from attack, and E. Miller in particular has pointed out that the number of ploughs and oxen at a man's disposal, even more so at the disposal of a group of men, does not necessarily tally with the amount of land directly at his or their disposal. An important element in the equation, the amount of plough-service that he or they might be called on to perform on the lord's demesne, is lacking. When all reservations have been made, however, Mr Lennard has opened up to us by his painstaking analysis a fresh line of approach which promises to modify the accepted conclusions of an earlier generation, and which leaves an impression of a peasantry more prosperous than had been realized.[23]

The main groups of peasants described in Domesday Book are four in number: the freemen, *liberi homines*, and sokemen; the *villani*; the cottagers, bordars and cottars; and the *servi*, or slaves. There is justification in an economic survey in taking the *liberi homines* and the sokemen together, though in the legal and social fields the liability to suit of court, which was the special mark of the sokeman, makes on occasion a significant point of division. *Liberi homines* are sometimes confused with sokemen in the Survey itself, and only in East Anglia do they assume special importance. About ninety-six per cent of the total number of *liberi homines* in Domesday Book appear in the entries for Norfolk and Suffolk.[24]

[23] R. Lennard, *Rural England, 1086–1135*, Oxford, 1959, and his earlier articles in the *Economic Journal* referred to below. E. Miller, *The Abbey and Bishopric of Ely*, p. 46. Economists are applying new computer techniques to this problem and appear to be reaching similar conclusions : J. McDonald and G.D. Snooks, *Domesday Economy : a new approach to Anglo-Norman history*, vol. i, Oxford, 1986.
[24] R. Lennard, *Rural England*, p. 349.

The mass of the peasantry, not far from three-quarters of the whole, were described as *villani*, or as cottars or bordars. The *villani* constituted the most numerous group of all, close on two-fifths of the recorded population, and they predominated in two out of three of the English shires. The point has already been made that the term was relatively unspecialized in the eleventh century, and that the *villanus* was not a villein as the thirteenth century would have understood it. The nearest English equivalent was *tunesman*, the inhabitant of a vill. Yet, according to the usage of Domesday Book, not all inhabitants of vills were *villani*. There was divergence, it is true, within the survey and from region to region. Some of the peculiarities of the Middlesex Domesday, for example, can best be explained on the grounds that *villanus* was used in a 'broad generic sense', rather as in the Exeter Domesday, to describe people who would have appeared elsewhere as bordars or cottars.[25] But, for the most part, the distinguishing mark of the *villanus* was clear enough. He held a more substantial share in the arable, and his holding in the arable normally had a direct relationship to the holding of other villeins. There is no need to talk too precisely of a typical villein holding of a virgate, of a quarter of a Domesday hide, of thirty Domesday acres. The variation from district to district, and from manor to manor was too pronounced to permit universal validity to such a generalization, though it must be added that once the conception of typical is legitimized there is no other figure that gives a more accurate picture than the virgate or thirty-acre unit. But within the manor a rough uniformity in distribution of arable was achieved at least within groups of villeins. In the Gloucestershire and Shropshire sections of Domesday Book the villein holding was so much a recognized feature of the agrarian landscape that it is used as a unit of account, and 'whole villeins' and 'half villeins' appear spasmodically in the survey.[26] The standardization of shares in the arable is as much a feature of unmanorialized villages in the east as of the compact manors in the west. It stems from the economic organization of the village community: the lord's discipline and the demands of the lord's demesne may have helped to depress the quantity of arable at the peasant's disposal; it left untouched the actual division of arable among peasant households.

[25] R. Lennard, 'The Economic Position of the Domesday Villani', *Economic Journal*, 1946, p. 248.
[26] R. Lennard, *Rural England*, pp. 341 ff. gives the best introduction to the problem of standard holdings.

Mr Lennard has brought out some exceptionally interesting facts concerning the ownership of plough-beasts by peasants who were called *villani*. From the sample that he is able to extract from the Domesday figures he shows that the average from the whole of the thirty-two counties examined is close on three oxen per villein, half again as much as we would expect from our 'normal' villein holding of a virgate. What is more, nearly a quarter of the villeins had on an average half a plough team, that is to say four oxen, or even more. In Herefordshire, Gloucestershire and Sussex the average was the highest. He concludes that 'villein holdings of two virgates or more were pretty common in England in 1086'.[27]

The distribution of well-to-do villeins is even more startling and unexpected. His three groups of counties with large villein holdings turn out to be: (1) Gloucestershire, Herefordshire, and probably Worcestershire; (2) Bedfordshire, Huntingdonshire and Hertfordshire; (3) Sussex and Hampshire. And it is in Lincoln and Norfolk, the traditional homes of a free and prosperous peasantry, that the predominance of small holdings is most marked. Terminological explanations have not been shown sufficient to account for these variations. The *villani* of Lincolnshire were not concealed bordars. The *villani* of Herefordshire were not concealed sokemen or *liberi homines*. Indeed the Lincolnshire sokemen themselves were particularly poorly off in the possession of recorded plough-beasts. Mr Lennard gives proper warning that it is difficult to learn much about the possession of individuals from the facts given to us in Domesday Book. Yet his arguments lead logically to the conclusion that some *villani* were substantial farmers, and that others held no more than very small patches of the arable. The neat lines drawn by Maitland of thirty acres to the villein, five to ten to the bordar, one to five to the cottar are irretrievably blurred by this modern investigation. But it is the blurring of legal generalizations, recognized by the master himself as approximations, under the friction of living social movement. If legal generalization is demanded, there is no better description of the *villanus* than that of the typical peasant member of a village community with a relatively uniform holding that will often be about a quarter of a hide, a virgate, in much of the country thirty acres, with a quarter of a plough team or two oxen in his own possession. What Mr Lennard has added to our knowledge is a sharpened awareness of variety of holding, and presumably of prosperity, among the Domesday *villani*.

[27] *Economic Journal*, 1946, p. 255.

The social implications of variety within this class must not be overlooked. At Fulham, for example, where the Bishop of London held a great manor assessed at forty hides, there were five *villani* who held a hide apiece, thirteen with a virgate and thirty-four with half a virgate.[28] Of course, there are many imponderables and unknowns connected with such entries. Even villeins grow old, and a villein with full-grown but unmarried sons to help him would be better fitted to look after a hide of land than one without such support. It is also obvious that a villein with no dependants and half a virgate of land might be better off than a villein with a virgate and ten lusty young children. Such speculation at least serves as a reminder that to attempt to read social history from concentrated and highly selective tax-returns is a perilous undertaking. Regularity of holding, and even irregularity in regular units, half-virgates, virgates and hides, show the strength of communal control of the arable. Where as much as a hide was held by one *villanus* it may well speak for vigour and mobility inside the peasant groups. Exact areal measurements cannot be given in modern terms but the respect in which a mere ten-acre field is held in a modern village gives some impression of the status of these villeins holding thirty, to say nothing of a hundred and twenty, Domesday acres. Nor were they necessarily bound to the performance of onerous service on the lord's demesne, though most clearly were. Money rents were sometimes rendered. In the north *censores*, or *censarii*, rent-payers, were not uncommon. The payment of rent did not exclude other services, but it is reasonable to suppose that where a high rent was exacted other services were light.[29] Perhaps typical of many were the peasants of Marcle in Herefordshire, who had to plough and sow with their own seed eighty acres of wheat and the same amount of oats on the lord's demesne, no intolerable burden, shared as it was among the forty peasant plough-teams on the manor.[30] There can be no doubt that regular week-work, occasional special services, notably ploughing-service and harvesting duties, and payments or renders in kind, were the normal demands made on the peasantry by the lord of the manor. The lord himself, the lessee of the manor or the *firmarius* when he was more than a ministerial reeve, moved in a different world from that of the *villanus* bound *ad opus domini*. The Norman Conquest, by emphasizing the difference between mobile lord and relatively immobile peasant, drew the red line of

[28] Ibid., pp. 251–2. D.B. I, 127b.
[29] *Rural England*, pp. 371–2.
[30] D.B. I, 179b.

significant social distinction somewhat higher than in Anglo-Saxon days. A ceorl who throve would take to the rights and obligations of a thegn. A *villanus* would not aspire to knighthood.

There are special problems to deal with in relation to a further class of peasantry, in relation to the sokeman. The features that impress the student of Domesday are two in number: his apparent freedom over against the *villani*, and his regional distribution. Sokemen are found even in Gloucestershire, but in significant number, that is to say exceeding a hundred, they are limited to eleven counties, and in great number, that is to say exceeding a thousand, it is the solid block of Danelaw and East Anglian counties, Nottinghamshire, Leicestershire, Northamptonshire, Lincolnshire, Norfolk and Suffolk that provide the heavy sokeman population. Indeed Lincolnshire provides, with a total of about 11,000 sokemen, nearly half the recorded number in the whole of the survey, and incidentally close on half, possibly a little more, possibly a little less, of its own recorded population were so described. Yet it is by no means certain that the conspicuous freedom of the sokeman was associated with prosperity in the possession of arable. Again Mr Lennard, in a penetrating study of the economic position of the sokeman, stresses the smallness of holding and the low average of plough-beasts in his possession. There were sokemen who owned a full team or more but they were exceptional. For the most part the sokeman of the free counties appeared little more prosperous than the *villani* among his neighbours, or indeed than the villeins of the more consolidated manorial counties. Economic heterogeneity was a feature of the sokeman population. In four of the most important shires, Lincolnshire, Norfolk, Essex and Suffolk, 'a large proportion of sokemen had either very few plough-beasts or none at all'.[31] But, as Mr Lennard suggests, the answer to the puzzle may be found purely in the economic field. Kent would also appear an area where the peasant, however described, had comparatively little arable under his direct control. Yet the prosperity and freedom of the Kentish peasant remained well-known throughout the Middle Ages. It seems likely that an economic reason lies behind the assumed prosperity, an emphasis on sheep-farming as well as on arable, a greater mobility and trade in agrarian products. The mints of London and East Anglia were not kept busy without some stimulus from the hinterland. There are two possibilities suggested

[31] R. Lennard, 'The Economic Position of the Domesday Sokemen', *Economic Journal*, 1947, p. 185.

by the apparent small holding of arable by the average free peasant in the eastern shires: the first would stress profits from sources other than arable, the other would suggest that the peasants were indeed poorer than elsewhere. Of the two possibilities the former seems much the more likely.

Villeins and sokemen were peasants who had a considerable share in the arable at the disposal of the community. Bordars and cottars comprised a very different class, though there is nothing to suggest that the one could not merge into the other. In some sections of the survey an attempt was made to distinguish between a bordar and a cottar, the former holding his five acres of land or more in the arable, but over the country as a whole the likenesses outstripped the differences. Both words had the same basic meaning of cottager, the former connected with the French *borde*, and the latter with the English *cote*. If modern terms are looked for, the bordar should be seen as more often akin to the smallholder, while the cottar more often retained his vague significance of cottager. But the fundamental distinction, in the eyes of the Domesday surveyors, lay between the true farmer, in the modern sense of the term, the *villanus*, and the other two groups. To the Domesday Commissioners a bordar or a cottar or a cosset was a peasant who did not hold a full share in the village fields. He had his cottage which gave him his name, his acres in the arable, rarely up to a virgate, his duties and responsibilities as part of the village community. He was a freeman. He could be prosperous, though possibly an extra function such as that of village smith was needed to account for such prosperity. But he did not hold a complete messuage with all the rights and burdens that involved.

Lowest of all in the scale of those referred to in the Domesday countryside came the *servi*, and it is likely that slave rather than serf makes the more acceptable rendering of the ambiguous *servus*. To the Domesday Commissioner the *servus* was very much an asset to be recorded in relation to the land of an estate. He was mentioned in connection with the ploughs on the lord's demesne. He could be sandwiched unhappily between a church and a mill, all equally sources of profit to a lord. He could be lumped together, as Maitland pointed out, with a nest of hawks or a pair of hunting dogs.[32] His work was at will. Little save custom and common sense could save him from exploitation.

---

[32] F.W. Maitland, *Domesday Book and Beyond*, p. 26.

In 1066 the number of *servi* was over 28,000, or more than one in ten of the recorded population. There were also some 706 *ancillae*, or female slaves, mostly in the West Midlands along the border with Wales.

Something has been said in an earlier chapter of how the *servus* arrived at his servile condition.[33] The taint was hereditary, though not without remedy. The manumissions of the late Anglo-Saxon period speak of constant activity, notably among the ecclesiastics, to redeem the servile, above all those who had 'sold their heads in return for food in hard times'.[34] It was possible, though exceptional, for a slave to rise into reasonable social prominence. For a thrall has been known to become a thegn, and a ceorl an eorl.

The general effects of the Norman Conquest upon this class were from the point of personal status distinctly upgrading. The number of *servi* had dropped between 1066 and 1086. In some districts, notably in Essex, the drop was not far short of sensational, and in this county it is clear that many who were *servi* in 1066 had become bordars in 1086.[35] The process was already initiated which was to lead to the virtual disappearance of Anglo-Saxon slavery. There is one clear case in Domesday Book of an emancipation of slaves, at *Heile* in Gloucestershire where there were twelve *servi* whom William (Leveric) made free.[36]

Historians have been at pains to discover reasons that would explain this gradual but pronounced alleviation in status of part of the servile population.[37] It has been suggested that the Normans were not used to the thoroughgoing slavery of Anglo-Saxon England. The newly vigorous and reformed Church may have had a part to play in the business. Moreover there were sound economic reasons for the change. The new lords would find it more expedient to have dependent peasants who fed themselves than to rely on notoriously fickle slave labour that had to be fed at the lord's expense. Here and there, as in Leicestershire, there is fragmentary evidence that the Normans perpetuated servile status as a means of supplying themselves with manorial officers; there are entries in the Leicestershire survey where a *servus* is mentioned alone and in front of the ordinary manorial peasantry. But the most satisfying explanation is that already hinted at in a graphic

[33] See above, pp. 90–1. The most reliable statistics are given by H.C. Darby, *Domesday England*, Cambridge, 1977, Appendix 2 and 3, pp. 337–45.
[34] *E.H.D.* I, pp. 607–11, notably no. 150.
[35] J.H. Round, V.C.H., *Essex*, vol. I, p. 362.
[36] D.B. I, 167b.
[37] See above, pp. 337–8. H.R. Loyn, *The Free Anglo-Saxon*, Cardiff, 1976.

phrase by Maitland when he stated that 'the gallows is a great leveller'.[38] It is in the wider field of law that true explanation may be found. Ideas of freedom changed, as ideas of felony grew more pronounced. A man's protection came to rest not on his personal status but on his standing before the royal-administered law. The old world of *wer* and *bot* disappeared, save in the memories of antiquarians. With it also disappeared the essence of Anglo-Saxon freedom. The peasantry could be treated as a class entire in itself. By the thirteenth century *servi* and *villani* had become virtually interchangeable terms to describe the manorial peasants. Serfs and villeins were rarely distinguished by even the most careful students of thirteenth-century institutions. The Domesday Commissioners took greater care. For in the eleventh century there was still need to distinguish between the servile and the *tunesman*. The movement towards a uniform serfdom was not far advanced. It still mattered that a man was oath-worthy, fit to bear arms, to act as suitor at a folk-court, to give free testimony with his fellows.

Of the distribution of *servi* regionally in the survey there are some important points to note. In some shires, notably those of the West Saxon heartlands, Wiltshire, Dorset, Devon and Gloucestershire, there was a strong tendency, already remarked upon, to associate the *servi* with the ploughs on the lord's demesne. Such a function seemed peculiarly the province of the unfree, and it may be that the grouping of the Leicester entries relating to *servi* points in the same direction. A certain unease in the recording of peripheral groups points to the difficulties faced by the commissioners as they attempted to record the *servi*.[39] In Hampshire, for example, there is reference to 113 so-called *bovarii* (ox-men), and to a further 11 free *bovarii*: it is a fair inference that the 113 were *servi* entered under their functional role as men bound to the plough rather than their status as unfree. The startling element in the distribution of the recorded *servi* is the variation between the north and the east on the one hand and the rest of England on the other. In the vast shires of Yorkshire and Lincolnshire no slaves are mentioned in the Domesday Book record for 1086. Indeed the proportion of slaves within the rural population north of the shire boundaries that run from the Wash to the Mersey and in the greater part of East Anglia is less than 5 per cent. In Norfolk and Suffolk, where the statistics are fuller than elsewhere, it is clear that many slaves had been

[38] *Domesday Book and Beyond*, p. 32.
[39] Figures in the following paragraph are based on the work of H.C.Darby, *Domesday England*, pp. 336–9, and on his maps, pp. 76–7.

emancipated between 1066 and 1086 and were now classified as bordars. We must be careful, of course, not to paint too rosy a picture. The silence of Domesday Book did not mean that slavery had ceased to exist over a large tract of England. Other sources, notably the records of great abbeys such as Ely and Ramsey, give evidence of the existence of slaves on estates where Domesday Book had none. But even after discounting such evidence and allowing for peculiarities in circuit practice the peasantry in the north and east appears to have enjoyed greater legal freedom than elsewhere.

Within the rest of England there are anomalies and puzzles but the main phenomenon is clearcut. The heaviest incidence of recorded slavery occurs for the most part in the west, in the shires adjoining the border with Wales, and in the south-west. On a shire basis (and one must allow for isolated topographical concentrations of slavery even in the east) Gloucestershire has the highest proportion with more than 25 per cent, 2,140 out of 8,249, described as servile. Shropshire (19.5%), Herefordshire (16.86%) and Worcestershire (15.59%) also contain large numbers of *servi*. In the south-west Cornwall (21.40%) and Devon (19.23%) have very high proportions with Somerset (16.32%) and Dorset (16.85%) not far behind. The number and the proportion remains impressive in the heartland of the ancient kingdom of Wessex. Wiltshire had 1,588 *servi* out of a recorded rural population of 9,944 (15.97%) and Hampshire 1,765 out of 9,780 (17.96%) with 22 out of 217 in the New Forest and 232 out of 1,124 in the Isle of Wight. The northern home counties of Bedfordshire, Berkshire and Hertfordshire average a modest 12–13 per cent with an increase in more servile Buckinghamshire to 16.50 per cent. A genuine and important difference arises from the figures for the south-east. Surrey has 12.25 per cent in line with its northern neighbours, and indeed with Essex at 12.92 per cent, but Kent has only 9.87 per cent, mostly heavily concentrated to the west of the county with very few slaves in the east and the south, Middlesex 5.14 per cent and Sussex the very low figure of 4.16 per cent, only 416 *servi* out of a rural population of 9,600. John Moore has given a clue to understanding the situation when he suggested that we have here evidence of differing policies towards demesne exploitation on the part of manorial lords.[40] His analysis is certainly patient of

[40] John Moore, 'Domesday Slavery', *Anglo-Norman Studies*, xi, ed. R.A. Brown, 1989, pp. 191–220. Moore presents a reasoned case for increasing the absolute and comparative number of slaves in England in 1086 and for assuming that many of the *servi* were married and the heads of households.

extension to parts of Kent. Can we already hint at a prosperous element in the south-east which is shedding slavery as an efficient means of managing a manorial based economy?

In the main the distribution of *servi* coincided well enough with the distribution of more consolidated manors and also, an odd point that could mean simply that the more elaborate manors were more likely to contain different classes of peasantry, with the distribution of bordars. It may be that an element of surveying technique enters into the question. The Commissioners found it easier to obtain figures for the men not directly responsible for geld and for a freeman's taxes and dues from the reeves of large estates. In the shires where smaller men predominated it may be that the *servus* was not an asset worthy of close and careful record, only a somewhat anomalous intruder into the normal agrarian pattern of free, though not necessarily prosperous, peasant communities. But however the figures are interpreted there is no escaping the fact that a substantial body of servile labour still existed in the fields of England in 1086, fewer in number than in 1066 but still enough to constitute an essential element in the agrarian economy. In strict law these *servi* were men from whom no right could be had – save their skins. In practice the Domesday survey shows that, provided the customary payments were made and services given, they could command resources, even to the point of sharing in the arable in the south-west, where their numbers were great. But for the most part their status was miserable and their economic resources negligible. According to the *Leges Henrici Primi* they possessed a wergeld, but it was no more than 40d. The corresponding penalty to their lord, the *manbot*, was six times as great[41]. A *servus* was no fit companion for a freeman. 'He stole alone who stole accompanied by a *servus*.'[42]

These four groups made up between them the vast bulk of the recorded rural population of 1086, but there are one or two special groups which have a particular interest in that they show both how the Domesday surveyors sought a proper terminology and also how regional peculiarities persisted in the England of King William's day. In the Western Midlands, notably in Gloucestershire, Herefordshire, Worcester and Shropshire, there appeared a number of superior peasants referred to as

[41] *Leges Henrici Primi*, 70.2: in Wessex, *si servus servum occidat, domino reddantur xxs pro manbota, parentibus interfecti servi xld*, See above, p. 305.
[42] *Leges Henrici Primi*, 59.24; 85.4a.

radmen or *radchistres*. They were freemen whose duties consisted essentially in honourable mounted service, as escorts and the like, riding-knights, corresponding quite closely to the *geneats* of the *Rectitudines Singularum Personarum*.[43] The needs of great ecclesiastical properties near a troubled western border may have helped them to develop into a specific ministerial class. At Deerhurst in Gloucestershire on the lands of the Abbot of Westminster reference is made to radmen, *id est liberi homines (T.R.E.)*, who nevertheless all plough and harrow and reap and mow at the lord's need.[44] Also in these western districts, and spread over most of Wessex and Western Mercia, were to be found a class of *coliberti*, who are on two occasions equated with the *buri*, though this may be an odd quirk on the part of the Domesday scribe in question.[45] The distinction between them and the rest of the peasantry appeared to be social in nature, and a likely explanation of the term in its English context lies in a greater awareness of servile origins in the larger estates of the west. One hundred and sixty four of the two hundred and eight *coliberti* of the Somerset survey are entered on royal manors. *Coliberti* were freedmen who had not yet achieved a fully free legal status. Even as early as the eighth century a *colibertus*, oppressed by the word and name, gave the Abbot of Gloucester a fishery in return for his freedom.[46] *Buri* was no more than a Latinized form of the Anglo-Saxon *gebur*. The presence of these groups helps to disclose the mobility, and to some degree the vitality, of social patterns underneath the recorded static surface.

5. SOURCES OF WEALTH OTHER THAN ARABLE

(a) Woodland

The available evidence leads naturally to an emphasis on the arable and on personal status. But Domesday Book in particular tells much, though at times obliquely, of ancillary sources of wealth, notably of woodland, mills and fisheries. It is true that the great survey is chiefly concerned with these tangible activities of an agrarian community inasmuch as they brought profit to an estate,

[43] See above, p. 197.
[44] D.B. I, 166: Radchen.
[45] Ibid., 38, 38b,*Domesday Book and Beyond*, p. 36.
[46] A point brought to notice by H.P.R. Finberg, and by T.H. Aston, 'The Origin of the Manor in England', *T.R. Hist S.*, 1958, p. 73.

and particularly to a lord of an estate. With origin of the dues and renders it is not concerned. Woods and fisheries were attributes essential to the well-being of most village communities, and yet particularly susceptible to usurpation on the part of a lord. As early as A.D. 825 there is record of reeves in charge of swine-herds brought to book through encroachments on such episcopal rights in Worcester.[47] Mills were also by their nature susceptible to lordly pressure. On the Continent rights over the mill were often symbolic of the lord's banal powers. The construction of a watermill demanded some deployment of capital resources, and the exercise of an initiative that could most easily come from a lord.

Extensive information is given concerning woodland in the course of the Domesday survey. As has already been said, it is the physical proximity of heavy woodland that so distinguishes the landscape of medieval England from that of modern England. Yet woodland was not only a bar to communications and to the plough. It was a source of profit. We neglect at peril the fondness of the king and nobility for hunting. From the time of Bede onwards references to the sport are frequent. According to Asser, King Alfred himself was a skilled huntsman. It was a hair-breadth escape while stag-hunting to the very edge of Cheddar Gorge that brought about Edmund's timely appreciation of the merits of St Dunstan. Edward the Confessor to the end of his days gloried in the chase. As for William the Conqueror the Chronicler flew into poetry to say that he loved 'the high harts as he were their very father'.[48] Hawking was also a popular sport, and there are frequent references to nests of hawks in the Domesday Book. Forest, that is to say land set aside from the ordinary laws of the realm, was not always wooded. But mostly it was. And the pleasure of the royal huntsmen was a prime reason for its creation.

Such spectacular sources of profit were not, however, the con-cern of the Domesday Commissioners. In Gloucestershire, for ex-ample, lay the great hunting preserve of the Forest of Dean, but the main reference to it is oblique. William FitzNorman held Mitcheldean (*Dene*) in place of three thegns who had been exempt from geld by King Edward *pro foresta custodienda*.[49] It is the more prosaic use of woodland, essential to the well-being and value of the villages and estates, that attracted the Commissioners' eyes.

[47] A.J. Robertson, *Anglo-Saxon Charters*, no. v.
[48] *Asser's Life of Alfred*, p. 59; *Memorials of St Dunstan*, ed. W. Stubbs, R.S., 1874, pp. 23–4. A.S. Chronicle, *sub anno* 1087.
[49] D.B. I, 167b.

The very methods of assessing extent of woodland indicate the use to which such wood was put. Often the measurements were given simply in leagues and furlongs. The exact method used for measuring is not known, and may never be known. A league was probably a mile and a half in most areas, but how the linear measurement was reckoned remains a mystery.[50] The other common method of assessment is much more interesting. Especially in the eastern counties, it was customary to measure woodland in terms of pannage for swine. 'Wood then [1066] for *x* swine: now for *y*' is one of the commonest types of entry for Norfolk and Suffolk. In most instances there was a marked drop in pannage, a fact which led Round to suggest a period of forest-clearing and extension of arable in the first generation of the Conquest. Later work has shown, however, that forest clearing could result not in more arable but in more waste.[51] Nevertheless the economic importance of pannage for swine is beyond dispute in the eastern counties. Elsewhere in Domesday Book there is further information to show how the method of assessment for pannage worked. In Sussex the entries for four important manors tell how each villein with seven swine gave one *de herbagio*, and a marginal note adds '*similiter per totum Sudsex*'. The same proportion was maintained in Surrey, but from the other end of England, at the great manor of Leominster in Herefordshire, each villein having ten swine gave one for the privilege of pannage. A pre-Conquest survey from the manor of Tidenham, at the junction of the Wye and the Severn, confirms this practice, in stating that there it was customary for a man who kept pigs to give three for the right to pasture the first seven, and one out of ten for the remainder.[52] Although pannage was often assessed in round numbers, entries suggesting woodland of sufficient extent to feed a thousand pigs being not unknown, the care with which assessments of pannage for three, four, seven, even for one poor pig, were recorded, shows that it had become a stereotyped method of measuring the extent of woodland, wood thick presumably in beech for mast and oak for acorns. Presumably, too, the community would take effective steps to protect the domestic

---

[50] Maitland reminds us in no uncertain terms 'how rude' these measurements were, *Domesday Book and Beyond*, pp. 432–3. Also P. Grierson, *Domesday Book : Studies* (Alecto), 1987, p. 82.

[51] R. Lennard, 'The Destruction of Woodland in the Eastern Counties, 1066–86,' *Econ H. R.*, 1949, p. 144.

[52] V.C.H., *Sussex*, vol. I, p. 365; *Surrey*, vol. I, p. 29.; D.B. I, 180 (Leominster); A.J. Robertson, *Anglo-Saxon Charters*, no. cix.

herd against the wild beasts that still infested the woodlands of England.

In Cambridgeshire, swine pasture was used as a standard of extent of woodland. But a further method of measurement was used, and mention is made of wood for fences, houses, repairs or fuel.[53] The essential part played by woodland in an agrarian community is well brought out by entries such as these. They serve, too, as reminders that we treat of a legalistic age. Anglo-Saxon law-codes had shown consistent interest in tree-felling. The axe is an informer but fire a thief, say the laws of Ine.[54] From the earliest time of which there is record, the village preserved jealously its rights over the appurtenant woodland.

(b) The mill

If wood was essential to the community, so by the end of the period was the mill. The grinding-slave of the earlier codes had been replaced by one of the technical triumphs of the age, the water-mill, driven by the power of the many streams which abound in England and grinding the corn for the whole or for a large part of the village community. To Aelfric in the late tenth century the mill-wheel was so familiar that he could liken it to the motion of the heavens around the earth, swifter than any mill-wheel and as deep under the earth as it is above.[55] The elaboration achieved by the eleventh century is illustrated in the archaeological finds at Old Windsor which reveal a mill with three vertical water-wheels turned by water flowing through a massive artificial ditch, twenty feet wide and twelve feet deep, running three-quarters of a mile across a bend in the Thames.[56]

There are features of the distribution of mills recorded in Domesday that call for comment. Some evidence suggests that the technical advance travelled from east to west, and had not reached the south-west peninsula in any strength by the time of the Domesday survey.[57] There is a great dearth of mills recorded in Devon, and above all in Cornwall where only six mills appear,

---

[53] Darby, *Eastern England*, pp. 297–8.
[54] Ine 43, 43.1. See above p. 165.
[55] *Aelfric, De Temporibus Anni*, ed. H. Henel, E.E.T.S., 1942, p. 4.
[56] D. Wilson, *The Anglo-Saxons*, London, 1960, p. 77.
[57] Margaret Hodgen, 'Domesday Water Mills', *Antiquity*, 1939, pp. 261–79; with note and comment by R. Lennard, *Rural England*, pp. 278 ff.

each with an average value below ten shillings. In some shires, particularly in Norfolk and Suffolk, districts with apparently the most arable were often badly served by mills, whereas other districts with few plough-teams in action abounded in them. So for example in the Norfolk double hundred of Flegg there were only two and a half mills to meet the needs of a prosperous arable district; in the Suffolk hundred of Lothingland only two to serve thirty villages.[58] Allowance must be made for the failure of the commissioners to record their existence. At times the very failure of the fractions of mills recorded to add up to reasonable integers proves that some have been left out. When three neighbouring villages are said to have enjoyed the fruits of one-fifth of a mill apiece, the inevitable query must be where was the other two-fifths. Domesday Book tells nothing about it. Yet in some respects the commissioners were scrupulous enough and accurate enough. They went to great lengths to state that there was a site for a mill, even if no mill then existed, that there was a mill that rendered nothing, or, for example, at Marcle in Herefordshire that there was a mill that rendered nothing beyond the sustenance of him who kept it.[59]

Specialization in the techniques of milling was probably further advanced than has always been recognized. Two features of the Domesday evidence point in this direction, namely that the range of values attributed to mills was very extensive, and that in some shires the tendency for mills to be grouped into veritable clusters was quite marked. To illustrate the first point, there was one miserable little mill in Staffordshire worth only 4d. There were many in all shires worth 16d. or 32d., or some such multiple of the Danish *ora* of 16d. The Domesday Commissioners, intent on discovering the revenue accruing to the lord, at times dismissed the very small mills as without rent. Their concern lay with the important mills that brought substantial financial return for capital sunk in them, profit that would pass both to the lord of a manor and to the farmer of a mill. Some rendered very large sums, like the two in Cambridgeshire, presumably at Grantchester, which paid between them 100s. in 1086, and which had paid no less than £8 in 1066.[60] Such mills must have served extensive areas in contrast to the modest contraptions that served a couple of poor upland villages, or which ground the corn for the *aula* of some

58 Darby, op. cit., p. 138 and p. 190.
59 D.B. I, 179b.
60 D.B. I, 194b.

equally modest manor. At Battersea the vast sum of £42 9s. 8d., or corn to that value, was the estimated revenue for seven mills that must have produced the flour for a substantial number of London bakeries.[61] Of course geographical position was especially important in determining the location of mills. There is no reason to marvel at the absence of recorded mills in the flat lands of Norfolk or the Fenlands of Cambridge. A slope was needed to give the force to drive a water-mill. But that mills were widespread and coveted is well illustrated by the Domesday entries that refer to winter-mills, that is to say to mills that could be used only in the wetter seasons of the year.

Geographical factors also apply in relation to the second point, that is to say to the presence of clusters of mills. In Lincolnshire at Tealby there were fourteen mills, at Louth thirteen, at Nettleton nine, which rendered only a pound between them, at Old Sleaford eight, which contributed ten pounds. In Norfolk fourteen places had five mills or more. There were eight mills at Ham in Essex and at Meldrith in Cambridgeshire. At Empingham in Rutland there were no fewer than eleven and a half recorded, and in Leicestershire there were seven apiece at Knipton and Battesford.[62] A similar concentration sometimes occurred in the West Country. At Leominster there were eight mills, divided among the groups of villages dependent upon the manor, although it is possible that these were not concentrated territorially at Leominster itself. The undistinguished little settlement of Blackley contained twelve mills, shared it is true with Ditchford and Icomb. Minchinhampton had eight mills at work in 1086.[63] The inference that favourable geographical conditions led to a concentration of this basic industry in some spots seems reasonable. On the other hand there are large stretches of country – Shropshire, Staffordshire, Warwickshire, Northamptonshire – where one finds few settlements with more than one or two mills recorded.

If the mills are numerous – and Miss Hodgen's figure of 5,624 actually recorded seems to have been too low[64] – the millers are elusive. They are occasionally mentioned, and common sense would suggest that the big mills at least must have been under the control of a more or less full-time specialist. In Shropshire, for example,

---

[61] Ibid., 32.
[62] Darby, *Midland England*, p. 346: D.B. I, 233b.
[63] D.B. I, 180, (Leominster) 173 (Blackley), 166b (Minchinhampton).
[64] R. Lennard, *Rural England*, p. 278; M. Hodgen, 'Domesday Water Mills', op. cit.

where renders in loads of corn, and malt, and sestiers of rye or eels are to be found, one entry adds, almost as an afterthought: 'the mill at Stokesay renders nine loads of corn, and there is a miller'.[65] Yet even though the building and techniques need not have been excessively elaborate, the task was too important to the community for it not to have been the preserve of men with special professional knowledge.

(c) The fisheries

Fisheries were often associated closely with Domesday mills. In many shires the mill's render was expressed in terms of money and of eels. Indeed, where resort was made to render in kind, eels were more frequent than grain or malt or rye. In Warwickshire, at Alveston, there were three mills 'of 40s. and 1,000 and 12 stitches of eels' (i.e. 1,300 eels).[66] The eel bulked large in the fisherman's economy, and was far and away the most frequently mentioned of his prizes. At times it was expressly stated that the render should be of *large* eels. Salmon and herring, though not ignored, received fitful treatment by the side of the eel, and it must be confessed that the treatment of fisheries itself is somewhat fitful. In places fractions of fisheries were recorded with no suggestion how the remaining fractions were made up. There was not a single fishery recorded in Warwickshire, for all the eels rendered by the mills. It may be that construction of weirs and the expense of maintaining them was a factor that determined entry or non-entry in Domesday Book. A Worcestershire charter tells of brushwood employed to build such a weir.[67] But more important than such a technical criterion is the mere existence of a source of profit which could be recorded and reported back to the king who had ordered the *descriptio* to be made.

The Fenlands area stands out as the most important centre of inland fishery in the survey. The Cambridgeshire Fens contained many fisheries, some of considerable size. Doddington rendered the fearsome cargo of 27,150 eels a year; Stuntney, 24,000 eels; Littleport, 17,000.[68] There was an industry of sizeable dimension here. It is from the Fens of the neighbouring county of

[65] D.B. I, 260b.
[66] Ibid., 238b.
[67] V.C.H., *Worcestershire*, vol. I, p. 272.
[68] D.B. I, 191b.

Huntingdonshire that the clearest insight is given into the organization of the industry. In Whittlesey Mere it is stated that:

> the abbot of Ramsey has one boat, and the abbot of Peterborough one
> boat, and the abbot of Thorney two boats. One of these two boats, and
> two fisheries and two fishermen and one virgate of land, the abbot of
> Peterborough holds of the abbot of Thorney, and for these he gives
> pasture sufficient for 120 swine, and if pasture fails, he feeds and
> fattens sixty pigs with corn. Moreover he finds timber for one house
> of sixty feet, and rods for the enclosure [*curia*] around the house.
> He also repairs the house and enclosure if they are in decay. This
> agreement was made between them in King Edward's time.[69]

The fisheries and meres of the Abbot of Ramsey in Huntingdonshire were valued at ten pounds, those of the Abbot of Thorney
at sixty shillings, those of the Abbot of Peterborough at four
pounds. These fisheries involved quite an expenditure of capital
and resources, and brought substantial returns to their monastic
owners and lessees.

From the other end of England there is one exceptionally interesting reference to fisheries, at the great royal manor of Tidenham
on the western fringe of Gloucestershire where the Wye meets
the Severn. No fewer than sixty-five fisheries existed there in
1086, at least fifty-three of which were in the Severn. At first
sight the extraordinary number of fisheries brings to mind the
possibility that Tidenham was the centre of a far-ranging fishing industry, spreading down the eminently fishable east bank
of the Severn, for which no Domesday fishery is recorded below
Longney. On the other hand, as Mr Seebohm was able to point
out long ago from his local knowledge, the fisheries were probably
simple basket-weirs, constructed to meet the difficulties of tide
and current in these swift-flowing rivers.[70] Exceptional interest is
aroused because of the fortunate survival, in a document to which
reference has already been made, of a survey of this manor taken
just a few years before the Conquest.[71] To the standard impositions
of labour-service on the peasantry were added also special services
in connection with the maintenance of the weirs. Every other fish
caught within the thirty hides of the manor, and every rare fish of
value, belonged to the lord of the manor. No one had the right of
selling any fish for money when the lord was on the estate without
telling him about it. The estate had belonged to the Abbot of Bath

[69] Darby, *Eastern England*, pp. 342–3; D.B. I, 205.
[70] D.B. I, 164; F. Seebohm, *The English Village Community*, pp. 152–3.
[71] A.J. Robertson, *Anglo-Saxon Charters*, no. cix; *E.H.D.*II, pp. 879–80.

in 956, and was leased to Archbishop Stigand at some date between 1061 and 1065. Wye salmon no doubt helped to make Fridays tolerable for the good men of eleventh-century Gloucestershire. A substantial portion of the render of six porpoises (*merswin*), thirty thousand herrings, and one mark of gold came from the archbishop's eastern properties.

On the question of sea-fisheries Domesday Book was communicative only spasmodically. Lewes in Sussex served as an important centre of a herring industry which brought in subsidiary manors strewn along the coast of Sussex. The manor of *Niworde* (Ilford), which contained twenty-six burgesses of Lewes, paid sixteen thousand herrings to the lord, William of Warenne, every year. Not to be outdone the church of St Peter, Winchester, received thirty-eight thousand five hundred herrings from the villeins on their manor at Lewes in Sussex. The Kentish port of Sandwich given by Canute to Christ Church, Canterbury, yielded annually forty thousand herrings for the refectory of the monks. Bury St Edmunds fared even better. From its manor of Beccles in Suffolk it had received thirty thousand herrings (*T.R.E.*). King William's day saw the impost doubled, and indeed the presence of burgesses enables Beccles to be classed as a small borough. The St Edmund's entries also give one of the rare glimpses of the methods employed when it refers to a *Heiemanis*, presumably a pitched net or a chall net.[72] Suffolk, unlike its northern neighbour, had many sea-fisheries, though even there the sheer number of fisheries was greater to the west of the county on the damp marshlands that guaranteed the isolation of East Anglia. But the Suffolk coast and to some extent the Essex coast and the Thames estuary, particularly at Ham (now East Ham and West Ham), was for fishermen primarily a herring coast.

(d) Waste and forest

There remain two features of social and agrarian life for which the Domesday evidence provides material for investigation: the waste and the forest. Waste in Domesday Book was a technical term meaning not any barren land, but specifically arable land that had fallen out of cultivation. Land could be waste yet still yield a profit. At Loynton in Staffordshire there was a waste half-hide that yielded two shillings.[73] Some entries show that profits from pasture

---

[72] D.B. I, 26, 17b (Lewes); 3 (Sandwich); II, 370 and 371b (Beccles).
[73] V.C.H., *Staffordshire*, vol. IV, p. 22; D.B. I, 249b.

or wood still belonged to manors that were technically waste. The prevalence of waste was often a temporary condition caused by economic or political disturbance but capable of repair, at times of quick repair. From the facts given by Domesday Book it is possible to suggest three principal causes of waste in the latter half of the eleventh century: border raids from the Welsh, political upheaval, and the creation of forest. There were also the natural hazards, rarely capable of analysis, the dying-out of old families, a series of bad harvests, even coast erosion as at Wrangle in Lincolnshire where in 1086 a tenement 'was waste on account of the acts of the sea'.[74]

Border raids from the Welsh left a deep impress on Hereford-shire, Shropshire and Cheshire, all of which were heavily scarred by the fighting of the Confessor's reign, as well as by the troubles of Edric the Wild's rebellion during the early years of the Norman Conquest. But in all districts there was a marked power of quick recuperation. In Herefordshire, there were in 1066 fifty-two vills described as waste, and fifteen as partly waste: twenty years later the number had been reduced to thirty-four waste, and sixteen part waste. Recovery came more quickly, as might be expected, in those vills furthest from the shifting Welsh frontier. The pattern of devastation would suggest short sharp sporadic raiding rather than large-scale carefully organized punitive expeditions.[75]

Shropshire, to the north, provided a more complicated picture. There is a firm record in this shire, not only of waste land in 1066 and in 1086, but also of waste land in 1070, an intermediate point where so many of the new Norman lords took over from tenants who had been foolish enough to support the old order against King William. For 1066 the figures of forty-three vills wasted, of which five were partly waste, correspond well enough with the Hereford situation. But in 1070 there were no fewer than 121 vills completely wasted, of which nine were partly waste.[76] The infer-ence is unmistakable. Welsh border troubles were overshadowed by the sweeping destruction that accompanied the Norman advent and the savage suppression of rebellion. Of course there may have been some exaggeration. An emphasis on the sad state of affairs in 1070 helped to offset the achievement of the new lords in 1086, when only forty-five vills were recorded as waste and fourteen as

[74] D.B. I, 367b.
[75] H.C. Darby, 'Devastated Land', *Domesday England*, pp. 232–59, provides the starting-point for modern analysis.
[76] Ibid., p. 145.

part waste. The year 1070 which fixed the new lords in their places was the very year when William was at his most remorseless and terrible in face of internal unrest.

The Shropshire evidence also has important things to say about the second principal cause of waste: political upheaval, rebellion and suppression of rebellion. This phenomenon was not confined to post-Conquest days. In connection with the overthrow of Earl Tostig of Northumbria in 1065, the northerners according to the Anglo-Saxon Chronicle (version D) did much harm about North-amptonshire (which was part of Tostig's midland earldom), 'slew men and burned houses and corn, and took all the cattle which they might come at, that was many thousand; and many hundred men they took and led north with them: so that the shire, and the other shires which are nigh were for many years the worse'. The truth of this entry is amply attested by the Domesday values for Northamptonshire vills in 1066, which were low, and also independently by the Northampton Geld Roll. This interesting document was a record of the geldable capacity of the shire during the first decade of the Conquest, and incidentally hints that some of the figures for 1066 conditions in Domesday Book may come from written documents long since lost. It stated that roughly a third of the number of vills in Northamptonshire were still waste, though by 1086 recovery was almost complete to judge from the small amount of waste recorded in Domesday Book itself.[77]

Such swift recovery was not characteristic of those devastations which may be attributed to William himself. The Norman was thorough. His campaign of 1069–70 was especially ruthless, and resulted in the so-called 'Harrying of the North', to say nothing of a large stretch of the north-west Midlands. From Stafford to Nottingham to York, where he spent Christmas, the track of his marauding armies can still be traced in the waste vills of Domesday. He employed a deliberate scorched-earth policy. The Deiran plain suffered the greatest severity. His return progress was equally rigorous, across to the Cheshire plains where he crushed the last of the Mercian resistance, to Chester and Stafford where tenements were destroyed to make way for the Norman castles, until at Easter he disbanded his mercenaries. Ordericus Vitalis tells how William on his deathbed felt remorse for the devastation inflicted on his kingdom. Domesday Book, treating of conditions as late as 1086,

---

[77] A.S. Chronicle, *sub anno* 1965; *E.H.D.* II, pp. 517–20; J.H. Round, *Feudal England*, p. 149.

suggests that he had good reason for remorse. Even peaceful and unspoiled Warwickshire had one vill at Harbury that was waste *per exercitum regis.*[78]

There remains a third source of waste, that associated with the creation of Norman forests. Probably no action of the early Norman kings is more notorious than their creation of the New Forest in Hampshire. The picture of prosperous settlements disrupted, houses burned, peasants evicted, all to serve the pleasure of the foreign tyrant, is a familiar element in the English national story. A more critical approach to the evident has whittled down the most extreme views, but even so the facts speak plain enough. The New Forest was treated as a separate area in Domesday Book, interpolated as a special entry after the description of the lands of the king's thegns and before the town of Southampton. The entry is not a success. Its editor made matters worse by inventing the forest Hundred of Truham. But it shows that the assessment in the area covered fell from 212½ hides to 72½, and the annual value of the land from £337 18s. to £133 4s. Some thirty vills suffered severely. On the other hand, it was the land of the King and his Norman followers that bore the brunt of this loss; the land in question was frequently of a somewhat marginal character; and where there was good arable within the forest the value could be maintained and even further increased. Aelfric held a hide at Brockenhurst which his father and uncle had held before him 'in parage'. The value had doubled between 1066 and 1086, from 40s. to £4, though the assessment had dropped from one hide to a half.[79] Peculiarities in assessment may well be explained by the introduction of new imposts in the more vigorously controlled forest lands. The extent and intensity of hardship and of depopulation have been exaggerated. Even so, it would be foolish to deny that the creation of the New Forest was an outstanding example of Norman high-handedness. William found 75,000 acres of very thinly populated woodland in Hampshire. To it he added 15,000–20,000 acres of inhabited land. There was some eviction, probably of about 2,000 persons. Later another 10,000–20,000 acres was added. The site was well chosen. But the impression of the heavy hand was so great that contemporaries could attribute

[78] *E.H.D.* II, pp. 309–10: D.B. I, 239: in *Edeuberie* where the church of Coventry had one hide and one virgate of land, and two acres of meadow. It had been worth ten shillings, now two shillings.
[79] V.C.H., *Hampshire*, vol. I, pp. 412–13, D.B. I, 51b.

the death of Rufus and of his brother Richard in the New Forest to divine vengeance falling on the sons for the sins of the father.[80]

The antecedents of the forest must unquestionably be sought in the Norman duchy and ultimately in the Carolingian Empire. Anglo-Saxon kings were great huntsmen but they did not hedge their preserves with the privilege that placed true forest outside (*foris*) the ordinary law of the realm, to the point that what is done legally in the forest 'is said not to be just absolutely but just according to the forest law'.[81] The principles of the forest were well understood by William and his sons and consistently enforced and extended during their reigns. Protection was given to venison and vert, to the red and fallow deer, the roe, the wild boar, and to the woodland and undergrowth that sheltered them. Inhabitants of forest land were subject to vexatious infringements of ancient rights and customs, to petty tyrannies at the hands of foresters and verderers, and to the threat of fearsome bodily penalties for some breaches of the forest law. The growth of the forest and its implications for medieval constitutional history are not our concern. But it may be in order to note that Henry I, despite the concessive mood customary on such occasions, was already anxious to record in his coronation charter of the year 1100 that 'with the common consent of my barons I have kept the forests in my hand, even as my father had them', though not, be it noted, as his brother had possessed them. William II indeed at one point promised to give up the forests in return for support against rebellious Norman barons.[82]

Apart from the unique entry relating to the New Forest, Domesday Book makes incidental reference to the king's forest. In Staffordshire, for example, there was an extraordinary number of waste vills in 1086, the vast majority being on either royal or ecclesiastical land. Many of these, particularly those on marginal land, had been hard hit by the campaigns of the early years of the reign and had not the resources to make swift recovery. But some owed their condition to a policy of afforestation that led ultimately to the creation of Cannock Chase. Catspelle (Chasepool) in the south-west of the county was 'in the king's forest, and waste'.

[80] *Florence of Worcester*, ed. B. Thorpe, pp. 44–5.
[81] Dialogus de Scaccario, I, xi, xii, C. Petit-Dutaillis, *Studies Supplementary to Stubbs' Constitutional History*, II, p. 149. There is a good account of the forest in D.M. Stenton, *English Society in the Early Middle Ages* (Pelican Books, London, 1951), pp. 98–119.
[82] Coronation Charter, Clause 10, *E.H.D.* II, p. 434. C. Petit-Dutaillis, op. cit., p. 172.

Most interesting of all, *Haswic* was described as 'waste because of [*propter*] the king's forest'. Richard the Forester, who held lands in Warwickshire as well as in Staffordshire, held his lands of the gift of the Conqueror according to a later authority by the service of keeping the forest of Cannock, and paying to the king ten marks yearly.[83] But for the most part, perhaps because the forests were so much out of the ordinary processes of law, only rare glimpses of the forest are given in the pages of Domesday Book. Essex was densely wooded, but the only reference to the forest which was to extend over the whole shire at one stage in the twelfth century comes from a mention of a swineherd at Writtle near Chelmsford who had been taken from his manor and made forester of the king's wood.[84] On his accession Henry II made the whole of Huntingdonshire forest land, but there were only two references to the king's forest in the Domesday survey. Of the Forest of Dean some information is given in the Gloucestershire and Herefordshire folios, but the evidence is on the whole distressingly jejune in the face of the tremendous twelfth-century agitation over the whole process. Huntsmen appear frequently as holders of land. The duty of *stabilitio*, that is to say the task of driving deer towards an agreed central point where they make their stand, was expressly laid on some of the citizens of Hereford, of Shrewsbury and of Berkshire.[85] Hays were frequently mentioned in the western shires, and have left their traces on the place-name structure of these areas. They were apparently hedged enclaves on forest land into which beasts could be driven, and may have been connected with the duty of constructing the *deorhege* mentioned earlier in another connection.[86] Parks were at this stage no more than enclosures, possibly extensive, for the preservation of beasts for the chase, and were referred to in Domesday Book as the possession of many of the greatest tenants-in-chief as well as of the king himself. Their connection with the special privileges associated with the possession of forest and forest right was indirect only. For hunting rights were the preserve of any powerful lord. It was as much part of the texture of his living as was the art of fighting on horseback itself. But the remorseless extension of arbitrary royal power which was so much a characteristic of the making of forests

---

[83] V.C.H., *Staffordshire*, vol. IV, pp. 34–5. D.B. I, 249b, 247b. *Book of Fees*, 1277.
[84] D.B. II, 5b.
[85] D.B. I, 179, 252 and 566. C. Petit-Dutaillis, op. cit., p. 173, discusses the annoyances suffered by holders of land under the forest law.
[86] See above, pp.196–7.

in Anglo-Norman days was quite another story. William I, when he established his 'baronies of the Forest' in Somersetshire, gave evidence of the political use to which these special reserves of power could be placed.

(e) Other aspects of rural life

Of other aspects of rural life fitful glimpses are given in the great surveys of the late eleventh century. There is surprisingly little told directly of sheep-farming, important as it was as an ancillary occupation to all the rural communities of England. In some parts of the country special reference was made to sheep-pasture which was detached from the main portion of the manor. In the Weald, Domesday entries relating to manors in Kent and Sussex tell of such 'denes' in the Weald. The salt-marshes of Essex, the fenlands of Norfolk and the upland pastures of western England were areas in which the evidence for large-scale sheep-farming was positive and detailed. Record of flocks exceeding two thousand sheep are to be found. Sometimes the facts of feudal geography can be brought in as circumstantial evidence. Suen of Essex inherited much of his land from his father Robert Fitz-Wimarc, who had settled in Essex during the reign of the Confessor. But he did not set up the *caput* of his feudal honour on his father's estates. He chose instead his new estate at Rayleigh where he made his castle. Round suggested that his chief reason for so doing may well have been economic. The greatest sheep-master in Essex was pleased to make his principal residence near the source of so much of his wealth, the salt-marshes of the Essex lowlands, on which he had grazing for over four thousand sheep in all.[87]

It seems likely that the ewe and the goat provided more milk, butter and cheese than did the cow. Dairy farming, as we understand it, was quite strange to eleventh-century England. The extent of meadow land, at least as recorded in Domesday Book, is less than one would expect. Vineyards have the appearance of recent importations, usually associated with the new Norman lords as at the castle of Rayleigh where Suen held a vineyard with a yield of twenty *modios* of wine in a good season.[88] This is the only reference to a yield of wine in Domesday Book. It may be assumed that what wine was produced was for immediate consumption by the lord and his household.

[87] V.C.H., *Essex*, vol. I, p. 346; R. Lennard, *Rural England*, pp. 260–4.
[88] D.B. II, 43b.

Important as the subsidiary rural crafts must have been, the skill of the bee-keeper, the hurdle-maker and so on, all seemed subordinate to the plough, to the arable, though renders in honey, for example, were quite common particularly in western districts. The records do not mislead. Their own emphasis reflects the importance of the corn-grower and of the bread-maker. Even the village itself, with its *tungerefa*, and the manor with its lord and reeve were only in one respect social manifestations of the agrarian reality: the open fields, the peasants diverse in equipment and wealth but united in their prime purpose, which was the cultivation of the arable wealth of England.

6. TOWNS AND BOROUGHS

(a) The differentiation of town and country

Last of all there is the question of the state of the towns in England at the end of the eleventh century. In general terms something has already been said in an earlier chapter concerning the existence, size and importance of the major towns of England. Discussion too has been made of some of the minting problems, and of the volume and significance of late Old English coinage and mints. The time has now come to attempt to deepen the analysis of urban life in the late eleventh century.

To begin with it is well to restate the proposition that towns virtually completely dependent on urban activity existed in late Anglo-Saxon and early Anglo-Norman England. London itself was outstanding in all ways, and a high proportion of its population must have depended for their sustenance on buying and selling or on the industrial activities associated with the life of a great seaport and centre of commerce. York in the north and Southampton, the seaport for Winchester, in the south, occupied a similar position on a smaller scale. Winchester itself, probably the second city of the realm, a knot of eastern towns, Norwich, Thetford and Lincoln, and Exeter and Chester to the west also supported populations that could not be sustained by local agrarian resources alone. All these towns owed prosperity and population to commercial activity and in some measure to trade overseas.

Yet to say so much should not lead to neglect of another important fact. Even the greatest of the towns, even London itself, was firmly wedded to the countryside it served. The sharp antithesis of urban to rural is a product of the society in which we live, and does not provide the surest of instruments to use in discussion of eleventh-century institutions. All Anglo-Saxon towns had some arable in their possession, and most important within their walls a substantial proportion of agricultural workers, who are often described in the Domesday survey as if they were normal manorial peasantry, bordars, cottars or the like. Cambridge was a substantial settlement with a total population of at least sixteen hundred. Nevertheless the burgesses lent the sheriff their plough-teams three times a year, a service which the sheriff was trying to increase threefold in 1086.[89] In the eleventh century there was still very slow differentiation of town from country. In some areas the process had reached an advanced stage, in others not.

Occasionally there is direct evidence of the initial break itself being made. At Tutbury, in Staffordshire, Domesday Book tells that there were in the *burh* in 1086 around the castle forty-two men living by their trade alone.[90] Tutbury was the head of the powerful honour of Henry de Ferrers. The very needs of the lord were sufficient to ensure its success in the lee of the *caput* of the honour. More illuminating still is the case of Bury St Edmunds. It was described as a *villa*, though it is known that coins were struck at Bury during the reigns of Harold I and of Edward the Confessor. No burgesses were mentioned. Even so the survey goes into great detail to describe what is truly the growth of a commercial centre. It had doubled its value, from ten to twenty pounds, between 1066 and 1086. Its proportions were given, apparently in linear measurements, one and a half leagues in length and the same in breadth, measurements that reveal Bury as no closely circumscribed enclosure, though the probability is that an areal measurement of some one hundred and eighty acres is what the scribe meant to imply, that is to say one and a half times the areal league of one hundred and twenty acres which occurs elsewhere in Domesday Book. But the energy of the ecclesiastical tenant-in-chief here, the great Abbot Baldwin, 1065–98, had as dramatic effect on this Suffolk village as had the coming of the lords of the honour of Eye or of Clare elsewhere in the county of Suffolk. For now, that is to say in 1086, it is stated that:

> the town is contained in a greater circuit, including land which used then to be ploughed and sown, on which there are altogether thirty

---

[89] D.B. I, 189.
[90] Ibid., 248b.

priests, deacons and clerks, twenty-eight nuns and poor people who daily utter prayers for the king and all Christian people; seventy-five millers [*pistores*], ale-brewers, tailors, washerwomen, shoemakers, robe-makers, cooks, carriers, dispensers altogether. And all these daily wait upon the Saint, the abbot and the brethren. Besides whom there are thirteen reeves over the land who have their houses in the said town, and under them five bordars. Now thirty-four knights, French and English together, and under them twenty-two bordars. Now altogether there are 342 houses on the demesne of the land of Saint Edmund which was under the plough in the time of King Edward.[91]

This is by no means a typical town, and Ballard was within his own rights in refusing to recognize it as a borough.[92] But it is a fine illustration of the way in which towns could be created. The four types of people directly mentioned in the analysis were all grouped around the great Abbey itself: clerks to serve the church, menials to serve the church, estate-managers to look after the lands of the church, knights to defend the lands. Norman administration provided a strong local centre. In such a circuit town life could flourish.

This centripetal attraction exercised by a new and energetic lord's household is well illustrated by another example from Suffolk. In the north of the county were the two little agricultural settlements of Hoxne and Eye. The former was the more important in 1066. It had been the *æcclesia sedes episcopatus de Sudfolc*, and it had a market which its neighbour, three miles distant to the south-west, had not. The Norman settlement brought harder times. The bishop moved to the border-town of Thetford. And at Eye William Malet made his castle, the *caput* of one of the great Honours of England. The result is best told in the sad words of the Domesday Book itself:

In this manor [Hoxne] there was a market in the days of King Edward and since King William came, it was held on a Saturday. And William Malet made his castle at Eye, and on the same day on which the market was held in the bishop's manor, William Malet held another market in his castle, and thereby the bishop's market had so deteriorated that it is worth little, and the market is now held on a Friday.[93]

This precious little insight into a squabble for local markets tells more than many lengthier documents of the state of the country. Eye itself had no great urban future, but its position in the feudal

[91] D.B. II, 372; for areal leagues cf. V.C.H., *Devon*, vol. I, p. 389.
[92] A. Ballard, *The Domesday Boroughs*, p. 10.
[93] D.B. II, 379.

world was sufficient to make it rather than Hoxne the economic fulcrum of the district.

(b) The market: contributory burgesses and town houses

   This brings to the forefront a problem of some complexity in relation to English urban institutions and to the Domesday survey. It has been argued earlier that a market was essential for the continued existence of a borough so that it could develop into a medieval town. Yet in the Domesday record references to markets in boroughs were often fleeting, oblique, or frankly non-existent. And references to markets in places that certainly had not attained burghal status were by no means infrequent. In Gloucestershire, for example, no market was recorded at Gloucester, Bristol or Winchcombe. Tewkesbury alone of the boroughs possessed a market 'which the queen had established there', and which rendered eleven shillings and eight-pence. Yet Berkeley, Cirencester and Thornbury all possessed recorded markets, that of Cirencester also being described as a new market.[94]

   The explanation offered for this state of affairs is not simple, nor is it certain. It is probably to be found in the limitations of our records and also in the partial failure of the burghal policy of the late Old English kings, a failure attendant upon a growth in local trade and local marketing. Markets are not mentioned in some of the big boroughs for the simple reason that they go without saying. The profits of the market would not need to be recorded separately unless there was something unusual about them, as in the case of Tewkesbury, where the Queen had recently taken steps to set up such a market at a fixed render. Normally marketing profits would pass to the lord of the borough in the form of tolls and of rents and dues from the burgesses. When an extra impost was levied, as in the case of the Sussex boroughs, then that extra impost was recorded, and it is stated, for example, that at Lewes a man selling a horse paid one penny to the reeve, a halfpenny for an ox, and if a slave were sold, fourpence. The purchaser also paid a similar sum.[95] Where the borough was farmed, the farmer was in a position to tap extra profits. If the burgesses were prosperous enough and possessed enough corporate sense they could take on the function of farmer themselves. In some instances they move towards a

[94] D.B. I, 163b, 163, 162b, 163b.
[95] Ibid., 26.

true conception of corporate ownership, buying churches, owning
pasture or arable, farming mints. But the Domesday record with its
dominical slant was not concerned with the detail of the payments
as much as with the results as they accrued to the lord. For example,
in all the detailed survey of the important borough of Hereford
there is no mention of a market. It is only from the entry relating
to Etune (Eaton Bishop) that it is possible to infer the presence of
a market, when it is said that Harold had held Eaton, and Earl
William after him had exchanged the manor with the bishop in
return for 'the land in which the market is now and for three
hides at Lydney'.[96] Eaton Bishop itself was assessed at five hides.
All boroughs of the size and importance of Hereford, the true
county boroughs, normally preceding the survey of the rest of the
county in Domesday Book, served as the greatest market in their
respective shires.

Strong evidence in support of this assertion comes from the presence of contributory burgesses scattered about the shire, entered
in Domesday Book under the particular manor which provided
them, an asset worthy of note in relation to a rural manor. Great
controversy has raged around the term 'burgess' itself in the past.
Some have said that the term meant little more than a dweller in
a town, or even more loosely a man who had a strong connection
with a town. Others have argued differently, pointing out that no
burgesses are known in Domesday Book who are not 'holders of
messuages either rendering customs to the king or to some other
lord or to both or in rare cases directly exempt from payment'.[97]
No one, of course, would suggest that all inhabitants of towns
were worthy to be called burgesses, and the weight of argument
appears to rest with those willing to admit a certain degree of
specialization in the term. A burgess was a man rendering borough
customs. References are made to lesser burgesses, even to minute
burgesses, as if some degree of affluence were anticipated from a
full burgess. But the immediate concern lies with those men, known
in our modern jargon as contributory burgesses, that is to say men
who were attached to and resident at a rural manor, but who
nevertheless were classed as burgesses of this town or that in the
Domesday Survey. The city of Gloucester provides a particularly
telling example of the activity of these men. Eighty-one burgesses
were recorded in all under the various manors of the shire, ranging

[96] Ibid., 181b.
[97] J. Tait, *The Medieval English Borough*, p. 96.

widely throughout the county and including eight burgesses from the borough of Tewkesbury itself who rendered 5s. 4d. and did service at the court, *ad curiam*. In Bisley there were eleven burgesses who contributed 66d. between them; in Deerhurst there were no fewer than thirty burgesses paying 15s. 8d; a single burgess at Bulley rendered 18d.; another from Quenington rendered four plough-shares, and one from Lechdale was a burgess at Gloucester *sine censu*. These payments were entered under the respective manors, and for some seventy of the eighty-one burgesses a flat rate of between 5d. and 8d. a head was exacted.[98] It is possible that the sums specified related to the money paid in order to buy the privilege of burgess status in Gloucester, and were therefore recorded as a source of direct profit to the lord of that borough, that is to the King himself. They were renders from the manors, rather than to the lords of the manors. On the other hand, as the payments were recorded under the individual manors, they can be taken to represent rents paid to the lords of the manor in return for the privilege of handling the trade associated with the manor at the market or fair; though in that case further payment unrecorded by itself must have been made to the lord of the borough.

Miss Bateson gave the most plausible definition of a contributory burgess when she stated that he was probably a non-resident burgess who had bought himself into the borough for purposes of gain, notably, it seems, for purposes of marketing.[99] The rural burgess of Domesday Book should then be identified with the foreign burgess of a later time, the upland burgess who may be attached to one or two boroughs, not necessarily very close to where he lived. Even so one cannot be sure, for example, that the thirty burgesses from Deerhurst were all non-resident. They were attached to the lands in Deerhurst Hundred, a fine fifty-hide estate, held by the royal abbey of St Denis near Paris, and there would be need for a concentration of burgesses in the city of Gloucester to deal with the doubtless complicated affairs relating to marketing and transmission of dues to far-distant masters. But the same argument will scarcely apply to Dunwich on the opposite side of England, where the Abbot of Ely had no fewer than eighty burgesses appurtenant to his single manor of Alneterne, enough, one would imagine, to man a complete fishing fleet of the little

[98] Darby, *Midland England*, p. 45, sets out the full list.
[99] *E.H.R.*, 1905, p. 148.

Suffolk seaport, and incidentally a strong reminder that there were contributory burgesses in small towns as well as great.[100] In Gloucestershire itself Winchcombe possessed thirty-two such burgesses, including two from the lands of St Denis. Attached to the manor of Drayton Bassett in Staffordshire there were eight burgesses of Tamworth who certainly resided on the manor. They performed labour service just as the other *villani*, an unusual feature obviously to be remarked on. It also happened on occasion that contributory burgesses moved across a shire border, from manors in Buckinghamshire and Berkshire to Oxford, or from Hereford manors to Worcester, never too far for the burgesses to lose touch, but nevertheless outside the shire limits.[101]

Another associated problem is also capable of solutions that support the view that would stress the importance of the market to the borough. Property within the borough could often be annexed to a county estate. Ballard in his account of Domesday boroughs has published maps indicating the extent of this close liaison between town and country for places as diverse as Leicester, Wallingford, Lewes and Arundel.[102] It is not a matter of an isolated phenomenon, or of a mere regional peculiarity, but of a characteristic common to many middle-sized and big towns, not only in England but also on the Continent. The origin of these appendant properties has already been discussed.[103] That their original purpose was in large part military cannot be denied. There were still *mansiones murales* at Oxford in 1086, connected with the defence of the city walls.[104] And although, as Miss Bateson reminded us long ago, borough houses 'were not merely tiresome evidences of a duty towards national defence', burgesses in Domesday Book often wore a most military aspect, some having, as at Hereford, the duty of serving the King on horseback as escorts and in hunting, the King retaining the horse and arms as a heriot on the burgess's death.[105] Military service on land or sea could be, and often was, composed for by money payment, but there is still a great difference from the comfortable, solid, peaceful bourgeois of the golden Middle Age.

[100] D.B. II, 385b.
[101] Darby, op. cit. (Winchcombe); D.B. I, 246b (Tamworth). Both Tait and Ballard deal with the problem in general terms.
[102] A. Ballard, op. cit.: lists, pp. 14–19; maps facing pp. 14, 22, 28.
[103] See above, p. 141.
[104] D.B. I, 154, *vocantur murales mansiones quia si opus fuerit et rex preceperit murum reficient.*
[105] *E.H.R.*, 1905, p. 149; on Hereford see below, pp. 392–4.

Yet a military and garrison purpose alone will not suffice to account for the widespread presence of these appendant tenements in 1086. They were profitable to the lords of the manor themselves. The most likely explanation that can be offered for their presence is that they served the estates in the economic field. A great estate could, in itself, be an elaborate economic institution, and could create its own market at the centre out of sheer economic and administrative need. But where fortified and well-placed centres flourished already, it was natural that county estates should tighten the bonds which had from the days of Alfred and Edward tied them to the *burhs* of the shires. At Leicester twenty-seven manors had attached to them 134 of the houses in the borough. At Chichester forty-four manors had 142 houses.[106] These houses brought in rents to their lords. But the fact that they are recorded with the manors in question suggests strongly that they were often used as store-houses, as places where the lord and his retinue could stay, if legal or financial business should bring him to the borough, where his reeve might supervise the marketing of his produce, and where his own burgesses might live. A powerful lord would find it much to his advantage to possess houses and men in the most important strategic centre of the shire. At Guildford an unscrupulous reeve of Odo of Bayeux robbed a poor widow, and his own dead friend, of their messuages in order to provide town houses for his master who was incidentally lord of the manor of Bromley.[107] The needs of the manor drove the reeve to violent action. It is a measure of the royal strength in England that the great boroughs remained so royal in composition. Nevertheless in all of them is evidence enough of the interest taken by the landed proprietors of the surrounding district in their functioning and their well-being. Indeed the Norman, with his love of order, tried to squeeze the complex pattern of Anglo-Saxon borough tenements into the 'land of the king' and the 'land of the barons'. In York the Archbishop possessed one of the seven shires into which the great city was divided. He held his shire 'with full custom' but often, in point of fact, the barons' land was subject to full custom just as was the ordinary burgess tenement.[108]

To concentrate exclusively on the finished product of the Domesday borough is to miss the real excitement which comes from the

---

[106] A. Ballard, op. cit., pp. 28–9, 14–15; D.B. I, 230, 23.
[107] D.B. I, 30,
[108] J. Tait, *The Medieval English Borough*, pp. 91, 94.

sight of institutions half-grown or in process of formation. In the face of economic necessity it was impossible to confine agricultural trade to the established boroughs. The legislation of the late Old English kings shows a gradual relaxation of the more vigorous enactments of early days. A farmer from the Severn estuary might find the long trail to Bristol or Gloucester too far for a regular journey. The growth of a market at Thornbury helped to meet his needs. There was no further move in that instance beyond the agrarian market stage, yet the potentiality remained. These little markets constituted a factor of great importance in the social life of the time, and a factor of considerable financial importance to whosoever exercised lordship over them.

(c) Norman lords and the boroughs

Nevertheless it might well be argued that from the point of view of the development of town life and urban institutions the small markets have an interest only in their capacity for growth. In many ways the Norman Conquest proved salutary in that it institutionalized some of these small and intermediate units by providing a feudal framework into which they could fit. It has already been emphasized that the boroughs as such were predominantly royal in Anglo-Saxon days. There were few mediatized boroughs of importance in 1066. Apart from Durham and Dunwich ,the permanently mediatized borough occurred only in Kent in 1066 where Sandwich, Hythe and Seasalter belonged to Christ Church, Canterbury, and Fordwich by a recent grant of royal rights by Edward himself, to St Augustine's.[109] The stronger lordly bond exercised by the Norman conquerors gave opportunity for further mediatization. Up to 1066 the secular aristocracy had taken its proceeds from the borough indirectly through control of some of the burgesses, and directly only through the earl's perquisite of the third penny, the enjoyment of which was in itself a consequence of office not of rank. It was because the earl was a royal officer of the first importance that he was able to lay claim to the privilege of receiving a third of the royal dues and customs presumably in return for his share in the construction and defence of the borough. But after 1066 more boroughs, some quite large, fell into the hands of secular lords. On a smaller scale the new barons discovered the financial advantages that would accrue from the

[109] J. Tait, *The Medieval English Borough*, pp. 140–1.

establishment of a market in the lee of a castle. The stage was reached by the twelfth century when by a stroke of the pen a lord would convert a little village like Burford into a borough, and his *villani* into burgesses.[110] The lords introduced alien customs from the Continent. They introduced burgesses from the Continent. On the Marches of Wales the laws of the little Norman town of Breteuil were enforced as a standard of good burghal privilege. At times, as at Norwich, the introduction of many foreigners brought about the formation of what was referred to as a new borough. It is not without note that Earl Ralph who was instrumental in bringing about this innovation in Norwich gave back some of his own land to the King so that his royal master could make the borough, the profits to be shared in the traditional manner, two parts to the king and one to the earl.[111]

(d) Waste and the boroughs

Yet the final impression received from Domesday Book is not of an urban economy flourishing and vitalized by the Norman Conquest. Perhaps the date itself, 1086, was too near the political troubles and unrest of the early part of William's reign not to have left its mark on the English town. The Domesday preoccupation with waste certainly showed up the state of the town to poor advantage. The Norman policy, for such it was, of consolidating their hold on urban strategic centres by castle-building led to much local disruption in old-established towns. In Cambridge twenty-seven houses were destroyed to make room for the castle; and in Gloucester, sixteen; in Huntingdon there were twenty waste messuages on account of the castle, and at Stamford five messuages were waste for the same reason. Lincoln was exceptionally hard hit. It has been estimated that there were 1,150 inhabited houses in 1066. This number had dropped to 900 twenty years later, no fewer than 166 having been destroyed 'on account of the castle'. There were also four more waste outside the castle boundary 'not because of oppression of sheriffs and officers but by reason of misfortune and poverty and ravage of fires'.[112] When notice is taken of the care with which the reeve of Hereford tried to avoid empty messuages, lest the king should lose his rent thereby, the subordination of immediate economic interest to immediate mili-

---

[110] A.L. Poole, *From Domesday Book to Magna Carta*, p. 66.
[111] D.B. II, 118,
[112] D.B. I, 189, 162, 336b (Stamford and Lincoln).

tary necessity is thrown sharply into relief.[113] Another indication that the presence of waste messuages could press hard on the remaining burgesses comes from the Shrewsbury entry, where it is said that in Shrewsbury and in the *nova domus et burgus Quatford* they pay the same geld as *T.R.E.*, though the Earl's castle occupied the place of fifty-one burgages, and another fifty were waste'. All in all, there were 193 burgages at Shrewsbury not rendering geld. No wonder the owners of the remaining burgages grumbled *multum grave sibi esse*.[114] A similar story must have often lain behind the laments of impoverishment that resound through the pages of Domesday Book. At Dunwich there were 178 *pauperes homines* in 1086, and at Winchester an early twelfth-century survey tells that there were many *boni cives* and *burgenses* who were reduced to poverty by the effects of the Conquest.[115] The addition of French burgesses and the imposition of new customs could not always mask the damage done by the heavy hand of Norman military settlement.

(e) The customs and the firma burgi

Last of all, a word is needed about two matters of great signifi-cance in the development of the medieval borough, the question of the *customs* themselves and the very complicated problem of the farm of the borough, of the *firma burgi*. Legally and socially the mark of membership of a borough group was participation in the burdens demanded by the *consuetudines*, or customs of the group. For some towns such as Chester and Hereford a full statement of customs has been preserved. For others there is no more than the bare mention that this tenement was held in custom, or that the land was held free from custom. Normally customs lay upon the tenements, or even fractions of tenements, rather than on the burgesses themselves. One fact is plain. To inhabit a customary tenement could be an expensive business. The fundamental cus-tom was the payment of land-gable or rent to the lord of the borough. This rent was normally fixed at a flat rate. In Hereford, for example, those who dwelt within the walls paid $7\frac{1}{2}$d.: those without, $4\frac{1}{2}$d.[116] It was the job of the bailiff or reeve to see that the tenements were fully occupied, lest the lord might suffer loss. The rents of which there is record varied considerably. In Lincoln,

[113] D.B. I, 179.
[114] Ibid., 252.
[115] D.B. II, 311b (Dunwich); *Liber Winton.*, D.B. IV, 532.
[116] Ibid., I, 179.

and possibly at Norwich, the gable was only a penny.[117] It became customary to demand a higher rent, and in the course of the twelfth century a shilling rent was quite common among new foundations. This high rent may have been offset to some extent by a quittance of other custom. In the main, land-gables do not seem to have been a heavy burden on the burgess tenements. Nor was the burden of geld excessive on boroughs in normal times. Some were treated as exclusively royal demesne and exempt. Exeter claimed the special privilege of paying geld only when London, York and Winchester also paid, that is presumably in moments of considerable crisis.[118]

It is when consideration is given to the burden of incidental custom, that it becomes clear how necessary it was for a town-dweller to live on resources greater than he could command from his arable plot, his meadow and pasture, his woodland and associated rights. Trade and steady trade alone could enable a man to sustain the position which the customs, in this sense primarily the obligations, of the borough demanded. There is something of a difference in this respect between the big boroughs of the east and those of the west. The western boroughs are treated fully in Domesday Book, but they do not appear to have been quite so far advanced as some of the big eastern boroughs. For the three key border boroughs of Shrewsbury, Hereford and Chester much detailed and interesting material is available. At Shrewsbury, where the new French settlers were exempt from the geld, special emphasis was given to legal forfeitures.[119] Outlawry was the penalty for infringement of the peace granted by the king's own hand; a hundred shillings was exacted for the infringement of the royal peace given by the hand of the sheriff, and the same penalty for ambush or forcible entry. King Edward had held these forfeitures on his royal land throughout England, and they had lain outside and apart from the farms (*extra firmas*). Personal service demanded of the burgesses was heavy when the king appeared in person. Twelve of the better of the burgesses were to serve him during his stay in the city. When he went hunting, a posse of the better burgesses, drawn from those who owned horses, was to accompany him. Further duties on foot were exacted for the king's hunting, and when he departed twenty-four men had to ride with him to

[117] Ibid., I, 336, 336b; Ibid., II, 116–18.
[118] Ibid., I, 100.
[119] Ibid., 252.

393

the borders of Staffordshire. A forty-shilling fine was imposed on any burgess failing to accompany the sheriff into Wales when summoned to do so. The burgesses were to pay a relief of ten shillings to enter their inheritance; a widow was to pay to the king twenty shillings on marriage, a girl was to pay ten shillings. Special forfeitures were exacted in case of bloodshed, and in case of fire when forty shillings passed to the king, and two shillings to each of the two nearest neighbours. The king's special peace and the king's special perquisites were prominent in this Shropshire borough. The burgesses, notably the *meliores* among them, were plainly men of substance.

The Hereford burgesses also appear to have been men of some standing and importance although, an unusual feature, they were subject to reaping service in August at a nearby royal manor.[120] Guard service, hunting duties and military service were prominent among their obligations, as might be expected from their position on a delicate and dangerous border. The burgess who owned a horse paid a formal heriot: on his death the king was to have his horse and his arms. If he died before dividing his goods, the king was to succeed to all his *pecunia*. In Chester military and hunting obligations were not discussed but a most elaborate and detailed description of the special judicial forfeitures of the borough was given, especially of those concerning a breach of the royal peace and outbreaks of violence.[121] For a delay in the payment of the gable or rent, a fine of ten shillings was exacted; if toll was not paid within three days then the penalty was forty shillings. For infringements of moral law a widow was fined twenty shillings, a girl ten shillings. The brewer of bad beer was to pay four shillings or to suffer the cucking-stool. Special thought was given to the control of trade in the seaport. Fines were levied on those ships which came or went without the royal permission, and a ship which came against the royal peace and in face of a royal prohibition was to be forfeit, the vessel itself and the men and the cargo. Even with royal permission granted, the king and the earl took a fourpenny toll from each lading (*lesth*). The king's reeve had a right to pre-emption in martens' pelts. The very full statement of the customs of Chester brings out well both the royal control and the complicated nature of these larger Domesday boroughs.

In the south-east and in the east of England the evidence is more clear-cut again for complicated urban life and for burgesses

120 Ibid., 179.
121 D.B. I, 262b.

who were men of property accustomed to the free use of money. It is there, too, that appear firmer hints of corporate effort on the part of townsmen and their guilds. In prosperous Kent, the burgesses of Canterbury held forty-five messuages outside the city of which they claimed the *gable* and the custom though the king retained sake and soke. Their guild held thirty-three acres of the king.[122] At Colchester the burgesses held land and pasture which brought in sixty shillings a year. This sixty shillings was to be paid for the king's service, if necessary. If not, then the burgesses would divide it in common. The royal burgesses paid what seems to have been a farm for all custom of two marks of silver a year, a considerable sum. They further paid sixpence from each house for the maintenance of the king's soldiers or for an expedition by sea or land.[123] This exaction takes a stage further the composition for military service which was open to burgesses of Warwick when ten of the burgesses did service for the rest when the king marched in person. If the king went against his enemies by sea then Warwick was to provide four *batsueins*, or four pounds in money.[124]

For ample demonstration of prosperity – and indeed of corporate endeavour in the collection of money – a great borough like Norwich provides good example. In 1086 the city paid £70 by weight to the King and 100s. by tale to the Queen, £20 of uncoined silver to the earl and 20s. as a free gift to Godric. The heavy render suggests some real increase in prosperity over against 1066 when Norwich paid £20 to the King and £10 to the earl; 21s. 4d. for measures of provender, six sextaries of honey, a bear and six bear-dogs.[125] Indeed to judge from the admirable table of farms given by Professor Tait, the demands made upon the burgesses of a town were consistently heavier in 1086 than had been the case twenty years earlier. Very large sums were involved. The farm of London was £300 in the reign of the Conqueror. York and Lincoln paid £100 apiece in 1086. Colchester paid £82 and £5 to the sheriffs; Chester and Thetford, £76 apiece; Gloucester, Hereford and Oxford, £60 each. Wallingford paid £80, though according to the survey £60 was the correct amount.[126]

Certainly the impression is given of townsmen fully capable of acting together corporately in financial matters. The struggle for

[122] Ibid., 2; J. Tait, op. cit., pp. 128–9.
[123] D.B. II, 107.
[124] Ibid. I, 238.
[125] Ibid. II, 116–18.
[126] J. Tait, op. cit., p. 184.

a farm of the borough that would completely exclude the sheriff, for a 'free borough' and ultimately for communal status lies in the twelfth century. The potentiality existed in the generation after the Conquest.

The most conspicuous way in which the borough asserted its freedom in the course of the twelfth century was by taking over the responsibility for the farming of the borough. That is to say the burgesses themselves elected to pay a fixed sum in composition of the customary revenue. In the case of London a charter of Henry I gave the citizens the right to render the farm of London and also of Middlesex for the sum of £300, to appoint their own sheriff and to have their own justiciar to keep the pleas of the Crown. A year or so earlier, in 1130, the burgesses of Lincoln were farming their borough direct from the king.[127] Already at the time of the Conquest the revenues were often farmed, but usually by the royal officer, town-reeve, port-reeve, or sometimes by the sheriff. The Norman Conquest threw much more authority on the sheriff's shoulders and by 1086 it was he, more often than not, who farmed the county borough, often combining it with his farm of the shire also. The sheriff may well have had the power to increase or to reduce the farm, and as sheriffs were usually men of high rank and often constables of the new castles they were in a remarkably fine position to assess the worth of the revenues that were compressed into the lump sum of the *firma burgi*. For not all the revenue was compounded for in the farm. Land-gable, itself the most regular though not the heaviest of the customs, seems to have remained outside it. Tolls, market-dues, and judicial perquisites must have accounted for the greater part, the variable portion of the revenue as opposed to the relatively fixed sums involved in gable and geld. And the sums involved were enough to suggest again that the volume of trade may have been considerable. The Norman sheriffs themselves paid the farm in no altruistic spirit. They expected to make a profit. It was a sad case worthy of emphatic mention in Domesday Book when the farmer of Reading lost seventeen shillings on his transaction.[128]

It was normal for an individual to farm a borough, if not the sheriff then a royal reeve, as at Dover, and possibly at Hereford. Yet already in Domesday Book there is some evidence of burgess

---

[127] Liebermann, I, p. 525, also J. Tait, op. cit., p. 140.
[128] D.B. I, 58. The King had twenty-eight haws rendering £4 3s., but he who was holding it paid £5.

participation. At Northampton it is said bluntly that the burgesses farmed the borough from the sheriff.[129] At Bath, though the wording of the entry is ambiguous, it is likely that the burgesses farmed both the mint and the borough.[130] Dover was, on strategic grounds alone, a special case. The burgesses of Dover did not control the *firma burgi*, but they were exempt from toll throughout the kingdom and, with Fordwich, Romney and Sandwich enjoyed sake and soke in direct return for annual service at sea, in equipping a naval vessel and escorting the king.[131] These privileges indicate the way in which corporate privilege could grow in return for corporate service. Indeed, in so many ways, the *consuetudines* or customs of all these boroughs represent little more in practice than the fruits of that celebrated jingle embodying the normal privileges granted to lords of rural estates. Sake and soke and *infangenetheof* represented the judicial perquisites: toll and team the marketing perquisites. It may not be too outrageous to suggest that the late-eleventh-century borough customs gave a commentary, in more complicated burghal context, on the vaguer attributes of royal control of trade and communications. Definition and more elaborate detail stem from the needs of a more elaborate society.

(f) Conclusion

At the end of this survey, the impression that we wish to leave is of a recognized norm in town life, to which the county boroughs in their varying degrees made rough correspondence. Such a borough would be owned by the king. Two-thirds of the proceeds of justice and dues and customs would go to him. Before 1066 one-third would go to the earl, but now normally this fraction also passed into royal hands. There would be a mint in the borough which, if farmed by the burgesses themselves, would bring in a very substantial sum to the royal coffers. The burgesses would live mostly on the proceeds of trade. A money rent would be paid for the burgage tenement. The burgess would be free to sell or mortgage his tenement. Customs would vary but would be binding on the particular boroughs. Fixed dues would be paid for rights of brewing, the forge and the like. Special legal penalties would fall on those infringing the law of the borough. A big town would be a network of jurisdictions where even the moneyers

---

[129] Ibid., I, 219.
[130] Exon. Domesday: D.B. IV, 106. J. Tait, op. cit., p. 150, n. 5.
[131] D.B. I, 1.

could enjoy rights of sake and soke. If the borough were big, subdivision might well be made for administrative purposes. At the highest level London provided the model with its shiremoot, its wardmoots and hustings. But below the norm lay a multitude of small boroughs that were more agricultural than urban in nature, and a host of villages with markets that nevertheless could not quite be classed as boroughs. Particularly in the south-west, historical reasons combined with the presence of larger and prosperous royal manors elevated little townships like Axbridge and Ilchester into the category of acceptable boroughs. The Conquest both simplified and complicated the pattern. Simplification came from the consolidation of church and lay administration in urban centres, so intensifying the separation of town and country. Complication came from the feudalization of the upper ranks of society, often providing an obscure village with a moment of burghal glory, as the cluster of traders' dwellings consolidated around the stone walls of a new Norman castle. If the economic background were vital enough, then the town survived as a town. And if not, then not. The moulds of urban development in their different shapes and sizes were prepared; but the urban metal had not yet set.

The very interest and complexity of the urban pattern must not, however, detract from the initial premise with which we began this survey. At a liberal estimate not more than one in ten of the inhabitants of England was a town-dweller in any sense of the word. If allowance is made for those bordars and cottars who are counted among the townsmen, the percentage is still smaller. The hard and monotonous daily round of the peasant was the lot of the vast majority of Englishmen. By their toil they had extended the hold of the plough on the lowlands of Britain. Their achievements were not perhaps spectacular, neither were they without merit. To dig foundations is wearisome work. But the foundations of the English economy were well laid.

Bibliography

The bibliography has been redrafted and simplified though the main structure of the equivalent section in the first edition has been retained. Following present-day practice the date of the latest edition of the work cited has been given but the publisher and place of publication mentioned only when such information seems especially useful. No attempt has been made at inclusiveness even on specific topics, but it is hoped that the studies selected will indicate the main lines of thought which the author found helpful in preparing both the first and the revised versions of the book.

PREVIOUS BIBLIOGRAPHIES

1. F.M. Stenton, *Anglo-Saxon England*, Oxford History of England, vol. II, 3rd ed., 1971. There is a fine analytical bibliography with critical notes.
2. D. Whitelock, ed., *English Historical Documents*, vol. I, *c.* A.D. 500–1042, 2nd ed., 1979. This exceptionally valuable volume contains full bibliographical guides to the secular and ecclesiastical history of the period with important bibliographical notes also to many of the individual documents.
3. D.C. Douglas and G.W. Greenway, ed., *English Historical Documents*, vol. II, A.D. 1042–1189, 2nd ed., 1981: the relevant bibliographies and bibliographical notes are valuable.
4. W. Bonser, *Anglo-Saxon and Celtic Bibliography* (450–1087), Oxford, 1957. This was the standard work of reference, and includes material published to the end of 1953. It contains no fewer than

11,975 items. Even so Mr Bonser has excluded 'all material dealing with literature and linguistics as such'. There is a useful supplementary volume of indexes.

5. N.R. Ker, *Catalogue of Manuscripts Containing Anglo-Saxon*, Oxford, 1957. This is indispensable for all advanced students of the period.

6. The best way of keeping abreast of modern writing is by consulting the full bibliographies published annually in *Anglo-Saxon England*, ed. Peter Clemoes, Cambridge U.P. 1972–. *The Old English Newsletter*, published twice yearly since 1967, Binghampton, N.Y. (current editor Paul Szarmach) also provides splendidly full information. The *Annual Bulletin of Historical Literature* published by the Historical Association offers a useful condensed guide to publication.

PRIMARY SOURCES

The task of the student has been lightened by the appearance of the first two volumes of *English Historical Documents*, mentioned above. Both volumes contain in translation a mass of documentation relevant to the social and economic history of the period. Where possible and convenient, footnote references in this book have been made to one or other of these volumes.

1. Laws

The authoritative edition is by the German scholar, F. Liebermann, *Die Gesetze der Angelsachsen* (3 vols., Halle, 1903–16). The text is given in vol. I; a glossary in vol. II, part I; introduction and notes in vol. III. To the social historian vol. II, part 2, is of great importance. In it Liebermann analyses the legal material, supplementing it where necessary from his vast store of knowledge of other sources, under headings such as 'Ehe (marriage), 'König' (the king), and the like. For the English student much work of importance has been done by F.L. Attenborough, *The Laws of the Earliest English Kings*, 1922, and by A.J. Robertson, *The Laws of the Kings of England from Edmund to Henry I*, 1925, and by D. Whitelock, *E.H.D.* I.

For ecclesiastical legislation the essential texts are given in *Councils and Ecclesiastical Documents relating to Great Britain and Ireland*, ed. A.W. Haddan and W. Stubbs, 3 vols, esp. vol. III (1871) which deals with the Anglo-Saxon Church to A.D. 870, and in *Councils and Synods with other documents relating to the English Church, 871–1204*, ed. D. Whitelock, R. Brett and C.N.L. Brooke, 2 vols., 1982.

2. *Charters, wills, writs and other such documents*

The basic collections of charters are those of J.H. Kemble, *Codex Diplomaticus Aevi Saxonici* (6 vols., London, 1839–48) and W. de G. Birch, *Cartularium Saxonicum* (3 vols., London, 1885–93); the latter deals with the period only to the death of Edgar. The best modern approach to such materials comes from a study of the introduction, bibliographies and documents in *E.H.D.* I (see above, and List of Abbrev.), pp. 369–89 and 479–611, from Sir Frank Stenton, *The Latin Charters of the Anglo-Saxon Period*, 1955, and from S.D. Keynes, *The Diplomas of King Æthelred the Unready, 978–1016*, 1980. Modern editions, arranged on an archival basis, in the British Academy *Anglo-Saxon Charters* series are useful (Rochester, 1973; Burton (especially valuable), 1979; Sherborne, 1988). The introductions and notes to the following works are all of a high order of excellence.

(a)   *The Crawford Collection of Early Charters and Documents*, ed. A.S. Napier and W.H. Stevenson, Oxford, 1895, the model of its kind.

(b)   F.E. Harmer, *Select Historical Documents of the Ninth and Tenth Centuries*, 1914.

(c)   D. Whitelock, *Anglo-Saxon Wills*, with preface by H.D. Hazeltine, Cambridge, 1930.

(d)   A.J. Robertson, *Anglo-Saxon Charters*, 1939.

(e)   F.E. Harmer, *Anglo-Saxon Writs*, 1952, reprinted 1989.

(f)   D. Whitelock (with Neil Ker and Lord Rennell) *The Will of Æthelgifu*, Roxburghe Club, Oxford, 1968.

3. *Narrative sources, lives of saints, etc.*

The two major sources of this type, Bede's 'Ecclesiastical History of the English People' and the Anglo-Saxon Chronicle, have both been edited by C. Plummer in works of enduring value: *The Anglo-Saxon Chronicle: Two of the Saxon Chronicles Parallel*, based on an edition by J. Earle, Oxford, 2 vols., 1892 and 1900, reprinted with bibliographical note by D. Whitelock, 1952; and *Venerabilis Baedae Opera Historica*, Oxford, 1896. The best translations appear in E.H.D. I and II; in the revised translation, *The Anglo-Saxon Chronicle*, ed. D. Whitelock, 1961; and in the splendid edition with translation of Bede's *Ecclesiastical History*, ed. B. Colgrave and R.A.B. Mynors, 1969. A good edition of the Peterborough Chronicle (1070–1155), with critical introduction and notes is given by Cecily Clark, Oxford, 2nd ed., 1970. For scholarly purposes the new multi-volumed edition, *The Anglo-Saxon Chronicle*, ed. D. Dumville and S.D. Keynes, 1983–, will be indispensable.

The following modern editions of 'Lives' of the saints are of great importance.

Adomnan's Life of St Columba, ed. A.O. and M.O. Anderson, 1961. The four authoritative editions by B. Colgrave are now available in paperback (1985): *The Life of Bishop Wilfrid by Eddius Stephanus* (1927); *Two Lives of St Cuthbert* (1940); *Felix's Life of St Guthlac* (1956); and *The Earliest Life of Gregory the Great* (1968).

Good guides to the 'Lives' of the eighth-century missionaries and their pupils are given in *E.H.D.* I, pp. 616–9. Most of the texts in question appear in the M.G.H. Alcuin's poem, 'De Pontificibus et Sanctis Ecclesiae Eboracensis', is also edited by J. Raine, *Historians of the Church of York* I, R.S., 1879. The three outstanding collections of eighth-century work (including letters) are part of the Monumenta Germaniae Historica series:

Aldhelm: *Aldhemi Opera*, ed. R. Ehwald, M.G.H., Auctores Antiquissimi XV, Berlin, 1919.

Boniface and Lul: *Bonifatii et Lulli Epistolae*, ed. M. Tangl, M.G.H., *Epistolae Selectae*, I, Berlin, 1916.

Alcuin: *Monumenta Alcuiniana*, ed. W. Wattenbach and E. Dümmler, M.G.H., Berlin, 1873.

The minor works of Bede are best known in the edition of J.A. Giles, *Venerabilis Bedae Opera*, London, 1843. A good edition of Bede's chronological work is given by C.W. Jones, *Bedae Opera de Temporibus*, Cambridge (Mass.), 1943. Peter Godman provides an excellent text with translation of *Alcuin: the bishops, kings and saints of York*, 1982.

For the later Anglo-Saxon period the following material is valuable:

Asser's Life of King Alfred, ed, W.H. Stevenson, 1904, 2nd imp. 1959.

S.D. Keynes and M. Lapidge, *Alfred the Great: Asser's 'Life of King Alfred' and other contemporary sources*, 1983.

The Memorials of St Dunstan, ed. W. Stubbs, R.S., 1874.

Regularis Concordia, ed. Dom T. Symons, 1953.

Frithegodi Monachi Breviloquium vitae beati Wilfredi et Wulfstani Cantoris Narratio Metrica de Sancto Swithuno, ed. A. Campbell, Zurich, 1950.

Encomium Emmae Reginae, ed. A. Campbell, 1949.

Vita Wulfstani, ed. R.R. Darlington, 1928.

From the twelfth-century chroniclers much material appears in the work of William of Malmesbury (*Gesta Pontificum*, ed. N.E.S.A. Hamilton, R.S., 1870, and *Gesta Regum*, ed. W. Stubbs, R.S., 1887–9), of Florence of Worcester (ed. B. Thorpe, 2 vols., London, 1848–9) and of Simeon of Durham (ed. T. Arnold, R.S., 1882–5). There is much of importance also in the *Historians of the Church of York and its Archbishops*, ed. J. Raine, R.S., 1879–94 (3 vols.), and in the *Chronicon Monasterii de Abingdon*, ed. J. Stevenson, R.S., 1858.

4. Anglo-Saxon poetry and prose in the vernacular

S.B. Greenfield and F.C. Robinson, *A Bibliography of Publications on Old English Literature*, 1980, is a good guide to the vernacular literature. A convenient collective edition of Anglo-Saxon poetry appears in the six-volume *The Anglo-Saxon Poetic Records*, ed. G.P. Krapp and E. van Kirk Dobbie, New York, 1931–51.

The following texts are important:

Widsith, ed. K. Malone, London, 1936.

Beowulf with the Finnsburg Fragment, ed. A.J. Wyatt and R.W. Chambers, 1933.

Beowulf and the Finnsburg Fragment, ed. F. Klaeber, rev. ed., Boston and London, 1950.

Beowulf with Finnsburg Fragment, ed. C.F. Wrenn, 1953.

The Exeter Book, part I, ed. I. Gollancz, E.E.T.S., 1895; part II, ed. W.S. Mackie, E.E.T.S., 1934; a facsimile with introductory chapters by R.W. Chambers, Max Förster and Robin Flower was published under the title *The Exeter Book of Old English Poetry*, 1933.

The Battle of Maldon, ed. E.V. Gordon, 1937.

The Life of Saint Chad, ed. R. Vleeskruyer, Amsterdam, 1953.

King Alfred's West Saxon Version of Gregory's Pastoral Care, ed. H. Sweet, E.E.T.S., 1871.

King Alfred's Orosius, ed. H. Sweet, E.E.T.S., 1883.

The Old English Version of Bede's Ecclesiastical History of the English People, ed. T. Miller, E.E.T.S., 1890.

The Benedictine Office: an Old English Text, ed. J.M. Ure, Edinburgh, 1957.

The Homilies of the Anglo-Saxon Church, part I, Catholic Homilies, ed. B. Thorpe, Aelfric Society, London, 1844.
Ælfric's Lives of the Saints, ed. W.W. Skeat, E.E.T.S., 1881–1900.
Ælfric's Grammatik und Glossar, ed. J. Zupitza, Berlin, 1880.
Ælfric's Colloquy, ed. G.N. Garmonsway, 1939.
Wulfstan: Sammlungen der ihm zugeschriebenen Homilien, ed. A.S. Napier, Berlin, 1883.
The Homilies of Wulfstan, ed. D. Betherum, 1957.
Sermo Lupi ad Anglos, ed. D. Whitelock, 2nd ed., 1952.
Die 'Institutes of Polity, Civil and Ecclesiastical', ein Werk Erzbischof Wulfstans von York, ed. K. Jost, Berne, 1959.
Byrhtferth's Manual, ed. S.J. Crawford, 1929.

5. Domesday Book

The authoritative edition was prepared by Abraham Farley and published in two volumes in 1783. Two further volumes, of indexes and of supplementary texts (including the Exon. Domesday), were published by the Record Commission (ed. Henry Ellis) in 1811 and 1816. See below (note on books used in preparing Chapters Eight and Nine), and also D.B. in the List of Abbreviations. In 1986 a facsimile edition of Greater D.B. was published, ed. R.W.H. Erskine, Alecto Historical Editions: county fascicules are in process of publication. The Farley text with translations has been published, ed. J. Morris *et al.*, by Phillimore, 1975–86.

SECONDARY SOURCES

This section of the bibliography has been divided into two parts, the first dealing with works of a general kind, the second dealing with works of special relevance to the particular chapters of the present volume.

1. General histories or works of outstanding importance on particular periods

The firmest general guides are the relevant volumes in the *Oxford History of England*:
Vol. Ia : P. Salway, *Roman Britain*, 1981.
Vol. Ib : J.N.L. Myres, *The English Settlements*, 1986.

Vol. II : F.M. Stenton, *Anglo-Saxon England*, 3rd ed., 1971.
Vol. III : A.L. Poole, *From Domesday Book to Magna Carta*, 1951.

Within their more limited scope the volumes in the *Pelican History of England* are valuable, especially D. Whitelock, *The Beginnings of English Society*, 1952.
Of books of an older generation F.W. Maitland, *Domesday Book and Beyond*, 1897 (Fontana reprint, intro. by Edward Miller, 1961), stands alone as a mine of thought and information. The standard works of J.H. Round, P. Vinogradoff, F. Seebohm, and E. Lipson (some of which are mentioned below) contain much of enduring value. The full implications of H.M. Chadwick, *Studies on Anglo-Saxon Institutions*, 1905, have still not been fully worked out.
In more recent generations the following surveys are especially valuable:
R.H. Hodgkin, *A History of the Anglo-Saxons*, 3rd ed. with note on Sutton Hoo by R.L.S. Bruce-Mitford, 1953.
P. Hunter Blair, *An Introduction to Anglo-Saxon England*, 2nd ed., 1977.
D.P. Kirby, *The Making of Early England*, 1967.
P.H. Sawyer, *From Roman Britain to Norman England*, 1978.
J. Campbell, P. Wormald and E. John, *The Anglo-Saxons*, ed. J. Campbell, 1982: splendidly illustrated, the best short guide to the period.
R. Hodges, *The Anglo-Saxon Achievement: Archaeology and the Beginnings of English Society*, 1989.
There is much of relevance and value in the appropriate volumes of the *Cambridge Economic History of Europe*, 3 vols., 1941–63, and the *Agrarian History of England and Wales*, Cambridge U.P. 1972–.

2. Works of importance relating to chapters of the present volume

(a)   *Settlement and peoples* (Chapter one)

Useful short critical guides to the two basic problems touched on in this chapter remain:

P. Lennard, 'From Roman Britain to Anglo-Saxon England', *Wirtschaft und Kultur* (Festschrift to Alfons Dopsch, Leipzig, 1938).
F.M. Stenton, 'The Danes in England', *Proc. British Academy*, 1927, and the relevant section in *Anglo Saxon England*.

Dark Age Britain, ed. D.B. Harden, 1956, provides a basic introduction to archaeological work on the period. The journals *Medieval Archaeology* (1957–) and on a more modest scale the *Archaeological News letter* and its successors, and *Current Archaeology* offer convenient ways of keeping in touch with archaeological discovery and interpretation. Volumes published by the English Place-Name Society are an indispensable means of entry to this important branch of study as are the works of the following scholars:

O.S. Anderson, *The English Hundred Names*, 3 parts, Lund, 1934–39.

K. Cameron, *English Place-Names*, 1961, and 'The Significance of English Place-Names', *Proc. British Academy*, 1976.

E. Ekwall, *English River-Names*, 1928, and the *Concise Oxford Dictionary of Place-Names*, 4th ed., 1960.

M. Gelling, *Signposts to the Past*, 1978, and *Place-Names in the Landscape*, 1984.

G. Fellows Jensen, 'Place-Name Research and Northern History', *Northern History* vii, Leeds, 1973: and a series of able specialist studies on personal and settlement names in the Danelaw, published Copenhagen, 1968–85.

A.H. Smith, *English Place-Name Elements*, E.P.N.S., 2 vols., 1956.

O. von Feilitzen, *The Pre-Conquest Personal Names of Domesday Book*, Uppsala, 1937.

Apart from studies mentioned in footnotes special attention is drawn to the following books or articles:

P.V. Addyman, 'York in its archaeological setting; *Archaeological Papers from York*, 1984.

L. Alcock, *Arthur's Britain*, 1971.

—*Economy, Society and Warfare among the Britons and Saxons*, c.400–800 A.D., 1987.

C.J. Arnold, *Roman Britain to Saxon England*, 1984.

—*An Archaeology of the Early Anglo-Saxon Kingdoms*, 1988.

S. Bassett, ed., *The Origin of Anglo-Saxon Kingdoms*, 1989, (a valuable survey, containing many original insights).

R.L.S. Bruce-Mitford, *The Sutton Hoo Ship Burial*, 3 vols., 1975–83 : magnificent and authoritative.

K. Cameron, ed., *Place-Name Evidence for the Anglo-Saxon Invasion and Scandinavian Settlements*, 1975.

W. Davies and H. Vierck, 'The contexts of the Tribal Hidage : Social aggregates and settlement patterns', *Frühmittelalterliche Studien*, viii, 1974.

J. McNeal Dodgson, 'The significance of the distribution of the English place-name in -*ingas*, -*inga*, in S.E. England', *M.A.*, x, 1966.

A. Dornier, ed., *Mercian Studies*, 1977.

A. Care Evans, *The Sutton Hoo Ship Burial*, 1986.

V.I. Evison, ed., *Angles, Saxons, and Jutes : Essays presented to J.N.L. Myres*, 1981.

M.L. Faull, ed. *Studies in Late Anglo-Saxon Settlement*, 1984.

H.P.R. Finberg, *Lucerna*, 1952.

M. Gelling, ed., *Offa's Dyke Reviewed*, *B.A.R.* 114, 1983.

R.A. Hall, ed., *Jorvik: Viking Age York*, 1980.

—'The Five Boroughs of the Danelaw', *A.S.E.*, 18, 1988.

D. Hill, *An Atlas of Anglo-Saxon England*, 1981 : skilfully arranged with problems of settlement in mind.

C. Hills, 'The Archaeology of Anglo-Saxon England in the pagan period', *A.S.E.*, 8, 1978.

—'The Anglo-Saxon Settlement of England', *The Northern World*, ed. D.M. Wilson, 1980, pp. 71–94.

R. Hodges, *The Anglo-Saxon Achievement : Archaeology and the Beginnings of English Society*, 1989.

Della Hooke, *The Anglo-Saxon Landscape : the Kingdom of the Hwicce*, 1985.

—ed., *Anglo-Saxon Settlements*, 1988.

B. Hope-Taylor, *Yeavering. An Anglo-British Centre of Early Northumbria*. 1977.

W.G. Hoskins and H.P.R. Finberg, *Devonshire Studies*, 1952.

K. Jackson, *Language and History in Early Britain*, 1953.

O. Jesperson, *Growth and Structure of the English Language*, 1935.

E. John, *Orbis Britanniae and Other Studies*, 1966.

A.K.G. Kristensen, 'Danelaw Institutions and Danish Society in the Viking Age', *Medieval Scandinavia*, 8, 1975.

H.R. Loyn, *The Vikings in Britain*, 1977.

J.N.L. Myres, *Anglo-Saxon Pottery and the Settlement of England*, 1969.

J. Percival, *The Roman Villa*, 1976.

P.H. Sawyer, 'The Two Viking Ages of Britain', *Medieval Scandinavia*, 1969.

—*The Age of the Vikings*, 2nd ed., 1971.

—*Early Medieval Settlement : Continuity and Change*, 1979.

P. Sims-Williams, 'The Settlement of England in Bede and the Chronicle', *A.S.E.*, 12, 1983.

A.H. Smith, 'Place-Names and the Anglo-Saxon Settlement', *Proc. British Academy*, 1956.

L. Smith, ed., *The Making of Britain : the Dark Ages*, 1984.

A.P. Smyth, *Scandinavian York and Dublin*, 2 vols., 1975–79.
—*Scandinavian Kings in the British Isles, 850–880*, 1977.
P. Stafford, *The East Midlands in the Early Middle Ages*, 1988.
F.M. Stenton, Presidential addresses to the Royal Historical Society
: *T.R. Hist. S.*, 1939–45, especially 1941, 'Anglo-Saxon Heathenism'
and 1942, 'The Danish Settlement of Eastern England'.
C.E. Stevens, 'Gildas Sapiens', *E.H.R.*, 1941.
F.T. Wainwright, 'Ingimund's Invasion', *E.H.R.*, 1948.

(b)   *The European setting and overseas trade* (Chapter two)

Good basic introductions to these problems come from the work
of P. Grierson and W. Levison mentioned below, supplemented
now by the recent investigations of R. Hodges and D. Whitehouse.
French or Francophone scholars have been greatly influential in
general interpretation of the evolution of the European economy
and the following studies, all available in English, remain fundamental:

Marc Bloch, *Feudal Society*, 1939–40, Eng. trs., 1961.
R. Latouche, *The Birth of Western Economy*, 1956, Eng. trs.,
1961.
G. Duby, *Rural Economy and Country Life in the Medieval West*,
Eng. trs., 1968.

The following books and articles are useful:

D. Bullough, *The Age of Charlemagne*, 1965.
R. Collins, *Early Medieval Spain*, 1983.
P. Grierson, *Dark Age Numismatics*, 1979.
P. Grierson and M. Blackburn, *Medieval European Coinage I :
Early Middle Ages (5th –10th Centuries)*, 1986 : work of massive
and fundamental importance (*M.E.C.* I).
F. Havighurst, *The Pirenne Thesis*, 1958.
J. Herrin, *The Formation of Christendom*, 1987.
R. Hodges and D. Whitehouse, *Mohammed, Charlemagne and
the Origins of Europe*, 1983.
R. Hodges and B. Hobley, eds., *The Rebirth of Towns in the
West, A.D. 700–1050, B.A.R.* 68, 1968.
E. James, *The Origins of France, 500–1000*, 1982.
—*The Franks*, 1988.

H.H. Lamb, *Climate, History and the Northern World*, 1982.

W. Levison, *England and the Continent in the Eighth Century*, 1946.

A.R. Lewis, *The Northern Seas*, 1958.

R.S. Lopez, 'Mohammed and Charlemagne, a Revision', *Speculum*, 1943.

D.M. Metcalf, 'The Prosperity of North-Western Europe in the Eighth and Ninth Centuries', *Econ. H.R.*, 1967.

J. Nelson and M. Gibson, eds., *Charles the Bald, Court and Kingdom*, 1981.

H. Pirenne, *Mahomet and Charlemagne*, 1939.

C.H.V. Sutherland, *Anglo-Saxon Gold Coinage in the Light of the Crondall Hoard*, 1948.

J.M. Wallace-Hadrill, *The Barbarian West*, 3rd ed., 1967.

C. Wickham, *Early Medieval Italy, 400–1000*, 1981.

P. Wormald, ed., *Ideal and Reality in Frankish and Anglo-Saxon Society*, 1983.

(c)   *Internal trade : the coinage and the towns* (Chapter three)

Internal trade

Apart from the evidence of the law-codes archaeological material offers the best hope of understanding the internal trade of Anglo-Saxon England. A convenient basic guide is given by D.M. Wilson, ed., *The Archaeology of Anglo-Saxon England*, 1976, which includes essays by Martin Biddle on Towns, J.G. Hurst on the pottery, and by Wilson himself on craft and industry. The periodical *Medieval Archaeology* (*M.A.*) presents regular discussion of pottery, metalwork, sculpture, carpentry etc.

Among specialist studies mention should be made of D.M. Wilson, *Anglo-Saxon Ornamental Metalwork, 700–1100, in the British Museum*, 1964; D.A. Hinton, *Catalogue of Anglo-Saxon Metalwork in the Ashmolean Museum*, 1974; R.N. Bailey, *Viking-Age Sculpture in Northern England*, 1980; and the authoritative and splendid volumes, gen. ed. Rosemary Cramp, of the *Corpus of Anglo-Saxon Stone Sculpture*, British Academy, 1984– .

Coinage

No field has been more active and the serious student must consult regularly *British Numismatic Journal* and the *Numismatic Chronicle*.

Anglo Saxon England and the Norman Conquest

More than forty volumes have been published in the last generation of the *Sylloge of Coins of the British Isles*, British Academy, 1958– , most of which deal with the Anglo-Saxon series. *Anglo-Saxon Coins*, ed. R.H.M. Dolley, 1961, a *festschrift* to Sir Frank Stenton, brought together several important studies on which modern work has been built. The best guide to much of the Anglo-Saxon coinage is now to be found in the sections by Mark Blackburn in *Medieval European Coinage* I, 1986 (above, section (b) : P. Grierson and M. Blackburn).

Other studies of exceptional importance are:

M. Blackburn, ed., *Anglo-Saxon Monetary History : Essays in Memorial of Michael Dolley*, 1986, with full bibliographical reference to Dolley's phenomenal output.

C.E. Blunt, 'The Anglo-Saxon Coinage and the Historian', *M.A.*, iv, 1961.

—'The Coinage of Athelstan, 924–39 : a Survey', *B.N.J.*, 42, 1974.

C.E. Blunt, B.H.I.H. Stewart, and C.S.S. Lyon, *Coinage in Tenth-Century England from Edward the Elder to Edgar's Reform*, 1989.

D. Hill and D.M. Metcalf, eds., *Sceattas in England and on the Continent*, *B.A.R.* 128, 1984.

K. Jonsson ed., *Studies in Late Anglo-Saxon Coinage*, Stockholm, 1990.

C.S.S. Lyon, 'Some Problems in Interpreting Anglo-Saxon Coinage', *A.S.E.*, 5, 1976 : also his valuable presidential addresses, *B.N.J.*, 36–39, 1967–70.

D.M. Metcalf, 'How Large was the Anglo-Saxon Currency?', *Econ. H.R.*, 18, 1965.

—'The Ranking of Boroughs : The Numismatic Evidence from the Reign of Æthelred II', *Ethelred the Unready : Papers from the Millenary Conference*, ed. D. Hill, *B.A.R.* 59, 1978.

—'Continuity and Change in English Monetary History, c.973–1086', *B.N.J.*, 50 and 51, 1981–82.

C.H.V. Sutherland, *Anglo-Saxon Gold Coinage in the Light of the Crondall Hoard*, 1948.

Trade and towns

J. Tait, *The Medieval English Borough*, 1936, still offers a powerful guide, as do the older works of F.W. Maitland and Mary Bateson. A useful general modern account is by S. Reynolds, *An Introduction to the History of the English Medieval Town*, 1977.

410

Important detailed studies include:

M. Biddle, 'Archaeology and the Beginnings of English Society', *England before the Conquest*, ed. P. Clemoes and K. Hughes, 1971.

—ed., *Winchester in the Early Middle Ages*, I, 1976 – further volumes forthcoming.

—'The Study of Winchester : Archaeology and History in a British Town, 1963–81', *Proc. British Academy*, 69, 1983.

J. Clark, *Saxon and Norman London*, 1989.

P. Grierson, 'The Relations between England and Flanders before the Norman Conquest', *T.R. Hist. S.*, 1941.

—'Commerce in the Dark Ages : a Critique of the Evidence', *T.R. Hist. S.*, 1959.

R.A. Hall, ed., *Viking Age York and the North*, 1978.

J. Haslam, ed., *Anglo-Saxon Towns in Southern England*, 1984.

D. Hill, 'The Burghal Hidage : the Establishment of a Text', *M.A.*, 13, 1969.

D. Hinton, *Alfred's Kingdom : Wessex and the South 800–1500*, 1977.

R. Hodges and B. Hobley, eds., *The Rebirth of Towns in the West, A.D. 700–1050*, 1988 : includes papers on London, York, Chester, Ipswich, and Southampton (*Hamwic*).

H.R. Loyn, 'Towns in Late Anglo-Saxon England', *England before the Conquest*, ed., P. Clemoes and K. Hughes, 1971.

F.W. Maitland, *Township and Borough*, 1898.

P. Nightingale, 'The Origin of the Court of Husting and Danish influence on London's development into a capital city', *E.H.R.*, 1987.

C.A. Ralegh Radford, 'The later pre-conquest boroughs and their defences', *M.A.*, xiv, 1970.

—'The pre-conquest boroughs of England, ninth-eleventh centuries', *Proc. British Academy*, 1980 (for 1978).

Carl Stephenson, 'The Anglo-Saxon borough', *E.H.R.*, 1930.

J.H. Williams, 'From 'palace' to 'town' : Northampton and Urban Origins', *A.S.E.* 13, 1984.

(d)   *The land* (Chapter four)

Of all topics in Anglo-Saxon social and economic history this perhaps is perhaps the most difficult to handle at the present stage of archaeological knowledge and technique. Older work of scholars such as F.W. Maitland, F. Seebohm, and P. Vinogradoff contains much of enduring value. The best single introduction to the working of rural society in the later phases of this period comes from R. Lennard, referred to below. On the controversial question of the open fields the third edition of the Orwins' classic study, listed below, remains the essential starting point.

R. Abels, *Lordship and Military Obligation in Anglo-Saxon England*, 1988.

P.V. Addyman, 'The Anglo-Saxon village at Chalton, Hampshire', *M.A.*, xvii, 1973.

T.H. Aston, 'The Origins of the Manor in England', *Social Relations and Ideas : essays in honour of R.H. Hilton*, ed. T.H. Aston *et al.*, 1983 : an elaboration of the author's important article of the same name, *T.R. Hist. S.*, 1958.

E. Barger, 'The present position of studies in English field-systems', *E.H.R.*, 1938.

R. Bennett and J. Elton, *History of Corn-Milling*, 4 vols., 1898–1904.

M.W. Beresford, *The Lost Villages of England*, 1954.

M.W. Beresford and J.K.S. St Joseph, *Medieval England : an Aerial Survey*, 1958.

M.W. Beresford and J.G. Hurst, eds., *Deserted Medieval Villages*, 1971.

N.P. Brooks, 'Anglo-Saxon Charters : the work of the last twenty years'. *A.S.E.*, 3, 1974.

M.L. Faull, ed., *Studies in Late Anglo-Saxon Settlement*, 1984.

P.J. Fowler, *Recent work on Rural Archaeology*, 1975.

'Farming in the Anglo-Saxon Landscape : an archaeologist's review', *A.S.E.*, 9, 1981.

H.L. Gray, *English Field Systems*, Cambridge (Mass.), 1915.

C.R. Hart, *The Hidation of Northamptonshire*, 1970.

H. Helbæk, 'Early Crops in Southern England', *Proceedings of the Prehistoric Society*, 1952.

D. Hooke, ed., *Medieval Villages*, 1985.

—ed., *Anglo-Saxon Settlements*, 1988.

K. Jessen and H. Helbæk, *Cereals in Great Britain and Ireland in Prehistoric and Early Historic Times*, Copenhagen, 1944.

J. Langdon, *Horses, Oxen and Technological Innovation*, 1986.

R. Lennard, *Rural England 1086–1135*, 1959.

F.W. Maitland, *Domesday Book and Beyond*, 1897 (reprinted with introduction by E. Miller, 1960).

C.S. and C.S. Orwin, *The Open Fields*, 3rd ed. with preface by J. Thirsk, 1967.

F.G. Payne, 'The Plough in Ancient Britain', *Archaeological Journal*, 1948.

—'The British Plough : some stages in its development', *Agricultural History Review*, 1957.

T.F.T. Plucknett, 'Bookland and Folkland', *Econ. H.R.*, vi, 1935.

H.G. Richardson, 'The Medieval Plough Team', *History*, 1942.

F. Seebohm, *The English Village Community*, 4th ed., 1905.

W.H. Stevenson, 'Trinoda Necessitas', *E.H.R.*, 1914.

C. Taylor, *Village and Farmstead: a History of Rural Settlement in England*, 1983.

G.J. Turner, 'Bookland and Folkland', *Historical Essays in honour of James Tait*, ed. J.G. Edwards, V. Galbraith and E.F. Jacob, 1933.

P. Vinogradoff, 'Folkland', *E.H.R.*, 1893.

—*The Growth of the Manor*, 2nd ed., 1911.

(e)   *Kingship and nobility* (Chapter five)

A convenient source for evidence relating to these problems remains H.M. Chadwick, *Studies on Anglo-Saxon Institutions*. Valuable general studies of the last generation include Marc Bloch, *The Royal Touch* (eng. trs. of *Les Rois Thaumaturges*, 1924), Fritz Kern, *Kingship and Law* (Eng. trs., 1939, of *Gottesgnadentum und Wiederstandsrechts . . .*, 1914), and P.E. Schramm, *A History of the English Coronation*, 1937.

The following books and articles are valuable:

S. Bassett, ed., *The Origin of Anglo-Saxon Kingdoms*, 1989.

D.A. Binchy, *Celtic and Anglo-Saxon Kingship*, 1970.

F.J. Byrne, *Irish Kings and High Kings*, 1973.

W.A. Chaney, *The Cult of Kingship in Anglo-Saxon England*, 1970.

P. Guilhiermoz, *Essai sur l'origine de la noblesse en France au moyen âge*, Paris, 1902.

S.D. Keynes, 'A Tale of Two Kings : Alfred the Great and Æthelred the Unready', *T.R. Hist. S.*, 1986.

L.M. Larson, *The King's Household in England before the Norman Conquest*, Wisconsin, 1904.

F. Liebermann, *The National Assembly in the Anglo-Saxon period*, Halle, 1913.

A.G. Little, 'Gesiths and Thegns', *E.H.R.*, 1889.

H.R. Loyn, 'The term *Ealdorman* in the Translations prepared at the time of King Alfred', *E.H.R.*, 1953.

—'Gesiths and Thegns in England from the Seventh to the Tenth Century', *E.H.R.*, 1955.

—'The Imperial Style of the Anglo-Saxon Kings', *History*, 1955.

J. Nelson, *Politics and Ritual in Early Medieval Europe*, 1986.

T.J. Oleson, *The Witenagemot in the Reign of Edward the Confessor*, Toronto, 1955.

P. Rahtz, 'The Saxon and Medieval Palaces at Cheddar', *B.A.R.*, 65, 1979.

S. Reynolds, *Kingdoms and Communities in Western Europe 900–1300*, 1984.

P.H. Sawyer and I.N. Wood, eds., *Early Medieval Kingship*, 1977.

K. Sisam, 'The Anglo-Saxon Royal Genealogies', *Proc. British Academy*, 39, 1953.

P. Stafford, *Queens, Concubines and Dowagers : the King's Wife in the Early Middle Ages*, 1983.

W. Ullmann, *The Carolingian Renaissance and the Idea of Kingship*, 1969.

H. Vollrath-Reichelt, *Königtum und Königsgedanke bei den Angelsachsen*, Cologne, 1971.

J.M. Wallace-Hadrill, *Early Germanic Kingship in England and on the Continent*, 1971.

J.H. Williams, *et. al.*, *Middle Saxon Palaces at Northampton*, 1985.

(f)   *The Church, learning and literature* (Chapter six)

The best introduction to the conversion of the Anglo-Saxons is H. Mayr-Harting, *The Coming of Christianity to Anglo-Saxon England*, 1972. For the work of the Anglo-Saxon missionaries on the Continent, W. Levison's study (section b above) remains indispensable. S.B. Greenfield and D.G. Calder provide a useful survey (with an account of the Anglo-Latin context by Michael Lapidge) in *A New Critical History of Old English Literature*, 1986. H.M. and J. Taylor, *Anglo-Saxon Architecture*, 3 vols, 1965–78, give a splendid detailed description of the standing churches from the period.

The following books and articles are useful:

J. Backhouse, *The Lindisfarne Gospels*, 1981.

J. Backhouse, D. Turner and L. Webster, eds., *The Golden Age of Anglo-Saxon Art 966–1066* (Introduction by S. Keynes), 1984.

F. Barlow, *The English Church, 1000–1066*, 2nd ed., 1972.

J. Bately, 'Old English Prose before and during the Reign of Alfred', *A.S.E.*, 17, 1988.

J. Blair, *Ministers and Parish Churches : the Local Church in Transition, 950–1200*, 1988.

P. Hunter Blair, *The World of Bede*, 1970.

G. Bonner, ed., *Famulus Christi*, 1976.

—ed., *St Cuthbert, his Cult and his Community to 1200*, 1989.

W. Bonser, *The Medical Background of Anglo-Saxon England*, 1963.

N.P. Brooks, *The Early History of the Church of Canterbury*, 1984 : exceptionally important.

G. Baldwin Brown, *The Arts in Early England*, 6 vols., 1903–37.

L.A.S. Butler and R.K. Morris, *The Anglo-Saxon Church*, C.B.A. 60, 1986.

J. Campbell, *Essays on Anglo-Saxon History*, 1986 : includes valuable studies on the Conversion.

A.G.I. Christie, *English Medieval Embroidery*, 1938.

A.W. Clapham, *English Romanesque Architecture before the Conquest*, 1930.

P. Clemes, ed., *Anglo-Saxon England* (Essays presented to Bruce Dickins), 1959.

R.R. Darlington, 'Ecclesiastical Reform in the Late Old English Period', *E.H.R.*, 1936.

M. Deanesley, *The Pre-Conquest Church in England*, 1961.

C.R. Dodwell, *Anglo-Saxon Art : a new perspective*, 1982.

E.S. Duckett, *Anglo-Saxon Saints and Scholars*, 1947 : and later readable biographies of *Alcuin* (1951), *Dunstan* (1955) and *Alfred* (1957).

E. Fernie, *The Architecture of the Anglo-Saxons*, 1983.

P. Grierson, 'Grimbald of St Bertins', *E.H.R.*, 1940.

G. Henderson, *From Durrow to Kells : the Insular Gospel Books, 650–800*, 1987.

K. Hughes, *The Church in Early Irish Society*, 1966.

D. Knowles, *The Monastic Order in England*, 1940 : indispensable and authoritative.

M.L.W. Laistner, *Thought and Letters in Western Europe*, 2nd ed., 1957.

M. Lapidge and H. Gneuss, eds., *Learning and Literature in Anglo-Saxon England*, 1985.

C.H. Lawrence, ed., *The English Church and the Papacy in the Middle Ages*, 1965.

C. Morris, 'William I and the Church Courts', *E.H.R.*, 1967.

J.D.A. Ogilvy, *Books well-known to Anglo-Latin writers from Aldhelm to Alcuin (670–804)*, Cambridge (Mass.), 1936.

R. Page, *An Introduction to English Runes*, 1973.

D. Parsons, ed., *Tenth-Century Studies*, 1975.

—'Sites and Monuments of the Anglo-Saxon Mission in Central Germany', *Archaeological Journal* 140, 1983

T. Reuter, ed., *The Greatest Englishman : Essays on St Boniface and the Church at Crediton*, 1980.

D. Talbot Rice, *English Art, 871–1100*, 1951.

J.A. Robinson, *The Times of St Dunstan*, 1923.

D.W. Rollason, *Saints, Shrines and Relics in Anglo-Saxon England*, 1991.

K. Sisam, *Studies in the History of Old English Literature*, 1953.

F.M. Stenton, *The Early History of the Abbey of Abingdon*, 1913.

T. Symons, 'The English Monastic Reform of the Tenth Century', *Downside Review*, 1942.

P.E. Szarmach, ed., *Sources of Anglo-Saxon Culture*, 1986.

C. Thomas, *Christianity in Roman Britain to A.D. 500*, 1981.

J.R.R. Tolkien, 'Beowulf, the Monsters, and the Critics, *Proc. British Academy*, 22, 1936.

D. Whitelock, 'The Conversion of the Eastern Danelaw', *Saga-book of the Viking Club*, 1941.

—'Archbishop Wulfstan, Homilist and Statesman', *T.R. Hist. S.*, 1942.

—*The Audience of Beowulf*, 1951.

D.M. Wilson and O. Klindt-Jensen, *Viking Art*, 1966.

F. Wormald, *English Drawings of the Tenth and Eleventh Centuries*, 1952.

P. Wormald, 'The Uses of Literacy in Anglo-Saxon England and its Neighbours', *T.R. Hist. S.*, 1977.

—ed., *Ideal and Reality in Frankish and Anglo-Saxon Society*, 1983.

C.E. Wright, *The Cultivation of Saga in Anglo-Saxon England*, 1939.

B. Yorke, ed., *Bishop Aethelwold : his career and influence*, 1988.

(g)   *The major social changes* (Chapter seven)

There is a good introduction to this topic in D. Whitelock, *The Beginnings of English Society*, 1952. Useful guides to the general state of late Old English society are given by R.R. Darlington, 'The last phase of Anglo-Saxon History', *History*, 1937, and by H.R.

Loyn, 'The King and the Structure of Society in Late Anglo-Saxon England', *History*, 1957.

The following books and articles are useful:

R. Abels, *Lordship and Military Organisation in Anglo-Saxon England*, 1988.

N.P. Brooks, 'England in the ninth century : the crucible of defeat', *T.R. Hist. S.*, 1979.

D. Bullough, 'Early Medieval Social Groupings : the terminology of kinship', *Past and Present*, 1969.

H.M. Cam, *Local Government in Francia and England*, 1912.

T.M. Charles-Edwards, 'Kinship status and the origins of the hide', *Past and Present*, 1972.

W. Davies and P. Fouracre, eds., *The Settlement of Disputes in Early Medieval Europe*, 1986.

S.T. Driscoll and M.R. Nieke, eds., *Power and Politics in Early Medieval Britain and Ireland*, 1988.

C. Fell, C. Clark and E. Williams, *Women in Anglo-Saxon England and the Impact of 1066*, 1984.

R. Fleming, 'Monastic Lands and England : Defence in the Viking Age', *E.H.R.*, 1985.

J.Gillingham, 'The Most Precious Jewel in the English Crown : levels of Danegeld and heregeld in the early eleventh century', *E.H.R.*, 1989.

C. R. Hart, 'The Tribal Hidage', *T.R. Hist. S.*, 1971.

J.E.A. Jolliffe, 'The Era of the Folk in English History', *Essays presented to H.E. Salter*, 1934.

M.K. Lawson, 'The Collection of Danegeld and heregeld in the reigns of Aethelred II and Cnut', *E.H.R.*, 1984.

H.R. Loyn, 'Kinship in Anglo-Saxon England', *A.S.E.*, 3, 1974.

—'The Hundred in England in the tenth and early eleventh centuries', *British Government and Administration*, eds., H. Hearder and H.R. Loyn, 1974.

D. Pelteret, 'Slave Raiding and Slave Trading in Early England', *A.S.E.*, 9, 1981.

W.G. Runciman, 'Accelerating Social Mobility : the case of Anglo-Saxon England', *Past and Present*, 1984.

P.A. Stafford, *Unification and Conquest : England in the Tenth and Eleventh Centuries*, 1989.

W.H. Stevenson, 'Trinoda Necessitas', *E.H.R.*, 1914.

C.S. Taylor, 'The Origin of the Mercian Shires', (Bristol, 1898), reprinted H.P.R. Finberg, *Gloucestershire Studies*, 1958.
A. Williams, 'Land and power in the eleventh century : the estates of Harold Godwineson', *Proceedings of the Battle Conference*, 1980.

(h)   *The Norman Conquest, and England at the end of the eleventh century* (Chapters eight and nine)

So much has been written on these topics since the first edition of this book that it would be ludicrous to attempt a full bibliography. The celebrations of the anniversaries of the Conquest itself in 1966 and then of Domesday Book in 1986 stimulated a massive production of literature of useful though variable quality. Of the work of the last generation the books of F.M. Stenton, D.C. Douglas, F. Barlow and J. Le Patourel remain valuable. F.M. Stenton, *The First Century of English Feudalism*, 2nd ed. 1961, provides the basic orthodox view of feudalism and the Norman Conquest. R. Allen Brown's series of Battle Abbey Conference papers (later produced under the title *Anglo-Norman Studies*) give the serious student the best opportunity of keeping in touch with current thought. D. Bates, *Bibliography of Domesday Book*, 1986, provides an indispensable guide. The completion of M. Chibnall's superb edition of *Ordericus Vitalis, Historia Ecclesiastica*, 6 vols., 1969–80, and of H.C. Darby's magisterial *Domesday Geography*, 6 vols., 1952–75, have added a new dimension to study of the period.

The following studies, many incorporating detailed bibliographical reference are specially commended:

F. Barlow, *William I and the Norman Conquest*, 1965.
—*The English Church, 1066–1154*, 1979.
D. Bates, *Normandy before 1066*, 1982.
—*William I*, 1989.
R. Allen Brown, ed., *Proceedings of the Battle Conference* and *Anglo-Norman Studies*, 1979–89.
—*The Normans and the Norman Conquest*, 2nd ed., 1985.
M. Chibnall, *The World of Orderic Vitalis*, 1984.
—*Anglo-Norman England, 1066–1166*, 1986.
R.H.M. Dolley, *The Norman Conquest and the English Coinage*, 1966.
D.C. Douglas, *The Social Structure of Medieval East Anglia*, 1927.

—*The Norman Conquest and British Historians*, 1946 : a good short guide to the historiography.
—*William the Conqueror*, 1964.
R.A Welldon Finn, *The Norman Conquest and its effects on the economy, 1066–86*, 1971.
V.H. Galbraith, *The Making of Domesday Book*, 1961.
—*Domesday Book : its place in administrative history*, 1974.
P. Grierson, 'Domesday Book, the Geld *De Moneta*, and *Monetagium* : a forgotten minting reform', *B.N.J.*, 55, 1986.
C. Harper-Bill, *et. al.*, eds., *Studies in Medieval History presented to R. Allen Brown*, 1989.
C.W. Hollister, *Anglo-Saxon Military Institutions on the Eve of the Norman Conquest*, 1962.
—*The Military Organisation of Norman England*, 1965.
J.C. Holt, ed., *Domesday Studies*, 1987 : valuable collection of papers read at the Winchester commemoration meeting of the Domesday Book anniversary.
N. Hurnard, 'The Anglo-Norman Franchises', *E.H.R.*, 1949.
R. Lennard, *Rural England, 1086–1135*, 1959 : an indispensable and authoritative guide.
J. Le Patourel, *The Norman Empire*, 1976.
H.R. Loyn, *The Norman Conquest*, 3rd ed., 1982.
J. MacDonald and G.D. Snooks, *Domesday Economy : a new approach to Anglo-Norman History, 1986* : and valuable contributions to new statistical approaches to Domesday Book in papers for the *Economic History Review*, 1985, and for the *Journal of Economic History*, 1985.
W.A. Morris, *The Medieval English Sheriff to 1300*, 1927.
J.O. Prestwich, 'Anglo-Norman feudalism and the problem of continuity', *Past and Present*, 1963.
J.H. Round, *Feudal England*, 1895, reissued 1964.
P.H. Sawyer, 'The Wealth of England in the Eleventh Century', *T.R. Hist. S.*, 1965.
—ed., *Domesday Book : a Reassessment*, 1985.
E. Searle, *Predatory Kinship and the Creation of Norman Power*, 1988.
F.M. Stenton, *Types of Manorial Structure in the Northern Danelaw*, 1910.
—'English Families and the Norman Conquest', *T.R. Hist. S.*, 1944.
—ed., *The Bayeux Tapestry*, 1957.
C. Stephenson, 'Feudalism and its antecedents in England', *American Historical Review*, xlviii, 1943.
P. Vinogradoff, *Villeinage in England*, 1892.
English Society in the Eleventh Century, 1908.

D. Whitelock *et al..*, The Norman Conquest : its setting and impact, 1966.
D.M. Wilson, ed., *The Bayeux Tapestry*, 1985.

Among titles published too late or not available for use in the preparation of this edition the following are of special interest:

H. Damico and A.H. Olsen, eds., *New Readings on Women in Old English Literature*, Indiana U.P., 1991.
Sonia Hawkes, ed., *Weapons and Warfare in Anglo-Saxon England* Oxford University Committee for Archaeology, 21, Oxford, 1989.
E. Mason, *St. Wulfstan of Worcester, c.1008–1097*, 1990.
P. Sims Williams, *Religion and Literature in Western England, 600–800*, 1990.
I. Wood and N. Lund, eds., *Peoples and Places in Northern Europe, 500–1600*, 1991.

Index

Index

architecture, 298
Aristotle, 279
Arundel, 288
Ashford, 106
Aspatria, 61
Asser, Bishop, 218, 223, 287, 291, 368
Aston, T.H., 170, 171, 193
Athelney, 251
Athelstan, Bishop, 189
Athelstan, Earl, Half-King, 177, 221
Athelstan, King, 50, 54, 60, 118, 125–7,
    130, 134, 137, 140, 204, 243, 247, 260,
    264, 274, 282, 285, 288, 311–12
Athelstan, Prince, 108, 133, 230
Athelstan of Sunbury, 119
Attila, 71
Augustine, St., Archbishop of
    Canterbury, 5, 67–8, 73, 143, 178,
    234, 237–8, 248, 267, 311
Augustine, St., Bishop of Hippo, 113,
    220, 239, 275–7, 279, 291–2
aulae, 228–9, 352–3, 371
Awre, 111
Axbridge, 398
Axminster, 50
Aylton, 190

Bakewell, 106, 139
Baldwin, Abbot, 383
Ballard, A., 384, 388
Balthild, 90
Barger, E., 19
barley, 156–7
Barnstaple, 148
barons, 331, 333, 390–1; *see also*
    lordship; noblemen
Bateson, 387, 388
Bath, 35, 149, 335, 397
Bath and Wells, 259
Battersea, 372
Battesford, 372
Bayeux Tapestry, 159, 336
Bebbanburh (Bamburgh), 142
Beccles, 375
Bede, 2, 12, 23–4, 27, 29, 38, 40, 48,
    67–8, 84–5, 90, 93, 108, 113, 115,
    142, 144, 173, 176, 178–9, 186, 188,
    217–18, 236–7, 249–50, 277, 279–81,
    283–5, 291–3, 296–7, 300, 317, 324;
    Ecclesiastical History, 67, 209, 232,
    279–80, 285
Bedford, 139
Bedwyn, 147
Benedict Biscop, 93, 115, 278
Benedict, St., of Nursia, 240, 251, 292
Beonna, 124

Beorhtric, King, 102
Beowulf, 102, 108, 114, 209, 215, 228,
    275, 278, 285–7, 289, 309, 317
berewick, 156–7, 195, 350, 353, 355
Berhtwold, Archbishop of Canterbury,
    278
Berkeley, 315, 385
Bernicia, 12, 23, 36, 54, 228, 248
Bibury, 183
Billingsgate, 96–7
bishops, 232–77 *passim*
Bisley, 387
Bjorko, 85
Blackley, 372
Bloch, M., 81, 91, 170
blood money, *see* wergeld
Boethius, 220, 279, 291, 292–3
Böhmer, H., 256, 257
Bohun, 333
Bokerly Junction, 20
Bolin, S., 134
Boniface, St., Archbishop of Mainz, 50,
    84, 239, 241, 250, 272
Book of Durrow, 282
Book of Kells, 282
bookland, 178–81, 227, 273, 304, 315
bordars, 109, 197, 338, 357–8, 362, 365,
    383, 398
borgbryce, 214
boroughs, *see* burh and towns
Bosham, 267
Botto, 83
Bourne (Brabourne), 191
bovarii, 338, 364
Bradwell-on-Sea, 30
Brailes, 111
Bremesbyrig, 139
Bridgnorth, 140
Bridstow, 13
Brihtric, 189
Brihtwulf, King, 315
Bristol, 90, 100, 385, 390
Britanny, 4
Brittia, 28
Brixworth, 116, 284
Brockenhurst, 378
Bromley, 389
Brooks, N. P., 42, 43
Brun, 190
Brunanburh, 288
Bruton, 129
bucellarii, 72, 76
Buckingham, 139–40
Bulley, 387
burgesses, 97, 149, 257, 375, 385–90,
    394–5, 397

422

Index

Index

freemen, 57, 180, 265, 307, 340, 350, 357ff., 367
Frisia, 28–9, 68, 83
Frisians, as traders, 85–6
Fulham, 360
fyrd, 90, 164, 196 (fyrd-service), 326

gafolgelda, 193, 216
Gaimar, 335
garrison theory, 141
Gaul, 17, 26, 71–2, 283
gebur, 193, 198ff., 202, 216, 367
gegildan, 146, 307
geld, 90, 182, 195, 203, 270, 314, 315–25, 353, 354, 393
geneat, 197, 202, 367
Geoffrey de Manneville, 350
Gerefa, 12, 106, 152, 200–1
Gervaldus, Abbot of St Wandrille, 87
gesett land, 170ff., 193, 202
gesith, 114, 178, 208–10, 218
Gilbert of Belvache, 350–1
Gildas, 1, 4, 12, 16, 29, 282
glassware, 86, 90, 99, 104, 106, 113–16
Glastonbury, 108, 116, 252, 258, 282, 298
Gloucester, 35, 104–5, 131, 144, 347, 385, 386, 387, 391, 395
goats, 381
Godmanchester, 39
Godric, 395
Godwin, Earl, 222, 275, 335
Godwin, thegn, 109
gold, 76–8, 99, 109, 114, 229–31
Goring, 26
Gower, 326
Grately, 125, 127, 149
graveyard, 262
Great Chesterford, 18
Green Norton, 105
Gregory I, St., Pope, 36, 67–8, 74, 77, 90, 133, 142–3, 145, 205, 220, 233, 237–40, 242, 248, 255, 267, 276–7, 279, 291–3
Gregory of Tours, 72, 279
Gretton, 105
Grierson, P., 122
Grimbald, 218, 291
Guildford, 389
guilds, 144, 146; thegn's, 147ff., 395
Gundulf, Bishop of Rochester, 259, 330, 332
Guthlac, St., 6, 11, 22, 186, 211, 240, 297

hall moots, 195
Halwell, 140
Ham, East and West, 372
hamlets, 19ff., 344, 346
Hampton Lucy, 316
Hamwih see Southampton
Harbury, 378
Harden, D.B., 115, 116
Harduin of Scalers, 350
Hardwell, 167
Harold, King, 129, 222, 386
harp, 115
Harpswell, 351
Harrow, 31
Harthacnut, King, 323
Hastings, 26, 32, 140; battle of, 224, 323, 327
Haswic, 380
Hatfield, 187, 235
Hatfield Chase, 324
Hawkes, C.F.C., 41
hawking, 368
hays, 380
Heahberht, 124
Hedeby, 85, 94
Helmstan, Bishop, 249
Hemming, 184, 196, 323
Hengest, 42, 43, 288
Henry de Ferrers, 383
Henry I, King, 129, 222, 305, 379, 396
Henry II, Emperor, 87
Henry II, King, 380
Henry IV, Emperor, 132
Hensingham, 31
Heptarchy, 5, 39, 67, 238
Hereford, 128, 129, 144, 248, 288, 386, 391–5
Herefordshire, 376
heregeld (army geld), 98, 320, 322–3
Hereward the Wake, 184
heriot, 108, 190, 226, 388, 394
Hertford, 139, 140, 235
Hessle, 105
Hexham, 248, 250
hide, definition of, 166, and *passim*
Hild, Abbess, 229
Hitchin, 48
Hlothere, King, 119, 212
Hodgen, M., 372
Hodgkin, R.H., 145
hold-oaths, 204, 310
honey, 382
Honorius, Pope, 74
Hope, 106
horses, 160, 190, 330
Hoskins, W.G., 49

426

Index

Index

Prudentius, 279
public burdens, 315
Pybba, 210

queens, 274–5, 335
Quenington, 387
Quentovic, 68, 77, 84, 87–8, 97

radcnihts, 197
radmen (radchistres), 367
Ralph, Earl, 391
Ramsbury, 260
Ramsey, 185, 252, 374
Rayleigh, 381
Reading, 25, 26, 169 (Readingas), 396
Rectitudines Singularum Personarum, 107,
    196–202, 204, 226–7, 367
Redwald, King of East Anglia, 236, 239
reeves, 200–1, 356, 368 passim
regional commands, 37
rent, 185, 190, 197–8, 203, 338–9, 360,
    385–6, 393
Repton, 116
revenue, 314ff., 396
Rhuddlan, 139
Richard, son of William I, 379
Richard the forester, 380
Richborough, 30
riddles, 281
Ripon, 254
river valleys, 22–3, 31
river-name evidence, 7–10
Robert, Archbishop of Canterbury, 247
Robert Fitz-Wimarc, 381
Robert German, 350
Robertson, A.J., 97
Rochester, 43, 143, 144, 191, 227, 259,
    278, 306
Roding, 26, 27
Roman roads, 22, 101
Roman tradition, 233–4, 283–4
Romney, 397
Romulus, Augustulus, 71
Rothwell, 39
Rouen, 52, 84, 97, 177, 332
Round, J.H., 337
royal exactions, 314–15
Rufus, 379
Ruthwell cross, 284
Rutland, 274, 335, 353, 372
rye, 156–7

Sabbé, E., 76, 88
St Albans, 11, 242, 259, 288, 332
St Benet's Holme, 255
St Denis, 83, 387

St Joseph, J.K.S., 153
Salford, 111
Salinus, 279
Salisbury, Bishop of, 180
Salisbury Plain, 20
salt, 109–13
Sampton, 110
Sandwich, 375, 390, 397
Sarauw, 156
Savory, H.N., 35
Sawyer, P.H., 57, 177
Saxons, 3, 24, 27ff., passim
Scandinavians, invasion, 51–5;
    settlement, 55–65
sceattas, 86, 122–3, 136, 213
Scergeat, 139
schools, 278, 295
scientific work, 296
scilling, see shilling
Seasalter, 390
Seaxneat, 238
Sedgebarrow, 316
Seebohm, F., 16, 158, 170–1, 300, 374
seisin, 177–8, 257
Selsey, 248
serfdom, 337
Servatus Lupus, 106
servi, see slaves
settlement, coastal, 32–3, 34; early
    routes and areas of, 31–8; economic
    and cultural development, 44–7;
    inland, 33–4; intensification of, 47–51;
    patterns of, 20–1; Scandinavian,
    55–65; sources of early 1–6; survival
    of institutions, 15–23; see also
    migrations
Shaftesbury, 21, 193, 251
sheep, 381
Sherborne, 248, 259, 260
sheriffs, 257, 338, 396
shilling, 122, 131–2, 135–6, 162
ship-building, 84–5, 93
Shrewsbury, 380, 392, 393
Sigebert, King of Essex, 210
Sigebert, King of East Anglia, 211
Sigeric, Archbishop, 322
Silchester, 18
silver, 105–6
slavery, 7, 11, 17, 36, 82, 337–8;
    Church's concern with, 91; trade, 68,
    78, 90–1, 100, 340, 365
slaves, 171, 173, 189, 199, 246, 265,
    337–8, 357, 362–6
Smeaton, 108
Smeeton, 108
Smethcote, 108

Index

432